2 0 0

HCPCS

MEDICODE®

Eleventh edition © 1999 Ingenix

First printing November 1999

All rights reserved. Printed in the United States of America. No part of this publication may be reproduced or transmitted in any form or by any means electronic or mechanical, including photocopy, recording or storage in a database or retrieval system, without the prior permission of the publisher.

Medicode's *HCPCS 2000* is designed to be an accurate and authoritative source of information about this government coding system. Every effort has been made to verify the accuracy of the listings, and all information is believed reliable at the time of publication. Absolute accuracy cannot be guaranteed, however. This publication is made available with the understanding that the publisher is not engaged in rendering legal or other services that require a professional license.

ISBN 1-56337-301-7

Medicode
5225 Wiley Post Way, Suite 500
Salt Lake City, UT 84116-2889

Medicode's 2000 Publications & Software For Coders

POWER TO MAKE THE RIGHT DECISIONS

Medicode, Inc. 5225 Wiley Post Way, Suite 500, Salt Lake City, UT 84116 • 801.536.1000 • FAX 801.536.1011

ORDER TOLL FREE OR CALL FOR A FREE CATALOG 800.999.4600
AVAILABLE FROM YOUR MEDICAL BOOKSTORE OR DISTRIBUTOR.

It's Easy to Tap into the Power of *Encoder Pro*

Encoder Pro
(Item #2717)   **$499.95**

Quickly look up ICD-9-CM, CPT and HCPCS Level II codes with the fastest, easiest and most powerful physician coding software available. Access Medicode's database of top selling publications instantaneously, to ensure all your claims are properly coded. See for yourself the advantages this invaluable resource will bring to your office:

- **[NEW!] View Index Results.** Instantaneously search ICD-9, CPT, and HCPCS indexes.
- **[NEW!] View CPT Assistant References.** See which editions of *CPT Assistant* have articles relating to CPT codes.
- **[NEW!] Alerts for deleted codes.** Deleted code alerts are displayed if a code is no longer valid. Provides cross-reference to valid codes where applicable.
- **[NEW!] Revised and New Code Icons.** New icons for ICD-9, CPT, and HCPCS Level II codes identify revised and new codes.
- **Easy to Use.** Using *Encoder Pro* is intuitive. Accessing information is just a click away.
- **Find the Right Code Fast.** *Encoder Pro's* powerful search engine guides you to the right code.
- **Save Time.** Search results display instantaneously. No more thumbing through various code books.
- **Interface Capability.** Active X technology allows *Encoder Pro* to be interfaced with practice management software.
- **HCFA-1500.** Enter claim information into electronic form. Save and or print.
- **Windows™ Compatible.** Copy codes and descriptions and reference information to the Windows clipboard for use in other Windows applications.

Medicode, Inc. 5225 Wiley Post Way, Suite 500, Salt Lake City, UT 84116 • 801.536.1000 • FAX 801.536.1011

Order Toll Free or Call for a Free Catalog 800.999.4600
Available From Your Medical Bookstore Or Distributor.

Capture Your Costs with *HCPCS* Codes

2000 HCPCS
ISBN 1-56337-301-7

(Item #2798) **$49⁹⁵**
Available December 1999

HCPCS ASCII File*

(Item #3906) **$229⁹⁵**
Available January 2000

This best-selling *HCPCS* book has many features to help you bill DME, pharmaceuticals, and select medical services easily and more accurately.

- EXCLUSIVE! **Payers Appendix.** We let you know which payers accept HCPCS Level II codes so you can file claims with confidence.
- EXCLUSIVE! **Flagged Quantity Codes.** Codes that require quantities are flagged to remind you to fill in the quantity when completing reimbursement forms.
- EXCLUSIVE! **Color tabs.** Color-coded index tabbing makes it easy to find the correct code quickly.
- **Expanded Index.** Helps you code accurately. We link brand name DME, like wheelchairs, diabetes supplies, and ostomy equipment, to their correct codes.
- **Color Coded Icons.** Codes with special Medicare instructions and coverage issues are flagged to curb claim denials.

Quick Reference Coding

2000 HCPCS Fast Finders
$24⁹⁵ per sheet

Drug Codes (HCPCS) (Item #3129)
Orthotics (Item #3172)
Prosthetics (Item #3173)
Home Health (Item #3171)
Vision and Hearing (Item #3174)
Physician Office Supplies (Item #3175)

Our *HCPCS Fast Finder* gives you the ability to quickly find the code that you need from among a list of more than 300 of the most commonly used codes. Each double-sided and laminated *Fast Finder* is durable, portable, and easy-to-use. Choose the one that best suits your specialty

- **Upated for 2000.** Provides current codes so that you have the most accurate information.
- **Easy-to-Use.** Lists more than 300 commonly used codes in one location.
- **Accurate.** All codes are valid and coded to the highest level of specificity.

POWER TO MAKE THE RIGHT DECISIONS™

Medicode, Inc. 5225 Wiley Post Way, Suite 500, Salt Lake City, UT 84116 • 801.536.1000 • FAX 801.536.1011

ORDER TOLL FREE OR CALL FOR A FREE CATALOG 800.999.4600
AVAILABLE FROM YOUR MEDICAL BOOKSTORE OR DISTRIBUTOR.

Don't Risk Filing with Obsolete CPT™ Codes

Available November 1999

Hundreds of CPT code changes will soon be in effect. Make sure you have a current CPT code book in your office — or risk rejected claims, delayed payments, and even charges of fraud and abuse!

CPT Professional Binder Version
Binder offers flexibility, color keys and illustrations.
ISBN 1-57947-019-X

(Item #2516) **$74.95**

CPT Professional Spiralbound Version
Durable and easy-to-use with color coding and illustrations.
ISBN 1-57947-018-1

(Item #2515) **$66.95**

CPT Standard Spiralbound
Economical, easy-to-use and durable
ISBN 1-57947-017-3

(Item #2518) **$51.95**

CPT Standard Softbound
AMA's economical classic
ISBN 1-57947-016-5

(Item #2517) **$47.95**

Medicodes Relative Values & CPT ASCII File*

(Item #3902) **$249.95**
Available January 2000

2000 CPT Minibooks
You can now order AMA Minibooks individually. Eight specialties to choose from for just **$29.95**

- **Dermatology, Plastic & Reconstructive Surgery**
  ISBN 1-57947-020-3
  (Item #3267)
- **General Surgery**
  ISBN 1-57947-021-1
  (Item #3264)
- **Gynecology, Obstetrics & Urology**
  ISBN 1-57947-022-X
  (Item #3261)
- **Head & Neck Surgery, Oral & Maxillofacial Surgery, Ophthalmology & Otorhinolaryngology**
  ISBN 1-57947-023-8
  (Item #3265)
- **Medical Specialties**
  ISBN 1-57947-024-6
  (Item #3266)
- **Neurological & Orthopaedic Surgery**
  ISBN 1-57947-025-4
  (Item #3262)
- **Pathology & Laboratory Medicine**
  ISBN 1-57947-026-2
  (Item #3260)
- **Radiology**
  ISBN 1-57947-027-0
  (Item #3263)

Shortcuts to Precision Coding

2000 CPT Specialty Fast Finders
Available November 1999

Each double-sided, laminated sheet provides a quick reference list of the most common CPT codes for each specialty.

- **NEW! Updated for 2000.** Prevents use of invalid codes. Only current codes are included.
- **Specialized and complete.** Includes 21 specialties on separate and laminated sheets.
- **Quick-Reference to CPT descriptions.** Condenses CPT descriptions in a format that ensures accurate coding.
- **All-inclusive code sets.** Covers the spectrum of CPT, including surgery, laboratory, radiology, medicine, E/M, and anesthesia.

$24.95 per sheet

Allergy and Immunology (Item #3150)
Cardiology (Item #3151)
Cardiovascular and Thoracic Surgery (Item #3152)
Dental/OMS (Item #3153)
Dermatology (Item #3154)
ENT (Item #3155)
Gastroenterology (Item #3156)
General Surgery (Item #3157)
Hematology/Oncology (Item #3158)
Laboratory and Pathology (Item #3159)
Neurology (Item #3160)
Obstetrics, Gynecology and Infertility (Item #3161)
Ophthalmology (Item #3162)
Orthopaedic Surgery (Item #3163)
Pediatrics (Item #3164)
Physical Medicine/Rehab/PT (Item #3165)
Plastic and Reconstructive Surgery (Item #3166)
Primary Care and Internal Medicine (Item #3167)
Psychiatry (Item #3168)
Radiology (Item #3169)
Urology and Nephrology (Item #3170)

MEDICODE®
POWER TO MAKE THE RIGHT DECISIONS™

Medicode, Inc. 5225 Wiley Post Way, Suite 500, Salt Lake City, UT 84116 • 801.536.1000 • FAX 801.536.1011

ORDER TOLL FREE OR CALL FOR A FREE CATALOG 800.999.4600
AVAILABLE FROM YOUR MEDICAL BOOKSTORE OR DISTRIBUTOR.

Manage Your DRG Selection Process

2000 DRG Guide
ISBN 1-56337-307-6

(Item #2530) $89.95
Available October 1999

Assigning correct DRGs is now easier than ever with *2000 DRG Guide*. This invaluable reference not only provides DRG information, but also contains DRG selection tips. All of the information you need is in one complete source.

- **EXCLUSIVE! DRG Information and Selection Tips.** Make sure you are assigning the correct DRG and receiving the highest payment to which you're entitled.
- **Indexes ICD-9-CM Codes.** Lists diagnoses and procedures numerically and alphabetically for fast lookup.
- **HCFA Rate Structure.** Identifies current relative weight, geometric mean length of stay, and average mean length of stay for each DRG.
- **DRG Drug List.** Alphabetically names brand and generic drugs that may be prescribed for conditions considered a CC.
- **DRG Decision Trees.** Easily select DRGs through flow chart type decision trees.

The Only Spiral Bound Hospital ICD-9-CM Available

1999-2000 Hospital & Payer ICD-9-CM
ISBN 1-56337-286-X

(Item #2924) $89.95
Available September 1999

ASCII File*

(Item #3900) $279.95
Available September 1999

This easy-to-use *ICD-9-CM* code book for hospitals and payers contains many valuable features to help you code accurately—all at a competitive price.

- **EXCLUSIVE! Note Saver System.** Space to write and a system to save important coding notes for next year's edition.
- **125+ Color Illustrations.** Anatomical differences are highlighted and coding issues explained.
- **2000+ Annotations.** Concise definitions aid in code selection.
- **Color Coded Tabular and Index.** Alerts coders to coding and reimbursement issues based on Medicare edits.
- **Highlighted Fourth and Fifth Digits.** Saves you from searching for the additional digit.
- **Flags Complications and Comorbidity.** Lets you know if a diagnosis could affect DRG selection.
- **AHA Coding Clinic References.** Listed next to codes to quickly find official guidelines.
- **ASCII File.** Includes ICD-9, Volumes 1 and 3 codes. Full, long, and short descriptions.

Medicode, Inc. 5225 Wiley Post Way, Suite 500, Salt Lake City, UT 84116 • 801.536.1000 • FAX 801.536.1011

ORDER TOLL FREE OR CALL FOR A FREE CATALOG 800.999.4600
AVAILABLE FROM YOUR MEDICAL BOOKSTORE OR DISTRIBUTOR.

The Best Features at the Best Prices

1999-2000 Deluxe Physician ICD-9-CM
Thumb tabs, spiral binding, free ICD-9 Fast Finder
ISBN 1-56337-314-9

(Item #2709) $69.95
Available August 1999

1999-2000 Compact Physician ICD-9-CM
Thumb tabs, convenient size
ISBN 1-56337-313-0

(Item #2708) $59.95
Available August 1999

1999-2000 Standard Physician ICD-9-CM
Medicode's economical classic
ISBN 1-56337-312-2

(Item #2687) $51.95
Available August 1999

Medicode's *ICD-9-CM* code books offer many features at a fantastic price. Varying editions of our code books are available to keep coders accurate and meet your specific needs.

- **EXCLUSIVE! Medicare Edits.** Large scopes of non-specific codes are identified and serve as guidelines for coding and audits.
- **Color Coded.** Tabular section and icons in the index are color coded to help you code quickly and easily.
- **Illustrations and Annotations.** Helps you code accurately.
- **Fourth and Fifth Digits.** Highlighted to help you find the additional digit.

Save Time and Money

1999-2000 ICD-9 Fast Finder
Available August 1999

Each double-sided, laminated *Fast Finder* contains more than 300 diagnosis codes based on actual frequencies for 20 specialties.

- **Accurate.** All codes are valid and coded to the highest level of specificity.
- **Specific Diagnoses.** We provide more than the .89 and .99 "dump" codes.
- **Secondary Diagnoses.** Included with each specialty to provide a complete coding resource.
- **Clinically and Statistically Sound.** Provides accurate, appropriate, and comprehensive code sets developed by clinical and records specialists.

$24.95 per sheet
Allergy/Immunology (Item #3120)
Cardiology (Item #3121)
Cardiovascular/Thoracic Surgery (Item #3122)
Dental/OMS (Item #3123)
Dermatology (Item #3124)
ENT (Item #3125)
Gastroenterology (Item #3126)
General Surgery (Item #3127)
Hematology/Oncology (Item #3128)
Neurology/Oncology (Item #3130)
Ob/Gyn (Item #3131)
Ophthalmology/Optometry (Item #3132)
Orthopedics (Item #3133)
Pediatrics (Item #3134)
Physical Medicine/Rehabilitation (Item #3135)
Plastic/Reconstructive Surgery (Item #3136)
Primary Care/Internal Medicine (Item #3137)
Psychiatry (Item #3138)
Urology/Nephrology (Item #3139)

Medicode, Inc. 5225 Wiley Post Way, Suite 500, Salt Lake City, UT 84116 • 801.536.1000 • FAX 801.536.1011

ORDER TOLL FREE OR CALL FOR A FREE CATALOG 800.999.4600
AVAILABLE FROM YOUR MEDICAL BOOKSTORE OR DISTRIBUTOR.

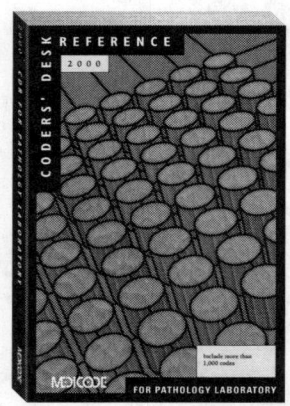

Get Instant Answers to Your Tough Coding Questions

2000 Coders' Desk Reference
ISBN 1-56337-324-6

(Item #2749) **$99.95**
Available December 1999

No matter how much experience you have using ICD-9, CPT, and HCPCS codes, there are always tough questions that hold up the billing process. And because billing errors can result in fines, you can't afford to guess. Now you can get easy-to-understand answers to your coding questions, without leaving your desk, with the *2000 Coders' Desk Reference*.

- **NEW! Improved explanations for surgical procedures.** Helps coders more accurately understand and determine CPT codes.
- **NEW! ICD-10-CM and ICD-10-PCS information.** Helps prepare for implementation in 2001.
- **NEW! 2000 CPT explanations.** CPT explanations are updated.
- **NEW! Extensive Glossary of Abbreviations, Acronyms, and Symbols—now with cross-references to applicable CPT codes.** Understand what the abbreviations, acronyms, and symbols mean and find out the CPT codes that use them.
- **Eponyms defined and linked.** Eponyms are cross-referenced to CPT codes.
- **Syndromes defined and coded.** Understand more than 1,000 syndromes explained and cross-referenced to *ICD-9-CM*.
- **Visual Help.** Find the right body area or incision length using the anatomical and metric conversion charts.
- **Anesthesia Crosswalk.** Outlines applicable anesthesia codes for CPT surgical procedures.

Get Fast Answers to Your Path/Lab Coding Questions

2000 Coders' Desk Reference for Pathology and Laboratory Services
ISBN 1-56337-334-3

(Item #5855) **$99.95**
Available February 2000

Code pathology and laboratory services right the first time. Increased scrutiny on path/lab claims can mean costly delays and denials... or worse. Having a resource dedicated to path/lab coding at your fingertips is essential.

The new *2000 Coders' Desk Reference for Pathology and Laboratory* gives you a wealth of information to answer your tough coding questions. You'll code more accurately, quickly, and confidently.

- **Easy-to-understand explanations of path/lab procedures.** Helps you quickly determine the appropriate CPT code.
- **Coding comments for hundreds of procedures.** Points you to more specific codes or other procedures that could apply, enabling you to code more accurately.
- **CLIA and HIPAA compliance information including detailed information on what constitutes fraud and abuse.** You can be confident that you are coding by the rules.

Medicode, Inc. 5225 Wiley Post Way, Suite 500, Salt Lake City, UT 84116 • 801.536.1000 • FAX 801.536.1011

MEDICODE PUBLISHING STAFF

Publisher	Susan P. Seare
Editorial Director	Lynn Speirs
Medical Director	Thomas G. Darr, MD, FACEP, Associate Medical Director, Clinical Content
Product Manager	Sheri Poe Bernard, CPC
Editors	Christine B. Fraizer, CPC
Clinical Editors	Charlene Neeshan, LPN, CCS, CPC, CPC-H
	Bonnie G. Schreck, CCS, CPC, CPC-H, CCS-P
	Lauri Gray, CPC, ART
Desktop Publisher	Kerrie Hornsby

Contents

Introduction ix
   The HCPCS System ix
   HCPCS Levels of Codes ix
   Modifiers ix
   Why You Should Be Using HCPCS xiii
   Why Our HCPCS? xiii
   How to Use HCPCS 2000 xiv
   New Codes xiv
   Changed Codes xx
   Deleted Codes xxii
   HCPCS Abbreviations and Acronyms xxii

A Codes 1
   Transportation Services Including Ambulance 1
   Medical and Surgical Supplies 3
      Miscellaneous Supplies 3
      Vascular Catheters 4
      Incontinence Appliances and Care Supplies 4
      External Urinary Supplies 5
      Ostomy Supplies 5
      Additional Miscellaneous Supplies 6
      Supplies for Oxygen and Related Respiratory Equipment 7
      Supplies for Other Durable Medical Equipment 7
      Supplies for Radiologic Procedures 8
      Supplies for ESRD 8
      Additional Ostomy Supplies 9
      Additional Incontinence Appliances/Supplies ... 10
      Supplies for Either Incontinence or Ostomy Appliances 10
      Diabetic Shoes, Fitting, and Modifications 10
      Dressings 11
   Administrative, Miscellaneous and Investigational 15

B Codes 16
   Enteral and Parenteral Therapy 16
      Enteral Formulae and Enteral Medical Supplies 16
      Parenteral Nutrition Solutions and Supplies 16
      Enteral and Parenteral Pumps 16

D Codes 18
   Dental Procedures — Diagnostic 18
      Clinical Oral Evaluation 18
      Radiographs/Diagnostic Imaging 18
      Test and Laboratory Examinations 18
      Oral Pathology Laboratory 18
   Dental Procedures — Preventive 19
      Dental Prophylaxis 19
      Topical Fluoride Treatment (Office Procedure) . 19
      Other Preventive Services 19
      Space Maintenance (Passive Appliances) 19
   Dental Procedures — Restorative 19
      Amalgam Restorations (Including Polishing) 19
      Resin-Based Composite Restorations 19
      Gold Foil Restorations 20
      Inlay/Onlay Restorations 20
      Crowns — Single Restorations Only 20
      Other Restorative Services 21
   Dental Procedures — Endodontics 21
      Pulp Capping 21
      Pulpotomy 21
      Endodontic Therapy on Primary Teeth 21
      Endodontic Therapy (Including Treatment Plan, Clinical Procedures and Follow-up Care) 21
      Endodontic Retreatment 22
      Apexification/Recalcification Procedures 22
      Apicoectomy/Periradicular Services 22
      Other Endodontic Procedures 22
   Dental Procedures – Periodontics 22
      Surgical Services (Including Usual Postoperative Care) 22
      Non-Surgical Periodontal Services 23
      Other Periodontal Services 23
   Dental Procedures – Prosthodontics (Removable) 23
      Complete Dentures (Including Routine Post-Delivery Care) 23
      Partial Dentures (Including Routine Post-Delivery Care) 23
      Adjustments to Dentures 23
      Repairs to Complete Dentures 23
      Repairs to Partial Dentures 23
      Denture Rebase Procedures 24
      Denture Reline Procedures 24
      Interim Prosthesis 24
      Other Removable Prosthetic Services 24
   Dental Procedures — Maxillofacial Prosthetics 24
   Dental Procedures — Implant Services 25
      Implant Supported Prosthetics 25
      Other Implant Services 26
   Dental Procedures — Prosthodontics (Fixed) 26
      Fixed Partial Denture Pontics 26
      Fixed Partial Denture Retainers — Inlays/Onlays 26

Fixed Partial Denture Retainers — Crowns 27
Other Fixed Partial Denture Services 27
Dental Procedures — Oral and Maxillofacial
  Surgery 28
  Extractions 28
  Surgical Extractions 28
  Other Surgical Procedures 28
  Alveoloplasty — Surgical Preparation of
    Ridge for Dentures 28
  Vestibuloplasty 28
  Surgical Excision of Reactive Inflammatory
    Lesions 28
  Removal of Tumors, Cysts and Neoplasms........28
  Excision of Bone Tissue 29
  Surgical Incision 29
  Treatment of Fractures — Simple 29
  Treatment of Fractures — Compound...............29
  Reduction of Dislocation and Management
    of Other Temporomandibular
    Joint Dysfunctions 29
  Repair of Traumatic Wounds 30
  Complicated Suturing 30
  Other Repair Procedures 30
Orthodontics..31
  Interceptive Orthodontic Treatment 31
  Comprehensive Orthodontic Treatment 31
  Minor Treatment to Control Harmful Habits 31
  Other Orthodontic Services 31
Adjunctive General Services 31
  Unclassified Treatment 31
  Anesthesia 31
  Professional Consultation 32
  Professional Visits 32
  Drugs 32
  Miscellaneous Services 32

E Codes..33
Durable Medical Equipment 33
  Canes 33
  Crutches 33
  Walkers 33
  Attachments 33
  Commodes 33
  Decubitus Care Equipment................................34
  Heat/Cold Application 35
  Bath and Toilet Aids 35
  Hospital Beds and Accessories 35
  Oxygen and Related Respiratory Equipment.....36
  IPPB Machines 37
  Humidifiers/Compressors/Nebulizers for
    Use with Oxygen IPPB Equipment 37
  Suction Pump/Room Vaporizers 37
  Monitoring Equipment 38
  Pacemaker Monitor 38
  Patient Lifts 38
  Pneumatic Compressor and Appliances 38
  Ultraviolet Cabinet 38

Safety Equipment 38
Restraints..38
Transcutaneous and/or Neuromuscular
  Electrical Nerve Stimulators — TENS 39
Infusion Supplies 39
Traction 39
  Cervical..39
  Overdoor..40
  Extremity 40
  Pelvic 40
Trapeze Equipment, Fracture Frame, and
  Other Orthopedic Devices 40
Wheelchairs..40
  Accessories 40
  Rollabout Chair 41
  Fully Reclining 41
  Semi-reclining 41
  Standard 41
  Amputee 42
  Power 42
  Special Size 42
  Lightweight 42
  Heavy-duty 42
Whirlpool — Equipment 43
Repairs and Replacement Supplies 43
Additional Oxygen Related Equipment 43
Artificial Kidney Machines and Accessories 43
Jaw Motion Rehabilitation System and
  Accessories 44
Other Orthopedic Devices 44

G Codes..45
PET Scan Modifiers 45

J Codes 49
Drugs Administered Other Than Oral Method.....49
Miscellaneous Drugs and Solutions 58
Inhalation Solutions 59
Chemotherapy Drugs 61

K Codes (Temporary) 64
K Codes Assigned to Durable Medical
  Equipment Regional Carriers (DMERC) 64
Wheelchair and Wheelchair Accessories 64
Spinal Orthotics 65
Immunosuppressive Drugs.................................65
Miscellaneous 66

L Codes 69
Orthotic Procedures 69
  Orthotic Devices — Spinal 69
    Cervical 69
    Multiple Post Collar 69
    Thoracic 69
  Thoracic-Lumbar-Sacral Orthosis (TLSO)........69
    Flexible 69
    Anterior-Posterior Control 69
    Anterior-Posterior-Lateral-Rotary Control 69
  Lumbar-Sacral Orthosis (LSO)..........................70

- Flexible 70
  - Anterior-Posterior-Lateral Control 70
  - Anterior-Posterior Control 70
  - Lumbar Flexion 70
- Sacroiliac 70
  - Flexible 70
  - Semi-Rigid 70
- Cervical-Thoracic-Lumbar-Sacral-Orthosis (CTLSO)
  - Anterior, Posterior-Lateral Control 70
- Halo Procedure 70
- Torso Supports 70
  - Ptosis Supports 70
  - Pendulous Abdomen Supports 70
  - Postsurgical Supports 70
  - Additions to Spinal Orthosis 70
- Orthotic Devices — Scoliosis Procedures 70
  - Cervical-Thoracic-Lumbar-Sacral Orthosis (CTLSO) (Milwaukee) 70
  - Thoracic-Lumbar-Sacral Orthosis (TLSO) (Low Profile) 71
  - Other Scoliosis Procedures 71
  - Thoracic-Hip-Knee-Ankle Orthosis (THKAO) 71
- Orthotic Devices — Lower Limb 71
  - Hip Orthosis (HO) — Flexible 71
  - Legg Perthes 71
  - Knee Orthosis (KO) 72
  - Ankle-Foot Orthosis (AFO) 72
  - Knee-Ankle-Foot Orthosis (KAFO) 72
  - Torsion Control: Hip-Knee-Ankle-Foot Orthosis (HKAFO) 73
  - Fracture Orthosis 73
  - Additions to Fracture Orthosis 73
  - Additions to Lower Extremity Orthosis: Shoe-Ankle-Shin-Knee 73
  - Additions to Straight Knee or Offset Knee Joints 74
  - Additions: Thigh/Weight Bearing — Gluteal/Ischial Weight Bearing 74
  - Additions: Pelvic and Thoracic Control 74
  - Additions: General 75
- Orthopedic Shoes 75
  - Inserts 75
  - Arch Support, Removable, Premolded 75
  - Arch Support, Nonremovable, Attached to Shoe 75
  - Abduction and Rotation Bars 75
  - Orthopedic Footwear 76
  - Shoe Modification — Lifts 76
  - Shoe Modification — Wedges 76
  - Shoe Modifications — Heels 77
  - Miscellaneous Shoe Additions 77
  - Transfer or Replacement 77
- Orthotic Devices — Upper Limb 77
  - Shoulder Orthosis (SO) 77
  - Elbow Orthosis (EO) 77
  - Wrist-Hand-Finger Orthosis (WHFO) 78
  - Additions 78
  - Dynamic Flexor Hinge, Reciprocal Wrist Extension/Flexion, Finger Flexion/Extension 78
- External Power 78
  - Other WHFOs — Custom Fitted 78
- Shoulder-Elbow-Wrist-Hand Orthosis (SEWHO) . 79
  - Abduction Positioning, Custom Fitted 79
  - Additions to Mobile Arm Supports 79
  - Fracture Orthosis 79
  - Specific Repair 79
  - Repairs 79
- Prosthetic Procedures 80
  - Lower Limb 80
    - Partial Foot 80
    - Ankle 80
    - Below Knee 80
    - Knee Disarticulation 80
    - Above Knee 80
    - Hip Disarticulation 80
    - Hemipelvectomy 80
    - Endoskeletal: Below Knee 80
    - Endoskeletal: Knee Disarticulation 80
    - Endoskeletal: Above Knee 80
    - Endoskeletal: Hip Disarticulation 80
    - Endoskeletal: Hemipelvectomy 80
    - Immediate Postsurgical or Early Fitting Procedures 80
    - Initial Prosthesis 81
    - Preparatory Prosthesis 81
    - Additions: Lower Extremity 81
    - Additions: Test Sockets 81
    - Additions: Socket Variations 81
    - Additions: Socket Insert and Suspension 82
    - Replacements 83
    - Additions: Exoskeletal Knee-Shin System 83
    - Component Modification 83
    - Additions: Endoskeletal Knee-Shin System ... 83
  - Upper Limb 84
    - Partial Hand 84
    - Wrist Disarticulation 84
    - Below Elbow 84
    - Elbow Disarticulation 85
    - Above Elbow 85
    - Shoulder Disarticulation 85
    - Interscapular Thoracic 85
    - Immediate and Early Postsurgical Procedures 85
    - Endoskeletal: Below Elbow 85
    - Endoskeletal: Elbow Disarticulation 85
    - Endoskeletal: Above Elbow 85
    - Endoskeletal: Shoulder Disarticulation .. 85
    - Endoskeletal: Interscapular Thoracic 85
    - Additions: Upper Limb 86
  - Terminal Devices 86
    - Hooks 86

  Hands 87
   Gloves for Above Hands 87
   Hand Restoration 88
  External Power 88
   Base Devices 88
   Elbow 88
   Battery Components 89
   Repairs 89
  General 89
   Breast Prosthesis 89
   Elastic Supports 89
   Trusses 89
   Prosthetic Socks 90
  Prosthetic Implants 90

M Codes 92
  Medical Services 92
   Other Medical Services 92
   Cardiovascular Services 92

P Codes 93
  Pathology and Laboratory Services 93
   Chemistry and Toxicology Tests 93
   Pathology Screening Tests 93
   Microbiology Tests 93
   Miscellaneous 93

Q Codes (Temporary) 94
  Injection Codes for Epoetin Alpha (EPO) 96

R Codes 98
  Diagnostic Radiology Services 98

S Codes (Temporary National Codes) 99

V Codes 102
  Vision Services 102
   Frames 102
   Spectacle Lenses 102
    Single Vision, Glass, or Plastic 102
    Bifocal, Glass, or Plastic 102
    Trifocal, Glass, or Plastic 103
    Variable Asphericity Lens, Glass, or
     Plastic 103
   Contact Lens 103
   Vision Aids 104
   Prosthetic Eye 104
   Intraocular Lenses 104
   Miscellaneous 104
  Hearing Services 105
   Speech-Language Pathology Services 105

Table of Drugs 107

Appendix 131
  Appendix A: Coverage Issues Manual (CIM)
   References 131
  Appendix B: Medicare Carriers Manual (MCM)
   References 171
  Appendix C: Medicare Statutes 227
  Appendix D: Payer Directory For HCPCS
   Level II Codes 233
  Appendix E: Medicare Carriers, Intermediaries,
   and Contacts 257

Index 275

Introduction

THE HCPCS SYSTEM

The HCPCS Level II National Codes found in *HCPCS 2000* include over 3,225 codes and represent just one part of a larger, three-level coding system called HCPCS.

HCPCS (pronounced "hick-picks") is the acronym for the HCFA (Health Care Financing Administration) Common Procedure Coding System. This system is a uniform method for healthcare providers and medical suppliers to report professional services, procedures, and supplies. HCFA developed this system in 1983 to:

- Meet the operational needs of Medicare/Medicaid.
- Coordinate government programs by uniform application of HCFA's policies.
- Allow providers and suppliers to communicate their services in a consistent manner.
- Ensure the validity of profiles and fee schedules through standardized coding.
- Enhance medical education and research by providing a vehicle for local, regional, and national utilization comparisons.

HCPCS LEVELS OF CODES

Each of the three HCPCS levels is its own unique coding system. The levels, I, II, and III, are also known by the names shown here with the level numbers.

Before applying the HCPCS Level II codes to your services, check for Level III codes assigned by your local Medicare carrier, state Medicaid office or private payer. Contact the carrier for a current listing of these codes and modifiers to ensure accurate billing and reimbursement. Also, pay attention to your carrier's newsletter for valuable information on appropriate coding, including using Level III. Normally, Level III codes override Level I and Level II codes.

If you cannot locate an appropriate code in Level III, check the nationally assigned Level II codes. If a Level II code fully describes the service performed, this code normally overrides the use of a Level I code.

Level I — CPT

Level I is the American Medical Association's *Physicians' Current Procedural Terminology* (CPT), which was developed and is maintained by the AMA. CPT lists five-digit codes with descriptive terms for reporting services performed by healthcare providers and is the country's most widely accepted coding reference. CPT was first published in 1966 and is updated annually.

Procedures are first grouped within six major sections: evaluation and management (E/M), anesthesiology, surgery, radiology, pathology and laboratory, and medicine. They are then broken into subsections according to body part, service, or diagnosis (e.g., mouth, amputation, or septal defect).

Level II — HCPCS /National Codes

CPT does not contain all the codes needed to report medical services and supplies, and HCFA developed the second level of codes — those found in this book.

As you will see in *HCPCS 2000,* the codes begin with a single letter (A through V) followed by four numeric digits. They are grouped by the type of service or supply they represent and are updated annually by HCFA.

HCPCS/National codes are now required for reporting most medical services and supplies provided to Medicare and Medicaid patients. An increasing number of private insurance carriers are also encouraging or requiring the use of HCPCS/National codes.

Level III — Local Codes

The third level contains codes assigned and maintained by individual state Medicare carriers. Like Level II, these codes begin with a letter (W through Z) followed by four numeric digits, but the most notable difference is that these codes are not common to all carriers.

Individual carriers assign these codes to describe new procedures that are not yet available in Level I or II. These codes can be introduced on an as-needed basis throughout the year, but carriers must send written notification to the physicians and suppliers in their area when these local codes are required. Reading and implementing the information received from these carriers will keep you up-to-date.

MODIFIERS

Modifiers should, or in some cases must, be used to identify circumstances that alter or enhance the description of a service or supply. There are also three levels of HCPCS modifiers — one for each level of codes.

Level I (CPT) modifiers are two numeric digits (e.g., -22 *Unusual Procedural Services*) and are described in detail in the

CPT book. They are also maintained and updated on an annual basis by the AMA.

Level II (HCPCS/National) modifiers are two alphabetic digits (AA–VP). They are recognized by carriers nationally and are updated annually by HCFA.

Level III (Local) modifiers are assigned by individual Medicare carriers and are distributed to physicians and suppliers through carrier newsletters. The carrier may change, add, or delete these local modifiers as needed.

HCPCS Level II National Modifiers

While all current Level II modifiers are listed here, many have specific or limited use.

- -AA Anesthesia services performed personally by anesthesiologist
- (-AB This modifier has been deleted)
- (-AC This modifier has been deleted)
- -AD Medical supervision by a physician: more than four concurrent anesthesia procedures
- (-AE This modifier has been deleted)
- (-AF This modifier has been deleted)
- (-AG This modifier has been deleted)
- -AH Clinical psychologist
- -AJ Clinical social worker
- -AM Physician, team member service
- -AP Determination of refractive state was not performed in the course of diagnostic ophthalmological examination
- -AS Physician assistant, nurse practitioner, or clinical nurse specialist services for assistant at surgery
- -AT Acute treatment (this modifier should be used when reporting service 98940, 98941, 98942)
- -BP The beneficiary has been informed of the purchase and rental options and has elected to purchase the item
- -BR The beneficiary has been informed of the purchase and rental options and has elected to rent the item
- -BU The beneficiary has been informed of the purchase and rental options and after 30 days has not informed the supplier of his/her decision
- -CC Procedure code change (use 'CC' when the procedure code submitted was changed either for administrative reasons or because an incorrect code was filed)
- -E1 Upper left, eyelid
- -E2 Lower left, eyelid
- -E3 Upper right, eyelid
- -E4 Lower right, eyelid

- ▲ -EJ Subsequent claims for a defined course of therapy, e.g., EPO, sodium hyaluronate, infliximab
- -EM Emergency reserve supply (for ESRD benefit only)
- -EP Service provided as part of medicaid early periodic screening diagnosis and treatment (EPSDT) program
- -ET Emergency treatment (dental procedures performed in emergency situations should show the modifier 'ET')
- -F1 Left hand, second digit
- -F2 Left hand, third digit
- -F3 Left hand, fourth digit
- -F4 Left hand, fifth digit
- -F5 Right hand, thumb
- -F6 Right hand, second digit
- -F7 Right hand, third digit
- -F8 Right hand, fourth digit
- -F9 Right hand, fifth digit
- -FA Left hand, thumb
- -FP Service provided as part of medicaid family planning program
- -G1 Most recent URR reading of less than 60
- -G2 Most recent URR reading of 60 to 64.9
- -G3 Most recent URR reading of 65 to 69.9
- -G4 Most recent URR reading of 70 to 74.9
- -G5 Most recent URR reading of 75 or greater
- -G6 ESRD patient for whom less than six dialysis sessions have been provided in a month
- ● -G7 Pregnancy resulted from rape or incest or pregnancy certified by physician as life threatening
- ● -G8 Monitored anesthesia care (MAC) for deep complex, complicated, or markedly invasive surgical procedure
- ● -G9 Monitored anesthesia care for patient who has history of severe cardio-pulmonary condition
- -GA Waiver of liability statement on file
- -GC This service has been performed in part by a resident under the direction of a teaching physician
- -GE This service has been performed by a resident without the presence of a teaching physician under the primary care exception
- -GH Diagnostic mammogram converted from screening mammogram on same day
- -GJ "OPT OUT" physician or practitioner emergency or urgent service

● New Code ▲ Revised Code HCPCS 1999

- -GN Service delivered personally by a speech-language pathologist or under an outpatient speech-language pathology plan of care
- -GO Service delivered personally by an occupational therapist or under an outpatient occupational therapy plan of care
- -GP Service delivered personally by a physical therapist or under an outpatient physical therapy plan of care
- -GT Via interactive audio and video telecommunication systems
- -GX Service not covered by Medicare
- -K0 Lower extremity prosthesis functional level 0 — does not have the ability or potential to ambulate or transfer safely with or without assistance and a prosthesis does not enhance their quality of life or mobility
- -K1 Lower extremity prosthesis functional level 1 — has the ability or potential to use a prosthesis for transfers or ambulation on level surfaces at fixed cadence. Typical of the limited and unlimited household ambulator
- -K2 Lower extremity prosthesis functional level 2 — has the ability or potential for ambulation with the ability to traverse low level environmental barriers such as curbs, stairs or uneven surfaces. Typical of the limited community ambulator
- -K3 Lower extremity prosthesis functional level 3 — has the ability or potential for ambulation with variable cadence. Typical of the community ambulator who has the ability to transverse most environmental barriers and may have vocational, therapeutic, or exercise activity that demands prosthetic utilization beyond simple locomotion
- -K4 Lower extremity prosthesis functional level 4 — has the ability or potential for prosthetic ambulation that exceeds the basic ambulation skills, exhibiting high impact, stress, or energy levels, typical of the prosthetic demands of the child, active adult, or athlete
- -KA Add on option/accessory for wheelchair
- -KH DMEPOS item, initial claim, purchase or first month rental
- -KI DMEPOS item, second or third month rental
- -KJ DMEPOS item, parenteral enteral nutrition (PEN) pump or capped rental, months four to fifteen
- -KK Inhalation solution compounded from an FDA approved formulation
- -KL Product characteristics defined in medical policy are met
- -KM Replacement of facial prosthesis including new impression/moulage
- -KN Replacement of facial prosthesis using previous master model
- -KO Single drug unit dose formulation
- -KP First drug of a multiple drug unit dose formulation
- -KQ Second or subsequent drug of a multiple drug unit dose formulation
- -KS Glucose monitor supply for diabetic beneficiary not treated with insulin
- -LC Left circumflex coronary artery
- -LD Left anterior descending coronary artery
- -LL Lease/rental (use the 'LL' modifier when DME equipment rental is to be applied against the purchase price)
- -LR Laboratory round trip
- -LS FDA-monitored intraocular lens implant
- -LT Left side (used to identify procedures performed on the left side of the body)
- -MS Six month maintenance and servicing fee for reasonable and necessary parts and labor which are not covered under any manufacturer or supplier warranty
- -NR New when rented (use the 'NR' modifier when DME which was new at the time of rental is subsequently purchased)
- -NU New equipment
- -PL Progressive addition lenses
- -Q2 HCFA/ORD demonstration project procedure/service
- -Q3 Live kidney donor: services associated with postoperative medical complications directly related to the donation
- -Q4 Service for ordering/referring physician qualifies as a service exemption
- -Q5 Service furnished by a substitute physician under a reciprocal billing arrangement
- -Q6 Service furnished by a locum tenens physician
- -Q7 One Class A finding
- -Q8 Two Class B findings
- -Q9 One Class B and two Class C findings
- -QA FDA investigational device exemption
- -QB Physician providing service in a rural HPSA
- -QC Single channel monitoring
- -QD Recording and storage in solid state memory by a digital recorder
- -QE Prescribed amount of oxygen is less than 1 liter per minute (LPM)
- -QF Prescribed amount of oxygen exceeds 4 liters per minute (LPM) and portable oxygen is prescribed

-QG Prescribed amount of oxygen is greater than 4 liters per minute (LPM)

-QH Oxygen conserving device is being used with an oxygen delivery system

-QK Medical direction of two, three, or four concurrent anesthesia procedures involving qualified individuals

-QL Patient pronounced dead after ambulance called

-QM Ambulance service provided under arrangement by a provider of services

-QN Ambulance service furnished directly by a provider of services

-QP Documentation is on file showing that the laboratory test(s) was ordered individually or ordered as a CPT-recognized panel other than automated profile codes 80002-80019, G0058, G0059, and G0060

(-QR This modifier has been deleted)

-QS Monitored anesthesia care service

-QT Recording and storage on tape by an analog tape recorder

-QU Physician providing service in an urban HPSA

-QW CLIA waived test

-QX CRNA service: with medical direction by a physician

-QY Medical direction of one certified registered nurse anesthetist (CRNA) by an anesthesiologist

-QZ CRNA service: without medical direction by a physician

-RC Right coronary artery

-RP Replacement and repair -RP may be used to indicate replacement of dme, orthotic and prosthetic devices which have been in use for sometime. The claim shows the code for the part, followed by the 'RP' modifier and the charge for the part

-RR Rental (use the 'RR' modifier when DME is to be rented)

-RT Right side (used to identify procedures performed on the right side of the body)

-SF Second opinion ordered by a professional review organization (PRO) per section 9401, p.l. 99-272 (100% reimbursement — no Medicare deductible or coinsurance)

-SG Ambulatory surgical center (ASC) facility service

-T1 Left foot, second digit

-T2 Left foot, third digit

-T3 Left foot, fourth digit

-T4 Left foot, fifth digit

-T5 Right foot, great toe

-T6 Right foot, second digit

-T7 Right foot, third digit

-T8 Right foot, fourth digit

-T9 Right foot, fifth digit

-TA Left foot, great toe

-TC Technical component. Under certain circumstances, a charge may be made for the technical component alone. Under those circumstances the technical component charge is identified by adding modifier 'TC' to the usual procedure number. Technical component charges are institutional charges and not billed separately by physicians. However, portable x-ray suppliers only bill for technical component and should utilize modifier TC. The charge data from portable x-ray suppliers will then be used to build customary and prevailing profiles.

-UE Used durable medical equipment

-VP Aphakic patient

Ambulance Origin and Destination Modifiers

Single-digit modifiers for ambulance transport are used in combination in reporting services to HCFA. The first digit indicates the transport's place of origin, and the destination is indicated by the second digit.

D Diagnostic or therapeutic site other than 'P' or 'H' when these codes are used as origin codes

E Residential, domiciliary, custodial facility (other than an 1819 facility)

G Hospital-based dialysis facility (hospital or hospital-related)

H Hospital

I Site of transfer (e.g., airport or helicopter pad) between types of ambulance vehicles

J Non hospital-based dialysis facility

N Skilled nursing facility (SNF) (1819 facility)

P Physician's office (includes HMO non-hospital facility, clinic, etc.)

R Residence

S Scene of accident or acute event

X (Destination code only) Intermediate stop at physician's office on the way to the hospital (includes HMO non-hospital facility, clinic, etc.)

PET Scan Modifiers

Use the following single digit alpha characters in combination as two-character modifiers to indicate the results of a current PET scan and a previous test.

N Negative

E Equivocal

P   Positive, but not suggestive of extensive ischemia

S   Positive and suggestive of extensive ischemia (>20 percent of the left ventricle)

WHY YOU SHOULD BE USING HCPCS

The following summarizes why your practice should be using HCPCS codes:

1. HCFA mandated the use of HCPCS codes on Medicare claims, and many Medicaid offices also require them.
2. HCPCS codes improve a provider's ability to communicate services or supplies correctly without resorting to narrative descriptors.
3. Using HCPCS reduces resubmission of claims for correction or review. When an inaccurate code or incomplete narrative description is submitted, the claim's adjudicator must assign a code or return the claim. This time delay can be costly, and the payer's reassignment of the code may be incorrect.
4. Using up-to-date and accurate HCPCS codes on office routing slips allows office staff to assign fees to services and supplies quickly and efficiently, saving you both time and money.
5. Making your coding system compatible with your carrier's helps expedite claims processing.
6. Consistent submission of "clean claims" (those with all information necessary for processing) will help avoid being targeted for an audit by your carrier for frequent development of your claims.
7. Using HCPCS is essential for:
    - If you bill Medicare for an injection using only a CPT code, you will not be reimbursed correctly. You must identify the drug administered with the correct Level II or III HCPCS code.
    - Supplies billed as "Over and above those usually included with the office visit" (CPT code 99070) will generally not be reimbursed unless identified with Level II or III HCPCS codes.

WHY OUR HCPCS?

With the array of coding books available to physician offices, you need solid reasons for choosing Medicode's *HCPCS 2000*.

Up-To-Date

Medicode's *HCPCS 2000* contains all mandated changes and new codes for use as of January 1, 2000. Deleted codes have also been indicated and cross-referenced to active codes when possible. All new codes have been added to the appropriate sections, eliminating the time-consuming step of looking in two places for the code you need.

Easy To Use

Simply refer to the Table of Contents for the type of service provided, and our convenient color tabs give you easy access to that range of codes.

Coding Tips

Information making code selection easier and more accurate is included with many codes. These coding tips provide information about government policy, direct the reader to the brand-name drugs associated with generic drug codes, and offer general coding guidelines. Medicode's *HCPCS 2000* coding tips are printed in blue to differentiate them from the official government HCPCS text, printed in black.

Medicare Carriers Manual and *Coverage Issues Manual* references are also listed with each code as appropriate.

Modifier Information

HCPCS Level II modifiers are listed on the line(s) following the code. This not only reminds coders to report modifiers with their HCPCS Level II codes, but also identifies which modifiers are appropriate for each HCPCS code. Again, these modifiers are printed in blue to differentiate them from official government text. HCPCS Level I (CPT) modifiers can also sometimes apply to HCPCS Level II codes, but because of AMA copyright, they are not presented here.

Expanded Index

Since HCPCS is organized by code number rather than by service or supply name, our extensive index allows you to locate the code you need without looking through individual ranges of codes. Just look up the medical or surgical supply, service, orthotic, prosthetic, or generic or brand name drug you need and you will be directed to the appropriate code(s). This index also references many of the brand names by which these items are known.

Table of Drugs and Cross-Referencing

You now have three methods to cross-reference from brand name to generic drugs with *HCPCS 2000*. In the listing of codes, brand name items are enclosed within parentheses following the generic name. The brand names listed are examples only and may not be inclusive of all products available for that type of drug.

Our new table of drugs lists all J, G, and K code generic drugs with amount, route of administration, and code numbers. Brand name drugs are also listed in the table with a reference to the appropriate generic drug.

Color-coded Coverage Instructions

Our HCPCS provides colored symbols for each coverage and reimbursement instruction. A legend to these symbols is provided on the bottom of each two-page spread.

⊘   Codes that are not covered by or valid for Medicare are preceded by this symbol. The pertinent *Coverage Issues Manual* (CIM) and *Medicare Carriers Manual* (MCM) reference numbers are also given explaining why a particular code is not covered. These numbers refer to appendixes A and B, where we have listed the CIM and MCM references, whenever possible.

➡ Issues that are left to "Carrier Discretion" are noted with this symbol. Contact your carrier for specific coverage information on those codes.

❓ This is the symbol for "Special Coverage Instructions" and means that special coverage instructions apply to that code. These special instructions are also typically given in the form of CIM and MCM reference numbers. Again, appendixes A and B list the CIM and MCM references.

☑ Many codes in HCPCS report quantities that may not coincide with quantities available in the marketplace. For instance, a HCPCS code for a disposable syringe reports one syringe, but the syringe is generally sold in a box of 100, and "100" must be indicated in the quantity box on the HCFA claim form to ensure proper reimbursement. This symbol indicates that care should be taken to verify quantities in this code.

Some codes are cross-referenced to other Level II codes, specific CPT codes, or to CPT in general. These are indicated with "Cross-reference" plus the CPT or Level II code(s).

HCPCS 2000 uses CPT conventions to indicate new, revised, and deleted codes. A black circle (●) precedes a new code to be used only for services or supplies provided on or after January 1, 2000; a black triangle (▲) precedes a code with revised terminology or rules; codes deleted from last year's active list appear in parentheses with a cross-reference to an active code if HCFA has determined one.

HOW TO USE HCPCS 2000

Using Medicode's *HCPCS 2000* is very simple because the majority of the codes listed in this book can be referenced in the Index. Check here for the name of the service, procedure, or supply provided to find the appropriate code or range of codes. If the service is not in the Index, refer to the Table of Contents at the front of the book where we have listed the general categories and subcategories of services to help you narrow your search for the proper codes.

NEW CODES

A4280	Adhesive skin support attachment for use with external breast prosthesis, each
A4369	Ostomy skin barrier, liquid (spray, brush, etc), per oz
A4370	Ostomy skin barrier, paste, per oz
A4371	Ostomy skin barrier, powder, per oz
A4372	Ostomy skin barrier, solid 4x4 or equivalent, standard wear, with built-in convexity, each
A4373	Ostomy skin barrier, with flange (solid, flexible or accordion), standard wear, with built-in convexity, any size, each
A4374	Ostomy skin barrier, with flange (solid, flexible or accordion), extended wear, with built-in convexity, any size, each
A4375	Ostomy pouch, drainable, with faceplate attached, plastic, each
A4376	Ostomy pouch, drainable, with faceplate attached, rubber, each
A4377	Ostomy pouch, drainable, for use on faceplate, plastic, each
A4378	Ostomy pouch, drainable, for use on faceplate, rubber, each
A4379	Ostomy pouch, urinary, with faceplate attached, plastic, each
A4380	Ostomy pouch, urinary, with faceplate attached, rubber, each
A4381	Ostomy pouch, urinary, for use on faceplate, plastic, each
A4382	Ostomy pouch, urinary, for use on faceplate, heavy plastic, each
A4383	Ostomy pouch, urinary, for use on faceplate, rubber, each
A4384	Ostomy faceplate equivalent, silicone ring, each
A4385	Ostomy skin barrier, solid 4x4 or equivalent, extended wear, without built-in convexity, each
A4386	Ostomy skin barrier, with flange (solid, flexible or accordion), extended wear, without built-in convexity, any size, each
A4387	Ostomy pouch closed, with standard wear barrier attached, with built-in convexity (1 piece), each
A4388	Ostomy pouch, drainable, with extended wear barrier attached, without built-in convexity (1 piece)
A4389	Ostomy pouch, drainable, with standard wear barrier attached, with built-in convexity (1 piece), each
A4390	Ostomy pouch, drainable, with extended wear barrier attached, with built-in convexity (1 piece), each
A4391	Ostomy pouch, urinary, with extended wear barrier attached, without built-in convexity (1 piece), each
A4392	Ostomy pouch, urinary, with standard wear barrier attached, with built-in convexity (1 piece), each
A4393	Ostomy pouch, urinary, with extended wear barrier attached, with built-in convexity (1 piece), each
A4394	Ostomy deodorant for use in ostomy pouch, liquid, per fluid ounce

A4395	Ostomy deodorant for use in ostomy pouch, solid, per tablet
A5508	For diabetics only, deluxe feature of off-the-shelf depth-inlay shoe or custom-molded shoe, per shoe
A7000	Canister, disposable, used with suction pump, each
A7001	Canister, non-disposable, used with suction pump, each
A7002	Tubing, used with suction pump, each
A7003	Administration set, with small volume nonfiltered pneumatic nebulizer, disposable
A7004	Small volume nonfiltered pneumatic nebulizer, disposable
A7005	Administration set, with small volume nonfiltered pneumatic nebulizer, non-disposable
A7006	Administration set, with small volume filtered pneumatic nebulizer
A7007	Large volume nebulizer, disposable, unfilled, used with aerosol compressor
A7008	Large volume nebulizer, disposable, prefilled, used with aerosol compressor
A7009	Reservoir bottle, non-disposable, used with large volume ultrasonic nebulizer
A7010	Corrugated tubing, disposable, used with large volume nebulizer, 100 feet
A7011	Corrugated tubing, non-disposable, used with large volume nebulizer, 10 feet
A7012	Water collection device, used with large volume nebulizer
A7013	Filter, disposable, used with aerosol compressor
A7014	Filter, nondisposable, used with aerosol compressor or ultrasonic generator
A7015	Aerosol mask, used with DME nebulizer
A7016	Dome and mouthpiece, used with small volume ultrasonic nebulizer
A7017	Nebulizer, durable, glass or autoclavable plastic, bottle type, not used with oxygen
A9504	Supply of radiopharmaceutical diagnostic imaging agent, technetium tc 99m apcitide
A9900	Miscellaneous supply, accessory, and/or service component of another HCPCS code
A9901	Delivery, set up, and/or dispensing service component of another HCPCS code
D0170	Re-evaluation — limited, problem focused (Established patient; not post-operative visit)
D0277	Vertical bitewings — 7 to 8 films
D0350	Oral/facial images (includes intra and extraoral images)
D0472	Accession of tissue, gross examination, preparation and transmission of written report
D0473	Accession of tissue, gross and microscopic examination, preparation and transmission of written report
D0474	Accession of tissue, gross and microscopic examination, including assessment of surgical margins for presence of disease, preparation and transmission of written report
D0480	Processing and interpretation of cytologic smears, including the preparation and transmission of written report
D2337	Resin-based composite crown, anterior — permanent
D2388	Resin-based composite — four or more surfaces, posterior — permanent
D2542	Onlay — metallic — two surfaces
D2780	Crown — 3/4 cast high noble metal
D2781	Crown — 3/4 cast predominately base metal
D2782	Crown — 3/4 cast noble metal
D2783	Crown — 3/4 porcelain/ceramic
D2799	Provisional crown
D2953	Each additional cast post — same tooth
D2957	Each additional prefabricated post — same tooth
D3221	Gross pulpal debridement, primary and permanent teeth
D3331	Treatment of root canal obstruction; non-surgical access
D3332	Incomplete endodontic therapy; inoperable or fractured tooth
D3333	Internal root repair of perforation defects
D4245	Apically positioned flap
D4268	Surgical revision procedure, per tooth
D5867	Replacement of replaceable part of semi-precision or precision attachment (male or female component)
D5875	Modification of removable prosthesis following implant surgery
D6056	Prefabricated abutment

D6057	Custom abutment
D6058	Abutment supported porcelain/ceramic crown
D6059	Abutment supported porcelain fused to metal crown (high noble metal)
D6060	Abutment supported porcelain fused to metal crown (predominantly base metal)
D6061	Abutment supported porcelain fused to metal crown (noble metal)
D6062	Abutment supported cast metal crown (high noble metal)
D6063	Abutment supported cast metal crown (predominantly base metal)
D6064	Abutment supported cast metal crown (noble metal)
D6065	Implant supported porcelain/ceramic crown
D6066	Implant supported porcelain fused to metal crown (titanium, titanium alloy, high noble metal)
D6067	Implant supported metal crown (titanium, titanium alloy, high noble metal)
D6068	Abutment supported retainer for porcelain/ceramic FPD
D6069	Abutment supported retainer for porcelain fused to metal FPD (high noble metal)
D6070	Abutment supported retainer for porcelain fused to metal FPD (predominately base metal)
D6071	Abutment supported retainer for porcelain fused to metal FPD (noble metal)
D6072	Abutment supported retainer for cast metal FPD (high noble metal)
D6073	Abutment supported retainer for cast metal FPD (predominately base metal)
D6074	Abutment supported retainer for cast metal FPD (noble metal)
D6075	Implant supported retainer for ceramic FPD
D6076	Implant supported retainer for porcelain fused to metal FPD (titanium, titanium alloy, or high noble metal)
D6077	Implant supported retainer for cast metal FPD (titanium, titanium alloy, or high noble metal)
D6078	Implant/abutment supported fixed denture for completely edentulous arch
D6079	Implant/abutment supported fixed denture for partially edentulous arch
D6245	Pontic — porcelain/ceramic
D6519	Inlay/onlay — porcelain/ceramic
D6548	Retainer — porcelain/ceramic for resin bonded fixed prosthesis
D6740	Crown — porcelain/ceramic
D6781	Crown — 3/4 cast predominately based metal
D6782	Crown — 3/4 cast noble metal
D6783	Crown — 3/4 porcelain/ceramic
D6976	Each additional cast post — same tooth
D6977	Each additional prefabricated post — same tooth
D7471	Removal of exostosis — per site
D7871	Non-arthroscopic lysis and lavage
D7997	Appliance removal (not by dentist who placed appliance), includes removal of archbar
D8691	Repair of orthodontic appliance
D8692	Replacement of lost or broken retainer
D9241	Intravenous sedation/analgesia — first 30 minutes
D9242	Intravenous sedation/analgesia — each additional 15 minutes
D9248	Non-intravenous conscious sedation
D9911	Application of desensitizing resin for cervical and/or root surface, per tooth
D9971	Odontoplasty 1–2 teeth; includes removal of enamel projections
D9972	External bleaching — per arch
D9973	External bleaching — per tooth
D9974	Internal bleaching — per tooth
E0144	Enclosed, framed folding walker, wheeled, with posterior seat
E0590	Dispensing fee covered drug administered through DME nebulizer suction pump, home model, portable
E0602	Breast pump, all types
E0616	Implantable cardiac event recorder with memory, activator and programmer
E0779	Ambulatory infusion pump, mechanical, reusable, for infusion 8 hours or greater
E0780	Ambulatory infusion pump, mechanical, reusable, for infusion less than 8 hours
E1390	Oxygen concentrator, capable of delivering 85 percent or greater oxygen concentration at the prescribed flow rate

E1900	Synthesized speech augmentative communication device with dynamic display routine venipuncture for collection of specimen(s)
G0102	Prostate cancer screening; digital rectal examination
G0103	Prostate cancer screening; prostate specific antigen test (PSA), total
G0129	Occupational therapy requiring the skills of a qualified occupational therapist, furnished as a component of a partial hospitalization treatment program, per day
G0151	Services of physical therapist in home health setting, each 15 minutes
G0152	Services of occupational therapist in home helth setting, each 15 minutes
G0153	Services of sppech and language pathologist in home health setting, each 15 minutes
G0154	Services of skilled nurse in home health setting, each 15 minutes
G0155	Services of clinical social worker in home health setting, each 15 minutes
G0156	Services of home health aide in home health setting, each 15 minutes
G0159	Percutaneous thrombectomy and/or revision, arteriovenous fistula, autogenous or nonautogenous dialysis graft
G0160	Cryosurgical ablation of localized prostate cancer, primary treatment only (post operative irrigations and aspiration of sloughing tissue included)
G0161	Ultrasonic guidance for interstitial placement of cyosurgical probes
G0163	Positron emission tomography (PET), whole body, for recurrence of colorectal metastatic cancer
G0164	Positron emission tomography (PET), whole body, for staging and characterization of lymphoma
G0165	Positron Emission tomography (PET), whole body, for recurrence of melanoma or melanoma metastatic cancer
G0166	External counterpulsation, per treatment session
G0167	Hyperbaric oxygen treatment not requiring physician attendance, per treatment session
G0168	Wound closure utilizing tissue adhesive(s) only
G0169	Removal of devitalized tissue, without use of anesthesia (conscious sedation, local, regional, general)
G0170	Application of tissue cultured skin grafts, including bilaminate skin substitutes or neodermis, including site preparation, initial 25 sq cm
G0171	Application of tissue cultured skin grafts, including bilaminate skin substitutes or neodermis, including site preparation, each additional 25 sq cm
G0172	Training and educational services furnished as a component of a partial hospitalization treatment program, per day
J0200	Injection, alatrofloxacin mesylate, 100 mg
J0456	Injection, azithromycin, 500 mg
J1327	Injection, eptifibatide, 5 mg
J1438	Injection, etanercept, 25 mg (Code may be used for Medicare when drug administered under the direct supervision of a physician, not for use when drug is self administered)
J1450	Injection fluconazole, 200 mg
J1745	Injection infliximab, 10 mg
J1750	Injection, iron dextran, 50 mg
J2352	Injection, octreotide acetate, 1 mg
J2500	Injection, paricalcitol, 5 mcg
J2543	Injection, piperacillin sodium 1g, with tazobactam sodium, 0.125 g; total injection, 1.125 gm
J2780	Injection, ranitidine hydrochloride, 25 mg
J3245	Injection, tirofiban hydrochloride, 12.5 mg
J7198	Anti-inhibitor, per i.u.
J7199	Hemophilia clotting factor, not otherwise classified
J7502	Cyclosporine, oral, 100 mg
J7515	Cyclosporine, oral, 25 mg
J7516	Cyclosporin, parenteral, 250 mg
J7517	Mycophenolate mofetil, oral, 250 mg
J7608	Acetylcysteine, inhalation solution administered through DME, unit dose form, per gram
J7618	Albuterol, inhalation solution administered through DME, concentrated form, per milligram
J7619	Albuterol, inhalation solution administered through DME, unit dose form, per milligram
J7628	Bitolterol mesylate, inhalation solution administered through DME, concentrated form, per milligram
J7629	Bitolterol mesylate, inhalation solution administered through DME, unit dose form, per milligram

J7631	Cromolyn sodium, inhalation solution administered through DME, unit dose form, per 10 milligrams
J7635	Atropine, inhalation solution administered through DME, concentrated form, per milligram
J7636	Atropine, inhalation solution administered through DME, unit dose form, per milligram
J7637	Dexamethasone, inhalation solution administered through DME, concentrated form, per milligram
J7638	Dexamethasone, inhalation solution administered through DME, unit dose form, per milligram
J7639	Dornase alpha, inhalation solution administered through DME, unit dose form, per milligram
J7642	Glycopyrrolate, inhalation solution administered through DME, concentrated form, per milligram
J7643	Glycopyrrolate, inhalation solution administered through DME, unit dose form, per milligram
J7644	Ipratropium bromide, inhalation solution administered through DME, unit dose form, per milligram
J7648	Isoetharine hcl, inhalation solution administered through DME, concentrated form, per milligram
J7649	Isoetharine hcl, inhalation solution administered through DME, unit dose form, per milligram
J7658	Isoproterenol HCl, inhalation solution administered through DME, concentrated form, per milligram
J7659	Isoproterenol HCl, inhalation solution administered through DME, unit dose form, per milligram
J7668	Metaproterenol sulfate, inhalation solution administered through DME, concentrated form, per 10 milligrams
J7669	Metaproterenol sulfate, inhalation solution administered through DME, unit dose form, per 10 milligrams
J7680	Terbutaline sulfate, inhalation solution administered through DME, concentrated form, per milligram
J7681	Terbutaline sulfate, inhalation solution administered through DME, unit dose form, per milligram
J7682	Tobramycin, unit dose form, 300 mg, inhalation solution, administered through DME
J7683	Triamcinolone, inhalation solution administered through DME, concentrated form, per milligram
J7684	Triamcinolone, inhalation solution administered through DME, unit dose form, per milligram
J8510	Bulsulfan; oral, 2 mg
J8520	Capecitabine, oral, 150 mg
J8521	Capecitabine, oral, 500 mg
J9001	Doxorubicin hydrochloride, all lipid formulations, 10 mg
J9355	Trastuzumab, 10 mg
J9357	Valrubicin, intravesical, 200 mg
L3807	WHFO, extension assist, with inflatable Palmer air support, with or without thumb extension
L9900	Orthotic and prosthetic supply, accessory, and/or service component of another HCPCS l code sales tax, orthotic/prosthetic/other office visits with two or more modalities to the same area, initial 30 minutes, each visit.
P9023	Plasma, pooled multiple donor, solvent/detergent treated, frozen, each unit
Q0187	Factor VIIa (coagulation factor, recombinant) per 1.2 mg
Q1001	New technology intraocular lense category 1 as defined in Federal Register notice
Q1002	New technology intraocular lense category 2 as defined in Federal Register notice
Q1003	New technology intraocular lense category 3 as defined in Federal Register notice
Q1004	New technology intraocular lense category 4 as defined in Federal Register notice
Q1005	New technology intraocular lense category 5 as defined in Federal Register notice
S0009	Injection, Butorphanol Tartrate, 1mg
S0010	Injection, somatrem, 5 mg
S0011	Injection, somatropin, 5 mg
S0012	Butorphanol tartrate, nasal spray, 25 mg
S0014	Tacrine hydrochloride, 10 mg
S0016	Injection, amikacin sulfate, 500 mg
S0017	Injection, aminocaproic acid, 5 grams
S0020	Injection, bupivicaine hydrochloride, 30 ml
S0021	Injection, ceftoperazone sodium, 1 gram
S0023	Injection, cimetidine hydrochloride, 300 mg
S0024	Injection, ciprofloxacin, 200 mg
S0028	Injection, famotidine, 20 mg
S0029	Injection, fluconazole, 400 mg

S0030	Injection, metronidazole, 500 mg
S0032	Injection, nafcillin sodium, 2 grams
S0034	Injection, ofloxacin, 400 mg
S0039	Injection, sulfamethoxazole and trimethoprim, 10 ml
S0040	Injection, ticarcillin disodium and clavulanate potassium, 3.1 grams
S0071	Injection, acyclovir sodium, 50 mg
S0072	Injection, amikacin sulfate, 100 mg
S0073	Injection, aztreonam, 500 mg
S0074	Injection, cefotetan disodium, 500 mg
S0077	Injection, clindamycin phosphate, 300 mg
S0078	Injection, fosphenytoin sodium, 750 mg
S0080	Injection, pentamidine isethionate, 300 mg
S0081	Injection, piperacillin sodium, 500 mg
S0090	Sildenafil citrate, 25 mg
S0096	Injection, itraconazole, 200 mg
S0097	Injection, ibutilide fumarate, 1 mg
S0098	Injection, sodium ferric gluconate complex in sucrose, 62.5 mg
S0601	Screening proctoscopy
S0605	Digital rectal examination, annual
S0610	Annual gynecological examination, new patient
S0612	Annual gynecological examination, established patient
S0620	Routine ophthalmological examination including refraction; new patient
S0621	Routine ophthalmological examination including refraction; established patient
S0800	Laser in situ keratomileusis (LASIK)
S0810	Photorefractive keratectomy (PRK)
S2050	Donor enterectomy, with preparation and maintenance of allograft; from cadaver donor
S2052	Transplantation of small intestine allograft
S2053	Transplantation of small intestine and liver allografts
S2054	Transplantation of multivisceral organs
S2055	Harvesting of donor multivisceral organs, with preparation and maintenance of allografts; from cadaver donor
S2109	Autologous chondrocyte transplantation (preparation of autologous cultured chondrocytes)
S2190	Subcutaneous implantation of medication pellet(s)
S2204	Transmyocardial laser revascularization
S2205	Minimally invasive direct coronary artery bypass surgery involving mini-thoracotomy or mini-sternotomy surgery, performed under direct vision; using arterial graft(s), single coronary arterial graft
S2206	Minimally invasive direct coronary artery bypass surgery involving mini-thoracotomy or mini-sternotomy surgery, performed under direct vision; using arterial graft(s), two coronary arterial grafts
S2207	Minimally invasive direct coronary artery bypass surgery involving mini-thoracotomy or mini-sternotomy surgery, performed under direct vision; using venous graft only, single coronary venous graft
S2208	Minimally invasive direct coronary artery bypass surgery involving mini-thoracotomy or mini-sternotomy surgery, performed under direct vision; using single arterial and venous graft(s), single venous graft
S2209	Minimally invasive direct coronary artery bypass surgery involving mini-thoracotomy or mini-sternotomy surgery, performed under direct vision; using two arterial grafts and single venous graft
S2210	Cryosurgical ablation (in situ destruction) of tumorous tissue, one or more lesions; liver
S2300	Arthroscopy, shoulder, surgical; with thermally-induced capsulorrhaphy
S2350	Diskectomy, anterior, with decompression of spinal cord and/or nerve root(s), including osteophytectomy; lumbar, single interspace
S2351	Diskectomy, anterior, with decompression of spinal cord and/or nerve root(s), including osteophytectomy; lumbar, each additional interspace (list separately in addition to code for primary procedure)
S3645	HIV-1 antibody testing of oral mucosal transudate
S3650	Saliva test, hormone level; during menopause
S3652	Saliva test, hormone level; to assess preterm labor risk
S8035	Magnetic source imaging
S8040	Topographic brain mapping
S8048	Isolated limb perfusion
S8049	Intraoperative radiation therapy (single administration)

S8060	Supply of contrast material for use in echocardiography (use in addition to echocardiography code)
S8092	Electron beam computed tomography (also known as ultrafast CT, cine CT)
S8095	Wig (for medically-induced hair loss)
S8096	Portable peak flow meter
S8110	Peak expiratory flow rate (physician services)
S8200	Chest compression vest
S8205	Chest compression system generator and hoses (for use with chest compression vest - S8200)
S8260	Oral orthotic for treatment of sleep apnea, includes fitting, fabrication, and materials
S8300	Sacral nerve stimulation test lead kit
S8950	Complex lymphedema therapy, each 15 minutes
S9001	Home uterine monitor with or without associated nursing services
S9022	Digital subtraction angiography (use in addition to CPT code for the procedure for further identification)
S9023	Xenon regional cerebral blood flow studies
S9024	Paranasal sinus ultrasound
S9033	Gait analysis
S9055	Procuren or other growth factor preparation to promote wound healing
S9056	Coma stimulation per diem
S9075	Smoking cessation treatment
S9085	Meniscal allograft transplantation
S9090	Vertebral axial decompression, per session
S9122	Home health aide or certified nurse assistant, providing care in the home; per hour
S9123	Nursing care, in the home; by registered nurse, per hour
S9124	Nursing care, in the home; by licensed practical nurse, per hour
S9125	Respite care, in the home, per diem
S9126	Hospice care, in the home, per diem
S9127	Social work visit, in the home, per diem
S9128	Speech therapy, in the home, per diem
S9129	Occupational therapy, in the home, per diem
S9140	Diabetic management program, follow-up visit to non-MD provider
S9141	Diabetic management program, follow-up visit to MD provider
S9455	Diabetic management program, group session
S9460	Diabetic management program, nurse visit
S9465	Diabetic management program, dietitian visit
S9470	Nutritional counseling, dietitian visit
S9472	Cardiac rehabilitation program, non-physician provider, per diem
S9473	Pulmonary rehabilitation program, non-physician provider, per diem
S9474	Enterostomal therapy by a registered nurse certified in enterostomal therapy, per diem
S9475	Ambulatory setting substance abuse treatment or detoxification services, per diem
S9480	Intensive outpatient psychiatric services, per diem
S9485	Crisis intervention mental health services, per diem
S9524	Nursing services related to home iv therapy, per diem
S9527	Insertion of a peripherally inserted central venous catheter (PICC), including nursing services and all supplies
S9528	Insertion of midline central venous catheter, including nursing services and all supplies
S9543	Administration of medication, intramuscularly, epidurally or subcutaneously, in the home setting, including all nursing care, equipment, and supplies; per diem
S9990	Services provided as part of a phase II clinical trial
S9991	Services provided as part of a phase III clinical trial
S9992	Transportation costs to and from trial location and local transportation costs (e.g., fares for taxicab or bus) for clinical trial participant and one caregiver/companion
S9994	Lodging costs (e.g., hotel charges) for clinical trial participant and one caregiver/companion
S9996	Meals for clinical trial participant and one caregiver/companion
S9999	Sales tax

CHANGED CODES

A4556	Electrodes, (e.g., Apnea monitor), per pair
A4557	Lead wires, (e.g., Apnea monitor), per pair

A5126	Adhesive or non-adhesive; disk or foam pad
D2650	Inlay — resin-based composite composite/resin — one surface
D2651	Inlay — resin-based composite composite/resin — two surfaces
D2652	Inlay — resin-based composite composite/resin — three or more surfaces
D2662	Onlay — resin-based composite composite/resin — two surfaces
D2663	Onlay — resin-based composite composite/resin — three surfaces
D2664	Onlay — resin-based composite composite/resin — four or more surfaces
D3220	Therapeutic pulpotomy (excluding final restoration) — removal of pulp coronal to the dentinocemental junction and application of medicament
D4266	Guided tissue regeneration — resorbable barrier, per site, per tooth
D4267	Guided tissue regeneration — nonresorbable barrier, per site, (includes membrane removal)
D7285	Biopsy of oral tissue — hard (bone, tooth) See also codes 20220, 20225, 20240, 20245.
D7286	Biopsy of oral tissue — soft (all others) See also code 40808.
D7670	Alveolus — stabilization of teeth, closed reduction splinting. See also CPT.
D7941	Osteotomy — mandibular rami. See also codes 21193, 21195, 21196.
D9230	Analgesia, anxiolysis, inhalation of nitrous oxide
D9410	House/extrended care facility call. See also CPT.
E0155	Wheel attachment, rigid pick-up walker, per pair seat attachment, walker
E0158	Leg extensions for walker, per set of four (4)
E0450	Volume ventilator, stationary or portable, with back-up rate feature, used with invasive interface (e.g., Tracheostomy tube)
E0781	Ambulatory infusion pump, single or multiple channels, electric or battery operated, with administrative equipment, worn by patient
J0270	Injection, alprostadil, 1.25 mcg (code may be used for Medicare when drug administered under direct supervision of a physician, not for use when drug is self-administered)
J0275	Alprostadil urethral suppository (code may be used for Medicare when drug administered under direct supervision of a physician, not for use when drug is self-administered)
J0290	Injection, ampicillin sodium, 500 mg
J0690	Injection, cefazolin sodium, 500 mg
J1100	Injection, dexamethosone sodium phosphate, up to 4 mg/ml
J1260	Injection, dolasetron mesylate, 10 mg
J1825	Injection, interferon beta-1a, 33 mcg (code may be used for Medicare when drug administered under direct supervision of a physician not for use when drug is self-administered)
J1830	Injection interferon beta-1b, 0.25 mg (code may be used for Medicare when drug administered under direct supervision of a physician not for use when drug is self-administered)
J3030	Injection, sumatriptan succinate, 6 mg (code may be used for Medicare when drug administered under direct supervision of a physician not for use when drug is self-administered)
J3240	Injection, thyrotropin alpha, 0.9 mg
J3370	Injection, vancomycin HCl, 500 mg
J7500	Azathioprine, oral, 50 mg
J7501	Azathioprine, parenteral, 100 mg
J7504	Lymphocyte immune globulin, antithymocyte globulin, parenteral, 250 mg
K0031	Safety belt/pelvic strap, each
K0065	Spoke protectors, each
K0100	Wheelchair adapter for amputee, pair (device used to compensate for transfer of weight due to lost limbs to maintain proper balance)
K0101	One-arm drive attachment, each
K0102	Crutch and cane holder, each
K0104	Cylinder tank carrier, each
K0105	IV hanger, each
L4392	Replace soft interface material, static AFO
L4396	Static AFO for positioning, pressure reduction, may be used for minimal ambulation
L5925	Addition, endoskeletal system, above knee, knee disarticulation or hip disarticulation, manual lock
L5968	Addition to lower limb prosthesis, multiaxial ankle with swing phase active dorsiflexion feature

L5988 Addition to lower limb prosthesis, vertical shock reducing pylon feature

L6693 Upper extremity addition, locking elbow, forearm counterbalance

L8435 Prosthetic sock, multiple ply, upper limb, each

DELETED CODES

A4363	D0471	D2210	D2810	D4250	D7470
D7942	D9240	E0452	E0453	E1400	E1401
E1402	E1403	E1404	G0133	J1760	J1770
J1780	J7196	J7503	K0109	K0119	K0120
K0121	K0122	K0123	K0137	K0138	K0139
K0168	K0169	K0170	K0171	K0172	K0173
K0174	K0175	K0176	K0177	K0178	K0179
K0180	K0181	K0190	K0191	K0192	K0193
K0194	K0277	K0278	K0279	K0284	K0400
K0401	K0412	K0417	K0418	K0419	K0420
K0421	K0422	K0423	K0424	K0425	K0426
K0427	K0428	K0429	K0430	K0431	K0432
K0433	K0434	K0435	K0436	K0437	K0438
K0439	K0453	K0503	K0504	K0505	K0506
K0507	K0508	K0509	K0511	K0512	K0513
K0514	K0515	K0516	K0518	K0519	K0520
K0521	K0522	K0523	K0524	K0525	K0526
K0527	K0528	K0530	L4310	L4320	L4390
M0101	P9014	P9015	P9610	Q0068	Q0132
Q0159	Q0162	Q0182			

HCPCS ABBREVIATIONS AND ACRONYMS

AMP	ampule
A-V	arteriovenous
AFO	ankle-foot orthosis
AICC	anti-inhibitor coagulant complex
AK	above the knee
ALS	advanced life support
ASC	ambulatory surgery center
AVF	arteriovenous fistula
BICROS	bilateral routing of signals
BK	below the knee
BLS	basic life support
CAPD	continuous ambulatory peritoneal dialysis
cc	cubic centimeter
CCPD	continuous cycling peritoneal dialysis
CIM	Coverage Issues Manual
cm	centimeter
CMN	certificate of medical necessity
CP	clinical psychologist
CPAP	continuous positive airway pressure
CPT	Current Procedural Terminology
CRF	chronic renal failure
CRNA	certified registered nurse anesthetist
CROS	contralateral routing of signals
CSW	clinical social worker
CTLSO	cervical-thoracic-lumbar-sacral orthosis
cu	cubic
DME	durable medical equipment
DMEPOS	durable medical equipment, prosthetics, orthotics and other supplies
DMERC	durable medical equipment regional carrier
ECF	extended care facility
ECG	electrocardiogram
EEG	electroencephalogram
EKG	electrocardiogram
EMG	electromyography
EO	elbow orthosis
EPO	epoetin alfa
EPSDT	early periodic screening, diagnosis and treatment
ESRD	end-stage renal disease
FDA	Food and Drug Administration
ft	foot
HCFA	Health Care Financing Administration
HCl	hydrochloric acid, hydrochloride
HCPCS	Health Care Financing Administration's Common Procedure Coding System
HCT, hct	hematocrit
HKAFO	hip-knee-ankle-foot orthosis
HPSA	health professional shortage area
HO	hip orthosis
ICF	intermediate care facility
ICU	intensive care unit
IM	intramuscular
INF	infusion
INH	inhalation solution
INJ	injection
IOL	intraocular lens
i.p.	interphalangeal
IPD	intermittent peritoneal dialysis
IPPB	intermittent positive pressure breathing
IT	intrathecal administration
IU	international units
IV	intravenous
KAFO	knee-ankle-foot orthosis
KO	knee orthosis
KOH	potassium hydroxide
lbs	pounds
LPM	liters per minute
LSO	lumbar-sacral orthosis
MCM	Medicare Carriers Manual
MCP	monthly capitation payment
mg	milligram
ml	milliliter
mm	millimeter
m.p.	metacarpophalangeal
MRI	magnetic resonance imaging
NCI	National Cancer Institute
NEC	not elsewhere classified
NH	nursing home
NMES	neuromuscular electrical stimulation

NOC	not otherwise classified
NOS	not otherwise specified
OBRA	Omnibus Budget Reconciliation Act
OMT	osteopathic manipulation therapy
OSA	obstructive sleep apnea
OTH	other routes of administration
oz	ounce
PA	physician's assistant
PAR	parenteral
PEN	parenteral and enteral nutrition
PENS	percutaneous electrical nerve stimulation
PRO	peer review organization
SACH	solid ankle, cushion heel
SC	subcutaneous
SEWHO	shoulder-elbow-wrist-hand orthosis
SNF	skilled nursing facility
SO	shoulder orthosis
TABS	tablets
TENS	transcutaneous electrical nerve stimulator
THAKO	thoracic-hip-knee-ankle orthosis
U	unit
VAR	various routes of administration
WAK	wearable artificial kidney
WHFO	wrist-hand-finger orthosis

Transportation Services Including Ambulance
A0000–A0999

Ambulance Origin and Destination modifiers used with Transportation Service codes are single-digit modifiers used in combination in boxes 12 and 13 of HCFA form 1491. The first digit indicates the transport's place of origin, and the destination is indicated by the second digit. The modifiers most commonly used are:

D	Diagnostic or therapeutic site other than 'P' or 'H' when these codes are used as origin codes
E	Residential, domiciliary, custodial facility (other than an 1819 facility)
G	Hospital-based dialysis facility (hospital or hospital-related)
H	Hospital
I	Site of transfer (e.g., airport or helicopter pad) between types of ambulance
J	Non hospital-based dialysis facility
N	Skilled nursing facility (SNF) (1819 facility)
P	Physician's office (includes HMO non-hospital facility, clinic, etc.)
R	Residence
S	Scene of accident or acute event
X	(Destination code only) Intermediate stop at physician's office on the way to the hospital (includes HMO non-hospital facility, clinic, etc.)

Claims for transportation services fall under the jurisdiction of the local carrier.

⊘ **A0021** Ambulance service, outside state per mile, transport (Medicaid only). See also code A0030.
Cross-reference A0030

? **A0030** Ambulance service, conventional air service, transport, one way
MCM 2120.4
Air ambulance may be covered if the aircraft is specially designed for medical transport, patient condition warrants immediacy, and land conditions are such that conventional EMS transport would require 30 to 60 minutes or more. Report disposable supplies separately.

? **A0040** Ambulance service, air, helicopter service, transport
MCM 2120.4
Air ambulance may be covered if the aircraft is specially designed for medical transport, patient condition warrants immediacy, and land conditions are such that conventional EMS transport would require 30 to 60 minutes or more. Report disposable supplies separately.

? **A0050** Ambulance service, emergency, water, special transportation services
MCM 2120.1, MCM 2125.1
Water ambulance may be covered if the craft is specially designed for medical transport and the EMS crew consists of at least two members charged with patient care. Report disposable supplies separately.

⊘ **A0080** Nonemergency transportation: per mile — volunteer, with no vested or personal interest

⊘ **A0090** Nonemergency transportation: per mile — volunteer, interested individual, neighbor

⊘ **A0100** Nonemergency transportation: taxi — intracity

⊘ **A0110** Nonemergency transportation and bus, intra- or interstate carrier

⊘ **A0120** Nonemergency transportation mini-bus, mountain area transports, other non-profit transportation systems

⊘ **A0130** Nonemergency transportation: wheelchair van

⊘ **A0140** Nonemergency transportation and air travel (private or commercial), intra- or interstate

⊘ **A0160** Nonemergency transportation: per mile — caseworker or social worker

⊘ **A0170** Nonemergency transportation: ancillary: parking fees, tolls, other

⊘ **A0180** Nonemergency transportation: ancillary: lodging — recipient

⊘ **A0190** Nonemergency transportation: ancillary: meals — recipient

⊘ **A0200** Nonemergency transportation: ancillary: lodging — escort

⊘ **A0210** Nonemergency transportation: ancillary: meals — escort

➥ **A0225** Ambulance service, neonatal transport, base rate, emergency transport, one way

➥ **A0300** Ambulance service, basic life support (BLS), non-emergency transport, all inclusive (mileage and supplies)

➥ **A0302** Ambulance service, BLS, emergency transport, all inclusive (mileage and supplies)

➥ **A0304** Ambulance service, advanced life support (ALS), nonemergency transport, no specialized ALS services rendered, all inclusive (mileage and supplies)

➥ **A0306** Ambulance service, ALS, nonemergency transport, specialized ALS services rendered, all inclusive (mileage and supplies)

➥ **A0308** Ambulance service, ALS, emergency transport, no specialized ALS services rendered, all inclusive (mileage and supplies)

➥ **A0310** Ambulance service, ALS, emergency transport, specialized ALS services rendered, all inclusive (mileage and supplies)

HCPCS 2000   ⊘ Not covered by or valid for Medicare   ? Special coverage instructions   ➥ Carrier discretion

TRANSPORTATION SERVICES INCLUDING AMBULANCE

➥ **A0320** Ambulance service, BLS, non-emergency transport, supplies included, mileage separately billed

➥ **A0322** Ambulance service, BLS, emergency transport, supplies included, mileage separately billed

➥ **A0324** Ambulance service, ALS, non-emergency transport, no specialized ALS services rendered, supplies included, mileage separately billed

➥ **A0326** Ambulance service, ALS, non-emergency transport, specialized ALS services rendered, supplies included, mileage separately billed

➥ **A0328** Ambulance service, ALS, emergency transport, no specialized ALS services rendered, supplies included, mileage separately billed

➥ **A0330** Ambulance service, ALS, emergency transport, specialized ALS services rendered, supplies included, mileage separately billed

➥ **A0340** Ambulance service, BLS, nonemergency transport, mileage included, disposable supplies separately billed

➥ **A0342** Ambulance service, BLS, emergency transport, mileage included, disposable supplies separately billed

➥ **A0344** Ambulance service, ALS, nonemergency transport, no specialized ALS services rendered, mileage included, disposable supplies separately billed

➥ **A0346** Ambulance service, ALS, nonemergency transport, specialized ALS services rendered, mileage included, disposable supplies separately billed

➥ **A0348** Ambulance service, ALS, emergency transport, no specialized ALS services rendered, mileage included, disposable supplies separately billed

➥ **A0350** Ambulance service, ALS, emergency transport, specialized ALS services rendered, mileage included, disposable supplies separately billed

➥ **A0360** Ambulance service, BLS, nonemergency transport, mileage and disposable supplies separately billed

➥ **A0362** Ambulance service, BLS, emergency transport, mileage and disposable supplies separately billed

➥ **A0364** Ambulance service, ALS, nonemergency transport, no specialized ALS services rendered, mileage and disposable supplies separately billed

➥ **A0366** Ambulance service, ALS, nonemergency transport, specialized ALS services rendered, mileage and disposable supplies separately billed

➥ **A0368** Ambulance service, ALS, emergency transport, no specialized ALS services rendered, mileage and disposable supplies separately billed

➥ **A0370** Ambulance service, ALS, emergency transport, specialized ALS services rendered, mileage and disposable supplies separately billed

➥ **A0380** BLS mileage (per mile)

➥ **A0382** BLS routine disposable supplies

➥ **A0384** BLS specialized service disposable supplies; defibrillation (used by ALS ambulances and BLS ambulances in jurisdictions where defibrillation is permitted in BLS ambulances)

➥ **A0390** ALS mileage (per mile)

➥ **A0392** ALS specialized service disposable supplies; defibrillation (to be used only in jurisdictions where defibrillation cannot be performed by BLS ambulances)

➥ **A0394** ALS specialized service disposable supplies; IV drug therapy

➥ **A0396** ALS specialized service disposable supplies; esophageal intubation

➥ **A0398** ALS routine disposable supplies

Waiting Time Table

Units	Time		
1	½	to	1 hr.
2	1	to	1½ hrs.
3	1½	to	2 hrs.
4	2	to	2½ hrs.
5	2½	to	3 hrs.
6	3	to	3½ hrs.
7	3½	to	4 hrs.
8	4	to	4½ hrs.
9	4½	to	5 hrs.
10	5	to	5½ hrs.

➥ **A0420** Ambulance waiting time (ALS or BLS), one-half (1/2) hour increments

➥ **A0422** Ambulance (ALS or BLS) oxygen and oxygen supplies, life sustaining situation

➥ **A0424** Extra ambulance attendant, ALS or BLS (requires medical review)
Pertinent documentation to evaluate medical appropriateness should be included when this code is reported.

MEDICAL AND SURGICAL SUPPLIES

⊘ **A0888** Non-covered ambulance mileage, per mile (e.g., for miles traveled beyond closest appropriate facility)
MCM 2125

? **A0999** Unlisted ambulance service
MCM 2120.1, MCM 2125.1
Determine if an alternative national HCPCS Level II code, a local HCPCS Level III code, or a CPT code better describes the service being reported. This code should be used only if a more specific code is unavailable.

Medical and Surgical Supplies A4000–A8999

This section covers a wide variety of medical and surgical supplies, and some Durable Medical Equipment (DME), supplies and accessories. DME and the supplies, accessories, maintenance, and repair required to ensure the proper functioning of this equipment is generally covered by Medicare under the Prosthetic Devices provision.

Unless otherwise noted, these codes are to be filed with the Medicare local carrier, unless they represent an incidental service or supplies.

Miscellaneous Supplies

⊘ ☑ **A4206** Syringe with needle, sterile 1 cc, each
This code specifies a 1cc syringe but is also used to report 3/10cc or 1/2cc syringes.

⊘ ☑ **A4207** Syringe with needle, sterile 2 cc, each

⊘ ☑ **A4208** Syringe with needle, sterile 3 cc, each

⊘ ☑ **A4209** Syringe with needle, sterile 5 cc or greater, each

⊘ **A4210** Needle-free injection device, each
CIM 60-9
Sometimes covered by commercial payers with preauthorization and physician letter stating need (e.g., for insulin injection in young children). Medicare jurisdiction: DME regional carrier.

? **A4211** Supplies for self-administered injections
MCM 2049
When a drug that is usually injected by the patient (e.g., insulin or calcitonin) is injected by the physician, it is excluded from Medicare coverage unless administered in an emergency situation (e.g., diabetic coma).

➡ **A4212** Non coring needle or stylet with or without catheter

⊘ **A4213** Syringe, sterile, 20 cc or greater, each
Medicare jurisdiction: DME regional carrier.

➡ ☑ **A4214** Sterile saline or water, 30 cc vial
Medicare jurisdiction: DME regional carrier.

⊘ **A4215** Needles only, sterile, any size, each
Medicare jurisdiction: DME regional carrier.

? **A4220** Refill kit for implantable infusion pump
CIM 60-14
Implantable infusion pumps are covered by Medicare for 5-FUdR therapy for unresected liver or colorectal cancer and for opioid drug therapy for intractable pain. They are not covered by Medicare for heparin therapy for thromboembolic disease. Report drugs separately.

➡ **A4221** Supplies for maintenance of drug infusion catheter, per week (list drug separately)
Medicare jurisdiction: DME regional carrier.

➡ **A4222** Supplies for external drug infusion pump, per cassette or bag (list drug separately)
Medicare jurisdiction: DME regional carrier.

?☑ **A4230** Infusion set for external insulin pump, nonneedle cannula type
CIM 60-14
Covered by some commercial payers as ongoing supply to preauthorized pump. Medicare jurisdiction: DME regional carrier.

?☑ **A4231** Infusion set for external insulin pump, needle type
CIM 60-14
Covered by some commercial payers as ongoing supply to preauthorized pump. Medicare jurisdiction: DME regional carrier.

?☑ **A4232** Syringe with needle for external insulin pump, sterile, 3cc
CIM 60-14
Covered by some commercial payers as ongoing supply to preauthorized pump. Medicare jurisdiction: DME regional carrier.

⊘ ☑ **A4244** Alcohol or peroxide, per pint
Medicare jurisdiction: DME regional carrier.

⊘ ☑ **A4245** Alcohol wipes, per box
Medicare jurisdiction: DME regional carrier.

⊘ ☑ **A4246** Betadine or pHisoHex solution, per pint
Medicare jurisdiction: DME regional carrier.

⊘ ☑ **A4247** Betadine or iodine swabs/wipes, per box
Medicare jurisdiction: DME regional carrier.

⊘ ☑ **A4250** Urine test or reagent strips or tablets (100 tablets or strips)
MCM 2100
Medicare jurisdiction: DME regional carrier.

?☑ **A4253** Blood glucose test or reagent strips for home blood glucose monitor, per 50 strips
CIM 60-11
Medicare covers glucose strips for diabetic patients using home glucose monitoring devices prescribed by their physicians. Medicare jurisdiction: DME regional carrier. Some commercial payers also provide this coverage to non-insulin dependent diabetics.

?☑ **A4254** Replacement battery, any type, for use with medically necessary home blood glucose monitor owned by patient, each
CIM 60-11
Medicare covers glucose strips for diabetic patients using home glucose monitoring devices prescribed by their physicians. Medicare jurisdiction: DME regional carrier. Some commercial payers also provide this coverage to non-insulin dependent diabetics.

MEDICAL AND SURGICAL SUPPLIES

➥ ☑ **A4255** Platforms for home blood glucose monitor, 50 per box
Some Medicare carriers cover monitor platforms for diabetic patients using home glucose monitoring devices prescribed by their physicians. Medicare jurisdiction: DME regional carrier. Some commercial payers also provide this coverage to non-insulin dependent diabetics.

➥ **A4256** Normal, low, and high calibrator solution/chips
Some Medicare carriers cover calibration solutions or chips for diabetic patients using home glucose monitoring devices prescribed by their physicians. Medicare jurisdiction: DME regional carrier. Some commercial payers also provide this coverage to non-insulin dependent diabetics.

➥ **A4258** Spring-powered device for lancet, each
Some Medicare carriers cover lancing devices for diabetic patients using home glucose monitoring devices prescribed by their physicians. Medicare jurisdiction: DME regional carrier. Some commercial payers also provide this coverage to non-insulin dependent diabetics.

? ☑ **A4259** Lancets, per box of 100
CIM 60-11
Medicare covers lancets for diabetic patients using home glucose monitoring devices prescribed by their physicians. Medicare jurisdiction: DME regional carrier. Some commercial payers also provide this coverage to non-insulin dependent diabetics.

⊘ **A4260** Levonorgestrel (contraceptive) implants system, including implants and supplies
Covered by some commercial payers. Always report concurrent to the implant procedure.

⊘ **A4261** Cervical cap for contraceptive use

? ☑ **A4262** Temporary, absorbable lacrimal duct implant, each
Always report concurrent to the implant procedure.

? ☑ **A4263** Permanent, long-term, nondissolvable lacrimal duct implant, each
MCM 15030
Always report concurrent to the implant procedure.

➥ ☑ **A4265** Paraffin, per pound
Medicare jurisdiction: DME regional carrier.

➥ ☑ **A4270** Disposable endoscope sheath, each

● ➥ **A4280** Adhesive skin support attachment for use with external breast prosthesis, each

Vascular Catheters

? **A4300** Implantable access catheter (venous, arterial, epidural, or peritoneal), external access
MCM 2130

➥ **A4301** Implantable access total system; catheter, port/reservoir (venous, arterial or epidural), percutaneous access

➥ **A4305** Disposable drug delivery system, flow rate of 50 ml or greater per hour
Medicare jurisdiction: DME regional carrier.

➥ **A4306** Disposable drug delivery system, flow rate of 5 ml or less per hour
Medicare jurisdiction: DME regional carrier.

Incontinence Appliances and Care Supplies

Covered by Medicare when the medical record indicates incontinence is permanent, or of long and indefinite duration.

Medicare claims fall under the jurisdiction of the DME regional carrier, unless otherwise noted.

? **A4310** Insertion tray without drainage bag and without catheter (accessories only)
MCM 2130

? **A4311** Insertion tray without drainage bag with indwelling catheter, Foley type, two-way latex with coating (Teflon, silicone, silicone elastomer or hydrophilic, etc.)
MCM 2130

? **A4312** Insertion tray without drainage bag with indwelling catheter, Foley type, two-way, all silicone
MCM 2130

? **A4313** Insertion tray without drainage bag with indwelling catheter, Foley type, three-way, for continuous irrigation
MCM 2130

? **A4314** Insertion tray with drainage bag with indwelling catheter, Foley type, two-way latex with coating (Teflon, silicone, silicone elastomer or hydrophilic, etc.)
MCM 2130

? **A4315** Insertion tray with drainage bag with indwelling catheter, Foley type, two-way, all silicone
MCM 2130

? **A4316** Insertion tray with drainage bag with indwelling catheter, Foley type, three-way, for continuous irrigation
MCM 2130

? **A4320** Irrigation tray with bulb or piston syringe, any purpose
MCM 2130

➥ **A4321** Therapeutic agent for urinary catheter irrigation

? ☑ **A4322** Irrigation syringe, bulb or piston, each
MCM 2130

? ☑ **A4323** Sterile saline irrigation solution, 1000 ml
MCM 2130

? ☑ **A4326** Male external catheter specialty type (e.g., inflatable, faceplate, etc.) each
MCM 2130

? ☑ **A4327** Female external urinary collection device; metal cup, each
MCM 2130

☑ Quantity Alert   ● New Code   ▲ Revised Code

? ☑ **A4328** Female external urinary collection device; pouch, each
MCM 2130

? ☑ **A4329** External catheter starter set, male/female, includes catheters/urinary collection device, bag/pouch and accessories (tubing, clamps, etc.), seven-day supply
MCM 2130

? ☑ **A4330** Perianal fecal collection pouch with adhesive, each
MCM 2130

? **A4335** Incontinence supply; miscellaneous
MCM 2130

? ☑ **A4338** Indwelling catheter; Foley type, two-way latex with coating (Teflon, silicone, silicone elastomer, or hydrophilic, etc.), each
MCM 2130

? ☑ **A4340** Indwelling catheter; specialty type, (e.g., coudé, mushroom, wing, etc.), each
MCM 2130

? ☑ **A4344** Indwelling catheter, Foley type, two-way, all silicone, each
MCM 2130A

? ☑ **A4346** Indwelling catheter; Foley type, three-way for continuous irrigation, each
MCM 2130

? ☑ **A4347** Male external catheter with or without adhesive, with or without anti-reflux device; per dozen
MCM 2130

? ☑ **A4351** Intermittent urinary catheter; straight tip, each
MCM 2130

? ☑ **A4352** Intermittent urinary catheter; coudé (curved) tip, each
MCM 2130

➡ **A4353** Intermittent urinary catheter, with insertion supplies

? **A4354** Insertion tray with drainage bag but without catheter
MCM 2130

? ☑ **A4355** Irrigation tubing set for continuous bladder irrigation through a three-way indwelling Foley catheter, each
MCM 2130

External Urinary Supplies
Medicare claims fall under the jurisdiction of the DME regional carrier, unless otherwise noted.

? ☑ **A4356** External urethral clamp or compression device (not to be used for catheter clamp), each
MCM 2130

? ☑ **A4357** Bedside drainage bag, day or night, with or without anti-reflux device, with or without tube, each
MCM 2130

? ☑ **A4358** Urinary leg bag; vinyl, with or without tube, each
MCM 2130

? ☑ **A4359** Urinary suspensory without leg bag, each
MCM 2130

Ostomy Supplies
Medicare claims fall under the jurisdiction of the DME regional carrier, unless otherwise noted.

? ☑ **A4361** Ostomy faceplate, each
MCM 2130A

? ☑ **A4362** Skin barrier; solid, four by four or equivalent; each
MCM 2130

(A4363 has been deleted)

? ☑ **A4364** Adhesive for ostomy or catheter; liquid (spray, brush, etc.), cement, powder or paste; any composition (e.g., silicone, latex, etc.), per oz.
MCM 2130

➡ ☑ **A4365** Ostomy adhesive remover wipes, 50 per box

? ☑ **A4367** Ostomy belt, each
MCM 2130A

➡ ☑ **A4368** Ostomy filter, any type, each

● ➡ ☑ **A4369** Ostomy skin barrier, liquid (spray, brush, etc), per oz

● ➡ ☑ **A4370** Ostomy skin barrier, paste, per oz

● ➡ ☑ **A4371** Ostomy skin barrier, powder, per oz

● ➡ ☑ **A4372** Ostomy skin barrier, solid 4x4 or equivalent, standard wear, with built-in convexity, each

● ➡ ☑ **A4373** Ostomy skin barrier, with flange (solid, flexible or accordion), standard wear, with built-in convexity, any size, each

● ➡ ☑ **A4374** Ostomy skin barrier, with flange (solid, flexible or accordion), extended wear, with built-in convexity, any size, each

● ➡ ☑ **A4375** Ostomy pouch, drainable, with faceplate attached, plastic, each

● ➡ ☑ **A4376** Ostomy pouch, drainable, with faceplate attached, rubber, each

● ➡ ☑ **A4377** Ostomy pouch, drainable, for use on faceplate, plastic, each

● ➡ ☑ **A4378** Ostomy pouch, drainable, for use on faceplate, rubber, each

● ➡ ☑ **A4379** Ostomy pouch, urinary, with faceplate attached, plastic, each

MEDICAL AND SURGICAL SUPPLIES

- ➡ ☑ **A4380** Ostomy pouch, urinary, with faceplate attached, rubber, each
- ➡ ☑ **A4381** Ostomy pouch, urinary, for use on faceplate, plastic, each
- ➡ ☑ **A4382** Ostomy pouch, urinary, for use on faceplate, heavy plastic, each
- ➡ ☑ **A4383** Ostomy pouch, urinary, for use on faceplate, rubber, each
- ➡ ☑ **A4384** Ostomy faceplate equivalent, silicone ring, each
- ➡ ☑ **A4385** Ostomy skin barrier, solid 4x4 or equivalent, extended wear, without built-in convexity, each
- ➡ ☑ **A4386** Ostomy skin barrier, with flange (solid, flexible or accordion), extended wear, without built-in convexity, any size, each
- ➡ ☑ **A4387** Ostomy pouch closed, with standard wear barrier attached, with built-in convexity (1 piece), each
- ➡ ☑ **A4388** Ostomy pouch, drainable, with extended wear barrier attached, without built-in convexity (1 piece)
- ➡ ☑ **A4389** Ostomy pouch, drainable, with standard wear barrier attached, with built-in convexity (1 piece), each
- ➡ ☑ **A4390** Ostomy pouch, drainable, with extended wear barrier attached, with built-in convexity (1 piece), each
- ➡ ☑ **A4391** Ostomy pouch, urinary, with extended wear barrier attached, without built-in convexity (1 piece), each
- ➡ ☑ **A4392** Ostomy pouch, urinary, with standard wear barrier attached, with built-in convexity (1 piece), each
- ➡ ☑ **A4393** Ostomy pouch, urinary, with extended wear barrier attached, with built-in convexity (1 piece), each
- ➡ ☑ **A4394** Ostomy deodorant for use in ostomy pouch, liquid, per fluid ounce
- ➡ ☑ **A4395** Ostomy deodorant for use in ostomy pouch, solid, per tablet
- ? ☑ **A4397** Irrigation supply; sleeve, each
  MCM 2130
- ? ☑ **A4398** Ostomy irrigation supply; bag, each
  MCM 2130A
- ? **A4399** Ostomy irrigation supply; cone/catheter, including brush
  MCM 2130A
- ? **A4400** Ostomy irrigation set
  MCM 2130
- ? ☑ **A4402** Lubricant, per ounce
  MCM 2130
- ? ☑ **A4404** Ostomy ring, each
  MCM 2130

- ? **A4421** Ostomy supply; miscellaneous
  MCM 2130
  Determine if an alternative national HCPCS Level II code or a local HCPCS Level III code better describes the supply being reported. This code should be used only if a more specific code is unavailable.

Additional Miscellaneous Supplies

- ? **A4454** Tape, all types, all sizes
  MCM 2130
  Medicare jurisdiction: DME regional carrier.
- ? ☑ **A4455** Adhesive remover or solvent (for tape, cement or other adhesive), per ounce
  MCM 2130
  Medicare jurisdiction: DME regional carrier.
- ? ☑ **A4460** Elastic bandage, per roll (e.g., compression bandage)
  MCM 2079
  Use this code to report compression bandages associated with lymphatic drainage.
- ➡ **A4462** Abdominal dressing holder/binder, each
  Dressings applied by a physician are included as part of the professional service. Surgical dressings obtained by the patient to perform homecare as prescribed by the physician are covered. Medicare jurisdiction: DME regional carrier.
- ➡ **A4465** Nonelastic binder for extremity
  Medicare jurisdiction: DME regional carrier.
- ? **A4470** Gravlee jet washer
  CIM 50-4
  The Gravlee jet washer is a disposable device used to detect endometrial cancer. It is covered only in patients exhibiting clinical symptoms or signs suggestive of endometrial disease. Medicare jurisdiction: local carrier.
- ? **A4480** VABRA aspirator
  CIM 50-4
  The VABRA aspirator is a disposable device used to detect endometrial cancer. It is covered only in patients exhibiting clinical symptoms or signs suggestive of endometrial disease. Medicare jurisdiction: local carrier.
- ➡ ☑ **A4481** Tracheostoma filter, any type, any size, each
  Medicare jurisdiction: DME regional carrier.
- ➡ **A4483** Moisture exchanger, disposable, for use with invasive mechanical ventilation
- ⊘ ☑ **A4490** Surgical stocking above knee length, each
  CIM 60-9, MCM 2133, MCM 2079
  Casts applied by a physician at the time of a fracture reduction are included as part of the professional service. Medicare jurisdiction: DME regional carrier.
- ⊘ ☑ **A4495** Surgical stocking thigh length, each
  CIM 60-9, MCM 2133, MCM 2079
  Although casts applied by a physician at the time of a fracture reduction are usually included as part of the professional service, specialty items like fiberglass may be reported separately. Medicare jurisdiction: DME regional carrier.

MEDICAL AND SURGICAL SUPPLIES

⊘ ☑ **A4500** Surgical stocking below knee length, each
CIM 60-9, MCM 2133, MCM 2079
Dressings applied by a physician are included as part of the professional service. Surgical dressings obtained by the patient to perform homecare as prescribed by the physician are covered. Medicare jurisdiction: DME regional carrier.

⊘ ☑ **A4510** Surgical stocking full-length, each
CIM 60-9, MCM 2133, MCM 2079
Dressings applied by a physician are included as part of the professional service. Surgical dressings obtained by the patient to perform homecare as prescribed by the physician are covered. Medicare jurisdiction: DME regional carrier.

? **A4550** Surgical trays
MCM 15030
Medicare jurisdiction: local carrier.

⊘ **A4554** Disposable underpads, all sizes (e.g., Chux's)
CIM 60-9, MCM 2130
Medicare jurisdiction: DME regional carrier.

▲ ➡ ☑ **A4556** Electrodes (e.g., Apnea monitor), per pair

▲ ➡ ☑ **A4557** Lead wires (e.g., Apnea monitor), per pair

➡ **A4558** Conductive paste or gel
Medicare jurisdiction: DME regional carrier.

➡ **A4560** Pessary
Medicare jurisdiction: DME regional carrier.

➡ **A4565** Slings
Dressings applied by a physician are included as part of the professional service. Surgical dressings obtained by the patient to perform homecare as prescribed by the physician are covered. Medicare jurisdiction: DME regional carrier.

? **A4570** Splint
MCM 2079
Dressings applied by a physician are included as part of the professional service. Medicare jurisdiction: DME regional carrier.

➡ **A4572** Rib belt
Medicare jurisdiction: DME regional carrier.

⊘ **A4575** Topical hyperbaric oxygen chamber, disposable
CIM 35-10
Medicare jurisdiction: local carrier.

? **A4580** Cast supplies (e.g., plaster)
MCM 2079
Dressings applied by a physician are included as part of the professional service. Medicare jurisdiction: local carrier.

➡ **A4590** Special casting material (e.g., fiberglass)
Dressings applied by a physician are included as part of the professional service. Medicare jurisdiction: local carrier.

➡ **A4595** TENS supplies, 2 lead, per month
Medicare jurisdiction: DME regional carrier.

Supplies for Oxygen and Related Respiratory Equipment

➡ **A4611** Battery, heavy duty; replacement for patient-owned ventilator
Medicare jurisdiction: DME regional carrier.

➡ **A4612** Battery cables; replacement for patient-owned ventilator
Medicare jurisdiction: DME regional carrier.

➡ **A4613** Battery charger; replacement for patient-owned ventilator
Medicare jurisdiction: DME regional carrier.

➡ **A4614** Peak expiratory flow rate meter, hand held

? **A4615** Cannula, nasal
CIM 60-4, MCM 3312
Medicare jurisdiction: DME regional carrier.

? ☑ **A4616** Tubing (oxygen), per foot
CIM 60-4, MCM 3312
Medicare jurisdiction: DME regional carrier.

? **A4617** Mouthpiece
CIM 60-4, MCM 3312
Medicare jurisdiction: DME regional carrier.

? **A4618** Breathing circuits
CIM 60-4, MCM 3312
Medicare jurisdiction: DME regional carrier.

? **A4619** Face tent
CIM 60-4, MCM 3312
Medicare jurisdiction: DME regional carrier.

? **A4620** Variable concentration mask
CIM 60-4, MCM 3312
Medicare jurisdiction: DME regional carrier.

➡ **A4621** Tracheostomy mask or collar
Medicare jurisdiction: DME regional carrier.

? **A4622** Tracheostomy or laryngectomy tube
CIM 65-16
Medicare jurisdiction: DME regional carrier.

? **A4623** Tracheostomy, inner cannula (replacement only)
CIM 65-16
Medicare jurisdiction: DME regional carrier.

➡ ☑ **A4624** Tracheal suction catheter, any type, each
Medicare jurisdiction: DME regional carrier.

➡ **A4625** Tracheostomy care kit for new tracheostomy
Medicare jurisdiction: DME regional carrier.

➡ ☑ **A4626** Tracheostomy cleaning brush, each
Medicare jurisdiction: DME regional carrier.

⊘ **A4627** Spacer, bag or reservoir, with or without mask, for use with metered dose inhaler
MCM 2100
Medicare jurisdiction: DME regional carrier.

➡ ☑ **A4628** Oropharyngeal suction catheter, each
Medicare jurisdiction: DME regional carrier.

➡ **A4629** Tracheostomy care kit for established tracheostomy
Medicare jurisdiction: DME regional carrier.

Supplies for Other Durable Medical Equipment

? **A4630** Replacement batteries for medically necessary transcutaneous electrical nerve stimulator (TENS) owned by patient
CIM 65-8
Medicare jurisdiction: DME regional carrier.

HCPCS 2000 ⊘ Not covered by or valid for Medicare ? Special coverage instructions ➡ Carrier discretion

MEDICAL AND SURGICAL SUPPLIES

? A4631 Replacement batteries for medically necessary electronic wheelchair owned by patient
CIM 60-9
Medicare jurisdiction: DME regional carrier.

? ☑ A4635 Underarm pad, crutch, replacement, each
CIM 60-9
Medicare jurisdiction: DME regional carrier.

? ☑ A4636 Replacement, handgrip, cane, crutch, or walker, each
CIM 60-9
Medicare jurisdiction: DME regional carrier.

? ☑ A4637 Replacement, tip, cane, crutch, walker, each
CIM 60-9
Medicare jurisdiction: DME regional carrier.

? A4640 Replacement pad for use with medically necessary alternating pressure pad owned by patient
CIM 60-9, MCM 4107.6
Medicare jurisdiction: DME regional carrier.

Supplies for Radiologic Procedures

➡ **A4641** Supply of radiopharmaceutical diagnostic imaging agent, not otherwise classified
MCM 15030
Medicare jurisdiction: local carrier.

➡ **☑ A4642** Supply of satumomab pendetide, radiopharmaceutical diagnostic imaging agent, per dose
MCM 15030
Medicare jurisdiction: local carrier.

➡ **A4643** Supply of additional high dose contrast material(s) during magnetic resonance imaging, e.g., gadoteridol injection
MCM 15030
Medicare jurisdiction: local carrier.

? ☑ A4644 Supply of low osmolar contrast material (100–199 mg of iodine)
MCM 15022, 15030
Medicare pays separately for low osmolar contrast material only for intrathecal injection, or for intra-articular or intravenous injection if the patient has a history of asthma, allergy to contrast material, or significant cardiac dysfunction. Medicare jurisdiction: local carrier.

? ☑ A4645 Supply of low osmolar contrast material (200–299 mg of iodine)
MCM 15022, 15030
Medicare pays separately for low osmolar contrast material only for intrathecal injection, or for intra-articular or intravenous injection if the patient has a history of asthma, allergy to contrast material, or significant cardiac dysfunction. Medicare jurisdiction: local carrier.

? ☑ A4646 Supply of low osmolar contrast material (300–399 mg of iodine)
MCM 15022, 15030
Medicare pays separately for low osmolar contrast material only for intrathecal injection, or for intra-articular or intravenous injection if the patient has a history of asthma, allergy to contrast material, or significant cardiac dysfunction. Medicare jurisdiction: local carrier.

? A4647 Supply of paramagnetic contrast material (e.g., gadolinium)
MCM 15022, 15030
Medicare jurisdiction: local carrier.

➡ **A4649** Surgical supply; miscellaneous
Determine if an alternative national HCPCS Level II code or a local HCPCS Level III code better describes the supply being reported. This code should be used only if a more specific code is unavailable. Medicare jurisdiction: local carrier.

Supplies for ESRD

For DME items for ESRD, see procedure codes E1550–E1669.

? A4650 Centrifuge (includes calibrated microcapillary tubes and sealease)
Medicare jurisdiction: DME regional carrier.

? A4655 Needles and syringes for dialysis
Medicare jurisdiction: DME regional carrier.

? A4660 Sphygmomanometer/blood pressure apparatus with cuff and stethoscope
Medicare jurisdiction: DME regional carrier.

? A4663 Blood pressure cuff only
Medicare jurisdiction: DME regional carrier.

⊘ **A4670** Automatic blood pressure monitor
CIM 50-42
Medicare jurisdiction: DME regional carrier.

? A4680 Activated carbon filters for dialysis
CIM 55-1
Medicare jurisdiction: DME regional carrier.

? ☑ A4690 Dialyzer (artificial kidneys) all brands, all sizes, per unit
Medicare jurisdiction: DME regional carrier.

? ☑ A4700 Standard dialysate solution, each
Medicare jurisdiction: DME regional carrier.

? ☑ A4705 Bicarbonate dialysate solution, each
Medicare jurisdiction: DME regional carrier.

? A4712 Water, sterile
Medicare jurisdiction: local carrier.

? A4714 Treated water (deionized, distilled, reverse osmosis) for use in dialysis system
CIM 55-1
Medicare jurisdiction: DME regional carrier.

? A4730 Fistula cannulation set for dialysis only
Medicare jurisdiction: DME regional carrier.

? A4735 Local/topical anesthetic for dialysis only
Medicare jurisdiction: DME regional carrier.

? A4740 Shunt accessory for dialysis only
Medicare jurisdiction: DME regional carrier.

? ☑ **A4750** Blood tubing, arterial or venous, each
Medicare jurisdiction: DME regional carrier.

? **A4755** Blood tubing, arterial and venous, combined
Medicare jurisdiction: DME regional carrier.

? **A4760** Dialysate standard testing solution, supplies
Medicare jurisdiction: DME regional carrier.

? ☑ **A4765** Dialysate concentrate additive, each
Medicare jurisdiction: DME regional carrier.

? **A4770** Blood testing supplies (e.g., vacutainers and tubes)
Medicare jurisdiction: DME regional carrier.

? ☑ **A4771** Serum clotting time tube, per box
Medicare jurisdiction: DME regional carrier.

? ☑ **A4772** Dextrostick or glucose test strips, per box
Medicare jurisdiction: DME regional carrier.

? ☑ **A4773** Hemostix, per bottle
Medicare jurisdiction: DME regional carrier.

? ☑ **A4774** Ammonia test paper, per box
Medicare jurisdiction: DME regional carrier.

? ☑ **A4780** Sterilizing agent for dialysis equipment, per gallon
Medicare jurisdiction: DME regional carrier.

? **A4790** Cleansing agent for equipment for dialysis only
Medicare jurisdiction: DME regional carrier.

? ☑ **A4800** Heparin for dialysis and antidote, any strength, porcine or beef, up to 1,000 units, 10–30 ml (for parenteral use, see code B4216)
Medicare jurisdiction: DME regional carrier.

? **A4820** Hemodialysis kit supply
Medicare jurisdiction: DME regional carrier.

? **A4850** Hemostats with rubber tips for dialysis
Medicare jurisdiction: DME regional carrier.

? **A4860** Disposable catheter caps
Medicare jurisdiction: DME regional carrier.

? **A4870** Plumbing and/or electrical work for home dialysis equipment
Medicaid suspend for medical review
Medicare jurisdiction: DME regional carrier.

? **A4880** Storage tank utilized in connection with water purification system, replacement tank for dialysis
CIM 55-1
Medicare jurisdiction: DME regional carrier.

? **A4890** Contracts, repair and maintenance, for home dialysis equipment (noncovered)
MCM 2100.4
Medicare jurisdiction: DME regional carrier.

? **A4900** Continuous ambulatory peritoneal dialysis (CAPD) supply kit
Medicare jurisdiction: DME regional carrier.

? **A4901** Continuous cycling peritoneal dialysis (CCPD) supply kit
Medicare jurisdiction: DME regional carrier.

? **A4905** Intermittent peritoneal dialysis (IPD) supply kit
Medicare jurisdiction: DME regional carrier.

? **A4910** Nonmedical supplies for dialysis, (i.e., scale, scissors, stop-watch, etc.) Note: For this procedure, "nonmedical supplies" include the following: scale, scissors, stopwatch, surgical brush, thermometer, tool kit, tourniquet, tube occluding forceps/clamps.
"Nonmedical supplies" includes the following; scale, scissors, stopwatch, surgical brush, thermometer tool kit, tourniquet, tube occluding forceps/clamps. Medicare jurisdiction: DME regional carrier.

? **A4912** Gomco drain bottle
Medicare jurisdiction: DME regional carrier.

? **A4913** Miscellaneous dialysis supplies, not identified elsewhere, by report
Pertinent documentation to evaluate medical appropriateness should be included when this code is reported. Determine if an alternative national HCPCS Level II code or a local HCPCS Level III code better describes the supplies being reported. This code should be used only if a more specific code is unavailable. Medicare jurisdiction: DME regional carrier.

? **A4914** Preparation kit
Medicare jurisdiction: DME regional carrier.

? ☑ **A4918** Venous pressure clamp, each
Medicare jurisdiction: DME regional carrier.

? ☑ **A4919** Dialyzer holder, each
Medicare jurisdiction: DME regional carrier.

? ☑ **A4920** Harvard pressure clamp, each
Medicare jurisdiction: DME regional carrier.

? ☑ **A4921** Measuring cylinder, any size, each
Medicare jurisdiction: DME regional carrier.

? ☑ **A4927** Gloves, sterile or nonsterile, per pair
Medicare jurisdiction: DME regional carrier.

Additional Ostomy Supplies
Medicare claims fall under the jurisdiction of the DME regional carrier, unless otherwise noted.

? **A5051** Pouch, closed; with barrier attached (one piece)
MCM 2130

? **A5052** Pouch, closed; without barrier attached (one piece)
MCM 2130

? **A5053** Pouch, closed; for use on faceplate
MCM 2130

? **A5054** Pouch, closed; for use on barrier with flange (two piece)
MCM 2130

- **? A5055** Stoma cap
  MCM 2130

- **? A5061** Pouch, drainable; with barrier attached (one piece)
  MCM 2130

- **? A5062** Pouch, drainable; without barrier attached (one piece)
  MCM 2130

- **? A5063** Pouch, drainable; for use on barrier with flange (two piece system)
  MCM 2130

- **⊘ A5064** Pouch, drainable; with faceplate attached; plastic or rubber
  MCM 2130

- **⊘ A5065** Pouch, drainable; for use on faceplate; plastic or rubber
  MCM 2130

- **? A5071** Pouch, urinary; with barrier attached (one piece)
  MCM 2130

- **? A5072** Pouch, urinary; without barrier attached (one piece)
  MCM 2130

- **? A5073** Pouch, urinary; for use on barrier with flange (two piece)
  MCM 2130

- **⊘ A5074** Pouch, urinary; with faceplate attached; plastic or rubber
  MCM 2130

- **⊘ A5075** Pouch, urinary; for use on faceplate; plastic or rubber
  MCM 2130

- **? A5081** Continent device; plug for continent stoma
  MCM 2130

- **? A5082** Continent device; catheter for continent stoma
  MCM 2130

- **? A5093** Ostomy accessory; convex insert
  MCM 2130
  Medicare jurisdiction: local carrier.

Additional Incontinence Appliances/Supplies

Medicare claims fall under the jurisdiction of the DME regional carrier, unless otherwise noted.

- **?☑ A5102** Bedside drainage bottle, with or without tubing, rigid or expandable, each
  MCM 2130

- **? A5105** Urinary suspensory; with leg bag, with or without tube
  MCM 2130

- **? A5112** Urinary leg bag; latex
  MCM 2130

- **?☑ A5113** Leg strap; latex, replacement only, per set
  MCM 2130

- **?☑ A5114** Leg strap; foam or fabric, replacement only, per set
  MCM 2130

Supplies for Either Incontinence or Ostomy Appliances

- **?☑ A5119** Skin barrier; wipes, box per 50
  MCM 2130

- **?☑ A5121** Skin barrier; solid, 6 x 6 or equivalent, each
  MCM 2130

- **?☑ A5122** Skin barrier; solid, 8 x 8 or equivalent, each
  MCM 2130

- **?☑ A5123** Skin barrier; with flange (solid, flexible or accordion), any size, each
  MCM 2130

- ▲ **? A5126** Adhesive or non-adhesive; disk or foam pad
  MCM 2130

- **?☑ A5131** Appliance cleaner, incontinence and ostomy appliances, per 16 oz.
  MCM 2130

- **? A5149** Incontinence/ostomy supply; miscellaneous
  MCM 2130
  Determine if an alternative national HCPCS Level II code or a local HCPCS Level III code better describes the supply being reported. This code should be used only if a more specific code is unavailable. Medicare jurisdiction: local carrier.

- ➡ **A5200** Percutaneous catheter/tube anchoring device, adhesive skin attachment

Diabetic Shoes, Fitting, and Modifications

According to Medicare, documentation from the prescribing physician must certify the diabetic patient has one of the following conditions: peripheral neuropathy with evidence of callus formation; history of preulcerative calluses; history of ulceration; foot deformity; previous amputation; or poor circulation. The footwear must be fitted and furnished by a podiatrist, pedorthist, orthotist, or prosthetist.

Medicare jurisdiction: DME regional carrier.

- **?☑ A5500** For diabetics only, fitting (including follow-up) custom preparation and supply of off-the-shelf depth-inlay shoe manufactured to accommodate multi-density insert(s), per shoe
  MCM 2134

- **?☑ A5501** For diabetics only, fitting (including follow-up) custom preparation and supply of shoe molded from cast(s) of patient's foot (custom molded shoe), per shoe
  MCM 2134

- **?☑ A5502** For diabetics only, multiple density insert(s), per shoe
  MCM 2134

- **?☑ A5503** For diabetics only, modification (including fitting) of off-the-shelf depth-inlay shoe or custom molded shoe with roller or rigid rocker bottom, per shoe
  MCM 2134

? ☑ **A5504** For diabetics only, modification (including fitting) of off-the-shelf depth-inlay shoe or custom molded shoe with wedge(s), per shoe
MCM 2134

? ☑ **A5505** For diabetics only, modification (including fitting) of off-the-shelf depth-inlay shoe or custom molded shoe with metatarsal bar, per shoe
MCM 2134

? ☑ **A5506** For diabetics only, modification (including fitting) of off-the-shelf depth-inlay shoe or custom molded shoe with off-set heel(s), per shoe
MCM 2134

? ☑ **A5507** For diabetics only, not otherwise specified modification (including fitting) of off-the-shelf depth-inlay shoe or custom molded shoe, per shoe
MCM 2134

● ➡ ☑ **A5508** For diabetics only, deluxe feature of off-the-shelf depth-inlay shoe or custom-molded shoe, per shoe

Dressings

Medicare claims fall under the jurisdiction of the DME regional carrier, unless otherwise noted.

➡ ☑ **A6020** Collagen based wound dressing, each dressing

⊘ ☑ **A6025** Silicone gel sheet, each

➡ ☑ **A6154** Wound pouch, each
Surgical dressings applied by a physician are included as part of the professional service. Surgical dressings obtained by the patient to perform homecare as prescribed by the physician are covered.

➡ ☑ **A6196** Alginate dressing, wound cover, pad size 16 sq. in. or less, each dressing
Surgical dressings applied by a physician are included as part of the professional service. Surgical dressings obtained by the patient to perform homecare as prescribed by the physician are covered.

➡ ☑ **A6197** Alginate dressing, wound cover, pad size more than 16 sq. in. but less than or equal to 48 sq. in., each dressing
Surgical dressings applied by a physician are included as part of the professional service. Surgical dressings obtained by the patient to perform homecare as prescribed by the physician are covered.

➡ ☑ **A6198** Alginate dressing, wound cover, pad size more then 48 sq. in., each dressing
Surgical dressings applied by a physician are included as part of the professional service. Surgical dressings obtained by the patient to perform homecare as prescribed by the physician are covered.

➡ ☑ **A6199** Alginate dressing, wound filler, per 6 inches
Surgical dressings applied by a physician are included as part of the professional service. Surgical dressings obtained by the patient to perform homecare as prescribed by the physician are covered.

➡ ☑ **A6200** Composite dressing, pad size 16 sq. in. or less, without adhesive border, each dressing
Surgical dressings applied by a physician are included as part of the professional service. Surgical dressings obtained by the patient to perform homecare as prescribed by the physician are covered.

➡ ☑ **A6201** Composite dressing, pad size more than 16 sq. in. but less than or equal to 48 sq. in., without adhesive border, each dressing
Surgical dressings applied by a physician are included as part of the professional service. Surgical dressings obtained by the patient to perform homecare as prescribed by the physician are covered.

➡ ☑ **A6202** Composite dressing, pad size more than 48 sq. in., without adhesive border, each dressing
Surgical dressings applied by a physician are included as part of the professional service. Surgical dressings obtained by the patient to perform homecare as prescribed by the physician are covered.

➡ ☑ **A6203** Composite dressing, pad size 16 sq. in. or less, with any size adhesive border, each dressing

➡ ☑ **A6204** Composite dressing, pad size more than 16 sq. in. but less than or equal to 48 sq. in., with any size adhesive border, each dressing

➡ ☑ **A6205** Composite dressing, pad size more than 48 sq. in., with any size adhesive border, each dressing

➡ ☑ **A6206** Contact layer, 16 sq. in. or less, each dressing
Surgical dressings applied by a physician are included as part of the professional service. Surgical dressings obtained by the patient to perform homecare as prescribed by the physician are covered.

➡ ☑ **A6207** Contact layer, more than 16 sq. in. but less than or equal to 48 sq. in., each dressing
Surgical dressings applied by a physician are included as part of the professional service. Surgical dressings obtained by the patient to perform homecare as prescribed by the physician are covered.

MEDICAL AND SURGICAL SUPPLIES

➡☑ **A6208** Contact layer, more than 48 sq. in., each dressing
Surgical dressings applied by a physician are included as part of the professional service. Surgical dressings obtained by the patient to perform homecare as prescribed by the physician are covered.

➡☑ **A6209** Foam dressing, wound cover, pad size 16 sq. in. or less, without adhesive border, each dressing
Surgical dressings applied by a physician are included as part of the professional service. Surgical dressings obtained by the patient to perform homecare as prescribed by the physician are covered.

➡☑ **A6210** Foam dressing, wound cover, pad size more than 16 sq. in. but less than or equal to 48 sq. in., without adhesive border, each dressing
Surgical dressings applied by a physician are included as part of the professional service. Surgical dressings obtained by the patient to perform homecare as prescribed by the physician are covered.

➡☑ **A6211** Foam dressing, wound cover, pad size more then 48 sq. in., without adhesive border, each dressing
Surgical dressings applied by a physician are included as part of the professional service. Surgical dressings obtained by the patient to perform homecare as prescribed by the physician are covered.

➡☑ **A6212** Foam dressing, wound cover, pad size 16 sq. in. or less, with any size adhesive border, each dressing
Surgical dressings applied by a physician are included as part of the professional service. Surgical dressings obtained by the patient to perform homecare as prescribed by the physician are covered.

➡☑ **A6213** Foam dressing, wound cover, pad size more than 16 sq. in. but less than or equal to 48 sq. in., with any size adhesive border, each dressing
Surgical dressings applied by a physician are included as part of the professional service. Surgical dressings obtained by the patient to perform homecare as prescribed by the physician are covered.

➡☑ **A6214** Foam dressing, wound cover, pad size more than 48 sq. in., with any size adhesive border, each dressing
Surgical dressings applied by a physician are included as part of the professional service. Surgical dressings obtained by the patient to perform homecare as prescribed by the physician are covered.

➡☑ **A6215** Foam dressing, wound filler, per gram
Surgical dressings applied by a physician are included as part of the professional service. Surgical dressings obtained by the patient to perform homecare as prescribed by the physician are covered.

➡☑ **A6216** Gauze, non-impregnated, non-sterile, pad size 16 sq. in. or less, without adhesive border, each dressing
Surgical dressings applied by a physician are included as part of the professional service. Surgical dressings obtained by the patient to perform homecare as prescribed by the physician are covered.

➡☑ **A6217** Gauze, non-impregnated, non-sterile, pad size more than 16 sq. in. but less than or equal to 48 sq. in., without adhesive border, each dressing
Surgical dressings applied by a physician are included as part of the professional service. Surgical dressings obtained by the patient to perform homecare as prescribed by the physician are covered.

➡☑ **A6218** Gauze, non-impregnated, non-sterile, pad size more than 48 sq. in., without adhesive border, each dressing
Surgical dressings applied by a physician are included as part of the professional service. Surgical dressings obtained by the patient to perform homecare as prescribed by the physician are covered.

➡☑ **A6219** Gauze, non-impregnated, pad size 16 sq. in. or less, with any size adhesive border, each dressing
Surgical dressings applied by a physician are included as part of the professional service. Surgical dressings obtained by the patient to perform homecare as prescribed by the physician are covered.

➡☑ **A6220** Gauze, non-impregnated, pad size more than 16 sq. in. but less than or equal to 48 sq. in., with any size adhesive border, each dressing
Surgical dressings applied by a physician are included as part of the professional service. Surgical dressings obtained by the patient to perform homecare as prescribed by the physician are covered.

➡☑ **A6221** Gauze, non-impregnated, pad size more than 48 sq. in., with any size adhesive border, each dressing
Surgical dressings applied by a physician are included as part of the professional service. Surgical dressings obtained by the patient to perform homecare as prescribed by the physician are covered.

➡☑ **A6222** Gauze, impregnated, other than water or normal saline, pad size 16 sq. in. or less, without adhesive border, each dressing
Surgical dressings applied by a physician are included as part of the professional service. Surgical dressings obtained by the patient to perform homecare as prescribed by the physician are covered.

MEDICAL AND SURGICAL SUPPLIES

➡ ☑ **A6223** Gauze, impregnated, other than water or normal saline, pad size more than 16 sq. in. but less than or equal to 48 sq. in., without adhesive border, each dressing
Surgical dressings applied by a physician are included as part of the professional service. Surgical dressings obtained by the patient to perform homecare as prescribed by the physician are covered.

➡ ☑ **A6224** Gauze, impregnated, other than water or normal saline, pad size more than 48 sq. in., without adhesive border, each dressing
Surgical dressings applied by a physician are included as part of the professional service. Surgical dressings obtained by the patient to perform homecare as prescribed by the physician are covered.

➡ ☑ **A6228** Gauze, impregnated, water or normal saline, pad size 16 sq. in. or less, without adhesive border, each dressing
Surgical dressings applied by a physician are included as part of the professional service. Surgical dressings obtained by the patient to perform homecare as prescribed by the physician are covered.

➡ ☑ **A6229** Gauze, impregnated, water or normal saline, pad size more than 16 sq. in. but less than or equal to 48 sq. in., without adhesive border, each dressing
Surgical dressings applied by a physician are included as part of the professional service. Surgical dressings obtained by the patient to perform homecare as prescribed by the physician are covered.

➡ ☑ **A6230** Gauze, impregnated, water or normal saline, pad size more than 48 sq. in., without adhesive border, each dressing
Surgical dressings applied by a physician are included as part of the professional service. Surgical dressings obtained by the patient to perform homecare as prescribed by the physician are covered.

➡ ☑ **A6234** Hydrocolloid dressing, wound cover, pad size 16 sq. in. or less, without adhesive border, each dressing

➡ ☑ **A6235** Hydrocolloid dressing, wound cover, pad size more than 16 sq. in. but less than or equal to 48 sq. in., without adhesive border, each dressing

➡ ☑ **A6236** Hydrocolloid dressing, wound cover, pad size more than 48 sq. in., without adhesive border, each dressing

➡ ☑ **A6237** Hydrocolloid dressing, wound cover, pad size 16 sq. in. or less, with any size adhesive border, each dressing

➡ ☑ **A6238** Hydrocolloid dressing, wound cover, pad size more than 16 sq. in. but less than or equal to 48 sq. in., with any size adhesive border, each dressing

➡ ☑ **A6239** Hydrocolloid dressing, wound cover, pad size more than 48 sq. in., with any size adhesive border, each dressing

➡ ☑ **A6240** Hydrocolloid dressing, wound filler, paste, per fluid ounce

➡ ☑ **A6241** Hydrocolloid dressing, wound filler, dry form, per gram

➡ ☑ **A6242** Hydrogel dressing, wound cover, pad size 16 sq. in. or less, without adhesive border, each dressing

➡ ☑ **A6243** Hydrogel dressing, wound cover, pad size more than 16 sq. in. but less than or equal to 48 sq. in., without adhesive border, each dressing

➡ ☑ **A6244** Hydrogel dressing, wound cover, pad size more than 48 sq. in., without adhesive border, each dressing

➡ ☑ **A6245** Hydrogel dressing, wound cover, pad size 16 sq. in. or less, with any size adhesive border, each dressing

➡ ☑ **A6246** Hydrogel dressing, wound cover, pad size more than 16 sq. in. but less than or equal to 48 sq. in., with any size adhesive border, each dressing

➡ ☑ **A6247** Hydrogel dressing, wound cover, pad size more than 48 sq. in., with any size adhesive border, each dressing

➡ ☑ **A6248** Hydrogel dressing, wound filler, gel, per fluid ounce

➡ **A6250** Skin sealants, protectants, moisturizers, ointments, any type, any size
Surgical dressings applied by a physician are included as part of the professional service. Surgical dressings obtained by the patient to perform homecare as prescribed by the physician are covered.

➡ ☑ **A6251** Specialty absorptive dressing, wound cover, pad size 16 sq. in. or less, without adhesive border, each dressing

➡ ☑ **A6252** Specialty absorptive dressing, wound cover, pad size more than 16 sq. in. but less than or equal to 48 sq. in., without adhesive border, each dressing

➡ ☑ **A6253** Specialty absorptive dressing, wound cover, pad size more than 48 sq. in., without adhesive border, each dressing

➡ ☑ **A6254** Specialty absorptive dressing, wound cover, pad size 16 sq. in. or less, with any size adhesive border, each dressing

➡ ☑ **A6255** Specialty absorptive dressing, wound cover, pad size more than 16 sq. in. but less than or equal to 48 sq. in., with any size adhesive border, each dressing

➡ ☑ **A6256** Specialty absorptive dressing, wound cover, pad size more than 48 sq. in., with any size adhesive border, each dressing

MEDICAL AND SURGICAL SUPPLIES

➡ ☑ **A6257** Transparent film, 16 sq. in. or less, each dressing
Surgical dressings applied by a physician are included as part of the professional service. Surgical dressings obtained by the patient to perform homecare as prescribed by the physician are covered. Use this code for Polyskin, Tegaderm, and Tegaderm HP.

➡ ☑ **A6258** Transparent film, more than 16 sq. in. but less than or equal to 48 sq. in., each dressing
Surgical dressings applied by a physician are included as part of the professional service. Surgical dressings obtained by the patient to perform homecare as prescribed by the physician are covered.

➡ ☑ **A6259** Transparent film, more than 48 sq. in., each dressing
Surgical dressings applied by a physician are included as part of the professional service. Surgical dressings obtained by the patient to perform homecare as prescribed by the physician are covered.

➡ **A6260** Wound cleansers, any type, any size
Surgical dressings applied by a physician are included as part of the professional service. Surgical dressings obtained by the patient to perform homecare as prescribed by the physician are covered.

➡ ☑ **A6261** Wound filler, gel/paste, per fluid ounce, not elsewhere classified
Surgical dressings applied by a physician are included as part of the professional service. Surgical dressings obtained by the patient to perform homecare as prescribed by the physician are covered.

➡ ☑ **A6262** Wound filler, dry form, per gram, not elsewhere classified

➡ ☑ **A6263** Gauze, elastic, non-sterile, all types, per linear yard
Surgical dressings applied by a physician are included as part of the professional service. Surgical dressings obtained by the patient to perform homecare as prescribed by the physician are covered.

➡ ☑ **A6264** Gauze, non-elastic, non-sterile, per linear yard
Surgical dressings applied by a physician are included as part of the professional service. Surgical dressings obtained by the patient to perform homecare as prescribed by the physician are covered.

➡ ☑ **A6265** Tape, all types, per 18 sq. in.
Surgical dressings applied by a physician are included as part of the professional service. Surgical dressings obtained by the patient to perform homecare as prescribed by the physician are covered.

➡ ☑ **A6266** Gauze, impregnated, other than water or normal saline, any width, per linear yard
Surgical dressings applied by a physician are included as part of the professional service. Surgical dressings obtained by the patient to perform homecare as prescribed by the physician are covered.

➡ ☑ **A6402** Gauze, non-impregnated, sterile, pad size 16 sq. in. or less, without adhesive border, each dressing
Surgical dressings applied by a physician are included as part of the professional service. Surgical dressings obtained by the patient to perform homecare as prescribed by the physician are covered.

➡ ☑ **A6403** Gauze, non-impregnated, sterile, pad size more than 16 sq. in. but less than or equal to 48 sq. in., without adhesive border, each dressing
Surgical dressings applied by a physician are included as part of the professional service. Surgical dressings obtained by the patient to perform homecare as prescribed by the physician are covered.

➡ ☑ **A6404** Gauze, non-impregnated, sterile, pad size more than 48 sq. in., without adhesive border, each dressing

➡ ☑ **A6405** Gauze, elastic, sterile, all types, per linear yard
Surgical dressings applied by a physician are included as part of the professional service. Surgical dressings obtained by the patient to perform homecare as prescribed by the physician are covered.

➡ ☑ **A6406** Gauze, non-elastic, sterile, all types, per linear yard
Surgical dressings applied by a physician are included as part of the professional service. Surgical dressings obtained by the patient to perform homecare as prescribed by the physician are covered.

● ➡ **A7000** Canister, disposable, used with suction pump, each

● ➡ **A7001** Canister, non-disposable, used with suction pump, each

● ➡ **A7002** Tubing, used with suction pump, each

● ➡ **A7003** Administration set, with small volume nonfiltered pneumatic nebulizer, disposable

● ➡ **A7004** Small volume nonfiltered pneumatic nebulizer, disposable

● ➡ **A7005** Administration set, with small volume nonfiltered pneumatic nebulizer, non-disposable

● ➡ **A7006** Administration set, with small volume filtered pneumatic nebulizer

● ➡ **A7007** Large volume nebulizer, disposable, unfilled, used with aerosol compressor

☑ Quantity Alert ● New Code ▲ Revised Code

- ● → **A7008** Large volume nebulizer, disposable, prefilled, used with aerosol compressor
- ● → **A7009** Reservoir bottle, non-disposable, used with large volume ultrasonic nebulizer
- ● → ☑ **A7010** Corrugated tubing, disposable, used with large volume nebulizer, 100 feet
- ● → ☑ **A7011** Corrugated tubing, non-disposable, used with large volume nebulizer, 10 feet
- ● → **A7012** Water collection device, used with large volume nebulizer
- ● → **A7013** Filter, disposable, used with aerosol compressor
- ● → **A7014** Filter, non-disposable, used with aerosol compressor or ultrasonic generator
- ● → **A7015** Aerosol mask, used with DME nebulizer
- ● → **A7016** Dome and mouthpiece, used with small volume ultrasonic nebulizer
- ● ? **A7017** Nebulizer, durable, glass or autoclavable plastic, bottle type, not used with oxygen
  CIM 60-9

Administrative, Miscellaneous and Investigational A9000–A9999

- ? **A9150** Nonprescription drug
  MCM 2050.5
  Medicare jurisdiction: local carrier.
- ⊘ **A9160** Noncovered service by podiatrist
  Medicare statute 1861.R3
  Medicare jurisdiction: local carrier.
- ⊘ **A9170** Noncovered service by chiropractor
  Medicare statute 1861.R5
  Medicare jurisdiction: local carrier.
- ⊘ **A9190** Personal comfort item
  Medicare jurisdiction: local or DME regional carrier.
- ⊘ **A9270** Noncovered item or service
  MCM 2303
  Medicare jurisdiction: local or DME regional carrier.
- ⊘ **A9300** Exercise equipment
  CIM 60-9, MCM 2100.1
  Medicare jurisdiction: DME regional carrier.
- ? ☑ **A9500** Supply of radiopharmaceutical diagnostic imaging agent, technetium Tc 99m sestamibi, per dose
  MCM 15022
  Medicare jurisdiction: local carrier.
- ? **A9502** Supply of radiopharmaceutical diagnostic imaging agent, technetium Tc 99m tetrofosmin, per unit dose
  MCM 15022
  Medicare jurisdiction: local carrier.
- ? ☑ **A9503** Supply of radiopharmaceutical diagnostic imaging agent, technetium Tc 99m, medronate, up to 30 mCi
  MCM 15022
  Medicare jurisdiction: local carrier.
- ● → **A9504** Supply of radiopharmaceutical diagnostic imaging agent, technetium Tc 99m apcitide
  MCM 15022
  Medicare jurisdiction: local carrier.
- ? ☑ **A9505** Supply of radiopharmaceutical diagnostic imaging agent, thallous chloride TL-201, per mCi
  MCM 15022
  Medicare jurisdiction: local carrier.
- ? **A9507** Supply of radiopharmaceutical diagnostic imaging agent, indium IN 111 capromab pendetide, per dose
  MCM 15022
  Medicare jurisdiction: local carrier.
- → **A9600** Supply of therapeutic radiopharmaceutical, strontium-89 chloride, per mCi
  Medicare jurisdiction: local carrier.
- → **A9605** Supply of therapeutic radiopharmaceutical, samarium sm 153 lexidronamm, 50 mCi
- ● → **A9900** Miscellaneous supply, accessory, and/or service component of another HCPCS code
- ● → **A9901** Delivery, set up, and/or dispensing service component of another HCPCS code

Enteral and Parenteral Therapy B4000–B9999

Certification of medical necessity is required for coverage. Submit a revision to the certification of medical necessity if the patient's daily volume changes by more than one liter; if there is a change in infusion method; or if there is a change from premix to home mix or parenteral to enteral therapy. Medicare claims fall under the jurisdiction of the DME regional carrier, unless otherwise noted.

Enteral Formulae and Enteral Medical Supplies

? **B4034** Enteral feeding supply kit; syringe, per day
CIM 65-10, MCM 2130, MCM 4450

? **B4035** Enteral feeding supply kit; pump fed, per day
CIM 65-10, MCM 2130, MCM 4450

? **B4036** Enteral feeding supply kit; gravity fed, per day
CIM 65-10, MCM 2130, MCM 4450

? **B4081** Nasogastric tubing with stylet
CIM 65-10, MCM 2130, MCM 4450

? **B4082** Nasogastric tubing without stylet
CIM 65-10, MCM 2130, MCM 4450

? **B4083** Stomach tube — Levine type
CIM 65-10, MCM 2130, MCM 4450

? **B4084** Gastrostomy/jejunostomy tubing
CIM 65-10, MCM 2130, MCM 4450

➥ ☑ **B4085** Gastronomy tube, silicone with sliding ring, each

? **B4150** Enteral formulae; category I; semi-synthetic intact protein/protein isolates, 100 calories = 1 unit
CIM 65-10, MCM 2130, MCM 4450
Use this code for Enrich, Ensure, Ensure HN, Ensure Powder, Isocal, Lonalac Powder, Meritene, Meritene Powder, Osmolite, Osmolite HN, Portagen Powder, Sustacal, Renu, Sustagen Powder, Travasorb.

? **B4151** Enteral formulae; category I: natural intact protein/protein isolates, 100 calories = 1 unit
CIM 65-10, MCM 2130, MCM 4450
Use this code for Compleat B, Vitaneed, Compleat B Modified.

? **B4152** Enteral formulae; category II: intact protein/protein isolates (calorically dense), 100 calories = 1 unit
CIM 65-10, MCM 2130, MCM 4450
Use this code for Magnacal, Isocal HCN, Sustacal HC, Ensure Plus, Ensure Plus HN.

? **B4153** Enteral formulae; category III: hydrolized protein/amino acids, 100 calories = 1 unit
CIM 65-10, MCM 2130, MCM 4450
Use this code for Criticare HN, Vivonex t.e.n. (Total Enteral Nutrition), Vivonex HN, Vital (Vital HN), Travasorb HN, Isotein HN, Precision HN, Precision Isotonic.

? **B4154** Enteral formulae; category IV: defined formula for special metabolic need, 100 calories = 1 unit
CIM 65-10, MCM 2130, MCM 4450
Use this code for Hepatic-aid, Travasorb Hepatic, Travasorb MCT, Travasorb Renal, Traum-aid, Tramacal, Aminaid.

? **B4155** Enteral formulae; category V: modular components, 100 calories = 1 unit
CIM 65-10, MCM 2130, MCM 4450
Use this code for Propac, Gerval Protein, Promix, Casec, Moducal, Controlyte, Polycose Liquid or Powder, Sumacal, Microlipids, MCT Oil, Nutri-source.

? **B4156** Enteral formulae; category VI: standardized nutrients, 100 calories = 1 unit
CIM 65-10, MCM 2130, MCM 4450
Use this code for Vivonex STD, Travasorb STD, Precision LR, Tolerex.

Parenteral Nutrition Solutions and Supplies

? **B4164** Parenteral nutrition solution; carbohydrates (dextrose), 50% or less (500 ml = 1 unit) — home mix
CIM 65-10, MCM 2130, MCM 4450

? **B4168** Parenteral nutrition solution; amino acid, 3.5%, (500 ml = 1 unit) — home mix
CIM 65-10, MCM 2130, MCM 4450

? **B4172** Parenteral nutrition solution; amino acid, 5.5% through 7%, (500 ml = 1 unit) — home mix
CIM 65-10, MCM 2130, MCM 4450

? **B4176** Parenteral nutrition solution; amino acid, 7% through 8.5%, (500 ml = 1 unit) — home mix
CIM 65-10, MCM 2130, MCM 4450

? **B4178** Parenteral nutrition solution; amino acid, greater than 8.5% (500 ml = 1 unit) — home mix
CIM 65-10, MCM 2130, MCM 4450

? **B4180** Parenteral nutrition solution; carbohydrates (dextrose), greater than 50% (500 ml = 1 unit) — home mix
CIM 65-10, MCM 2130, MCM 4450

? **B4184** Parenteral nutrition solution; lipids, 10% with administration set (500 ml = 1 unit)
CIM 65-10, MCM 2130, MCM 4450

? **B4186** Parenteral nutrition solution; lipids, 20% with administration set (500 ml = 1 unit)
CIM 65-10, MCM 2130, MCM 4450

?☑ **B4189** Parenteral nutrition solution; compounded amino acid and carbohydrates with electrolytes, trace elements, and vitamins, including preparation, any strength, 10 to 51 grams of protein — premix
CIM 65-10, MCM 2130, MCM 4450

ENTERAL AND PARENTERAL THERAPY

? ☑ B4193 Parenteral nutrition solution; compounded amino acid and carbohydrates with electrolytes, trace elements, and vitamins, including preparation, any strength, 52 to 73 grams of protein — premix
CIM 65-10, MCM 2130, MCM 4450

? ☑ B4197 Parenteral nutrition solution; compounded amino acid and carbohydrates with electrolytes, trace elements and vitamins, including preparation, any strength, 74 to 100 grams of protein — premix
CIM 65-10, MCM 2130, MCM 4450

? ☑ B4199 Parenteral nutrition solution; compounded amino acid and carbohydrates with electrolytes, trace elements and vitamins, including preparation, any strength, over 100 grams of protein — premix
CIM 65-10, MCM 2130, MCM 4450

? B4216 Parenteral nutrition; additives (vitamins, trace elements, heparin, electrolytes) — home mix, per day
CIM 65-10, MCM 2130, MCM 4450

? B4220 Parenteral nutrition supply kit; premix, per day
CIM 65-10, MCM 2130, MCM 4450

? B4222 Parenteral nutrition supply kit; home mix, per day
CIM 65-10, MCM 2130, MCM 4450

? B4224 Parenteral nutrition administration kit, per day
CIM 65-10, MCM 2130, MCM 4450

? B5000 Parenteral nutrition solution; compounded amino acid and carbohydrates with electrolytes, trace elements, and vitamins, including preparation, any strength, renal — amirosyn RF, nephramine, renamine — premix
CIM 65-10, MCM 2130, MCM 4450
Use this code for Amirosyn-RF, NephrAmine, RenAmin.

? B5100 Parenteral nutrition solution; compounded amino acid and carbohydrates with electrolytes, trace elements, and vitamins, including preparation, any strength, hepatic — freamine HBC, hepatamine — premix
CIM 65-10, MCM 2130, MCM 4450
Use this code for FreAmine HBC, HepatAmine.

? B5200 Parenteral nutrition solution; compounded amino acid and carbohydrates with electrolytes, trace elements, and vitamins, including preparation, any strength, stress — branch chain amino acids — premix
CIM 65-10, MCM 2130, MCM 4450

Enteral and Parenteral Pumps

Submit documentation of the need for the infusion pump. Medicare will reimburse for the simplest model that meets the patient's needs.

? B9000 Enteral nutrition infusion pump — without alarm
CIM 65-10, MCM 2130, MCM 4450

? B9002 Enteral nutrition infusion pump — with alarm
CIM 65-10, MCM 2130, MCM 4450

? B9004 Parenteral nutrition infusion pump, portable
CIM 65-10, MCM 2130, MCM 4450

? B9006 Parenteral nutrition infusion pump, stationary
CIM 65-10, MCM 2130, MCM 4450

? B9998 NOC for enteral supplies
CIM 65-10, MCM 2130, MCM 4450

? B9999 NOC for parenteral supplies
CIM 65-10, MCM 2130, MCM 4450
Determine if an alternative national HCPCS Level II code or a local HCPCS Level III code better describes the supplies being reported. This code should be used only if a more specific code is unavailable.

Dental Procedures D0000–D9999

Items and services, in connection with the care, treatment, filling, removal, or replacement of teeth, or structures directly supporting the teeth, are not covered by Medicare. Prosthetic devices that replace the function of a permanently inoperative or malfunctioning internal body organ are, however, a covered service under the Prosthetic Devices guidelines.

The hospitalization or nonhospitalization of a patient has no direct bearing on the coverage or exclusion of a given dental procedure.

This section (codes D0100-D9999) incorporates numeric codes and descriptors from CDT-3, which is copyright American Dental Association.

Participants are authorized to use copies of CDT-3 material in HCPCS only for purposes directly related to participating in HCFA programs. Permission for any other use must be obtained from the American Dental Association.

All dental codes fall under the jurisdiction of the Medicare local carrier.

Diagnostic D0100–D0999

Clinical Oral Evaluations

D0120 Periodic oral examination
CIM 50-26, Medicare statute 1862A (12)
This procedure is covered if its purpose is to identify a patient's existing infections prior to kidney transplantation.

D0140 Limited oral evaluation — problem focused
Medicare statute 1862A (12)

D0150 Comprehensive oral evaluation
CIM 50-26, MCM 2136, MCM 2336
This procedure is covered if its purpose is to identify a patient's existing infections prior to kidney transplantation.

D0160 Detailed and extensive oral evaluation — problem focused, by report
Medicare statute 1862A (12)
Pertinent documentation to evaluate medical appropriateness should be included when this code is reported.

D0170 Re-evaluation — limited, problem focused (Established patient; not post-operative visit)

Radiographs/Diagnostic Imaging

D0210 Intraoral — complete series (including bitewings)
Cross-reference CPT 70320

D0220 Intraoral — periapical, first film
Cross-reference CPT 70300

D0230 Intraoral — periapical, each additional film
Cross-reference CPT 70310

D0240 Intraoral — occlusal film
MCM 2136, MCM 2336

D0250 Extraoral — first film
MCM 2136, MCM 2336

D0260 Extraoral — each additional film
MCM 2136, MCM 2336

D0270 Bitewing — single film
MCM 2136, MCM 2336

D0272 Bitewings — two films
MCM 2136, MCM 2336

D0274 Bitewings — four films
MCM 2136, MCM 2336

D0277 Vertical bitewings — 7 to 8 films

D0290 Posterior-anterior or lateral skull and facial bone survey film
Cross-reference CPT 70150

D0310 Sialography
Cross-reference CPT 70390

D0320 Temporomandibular joint arthrogram, including injection
Cross-reference CPT 70332

D0321 Other temporomandibular joint films, by report
Cross-reference 76499

D0322 Tomographic survey
CIM 50-26

D0330 Panoramic film
Cross-reference CPT 70320

D0340 Cephalometric film
Cross-reference CPT 70350

D0350 Oral/facial images (includes intra and extraoral images)
This code excludes conventional radiographs.

Test and Laboratory Examinations

D0415 Bacteriologic studies for determination of pathologic agents
CIM 50-26, Medicare statute 1862A (12)
This procedure is covered if its purpose is to identify a patient's existing infections prior to kidney transplantation.

D0425 Caries susceptibility tests
CIM 50-26, Medicare statute 1862A (12)
This procedure is covered by Medicare if its purpose is to identify a patient's existing infections prior to kidney transplantation.

D0460 Pulp vitality tests
CIM 50-26, MCM 2136, MCM 2336
This procedure is covered by Medicare if its purpose is to identify a patient's existing infections prior to kidney transplantation.

D0470 Diagnostic casts
Medicare statute 1862A (12)

(D0471 has been deleted)

Oral Pathology Laboratory

For removal of tissue sample, see codes D7285, D7286

D0472 Accession of tissue, gross examination, preparation and transmission of written report

- ● **D0473** Accession of tissue, gross and microscopic examination, preparation and transmission of written report

- ● **D0474** Accession of tissue, gross and microscopic examination, including assessment of surgical margins for presence of disease, preparation and transmission of written report

- ● **D0480** Processing and interpretation of cytologic smears, including the preparation and transmission of written report

- ? **D0501** Histopathologic examinations
  CIM 50-26, MCM 2136, MCM 2336
  This procedure is covered by Medicare if its purpose is to identify a patient's existing infections prior to kidney transplantation.

- ? **D0502** Other oral pathology procedures, by report
  CIM 50-26, MCM 2136, MCM 2336
  Pertinent documentation to evaluate medical appropriateness should be included when this code is reported. This procedure is covered by Medicare if its purpose is to identify a patient's existing infections prior to kidney transplantation.

- ? **D0999** Unspecified diagnostic procedure, by report
  CIM 50-26, MCM 2136, MCM 2336
  Determine if an alternative national HCPCS Level II, a local HCPCS Level III code, or a CPT code better describes the service being reported. This code should be used only if a more specific code is unavailable.

Preventive D1000–D1999

Dental Prophylaxis

- ⊘ **D1110** Prophylaxis — adult
  Medicare statute 1862A (12)

- ⊘ **D1120** Prophylaxis — child
  Medicare statute 1862A (12)

Topical Fluoride Treatment (Office Procedure)

- ⊘ **D1201** Topical application of fluoride (including prophylaxis) — child
  Medicare statute 1862A (12)

- ⊘ **D1203** Topical application of fluoride (prophylaxis not included) — child
  Medicare statute 1862A (12)

- ⊘ **D1204** Topical application of fluoride (prophylaxis not included) — adult
  Medicare statute 1862A (12)

- ⊘ **D1205** Topical application of fluoride (including prophylaxis) — adult
  Medicare statute 1862A (12)

Other Preventive Services

- ⊘ **D1310** Nutritional counseling for control of dental disease
  MCM 2300

- ⊘ **D1320** Tobacco counseling for the control and prevention of oral disease
  MCM 2300

- ⊘ **D1330** Oral hygiene instructions
  MCM 2300

- ⊘ ☑ **D1351** Sealant — per tooth
  Medicare statute 1862A (12)

Space Maintenance (Passive Appliances)

- ? **D1510** Space maintainer — fixed-unilateral
  MCM 2336

- ? **D1515** Space maintainer — fixed-bilateral
  MCM 2336, MCM 2136

- ? **D1520** Space maintainer — removable-unilateral
  MCM 2336, MCM 2136

- ? **D1525** Space maintainer — removable-bilateral
  MCM 2336, MCM 2136

- ? **D1550** Recementation of space maintainer
  MCM 2336, MCM 2136

Restorative D2000–D2999

Amalgam Restorations (Including Polishing)

- ⊘ ☑ **D2110** Amalgam — one surface, primary
  Medicare statute 1862A (12)

- ⊘ ☑ **D2120** Amalgam — two surfaces, primary
  Medicare statute 1862A (12)

- ⊘ ☑ **D2130** Amalgam — three surfaces, primary
  Medicare statute 1862A (12)

- ⊘ ☑ **D2131** Amalgam — four or more surfaces, primary
  Medicare statute 1862A (12)

- ⊘ ☑ **D2140** Amalgam — one surface, permanent
  Medicare statute 1862A (12)

- ⊘ ☑ **D2150** Amalgam — two surfaces, permanent
  Medicare statute 1862A (12)

- ⊘ ☑ **D2160** Amalgam — three surfaces, permanent
  Medicare statute 1862A (12)

- ⊘ ☑ **D2161** Amalgam — four or more surfaces, permanent
  Medicare statute 1862A (12)

(D2210 has been deleted)

Resin-Based Composite Restorations

- ⊘ ☑ **D2330** Resin-based composite — one surface, anterior
  Medicare statute 1862A (12)

- ⊘ ☑ **D2331** Resin-based composite — two surfaces, anterior
  Medicare statute 1862A (12)

- ⊘ ☑ **D2332** Resin-based composite — three surfaces, anterior
  Medicare statute 1862A (12)

- ⊘ ☑ **D2335** Resin-based composite — four or more surfaces or involving incisal angle (anterior)
  Medicare statute 1862A (12)

- ⊘ **D2336** Resin-based composite crown, anterior — primary
  Medicare statute 1862A (12)

- ● **D2337** Resin-based composite crown, anterior — permanent

- ⊘ ☑ **D2380** Resin-based composite — one surface, posterior — primary
  Medicare statute 1862A (12)

- ⊘ ☑ **D2381** Resin-based composite — two surfaces, posterior — primary
  Medicare statute 1862A (12)

- ⊘ ☑ **D2382** Resin-based composite — three or more surfaces, posterior — primary
  Medicare statute 1862A (12)

- ⊘ ☑ **D2385** Resin-based composite — one surface, posterior — permanent
  Medicare statute 1862A (12)

- ⊘ ☑ **D2386** Resin-based composite — two surfaces, posterior — permanent
  Medicare statute 1862A (12)

- ⊘ ☑ **D2387** Resin-based composite — three surfaces, posterior — permanent
  Medicare statute 1862A (12)

- ● **D2388** Resin-based composite — four or more surfaces, posterior — permanent

Gold Foil Restorations

- ⊘ ☑ **D2410** Gold foil — one surface
  Medicare statute 1862A (12)

- ⊘ ☑ **D2420** Gold foil — two surfaces
  Medicare statute 1862A (12)

- ⊘ ☑ **D2430** Gold foil — three surfaces
  Medicare statute 1862A (12)

Inlay/Onlay Restorations

- ⊘ ☑ **D2510** Inlay — metallic — one surface
  Medicare statute 1862A (12)

- ⊘ ☑ **D2520** Inlay — metallic — two surfaces
  Medicare statute 1862A (12)

- ⊘ ☑ **D2530** Inlay — metallic — three or more surfaces
  Medicare statute 1862A (12)

- ● ☑ **D2542** Onlay — metallic — two surfaces

- ⊘ ☑ **D2543** Onlay — metallic — three surfaces
  Medicare statute 1862A (12)

- ⊘ ☑ **D2544** Onlay — metallic — four or more surfaces
  Medicare statute 1862A (12)

- ⊘ ☑ **D2610** Inlay — porcelain/ceramic — one surface
  Medicare statute 1862A (12)

- ⊘ ☑ **D2620** Inlay — porcelain/ceramic — two surfaces
  Medicare statute 1862A (12)

- ⊘ ☑ **D2630** Inlay — porcelain/ceramic — three or more surfaces
  Medicare statute 1862A (12)

- ⊘ ☑ **D2642** Onlay — porcelain/ceramic — two surfaces
  Medicare statute 1862A (12)

- ⊘ ☑ **D2643** Onlay — porcelain/ceramic — three surfaces
  Medicare statute 1862A (12)

- ⊘ ☑ **D2644** Onlay — porcelain/ceramic — four or more surfaces
  Medicare statute 1862A (12)

- ▲ ⊘ ☑ **D2650** Inlay — resin-based composite composite/resin — one surface
  Medicare statute 1862A (12)

- ▲ ⊘ ☑ **D2651** Inlay — resin-based composite composite/resin — two surfaces
  Medicare statute 1862A (12)

- ▲ ⊘ ☑ **D2652** Inlay — resin-based composite composite/resin — three or more surfaces
  Medicare statute 1862A (12)

- ▲ ⊘ ☑ **D2662** Onlay — resin-based composite composite/resin — two surfaces
  Medicare statute 1862A (12)

- ▲ ⊘ ☑ **D2663** Onlay — resin-based composite composite/resin — three surfaces
  Medicare statute 1862A (12)

- ▲ ⊘ ☑ **D2664** Onlay — resin-based composite composite/resin — four or more surfaces
  Medicare statute 1862A (12)

Crowns — Single Restorations Only

- ⊘ **D2710** Crown — resin (laboratory)
  Medicare statute 1862A (12)

- ⊘ **D2720** Crown — resin with high noble metal
  Medicare statute 1862A (12)

- ⊘ **D2721** Crown — resin with predominantly base metal
  Medicare statute 1862A (12)

- ⊘ **D2722** Crown — resin with noble metal
  Medicare statute 1862A (12)

- ⊘ **D2740** Crown — porcelain/ceramic substrate
  Medicare statute 1862A (12)

- ⊘ **D2750** Crown — porcelain fused to high noble metal
  Medicare statute 1862A (12)

- ⊘ **D2751** Crown — porcelain fused to predominantly base metal
  Medicare statute 1862A (12)

- ⊘ **D2752** Crown — porcelain fused to noble metal
  Medicare statute 1862A (12)

- ● **D2780** Crown — 3/4 cast high noble metal

- ● **D2781** Crown — 3/4 cast predominately base metal

- ● **D2782** Crown — 3/4 cast noble metal

- ● **D2783** Crown — 3/4 porcelain/ceramic

DENTAL PROCEDURES — ENDODONTICS

- ⊘ **D2790** Crown — full cast high noble metal
  Medicare statute 1862A (12)

- ⊘ **D2791** Crown — full cast predominantly base metal
  Medicare statute 1862A (12)

- ⊘ **D2792** Crown — full cast noble metal
  Medicare statute 1862A (12)

- ● **D2799** Provisional crown
  Do not use this code to report a temporary crown for a routine prosthetic restoration.

Other Restorative Services

- ⊘ **D2910** Recement inlay
  Medicare statute 1862A (12)

- ⊘ **D2920** Recement crown
  Medicare statute 1862A (12)

- ⊘ **D2930** Prefabricated stainless steel crown — primary tooth
  Medicare statute 1862A (12)

- ⊘ **D2931** Prefabricated stainless steel crown — permanent tooth
  Medicare statute 1862A (12)

- ⊘ **D2932** Prefabricated resin crown
  Medicare statute 1862A (12)

- ⊘ **D2933** Prefabricated stainless steel crown with resin window
  Medicare statute 1862A (12)

- ⊘ **D2940** Sedative filling
  Medicare statute 1862A (12)

- ⊘ **D2950** Core buildup, including any pins
  Medicare statute 1862A (12)

- ⊘ **D2951** Pin retention — per tooth, in addition to restoration
  Medicare statute 1862A (12)

- ⊘ **D2952** Cast post and core in addition to crown
  Medicare statute 1862A (12)

- ● ⊘ **D2953** Each additional cast post — same tooth
  Report in addition to code D2952.

- ⊘ **D2954** Prefabricated post and core in addition to crown
  Medicare statute 1862A (12)

- ⊘ **D2955** Post removal (not in conjunction with endodontic therapy)

- ● **D2957** Each additional prefabricated post — same tooth
  Report in addition to code D2954.

- ⊘ **D2960** Labial veneer (resin laminate) — chairside
  Medicare statute 1862A (12)

- ⊘ **D2961** Labial veneer (resin laminate) — laboratory
  Medicare statute 1862A (12)

- ⊘ **D2962** Labial veneer (porcelain laminate) — laboratory
  Medicare statute 1862A (12)

- ? **D2970** Temporary crown (fractured tooth)
  MCM 2336, MCM 2136

- ⊘ **D2980** Crown repair, by report
  Medicare statute 1862A (12)
  Pertinent documentation to evaluate medical appropriateness should be included when this code is reported.

- ? **D2999** Unspecified restorative procedure, by report
  MCM 2336, MCM 2136
  Determine if an alternative national HCPCS Level II code, a local HCPCS Level III code, or a CPT code better describes the service being reported. This code should be used only if a more specific code is unavailable.

Endodontics D3000–D3999

Pulp Capping

- ⊘ **D3110** Pulp cap — direct (excluding final restoration)
  Medicare statute 1862A (12)

- ⊘ **D3120** Pulp cap — indirect (excluding final restoration)
  Medicare statute 1862A (12)

Pulpotomy

- ▲ ⊘ **D3220** Therapeutic pulpotomy (excluding final restoration) — removal of pulp coronal to the dentinocemental junction and application of medicament
  Medicare statute 1862A (12)
  Do not use this code to report the first stage of root canal therapy.

- ● **D3221** Gross pulpal debridement, primary and permanent teeth

Endodontic Therapy on Primary Teeth

- ⊘ **D3230** Pulpal therapy (resorbable filling) — anterior, primary tooth (excluding final restoration)
  Medicare statute 1862A (12)

- ⊘ **D3240** Pulpal therapy (resorbable filling) — posterior, primary tooth (excluding final restoration)
  Medicare statute 1862A (12)

Endodontic Therapy (Including Treatment Plan, Clinical Procedures and Follow-up Care)

- ⊘ **D3310** Anterior (excluding final restoration)
  Medicare statute 1862A (12)

- ⊘ **D3320** Bicuspid (excluding final restoration)
  Medicare statute 1862A (12)

- ⊘ **D3330** Molar (excluding final restoration)
  Medicare statute 1862A (12)

- ● **D3331** Treatment of root canal obstruction; non-surgical access

- ● **D3332** Incomplete endodontic therapy; inoperable or fractured tooth

- ● **D3333** Internal root repair of perforation defects

⊘ Not covered by or valid for Medicare   ? Special coverage instructions   ➡ Carrier discretion

DENTAL PROCEDURES — PERIODONTICS

Endodontic Retreatment

⊘ **D3346** Retreatment of previous root canal therapy — anterior
Medicare statute 1862A (12)

⊘ **D3347** Retreatment of previous root canal therapy — bicuspid
Medicare statute 1862A (12)

⊘ **D3348** Retreatment of previous root canal therapy — molar
Medicare statute 1862A (12)

Apexification/Recalcification Procedures

⊘ **D3351** Apexification/recalcification — initial visit (apical closure/calcific repair of perforations, root resorption, etc.)
Medicare statute 1862A (12)

⊘ **D3352** Apexification/recalcification — interim medication replacement (apical closure/calcific repair of perforations, root resorption, etc.)
Medicare statute 1862A (12)

⊘ **D3353** Apexification/recalcification – final visit (includes completed root canal therapy — apical closure/calcific repair of perforations, root resorption, etc.)
Medicare statute 1862A (12)

Apicoectomy/Periradicular Services

⊘ **D3410** Apicoectomy/periradicular surgery — anterior
Medicare statute 1862A (12)

⊘ **D3421** Apicoectomy/periradicular surgery — bicuspid (first root)
Medicare statute 1862A (12)

⊘ **D3425** Apicoectomy/periradicular surgery — molar (first root)
Medicare statute 1862A (12)

⊘ ☑ **D3426** Apicoectomy/periradicular surgery (each additional root)
Medicare statute 1862A (12)

⊘ ☑ **D3430** Retrograde filling — per root
Medicare statute 1862A (12)

⊘ ☑ **D3450** Root amputation — per root
Medicare statute 1862A (12)

? **D3460** Endodontic endosseous implant
Medicare statute 1862A (12)

⊘ **D3470** Intentional reimplantation (including necessary splinting)
Medicare statute 1862A (12)

Other Endodontic Procedures

⊘ **D3910** Surgical procedure for isolation of tooth with rubber dam
Medicare statute 1862A (12)

⊘ **D3920** Hemisection (including any root removal), not including root canal therapy
Medicare statute 1862A (12)

⊘ **D3950** Canal preparation and fitting of preformed dowel or post
Medicare statute 1862A (12)

(D3960 has been deleted)

? **D3999** Unspecified endodontic procedure, by report
MCM 2336, MCM 2136
Determine if an alternative national HCPCS Level II code, a local HCPCS Level III code, or a CPT code better describes the service being reported. This code should be used only if a more specific code is unavailable.

Periodontics D4000–D4999

Surgical Services (Including Usual Postoperative Care)

⊘ ☑ **D4210** Gingivectomy or gingivoplasty — per quadrant. See also code 41820.
Cross-reference CPT 41820

⊘ ☑ **D4211** Gingivectomy or gingivoplasty — per tooth. See also code 41820 or 41872.
Cross-reference CPT

⊘ ☑ **D4220** Gingival curettage, surgical — per quadrant, by report
Medicare statute 1862A (12)
Pertinent documentation to evaluate medical appropriateness should be included when this code is reported.

⊘ ☑ **D4240** Gingival flap procedure, including root planing — per quadrant
Medicare statute 1862A (12)

● **D4245** Apically positioned flap

⊘ **D4249** Clinical crown lengthening — hard tissue
Medicare statute 1862A (12)

(D 4250 has been deleted)

? ☑ **D4260** Osseous surgery (including flap entry and closure) — per quadrant
MCM 2336, MCM 2136

? ☑ **D4263** Bone replacement graft — first site in quadrant
CIM 50-26, MCM 2336, MCM 2136

? ☑ **D4264** Bone replacement graft — each additional site in quadrant (use if performed on same date of service as D4263)
CIM 50-26, MCM 2336, MCM 2136

▲ ⊘ ☑ **D4266** Guided tissue regeneration — resorbable barrier, per site
Medicare statute 1862A (12)

▲ ⊘ ☑ **D4267** Guided tissue regeneration — nonresorbable barrier, per site (includes membrane removal)
Medicare statute 1862A (12)

● ☑ **D4268** Surgical revision procedure, per tooth

? **D4270** Pedicle soft tissue graft procedure
MCM 2336, MCM 2136

DENTAL PROCEDURES — PROSTHODONTICS (REMOVABLE)

? **D4271** Free soft tissue graft procedure (including donor site surgery)
MCM 2336, MCM 2136

? **D4273** Subepithelial connective tissue graft procedure (including donor site surgery)
CIM 50-26, MCM 2336, MCM 2136

⊘ **D4274** Distal or proximal wedge procedure (when not performed in conjunction with surgical procedures in the same anatomical area)

Non-Surgical Periodontal Services

⊘ **D4320** Provisional splinting — intracoronal
Medicare statute 1862A (12)

⊘ **D4321** Provisional splinting — extracoronal
Medicare statute 1862A (12)

⊘ ☑ **D4341** Periodontal scaling and root planing, per quadrant
Medicare statute 1862A (12)

? **D4355** Full mouth debridement to enable comprehensive periodontal evaluation and diagnosis
Medicare statute 1862A (12)
This procedure is covered by Medicare if its purpose is to identify a patient's existing infections prior to kidney transplantation.

? **D4381** Localized delivery of chemotherapeutic agents via a controlled release vehicle into diseased crevicular tissue, per tooth, by report
CIM 50-26, MCM 2336, MCM 2136
Pertinent documentation to evaluate medical appropriateness should be included when this code is reported.

Other Periodontal Services

⊘ **D4910** Periodontal maintenance procedures (following active therapy)
Medicare statute 1862A (12)

⊘ **D4920** Unscheduled dressing change (by someone other than treating dentist)
Medicare statute 1862A (12)

⊘ **D4999** Unspecified periodontal procedure, by report
Medicare statute 1862A (12)
Determine if an alternative national HCPCS Level II code, a local HCPCS Level III code, or a CPT code better describes the service being reported. This code should be used only if a more specific code is unavailable.

Prosthodontics (Removable) D5000–D5899

Complete Dentures (Including Routine Post-Delivery Care)

⊘ **D5110** Complete denture — maxillary
Medicare statute 1862A (12)

⊘ **D5120** Complete denture — mandibular
Medicare statute 1862A (12)

⊘ **D5130** Immediate denture — maxillary
Medicare statute 1862A (12)

⊘ **D5140** Immediate denture — mandibular
Medicare statute 1862A (12)

Partial Dentures (Including Routine Post-Delivery Care)

⊘ **D5211** Maxillary partial denture — resin base (including any conventional clasps, rests and teeth)
Medicare statute 1862A (12)

⊘ **D5212** Mandibular partial denture — resin base (including any conventional clasps, rests and teeth)
Medicare statute 1862A (12)

⊘ **D5213** Maxillary partial denture — cast metal framework with resin denture bases (including any conventional clasps, rests and teeth)
Medicare statute 1862A (12)

⊘ **D5214** Mandibular partial denture — cast metal framework with resin denture bases (including any conventional clasps, rests and teeth)
Medicare statute 1862A (12)

⊘ **D5281** Removable unilateral partial denture — one piece cast metal (including clasps and teeth)
Medicare statute 1862A (12)

Adjustments to Dentures

⊘ **D5410** Adjust complete denture — maxillary
Medicare statute 1862A (12)

⊘ **D5411** Adjust complete denture — mandibular
Medicare statute 1862A (12)

⊘ **D5421** Adjust partial denture — maxillary
Medicare statute 1862A (12)

⊘ **D5422** Adjust partial denture — mandibular
Medicare statute 1862A (12)

Repairs to Complete Dentures

⊘ **D5510** Repair broken complete denture base
Medicare statute 1862A (12)

⊘ **D5520** Replace missing or broken teeth — complete denture (each tooth)
Medicare statute 1862A (12)

Repairs to Partial Dentures

⊘ **D5610** Repair resin denture base
Medicare statute 1862A (12)

⊘ **D5620** Repair cast framework
Medicare statute 1862A (12)

⊘ **D5630** Repair or replace broken clasp
Medicare statute 1862A (12)

⊘ ☑ **D5640** Replace broken teeth — per tooth
Medicare statute 1862A (12)

⊘ **D5650** Add tooth to existing partial denture
Medicare statute 1862A (12)

⊘ **D5660** Add clasp to existing partial denture
Medicare statute 1862A (12)

DENTAL PROCEDURES — PROSTHODONTICS (REMOVABLE)

Denture Rebase Procedures

⊘ **D5710** Rebase complete maxillary denture
Medicare statute 1862A (12)

⊘ **D5711** Rebase complete mandibular denture
Medicare statute 1862A (12)

⊘ **D5720** Rebase maxillary partial denture
Medicare statute 1862A (12)

⊘ **D5721** Rebase mandibular partial denture
Medicare statute 1862A (12)

Denture Reline Procedures

⊘ **D5730** Reline complete maxillary denture (chairside)
Medicare statute 1862A (12)

⊘ **D5731** Reline complete mandibular denture (chairside)
Medicare statute 1862A (12)

⊘ **D5740** Reline maxillary partial denture (chairside)
Medicare statute 1862A (12)

⊘ **D5741** Reline mandibular partial denture (chairside)
Medicare statute 1862A (12)

⊘ **D5750** Reline complete maxillary denture (laboratory)
Medicare statute 1862A (12)

⊘ **D5751** Reline complete mandibular denture (laboratory)
Medicare statute 1862A (12)

⊘ **D5760** Reline maxillary partial denture (laboratory)
Medicare statute 1862A (12)

⊘ **D5761** Reline mandibular partial denture (laboratory)
Medicare statute 1862A (12)

Interim Prosthesis

⊘ **D5810** Interim complete denture (maxillary)
Medicare statute 1862A (12)

⊘ **D5811** Interim complete denture (mandibular)
Medicare statute 1862A (12)

⊘ **D5820** Interim partial denture (maxillary)
Medicare statute 1862A (12)

⊘ **D5821** Interim partial denture (mandibular)
Medicare statute 1862A (12)

Other Removable Prosthetic Services

⊘ **D5850** Tissue conditioning, maxillary
Medicare statute 1862A (12)

⊘ **D5851** Tissue conditioning, mandibular
Medicare statute 1862A (12)

⊘ **D5860** Overdenture — complete, by report
Medicare statute 1862A (12)
Pertinent documentation to evaluate medical appropriateness should be included when this code is reported.

⊘ **D5861** Overdenture — partial, by report
Medicare statute 1862A (12)
Pertinent documentation to evaluate medical appropriateness should be included when this code is reported.

⊘ **D5862** Precision attachment, by report
Medicare statute 1862A (12)
Pertinent documentation to evaluate medical appropriateness should be included when this code is reported.

● **D5867** Replacement of replaceable part of semi-precision or precision attachment (male or female component)

● **D5875** Modification of removable prosthesis following implant surgery

⊘ **D5899** Unspecified removable prosthodontic procedure, by report
Medicare statute 1862A (12)
Determine if an alternative national HCPCS Level II code, a local HCPCS Level III code, or a CPT code better describes the service being reported. This code should be used only if a more specific code is unavailable.

Maxillofacial Prosthetics D5900–D5999

?D5911 Facial moulage (sectional)
MCM 2136, MCM 2130A

?D5912 Facial moulage (complete)
MCM 2130A

⊘ **D5913** Nasal prosthesis
Cross-reference CPT 21087

⊘ **D5914** Auricular prosthesis
Cross-reference CPT 21086

⊘ **D5915** Orbital prosthesis
Cross-reference L8611

⊘ **D5916** Ocular prosthesis
Cross-reference V2626, V2629

⊘ **D5919** Facial prosthesis
Cross-reference CPT 21088

⊘ **D5922** Nasal septal prosthesis
Cross-reference CPT 30220

⊘ **D5923** Ocular prosthesis, interim
Cross-reference CPT 92330

⊘ **D5924** Cranial prosthesis
Cross-reference CPT 62143

⊘ **D5925** Facial augmentation implant prosthesis
Cross-reference CPT 21208

⊘ **D5926** Nasal prosthesis, replacement
Cross-reference CPT 21087

⊘ **D5927** Auricular prosthesis, replacement
Cross-reference CPT 21086

⊘ **D5928** Orbital prosthesis, replacement
Cross-reference CPT 67550

⊘ **D5929** Facial prosthesis, replacement
Cross-reference CPT 21088

⊘ **D5931** Obturator prosthesis, surgical
Cross-reference CPT 21079

- ⊘ **D5932** Obturator prosthesis, definitive
  Cross-reference CPT 21080
- ⊘ **D5933** Obturator prosthesis, modification
  Cross-reference CPT 21080
- ⊘ **D5934** Mandibular resection prosthesis with guide flange
  Cross-reference CPT 21081
- ⊘ **D5935** Mandibular resection prosthesis without guide flange
  Cross-reference CPT 21081
- ⊘ **D5936** Obturator/prosthesis, interim
  Cross-reference CPT 21079
- ⊘ **D5937** Trismus appliance (not for TMD treatment)
  MCM 2130
- ? **D5951** Feeding aid
  MCM 2336, MCM 2130
- ⊘ **D5952** Speech aid prosthesis, pediatric
  Cross-reference CPT 21084
- ⊘ **D5953** Speech aid prosthesis, adult
  Cross-reference CPT 21084
- ⊘ **D5954** Palatal augmentation prosthesis
  Cross-reference CPT 21082
- ⊘ **D5955** Palatal lift prosthesis, definitive
  Cross-reference CPT 21083
- ⊘ **D5958** Palatal lift prosthesis, interim
  Cross-reference CPT 21083
- ⊘ **D5959** Palatal lift prosthesis, modification
  Cross-reference CPT 21083
- ⊘ **D5960** Speech aid prosthesis, modification
  Cross-reference CPT 21084
- ⊘ **D5982** Surgical stent
  Cross-reference CPT 21085
- ? **D5983** Radiation carrier
  MCM 2336, MCM 2136
- ? **D5984** Radiation shield
  MCM 2336, MCM 2136
- ? **D5985** Radiation cone locator
  MCM 2336, MCM 2136
- ⊘ **D5986** Fluoride gel carrier
  MCM 2336, MCM 2136
- ? **D5987** Commissure splint
  MCM 2336, MCM 2136
- ⊘ **D5988** Surgical splint
  Cross-reference CPT
- ⊘ **D5999** Unspecified maxillofacial prosthesis, by report
  Cross-reference CPT
  Determine if an alternative national HCPCS Level II code, a local HCPCS Level III code, or a CPT code better describes the service being reported. This code should be used only if a more specific code is unavailable.

Implant Services D6000–D6199

- ⊘ **D6010** Surgical placement of implant body: endosteal implant
  Cross-reference CPT 21248
- ⊘ **D6020** Abutment placement or substitution: endosteal implant
  Cross-reference CPT 21248
- ⊘ **D6040** Surgical placement: eposteal implant
  Cross-reference CPT 21245
- ⊘ **D6050** Surgical placement: transosteal implant
  Cross-reference CPT 21244

Implant Supported Prosthetics

- ⊘ **D6055** Dental implant supported connecting bar
  MCM 2136
- ● **D6056** Prefabricated abutment
- ● **D6057** Custom abutment
- ● **D6058** Abutment supported porcelain/ceramic crown
- ● **D6059** Abutment supported porcelain fused to metal crown (high noble metal)
- ● **D6060** Abutment supported porcelain fused to metal crown (predominantly base metal)
- ● **D6061** Abutment supported porcelain fused to metal crown (noble metal)
- ● **D6062** Abutment supported cast metal crown (high noble metal)
- ● **D6063** Abutment supported cast metal crown (predominantly base metal)
- ● **D6064** Abutment supported cast metal crown (noble metal)
- ● **D6065** Implant supported porcelain/ceramic crown
- ● **D6066** Implant supported porcelain fused to metal crown (titanium, titanium alloy, high noble metal)
- ● **D6067** Implant supported metal crown (titanium, titanium alloy, high noble metal)
- ● **D6068** Abutment supported retainer for porcelain/ceramic FPD
- ● **D6069** Abutment supported retainer for porcelain fused to metal FPD (high noble metal)
- ● **D6070** Abutment supported retainer for porcelain fused to metal FPD (predominately base metal)
- ● **D6071** Abutment supported retainer for porcelain fused to metal FPD (noble metal)
- ● **D6072** Abutment supported retainer for cast metal FPD (high noble metal)
- ● **D6073** Abutment supported retainer for cast metal FPD (predominately base metal)

DENTAL PROCEDURES — IMPLANT SERVICES

- **D6074** Abutment supported retainer for cast metal FPD (noble metal)
- **D6075** Implant supported retainer for ceramic FPD
- **D6076** Implant supported retainer for porcelain fused to metal FPD (titanium, titanium alloy, or high noble metal)
- **D6077** Implant supported retainer for cast metal FPD (titanium, titanium alloy, or high noble metal)
- **D6078** Implant/abutment supported fixed denture for completely edentulous arch
- **D6079** Implant/abutment supported fixed denture for partially edentulous arch

Other Implant Services

⊘ **D6080** Implant maintenance procedures, including removal of prosthesis, cleansing of prosthesis and abutments, reinsertion of prosthesis
MCM 2136

⊘ **D6090** Repair implant supported prosthesis, by report
Cross-reference CPT 21299
Pertinent documentation to evaluate medical appropriateness should be included when this code is reported.

⊘ **D6095** Repair implant abutment, by report
Cross-reference CPT 21299
Pertinent documentation to evaluate medical appropriateness should be included when this code is reported.

⊘ **D6100** Implant removal, by report
Cross-reference CPT 21299
Pertinent documentation to evaluate medical appropriateness should be included when this code is reported.

⊘ **D6199** Unspecified implant procedure, by report
Cross-reference CPT 21299
Pertinent documentation to evaluate medical appropriateness should be included when this code is reported. Determine if an alternative national HCPCS Level II code, a local HCPCS Level III code, or a CPT code better describes the service being reported. This code should be used only if a more specific code is unavailable.

Prosthodontics Fixed (each retainer and each pontic constitutes a unit in a fixed partial denture)
D6200–D6999

Fixed Partial Denture Pontics

⊘ **D6210** Pontic — cast high noble metal
Medicare statute 1862A (12)
Each abutment and each pontic constitute a unit in a prosthesis. An alloy of at least 60 percent gold (Au), palladium (Pd), or platinum (Pt) is considered a high noble metal.

⊘ **D6211** Pontic — cast predominantly base metal
Medicare statute 1862A (12)
Each abutment and each pontic constitute a unit in a prosthesis. An alloy of less than 25 percent gold (Au), palladium (Pd), or platinum (Pt) is considered a base metal.

⊘ **D6212** Pontic — cast noble metal
Medicare statute 1862A (12)
Each abutment and each pontic constitute a unit in a prosthesis. An alloy of at least 25 percent gold (Au), palladium (Pd), or platinum (Pt) is considered a noble metal.

⊘ **D6240** Pontic — porcelain fused to high noble metal
Medicare statute 1862A (12)
Each abutment and each pontic constitute a unit in a prosthesis. An alloy of at least 60 percent gold (Au), palladium (Pd), or platinum (Pt) is considered a high noble metal.

⊘ **D6241** Pontic — porcelain fused to predominantly base metal
Medicare statute 1862A (12)
Each abutment and each pontic constitute a unit in a prosthesis. An alloy of less than 25 percent gold (Au), palladium (Pd), or platinum (Pt) is considered a base metal.

⊘ **D6242** Pontic — porcelain fused to noble metal
Medicare statute 1862A (12)
Each abutment and each pontic constitute a unit in a prosthesis. An alloy of at least 60 percent gold (Au), palladium (Pd), or platinum (Pt) is considered a high noble metal.

- **D6245** Pontic — porcelain/ceramic

⊘ **D6250** Pontic — resin with high noble metal
Medicare statute 1862A (12)
Each abutment and each pontic constitute a unit in a prosthesis. An alloy of at least 60 percent gold (Au), palladium (Pd), or platinum (Pt) is considered a high noble metal.

⊘ **D6251** Pontic — resin with predominantly base metal
Medicare statute 1862A (12)
Each abutment and each pontic constitute a unit in a prosthesis. An alloy of less than 25 percent gold (Au), palladium (Pd), or Platinum (Pt) is considered a base metal.

⊘ **D6252** Pontic — resin with noble metal
Medicare statute 1862A (12)
Each abutment and each pontic constitute a unit in a prosthesis. An alloy of at least 25 percent gold (Au), palladium (Pd), or platinum (Pt) is considered a noble metal.

Fixed Partial Denture Retainers — Inlays/Onlays

- **D6519** Inlay/onlay — porcelain/ceramic

⊘ ☑ **D6520** Inlay — metallic — two surfaces
Medicare statute 1862A (12)

⊘ ☑ **D6530** Inlay — metallic — three or more surfaces
Medicare statute 1862A (12)

⊘ ☑ **D6543** Onlay — metallic — three surfaces
Medicare statute 1862A (12)

DENTAL PROCEDURES — PROSTHODONTICS FIXED

- ⊘ ☑ **D6544** Onlay — metallic — four or more surfaces
  Medicare statute 1862A (12)

- ⊘ **D6545** Retainer — cast metal for resin bonded fixed prosthesis
  Medicare statute 1862A (12)

- **D6548** Retainer — porcelain/ceramic for resin bonded fixed prosthesis

Fixed Partial Denture Retainers — Crowns

- ⊘ **D6720** Crown — resin with high noble metal
  Medicare statute 1862A (12)
  An alloy of at least 60 percent gold (Au), palladium (Pd), or platinum (Pt) is considered a high noble metal.

- ⊘ **D6721** Crown — resin with predominantly base metal
  Medicare statute 1862A (12)
  An alloy of less than 25 percent gold (Au), palladium (Pd), or Platinum (Pt) is considered a base metal.

- ⊘ **D6722** Crown — resin with noble metal
  Medicare statute 1862A (12)
  An alloy of at least 25 percent gold (Au), palladium (Pd), or platinum (Pt) is considered a noble metal.

- **D6740** Crown — porcelain/ceramic

- ⊘ **D6750** Crown — porcelain fused to high noble metal
  Medicare statute 1862A (12)
  An alloy of at least 60 percent gold (Au), palladium (Pd), or platinum (Pt) is considered a high noble metal.

- ⊘ **D6751** Crown — porcelain fused to predominantly base metal
  Medicare statute 1862A (12)
  An alloy of less than 25 percent gold (Au), palladium (Pd), or Platinum (Pt) is considered a base metal.

- ⊘ **D6752** Crown — porcelain fused to noble metal
  Medicare statute 1862A (12)
  An alloy of at least 25 percent gold (Au), palladium (Pd), or platinum (Pt) is considered a noble metal.

- ⊘ **D6780** Crown — 3/4 cast high noble metal
  Medicare statute 1862A (12)
  An alloy of at least 60 percent gold (Au), palladium (Pd), or platinum (Pt) is considered a high noble metal.

- **D6781** Crown — 3/4 cast predominately based metal

- **D6782** Crown — 3/4 cast noble metal

- **D6783** Crown — 3/4 porcelain/ceramic

- ⊘ **D6790** Crown — full cast high noble metal
  Medicare statute 1862A (12)
  An alloy of at least 60 percent gold (Au), palladium (Pd), or platinum (Pt) is considered a high noble metal.

- ⊘ **D6791** Crown — full cast predominantly base metal
  Medicare statute 1862A (12)
  An alloy of less than 25 percent gold (Au), palladium (Pd), or Platinum (Pt) is considered a base metal.

- ⊘ **D6792** Crown — full cast noble metal
  Medicare statute 1862A (12)
  An alloy of at least 25 percent gold (Au), palladium (Pd), or platinum (Pt) is considered a noble metal.

Other Fixed Partial Denture Services

- ⊘ **D6920** Connector bar
  CIM 50-26, MCM 2136, MCM 2336

- ⊘ **D6930** Recement fixed partial denture
  Medicare statute 1862A (12)

- ⊘ **D6940** Stress breaker
  Medicare statute 1862A (12)

- ⊘ **D6950** Precision attachment
  Medicare statute 1862A (12)

- ⊘ **D6970** Cast post and core in addition to fixed partial denture retainer
  Medicare statute 1862A (12)

- ⊘ **D6971** Cast post as part of fixed partial denture retainer
  Medicare statute 1862A (12)

- ⊘ **D6972** Prefabricated post and core in addition to fixed partial denture retainer
  Medicare statute 1862A (12)

- ⊘ **D6973** Core build up for retainer, including any pins
  Medicare statute 1862A (12)

- ⊘ **D6975** Coping — metal
  Medicare statute 1862A (12)

- ⊘ **D6976** Each additional cast post — same tooth
  Report this code in addition to codes D6970 or D6971.

- ⊘ **D6977** Each additional prefabricated post — same tooth
  Report this code in addition to code D6972.

- ⊘ **D6980** Fixed partial denture repair, by report
  Medicare statute 1862A (12)
  Pertinent documentation to evaluate medical appropriateness should be included when this code is reported.

- ⊘ **D6999** Unspecified, fixed prosthodontic procedure, by report
  Medicare statute 1862A (12)
  Determine if an alternative national HCPCS Level II code, a local HCPCS Level III code, or a CPT code better describes the service being reported. This code should be used only if a more specific code is unavailable.

Oral and Maxillofacial Surgery D7000–D7999

Extractions (Includes Local Anesthesia, Suturing, if Needed, and Routine Postoperative Care)

D7110 Extraction — single tooth
MCM 2336, MCM 2136

D7120 Extraction — each additional tooth
MCM 2336, MCM 2136

D7130 Root removal — exposed roots
MCM 2336, MCM 2136

Surgical Extractions (Includes Local Anesthesia, Suturing, if Needed, and Routine Postoperative Care)

D7210 Surgical removal of erupted tooth requiring elevation of mucoperiosteal flap and removal of bone and/or section of tooth
MCM 2336, MCM 2136

D7220 Removal of impacted tooth — soft tissue
MCM 2336, MCM 2136

D7230 Removal of impacted tooth — partially bony

D7240 Removal of impacted tooth — completely bony
MCM 2336, MCM 2136

D7241 Removal of impacted tooth — completely bony, with unusual surgical complications
MCM 2336, MCM 2136

D7250 Surgical removal of residual tooth roots (cutting procedure)
MCM 2336, MCM 2136

Other Surgical Procedures

D7260 Oroantral fistula closure
MCM 2336, MCM 2136

D7270 Tooth reimplantation and/or stabilization of accidentally evulsed or displaced tooth and/or alveolus
MCM 2336, MCM 2136

D7272 Tooth transplantation (includes reimplantation from one site to another and splinting and/or stabilization)
Medicare statute 1862A (12)

D7280 Surgical exposure of impacted or unerupted tooth for orthodontic reasons (including orthodontic attachments)
Medicare statute 1862A (12)

D7281 Surgical exposure of impacted or unerupted tooth to aid eruption
Medicare statute 1862A (12)

D7285 Biopsy of oral tissue — hard (bone, tooth)
Cross-reference CPT 20220, 20225, 20240, 20245

D7286 Biopsy of oral tissue — soft (all others)
Cross-reference CPT 40808

D7290 Surgical repositioning of teeth
Medicare statute 1862A (12)

D7291 Transseptal fiberotomy, by report
MCM 2336, MCM 2136
Pertinent documentation to evaluate medical appropriateness should be included when this code is reported.

Alveoloplasty — Surgical Preparation of Ridge for Dentures

D7310 Alveoloplasty in conjunction with extractions — per quadrant
Cross-reference CPT 41874

D7320 Alveoloplasty not in conjunction with extractions — per quadrant
Cross-reference CPT 41870

Vestibuloplasty

D7340 Vestibuloplasty — ridge extension (second epithelialization)
Cross-reference CPT 40840, 40842, 40843, 40844

D7350 Vestibuloplasty — ridge extension (including soft tissue grafts, muscle reattachments, revision of soft tissue attachment and management of hypertrophied and hyperplastic tissue)
Cross-reference CPT 40845

Surgical Excision of Reactive Inflammatory Lesions (Scar Tissue or Localized Congenital Lesions)

D7410 Radical excision — lesion diameter up to 1.25 cm
Cross-reference CPT

D7420 Radical excision — lesion diameter greater than 1.25 cm
Cross-reference CPT

Removal of Tumors, Cysts and Neoplasms

D7430 Excision of benign tumor – lesion diameter up to 1.25 cm
Cross-reference CPT

D7431 Excision of benign tumor – lesion diameter greater than 1.25 cm
Cross-reference CPT

D7440 Excision of malignant tumor – lesion diameter up to 1.25 cm
Cross-reference CPT

D7441 Excision of malignant tumor – lesion diameter greater than 1.25 cm
Cross-reference CPT

D7450 Removal of odontogenic cyst or tumor – lesion diameter up to 1.25 cm
Cross-reference CPT

D7451 Removal of odontogenic cyst or tumor – lesion diameter greater than 1.25 cm
Cross-reference CPT

DENTAL PROCEDURES — ORAL AND MAXILLOFACIAL SURGERY

- ⊘ ☑ **D7460** Removal of nonodontogenic cyst or tumor – lesion diameter up to 1.25 cm
  Cross-reference CPT
- ⊘ ☑ **D7461** Removal of nonodontogenic cyst or tumor – lesion diameter greater than 1.25 cm
  Cross-reference CPT
- ⊘ **D7465** Destruction of lesion(s) by physical or chemical method, by report
  Cross-reference CPT 41850
  Pertinent documentation to evaluate medical appropriateness should be included when this code is reported.

Excision of Bone Tissue

- ● ☑ **D7471** Removal of exostosis — per site
- ⊘ **D7480** Partial ostectomy (guttering or saucerization)
  Cross-reference CPT 21025
- ⊘ **D7490** Radical resection of mandible with bone graft
  Cross-reference CPT 21095

Surgical Incision

- ⊘ **D7510** Incision and drainage of abscess – intraoral soft tissue
  Cross-reference CPT 41800
- ⊘ **D7520** Incision and drainage of abscess – extraoral soft tissue
  Cross-reference CPT 40800
- ⊘ **D7530** Removal of foreign body, skin, or subcutaneous alveolar tissue
  Cross-reference CPT 41805, 41828
- ⊘ **D7540** Removal of reaction-producing foreign bodies, musculoskeletal system
  Cross-reference CPT 20520, 41800, 41806
- ⊘ **D7550** Sequestrectomy for osteomyelitis
  Cross-reference CPT 20999
- ⊘ **D7560** Maxillary sinusotomy for removal of tooth fragment or foreign body
  Cross-reference CPT 31020

Treatment of Fractures — Simple

- ⊘ **D7610** Maxilla — open reduction (teeth immobilized, if present)
  Cross-reference CPT
- ⊘ **D7620** Maxilla — closed reduction (teeth immobilized, if present)
  Cross-reference CPT
- ⊘ **D7630** Mandible — open reduction (teeth immobilized, if present)
  Cross-reference CPT
- ⊘ **D7640** Mandible — closed reduction (teeth immobilized, if present)
  Cross-reference CPT
- ⊘ **D7650** Malar and/or zygomatic arch — open reduction
  Cross-reference CPT
- ⊘ **D7660** Malar and/or zygomatic arch — closed reduction
  Cross-reference CPT
- ▲ ⊘ **D7670** Alveolus — stabilization of teeth, closed reduction splinting
  Cross-reference CPT
- ⊘ **D7680** Facial bones — complicated reduction with fixation and multiple surgical approaches
  Cross-reference CPT

Treatment of Fractures — Compound

- ⊘ **D7710** Maxilla — open reduction
  Cross-reference CPT 21346
- ⊘ **D7720** Maxilla — closed reduction
  Cross-reference CPT 21345
- ⊘ **D7730** Mandible — open reduction
  Cross-reference CPT 21461, 21462
- ⊘ **D7740** Mandible — closed reduction
  Cross-reference CPT 21455
- ⊘ **D7750** Malar and/or zygomatic arch — open reduction
  Cross-reference CPT 21360, 21365
- ⊘ **D7760** Malar and/or zygomatic arch — closed reduction
  Cross-reference CPT 21355
- ⊘ **D7770** Alveolus — stabilization of teeth, open reduction splinting
  Cross-reference CPT 21422
- ⊘ **D7780** Facial bones — complicated reduction with fixation and multiple surgical approaches
  Cross-reference CPT 21433, 21435, 21436

Reduction of Dislocation and Management of Other Temporomandibular Joint Dysfunctions

Procedures which are an integral part of a primary procedure should not be reported separately.

- ⊘ **D7810** Open reduction of dislocation
  Cross-reference CPT 21490
- ⊘ **D7820** Closed reduction of dislocation
  Cross-reference CPT 21480
- ⊘ **D7830** Manipulation under anesthesia
  Cross-reference CPT 00190
- ⊘ **D7840** Condylectomy
  Cross-reference CPT 21050
- ⊘ **D7850** Surgical discectomy, with/without implant
  Cross-reference CPT 21060
- ⊘ **D7852** Disc repair
  Cross-reference CPT 21299
- ⊘ **D7854** Synovectomy
  Cross-reference CPT 21299
- ⊘ **D7856** Myotomy
  Cross-reference CPT 21299

DENTAL PROCEDURES — ORAL AND MAXILLOFACIAL SURGERY

⊘ **D7858** Joint reconstruction
Cross-reference CPT 21242, 21243

⊘ **D7860** Arthrotomy
MCM 2336, MCM 2136

⊘ **D7865** Arthroplasty
Cross-reference CPT 21240

⊘ **D7870** Arthrocentesis
Cross-reference CPT 21060

● **D7871** Non-arthroscopic lysis and lavage

⊘ **D7872** Arthroscopy — diagnosis, with or without biopsy
Cross-reference CPT 29800

⊘ **D7873** Arthroscopy — surgical: lavage and lysis of adhesions
Cross-reference CPT 29804

⊘ **D7874** Arthroscopy — surgical: disc repositioning and stabilization
Cross-reference CPT 29804

⊘ **D7875** Arthroscopy — surgical: synovectomy
Cross-reference CPT 29804

⊘ **D7876** Arthroscopy — surgical: discectomy
Cross-reference CPT 29804

⊘ **D7877** Arthroscopy — surgical: debridement
Cross-reference CPT 29804

⊘ **D7880** Occlusal orthotic device, by report
Cross-reference CPT 21499

⊘ **D7899** Unspecified TMD therapy, by report
Cross-reference CPT 21499
Determine if an alternative national HCPCS Level II code, a local HCPCS Level III code, or a CPT code better describes the service being reported. This code should be used only if a more specific code is unavailable.

Repair of Traumatic Wounds

⊘ ☑ **D7910** Suture of recent small wounds up to 5 cm
Cross-reference CPT 12011, 12013

Complicated Suturing (Reconstruction Requiring Delicate Handling of Tissues and Wide Undermining for Meticulous Closure)

⊘ **D7911** Complicated suture — up to 5 cm
Cross-reference CPT 12051, 12052

⊘ **D7912** Complicated suture — greater than 5 cm
Cross-reference CPT 13132

Other Repair Procedures

⊘ **D7920** Skin graft (identify defect covered, location and type of graft)
Cross-reference CPT

⊘ **D7940** Osteoplasty — for orthognathic deformities
MCM 2336, MCM 2136

▲ ⊘ **D7941** Osteotomy — mandibular rami
Cross-reference CPT 21193, 21195, 21196

(D7942 has been deleted)

▲ **D7943** Osteotomy — mandibular rami with bone graft; includes obtaining the graft
Cross-reference CPT 21194

⊘ ☑ **D7944** Osteotomy — segmented or subapical — per sextant or quadrant
Cross-reference CPT 21198, 21206

⊘ **D7945** Osteotomy — body of mandible
Cross-reference CPT 21193, 21194, 21195, 21196

⊘ **D7946** LeFort I (maxilla — total)
Cross-reference CPT 21147

⊘ **D7947** LeFort I (maxilla — segmented)
Cross-reference CPT 21145, 21146

⊘ **D7948** LeFort II or LeFort III (osteoplasty of facial bones for midface hypoplasia or retrusion) — without bone graft
Cross-reference CPT 21150

⊘ **D7949** LeFort II or LeFort III — with bone graft
Cross-reference CPT

⊘ **D7950** Osseous, osteoperiosteal, or cartilage graft of the mandible or facial bones— autogenous or nonautogenous, by report
Cross-reference CPT 21247
Pertinent documentation to evaluate medical appropriateness should be included when this code is reported.

⊘ **D7955** Repair of maxillofacial soft and hard tissue defect
Cross-reference CPT 21299

⊘ **D7960** Frenulectomy (frenectomy or frenotomy) — separate procedure
Cross-reference CPT 40819, 41010, 41115

⊘ ☑ **D7970** Excision of hyperplastic tissue — per arch
Cross-reference CPT

⊘ **D7971** Excision of pericoronal gingiva
Cross-reference CPT 41821

⊘ **D7980** Sialolithotomy
Cross-reference CPT 42330, 42335, 42340

⊘ **D7981** Excision of salivary gland, by report
Cross-reference CPT 42408
Pertinent documentation to evaluate medical appropriateness should be included when this code is reported.

⊘ **D7982** Sialodochoplasty
Cross-reference CPT 42500

⊘ **D7983** Closure of salivary fistula
Cross-reference CPT 42600

⊘ **D7990** Emergency tracheotomy
Cross-reference CPT 31603, 31605

⊘ **D7991** Coronoidectomy
Cross-reference CPT 21070

⊘ **D7995** Synthetic graft — mandible or facial bones, by report
Cross-reference CPT 21299
Pertinent documentation to evaluate medical appropriateness should be included when this code is reported.

DENTAL PROCEDURES — ADJUNCTIVE GENERAL SERVICES

⊘ **D7996** Implant — mandible for augmentation purposes (excluding alveolar ridge), by report
Cross-reference CPT 21299
Pertinent documentation to evaluate medical appropriateness should be included when this code is reported.

● **D7997** Appliance removal (not by dentist who placed appliance), includes removal of archbar

⊘ **D7999** Unspecified oral surgery procedure, by report
Cross-reference CPT 21299
Determine if an alternative national HCPCS Level II code, a local HCPCS Level III code, or a CPT code better describes the service being reported. This code should be used only if a more specific code is unavailable.

Orthodontics D8000–D8999

⊘ **D8010** Limited orthodontic treatment of the primary dentition
Medicare statute 1862A (12)

⊘ **D8020** Limited orthodontic treatment of the transitional dentition
Medicare statute 1862A (12)

⊘ **D8030** Limited orthodontic treatment of the adolescent dentition
Medicare statute 1862A (12)

⊘ **D8040** Limited orthodontic treatment of the adult dentition
Medicare statute 1862A (12)

Interceptive Orthodontic Treatment

⊘ **D8050** Interceptive orthodontic treatment of the primary dentition
Medicare statute 1862A (12)

⊘ **D8060** Interceptive orthodontic treatment of the transitional dentition
Medicare statute 1862A (12)

Comprehensive Orthodontic Treatment

⊘ **D8070** Comprehensive orthodontic treatment of the transitional dentition
Medicare statute 1862A (12)

⊘ **D8080** Comprehensive orthodontic treatment of the adolescent dentition
Medicare statute 1862A (12)

⊘ **D8090** Comprehensive orthodontic treatment of the adult dentition
Medicare statute 1862A (12)

Minor Treatment to Control Harmful Habits

⊘ **D8210** Removable appliance therapy
Medicare statute 1862A (12)

⊘ **D8220** Fixed appliance therapy
Medicare statute 1862A (12)

Other Orthodontic Services

⊘ **D8660** Pre-orthodontic treatment visit
Medicare statute 1862A (12)

⊘ **D8670** Periodic orthodontic treatment visit (as part of contract)
Medicare statute 1862A (12)

⊘ **D8680** Orthodontic retention (removal of appliances, construction and placement of retainer(s))
Medicare statute 1862A (12)

⊘ **D8690** Orthodontic treatment (alternative billing to a contract fee)
Medicare statute 1862A (12)

● **D8691** Repair of orthodontic appliance

● **D8692** Replacement of lost or broken retainer

⊘ **D8999** Unspecified orthodontic procedure, by report
Medicare statute 1862A (12)
Determine if an alternative national HCPCS Level II code, a local HCPCS Level III code, or a CPT code better describes the service being reported. This code should be used only if a more specific code is unavailable.

Adjunctive General Services D9000–D9999

Unclassified Treatment

? **D9110** Palliative (emergency) treatment of dental pain — minor procedure
MCM 2336, MCM 2136

Anesthesia

⊘ **D9210** Local anesthesia not in conjunction with operative or surgical procedures
Cross-reference CPT 90784

⊘ **D9211** Regional block anesthesia
Cross-reference CPT 01995

⊘ **D9212** Trigeminal division block anesthesia
Cross-reference CPT 64400

⊘ **D9215** Local anesthesia
Cross-reference CPT 90784

⊘ ☑**D9220** General anesthesia — first 30 minutes
Cross-reference CPT

⊘ ☑**D9221** General anesthesia — each additional 15 minutes
MCM 2336, MCM 2136

▲ ? **D9230** Analgesia, anxiolysis, inhalation of nitrous oxide
MCM 2336, MCM 2136

● ☑**D9241** Intravenous sedation/analgesia — first 30 minutes

● ☑**D9242** Intravenous sedation/analgesia — each additional 15 minutes

● **D9248** Non-intravenous conscious sedation

HCPCS 2000 ⊘ Not covered by or valid for Medicare ? Special coverage instructions ➥ Carrier discretion **31**

DENTAL PROCEDURES — ADJUNCTIVE GENERAL SERVICES

Professional Consultation

⊘ **D9310** Consultation (diagnostic service provided by dentist or physician other than practitioner providing treatment)
Cross-reference CPT

Professional Visits

▲ ⊘ **D9410** House/extrended care facility call
Cross-reference CPT

⊘ **D9420** Hospital call
Cross-reference CPT

⊘ **D9430** Office visit for observation (during regularly scheduled hours) — no other services performed
Cross-reference CPT

⊘ **D9440** Office visit — after regularly scheduled hours
Cross-reference CPT 99050

Drugs

⊘ **D9610** Therapeutic drug injection, by report
Cross-reference CPT 90784, 90788
Pertinent documentation to evaluate medical appropriateness should be included when this code is reported.

? **D9630** Other drugs and/or medicaments, by report
MCM 2336, MCM 2136
Determine if an alternative national HCPCS Level II or a local HCPCS Level III code better describes the supplies being reported. This code should be used only if a more specific code is unavailable.

Miscellaneous Services

⊘ **D9910** Application of desensitizing medicament
Medicare statute 1862A (12)

● ☑ **D9911** Application of desensitizing resin for cervical and/or root surface, per tooth

⊘ **D9920** Behavior management, by report
Medicare statute 1862A (12)
Pertinent documentation to evaluate medical appropriateness should be included when this code is reported.

? **D9930** Treatment of complications (post-surgical) — unusual circumstances, by report
MCM 2336, MCM 2136

? **D9940** Occlusal guard, by report
MCM 2336, MCM 2136
Pertinent documentation to evaluate medical appropriateness should be included when this code is reported.

⊘ **D9941** Fabrication of athletic mouthguard. See also code 21089.
Medicare statute 1862A (12); Cross-reference CPT 21089

? **D9950** Occlusion analysis — mounted case
MCM 2336, MCM 2136

? **D9951** Occlusal adjustment — limited
MCM 2336, MCM 2136

? **D9952** Occlusal adjustment — complete
MCM 2336, MCM 2136

⊘ **D9970** Enamel microabrasion
Medicare statute 1862A (12)

● ☑ **D9971** Odontoplasty 1–2 teeth; includes removal of enamel projections

● ☑ **D9972** External bleaching — per arch

● ☑ **D9973** External bleaching — per tooth

● ☑ **D9974** Internal bleaching — per tooth

(D9999 has been deleted)

Durable Medical Equipment E0100–E9999

Before an item can be considered to be durable medical equipment, it must meet all the following requirements: it must be able to withstand repeated use; be primarily and customarily used to serve a medical purpose; generally not useful to a person in the absence of an illness or injury; and appropriate for use in the home.

All E codes fall under the jurisdiction of the DME regional carrier unless otherwise noted.

Canes

? E0100 Cane, includes canes of all materials, adjustable or fixed, with tip
CIM 60-3, CIM 60-9, MCM 2100.1
White canes for the blind are not covered under Medicare.

? E0105 Cane, quad or three-prong, includes canes of all materials, adjustable or fixed, with tips
CIM 60-15, CIM 60-9, MCM 2100.1

Crutches

? ☑ E0110 Crutches, forearm, includes crutches of various materials, adjustable or fixed, pair, complete with tips and handgrips
CIM 60-9, MCM 2100.1

? ☑ E0111 Crutch, forearm, includes crutches of various materials, adjustable or fixed, each, with tip and handgrip
CIM 60-9, MCM 2100.1

? ☑ E0112 Crutches, underarm, wood, adjustable or fixed, pair, with pads, tips and handgrips
CIM 60-9, MCM 2100.1

? ☑ E0113 Crutch, underarm, wood, adjustable or fixed, each, with pad, tip and handgrip
CIM 60-9, MCM 2100.1

? E0114 Crutches, underarm, other than wood, adjustable or fixed, pair, with pads, tips and handgrips
CIM 60-9, MCM 2100.1

? E0116 Crutch, underarm, other than wood, adjustable or fixed, each, with pad, tip and handgrip
CIM 60-9, MCM 2100.1

Walkers

? E0130 Walker, rigid (pickup), adjustable or fixed height
CIM 60-9, MCM 2100.1
Medicare covers walkers if patient's ambulation is impaired.

? E0135 Walker, folding (pickup), adjustable or fixed height
CIM 60-9, MCM 2100.1
Medicare covers walkers if patient's ambulation is impaired.

? E0141 Rigid walker, wheeled, without seat
CIM 60-9, MCM 2100.1
Medicare covers walkers if patient's ambulation is impaired.

? E0142 Rigid walker, wheeled, with seat
CIM 60-9, MCM 2100.1
Medicare covers walkers if patient's ambulation is impaired.

? E0143 Folding walker, wheeled, without seat
CIM 60-9, MCM 2100.1
Medicare covers walkers if patient's ambulation is impaired.

● ? E0144 Enclosed, framed folding walker, wheeled, with posterior seat
CIM 60-9, MCM 2100.1

? E0145 Walker, wheeled, with seat and crutch attachments
CIM 60-9, MCM 2100.1
Medicare covers walkers if patient's ambulation is impaired.

? E0146 Folding walker, wheeled, with seat
CIM 60-9, MCM 2100.1
Medicare covers walkers if patient's ambulation is impaired.

? E0147 Heavy duty, multiple breaking system, variable wheel resistance walker
CIM 60-15, MCM 2100.1
Medicare covers "safety roller" walkers only in patients with severe neurological disorders or restricted use of one hand. In some cases, coverage will be extended to patients with a weight exceeding the limits of a standard wheeled walker.

➡ ☑ E0153 Platform attachment, forearm crutch, each

➡ ☑ E0154 Platform attachment, walker, each

▲ ➡ E0155 Wheel attachment, rigid pick-up walker, per pair

Attachments

➡ E0156 Seat attachment, walker

➡ ☑ E0157 Crutch attachment, walker, each

▲ ➡ ☑ E0158 Leg extensions for walker, per set of four (4)

➡ ☑ E0159 Brake attachment for wheeled walker, replacement, each

Commodes

? E0160 Sitz type bath or equipment, portable, used with or without commode
CIM 60-9
Medicare covers sitz baths if medical record indicates that the patient has an infection or injury of the perineal area and the sitz bath is prescribed by the physician.

HCPCS 2000   ⊘ Not covered by or valid for Medicare   ? Special coverage instructions   ➡ Carrier discretion   33

DURABLE MEDICAL EQUIPMENT

? **E0161** Sitz type bath or equipment, portable, used with or without commode, with faucet attachment/s
CIM 60-9
Medicare covers sitz baths if medical record indicates that the patient has an infection or injury of the perineal area and the sitz bath is prescribed by the physician.

? **E0162** Sitz bath chair
CIM 60-9
Medicare covers sitz baths if medical record indicates that the patient has an infection or injury of the perineal area and the sitz bath is prescribed by the physician.

? **E0163** Commode chair, stationary, with fixed arms
CIM 60-9, MCM 2100.1
Medicare covers commodes for patients confined to their beds or rooms, for patients without indoor bathroom facilities, and to patients who cannot climb or descend the stairs necessary to reach the bathrooms in their homes.

? **E0164** Commode chair, mobile, with fixed arms
CIM 60-9, MCM 2100.1
Medicare covers commodes for patients confined to their beds or rooms, for patients without indoor bathroom facilities, and to patients who cannot climb or descend the stairs necessary to reach the bathrooms in their homes.

? **E0165** Commode chair, stationary, with detachable arms
CIM 60-9, MCM 2100.1
Medicare covers commodes for patients confined to their beds or rooms, for patients without indoor bathroom facilities, and to patients who cannot climb or descend the stairs necessary to reach the bathrooms in their homes.

? **E0166** Commode chair, mobile, with detachable arms
CIM 60-9, MCM 2100.1
Medicare covers commodes for patients confined to their beds or rooms, for patients without indoor bathroom facilities, and to patients who cannot climb or descend the stairs necessary to reach the bathrooms in their homes.

? **E0167** Pail or pan for use with commode chair
CIM 60-9
Medicare covers commodes for patients confined to their beds or rooms, for patients without indoor bathroom facilities, and to patients who cannot climb or descend the stairs necessary to reach the bathrooms in their homes.

➡ ☑ **E0175** Foot rest, for use with commode chair, each

? **E0176** Air pressure pad or cushion, nonpositioning
CIM 60-9

? **E0177** Water pressure pad or cushion, nonpositioning
CIM 60-9

? **E0178** Gel or gel-like pressure pad or cushion, nonpositioning
CIM 60-9

? **E0179** Dry pressure pad or cushion, nonpositioning
CIM 60-9

Decubitus Care Equipment

? **E0180** Pressure pad, alternating with pump
CIM 60-9, MCM 4107.6
Medicare covers pads if physicians supervise their use in patients who have decubitus ulcers or susceptibility to them. Prior authorization is required by Medicare for this item.

? **E0181** Pressure pad, alternating with pump, heavy duty
CIM 60-9, MCM 4107.6
Medicare covers pads if physicians supervise their use in patients who have decubitus ulcers or susceptibility to them. Prior authorization is required by Medicare for this item.

? **E0182** Pump for alternating pressure pad
CIM 60-9, MCM 4107.6
Medicare covers pads if physicians supervise their use in patients who have decubitus ulcers or susceptibility to them. Prior authorization is required by Medicare for this item.

? **E0184** Dry pressure mattress
CIM 60-9, MCM 4107.6
Medicare covers pads if physicians supervise their use in patients who have decubitus ulcers or susceptibility to them. Prior authorization is required by Medicare for this item.

? **E0185** Gel or gel-like pressure pad for mattress, standard mattress length and width
CIM 60-9, MCM 4107.6
Medicare covers pads if physicians supervise their use in patients who have decubitus ulcers or susceptibility to them. Prior authorization is required by Medicare for this item.

? **E0186** Air pressure mattress
CIM 60-9
Medicare covers pads if physicians supervise their use in patients who have decubitus ulcers or susceptibility to them.

? **E0187** Water pressure mattress
CIM 60-9
Medicare covers pads if physicians supervise their use in patients who have decubitus ulcers or susceptibility to them.

? **E0188** Synthetic sheepskin pad
CIM 60-9, MCM 4107.6
Medicare covers pads if physicians supervise their use in patients who have decubitus ulcers or susceptibility to them. Prior authorization is required by Medicare for this item.

? **E0189** Lambswool sheepskin pad, any size
CIM 60-9, MCM 4107.6
Medicare covers pads if physicians supervise their use in patients who have decubitus ulcers or susceptibility to them. Prior authorization is required by Medicare for this item.

➡ ☑ **E0191** Heel or elbow protector, each

? **E0192** Low pressure and positioning equalization pad, for wheelchair
CIM 60-9, MCM 4107.6
Medicare covers pads if physicians supervise their use in patients who have decubitus ulcers or susceptibility to them. Prior authorization and a written order is required by Medicare for this item.

➡ **E0193** Powered air flotation bed (low air loss therapy)

? **E0194** Air fluidized bed
CIM 60-9
An air fluidized bed is covered by Medicare if the patient has a stage 3 or stage 4 pressure sore and, without the bed, would require institutionalization. A physician's prescription is required.

? **E0196** Gel pressure mattress
CIM 60-9
Medicare covers pads if physicians supervise their use in patients who have decubitus ulcers or susceptibility to them.

? **E0197** Air pressure pad for mattress, standard mattress length and width
CIM 60-9
Medicare covers pads if physicians supervise their use in patients who have decubitus ulcers or susceptibility to them.

? **E0198** Water pressure pad for mattress, standard mattress length and width
CIM 60-9
Medicare covers pads if physicians supervise their use in patients who have decubitus ulcers or susceptibility to them.

? **E0199** Dry pressure pad for mattress, standard mattress length and width
CIM 60-9
Medicare covers pads if physicians supervise their use in patients who have decubitus ulcers or susceptibility to them.

Heat/Cold Application

? **E0200** Heat lamp, without stand (table model), includes bulb, or infrared element
CIM 60-9, MCM 2100.1

➡ **E0202** Phototherapy (bilirubin) light with photometer

? **E0205** Heat lamp, with stand, includes bulb, or infrared element
CIM 60-9, MCM 2100.1

? **E0210** Electric heat pad, standard
CIM 60-9

? **E0215** Electric heat pad, moist
CIM 60-9

? **E0217** Water circulating heat pad with pump
CIM 60-9

? **E0218** Water circulating cold pad with pump
CIM 60-9

➡ **E0220** Hot water bottle

? **E0225** Hydrocollator unit, includes pads
CIM 60-9, MCM 2210.3

➡ **E0230** Ice cap or collar

? **E0235** Paraffin bath unit, portable (see medical supply code A4265 for paraffin)
CIM 60-9, MCM 2210.3

? **E0236** Pump for water circulating pad
CIM 60-9

? **E0238** Nonelectric heat pad, moist
CIM 60-9

? **E0239** Hydrocollator unit, portable
CIM 60-9 MCM 2210.3

Bath and Toilet Aids

⊘ ☑ **E0241** Bathtub wall rail, each
CIM 60-9, MCM 2100.1

⊘ **E0242** Bathtub rail, floor base
CIM 60-9, MCM 2100.1

⊘ ☑ **E0243** Toilet rail, each
CIM 60-9, MCM 2100.1

⊘ **E0244** Raised toilet seat
CIM 60-9

⊘ **E0245** Tub stool or bench
CIM 60-9

➡ **E0246** Transfer tub rail attachment

? **E0249** Pad for water circulating heat unit
CIM 60-9

Hospital Beds and Accessories

? **E0250** Hospital bed, fixed height, with any type side rails, with mattress
CIM 60-18, MCM 2100.1

? **E0251** Hospital bed, fixed height, with any type side rails, without mattress
CIM 60-18 MCM 2100.1

? **E0255** Hospital bed, variable height, hi-lo, with any type side rails, with mattress
CIM 60-18, MCM 2100.1

? **E0256** Hospital bed, variable height, hi-lo, with any type side rails, without mattress
CIM 60-18, MCM 2100.1

? **E0260** Hospital bed, semi-electric (head and foot adjustment), with any type side rails, with mattress
CIM 60-18, MCM 2100.1

? **E0261** Hospital bed, semi-electric (head and foot adjustment), with any type side rails, without mattress
CIM 60-18 MCM 2100.1

? **E0265** Hospital bed, total electric (head, foot, and height adjustments), with any type side rails, with mattress
CIM 60-18 MCM 2100.1

? **E0266** Hospital bed, total electric (head, foot, and height adjustments), with any type side rails, without mattress
CIM 60-18, MCM 2100.1

DURABLE MEDICAL EQUIPMENT

⊘ **E0270** Hospital bed, institutional type includes: oscillating, circulating and stryker frame, with mattress
CIM 60-9

? **E0271** Mattress, inner spring
CIM 60-18, CIM 60-9

? **E0272** Mattress, foam rubber
CIM 60-18, CIM 60-9

⊘ **E0273** Bed board
CIM 60-9

⊘ **E0274** Over-bed table
CIM 60-9

? **E0275** Bed pan, standard, metal or plastic
CIM 60-9
Reusable, autoclavable bedpans are covered by Medicare for bed-confined patients.

? **E0276** Bed pan, fracture, metal or plastic
CIM 60-9
Reusable, autoclavable bedpans are covered by Medicare for bed-confined patients.

? **E0277** Powered pressure-reducing air mattress
CIM 60-9

➡ **E0280** Bed cradle, any type

? **E0290** Hospital bed, fixed height, without side rails, with mattress
CIM 60-18, MCM 2100.1

? **E0291** Hospital bed, fixed height, without side rails, without mattress
CIM 60-18, MCM 2100.1

? **E0292** Hospital bed, variable height, hi-lo, without side rails, with mattress
CIM 60-18, MCM 2100.1

? **E0293** Hospital bed, variable height, hi-lo, without side rails, without mattress
CIM 60-18, MCM 2100.1

? **E0294** Hospital bed, semi-electric (head and foot adjustment), without side rails, with mattress
CIM 60-18, MCM 2100.1

? **E0295** Hospital bed, semi-electric (head and foot adjustment), without side rails, without mattress
CIM 60-18, MCM 2100.1

? **E0296** Hospital bed, total electric (head, foot, and height adjustments), without side rails, with mattress
CIM 60-18, MCM 2100.1

? **E0297** Hospital bed, total electric (head, foot, and height adjustments), without side rails, without mattress
CIM 60-18, MCM 2100.1

? **E0305** Bedside rails, half-length
CIM 60-18

? **E0310** Bedside rails, full-length
CIM 60-18

⊘ **E0315** Bed accessory: board, table, or support device, any type
CIM 60-9

? **E0325** Urinal; male, jug-type, any material
CIM 60-9

? **E0326** Urinal; female, jug-type, any material
CIM 60-9

➡ **E0350** Control unit for electronic bowel irrigation/evacuation system

➡ **E0352** Disposable pack (water reservoir bag, speculum, valving mechanism and collection bag/box) for use with the electronic bowel irrigation/evacuation system

➡ **E0370** Air pressure elevator for heel

➡ **E0371** Nonpowered advanced pressure reducing overlay for mattress, standard mattress length and width

➡ **E0372** Powered air overlay for mattress, standard mattress length and width

➡ **E0373** Nonpowered advanced pressure reducing mattress

Oxygen and Related Respiratory Equipment

? **E0424** Stationary compressed gaseous oxygen system, rental; includes contents (per unit), regulator, flowmeter, humidifier, nebulizer, cannula or mask, and tubing; 1 unit = 50 cubic ft
CIM 60-4, MCM 4107.9
For the first claim filed for home oxygen equipment or therapy, submit a certificate of medical necessity that includes the oxygen flow rate, anticipated frequency and duration of oxygen therapy, and physician signature. Medicare accepts oxygen therapy as medically necessary in cases documenting any of the following: erythrocythemia with a hematocrit greater than 56 percent; a P pulmonale on EKG; or dependent edema consistent with congestive heart failure.

? **E0425** Stationary compressed gas system, purchase; includes regulator, flowmeter, humidifier, nebulizer, cannula or mask, and tubing
CIM 60-4, MCM 4107.9

? **E0430** Portable gaseous oxygen system, purchase; includes regulator, flowmeter, humidifier, cannula or mask, and tubing
CIM 60-4, MCM 4107.9

? **E0431** Portable gaseous oxygen system, rental; includes regulator, flowmeter, humidifier, cannula or mask, and tubing
CIM 60-4, MCM 4107.9

? **E0434** Portable liquid oxygen system, rental; includes portable container, supply reservoir, humidifier, flowmeter, refill adaptor, contents gauge, cannula or mask, and tubing
CIM 60-4, MCM 4107.9

DURABLE MEDICAL EQUIPMENT

? E0435 Portable liquid oxygen system, purchase; includes portable container, supply reservoir, flowmeter, humidifier, contents gauge, cannula or mask, tubing, and refill adapter
CIM 60-4, MCM 4107.9

? ☑ E0439 Stationary liquid oxygen system, rental; includes use of reservoir, contents (per unit), regulator, flowmeter, humidifier, nebulizer, cannula or mask, and tubing; 1 unit = 10 lbs
CIM 60-4, MCM 4107.9

? E0440 Stationary liquid oxygen system, purchase; includes use of reservoir, contents indicator, regulator, flowmeter, humidifier, nebulizer, cannula or mask, and tubing
CIM 60-4, MCM 4107.9

? ☑ E0441 Oxygen contents, gaseous, per unit (for use with owned gaseous stationary systems or when both a stationary and portable gaseous system are owned; 1 unit = 50 cubic ft)
CIM 60-4, MCM 4107.9

? ☑ E0442 Oxygen contents, liquid, per unit (for use with owned liquid stationary systems or when both a stationary and portable liquid system are owned; 1 unit = 10 lbs)
CIM 60-4, MCM 4107.9

? ☑ E0443 Portable oxygen contents, gaseous, per unit (for use only with portable gaseous systems when no stationary gas or liquid system is used; 1 unit = 5 cubic ft)
CIM 60-4, MCM 4107.9

? ☑ E0444 Portable oxygen contents, liquid, per unit (for use only with portable liquid systems when no stationary gas or liquid system is used; 1 unit = 1 lb)
CIM 60-4, MCM 4107.9

▲ **? E0450** Volume ventilator, stationary or portable, with backup rate feature, used with invasive interface (e.g., Tracheostomy tube)
CIM 60-9

(E0452 has been deleted)

(E0453 has been deleted)

? E0455 Oxygen tent, excluding croup or pediatric tents
CIM 60-4, MCM 4107.9

➡ E0457 Chest shell (cuirass)

➡ E0459 Chest wrap

? E0460 Negative pressure ventilator; portable or stationary
CIM 60-9

➡ E0462 Rocking bed, with or without side rails

? E0480 Percussor, electric or pneumatic, home model
CIM 60-9

IPPB Machines

? E0500 IPPB machine, all types, with built-in nebulization; manual or automatic valves; internal or external power source
CIM 60-9

Humidifiers/Compressors/Nebulizers for Use with Oxygen IPPB Equipment

? E0550 Humidifier, durable for extensive supplemental humidification during IPPB treatments or oxygen delivery
CIM 60-9

? E0555 Humidifier, durable, glass or autoclavable plastic bottle type, for use with regulator or flowmeter
CIM 60-9

? E0560 Humidifier, durable for supplemental humidification during IPPB treatment or oxygen delivery
CIM 60-9

➡ E0565 Compressor, air power source for equipment which is not self-contained or cylinder driven

? E0570 Nebulizer, with compressor
CIM 60-9, MCM 4107.9

? E0575 Nebulizer, ultrasonic
CIM 60-9

? E0580 Nebulizer, durable, glass or autoclavable plastic, bottle type, for use with regulator or flowmeter
CIM 60-9, MCM 4107.9

? E0585 Nebulizer, with compressor and heater
CIM 60-9, MCM 4107.9

● **➡ E0590** Dispensing fee covered drug administered through DME nebulizer

Suction Pump/Room Vaporizers

? E0600 Suction pump, home model, portable
CIM 60-9

? E0601 Continuous airway pressure (CPAP) device
CIM 60-17

● **⊘ E0602** Breast pump, all types

? E0605 Vaporizer, room type
CIM 60-9

? E0606 Postural drainage board
CIM 60-9

HCPCS 2000   ⊘ Not covered by or valid for Medicare   ? Special coverage instructions   ➡ Carrier discretion

Monitoring Equipment

? **E0607** Home blood glucose monitor
CIM 60-11
Medicare covers home blood testing devices for diabetic patients when the devices are prescribed by the patients' physicians. Many commercial payers provide this coverage to non-insulin dependent diabetics as well.

? **E0608** Apnea monitor
CIM 60-17

? **E0609** Blood glucose monitor with special features (e.g., voice synthesizers, automatic timers, etc.)
CIM 60-11
Medicare covers the additional cost of specialty home blood testing devices for diabetic patients who are visually impaired, when the diabetes and the visual impairment are documented and the device is prescribed by the patient's physician.

Pacemaker Monitor

? **E0610** Pacemaker monitor, self-contained, checks battery depletion, includes audible and visible check systems
CIM 50-1, CIM 60-7

? **E0615** Pacemaker monitor, self-contained, checks battery depletion and other pacemaker components, includes digital/visible check systems
CIM 50-1, CIM 60-7

● ➡ **E0616** Implantable cardiac event recorder with memory, activator and programmer

Patient Lifts

? **E0621** Sling or seat, patient lift, canvas or nylon
CIM 60-9

⊘ **E0625** Patient lift, Kartop, bathroom or toilet
CIM 60-9

? **E0627** Seat lift mechanism incorporated into a combination lift-chair mechanism
CIM 60-8, MCM 4107.8

? **E0628** Separate seat lift mechanism for use with patient owned furniture — electric
CIM 60-9, MCM 4107.8

? **E0629** Separate seat lift mechanism for use with patient owned furniture — nonelectric
MCM 4107.8

? **E0630** Patient lift, hydraulic, with seat or sling
CIM 60-9

? **E0635** Patient lift, electric, with seat or sling
CIM 60-9

Pneumatic Compressor and Appliances

? **E0650** Pneumatic compressor, nonsegmental home model
CIM 60-16

? **E0651** Pneumatic compressor, segmental home model without calibrated gradient pressure
CIM 60-16

? **E0652** Pneumatic compressor, segmental home model with calibrated gradient pressure
CIM 60-16

? **E0655** Nonsegmental pneumatic appliance for use with pneumatic compressor, half arm
CIM 60-16

? **E0660** Nonsegmental pneumatic appliance for use with pneumatic compressor, full leg
CIM 60-16

? **E0665** Nonsegmental pneumatic appliance for use with pneumatic compressor, full arm
CIM 60-16

? **E0666** Nonsegmental pneumatic appliance for use with pneumatic compressor, half leg
CIM 60-16

? **E0667** Segmental pneumatic appliance for use with pneumatic compressor, full leg
CIM 60-16

? **E0668** Segmental pneumatic appliance for use with pneumatic compressor, full arm
CIM 60-16

? **E0669** Segmental pneumatic appliance for use with pneumatic compressor, half leg
CIM 60-16

? **E0671** Segmental gradient pressure pneumatic appliance, full leg
CIM 60-16

? **E0672** Segmental gradient pressure pneumatic appliance, full arm
CIM 60-16

? **E0673** Segmental gradient pressure pneumatic appliance, half leg
CIM 60-16

Ultraviolet Cabinet

? **E0690** Ultraviolet cabinet, appropriate for home use
CIM 60-9

Safety Equipment

➡ **E0700** Safety equipment (e.g., belt, harness or vest)

Restraints

➡ **E0710** Restraint, any type (body, chest, wrist or ankle)

Transcutaneous and/or Neuromuscular Electrical Nerve Stimulators — TENS

? **E0720** TENS, two lead, localized stimulation
CIM 35-20, CIM 35-46, MCM 4107.6
While TENS is covered when employed to control chronic pain, it is not covered for experimental treatment, as in motor function disorders like MS. Prior authorization is required by Medicare for this item.

? **E0730** TENS, four lead, larger area/multiple nerve stimulation
CIM 35-20, CIM 35-46, MCM 4107.6
While TENS is covered when employed to control chronic pain, it is not covered for experimental treatment, as in motor function disorders like MS. Prior authorization is required by Medicare for this item.

? **E0731** Form-fitting conductive garment for delivery of TENS or NMES (with conductive fibers separated from the patient's skin by layers of fabric)
CIM 45-25

⊘ **E0740** Incontinence treatment system, pelvic floor stimulator, monitor, sensor and/or trainer
CIM 65-11

➡ **E0744** Neuromuscular stimulator for scoliosis

? **E0745** Neuromuscular stimulator, electronic shock unit
CIM 35-77

? **E0746** Electromyography (EMG), biofeedback device
CIM 35-27
Biofeedback therapy is covered by Medicare only for re-education of specific muscles or for treatment of incapacitating muscle spasm or weakness. Medicare jurisdiction: local carrier.

? **E0747** Osteogenesis stimulator, electrical, noninvasive, other than spinal applications
CIM 35-48
Medicare covers noninvasive osteogenic stimulation for nonunion of long bone fractures, failed fusion, or congenital pseudoarthroses.

? **E0748** Osteogenesis stimulator, electrical, noninvasive, spinal applications
CIM 35-48
Medicare covers noninvasive osteogenic stimulation as an adjunct to spinal fusion surgery for patients at high risk of pseudoarthroses due to previously failed spinal fusion, or for those undergoing fusion of three or more vertebrae.

? **E0749** Osteogenesis stimulator, electrical (surgically implanted)
CIM 35-48
Medicare covers invasive osteogenic stimulation for nonunion of long bone fractures or as an adjunct to spinal fusion surgery for patients at high risk of pseudoarthroses due to previously failed spinal fusion, or for those undergoing fusion of three or more vertebrae.

? **E0751** Implantable neurostimulator pulse generator or combination of external transmitter with implantable receiver (includes extension)
CIM 65-8
Medicare jurisdiction: local carrier.

? **E0753** Implantable neurostimulator electrodes, per group of four
CIM 65-8
Medicare jurisdiction: local carrier.

➡ **E0755** Electronic salivary reflex stimulator (intraoral/noninvasive)

⊘ **E0760** Osteogenesis stimulator, low intensity ultrasound, non-invasive
CIM 35-48

Infusion Supplies

➡ **E0776** IV pole

● ➡ **E0779** Ambulatory infusion pump, mechanical, reusable, for infusion 8 hours or greater

● ➡ **E0780** Ambulatory infusion pump, mechanical, reusable, for infusion less than 8 hours

▲ ? **E0781** Ambulatory infusion pump, single or multiple channels, electric or battery operated, with administrative equipment, worn by patient
CIM 60-14

? **E0782** Infusion pump, implantable, non-programmable
CIM 60-14
Medicare jurisdiction: local carrier.

? **E0783** Infusion pump system, implantable, programmable (includes all components, e.g., pump, catheter, connectors, etc.)
CIM 60-14
Medicare jurisdiction: local carrier.

? **E0784** External ambulatory infusion pump, insulin
CIM 60-14
Covered by some commercial payers with preauthorization.

? **E0785** Implantable intraspinal (epidural/intrathecal) catheter used with implantable infusion pump, replacement
CIM 60-14

? **E0791** Parenteral infusion pump, stationary, single or multichannel
CIM 65-10, MCM 2130, MCM 4450

Traction — Cervical

? **E0840** Traction frame, attached to headboard, cervical traction
CIM 60-9

? **E0850** Traction stand, freestanding, cervical traction
CIM 60-9

➡ **E0855** Cervical traction equipment not requiring additional stand or frame

Traction — Overdoor

? **E0860** Traction equipment, overdoor, cervical
CIM 60-9

Traction — Extremity

? **E0870** Traction frame, attached to footboard, extremity traction (e.g., Buck's)
CIM 60-9

? **E0880** Traction stand, freestanding, extremity traction (e.g., Buck's)
CIM 60-9

Traction — Pelvic

? **E0890** Traction frame, attached to footboard, pelvic traction
CIM 60-9

? **E0900** Traction stand, freestanding, pelvic traction (e.g., Buck's)
CIM 60-9

Trapeze Equipment, Fracture Frame, and Other Orthopedic Devices

? **E0910** Trapeze bars, also known as Patient Helper, attached to bed, with grab bar
CIM 60-9

? **E0920** Fracture frame, attached to bed, includes weights
CIM 60-9

? **E0930** Fracture frame, freestanding, includes weights
CIM 60-9

? **E0935** Passive motion exercise device
CIM 60-9

? **E0940** Trapeze bar, freestanding, complete with grab bar
CIM 60-9

? **E0941** Gravity assisted traction device, any type
CIM 60-9

➡ **E0942** Cervical head harness/halter

➡ **E0943** Cervical pillow

➡ **E0944** Pelvic belt/harness/boot

➡ **E0945** Extremity belt/harness

? **E0946** Fracture, frame, dual with cross bars, attached to bed (e.g., Balken, Four Poster)
CIM 60-9

? **E0947** Fracture frame, attachments for complex pelvic traction
CIM 60-9

? **E0948** Fracture frame, attachments for complex cervical traction
CIM 60-9

Wheelchairs

Note: See also K0001–K0109.

➡ **E0950** Tray

➡ ☑ **E0951** Loop heel, each

➡ ☑ **E0952** Loop toe, each

? ☑ **E0953** Pneumatic tire, each
CIM 60-9

? ☑ **E0954** Semi-pneumatic caster, each
CIM 60-9

Wheelchair Accessories

? **E0958** Wheelchair attachment to convert any wheelchair to one arm drive
CIM 60-9

? **E0959** Amputee adapter (device used to compensate for transfer of weight due to lost limbs to maintain proper balance)
CIM 60-9

? **E0961** Brake extension, for wheelchair
CIM 60-9

? **E0962** One-inch cushion, for wheelchair
CIM 60-9

? **E0963** Two-inch cushion, for wheelchair
CIM 60-9

? **E0964** Three-inch cushion, for wheelchair
CIM 60-9

? **E0965** Four-inch cushion, for wheelchair
CIM 60-9

? **E0966** Hook on headrest extension
CIM 60-9

? ☑ **E0967** Wheelchair hand rims with eight vertical rubber-tipped projections, pair
CIM 60-9

? **E0968** Commode seat, wheelchair
CIM 60-9

? **E0969** Narrowing device, wheelchair
CIM 60-9

? **E0970** No. 2 footplates, except for elevating legrest
CIM 60-9

? **E0971** Anti-tipping device, wheelchair
CIM 60-9

➡ **E0972** Transfer board or device

? **E0973** Adjustable height detachable arms, desk or full-length, wheelchair
CIM 60-9

➡ **E0974** "Grade-aid" (device to prevent rolling back on an incline) for wheelchair

? **E0975** Reinforced seat upholstery, wheelchair
CIM 60-9

? **E0976** Reinforced back, wheelchair, upholstery or other material
CIM 60-9

➡ **E0977** Wedge cushion, wheelchair

➡ **E0978** Belt, safety with airplane buckle, wheelchair

➡ **E0979** Belt, safety with Velcro closure, wheelchair

➡ **E0980** Safety vest, wheelchair

? ☑ **E0990** Elevating leg rest, each
CIM 60-9

? **E0991** Upholstery seat
CIM 60-9

? **E0992** Solid seat insert
CIM 60-9

? **E0993** Back, upholstery
CIM 60-9

? ☑ **E0994** Armrest, each
CIM 60-9

? ☑ **E0995** Calf rest, each
CIM 60-9

? ☑ **E0996** Tire, solid, each
CIM 60-9

? **E0997** Caster with fork
CIM 60-9

? **E0998** Caster without fork
CIM 60-9

? **E0999** Pneumatic tire with wheel
CIM 60-9

? **E1000** Tire, pneumatic caster
CIM 60-9

? ☑ **E1001** Wheel, single
CIM 60-9

Rollabout Chair

? **E1031** Rollabout chair, any and all types with casters five inches or greater
CIM 60-9

Wheelchairs — Fully Reclining

? **E1050** Fully reclining wheelchair; fixed full-length arms, swing-away, detachable, elevating legrests
CIM 60-9

? **E1060** Fully reclining wheelchair; detachable arms, desk or full-length, swing-away, detachable, elevating legrests
CIM 60-9

? **E1065** Power attachment (to convert any wheelchair to motorized wheelchair, e.g., Solo)
CIM 60-9

? **E1066** Battery charger
CIM 60-9

? **E1069** Deep cycle battery
CIM 60-9

? **E1070** Fully reclining wheelchair; detachable arms, desk or full-length, swing-away, detachable footrests
CIM 60-9

? **E1083** Hemi-wheelchair; fixed full-length arms, swing-away, detachable, elevating legrests
CIM 60-9

? **E1084** Hemi-wheelchair; detachable arms, desk or full-length, swing-away, detachable, elevating legrests
CIM 60-9

? **E1085** Hemi-wheelchair; fixed full-length arms, swing-away, detachable footrests
CIM 60-9

? **E1086** Hemi-wheelchair; detachable arms, desk or full-length, swing-away, detachable footrests
CIM 60-9

? **E1087** High-strength lightweight wheelchair; fixed full-length arms, swing-away, detachable, elevating legrests
CIM 60-9

? **E1088** High-strength lightweight wheelchair; detachable arms, desk or full-length, swing-away, detachable, elevating legrests
CIM 60-9

? **E1089** High-strength lightweight wheelchair; fixed-length arms, swing-away, detachable footrests
CIM 60-9

? **E1090** High-strength lightweight wheelchair; detachable arms, desk or full-length, swing-away, detachable footrests
CIM 60-9

? **E1091** Youth wheelchair; any type
CIM 60-9

? **E1092** Wide, heavy-duty wheelchair; detachable arms, desk or full-length, swing-away, detachable, elevating legrests
CIM 60-9

? **E1093** Wide, heavy-duty wheelchair; detachable arms, desk or full-length arms, swing-away, detachable footrests
CIM 60-9

Wheelchair — Semi-reclining

? **E1100** Semi-reclining wheelchair; fixed full-length arms, swing-away, detachable, elevating legrests
CIM 60-9

? **E1110** Semi-reclining wheelchair; detachable arms, desk or full-length, elevating legrest
CIM 60-9

Wheelchair — Standard

? **E1130** Standard wheelchair; fixed full-length arms, fixed or swing-away, detachable footrests
CIM 60-9

? **E1140** Wheelchair; detachable arms, desk or full-length, swing-away, detachable footrests
CIM 60-9

? **E1150** Wheelchair; detachable arms, desk or full-length, swing-away, detachable, elevating legrests
CIM 60-9

? **E1160** Wheelchair; fixed full-length arms, swing-away, detachable, elevating legrests
CIM 60-9

Wheelchair — Amputee

? **E1170** Amputee wheelchair; fixed full-length arms, swing-away, detachable, elevating legrests
CIM 60-9

? **E1171** Amputee wheelchair; fixed full-length arms, without footrests or legrests
CIM 60-9

? **E1172** Amputee wheelchair; detachable arms, desk or full-length, without footrests or legrests
CIM 60-9

? **E1180** Amputee wheelchair; detachable arms, desk or full-length, swing-away, detachable footrests
CIM 60-9

? **E1190** Amputee wheelchair; detachable arms, desk or full-length, swing-away, detachable, elevating legrests
CIM 60-9

? **E1195** Heavy duty wheelchair; fixed full-length arms, swing-away, detachable, elevating legrests
CIM 60-9

? **E1200** Amputee wheelchair; fixed full-length arms, swing-away, detachable footrests
CIM 60-9

Wheelchair — Power

? **E1210** Motorized wheelchair; fixed full-length arms, swing-away, detachable, elevating legrests
CIM 60-5, CIM 60-9

? **E1211** Motorized wheelchair; detachable arms, desk or full-length, swing-away, detachable, elevating legrests
CIM 60-5, CIM 60-9

? **E1212** Motorized wheelchair; fixed full-length arms, swing-away, detachable footrests
CIM 60-5, CIM 60-9

? **E1213** Motorized wheelchair; detachable arms, desk or full-length, swing-away, detachable footrests
CIM 60-5, CIM 60-9

Wheelchair — Special Size

? **E1220** Wheelchair; specially sized or constructed (indicate brand name, model number, if any, and justification)
Medicaid suspend for medical review, CIM 60-6

? **E1221** Wheelchair with fixed arm, footrests
CIM 60-6

? **E1222** Wheelchair with fixed arm, elevating legrests
CIM 60-6

? **E1223** Wheelchair with detachable arms, footrests
CIM 60-6

? **E1224** Wheelchair with detachable arms, elevating legrests
CIM 60-6

? **E1225** Semi-reclining back for customized wheelchair
CIM 60-6

? **E1226** Full reclining back for customized wheelchair
CIM 60-6

? **E1227** Special height arms for wheelchair
CIM 60-6

? **E1228** Special back height for wheelchair
CIM 60-6

? **E1230** Power operated vehicle (three- or four-wheel nonhighway), specify brand name and model number
Medicaid suspend for medical review, CIM 60-5, MCM 4107.6
Prior authorization is required by Medicare for this item.

Wheelchair — Lightweight

? **E1240** Lightweight wheelchair; detachable arms, desk or full-length, swing-away, detachable, elevating legrest
CIM 60-9

? **E1250** Lightweight wheelchair; fixed full-length arms, swing-away, detachable footrests
CIM 60-9

? **E1260** Lightweight wheelchair; detachable arms, desk or full-length, swing-away, detachable footrests
CIM 60-9

? **E1270** Lightweight wheelchair; fixed full-length arms, swing-away, detachable elevating legrests
CIM 60-9

Wheelchair — Heavy-duty

? **E1280** Heavy-duty wheelchair; detachable arms, desk or full-length, elevating legrests
CIM 60-9

? **E1285** Heavy-duty wheelchair; fixed full-length arms, swing-away, detachable footrests
CIM 60-9

? **E1290** Heavy-duty wheelchair; detachable arms, desk or full-length, swing-away, detachable footrests
CIM 60-9

? **E1295** Heavy-duty wheelchair; fixed full-length arms, elevating legrests
CIM 60-9

? **E1296** Special wheelchair seat height from floor
CIM 60-6

? **E1297** Special wheelchair seat depth, by upholstery
CIM 60-6

? **E1298** Special wheelchair seat depth and/or width, by construction
CIM 60-6

Whirlpool — Equipment

⊘ **E1300** Whirlpool, portable (overtub type)
CIM 60-9

? **E1310** Whirlpool, nonportable (built-in type)
CIM 60-9

Repairs and Replacement Supplies

? ☑ **E1340** Repair or nonroutine service for durable medical equipment requiring the skill of a technician, labor component, per 15 minutes
MCM 2100.4
Medicare jurisdiction: local carrier if repair or implanted DME.

Additional Oxygen Related Equipment

? **E1353** Regulator
CIM 60-4, MCM 4107.9

? **E1355** Stand/rack
CIM 60-4

? **E1372** Immersion external heater for nebulizer
CIM 60-4

? **E1375** Nebulizer portable with small compressor, with limited flow
CIM 60-4, CIM 60-9

? ☑ **E1377** Oxygen concentrator, high humidity system equiv. to 244 cu. ft.
CIM 60-4, MCM 4107.9

? ☑ **E1378** Oxygen concentrator, high humidity system equiv. to 488 cu. ft.
CIM 60-4, MCM 4107.9

? ☑ **E1379** Oxygen concentrator, high humidity system equiv. to 732 cu. ft.
CIM 60-4, MCM 4107.9

? ☑ **E1380** Oxygen concentrator, high humidity system equiv. to 976 cu. ft.
CIM 60-4, MCM 4107.9

? ☑ **E1381** Oxygen concentrator, high humidity system equiv. to 1220 cu. ft.
CIM 60-4, MCM 4107.9

? ☑ **E1382** Oxygen concentrator, high humidity system equiv. to 1464 cu. ft.
CIM 60-4, MCM 4107.9

? ☑ **E1383** Oxygen concentrator, high humidity system equiv. to 1708 cu. ft.
CIM 60-4, MCM 4107.9

? ☑ **E1384** Oxygen concentrator, high humidity system equiv. to 1952 cu. ft.
CIM 60-4, MCM 4107.9

? ☑ **E1385** Oxygen concentrator, high humidity system equiv. to over 1952 cu. ft.
CIM 60-4, MCM 4107.9

● ? **E1390** Oxygen concentrator, capable of delivering 85 percent or greater oxygen concentration at the prescribed flow rate
CIM 60-4, MCM 4107.9

➡ **E1399** Durable medical equipment, miscellaneous
Determine if an alternative national HCPCS Level II or a local HCPCS Level III code better describes the equipment being reported. This code should be used only if a more specific code is unavailable. Medicare jurisdiction: local carrier if repair or implanted DME.

(E1400 has been deleted)

(E1401 has been deleted)

(E1402 has been deleted)

(E1403 has been deleted)

(E1404 has been deleted)

? **E1405** Oxygen and water vapor enriching system with heated delivery
CIM 60-4, MCM 4107

? **E1406** Oxygen and water vapor enriching system without heated delivery
CIM 60-4, MCM 4107

Artificial Kidney Machines and Accessories

For suppplies for ESRD, see procedure codes A4650–A4999.

? **E1510** Kidney, dialysate delivery system kidney machine, pump recirculating, air removal system, flowrate meter, power off, heater and temp control with alarm, IV poles, pressure gauge, concentrate container

? **E1520** Heparin infusion pump for dialysis

? **E1530** Air bubble detector for dialysis

? **E1540** Pressure alarm for dialysis

? **E1550** Bath conductivity meter for dialysis

? **E1560** Blood leak detector for dialysis

? **E1570** Adjustable chair, for ESRD patients

? ☑ **E1575** Transducer protector/fluid barrier, any size, each

? **E1580** Unipuncture control system for dialysis

? **E1590** Hemodialysis machine

DURABLE MEDICAL EQUIPMENT

? **E1592** Automatic intermittent peritoneal dialysis system

? **E1594** Cycler dialysis machine for peritoneal dialysis

? **E1600** Delivery and/or installation charges for renal dialysis equipment
Medicaid suspend for medical review

? **E1610** Reverse osmosis water purification system
CIM 55-1 A

? **E1615** Deionizer water purification system
CIM 55-1 A

? **E1620** Blood pump for dialysis

? **E1625** Water softening system
CIM 55-1 B

➥ **E1630** Reciprocating peritoneal dialysis system

? **E1632** Wearable artificial kidney

? **E1635** Compact (portable) travel hemodialyzer system
Medicaid suspend for medical review

?☑ **E1636** Sorbent cartridges, per case

? **E1640** Replacement components for hemodialysis and/or peritoneal dialysis machines that are owned or being purchased by the patient

? **E1699** Dialysis equipment, unspecified, by report
Determine if an alternative national HCPCS Level II or a local HCPCS Level III code better describes the equipment being reported. This code should be used only if a more specific code is unavailable. Pertinent documentation to evaluate medical appropriateness should be included when this code is reported.

Jaw Motion Rehabilitation System and Accessories

➥ **E1700** Jaw motion rehabilitation system
Medicare jurisdiction: local carrier.

➥☑ **E1701** Replacement cushions for jaw motion rehabilitation system, package of six
Medicare jurisdiction: local carrier.

➥☑ **E1702** Replacement measuring scales for jaw motion rehabilitation system, package of 200
Medicare jurisdiction: local carrier.

Other Orthopedic Devices

➥ **E1800** Dynamic adjustable elbow extension/flexion device

➥ **E1805** Dynamic adjustable wrist extension/flexion device

➥ **E1810** Dynamic adjustable knee extension/flexion device

➥ **E1815** Dynamic adjustable ankle extension/flexion device

➥ **E1820** Soft interface material, dynamic adjustable extension/flexion device

➥ **E1825** Dynamic adjustable finger extension/flexion device

➥ **E1830** Dynamic adjustable toe extension/flexion device

● ? **E1900** Synthesized speech augmentative communication device with dynamic display
CIM 60-9

Procedures/Professional Services (Temporary)
G0000–G9999

HCFA assigns temporary G codes to procedures and services which are being reviewed prior to inclusion in the American Medical Association's Current Procedural Terminology (CPT). Once CPT codes for these services and procedures are assigned, the G codes are removed from this section.

G codes fall under the jurisdiction of the local carrier.

PET Scan Modifiers

Use the following single digit alpha characters, in combination as two-character modifiers to indicate the results of a current PET scan and a previous test.

- **N** Negative
- **E** Equivocal
- **P** Positive, but not suggestive of extensive ischemia
- **S** Positive and suggestive of extensive ischemia (>20% of the left ventricle)

➡ **G0001** Routine venipuncture for collection of specimen(s)
This code should be reported instead of 36415 on Medicare claims.

➡ **G0002** Office procedure, insertion of temporary indwelling catheter, Foley type (separate procedure)

? ☑ **G0004** Patient demand single or multiple event recording with presymptom memory loop and 24-hour attended monitoring, per 30-day period; includes transmission, physician review and interpretation
CIM 50-15

? ☑ **G0005** Patient demand single or multiple event recording with presymptom memory loop and 24-hour attended monitoring, per 30-day period; recording (includes hookup, recording and disconnection)
CIM 50-15

? ☑ **G0006** Patient demand single or multiple event recording with presymptom memory loop and 24-hour attended monitoring, per 30-day period; 24-hour attended monitoring, receipt of transmissions, and analysis
CIM 50-15

? ☑ **G0007** Patient demand single or multiple event recording with presymptom memory loop and 24-hour attended monitoring, per 30-day period; physician review and interpretation only
CIM 50-15

➡ **G0008** Administration of influenza virus vaccine when no physician fee schedule service on the same day

➡ **G0009** Administration of pneumococcal vaccine when no physician fee schedule service on the same day

➡ **G0010** Administration of hepatitis B vaccine when no physician fee schedule service on the same day

? ☑ **G0015** Post-symptom telephonic transmission of electrocardiogram rhythm strip(s) and 24-hour attended monitoring, per 30-day period: Tracing only
CIM 50-15

? ☑ **G0016** Post-symptom telephonic transmission of electrocardiogram rhythm strip(s) and 24-hour attended monitoring, per 30-day period: Physician review and interpretation only
CIM 50-15

? **G0025** Collagen skin test kit
CIM 65-9

➡ **G0026** Fecal leukocyte examination

➡ **G0027** Semen analysis; presence and/or motility of sperm excluding Huhner test

? **G0030** PET myocardial perfusion imaging, (following previous PET, G0030–G0047); single study, rest or stress (exercise and/or pharmacologic)
CIM 50-36

? **G0031** PET myocardial perfusion imaging, (following previous PET, G0030–G0047); multiple studies, rest or stress (exercise and/or pharmacologic)
CIM 50-36

? **G0032** PET myocardial perfusion imaging, (following rest SPECT, 78464); single study, rest or stress (exercise and/or pharmacologic)
CIM 50-36

? **G0033** PET myocardial perfusion imaging, (following rest SPECT, 78464); multiple studies, rest or stress (exercise and/or pharmacologic)
CIM 50-36

? **G0034** PET myocardial perfusion imaging, (following stress SPECT, 78465); single study, rest or stress (exercise and/or pharmacologic)
CIM 50-36

? **G0035** PET myocardial perfusion imaging, (following stress SPECT, 78465); multiple studies, rest or stress (exercise and/or pharmacologic)
CIM 50-36

? **G0036** PET myocardial perfusion imaging, (following coronary angiography, 93510–93529); single study, rest or stress (exercise and/or pharmacologic)
CIM 50-36

? **G0037** PET myocardial perfusion imaging, (following coronary angiography, 93510–93529); multiple studies, rest or stress (exercise and/or pharmacologic)
CIM 50-36

PROCEDURES/PROFESSIONAL SERVICES (TEMPORARY)

? **G0038** PET myocardial perfusion imaging, (following stress planar myocardial perfusion, 78460); single study, rest or stress (exercise and/or pharmacologic)
CIM 50-36

? **G0039** PET myocardial perfusion imaging, (following stress planar myocardial perfusion, 78460); multiple studies, rest or stress (exercise and/or pharmacologic)
CIM 50-36

? **G0040** PET myocardial perfusion imaging, (following stress echocardiogram, 93350); single study, rest or stress (exercise and/or pharmacologic)
CIM 50-36

? **G0041** PET myocardial perfusion imaging, (following stress echocardiogram, 93350); multiple studies, rest or stress (exercise and/or pharmacologic)
CIM 50-36

? **G0042** PET myocardial perfusion imaging, (following stress nuclear ventriculogram, 78481 or 78483); single study, rest or stress (exercise and/or pharmacologic)
CIM 50-36

? **G0043** PET myocardial perfusion imaging, (following stress nuclear ventriculogram, 78481 or 78483); multiple studies, rest or stress (exercise and/or pharmacologic)
CIM 50-36

? **G0044** PET myocardial perfusion imaging, (following rest ECG, 93000); single study, rest or stress (exercise and/or pharmacologic)
CIM 50-36

? **G0045** PET myocardial perfusion imaging, (following rest ECG, 93000); multiple studies, rest or stress (exercise and/or pharmacologic)
CIM 50-36

? **G0046** PET myocardial perfusion imaging, (following stress ECG, 93015); single study, rest or stress (exercise and/or pharmacologic)
CIM 50-36

? **G0047** PET myocardial perfusion imaging, (following stress ECG, 93015); multiple studies, rest or stress (exercise and/or pharmacologic)
CIM 50-36

➡ **G0050** Measurement of post-voiding residual urine and/or bladder capacity by ultrasound

? **G0101** Cervical or vaginal cancer screening; pelvic and clinical breast examination
G0101 can be reported with an E/M code when a separately identifiable E/M service is provided.

● ? **G0102** Prostate cancer screening; digital rectal examination
CIM 50-55, MCM 4182

● ? **G0103** Prostate cancer screening; prostate specific antigen test (PSA), total
CIM 50-55, MCM 4182

? **G0104** Colorectal cancer screening; flexible sigmoidoscopy
Medicare covers colorectal screening for cancer via flexible sigmoidoscopy once every four years for patients 50 years or older.

? **G0105** Colorectal cancer screening; colonoscopy on individual at high risk
An individual with ulcerative enteritis or a history of a malignant neoplasm of the lower gastrointestinal tract is considered at high-risk for colorectal cancer, as defined by HCFA.

? **G0106** Colorectal cancer screening; alternative to G0104, screening sigmoidoscopy, barium enema
Medicare covers colorectal screening for cancer via barium enema once every four years for patients 50 years or older.

? **G0107** Colorectal cancer screening; fecal-occult blood test, 1-3 simultaneous determinations
Medicare covers colorectal screening for cancer via fecal-occult blood test once every year for patients 50 years or older.

➡ **G0108** Diabetes outpatient self-management training services, individual, per session

➡ **G0109** Diabetes self-management training services, group session, per individual

? **G0110** NETT pulmonary rehabilitation; education/skills training, individual
CIM 35-93
This code is for use only by physicians participating in the National Emphysema Treatment Trials (NETT).

? **G0111** NETT pulmonary rehabilitation; education/skills, group
This code is for use only by physicians participating in the National Emphysema Treatment Trials (NETT).

? **G0112** NETT pulmonary rehabilitation; nutritional guidance, initial
This code is for use only by physicians participating in the National Emphysema Treatment Trials (NETT).

? **G0113** NETT pulmonary rehabilitation; nutritional guidance, subsequent
This code is for use only by physicians participating in the National Emphysema Treatment Trials (NETT).

? **G0114** NETT pulmonary rehabilitation; psychosocial consultation
This code is for use only by physicians participating in the National Emphysema Treatment Trials (NETT).

PROCEDURES/PROFESSIONAL SERVICES (TEMPORARY)

? **G0115** NETT pulmonary rehabilitation; psychological testing
This code is for use only by physicians participating in the National Emphysema Treatment Trials (NETT).

? **G0116** NETT pulmonary rehabilitation; psychosocial counselling
This code is for use only by physicians participating in the National Emphysema Treatment Trials (NETT).

? **G0120** Colorectal cancer screening; alternative to G0105, screening colonoscopy, barium enema

⊘ **G0121** Colorectal cancer screening; colonoscopy on individual not meeting criteria for high risk

⊘ **G0122** Colorectal cancer screening; barium enema

? **G0123** Screening cytopathology, cervical or vaginal (any reporting system), collected in preservative fluid, automated thin layer preparation, screening by cytotechnologist under physician supervision
CIM 50-20

? **G0124** Screening cytopathology, cervical or vaginal (any reporting system), collected in preservative fluid, automated thin layer preparation, requiring interpretation by physician
CIM 50-20

? **G0125** PET lung imaging of solitary pulmonary nodules, using 2-(fluorine-18)-fluoro-2-deoxy-d-glucose (FDG), following CT (71250/71260 or 71270)
CIM 50-16, MCM 4173

? **G0126** PET lung imaging of solitary pulmonary nodules, using 2-(fluorine-18)-fluoro-2-deoxy-d-glucose (FDG), following CT (71250/71260 or 71270); initial staging of pathologically diagnosed non-small cell lung cancer
CIM 50-36, MCM 4173

? **G0127** Trimming of dystrophic nails, any number
MCM 2323, MCM 4120

? **G0128** Direct (face-to-face with patient) skilled nursing services of a registered nurse provided in a comprehensive outpatient rehabilitation facility, each 10 minutes beyond the first 5 minutes
Medicare Statute 1833(a)

● ➡ **G0129** Occupational therapy requiring the skills of a qualified occupational therapist, furnished as a component of a partial hospitalization treatment program, per day

? **G0130** Single energy x-ray absorptiometry (SEXA) bone density study, one or more sites; appendicular skeleton (peripheral) (e.g., radius, wrist, heel)
CIM 50-44

? **G0131** Computerized tomography bone mineral density study, one or more sites; axial skeleton (e.g., hips, pelvis, spine)
CIM 50-44

? **G0132** Computerized tomography bone mineral density study, one or more sites; appendicular skeleton (peripheral) (e.g., radius, wrist, heel)
CIM 50-44

(G0133 has been deleted. See code 76977)

➡ **G0141** Screening cytopathology smears, cervical or vaginal, performed by automated system, with manual rescreening, requiring interpretation by physician

➡ **G0143** Screening cytopathology, cervical or vaginal (any reporting system), collected in preservative fluid, automated thin layer preparation, with manual screening and rescreening by cytotechnologist under physician supervision

➡ **G0144** Screening cytopathology, cervical or vaginal (any reporting system), collected in preservative fluid, automated thin layer preparation, with manual screening and computer-assisted rescreening by cytotechnologist under physician supervision

➡ **G0145** Screening cytopathology, cervical or vaginal (any reporting system), collected in preservative fluid, automated thin layer preparation, with manual screening and computer-assisted rescreening using cell selection and review under physician supervision

➡ **G0147** Screening cytopathology smears, cervical or vaginal, performed by automated system under physician supervision

➡ **G0148** Screening cytopathology smears, cervical or vaginal, performed by automated system with manual rescreening

● ➡ **G0151** Services of physical therapist in home health setting, each 15 minutes

● ➡ **G0152** Services of occupational therapist in home health setting, each 15 minutes

● ➡ **G0153** Services of speech and language pathologist in home health setting, each 15 minutes

● ➡ **G0154** Services of skilled nurse in home health setting, each 15 minutes

● ➡ **G0155** Services of clinical social worker in home health setting, each 15 minutes

PROCEDURES/PROFESSIONAL SERVICES (TEMPORARY)

- ➥ **G0156** Services of home health aide in home health setting, each 15 minutes

- ➥ **G0159** Percutaneous thrombectomy and/or revision, arteriovenous fistula, autogenous or nonautogenous dialysis graft

- ? **G0160** Cryosurgical ablation of localized prostate cancer, primary treatment only (post operative irrigations and aspiration of sloughing tissue included)
  CIM 35-96

- ? **G0161** Ultrasonic guidance for interstitial placement of cyosurgical probes
  CIM 35-96

- ? **G0163** Positron emission tomography (PET), whole body, for recurrence of colorectal metastatic cancer
  CIM 50-36, MCM 4173

- ? **G0164** Positron emission tomography (PET), whole body, for staging and characterization of lymphoma
  CIM 50-36, MCM 4173

- ? **G0165** Positron emission tomography (PET), whole body, for recurrence of melanoma or melanoma metastatic cancer
  CIM 50-36, MCM 4173

- ➥ **G0166** External counterpulsation, per treatment session
  CIM 35-74

- ➥ **G0167** Hyperbaric oxygen treatment not requiring physician attendance, per treatment session
  CIM 35-10

- ➥ **G0168** Wound closure utilizing tissue adhesive(s) only

- ➥ **G0169** Removal of devitalized tissue, without use of anesthesia (conscious sedation, local, regional, general)

- ➥ ☑ **G0170** Application of tissue cultured skin grafts, including bilaminate skin substitutes or neodermis, including site preparation, initial 25 sq cm

- ➥ ☑ **G0171** Application of tissue cultured skin grafts, including bilaminate skin substitutes or neodermis, including site preparation, each additional 25 sq cm
  Report this code in conjunction with code G0170.

- ➥ **G0172** Training and educational services furnished as a component of a partial hospitalization treatment program, per day

Drugs Administered Other Than Oral Method
J0000–J8999

Drugs and biologicals are usually covered by Medicare if: they are of the type that cannot be self-administered; they are not excluded by being immunizations; they are reasonable and necessary for the diagnosis or treatment of the illness or injury for which they are administered; and they have not been determined by the FDA to be less than effective. In addition they must meet all the general requirements for coverage of items as incident to a physician's services. Generally, prescription and nonprescription drugs and biologicals purchased by or dispensed to a patient are not covered.

The following list of drugs can be injected either subcutaneously, intramuscularly, or intravenously. Third-party payers may wish to determine a threshold and pay up to a certain dollar limit before developing for the drug.

J codes fall under the jurisdiction of the DME Regional office for Medicare, unless incidental or otherwise noted.

Exception: Oral Immunosuppressive Drugs

J0120 Injection, tetracycline, up to 250 mg
MCM 2049
Use this code for Achromycin.

J0130 Injection abciximab, 10 mg
MCM 2049

J0150 Injection, adenosine, 6 mg (not to be used to report any adenosine phosphate compounds; instead use A9270)
MCM 2049
Use this code for Adenocard.

J0151 Injection, adenosine, 90 mg (not to be used to report any adenosine phosphate compounds; instead use A9270)
MCM 2049

J0170 Injection, adrenalin, epinephrine, up to 1 ml ampule
MCM 2049
Use this code for Adrenalin Chloride, Sus-Phrine.

J0190 Injection, biperiden lactate, per 5 mg
MCM 2049
Use this code for Akineton.

J0200 Injection, alatrofloxacin mesylate, 100 mg
MCM 2049.5

J0205 Injection, alglucerase, per 10 units
MCM 2049
Use this code for Ceredase.

J0207 Injection, amifostine, 500 mg
MCM 2049

J0210 Injection, methyldopate HCl, up to 250 mg
MCM 2049
Use this code for Aldomet.

J0256 Injection, alpha 1-proteinase inhibitor — human, 10 mg
MCM 2049
Use this code for Prolastin.

J0270 Injection, alprostadil, 1.25 mcg (code may be used for Medicare when drug administered under direct supervision of a physician, not for use when drug is self-administered)

J0275 Alprostadil urethral suppository (code may be used for Medicare when drug administered under direct supervision of a physician, not for use when drug is self-administered)

J0280 Injection, aminophyllin, up to 250 mg
MCM 2049

J0285 Injection, amphotericin B, 50 mg
MCM 2049

J0286 Injection, amphotericin B, any lipid formulation, 50 mg
MCM 2049

J0290 Injection, ampicillin sodium, 500 mg
MCM 2049

J0295 Injection, ampicillin sodium/sulbactam sodium, per 1.5 g
MCM 2049
Use this code for Unasyn.

J0300 Injection, amobarbital, up to 125 mg
MCM 2049
Use this code for Amytal.

J0330 Injection, succinylcholine chloride, up to 20 mg
MCM 2049
Use this code for Anectine, Quelicin, Sucostrin.

J0340 Injection, nandrolone phenpropionate, up to 50 mg
MCM 2049
Use this code for Durabolin, Androlone, Androlone-50, Hybolin Improved, Nandrobolic.

J0350 Injection, anistreplase, per 30 units
MCM 2049
Use this code for Eminase.

J0360 Injection, hydralazine HCl, up to 20 mg
MCM 2049
Use this code for Apresoline.

J0380 Injection, metaraminol bitartrate, per 10 mg
MCM 2049
Use this code for Aramine.

J0390 Injection, chloroquine HCl, up to 250 mg
MCM 2049
Use this code for Aralen.

J0395 Injection, arbutamine HCl, 1 mg
MCM 2049

J0400 Injection, trimethaphan camsylate, up to 500 mg
MCM 2049
Use this code for Arfonad.

J0456 Injection, azithromycin, 500 mg
MCM 2049.5

J0460 Injection, atropine sulfate, up to 0.3 mg
MCM 2049

J0470 Injection, dimercaprol, per 100 mg
MCM 2049
Use this code for BAL in oil.

J0475 Injection, baclofen, 10 mg
MCM 2049
Use this code for Lioresal.

J0476 Injection, baclofen, 50 mcg for intrathecal trial
MCM 2049

J0500 Injection, dicyclomine HCl, up to 20 mg
MCM 2049
Use this code for Bentyl, Dilomine, Antispas, Dibent, Di-Spaz, Neoquess, Or-Tyl, Spasmoject.

J0510 Injection, benzquinamide HCl, up to 50 mg
MCM 2049
Use this code for Emete-con.

J0515 Injection, benztropine mesylate, per 1 mg
MCM 2049
Use this code for Cogentin.

J0520 Injection, bethanechol chloride, mytonachol or urecholine, up to 5 mg
MCM 2049
Use this code for Urecholine.

J0530 Injection, penicillin G benzathine and penicillin G procaine, up to 600,000 units
MCM 2049
Use this code for Bicillin C-R.

J0540 Injection, penicillin G benzathine and penicillin G procaine, up to 1,200,000 units
MCM 2049
Use this code for Bicillin C-R, Bicillin C-R 900/300.

J0550 Injection, penicillin G benzathine and penicillin G procaine, up to 2,400,000 units
MCM 2049
Use this code for Bicillin C-R.

J0560 Injection, penicillin G benzathine, up to 600,000 units
MCM 2049
Use this code for Bicillin L-A, Permapen.

J0570 Injection, penicillin G benzathine, up to 1,200,000 units
MCM 2049
Use this code for Bicillin L-A, Permapen.

J0580 Injection, penicillin G benzathine, up to 2,400,000 units
MCM 2049
Use this code for Bicillin L-A, Permapen.

J0585 Botulinum toxin type A, per unit
MCM 2049

J0590 Injection, ethylnorepinephrine HCl, 1 ml
MCM 2049
Use this code for Bronkephrine.

J0600 Injection, edetate calcium disodium, up to 1000 mg
MCM 2049
Use this code for Calcium Disodium Versenate, Calcium EDTA).

J0610 Injection, calcium gluconate, per 10 ml
MCM 2049
Use this code for Kaleinate.

J0620 Injection, calcium glycerophosphate and calcium lactate, per 10 ml
MCM 2049
Use this code for Calphosan.

J0630 Injection, calcitonin-salmon, up to 400 units
MCM 2049
Use this code for Calcimar, Miacalcin.

J0635 Injection, calcitriol, 1 mcg ampule
MCM 2049
Use this code for Calcijex.

J0640 Injection, leucovorin calcium, per 50 mg
MCM 2049
Use this code for Wellcovorin.

J0670 Injection, mepivacaine HCl, per 10 ml
MCM 2049
Use this code for Carbocaine, Polocaine, Isocaine HCl.

▲ **J0690** Injection, cefazolin sodium, 500 mg

J0694 Injection, cefoxitin sodium, 1 g
MCM 2049
Use this code for Mefoxin.

J0695 Injection, cefonicid sodium, 1 g
MCM 2049
Use this code for Monocid.

J0696 Injection, ceftriaxone sodium, per 250 mg
MCM 2049
Use this code for Rocephin.

J0697 Injection, sterile cefuroxime sodium, per 750 mg
MCM 2049
Use this code for Kefurox, Zinacef.

J0698 Cefotaxime sodium, per g
MCM 2049
Use this code for Claforan.

J0702 Injection, betamethasone acetate and betamethasone sodium phosphate, per 3 mg
MCM 2049

J0704 Injection, betamethasone sodium phosphate, per 4 mg
MCM 2049
Use this code for Betameth, Celestone Phosphate, Cel-U-Jec, Selestoject.

J0710 Injection, cephapirin sodium, up to 1 g
MCM 2049
Use this code for Cefadyl.

J0713 Injection, ceftazidime, per 500 mg
MCM 2049
Use this code for Fortaz, Tazidime.

J0715 Injection, ceftizoxime sodium, per 500 mg
MCM 2049
Use this code for Cefizox.

J0720 Injection, chloramphenicol sodium succinate, up to 1 g
MCM 2049
Use this code for Chloromycetin Sodium Succinate.

J0725 Injection, chorionic gonadotropin, per 1,000 USP units
MCM 2049
Use this code for Glukor, Follutein, Chorex-5, Corgonject-5, Profasi HP, A.P.L., Pregnyl, Gonic, Choron 10, Chorex-10, Chorignon.

J0730 Injection, chlorpheniramine maleate, per 10 mg
MCM 2049
Use this code for Chlortrimeton, Chlor-Pro, Chlor-pro 10, Chlor-100.

J0735 Injection, clonidine hydrochloride, 1 mg
MCM 2049

J0740 Injection, cidofovir, 375 mg
MCM 2049

J0743 Injection, cilastatin sodium imipenem, per 250 mg
MCM 2049
Use this code for Primaxin I.M., Primaxin I.V.

J0745 Injection, codeine phosphate, per 30 mg
MCM 2049

J0760 Injection, colchicine, per 1 mg
MCM 2049

J0770 Injection, colistimethate sodium, up to 150 mg
MCM 2049
Use this code for Coly-Mycin M.

J0780 Injection, prochlorperazine, up to 10 mg
MCM 2049
Use this code for Compazine, Cotranzine, Compa-Z, Ultrazine-10.

J0800 Injection, corticotropin, up to 40 units
MCM 2049
Use this code for Acthar, ACTH.

J0810 Injection, cortisone, up to 50 mg
MCM 2049
Use this code for Cortisone Acetate, Cortone Acetate.

J0835 Injection, cosyntropin, per 0.25 mg
MCM 2049
Use this code for Cortrosyn.

J0850 Injection, cytomegalovirus immune globulin intravenous (human), per vial
MCM 2049

J0895 Injection, deferoxamine mesylate, 500 mg per 5 cc
MCM 2049
Use this code for Desferal.

J0900 Injection, testosterone enanthate and estradiol valerate, up to 1 cc
MCM 2049
Use this code for Deladumone, Andrest 90-4, Andro-Estro 90-4, Androgyn L.A., Delatestadiol, Dua-Gen L.A., Duoval P.A., Estra-Testrin, TEEV, Testadiate, Testradiol 90/4, Valertest No. 1, Valertest No. 2, Deladumone OB, Ditate-DS.

J0945 Injection, brompheniramine maleate, per 10 mg
MCM 2049
Use this code for Histaject, Cophene-B, Dehist, Nasahist B, ND Stat, Oraminic II, Sinusol-B.

J0970 Injection, estradiol valerate, up to 40 mg
MCM 2049
Use this code for Delestrogen, Dioval, Dioval XX, Dioval 40, Duragen-10, Duragen-20, Duragen-40, Estradiol L.A., Estradiol L.A. 20, Estradiol L.A. 40, Gynogen L.A. "10," Gynogen L.A. "20," Gynogen L.A. "40," Valergen 10, Valergen 20, Valergen 40, Estra-L 20, Estra-L 40, L.A.E. 20.

J1000 Injection, depo-estradiol cypionate, up to 5 mg
MCM 2049
Use this code for Estradiol Cypionate, depGynogen, Depogen, Dura-Estrin, Estra-D, Estro-Cyp, Estroject L.A., Estronol-L.A.

J1020 Injection, methylprednisolone acetate, 20 mg
MCM 2049
Use this code for Depo-Medrol.

J1030 Injection, methylprednisolone acetate, 40 mg
MCM 2049
Use this code for Depo-Medrol, depMedalone 40, Depoject, Depopred-40, Duralone-40, Medralone 40, M-Prednisol-40, Rep-Pred 40.

J1040 Injection, methylprednisolone acetate, 80 mg
MCM 2049
Use this code for Depo-Medrol, depMedalone 80, Depoject, Depopred-80, D-Med 80, Duralone-80, Medralone 80, M-Prednisol-80, Rep-Pred 80.

J1050 Injection, medroxyprogesterone acetate, 100 mg
MCM 2049
Use this code for Depo-Provera.

J1055 Injection, medroxyprogesterone acetate for contraceptive use, 150 mg
Medicare statute 1862.A1
Use this code for Depo-Provera.

J1060 Injection, testosterone cypionate and estradiol cypionate, up to 1 ml
MCM 2049
Use this code for Depo-Testadiol, Andro/Fem, De-Comberol, depAndrogyn, Depotestogen, Duo-Cyp, Duratestrin, Menoject LA, Test-Estro-C, Test-Estro Cypionates.

J1070 Injection, testosterone cypionate, up to 100 mg
MCM 2049
Use this code for Depo-Testosterone, Duratest-100, Andro-Cyp, Andronaq-LA, Andronate-100, depAndro 100, Depotest, Testoject-LA.

J1080 Injection, testosterone cypionate, 1 cc, 200 mg
MCM 2049
Use this code for Depo-Testosterone, Andro-Cyp 200, Andronate 200, depAndro 200, Depotest, Duratest-200, Testa-C, Testadiate-Depo, Testoject-LA.

J1090 Injection, testosterone cypionate, 1 cc, 50 mg
MCM 2049
Use this code for Depo-Testosterone.

➡ **J1095** Injection, dexamethasone acetate, per 8 mg
MCM 2049
Use this code for Dalalone L.A., Decadron-LA, Decaject-L.A., Dexasone L.A., Dexone LA, Solurex LA. For dexamethasone acetate in inhalation solution, see K0512 and K0513.

▲ **J1100** Injection, dexamethosone sodium phosphate, up to 4 mg/ml
MCM 2049

J1110 Injection, dihydroergotamine mesylate, per 1 mg
MCM 2049
Use this code for D.H.E. 45.

J1120 Injection, acetazolamide sodium, up to 500 mg
MCM 2049
Use this code for Diamox.

J1160 Injection, digoxin, up to 0.5 mg
MCM 2049
Use this code for Lanoxin.

J1165 Injection, phenytoin sodium, per 50 mg
MCM 2049
Use this code for Dilantin.

J1170 Injection, hydromorphone, up to 4 mg
MCM 2049
Use this code for Dilaudid.

J1180 Injection, dyphylline, up to 500 mg
MCM 2049
Use this code for Lufyllin, Dilor.

J1190 Injection, dexrazoxane hydrochloride, per 250 mg
MCM 2049
Use this code for Zinecard.

J1200 Injection, diphenhydramine HCl, up to 50 mg
MCM 2049
Use this code for Benadryl, Benahist 10, Benahist 50, Benoject-10, Benoject-50, Bena-D 10, Bena-D 50, Nordryl, Ben-Allergin-50, Dihydrex, Diphenacen-50, Hyrexin-50, Wehdryl.

J1205 Injection, chlorothiazide sodium, per 500 mg
MCM 2049
Use this code for Diuril Sodium.

J1212 Injection, DMSO, dimethyl sulfoxide, 50%, 50 ml
MCM 2049
Use this code for Rimso. DMSO is covered only as a treatment of interstitial cystitis.

J1230 Injection, methadone HCl, up to 10 mg
MCM 2049
Use this code for Dolophine HCl.

J1240 Injection, dimenhydrinate, up to 50 mg
MCM 2049
Use this code for Dramamine, Dinate, Dommanate, Dramanate, Dramilin, Dramocen, Dramoject, Dymenate, Hydrate, Marmine, Wehamine.

J1245 Injection, dipyridamole, per 10 mg
MCM 2049, 15030
Use this code for Persantine IV.

J1250 Injection, dobutamine HCl, per 250 mg
MCM 2049
Use this code for Dobutrex.

▲ **J1260** Injection, dolasetron mesylate, 10 mg
MCM 2049

J1320 Injection, amitriptyline HCl, up to 20 mg
MCM 2049
Use this code for Elavil, Enovil.

J1325 Injection, epoprostenol, 0.5 mg
MCM 2049

● **J1327** Injection, eptifibatide, 5 mg
MCM 2049

J1330 Injection, ergonovine maleate, up to 0.2 mg
MCM 2049
Use this code for Ergotrate Maleate.

J1362 Injection, erythromycin gluceptate, per 250 mg
MCM 2049
Use this code for Ilotycin.

J1364 Injection, erythromycin lactobionate, per 500 mg
MCM 2049

J1380 Injection, estradiol valerate, up to 10 mg
MCM 2049
Use this code for Delestrogen, Dioval, Dioval XX, Dioval 40, Duragen-10, Duragen-20, Duragen-40, Estradiol L.A., Estradiol L.A. 20, Estradiol L.A. 40, Gynogen L.A. "10," Gynogen L.A. "20," Gynogen L.A. "40," Valergen 10, Valergen 20, Valergen 40, Estra-L 20, Estra-L 40, L.A.E. 20.

J1390 Injection, estradiol valerate, up to 20 mg
MCM 2049
Use this code for Delestrogen, Dioval, Dioval XX, Dioval 40, Duragen-10, Duragen-20, Duragen-40, Estradiol L.A., Estradiol L.A. 20, Estradiol L.A. 40, Gynogen L.A. "10," Gynogen L.A. "20," Gynogen L.A. "40," Valergen 10, Valergen 20, Valergen 40, Estra-L 20, Estra-L 40, L.A.E. 20.

J1410 Injection, estrogen conjugated, per 25 mg
MCM 2049
Use this code for Premarin Intravenous.

J1435 Injection, estrone, per 1 mg
MCM 2049
Use this code for Estone Aqueous, Estronol, Theelin Aqueous, Estone 5, Kestrone 5.

J1436 Injection, etidronate disodium, per 300 mg
MCM 2049
Use this code for Didronel.

DRUGS ADMINISTERED OTHER THAN ORAL METHOD

- ? **J1438** Injection, etanercept, 25 mg (code may be used for Medicare when drug administered under the direct supervision of a physician, not for use when drug is self administered)
  MCM 2049

  ? ☑ **J1440** Injection, filgrastim (G-CSF), 300 mcg
  MCM 2049
  Use this code for Neupogen.

  ? ☑ **J1441** Injection, filgrastim (G-CSF), 480 mcg
  MCM 2049
  Use this code for Neupogen.

- ? ☑ **J1450** Injection, fluconazole, 200 mg
  MCM 2049.5

  ? ☑ **J1455** Injection, foscarnet sodium, per 1,000 mg
  MCM 2049
  Use this code for Foscavir.

  ? ☑ **J1460** Injection, gamma globulin, intramuscular, 1 cc
  MCM 2049
  Use this code for Gammar, Gamastan.

  ? ☑ **J1470** Injection, gamma globulin, intramuscular, 2 cc
  MCM 2049
  Use this code for Gammar, Gamastan.

  ? ☑ **J1480** Injection, gamma globulin, intramuscular, 3 cc
  MCM 2049
  Use this code for Gammar, Gamastan.

  ? ☑ **J1490** Injection, gamma globulin, intramuscular, 4 cc
  MCM 2049
  Use this code for Gammar, Gamastan.

  ? ☑ **J1500** Injection, gamma globulin, intramuscular, 5 cc
  MCM 2049
  Use this code for Gammar, Gamastan.

  ? ☑ **J1510** Injection, gamma globulin, intramuscular, 6 cc
  MCM 2049
  Use this code for Gammar, Gamastan.

  ? ☑ **J1520** Injection, gamma globulin, intramuscular, 7 cc
  MCM 2049
  Use this code for Gammar, Gamastan.

  ? ☑ **J1530** Injection, gamma globulin, intramuscular, 8 cc
  MCM 2049
  Use this code for Gammar, Gamastan.

  ? ☑ **J1540** Injection, gamma globulin, intramuscular, 9 cc
  MCM 2049
  Use this code for Gammar, Gamastan.

  ? ☑ **J1550** Injection, gamma globulin, intramuscular, 10 cc
  MCM 2049
  Use this code for Gammar, Gamastan.

  ? ☑ **J1560** Injection, gamma globulin, intramuscular, over 10 cc
  MCM 2049
  Use this code for Gammar, Gamastan.

  ? ☑ **J1561** Injection, immune globulin, intravenous, 500 mg
  MCM 2049
  Use this code for Gammar.

  ? ☑ **J1562** Injection, immune globulin, intravenous 5 g
  MCM 2049
  Use this code for Panglobulin or Polygam SD.

  ? ☑ **J1565** Injection, respiratory syncytial virus immune globulin, intravenous, 50 mg
  MCM 2049

  ? ☑ **J1570** Injection, ganciclovir sodium, 500 mg
  MCM 2049
  Use this code for Cytovene.

  ? ☑ **J1580** Injection, Garamycin, gentamicin, up to 80 mg
  MCM 2049
  Use this code for Gentamicin Sulfate, Jenamicin.

  ? ☑ **J1600** Injection, gold sodium thiomalate, up to 50 mg
  MCM 2049
  Use this code for Myochrysine.

  ? ☑ **J1610** Injection, glucagon hydrochloride, per 1 mg
  MCM 2049

  ? ☑ **J1620** Injection, gonadorelin hydrochloride, per 100 mcg
  MCM 2049
  Use this code for Factrel.

  ? ☑ **J1626** Injection, granisetron hydrochloride, 100 mcg
  MCM 2049

  ? ☑ **J1630** Injection, haloperidol, up to 5 mg
  MCM 2049
  Use this code for Haldol.

  ? ☑ **J1631** Injection, haloperidol decanoate, per 50 mg
  MCM 2049
  Use this code for aldol Decanoate-50, Haldol Decanoate-100.

  ? ☑ **J1642** Injection, heparin sodium, (Heparin Lock Flush), per 10 units
  MCM 2049
  Use this code for Hep-Lock, Hep-Lock U/P.

  ? ☑ **J1644** Injection, heparin sodium, per 1,000 units
  MCM 2049
  Use this code for Heparin Sodium, Liquaemin Sodium.

  ? ☑ **J1645** Injection, dalteparin sodium, per 2500 IU
  MCM 2049
  Use this code for Fragmin.

  ? ☑ **J1650** Injection, enoxaparin sodium, 10 mg
  MCM 2049
  Use this code for Lovenox.

HCPCS 2000   ⊘ Not covered by or valid for Medicare   ? Special coverage instructions   ➡ Carrier discretion

Drugs Administered Other Than Oral Method

? ☑ **J1670** Injection, tetanus immune globulin, human, up to 250 units
MCM 2049

? ☑ **J1690** Injection, prednisolone tebutate, up to 20 mg
MCM 2049
Use this code for Hydeltra-T.B.A., Predalone T.B.A., Prednisol TBA.

? ☑ **J1700** Injection, hydrocortisone acetate, up to 25 mg
MCM 2049
Use this code for Hydrocortone Acetate.

? ☑ **J1710** Injection, hydrocortisone sodium phosphate, up to 50 mg
MCM 2049
Use this code for Hydrocortone Phosphate.

? ☑ **J1720** Injection, hydrocortisone sodium succinate, up to 100 mg
MCM 2049
Use this code for Solu-Cortef, A-Hydrocort.

? ☑ **J1730** Injection, diazoxide, up to 300 mg
MCM 2049
Use this code for Hyperstat IV.

? ☑ **J1739** Injection, hydroxyprogesterone caproate, 125 mg/ml
MCM 2049
Use this code for Pro-Depo.

? ☑ **J1741** Injection, hydroxyprogesterone caproate, 250 mg/ml
MCM 2049
Use this code for Duralutin, Gesterol L.A. 250, Hylutin, Hyprogest 250, Pro-Depo.

? ☑ **J1742** Injection, ibutilide fumarate, 1 mg
MCM 2049

● ? ☑ **J1745** Injection, infliximab, 10 mg
MCM 2049

● ? ☑ **J1750** Injection, iron dextran, 50 mg
MCM 2049.5

(J1760 has been deleted)

(J1770 has been deleted)

(J1780 has been deleted)

? ☑ **J1785** Injection, imiglucerase, per unit
MCM 2049
Use this code for Cerezyme.

? ☑ **J1790** Injection, droperidol, up to 5 mg
MCM 2049
Use this code for Inapsine.

? ☑ **J1800** Injection, propranolol HCl, up to 1 mg
MCM 2049
Use this code for Inderal.

? ☑ **J1810** Injection, droperidol and fentanyl citrate, up to 2 ml ampule
MCM 2049
Use this code for Innovar.

? ☑ **J1820** Injection, insulin, up to 100 units
CIM 60-14, MCM 2049
Use this code for Humalog, Regular, NPH, Lente, or Ultralente insulin.

▲ ? **J1825** Injection, interferon beta-1a, 33 mcg (code may be used for Medicare when drug administered under direct supervision of a physician not for use when drug is self-administered)
MCM 2049

▲ ? **J1830** Injection interferon beta-1b, 0.25 mg (code may be used for Medicare when drug administered under direct supervision of a physician not for use when drug is self-administered)
MCM 2049

? ☑ **J1840** Injection, kanamycin sulfate, up to 500 mg
MCM 2049
Use this code for Kantrex, Klebcil.

? ☑ **J1850** Injection, kanamycin sulfate, up to 75 mg
MCM 2049
Use this code for Kantrex, Klebcil.

? ☑ **J1885** Injection, ketorolac tromethamine, per 15 mg
MCM 2049
Use this code for Toradol.

? ☑ **J1890** Injection, cephalothin sodium, up to 1 g
MCM 2049
Use this code for Cephalothin Sodium, Keflin.

? ☑ **J1910** Injection, kutapressin, up to 2 ml
MCM 2049

? **J1930** Injection, propiomazine HCl, up to 20 mg
MCM 2049
Use this code for Largon.

? ☑ **J1940** Injection, furosemide, up to 20 mg
MCM 2049
Use this code for Lasix, Furomide M.D.

? ☑ **J1950** Injection, leuprolide acetate (for depot suspension), per 3.75 mg
MCM 2049
Use this code for Lupron.

? ☑ **J1955** Injection, levocarnitine, per 1 g
MCM 2049
Use this code for Carnitor.

? ☑ **J1956** Injection, levofloxacin, 250 mg
MCM 2049

? ☑ **J1960** Injection, levorphanol tartrate, up to 2 mg
MCM 2049
Use this code for Levo-Dromoran.

? ☑ **J1970** Injection, methotrimeprazine, up to 20 mg
MCM 2049
Use this code for Levoprome.

? ☑ **J1980** Injection, hyoscyamine sulfate, up to 0.25 mg
MCM 2049
Use this code for Levsin.

DRUGS ADMINISTERED OTHER THAN ORAL METHOD

J1990 Injection, chlordiazepoxide HCl, up to 100 mg
MCM 2049
Use this code for Librium.

J2000 Injection, lidocaine HCl, 50 cc
MCM 2049
Use this code for Xylocaine HCl, Lidoject-1, Lidoject-2, Dilocaine, Caine-1, Caine-2, L-Caine, Nervocaine 1%, Nervocaine 2%, Nulicaine.

J2010 Injection, lincomycin HCl, up to 300 mg
MCM 2049
Use this code for Lincocin.

➡ **J2060** Injection, lorazepam, 2 mg
MCM 2049
Use this code for Ativan.

J2150 Injection, mannitol, 25% in 50 ml
MCM 2049

J2175 Injection, meperidine HCl, per 100 mg
MCM 2050.5
Use this code for Demerol HCl.

J2180 Injection, meperidine and promethazine HCl, up to 50 mg
MCM 2049
Use this code for Mepergan Injection.

J2210 Injection, methylergonovine maleate, up to 0.2 mg
MCM 2049
Use this code for Methergine.

J2240 Injection, metocurine iodide, up to 2 mg
MCM 2049
Use this code for Metubine Iodide.

J2250 Injection, midazolam HCl, per 1 mg
MCM 2049
Use this code for Versed.

J2260 Injection, milrinone lactate, per 5 ml
MCM 2049
Use this code for Primacor.

J2270 Injection, morphine sulfate, up to 10 mg
MCM 2049

J2271 Injection, morphine sulfate, 100 mg
CIM 60-14, MCM 2049

J2275 Injection, morphine sulfate (preservative-free sterile solution), per 10 mg
MCM 2049
Use this code for Astramorph PF, Duramorph.

J2300 Injection, nalbuphine HCl, per 10 mg
MCM 2049
Use this code for Nubain.

J2310 Injection, naloxone HCl, per 1 mg
MCM 2049
Use this code for Narcan.

J2320 Injection, nandrolone decanoate, up to 50 mg
MCM 2049
Use this code for Deca-Durabolin, Hybolin Decanoate, Decolone-50, Neo-Durabolic.

J2321 Injection, nandrolone decanoate, up to 100 mg
MCM 2049
Use this code for Deca-Durabolin, Hybolin Decanoate, Decolone-100, Neo-Durabolic, Anabolin LA 100, Androlone-D 100, Nandrobolic L.A.

J2322 Injection, nandrolone decanoate, up to 200 mg
MCM 2049
Use this code for Deca-Durabolin, Neo-Durabolic.

J2330 Injection, thiothixene, up to 4 mg
MCM 2049
Use this code for Navane.

J2350 Injection, niacinamide, niacin, up to 100 mg
MCM 2049
Use this code for Nicotinamide, Nicotinic Acid.

● **J2352** Injection, octreotide acetate, 1 mg

J2355 Injection, oprelvekin, 5 mg
MCM 2049

J2360 Injection, orphenadrine citrate, up to 60 mg
MCM 2049
Use this code for Norflex, Banflex, Flexoject, Flexon, K-Flex, Myolin, Neocyten, O-Flex, Orphenate.

J2370 Injection, phenylephrine HCl, up to 1 ml
MCM 2049
Use this code for Neo-Synephrine.

J2400 Injection, chloroprocaine HCl, per 30 ml
MCM 2049
Use this code for Nesacaine, Nesacaine-MPF.

J2405 Injection, ondansetron HCl, per 1 mg
MCM 2049
Use this code for Zofran.

J2410 Injection, oxymorphone HCl, up to 1 mg
MCM 2049
Use this code for Numorphan, Numorphan H.P.

J2430 Injection, pamidronate disodium, per 30 mg
MCM 2049
Use this code for Aredia.

J2440 Injection, papaverine HCl, up to 60 mg
MCM 2049

J2460 Injection, oxytetracycline HCl, up to 50 mg
MCM 2049
Use this code for Terramycin IM.

J2480 Injection, hydrochlorides of opium alkaloids, up to 20 mg
MCM 2049
Use this code for Pantopon.

● **J2500** Injection, paricalcitol, 5 mcg
MCM 2049

J2510 Injection, penicillin G procaine, aqueous, up to 600,000 units
MCM 2049
Use this code for Wycillin, Duracillin A.S., Pfizerpen A.S., Crysticillin 300 A.S., Crysticillin 600 A.S.

DRUGS ADMINISTERED OTHER THAN ORAL METHOD

J2512 Injection, pentagastrin, per 2 ml
MCM 2049
Use this code for Peptavlon.

J2515 Injection, pentobarbital sodium, per 50 mg
MCM 2049
Use this code for Nembutal Sodium Solution.

J2540 Injection, penicillin G potassium, up to 600,000 units
MCM 2049
Use this code for Pfizerpen.

● **J2543** Injection, piperacillin sodium/tazobactam sodium, 1.125 grams
MCM 2049

J2545 Pentamidine isethionate, inhalation solution, per 300 mg, administered through a DME
MCM 2049

J2550 Injection, promethazine HCl, up to 50 mg
MCM 2049
Use this code for Phenergan, Anergan 25, Anergan 50, Phenazine 25, Phenazine 50, Prorex-25, Prorex-50, Prothazine, V-Gan 25, V-Gan 50.

J2560 Injection, phenobarbital sodium, up to 120 mg
MCM 2049

J2590 Injection, oxytocin, up to 10 units
MCM 2049
Use this code for Pitocin, Syntocinon.

J2597 Injection, desmopressin acetate, per 1 mcg
MCM 2049
Use this code for DDAVP.

J2640 Injection, prednisolone sodium phosphate, up to 20 mg
MCM 2049
Use this code for Hydeltrasol, Key-Pred-SP.

J2650 Injection, prednisolone acetate, up to 1 ml
MCM 2049
Use this code for Key-Pred 25, Key-Pred 50, Predcor-25, Predcor-50, Predoject-50, Predalone-50, Predicort-50.

J2670 Injection, tolazoline HCl, up to 25 mg
MCM 2049
Use this code for Priscoline HCl.

J2675 Injection, progesterone, per 50 mg
MCM 2049
Use this code for (Gesterol 50, Progestaject) per 50 mg.

J2680 Injection, fluphenazine decanoate, up to 25 mg
MCM 2049
Use this code for Prolixin Decanoate.

J2690 Injection, procainamide HCl, up to 1 g
MCM 2049
Use this code for Pronestyl.

J2700 Injection, oxacillin sodium, up to 250 mg
MCM 2049
Use this code for Bactocill, Prostaphlin.

J2710 Injection, neostigmine methylsulfate, up to 0.5 mg
MCM 2049
Use this code for Prostigmin.

J2720 Injection, protamine sulfate, per 10 mg
MCM 2049

J2725 Injection, protirelin, per 250 mcg
MCM 2049
Use this code for Relefact TRH, Thypinone.

J2730 Injection, pralidoxime chloride, up to 1 g
MCM 2049
Use this code for Protopam Chloride.

J2760 Injection, phentolamine mesylate, up to 5 mg
MCM 2049
Use this code for Regitine.

J2765 Injection, metoclopramide HCl, up to 10 mg
MCM 2049
Use this code for Reglan.

● **J2780** Injection, ranitidine hydrochloride, 25 mg
MCM 2049

J2790 Injection, Rho (D) immune globulin, human, one dose package
MCM 2049
Use this code for Gamulin RH, HypRho-D.

J2792 Injection, rho D immune globulin, intravenous, human, solvent detergent, 100 I.U.
MCM 2049

J2800 Injection, methocarbamol, up to 10 ml
MCM 2050.5
Use this code for Robaxin.

J2810 Injection, theophylline, per 40 mg
MCM 2050.5

J2820 Injection, sargramostim (GM-CSF), 50 mcg
MCM 2049
Use this code for Leukine, Prokine.

J2860 Injection, secobarbital sodium, up to 250 mg
MCM 2049
Use this code for Seconal.

J2910 Injection, aurothioglucose, up to 50 mg
MCM 2049
Use this code for Solganal.

J2912 Injection, sodium chloride, 0.9%, per 2 ml
MCM 2049

J2920 Injection, methylprednisolone sodium succinate, up to 40 mg
MCM 2049
Use this code for Solu-Medrol, A-methaPred.

J2930 Injection, methylprednisolone sodium succinate, up to 125 mg
MCM 2049
Use this code for Solu-Medrol, A-methaPred.

J2950 Injection, promazine HCl, up to 25 mg
MCM 2049
Use this code for Sparine, Prozine-50.

Drugs Administered Other Than Oral Method

- ? ☑ **J2970** Injection, methicillin sodium, up to 1 g
  MCM 2049
  Use this code for Staphcillin.

- ? ☑ **J2994** Injection reteplase, 37.6 mg (two single-use vials)
  MCM 2049

- ? ☑ **J2995** Injection, streptokinase, per 250,000 IU
  MCM 2049
  Use this code for Kabikinase, Streptase.

- ? ☑ **J2996** Injection, alteplase recombinant, per 10 mg
  MCM 2049
  Use this code for Activase.

- ? ☑ **J3000** Injection, streptomycin, up to 1 g
  MCM 2049
  Use this code for Streptomycin Sulfate.

- ? ☑ **J3010** Injection, fentanyl citrate, up to 2 ml
  MCM 2049
  Use this code for Sublimaze.

- ▲ **J3030** Injection, sumatriptan succinate, 6 mg (code may be used for Medicare when drug administered under direct supervision of a physician not for use when drug is self-administered)

- ? ☑ **J3070** Injection, pentazocine HCl, up to 30 mg
  MCM 2049
  Use this code for Talwin.

- ? ☑ **J3080** Injection, chlorprothixene, up to 50 mg
  MCM 2049
  Use this code for Taractan.

- ? ☑ **J3105** Injection, terbutaline sulfate, up to 1 mg
  MCM 2049
  Use this code for Brethine, Bricanyl Subcutaneous. For terbutaline in inhalation solution, see K0525 and K0526.

- ? ☑ **J3120** Injection, testosterone enanthate, up to 100 mg
  MCM 2049
  Use this code for Everone, Delatest, Delatestryl, Andropository 100, Testone LA 100.

- ? ☑ **J3130** Injection, testosterone enanthate, up to 200 mg
  MCM 2049
  Use this code for Everone, Delatestryl, Andro L.A. 200, Andryl 200, Durathate-200, Testone LA 200, Testrin PA.

- ? ☑ **J3140** Injection, testosterone suspension, up to 50 mg
  MCM 2049
  Use this code for Andronaq 50, Testosterone Aqueous, Testaqua, Testoject-50, Histerone 50, Histerone 100.

- ? ☑ **J3150** Injection, testosterone propionate, up to 100 mg
  MCM 2049
  Use this code for Testex.

- ? ☑ **J3230** Injection, chlorpromazine HCl, up to 50 mg
  MCM 2049
  Use this code for Thorazine, Ormazine.

- ▲ **J3240** Injection, thyrotropin alpha, 0.9 mg
  MCM 2049

- ● **J3245** Injection, tirofiban hydrochloride, 12.5 mg
  MCM 2049

- ? ☑ **J3250** Injection, trimethobenzamide HCl, up to 200 mg
  MCM 2049
  Use this code for Tigan, Ticon, Tiject-20, Arrestin.

- ? ☑ **J3260** Injection, tobramycin sulfate, up to 80 mg
  MCM 2049
  Use this code for Nebcin.

- ? ☑ **J3265** Injection, torsemide, 10 mg/ml
  MCM 2049
  Use this code for Demadex.

- ? ☑ **J3270** Injection, imipramine HCl, up to 25 mg
  MCM 2049
  Use this code for Tofranil.

- ? ☑ **J3280** Injection, thiethylperazine maleate, up to 10 mg
  MCM 2049
  Use this code for Norzine, Torecan.

- ? ☑ **J3301** Injection, triamcinolone acetonide, per 10 mg
  MCM 2049
  Use this code for Kenalog-10, Kenalog-40, Tri-Kort, Kenaject-40, Cenacort A-40, Triam-A, Trilog. For triamcinolone in inhalation solution, see K0527 and K0528.

- ? ☑ **J3302** Injection, triamcinolone diacetate, per 5 mg
  MCM 2049
  Use this code for Aristocort Intralesional, Aristocort Forte, Amcort, Trilone, Cenacort Forte.

- ? ☑ **J3303** Injection, triamcinolone hexacetonide, per 5 mg
  MCM 2049
  Use this code for Aristospan Intralesional, Aristospan Intra-articular.

- ? ☑ **J3305** Injection, trimetrexate glucoronate, per 25 mg
  MCM 2049
  Use this code for Neutrexin.

- ? ☑ **J3310** Injection, perphenazine, up to 5 mg
  MCM 2049
  Use this code for Trilafon.

- ? ☑ **J3320** Injection, spectinomycin dihydrochloride, up to 2 g
  MCM 2049
  Use this code for Trobicin.

- ? ☑ **J3350** Injection, urea, up to 40 g
  MCM 2049
  Use this code for Ureaphil.

- ? ☑ **J3360** Injection, diazepam, up to 5 mg
  MCM 2049
  Use this code for Valium, Zetran.

- ? ☑ **J3364** Injection, urokinase, 5,000 IU vial
  MCM 2049
  Use this code for Abbokinase Open-Cath.

J3365 Injection, IV, urokinase, 250,000 IU vial
MCM 2049
Use this code for Abbokinase.

▲ **J3370** Injection, vancomycin HCl, 500 mg
CIM 60-14, MCM 2049

J3390 Injection, methoxamine HCl, up to 20 mg
MCM 2049
Use this code for Vasoxyl.

J3400 Injection, triflupromazine HCl, up to 20 mg
MCM 2049
Use this code for Vesprin.

J3410 Injection, hydroxyzine HCl, up to 25 mg
MCM 2049
Use this code for Vistaril, Vistaject-25, Hyzine-50.

J3420 Injection, vitamin B-12 cyanocobalamin, up to 1,000 mcg
CIM 45-4, MCM 2049
Use this code for Sytobex, Redisol, Rubramin PC, Betalin 12, Berubigen, Cobex.

J3430 Injection, phytonadione (vitamin K), per 1 mg
MCM 2049
Use this code for AquaMephyton, Konakion.

J3450 Injection, mephentermine sulfate, up to 30 mg
MCM 2049
Use this code for Wyamine Sulfate.

J3470 Injection, hyaluronidase, up to 150 units
MCM 2049
Use this code for Wydase.

J3475 Injection, magnesium sulphate, per 500 mg
MCM 2049

J3480 Injection, potassium chloride, per 2 mEq
MCM 2049

J3490 Unclassified drugs
MCM 2049

J3520 Edetate disodium, per 150 mg
Medicaid suspend for medical review, CIM 35-64, 45-20
Use this code for Endrate, Disotate. This drug is used in chelation therapy, a treatment for atherosclerosis that is not covered by Medicare.

J3530 Nasal vaccine inhalation
MCM 2049

J3535 Drug administered through a metered dose inhaler
MCM 2050.5

J3570 Laetrile, amygdalin, vitamin B-17
CIM 45-10
The FDA has found Laetrile to have no safe or effective therapeutic purpose.

Miscellaneous Drugs and Solutions

J7030 Infusion, normal saline solution, 1,000 cc
MCM 2049

J7040 Infusion, normal saline solution, sterile (500 ml = 1 unit)
MCM 2049

J7042 5% dextrose/normal saline (500 ml = 1 unit)
MCM 2049

J7050 Infusion, normal saline solution, 250 cc
MCM 2049

J7051 Sterile saline or water, up to 5 cc
MCM 2049

J7060 5% dextrose/water (500 ml = 1 unit)
MCM 2049

J7070 Infusion, D-5-W, 1,000 cc
MCM 2049

J7100 Infusion, dextran 40, 500 ml
MCM 2049
Use this code for Gentran, 10% LMD, Rheomacrodex.

J7110 Infusion, dextran 75, 500 ml
MCM 2049
Use this code for Gentran 75.

J7120 Ringer's lactate infusion, up to 1,000 cc
MCM 2049

J7130 Hypertonic saline solution, 50 or 100 mEq, 20 cc vial
MCM 2049

J7190 Factor VIII (antihemophilic factor, human) per I.U.
MCM 2049
Use this code for Monarc-M. Medicare jurisdiction: local carrier.

J7191 Factor VIII (anti-hemophilic factor (porcine)), per I.U.
Medicare jurisdiction: local carrier.

J7192 Factor VIII (antihemophilic factor, recombinant) per I.U.
MCM 2049
Use this code for Recombinate, Kogenate. Medicare jurisdiction: local carrier.

J7194 Factor IX complex, per IU
MCM 2049
Use this code for Konyne-80, Profilnine Heat-Treated, Proplex T, Proplex SX-T. Medicare jurisdiction: local carrier.

(J7196 has been deleted)

J7197 Antithrombin III (human), per IU
MCM 2049
Medicare jurisdiction: local carrier.

● **J7198** Anti-inhibitor, per i.u.
CIM 45-24, MCM 2049

● **J7199** Hemophilia clotting factor, not otherwise classified
CIM 45-24, MCM 2049

J7300 Intrauterine copper contraceptive
Medicare statute 1862.A1
Use this code for Paragard T380A.

J7310 Ganciclovir, 4.5 mg, long-acting implant
MCM 2049
Use this code for Vitrasert.

DRUGS ADMINISTERED OTHER THAN ORAL METHOD

➥ ☑ **J7315** Sodium hyaluronate, 20 mg, for intra-articular injection

➥ ☑ **J7320** Hylan G-F 20, 16 mg, for intra-articular injection

▲ ? ☑ **J7500** Azathioprine, oral, 50 mg
MCM 2049.5

▲ ? ☑ **J7501** Azathioprine, parenteral, 100 mg
MCM 2049

● ? ☑ **J7502** Cyclosporine, oral, 100 mg
MCM 2049.5

(J7503 has been deleted)

▲ ? ☑ **J7504** Lymphocyte immune globulin, antithymocyte globulin, parenteral, 250 mg
CIM 45-22, MCM 2049

? ☑ **J7505** Monoclonal antibodies - parenteral, 5 mg
MCM 2049

? ☑ **J7506** Prednisone, oral, per 5 mg
MCM 2049.5

? ☑ **J7507** Tacrolimus, oral, per 1 mg
MCM 2049.5
Use this code for Prograf.

? ☑ **J7508** Tacrolimus, oral, per 5 mg
MCM 2049.5
Use this code for Prograf.

➥ ☑ **J7509** Methylprednisolone, oral, per 4 mg
MCM 2049.5
Use this code for Medrol.

➥ ☑ **J7510** Prednisolone, oral, per 5 mg
MCM 2049.5
Use this code for Delta-Cortef.

? ☑ **J7513** Daclizumab, parenteral, 25 mg
MCM 2049.5

● ➥ ☑ **J7515** Cyclosporine, oral, 25 mg

● ➥ ☑ **J7516** Cyclosporine, parenteral, 250 mg

● ➥ ☑ **J7517** Mycophenolate mofetil, oral, 250 mg

? **J7599** Immunosuppressive drug, not otherwise classified
MCM 2049.5
Determine if an alternative national HCPCS Level II or a local HCPCS Level III code better describes the service being reported. This code should be used only if a more specific code is unavailable.

● ? ☑ **J7608** Acetylcysteine, inhalation solution administered through DME, unit dose form, per gram
MCM 2100.5

Inhalation Solutions

? ☑ **J7610** Acetylcysteine, 10%, per ml, inhalation solution administered through DME
MCM 2100.5
Use this code for Mucomyst, Mucosol. For acetylcysteine in inhalation solution, see K0503.

? ☑ **J7615** Acetylcysteine, 20%, per ml, inhalation solution administered through DME
MCM 2100.5
Use this code for Mucomyst, Mucosol. For acetylcysteine in inhalation solution, see K0503.

● ? ☑ **J7618** Albuterol, inhalation solution administered through DME, concentrated form, per milligram
MCM 2100.5

● ? ☑ **J7619** Albuterol, inhalation solution administered through DME, unit dose form, per milligram
MCM 2100.5

? ☑ **J7620** Albuterol sulfate, 0.083%, per ml, inhalation solution administered through DME
MCM 2100.5, MCM 2049
Use this code for Proventil. For albuterol in inhalation solution, see K0504 and K0505.

? ☑ **J7625** Albuterol sulfate, 0.5%, per ml, inhalation solution administered through DME
MCM 2100.5, MCM 2049
Use this code for Proventil, Ventolin. For albuterol in inhalation solution, see K0504 and K0505.

➥ ☑ **J7627** Bitolterol mesylate, 0.2%, per 10 ml, inhalation solution administered through DME
Use this code for Tornalate. For bitolterol mesylate in inhalation solution, see K0508 and K0809.

● ? ☑ **J7628** Bitolterol mesylate, inhalation solution administered through DME, concentrated form, per milligram
MCM 2100.5

● ? ☑ **J7629** Bitolterol mesylate, inhalation solution administered through DME, unit dose form, per milligram
MCM 2100.5

? ☑ **J7630** Cromolyn sodium, per 20 mg, inhalation solution administered through DME
MCM 2100.5, MCM 2049
Use this code for Intal. For cromolyn sodium in inhalation solution, see K0511.

● ? ☑ **J7631** Cromolyn sodium, inhalation solution administered through DME, unit dose form, per 10 milligrams
MCM 2100.5

● ? ☑ **J7635** Atropine, inhalation solution administered through DME, concentrated form, per milligram
MCM 2100.5

● ? ☑ **J7636** Atropine, inhalation solution administered through DME, unit dose form, per milligram
MCM 2100.5

● ? ☑ **J7637** Dexamethasone, inhalation solution administered through DME, concentrated form, per milligram
MCM 2100.5

DRUGS ADMINISTERED OTHER THAN ORAL METHOD

- ?☑ **J7638** Dexamethasone, inhalation solution administered through DME, unit dose form, per milligram
  MCM 2100.5

- ?☑ **J7639** Dornase alpha, inhalation solution administered through DME, unit dose form, per milligram
  MCM 2100.5

  ?☑ **J7640** Epinephrine, 2.25%, per ml, inhalation solution administered through DME
  MCM 2100.5

- ?☑ **J7642** Glycopyrrolate, inhalation solution administered through DME, concentrated form, per milligram
  MCM 2100.5

- ?☑ **J7643** Glycopyrrolate, inhalation solution administered through DME, unit dose form, per milligram
  MCM 2100.5

- ?☑ **J7644** Ipratropium bromide, inhalation solution administered through DME, unit dose form, per milligram
  MCM 2100.5

  ?☑ **J7645** Ipratropium bromide 0.02%, per ml, inhalation solution, administered through a DME
  MCM 2100.5
  Use this code for Atrovent. For ipratropium bromide in inhalation solution, see K0518.

- ?☑ **J7648** Isoetharine HCl, inhalation solution administered through DME, concentrated form, per milligram
  MCM 2100.5

- ?☑ **J7649** Isoetharine HCl, inhalation solution administered through DME, unit dose form, per milligram
  MCM 2100.5

  ?☑ **J7650** Isoetharine HCl, 0.1%, per ml, inhalation solution administered through DME
  MCM 2100.5, MCM 2049

  ?☑ **J7651** Isoetharine HCl, 0.125%, per ml, inhalation solution administered through DME
  MCM 2100.5, MCM 2049

  ?☑ **J7652** Isoetharine HCl, 0.167%, per ml, inhalation solution administered through DME
  MCM 2100.5, MCM 2049

  ?☑ **J7653** Isoetharine HCl, 0.2%, per ml, inhalation solution administered through DME
  MCM 2100.5, MCM 2049

  ?☑ **J7654** Isoetharine HCl, 0.25%, per ml, inhalation solution administered through DME
  MCM 2100.5, MCM 2049
  Use this code for Bronkosol Unijet, Arm-a-Med.

  ?☑ **J7655** Isoetharine HCl, 1.0%, per ml, inhalation solution administered through DME
  MCM 2100.5, MCM 2049
  Use this code for Bronkosol.

- ?☑ **J7658** Isoproterenol HCl, inhalation solution administered through DME, concentrated form, per milligram
  MCM 2100.5

- ?☑ **J7659** Isoproterenol HCl, inhalation solution administered through DME, unit dose form, per milligram
  MCM 2100.5

  ?☑ **J7660** Isoproterenol HCl, 0.5%, per ml, inhalation solution administered through DME
  MCM 2100.5
  Use this code for Isuprel. For isoproterenol in inhalation solution, see K0521 and K0522.

  ?☑ **J7665** Isoproterenol HCl, 1.0%, per ml, inhalation solution administered through DME
  MCM 2100.5
  Use this code for Isuprel. For isoproterenol in inhalation solution, see K0521 and K0522.

- ?☑ **J7668** Metaproterenol sulfate, inhalation solution administered through DME, concentrated form, per 10 milligrams
  MCM 2100.5

- ?☑ **J7669** Metaproterenol sulfate, inhalation solution administered through DME, unit dose form, per 10 milligrams
  MCM 2100.5

  ?☑ **J7670** Metaproterenol sulfate, 0.4%, per 2.5 ml, inhalation solution administered through DME
  MCM 2100.5, MCM 2049
  Use this code for Alupent. For metaproterenol in inhalation solution, see K0523 and K0524.

  ?☑ **J7672** Metaproterenol sulfate, 0.6%, per 2.5 ml, inhalation solution administered through DME
  MCM 2100.5, MCM 2049
  Use this code for Alupent.

  ?☑ **J7675** Metaproterenol sulfate, 5.0%, per ml, inhalation solution administered through DME
  MCM 2100.5, MCM 2049
  Use this code for Alupent, Metaprel. For metaproterenol in inhalation solution, see K0523 and K0524.

- ?☑ **J7680** Terbutaline sulfate, inhalation solution administered through DME, concentrated form, per milligram
  MCM 2100.5

- ?☑ **J7681** Terbutaline sulfate, inhalation solution administered through DME, unit dose form, per milligram
  MCM 2100.5

- ?☑ **J7682** Tobramycin, unit dose form, 300 mg, inhalation solution, administered through DME
  MCM 2100.5

Drugs Administered Other Than Oral Method

- ? ☑ **J7683** Triamcinolone, inhalation solution administered through DME, concentrated form, per milligram
  MCM 2100.5

- ? ☑ **J7684** Triamcinolone, inhalation solution administered through DME, unit dose form, per milligram
  MCM 2100.5

? **J7699** NOC drugs, inhalation solution administered through DME
MCM 2100.5

? **J7799** NOC drugs, other than inhalation drugs, administered through DME
MCM 2100.5

⊘ **J8499** Prescription drug, oral, nonchemotherapeutic, not otherwise specified
MCM 2049

- ? ☑ **J8510** Bulsulfan; oral, 2 mg
  MCM 2049.5

- ? ☑ **J8520** Capecitabine, oral, 150 mg
  MCM 2049.5

- ? ☑ **J8521** Capecitabine, oral, 500 mg
  MCM 2049.5

? ☑ **J8530** Cyclophosphamide, oral, 25 mg
MCM 2049.5
Use this code for Cytoxan.

? ☑ **J8560** Etoposide, oral, 50 mg
MCM 2049.5
Use this code for VePesid.

? ☑ **J8600** Melphalan, oral 2 mg
MCM 2049.5
Use this code for Alkeran.

? ☑ **J8610** Methotrexate, oral, 2.5 mg
MCM 2049.5
Use this code for Rheumatrex Dose Pack.

? **J8999** Prescription drug, oral, chemotherapeutic, not otherwise specified
MCM 2049.5
Determine if an alternative national HCPCS Level II or a local HCPCS Level III code better describes the service being reported. This code should be used only if a more specific code is unavailable.

Chemotherapy Drugs J9000–J9999

These codes cover the cost of the chemotherapy drug only, not the administration. See also J8999.

? ☑ **J9000** Doxorubicin HCl, 10 mg
MCM 2049
Use this code for Adriamycin PFS, Adriamycin RDF, Rubex.

- ? ☑ **J9001** Doxorubicin hydrochloride, all lipid formulations, 10 mg
  MCM 2049

? ☑ **J9015** Aldesleukin, per single use vial
MCM 2049
Use this code for Proleukin, IL-2, Interleukin.

? ☑ **J9020** Asparaginase, 10,000 units
MCM 2049
Use this code for Elspar.

? ☑ **J9031** BCG live (intravesical), per installation
MCM 2049
Use this code for Tice BCG, TheraCys.

? ☑ **J9040** Bleomycin sulfate, 15 units
MCM 2049
Use this code for lenoxane.

? ☑ **J9045** Carboplatin, 50 mg
MCM 2049
Use this code for Paraplatin.

? ☑ **J9050** Carmustine, 100 mg
MCM 2049
Use this code for BiCNU.

? ☑ **J9060** Cisplatin, powder or solution, per 10 mg
MCM 2049
Use this code for Platinol, Plantinol AQ.

? ☑ **J9062** Cisplatin, 50 mg
MCM 2049
Use this code for Platinol, Plantinol AQ.

? ☑ **J9065** Injection, cladribine, per 1 mg
MCM 2049
Use this code for Leustatin.

? ☑ **J9070** Cyclophosphamide, 100 mg
MCM 2049
Use this code for Cytoxan, Neosar.

? ☑ **J9080** Cyclophosphamide, 200 mg
MCM 2049
Use this code for Cytoxan, Neosar.

? ☑ **J9090** Cyclophosphamide, 500 mg
MCM 2049
Use this code for Cytoxan, Neosar.

? ☑ **J9091** Cyclophosphamide, 1 g
MCM 2049
Use this code for Cytoxan, Neosar.

? ☑ **J9092** Cyclophosphamide, 2 g
MCM 2049
Use this code for Cytoxan, Neosar.

? ☑ **J9093** Cyclophosphamide, lyophilized, 100 mg
MCM 2049
Use this code for Cytoxan Lyophilized.

? ☑ **J9094** Cyclophosphamide, lyophilized, 200 mg
MCM 2049
Use this code for Cytoxan Lyophilized.

? ☑ **J9095** Cyclophosphamide, lyophilized, 500 mg
MCM 2049
Use this code for Cytoxan Lyophilized.

? ☑ **J9096** Cyclophosphamide, lyophilized, 1 g
MCM 2049
Use this code for Cytoxan Lyophilized.

? ☑ **J9097** Cyclophosphamide, lyophilized, 2 g
MCM 2049
Use this code for Cytoxan, Lyophilized.

? ☑ **J9100** Cytarabine, 100 mg
MCM 2049
Use this code for Cytosar-U.

Drugs Administered Other Than Oral Method

- **J9110** Cytarabine, 500 mg
  MCM 2049
  Use this code for Cytosar-U.

- **J9120** Dactinomycin, 0.5 mg
  MCM 2049
  Use this code for Cosmegen.

- **J9130** Dacarbazine, 100 mg
  MCM 2049
  Use this code for DTIC-Dome.

- **J9140** Dacarbazine, 200 mg
  MCM 2049
  Use this code for DTIC-Dome.

- **J9150** Daunorubicin HCl, 10 mg
  MCM 2049
  Use this code for Cerubidine.

- **J9151** Daunorubicin citrate, liposomal formulation, 10 mg
  MCM 2049

- **J9165** Diethylstilbestrol diphosphate, 250 mg
  MCM 2049
  Use this code for Stilphostrol.

- **J9170** Docetaxel, 20 mg
  MCM 2049

- **J9181** Etoposide, 10 mg
  MCM 2049
  Use this code for VePesid.

- **J9182** Etoposide, 100 mg
  MCM 2049
  Use this code for VePesid.

- **J9185** Fludarabine phosphate, 50 mg
  MCM 2049
  Use this code for Fludara.

- **J9190** Fluorouracil, 500 mg
  MCM 2049
  Use this code for Adrucil.

- **J9200** Floxuridine, 500 mg
  MCM 2049
  Use this code for FUDR.

- **J9201** Gemcitabine HCl, 200 mg
  MCM 2049

- **J9202** Goserelin acetate implant, per 3.6 mg
  MCM 2049
  Use this code for Zoladex.

- **J9206** Irinotecan, 20 mg
  MCM 2049

- **J9208** Ifosfamide, per 1 g
  MCM 2049
  Use this code for Ifex.

- **J9209** Mesna, 200 mg
  MCM 2049
  Use this code for Mesnex.

- **J9211** Idarubicin HCl, 5 mg
  MCM 2049
  Use this code for Idamycin.

- **J9212** Injection, interferon Alfacon-1, recombinant, 1 mcg
  MCM 2049

- **J9213** Interferon alfa-2A, recombinant, 3 million units
  MCM 2049
  Use this code for Roferon-A.

- **J9214** Interferon alfa-2B, recombinant, 1 million units
  MCM 2049
  Use this code for Intron A.

- **J9215** Interferon alfa-N3, (human leukocyte derived), 250,000 IU
  MCM 2049
  Use this code for Alferon N.

- **J9216** Interferon gamma-1B, 3 million units
  MCM 2049
  Use this code for Actimmune.

- **J9217** Leuprolide acetate (for depot suspension), 7.5 mg
  MCM 2049
  Use this code for Lupron.

- **J9218** Leuprolide acetate, per 1 mg
  MCM 2049
  Use this code for Lupron.

- **J9230** Mechlorethamine HCl, (nitrogen mustard), 10 mg
  MCM 2049
  Use this code for Mustargen.

- **J9245** Injection, melphalan HCl, 50 mg
  MCM 2049

- **J9250** Methotrexate sodium, 5 mg
  MCM 2049
  Use this code for Folex, Folex PFS, Methotrexate LPF.

- **J9260** Methotrexate sodium, 50 mg
  MCM 2049
  Use this code for Folex, Folex PFS, Methotrexate LPF.

- **J9265** Paclitaxel, 30 mg
  MCM 2049
  Use this code for Taxol.

- **J9266** Pegaspargase, per single dose vial
  MCM 2049
  Use this code for Oncaspar, Peg-L-asparaginase.

- **J9268** Pentostatin, per 10 mg
  MCM 2049

- **J9270** Plicamycin, 2.5 mg
  MCM 2049

- **J9280** Mitomycin, 5 mg
  MCM 2049

- **J9290** Mitomycin, 20 mg
  MCM 2049

- **J9291** Mitomycin, 40 mg
  MCM 2049

- **J9293** Injection, mitoxantrone HCl, per 5 mg
  MCM 2049

- **J9310** Rituximab, 100 mg
  MCM 2049

- **J9320** Streptozocin, 1 g
  MCM 2049

CHEMOTHERAPY DRUGS

? ☑ **J9340** Thiotepa, 15 mg
MCM 2049

? ☑ **J9350** Topotecan, 4 mg
MCM 2049

● ➡ ☑ **J9355** Trastuzumab, 10 mg

● ? ☑ **J9357** Valrubicin, intravesical, 200 mg
MCM 2049

? ☑ **J9360** Vinblastine sulfate, 1 mg
MCM 2049

? ☑ **J9370** Vincristine sulfate, 1 mg
MCM 2049

? ☑ **J9375** Vincristine sulfate, 2 mg
MCM 2049

? ☑ **J9380** Vincristine sulfate, 5 mg
MCM 2049

? ☑ **J9390** Vinorelbine tartrate, per 10 mg
MCM 2049

? ☑ **J9600** Porfimer sodium, 75 mg
MCM 2049

? **J9999** Not otherwise classified, antineoplastic drug
CIM 45-16, MCM 2049
Determine if an alternative national HCPCS Level II or a local HCPCS Level III code better describes the service being reported. This code should be used only if a more specific code is unavailable.

K Codes (Temporary) K0000–K9999

Medicare claims for K codes fall under the jurisdiction of the DME regional carrier, unless otherwise noted.

K Codes Assigned to Durable Medical Equipment Regional Carriers (DMERC)

Wheelchair and Wheelchair Accessories

➥ **K0001** Standard wheelchair

➥ **K0002** Standard hemi (low seat) wheelchair

➥ **K0003** Lightweight wheelchair

➥ **K0004** High strength, lightweight wheelchair

➥ **K0005** Ultralightweight wheelchair

➥ **K0006** Heavy-duty wheelchair

➥ **K0007** Extra heavy-duty wheelchair

➥ **K0008** Custom manual wheelchair/base

➥ **K0009** Other manual wheelchair/base

➥ **K0010** Standard-weight frame motorized/power wheelchair

➥ **K0011** Standard-weight frame motorized/power wheelchair with programmable control parameters for speed adjustment, tremor dampening, acceleration control and braking

➥ **K0012** Lightweight portable motorized/power wheelchair

➥ **K0013** Custom motorized/power wheelchair base

➥ **K0014** Other motorized/power wheelchair base

➥ ☑ **K0015** Detachable, nonadjustable height armrest, each

➥ ☑ **K0016** Detachable, adjustable height armrest, complete assembly, each

➥ ☑ **K0017** Detachable, adjustable height armrest, base, each

➥ ☑ **K0018** Detachable, adjustable height armrest, upper portion, each

➥ ☑ **K0019** Arm pad, each

➥ ☑ **K0020** Fixed, adjustable height armrest, pair

➥ ☑ **K0021** Antitipping device, each

➥ **K0022** Reinforced back upholstery

➥ **K0023** Solid back insert, planar back, single density foam, attached with straps

➥ **K0024** Solid back insert, planar back, single density foam, with adjustable hook-on hardware

➥ **K0025** Hook-on headrest extension

➥ **K0026** Back upholstery for ultralightweight or high-strength lightweight wheelchair

➥ **K0027** Back upholstery for wheelchair type other than ultralightweight or high-strength lightweight wheelchair

➥ **K0028** Fully reclining back

➥ **K0029** Reinforced seat upholstery

➥ **K0030** Solid seat insert, planar seat, single density foam

▲ ➥ ☑ **K0031** Safety belt/pelvic strap, each

➥ **K0032** Seat upholstery for ultralightweight or high-strength lightweight wheelchair

➥ **K0033** Seat upholstery for wheelchair type other than ultralightweight or high-strength lightweight wheelchair

➥ ☑ **K0034** Heel loop, each

➥ ☑ **K0035** Heel loop with ankle strap, each

➥ ☑ **K0036** Toe loop, each

➥ ☑ **K0037** High mount flip-up footrest, each

➥ ☑ **K0038** Leg strap, each

➥ ☑ **K0039** Leg strap, H style, each

➥ ☑ **K0040** Adjustable angle footplate, each

➥ ☑ **K0041** Large size footplate, each

➥ ☑ **K0042** Standard size footplate, each

➥ ☑ **K0043** Footrest, lower extension tube, each

➥ ☑ **K0044** Footrest, upper hanger bracket, each

➥ **K0045** Footrest, complete assembly

➥ ☑ **K0046** Elevating legrest, lower extension tube, each

➥ ☑ **K0047** Elevating legrest, upper hanger bracket, each

➥ **K0048** Elevating legrest, complete assembly

➥ ☑ **K0049** Calf pad, each

➥ **K0050** Ratchet assembly

➥ ☑ **K0051** Cam release assembly, footrest or legrest, each

➥ ☑ **K0052** Swingaway, detachable footrests, each

➥ ☑ **K0053** Elevating footrests, articulating (telescoping), each

➥ ☑ **K0054** Seat width of 10, 11, 12, 15, 17, or 20 inches for a high-strength, lightweight or ultralightweight wheelchair

➥ ☑ **K0055** Seat depth of 15, 17, or 18 inches for a high strength, lightweight or ultralightweight wheelchair

➥ ☑ **K0056** Seat height less than 17 inches or equal to or greater than 21 inches for a high strength, lightweight, or ultralightweight wheelchair

☑ Quantity Alert ● New Code ▲ Revised Code

- **K0057** Seat width 19 or 20 inches for heavy duty or extra heavy-duty chair
- **K0058** Seat depth 17 or 18 inches for a motorized/power wheelchair
- **K0059** Plastic coated handrim, each
- **K0060** Steel handrim, each
- **K0061** Aluminum handrim, each
- **K0062** Handrim with 8 to 10 vertical or oblique projections, each
- **K0063** Handrim with 12 to 16 vertical or oblique projections, each
- **K0064** Zero pressure tube (flat free insert), any size, each
- ▲ **K0065** Spoke protectors, each
- **K0066** Solid tire, any size, each
- **K0067** Pneumatic tire, any size, each
- **K0068** Pneumatic tire tube, each
- **K0069** Rear wheel assembly, complete, with solid tire, spokes or molded, each
- **K0070** Rear wheel assembly, complete with pneumatic tire, spokes or molded, each
- **K0071** Front caster assembly, complete, with pneumatic tire, each
- **K0072** Front caster assembly, complete, with semipneumatic tire, each
- **K0073** Caster pin lock, each
- **K0074** Pneumatic caster tire, any size, each
- **K0075** Semipneumatic caster tire, any size, each
- **K0076** Solid caster tire, any size, each
- **K0077** Front caster assembly, complete, with solid tire, each
- **K0078** Pneumatic caster tire tube, each
- **K0079** Wheel lock extension, pair
- **K0080** Antirollback device, pair
- **K0081** Wheel lock assembly, complete, each
- **K0082** 22 NF deep cycle lead acid battery, each
- **K0083** 22 NF gel cell battery, each
- **K0084** Group 24 deep cycle lead acid battery, each
- **K0085** Group 24 gel cell battery, each
- **K0086** U-1 lead acid battery, each
- **K0087** U-1 gel cell battery, each
- **K0088** Battery charger, lead acid or gel cell
- **K0089** Battery charger, dual mode
- **K0090** Rear wheel tire for power wheelchair, any size, each
- **K0091** Rear wheel tire tube other than zero pressure for power wheelchair, any size, each
- **K0092** Rear wheel assembly for power wheelchair, complete, each
- **K0093** Rear wheel zero pressure tire tube (flat free insert) for power wheelchair, any size, each
- **K0094** Wheel tire for power base, any size, each
- **K0095** Wheel tire tube other than zero pressure for each base, any size, each
- **K0096** Wheel assembly for power base, complete, each
- **K0097** Wheel zero-pressure tire tube (flat free insert) for power base, any size, each
- **K0098** Drive belt for power wheelchair
- **K0099** Front caster for power wheelchair
- ▲ **K0100** Wheelchair adapter for amputee, pair
- ▲ **K0101** One-arm drive attachment, each
- ▲ **K0102** Crutch and cane holder, each
- **K0103** Transfer board, less than 25 inches
- ▲ **K0104** Cylinder tank carrier, each
- ▲ **K0105** IV hanger, each
- **K0106** Arm trough, each
- **K0107** Wheelchair tray
- **K0108** Other accessories

(K0109 has been deleted)

Spinal Orthotics

- **K0112** Trunk support device, vest type, with inner frame, prefabricated
- **K0113** Trunk support device, vest type, without inner frame, prefabricated
- **K0114** Back support system for use with a wheelchair, with inner frame, prefabricated
- **K0115** Seating system, back module, posterior-lateral control, with or without lateral supports, custom fabricated for attachment to wheelchair base
- **K0116** Seating system, combined back and seat module, custom fabricated for attachment to wheelchair base

Immunosuppressive Drugs

(K0119 has been deleted)
(K0120 has been deleted)
(K0121 has been deleted)
(K0122 has been deleted)
(K0123 has been deleted)

(K0137 has been deleted)
(K0138 has been deleted)
(K0139 has been deleted)
(K0168 has been deleted)
(K0169 has been deleted)
(K0170 has been deleted)
(K0171 has been deleted)
(K0172 has been deleted)
(K0173 has been deleted)
(K0174 has been deleted)
(K0175 has been deleted)
(K0176 has been deleted)
(K0177 has been deleted)
(K0178 has been deleted)
(K0179 has been deleted)
(K0180 has been deleted)
(K0181 has been deleted)

➥ ☑ **K0182** Water, distilled, used with large volume nebulizer, 1000 ml

➥ **K0183** Nasal application device used with positive airway pressure device

➥ ☑ **K0184** Nasal pillows/seals, replacement for nasal application device, pair

➥ **K0185** Headgear used with positive airway pressure device

➥ **K0186** Chin strap used with positive airway pressure device

➥ **K0187** Tubing used with positive airway pressure device

➥ **K0188** Filter, disposable, used with positive airway pressure device

➥ **K0189** Filter, nondisposable, used with positive airway pressure device

(K0190 has been deleted)
(K0191 has been deleted)
(K0192 has been deleted)
(K0193 has been deleted)
(K0194 has been deleted)

? **K0195** Elevating legrest, pair (for use with capped rental wheelchair base)
CIM 60-9

Miscellaneous

➥ **K0268** Humidifier, nonheated, used with positive airway pressure device

➥ **K0269** Aerosol compressor, adjustable pressure, light duty for intermittent use

➥ **K0270** Ultrasonic generator with small volume ultrasonic nebulizer

(K0277 has been deleted)
(K0278 has been deleted)
(K0279 has been deleted)

➥ ☑ **K0280** Extension drainage tubing, any type, any length, with connector/adaptor, for use with urinary leg bag or urostomy pouch, each

➥ ☑ **K0281** Lubricant, individual sterile packet, for insertion of urinary catheter, each

➥ ☑ **K0283** Saline solution, per 10 ml, metered dose dispenser, for use with inhalation drugs

(K0284 has been deleted)
(K0400 has been deleted)
(K0401 has been deleted)

➥ **K0407** Urinary catheter anchoring device, adhesive skin attachment

➥ **K0408** Urinary catheter anchoring device, leg strap

➥ ☑ **K0409** Sterile water irrigation solution, 1000 ml

➥ ☑ **K0410** Male external catheter, with adhesive coating, each

➥ ☑ **K0411** Male external catheter, with adhesive strip, each

(K0412 has been deleted)

? ☑ **K0415** Prescription antiemetic drug, oral, per 1 mg, for use in conjunction with oral anti-cancer drug, not otherwise specified
MCM 2049.5c
CC, KL, Q5, Q6

? ☑ **K0416** Prescription antiemetic drug, rectal, per 1 mg, for use in conjunction with oral anti-cancer drug, not otherwise specified
MCM 2049.5c
CC, KL, Q5, Q6

(K0417 has been deleted)
(K0418 has been deleted)
(K0419 has been deleted)
(K0420 has been deleted)
(K0421 has been deleted)
(K0422 has been deleted)
(K0423 has been deleted)
(K0424 has been deleted)
(K0425 has been deleted)
(K0426 has been deleted)
(K0427 has been deleted)
(K0428 has been deleted)

K CODES (TEMPORARY)

(K0429 has been deleted)
(K0430 has been deleted)
(K0431 has been deleted)
(K0432 has been deleted)
(K0433 has been deleted)
(K0434 has been deleted)
(K0435 has been deleted)
(K0436 has been deleted)
(K0437 has been deleted)
(K0438 has been deleted)
(K0439 has been deleted)

➡ **K0440** Nasal prosthesis, provided by a non-physician

➡ **K0441** Midfacial prosthesis, provided by a non-physician

➡ **K0442** Orbital prosthesis, provided by a non-physician

➡ **K0443** Upper facial prosthesis, provided by a non-physician

➡ **K0444** Hemi-facial prosthesis, provided by a non-physician

➡ **K0445** Auricular prosthesis, provided by a non-physician

➡ **K0446** Partial facial prosthesis, provided by a non-physician

➡ **K0447** Nasal septal prosthesis, provided by a non-physician

➡ **K0448** Unspecified maxillofacial prosthesis, by report, provided by a non-physician
  Pertinent documentation to evaluate medical appropriateness should be included when this code is reported.

➡ ☑ **K0449** Repair or modification of maxillofacial prosthesis, labor component, 15 minute increments, provided by a non-physician

➡ ☑ **K0450** Adhesive liquid, for use with facial prosthesis only, per ounce

➡ ☑ **K0451** Adhesive remover, wipes, for use with facial prosthesis, per box of 50

➡ **K0452** Wheelchair bearings, any type

(K0453 has been deleted. See code J0285)

? **K0455** Infusion pump used for uninterrupted administration of epoprostenol
  CIM 60-14

➡ **K0456** Hospital bed, heavy duty, extra wide, with any type side rails, with mattress

➡ **K0457** Extra wide/heavy duty commode chair, each

➡ **K0458** Heavy duty walker, without wheels, each

➡ **K0459** Heavy duty wheeled walker, each

➡ **K0460** Power add-on, to convert manual wheelchair to motorized wheelchair, joystick control

➡ **K0461** Power add-on, to convert manual wheelchair to power operated vehicle, tiller control

? **K0462** Temporary replacement for patient owned equipment being repaired, any type
  MCM 5102.3

? **K0501** Aerosol compressor, battery powered, for use with small volume nebulizer
  CIM 60-9

(K0503 has been deleted)
(K0504 has been deleted)
(K0505 has been deleted)
(K0506 has been deleted)
(K0507 has been deleted)
(K0508 has been deleted)
(K0509 has been deleted)
(K0511 has been deleted)
(K0512 has been deleted)
(K0513 has been deleted)
(K0514 has been deleted)
(K0515 has been deleted)
(K0516 has been deleted)
(K0518 has been deleted)
(K0519 has been deleted)
(K0520 has been deleted)
(K0521 has been deleted)
(K0522 has been deleted)
(K0523 has been deleted)
(K0524 has been deleted)
(K0525 has been deleted)
(K0526 has been deleted)
(K0527 has been deleted)
(K0528 has been deleted)

➡ ☑ **K0529** Sterile water or sterile saline, 1,000 ml, used with large volume nebulizer

(K0530 has been deleted)

● ? **K0531** Humidifier, heated, used with positive airway pressure device
  CIM 60-9

● ? **K0532** Respiratory assist device, bi-level pressure capability, without backup rate feature, used with noninvasive interface, e.g., nasal or facial mask (intermittent assist device with continuous positive airway pressure device)
CIM 60-9

● ? **K0533** Respiratory assist device, bi-level pressure capability, with backup rate feature, used with noninvasive interface, e.g., nasal or facial mask (intermittent assist device with continuous positive airway pressure device)
CIM 60-9

● ? **K0534** Respiratory assist device, bi-level pressure capacity, with backup rate feature, used with invasive interface, e.g., tracheostomy tube (intermittent assist device with continuous positive airway pressure device)
CIM 60-9

Orthotic Procedures L0000–L4999

Braces, trusses, and artificial legs, arms, and eyes are covered when furnished incident to a physician's services or on a physician's order. A brace includes rigid and semi-rigid devices used for the purpose of supporting a weak or deformed body member or restricting or eliminating motion in a diseased or injured part of the body. Back braces include, but are not limited to, sacroiliac, sacrolumbar, dorsolumbar corsets and belts. Stump stockings and harnesses (including replacements) are also covered when these appliances are essential to the effective use of an artificial limb. Adjustments to an artificial limb or other appliance required by wear or by a change in the patient's condition are covered when ordered by a physician. Adjustments, repairs and replacements are covered so long as the device continues to be medically required.

Medicare claims for L codes fall under the jurisdiction of the DME regional carrier, unless otherwise noted.

Orthotic Devices — Spinal

Cervical

- **L0100** Cervical, craniostenosis, helmet molded to patient model
- **L0110** Cervical, craniostenosis, helmet, nonmolded
- **L0120** Cervical, flexible, nonadjustable (foam collar)
- **L0130** Cervical, flexible, thermoplastic collar, molded to patient
- **L0140** Cervical, semi-rigid, adjustable (plastic collar)
- **L0150** Cervical, semi-rigid, adjustable molded chin cup (plastic collar with mandibular/occipital piece)
- **L0160** Cervical, semi-rigid, wire frame occipital/mandibular support
- **L0170** Cervical, collar, molded to patient model
- ☑ **L0172** Cervical, collar, semi-rigid thermoplastic foam, two piece
- ☑ **L0174** Cervical, collar, semi-rigid, thermoplastic foam, two piece with thoracic extension

Multiple Post Collar

- **L0180** Cervical, multiple post collar, occipital/mandibular supports, adjustable
- **L0190** Cervical, multiple post collar, occipital/mandibular supports, adjustable cervical bars (Somi, Guilford, Taylor types)
- **L0200** Cervical, multiple post collar, occipital/mandibular supports, adjustable cervical bars, and thoracic extension

Thoracic

- **L0210** Thoracic, rib belt
- **L0220** Thoracic, rib belt, custom fabricated

Thoracic-Lumbar-Sacral Orthosis (TLSO)

Flexible

- **L0300** TLSO, flexible (dorso-lumbar surgical support)
- **L0310** TLSO, flexible (dorso-lumbar surgical support), custom fabricated
- **L0315** TLSO, flexible (dorso-lumbar surgical support), elastic type, with rigid posterior panel
- **L0317** TLSO, flexible (dorso-lumbar surgical support), hyperextension, elastic type, with rigid posterior panel

Anterior-Posterior Control

- **L0320** TLSO, anterior-posterior control (Taylor type), with apron front
- **L0330** TLSO, anterior-posterior-lateral control (Knight-Taylor type), with apron front

Anterior-Posterior-Lateral-Rotary Control

- **L0340** TLSO, anterior-posterior-lateral-rotary control (Arnold, Magnuson, Steindler types), with apron front
- **L0350** TLSO, anterior-posterior-lateral-rotary control, flexion compression jacket, custom fitted
- **L0360** TLSO, anterior-posterior-lateral-rotary control, flexion compression jacket molded to patient model
- **L0370** TLSO, anterior-posterior-lateral-rotary control, hyperextension (Jewett, Lennox, Baker, Cash types)
- **L0380** TLSO, anterior-posterior-lateral-rotary control, with extensions
- **L0390** TLSO, anterior-posterior-lateral control molded to patient model
- **L0400** TLSO, anterior-posterior-lateral control molded to patient model, with interface material
- **L0410** TLSO, anterior-posterior-lateral control, two-piece construction, molded to patient model
- **L0420** TLSO, anterior-posterior-lateral control, two-piece construction, molded to patient model, with interface material
- **L0430** TLSO, anterior-posterior-lateral control, with interface material, custom fitted
- **L0440** TLSO, anterior-posterior-lateral control, with overlapping front section, spring steel front, custom fitted

Lumbar-Sacral Orthosis (LSO)

Flexible

- **L0500** LSO, flexible (lumbo-sacral surgical support)
- **L0510** LSO, flexible (lumbo-sacral surgical support), custom fabricated
- **L0515** LSO, flexible (lumbo-sacral surgical support) elastic type, with rigid posterior panel

Anterior-Posterior-Lateral Control

- **L0520** LSO, anterior-posterior-lateral control (Knight, Wilcox types), with apron front

Anterior-Posterior Control

- **L0530** LSO, anterior-posterior control (Macausland type), with apron front

Lumbar Flexion

- **L0540** LSO, lumbar flexion (Williams flexion type)
- **L0550** LSO, anterior-posterior-lateral control, molded to patient model
- **L0560** LSO, anterior-posterior-lateral control, molded to patient model, with interface material
- **L0565** LSO, anterior-posterior-lateral control, custom fitted

Sacroiliac

Flexible

- **L0600** Sacroiliac, flexible (sacroiliac surgical support)
- **L0610** Sacroiliac, flexible (sacroiliac surgical support), custom fabricated

Semi-Rigid

- **L0620** Sacroiliac, semi-rigid (Goldthwaite, Osgood types), with apron front

Cervical-Thoracic-Lumbar-Sacral Orthosis (CTLSO)

Anterior-Posterior-Lateral Control

- **L0700** CTLSO, anterior-posterior-lateral control, molded to patient model (Minerva type)
- **L0710** CTLSO, anterior-posterior-lateral control, molded to patient model, with interface material (Minerva type)

Halo Procedure

- **L0810** Halo procedure, cervical halo incorporated into jacket vest
- **L0820** Halo procedure, cervical halo incorporated into plaster body jacket
- **L0830** Halo procedure, cervical halo incorporated into Milwaukee type orthosis
- **L0860** Addition to halo procedure, magnetic resonance image compatible system

Torso Supports

Ptosis Supports

- **L0900** Torso support, ptosis support
- **L0910** Torso support, ptosis support, custom fabricated

Pendulous Abdomen Supports

- **L0920** Torso support, pendulous abdomen support
- **L0930** Torso support, pendulous abdomen support, custom fabricated

Postsurgical Supports

- **L0940** Torso support, postsurgical support
- **L0950** Torso support, postsurgical support, custom fabricated
- **L0960** Torso support, postsurgical support, pads for postsurgical support

Additions to Spinal Orthosis

- **L0970** TLSO, corset front
- **L0972** LSO, corset front
- **L0974** TLSO, full corset
- **L0976** LSO, full corset
- **L0978** Axillary crutch extension
- ☑ **L0980** Peroneal straps, pair
- ☑ **L0982** Stocking supporter grips, set of four (4)
- ☑ **L0984** Protective body sock, each
- **L0999** Addition to spinal orthosis, not otherwise specified
  Determine if an alternative national HCPCS Level II or a local HCPCS Level III code better describes the service being reported. This code should be used only if a more specific code is unavailable.

Orthotic Devices — Scoliosis Procedures

The orthotic care of scoliosis differs from other orthotic care in that the treatment is more dynamic in nature and uses ongoing continual modification of the orthosis to the patient's changing condition. This coding structure uses the proper names — or eponyms — of the procedures because they have historic and universal acceptance in the profession. It should be recognized that variations to the basic procedures described by the founders/developers are accepted in various medical and orthotic practices throughout the country. All procedures include model of patient when indicated.

Cervical-Thoracic-Lumbar-Sacral Orthosis (CTLSO) (Milwaukee)

- **L1000** CTLSO (Milwaukee), inclusive of furnishing initial orthosis, including model

ORTHOTIC PROCEDURES

- **L1010** Addition to CTLSO or scoliosis orthosis, axilla sling
- **L1020** Addition to CTLSO or scoliosis orthosis, kyphosis pad
- **L1025** Addition to CTLSO or scoliosis orthosis, kyphosis pad, floating
- **L1030** Addition to CTLSO or scoliosis orthosis, lumbar bolster pad
- **L1040** Addition to CTLSO or scoliosis orthosis, lumbar or lumbar rib pad
- **L1050** Addition to CTLSO or scoliosis orthosis, sternal pad
- **L1060** Addition to CTLSO or scoliosis orthosis, thoracic pad
- **L1070** Addition to CTLSO or scoliosis orthosis, trapezius sling
- **L1080** Addition to CTLSO or scoliosis orthosis, outrigger
- **L1085** Addition to CTLSO or scoliosis orthosis, outrigger, bilateral with vertical extensions
- **L1090** Addition to CTLSO or scoliosis orthosis, lumbar sling
- **L1100** Addition to CTLSO or scoliosis orthosis, ring flange, plastic or leather
- **L1110** Addition to CTLSO or scoliosis orthosis, ring flange, plastic or leather, molded to patient model
- ☑ **L1120** Addition to CTLSO, scoliosis orthosis, cover for upright, each

Thoracic-Lumbar-Sacral Orthosis (TLSO) (Low Profile)

- **L1200** TLSO, inclusive of furnishing initial orthosis only
- **L1210** Addition to TLSO, (low profile), lateral thoracic extension
- **L1220** Addition to TLSO, (low profile), anterior thoracic extension
- **L1230** Addition to TLSO, (low profile), Milwaukee type superstructure
- **L1240** Addition to TLSO, (low profile), lumbar derotation pad
- **L1250** Addition to TLSO, (low profile), anterior ASIS pad
- **L1260** Addition to TLSO, (low profile), anterior thoracic derotation pad
- **L1270** Addition to TLSO, (low profile), abdominal pad
- ☑ **L1280** Addition to TLSO, (low profile), rib gusset (elastic), each
- **L1290** Addition to TLSO, (low profile), lateral trochanteric pad

Other Scoliosis Procedures

- **L1300** Other scoliosis procedure, body jacket molded to patient model
- **L1310** Other scoliosis procedure, postoperative body jacket
- **L1499** Spinal orthosis, not otherwise specified
  Determine if an alternative national HCPCS Level II or a local HCPCS Level III code better describes the orthosis being reported. This code should be used only if a more specific code is unavailable.

Thoracic-Hip-Knee-Ankle Orthosis (THKAO)

- **L1500** THKAO, mobility frame (Newington, Parapodium types)
- **L1510** THKAO, standing frame
- **L1520** THKAO, swivel walker

Orthotic Devices — Lower Limb

The procedures in L1600-L2999 are considered as "base" or "basic procedures" and may be modified by listing procedure from the "additions" sections and adding them to the base procedures.

Hip Orthosis (HO) — Flexible

- **L1600** HO, abduction control of hip joints, flexible, Frejka type with cover
- **L1610** HO, abduction control of hip joints, flexible, (Frejka cover only)
- **L1620** HO, abduction control of hip joints, flexible, (Pavlik harness)
- **L1630** HO, abduction control of hip joints, semi-flexible (Von Rosen type)
- **L1640** HO, abduction control of hip joints, static, pelvic band or spreader bar, thigh cuffs
- **L1650** HO, abduction control of hip joints, static, adjustable (Ilfled type)
- **L1660** HO, abduction control of hip joints, static, plastic
- **L1680** HO, abduction control of hip joints, dynamic, pelvic control, adjustable hip motion control, thigh cuffs (Rancho hip action type)
- **L1685** HO, abduction control of hip joint, postoperative hip abduction type, custom fabricated
- **L1686** HO, abduction control of hip joint, postoperative hip abduction type
- **L1690** Combination, bilateral, lumbo-sacral, hip, femur orthosis providing adduction and internal rotation control

Legg Perthes

- **L1700** Legg Perthes orthosis, (Toronto type)
- **L1710** Legg Perthes orthosis, (Newington type)

- **L1720** Legg Perthes orthosis, trilateral, (Tachdijan type)
- **L1730** Legg Perthes orthosis, (Scottish Rite type)
- **L1750** Legg Perthes orthosis, Legg Perthes sling (Sam Brown type)
- **L1755** Legg Perthes orthosis, (Patten bottom type)

Knee Orthosis (KO)

- **L1800** KO, elastic with stays
- **L1810** KO, elastic with joints
- **L1815** KO, elastic or other elastic type material with condylar pad(s)
- **L1820** KO, elastic with condylar pads and joints
- **L1825** KO, elastic knee cap
- **L1830** KO, immobilizer, canvas longitudinal
- **L1832** KO, adjustable knee joints, positional orthosis, rigid support
- **L1834** KO, without knee joint, rigid, molded to patient model
- **L1840** KO, derotation, medial-lateral, anterior cruciate ligament, custom fabricated to patient model
- **L1843** KO, single upright, thigh and calf, with adjustable flexion and extension joint, medial-lateral and rotation control, custom fitted
- **L1844** KO, single upright, thigh and calf, with adjustable flexion and extension joint, medial-lateral and rotation control, molded to patient model
- **L1845** KO, double upright, thigh and calf, with adjustable flexion and extension joint, medial-lateral and rotation control, custom fitted
- **L1846** KO, double upright, thigh and calf, with adjustable flexion and extension joint, medial-lateral and rotation control, molded to patient model
- **L1847** Knee orthosis, double upright with adjustable joint, with inflatable air support chamber(s)
- **L1850** KO, Swedish type
- **L1855** KO, molded plastic, thigh and calf sections, with double upright knee joints, molded to patient model
- **L1858** KO, molded plastic, polycentric knee joints, pneumatic knee pads (CTI)
- **L1860** KO, modification of supracondylar prosthetic socket, molded to patient model (SK)
- **L1870** KO, double upright, thigh and calf lacers, molded to patient model with knee joints
- **L1880** KO, double upright, nonmolded thigh and calf cuffs/lacers with knee joints
- **L1885** KO, single or double upright, thigh and calf, with funtional active resistance control

Ankle-Foot Orthosis (AFO)

- **L1900** AFO, spring wire, dorsiflexion assist calf band
- **L1902** AFO, ankle gauntlet
- **L1904** AFO, molded ankle gauntlet, molded to patient model
- **L1906** AFO, multiligamentus ankle support
- **L1910** AFO, posterior, single bar, clasp attachment to shoe counter
- **L1920** AFO, single upright with static or adjustable stop (Phelps or Perlstein type)
- **L1930** AFO, plastic
- **L1940** AFO, molded to patient model, plastic
- **L1945** AFO, molded to patient model, plastic, rigid anterior tibial section (floor reaction)
- **L1950** AFO, spiral, molded to patient model (IRM type), plastic
- **L1960** AFO, posterior solid ankle, molded to patient model, plastic
- **L1970** AFO, plastic molded to patient model, with ankle joint
- **L1980** AFO, single upright free plantar dorsiflexion, solid stirrup, calf band/cuff (single bar "BK" orthosis)
- **L1990** AFO, double upright free plantar dorsiflexion, solid stirrup, calf band/cuff (double bar "BK" orthosis)

Knee-Ankle-Foot Orthosis (KAFO) — Or Any Combination

L2000, L2020, L2036 are base procedures to be used with any knee joint, L2010 and L2030 are to be used only with no knee joint.

- **L2000** KAFO, single upright, free knee, free ankle, solid stirrup, thigh and calf bands/cuffs (single bar "AK" orthosis)
- **L2010** KAFO, single upright, free ankle, solid stirrup, thigh and calf bands/cuffs (single bar "AK" orthosis), without knee joint
- **L2020** KAFO, double upright, free knee, free ankle, solid stirrup, thigh and calf bands/cuffs (double bar "AK" orthosis)
- **L2030** KAFO, double upright, free ankle, solid stirrup, thigh and calf bands/cuffs, (double bar "AK" orthosis), without knee joint
- **L2035** KAFO, full plastic, static, prefabricated (pediatric size)

➡ **L2036** KAFO, full plastic, double upright, free knee, molded to patient model

➡ **L2037** KAFO, full plastic, single upright, free knee, molded to patient model

➡ **L2038** KAFO, full plastic, without knee joint, multiaxis ankle, molded to patient model (Lively orthosis or equal)

➡ **L2039** KAFO, full plastic, single upright, polyaxial hinge, medial lateral rotation control, molded to patient model

Torsion Control: Hip-Knee-Ankle-Foot Orthosis (HKAFO)

➡ **L2040** HKAFO, torsion control, bilateral rotation straps, pelvic band/belt

➡ **L2050** HKAFO, torsion control, bilateral torsion cables, hip joint, pelvic band/belt

➡ **L2060** HKAFO, torsion control, bilateral torsion cables, ball bearing hip joint, pelvic band/belt

➡ **L2070** HKAFO, torsion control, unilateral rotation straps, pelvic band/belt

➡ **L2080** HKAFO, torsion control, unilateral torsion cable, hip joint, pelvic band/belt

➡ **L2090** HKAFO, torsion control, unilateral torsion cable, ball bearing hip joint, pelvic band/belt

Fracture Orthosis

➡ **L2102** AFO, fracture orthosis, tibial fracture cast orthosis, plaster type casting material, molded to patient

➡ **L2104** AFO, fracture orthosis, tibial fracture cast orthosis, synthetic type casting material, molded to patient

➡ **L2106** AFO, fracture orthosis, tibial fracture cast orthosis, thermoplastic type casting material, molded to patient

➡ **L2108** AFO, fracture orthosis, tibial fracture cast orthosis, molded to patient model

➡ **L2112** AFO, fracture orthosis, tibial fracture orthosis, soft

➡ **L2114** AFO, fracture orthosis, tibial fracture orthosis, semi-rigid

➡ **L2116** AFO, fracture orthosis, tibial fracture orthosis, rigid

➡ **L2122** KAFO, fracture orthosis, femoral fracture cast orthosis, plaster type casting material, molded to patient

➡ **L2124** KAFO, fracture orthosis, femoral fracture cast orthosis, synthetic type casting material, molded to patient

➡ **L2126** KAFO, fracture orthosis, femoral fracture cast orthosis, thermoplastic type casting material, molded to patient

➡ **L2128** KAFO, fracture orthosis, femoral fracture cast orthosis, molded to patient model

➡ **L2132** KAFO, fracture orthosis, femoral fracture cast orthosis, soft

➡ **L2134** KAFO, fracture orthosis, femoral fracture cast orthosis, semi-rigid

➡ **L2136** KAFO, fracture orthosis, femoral fracture cast orthosis, rigid

Additions to Fracture Orthosis

➡ **L2180** Addition to lower extremity fracture orthosis, plastic shoe insert with ankle joints

➡ **L2182** Addition to lower extremity fracture orthosis, drop lock knee joint

➡ **L2184** Addition to lower extremity fracture orthosis, limited motion knee joint

➡ **L2186** Addition to lower extremity fracture orthosis, adjustable motion knee joint, Lerman type

➡ **L2188** Addition to lower extremity fracture orthosis, quadrilateral brim

➡ **L2190** Addition to lower extremity fracture orthosis, waist belt

➡ **L2192** Addition to lower extremity fracture orthosis, hip joint, pelvic band, thigh flange, and pelvic belt

Additions to Lower Extremity Orthosis: Shoe-Ankle-Shin-Knee

➡ ☑ **L2200** Addition to lower extremity, limited ankle motion, each joint

➡ ☑ **L2210** Addition to lower extremity, dorsiflexion assist (plantar flexion resist), each joint

➡ ☑ **L2220** Addition to lower extremity, dorsiflexion and plantar flexion assist/resist, each joint

➡ **L2230** Addition to lower extremity, split flat caliper stirrups and plate attachment

➡ **L2240** Addition to lower extremity, round caliper and plate attachment

➡ **L2250** Addition to lower extremity, foot plate, molded to patient model, stirrup attachment

➡ **L2260** Addition to lower extremity, reinforced solid stirrup (Scott-Craig type)

➡ **L2265** Addition to lower extremity, long tongue stirrup

➡ **L2270** Addition to lower extremity, varus/valgus correction ("T") strap, padded/lined or malleolus pad

➡ **L2275** Addition to lower extremity, varus/vulgus correction, plastic modification, padded/lined

ORTHOTIC PROCEDURES

➡ **L2280** Addition to lower extremity, molded inner boot

➡ **L2300** Addition to lower extremity, abduction bar (bilateral hip involvement), jointed, adjustable

➡ **L2310** Addition to lower extremity, abduction bar, straight

➡ **L2320** Addition to lower extremity, nonmolded lacer

➡ **L2330** Addition to lower extremity, lacer molded to patient model

➡ **L2335** Addition to lower extremity, anterior swing band

➡ **L2340** Addition to lower extremity, pretibial shell, molded to patient model

➡ **L2350** Addition to lower extremity, prosthetic type, (BK) socket, molded to patient model, (used for "PTB," "AFO" orthoses)

➡ **L2360** Addition to lower extremity, extended steel shank

➡ **L2370** Addition to lower extremity, Patten bottom

➡ **L2375** Addition to lower extremity, torsion control, ankle joint and half solid stirrup

➡ ☑ **L2380** Addition to lower extremity, torsion control, straight knee joint, each joint

➡ ☑ **L2385** Addition to lower extremity, straight knee joint, heavy duty, each joint

➡ ☑ **L2390** Addition to lower extremity, offset knee joint, each joint

➡ ☑ **L2395** Addition to lower extremity, offset knee joint, heavy duty, each joint

➡ **L2397** Addition to lower extremity orthosis, suspension sleeve

Additions to Straight Knee or Offset Knee Joints

➡ ☑ **L2405** Addition to knee joint, drop lock, each joint

➡ ☑ **L2415** Addition to knee joint, cam lock (Swiss, French, bail types) each joint

➡ ☑ **L2425** Addition to knee joint, disc or dial lock for adjustable knee flexion, each joint

➡ ☑ **L2430** Addition to knee joint, ratchet lock for active and progressive knee extension, each joint

➡ ☑ **L2435** Addition to knee joint, polycentric joint, each joint

➡ **L2492** Addition to knee joint, lift loop for drop lock ring

Additions: Thigh/Weight Bearing — Gluteal/Ischial Weight Bearing

➡ **L2500** Addition to lower extremity, thigh/weight bearing, gluteal/ischial weight bearing, ring

➡ **L2510** Addition to lower extremity, thigh/weight bearing, quadri-lateral brim, molded to patient model

➡ **L2520** Addition to lower extremity, thigh/weight bearing, quadri-lateral brim, custom fitted

➡ **L2525** Addition to lower extremity, thigh/weight bearing, ischial containment/narrow M-L brim molded to patient model

➡ **L2526** Addition to lower extremity, thigh/weight bearing, ischial containment/narrow M-L brim, custom fitted

➡ **L2530** Addition to lower extremity, thigh/weight bearing, lacer, nonmolded

➡ **L2540** Addition to lower extremity, thigh/weight bearing, lacer, molded to patient model

➡ **L2550** Addition to lower extremity, thigh/weight bearing, high roll cuff

Additions: Pelvic and Thoracic Control

➡ ☑ **L2570** Addition to lower extremity, pelvic control, hip joint, Clevis type, two position joint, each

➡ **L2580** Addition to lower extremity, pelvic control, pelvic sling

➡ ☑ **L2600** Addition to lower extremity, pelvic control, hip joint, Clevis type, or thrust bearing, free, each

➡ ☑ **L2610** Addition to lower extremity, pelvic control, hip joint, Clevis or thrust bearing, lock, each

➡ ☑ **L2620** Addition to lower extremity, pelvic control, hip joint, heavy-duty, each

➡ ☑ **L2622** Addition to lower extremity, pelvic control, hip joint, adjustable flexion, each

➡ ☑ **L2624** Addition to lower extremity, pelvic control, hip joint, adjustable flexion, extension, abduction control, each

➡ **L2627** Addition to lower extremity, pelvic control, plastic, molded to patient model, reciprocating hip joint and cables

➡ **L2628** Addition to lower extremity, pelvic control, metal frame, reciprocating hip joint and cables

➡ **L2630** Addition to lower extremity, pelvic control, band and belt, unilateral

➡ **L2640** Addition to lower extremity, pelvic control, band and belt, bilateral

➡ ☑ **L2650** Addition to lower extremity, pelvic and thoracic control, gluteal pad, each

ORTHOTIC PROCEDURES

➡ **L2660** Addition to lower extremity, thoracic control, thoracic band

➡ **L2670** Addition to lower extremity, thoracic control, paraspinal uprights

➡ **L2680** Addition to lower extremity, thoracic control, lateral support uprights

Additions: General

➡ ☑ **L2750** Addition to lower extremity orthosis, plating chrome or nickel, per bar

➡ **L2755** Addition to lower extremity orthosis, carbon graphite lamination

➡ ☑ **L2760** Addition to lower extremity orthosis, extension, per extension, per bar (for lineal adjustment for growth)

➡ ☑ **L2770** Addition to lower extremity orthosis, any material, per bar or joint

➡ ☑ **L2780** Addition to lower extremity orthosis, noncorrosive finish, per bar

➡ ☑ **L2785** Addition to lower extremity orthosis, drop lock retainer, each

➡ **L2795** Addition to lower extremity orthosis, knee control, full kneecap

➡ **L2800** Addition to lower extremity orthosis, knee control, kneecap, medial or lateral pull

➡ **L2810** Addition to lower extremity orthosis, knee control, condylar pad

➡ **L2820** Addition to lower extremity orthosis, soft interface for molded plastic, below knee section

➡ **L2830** Addition to lower extremity orthosis, soft interface for molded plastic, above knee section

➡ ☑ **L2840** Addition to lower extremity orthosis, tibial length sock, fracture or equal, each

➡ ☑ **L2850** Addition to lower extremity orthosis, femoral length sock, fracture or equal, each

➡ ☑ **L2860** Addition to lower extremity joint, knee or ankle, concentric adjustable torsion style mechanism, each

➡ **L2999** Lower extremity orthoses, not otherwise specified
Determine if an alternative national HCPCS Level II or a local HCPCS Level III code better describes the orthosis being reported. This code should be used only if a more specific code is unavailable.

Orthopedic Shoes

Inserts

? ☑ **L3000** Foot insert, removable, molded to patient model, "UCB" type, Berkeley shell, each
CIM 70-3, MCM 2323

? ☑ **L3001** Foot insert, removable, molded to patient model, Spenco, each
MCM 2323

? ☑ **L3002** Foot insert, removable, molded to patient model, Plastazote or equal, each
MCM 2323

? ☑ **L3003** Foot insert, removable, molded to patient model, silicone gel, each
MCM 2323

? ☑ **L3010** Foot insert, removable, molded to patient model, longitudinal arch support, each
MCM 2323

? ☑ **L3020** Foot insert, removable, molded to patient model, longitudinal/metatarsal support, each
MCM 2323

? ☑ **L3030** Foot insert, removable, formed to patient foot, each
MCM 2323

Arch Support, Removable, Premolded

? ☑ **L3040** Foot, arch support, removable, premolded, longitudinal, each
MCM 2323

? ☑ **L3050** Foot, arch support, removable, premolded, metatarsal, each
MCM 2323

? ☑ **L3060** Foot, arch support, removable, premolded, longitudinal/metatarsal, each
MCM 2323

Arch Support, Nonremovable, Attached to Shoe

? ☑ **L3070** Foot, arch support, nonremovable, attached to shoe, longitudinal, each
MCM 2323

? ☑ **L3080** Foot, arch support, nonremovable, attached to shoe, metatarsal, each
MCM 2323

? ☑ **L3090** Foot, arch support, nonremovable, attached to shoe, longitudinal/metatarsal, each
MCM 2323

? **L3100** Hallus-Valgus night dynamic splint
MCM 2323

Abduction and Rotation Bars

? **L3140** Foot, abduction rotation bar, including shoes
MCM 2323

? **L3150** Foot, abduction rotation bar, without shoes
MCM 2323

➡ **L3160** Foot, adjustable shoe-styled positioning device

? **L3170** Foot, plastic heel stabilizer
MCM 2323

ORTHOTIC PROCEDURES

Orthopedic Footwear

? L3201 Orthopedic shoe, oxford with supinator or pronator, infant
MCM 2323

? L3202 Orthopedic shoe, oxford with supinator or pronator, child
MCM 2323

? L3203 Orthopedic shoe, oxford with supinator or pronator, junior
MCM 2323

? L3204 Orthopedic shoe, hightop with supinator or pronator, infant
MCM 2323

? L3206 Orthopedic shoe, hightop with supinator or pronator, child
MCM 2323

? L3207 Orthopedic shoe, hightop with supinator or pronator, junior
MCM 2323

?☑ L3208 Surgical boot, each, infant
MCM 2079

?☑ L3209 Surgical boot, each, child
MCM 2079

?☑ L3211 Surgical boot, each, junior
MCM 2079

?☑ L3212 Benesch boot, pair, infant
MCM 2079

?☑ L3213 Benesch boot, pair, child
MCM 2079

?☑ L3214 Benesch boot, pair, junior
MCM 2079

⊘ L3215 Orthopedic footwear, woman's shoes, oxford
Medicare statute 1862.A8

⊘ L3216 Orthopedic footwear, woman's shoes, depth inlay
Medicare statute 1862.A8

⊘ L3217 Orthopedic footwear, woman's shoes, hightop, depth inlay
Medicare statute 1862.A8

?☑ L3218 Orthopedic footwear, woman's surgical boot, each
MCM 2323

⊘ L3219 Orthopedic footwear, man's shoes, oxford
Medicare statute 1862.A8

⊘ L3221 Orthopedic footwear, man's shoes, depth inlay
Medicare statute 1862.A8

⊘ L3222 Orthopedic footwear, man's shoes, hightop, depth inlay
Medicare statute 1862.A8

?☑ L3223 Orthopedic footwear, man's surgical boot, each
MCM 2323

? L3224 Orthopedic footwear, woman's shoe, oxford, used as an integral part of a brace (orthosis)
MCM 2323D
CC, KL, LT, RP, RT

? L3225 Orthopedic footwear, man's shoe, oxford, used as an integral part of a brace (orthosis)
MCM 2323D
CC, KL, LT, RP, RT

? L3230 Orthopedic footwear, custom shoes, depth inlay
MCM 2323

?☑ L3250 Orthopedic footwear, custom molded shoe, removable inner mold, prosthetic shoe, each
MCM 2323

?☑ L3251 Foot, shoe molded to patient model, silicone shoe, each
MCM 2323

?☑ L3252 Foot, shoe molded to patient model, Plastazote (or similar), custom fabricated, each
MCM 2323

?☑ L3253 Foot, molded shoe Plastazote (or similar), custom fitted, each
MCM 2323

? L3254 Nonstandard size or width
MCM 2323

? L3255 Nonstandard size or length
MCM 2323

? L3257 Orthopedic footwear, additional charge for split size
MCM 2323

?☑ L3260 Ambulatory surgical boot, each
MCM 2079

➡☑ L3265 Plastazote sandal, each

Shoe Modification — Lifts

?☑ L3300 Lift, elevation, heel, tapered to metatarsals, per inch
MCM 2323

?☑ L3310 Lift, elevation, heel and sole, neoprene, per inch
MCM 2323

?☑ L3320 Lift, elevation, heel and sole, cork, per inch
MCM 2323

? L3330 Lift, elevation, metal extension (skate)
MCM 2323

?☑ L3332 Lift, elevation, inside shoe, tapered, up to one-half inch
MCM 2323

?☑ L3334 Lift, elevation, heel, per inch
MCM 2323

Shoe Modification — Wedges

? L3340 Heel wedge, SACH
MCM 2323

? **L3350** Heel wedge
MCM 2323

? **L3360** Sole wedge, outside sole
MCM 2323

? **L3370** Sole wedge, between sole
MCM 2323

? **L3380** Clubfoot wedge
MCM 2323

? **L3390** Outflare wedge
MCM 2323

? **L3400** Metatarsal bar wedge, rocker
MCM 2323

? **L3410** Metatarsal bar wedge, between sole
MCM 2323

? **L3420** Full sole and heel wedge, between sole
MCM 2323

Shoe Modifications — Heels

? **L3430** Heel, counter, plastic reinforced
MCM 2323

? **L3440** Heel, counter, leather reinforced
MCM 2323

? **L3450** Heel, SACH cushion type
MCM 2323

? **L3455** Heel, new leather, standard
MCM 2323

? **L3460** Heel, new rubber, standard
MCM 2323

? **L3465** Heel, Thomas with wedge
MCM 2323

? **L3470** Heel, Thomas extended to ball
MCM 2323

? **L3480** Heel, pad and depression for spur
MCM 2323

? **L3485** Heel, pad, removable for spur
MCM 2323

Miscellaneous Shoe Additions

? **L3500** Orthopedic shoe addition, insole, leather
MCM 2323

? **L3510** Orthopedic shoe addition, insole, rubber
MCM 2323

? **L3520** Orthopedic shoe addition, insole, felt covered with leather
MCM 2323

? **L3530** Orthopedic shoe addition, sole, half
MCM 2323

? **L3540** Orthopedic shoe addition, sole, full
MCM 2323

? **L3550** Orthopedic shoe addition, toe tap, standard
MCM 2323

? **L3560** Orthopedic shoe addition, toe tap, horseshoe
MCM 2323

? **L3570** Orthopedic shoe addition, special extension to instep (leather with eyelets)
MCM 2323

? **L3580** Orthopedic shoe addition, convert instep to velcro closure
MCM 2323

? **L3590** Orthopedic shoe addition, convert firm shoe counter to soft counter
MCM 2323

? **L3595** Orthopedic shoe addition, March bar
MCM 2323

Transfer or Replacement

? **L3600** Transfer of an orthosis from one shoe to another, caliper plate, existing
MCM 2323

? **L3610** Transfer of an orthosis from one shoe to another, caliper plate, new
MCM 2323

? **L3620** Transfer of an orthosis from one shoe to another, solid stirrup, existing
MCM 2323

? **L3630** Transfer of an orthosis from one shoe to another, solid stirrup, new
MCM 2323

? **L3640** Transfer of an orthosis from one shoe to another, Dennis Browne splint (Riveton), both shoes
MCM 2323

? **L3649** Orthopedic shoe, modification, addition or transfer, not otherwise specified
MCM 2323
Determine if an alternative national HCPCS Level II or a local HCPCS Level III code better describes the service being reported. This code should be used only if a more specific code is unavailable.

Orthotic Devices — Upper Limb

The procedures in this section are considered as "base" or "basic procedures" and may be modified by listing procedures from the "additions" sections and adding them to the base procedure.

Shoulder Orthosis (SO)

➡ **L3650** SO, figure of eight design abduction restrainer

➡ **L3660** SO, figure of eight design abduction restrainer, canvas and webbing

➡ **L3670** SO, acromio/clavicular (canvas and webbing type)

➡ **L3675** SO, vest type abduction restrainer, canvas webbing type, or equal

Elbow Orthosis (EO)

➡ **L3700** EO, elastic with stays

➡ **L3710** EO, elastic with metal joints

➡ **L3720** EO, double upright with forearm/arm cuffs, free motion

ORTHOTIC PROCEDURES

- **L3730** EO, double upright with forearm/arm cuffs, extension/flexion assist
- **L3740** EO, double upright with forearm/arm cuffs, adjustable position lock with active control

Wrist-Hand-Finger Orthosis (WHFO)

- **L3800** WHFO, short opponens, no attachment
- **L3805** WHFO, long opponens, no attachment
- ● **L3807** WHFO, extension assist, with inflatable Palmer air support, with or without thumb extension

Additions

- **L3810** WHFO, addition to short and long opponens, thumb abduction ("C") bar
- **L3815** WHFO, addition to short and long opponens, second M.P. abduction assist
- **L3820** WHFO, addition to short and long opponens, I.P. extension assist, with M.P. extension stop
- **L3825** WHFO, addition to short and long opponens, M.P. extension stop
- **L3830** WHFO, addition to short and long opponens, M.P. extension assist
- **L3835** WHFO, addition to short and long opponens, M.P. spring extension assist
- **L3840** WHFO, addition to short and long opponens, spring swivel thumb
- **L3845** WHFO, addition to short and long opponens, thumb I.P. extension assist, with M.P. stop
- **L3850** WHO, addition to short and long opponens, action wrist, with dorsiflexion assist
- **L3855** WHFO, addition to short and long opponens, adjustable M.P. flexion control
- **L3860** WHFO, addition to short and long opponens, adjustable M.P. flexion control and I.P.
- **L3890** Addition to upper extremity joint, wrist or elbow, concentric adjustable torsion style mechanism, each

Dynamic Flexor Hinge, Reciprocal Wrist Extension/Flexion, Finger Flexion/Extension

- **L3900** WHFO, dynamic flexor hinge, reciprocal wrist extension/flexion, finger flexion/extension, wrist or finger driven
- **L3901** WHFO, dynamic flexor hinge, reciprocal wrist extension/flexion, finger flexion/extension, cable driven

External Power

- **L3902** WHFO, external powered, compressed gas
- **L3904** WHFO, external powered, electric

Other WHFOs — Custom Fitted

- **L3906** WHO, wrist gauntlet, molded to patient model
- **L3907** WHFO, wrist gauntlet with thumb spica, molded to patient model
- **L3908** WHO, wrist extension control cock-up, nonmolded
- **L3910** WHFO, Swanson design
- **L3912** HFO, flexion glove with elastic finger control
- **L3914** WHO, wrist extension cock-up
- **L3916** WHFO, wrist extension cock-up, with outrigger
- **L3918** HFO, knuckle bender
- **L3920** HFO, knuckle bender, with outrigger
- **L3922** HFO, knuckle bender, two segment to flex joints
- **L3924** WHFO, Oppenheimer
- **L3926** WHFO, Thomas suspension
- **L3928** HFO, finger extension, with clock spring
- **L3930** WHFO, finger extension, with wrist support
- **L3932** FO, safety pin, spring wire
- **L3934** FO, safety pin, modified
- **L3936** WHFO, Palmer
- **L3938** WHFO, dorsal wrist
- **L3940** WHFO, dorsal wrist, with outrigger attachment
- **L3942** HFO, reverse knuckle bender
- **L3944** HFO, reverse knuckle bender, with outrigger
- **L3946** HFO, composite elastic
- **L3948** FO, finger knuckle bender
- **L3950** WHFO, combination Oppenheimer, with knuckle bender and two attachments
- **L3952** WHFO, combination Oppenheimer, with reverse knuckle and two attachments
- **L3954** HFO, spreading hand
- ☑ **L3956** Addition of joint to upper extremity orthosis, any material; per joint

Shoulder-Elbow-Wrist-Hand Orthosis (SEWHO)

Abduction Position, Custom Fitted

- **L3960** SEWHO, abduction positioning, airplane design
- **L3962** SEWHO, abduction positioning, Erbs palsey design
- **L3963** SEWHO, molded shoulder, arm, forearm, and wrist, with articulating elbow joint
- **L3964** SEO, mobile arm support attached to wheelchair, balanced, adjustable
- **L3965** SEO, mobile arm support attached to wheelchair, balanced, adjustable Rancho type
- **L3966** SEO, mobile arm support attached to wheelchair, balanced, reclining
- **L3968** SEO, mobile arm support attached to wheelchair, balanced, friction arm support (friction dampening to proximal and distal joints)
- **L3969** SEO, mobile arm support, monosuspension arm and hand support, overhead elbow forearm hand sling support, yoke type arm suspension support

Additions to Mobile Arm Supports

- **L3970** SEO, addition to mobile arm support, elevating proximal arm
- **L3972** SEO, addition to mobile arm support, offset or lateral rocker arm with elastic balance control
- **L3974** SEO, addition to mobile arm support, supinator

Fracture Orthosis

- **L3980** Upper extremity fracture orthosis, humeral
- **L3982** Upper extremity fracture orthosis, radius/ulnar
- **L3984** Upper extremity fracture orthosis, wrist
- **L3985** Upper extremity fracture orthosis, forearm, hand with wrist hinge
- **L3986** Upper extremity fracture orthosis, combination of humeral, radius/ulnar, wrist (example: Colles' fracture)
- **L3995** Addition to upper extremity orthosis, sock, fracture or equal, each
- **L3999** Upper limb orthosis, not otherwise specified

Specific Repair

- **L4000** Replace girdle for Milwaukee orthosis
- **L4010** Replace trilateral socket brim
- **L4020** Replace quadrilateral socket brim, molded to patient model
- **L4030** Replace quadrilateral socket brim, custom fitted
- **L4040** Replace molded thigh lacer
- **L4045** Replace nonmolded thigh lacer
- **L4050** Replace molded calf lacer
- **L4055** Replace nonmolded calf lacer
- **L4060** Replace high roll cuff
- **L4070** Replace proximal and distal upright for KAFO
- **L4080** Replace metal bands KAFO, proximal thigh
- **L4090** Replace metal bands KAFO-AFO, calf or distal thigh
- **L4100** Replace leather cuff KAFO, proximal thigh
- **L4110** Replace leather cuff KAFO-AFO, calf or distal thigh
- **L4130** Replace pretibial shell

Repairs

- **L4205** Repair of orthotic device, labor component, per 15 minutes
  MCM 2100.4
- **L4210** Repair of orthotic device, repair or replace minor parts
  MCM 2100.4, MCM 2130D, MCM 2133
- **L4350** Pneumatic ankle control splint (e.g., aircast)
- **L4360** Pneumatic walking splint (e.g., aircast)
- **L4370** Pneumatic full leg splint (e.g., aircast)
- **L4380** Pneumatic knee splint (e.g., aircast)
- **L4392** Replace soft interface material, static AFO
- **L4394** Replace soft interface material, foot drop splint
- **L4396** Static AFO for positioning, pressure reduction, may be used for minimal ambulation
- **L4398** Foot drop splint, recumbent positioning device

Prosthetic Procedures L5000–L9999

Lower Limb

The procedures in this section are considered as "base" or "basic procedures" and may be modified by listing items/procedures or special materials from the "additions" sections and adding them to the base procedure.

Partial Foot

? **L5000** Partial foot, shoe insert with longitudinal arch, toe filler
MCM 2323

? **L5010** Partial foot, molded socket, ankle height, with toe filler
MCM 2323

? **L5020** Partial foot, molded socket, tibial tubercle height, with toe filler
MCM 2323

Ankle

➡ **L5050** Ankle, Symes, molded socket, SACH foot

➡ **L5060** Ankle, Symes, metal frame, molded leather socket, articulated ankle/foot

Below Knee

➡ **L5100** Below knee, molded socket, shin, SACH foot

➡ **L5105** Below knee, plastic socket, joints and thigh lacer, SACH foot

Knee Disarticulation

➡ **L5150** Knee disarticulation (or through knee), molded socket, external knee joints, shin, SACH foot

➡ **L5160** Knee disarticulation (or through knee), molded socket, bent knee configuration, external knee joints, shin, SACH foot

Above Knee

➡ **L5200** Above knee, molded socket, single axis constant friction knee, shin, SACH foot

➡ ☑ **L5210** Above knee, short prosthesis, no knee joint ("stubbies"), with foot blocks, no ankle joints, each

➡ ☑ **L5220** Above knee, short prosthesis, no knee joint ("stubbies"), with articulated ankle/foot, dynamically aligned, each

➡ **L5230** Above knee, for proximal femoral focal deficiency, constant friction knee, shin, SACH foot

Hip Disarticulation

➡ **L5250** Hip disarticulation, Canadian type; molded socket, hip joint, single axis constant friction knee, shin, SACH foot

➡ **L5270** Hip disarticulation, tilt table type; molded socket, locking hip joint, single axis constant friction knee, shin, SACH foot

Hemipelvectomy

➡ **L5280** Hemipelvectomy, Canadian type; molded socket, hip joint, single axis constant friction knee, shin, SACH foot

Endoskeletal: Below Knee

➡ **L5300** Below knee, molded socket, SACH foot, endoskeletal system, including soft cover and finishing

Endoskeletal: Knee Disarticulation

➡ **L5310** Knee disarticulation (or through knee), molded socket, SACH foot endoskeletal system, including soft cover and finishing

Endoskeletal: Above Knee

➡ **L5320** Above knee, molded socket, open end, SACH foot, endoskeletal system, single axis knee, including soft cover and finishing

Endoskeletal: Hip Disarticulation

➡ **L5330** Hip disarticulation, Canadian type; molded socket, endo-skeletal system, hip joint, single axis knee, SACH foot, including soft cover and finishing

Endoskeletal: Hemipelvectomy

➡ **L5340** Hemipelvectomy, Canadian type; molded socket, endoskeletal system, hip joint, single axis knee, SACH foot, including soft cover and finishing

Immediate Postsurgical or Early Fitting Procedures

➡ ☑ **L5400** Immediate postsurgical or early fitting, application of initial rigid dressing, including fitting, alignment, suspension, and one cast change, below knee

➡ ☑ **L5410** Immediate postsurgical or early fitting, application of initial rigid dressing, including fitting, alignment and suspension, below knee, each additional cast change and realignment

➡ ☑ **L5420** Immediate postsurgical or early fitting, application of initial rigid dressing, including fitting, alignment and suspension and one cast change "AK" or knee disarticulation

➡ ☑ **L5430** Immediate postsurgical or early fitting, application of initial rigid dressing, including fitting, alignment and suspension, "AK" or knee disarticulation, each additional cast change and realignment

➡ **L5450** Immediate postsurgical or early fitting, application of nonweight bearing rigid dressing, below knee

➡ **L5460** Immediate postsurgical or early fitting, application of nonweight bearing rigid dressing, above knee

Initial Prosthesis

➥ **L5500** Initial, below knee "PTB" type socket, non-alignable system, pylon, no cover, SACH foot, plaster socket, direct formed

➥ **L5505** Initial, above knee — knee disarticulation, ischial level socket, non-alignable system, pylon, no cover, SACH foot plaster socket, direct formed

Preparatory Prosthesis

➥ **L5510** Preparatory, below knee "PTB" type socket, non-alignable system, pylon, no cover, SACH foot, plaster socket, molded to model

➥ **L5520** Preparatory, below knee "PTB" type socket, non-alignable system, pylon, no cover, SACH foot, thermoplastic or equal, direct formed

➥ **L5530** Preparatory, below knee "PTB" type socket, non-alignable system, pylon, no cover, SACH foot, thermoplastic or equal, molded to model

➥ **L5535** Preparatory, below knee "PTB" type socket, non-alignable system, pylon, no cover, SACH foot, prefabricated, adjustable open end socket

➥ **L5540** Preparatory, below knee "PTB" type socket, non-alignable system, pylon, no cover, SACH foot, laminated socket, molded to model

➥ **L5560** Preparatory, above knee — knee disarticulation, ischial level socket, non-alignable system, pylon, no cover, SACH foot, plaster socket, molded to model

➥ **L5570** Preparatory, above knee — knee disarticulation, ischial level socket, non-alignable system, pylon, no cover, SACH foot, thermoplastic or equal, direct formed

➥ **L5580** Preparatory, above knee — knee disarticulation, ischial level socket, non-alignable system, pylon, no cover, SACH foot, thermoplastic or equal, molded to model

➥ **L5585** Preparatory, above knee — knee disarticulation, ischial level socket, non-alignable system, pylon, no cover, SACH foot, prefabricated adjustable open end socket

➥ **L5590** Preparatory, above knee — knee disarticulation, ischial level socket, non-alignable system, pylon, no cover, SACH foot, laminated socket, molded to model

➥ **L5595** Preparatory, hip disarticulation — hemipelvectomy, pylon, no cover, SACH foot, thermoplastic or equal, molded to patient model

Additions: Lower Extremity

➥ **L5600** Preparatory, hip disarticulation — hemipelvectomy, pylon, no cover, SACH foot, laminated socket, molded to patient model

➥ **L5610** Addition to lower extremity, endoskeletal system, above knee, hydracadence system

➥ **L5611** Addition to lower extremity, endoskeletal system, above knee — knee disarticulation, 4-bar linkage, with friction swing phase control

➥ **L5613** Addition to lower extremity, endoskeletal system, above knee — knee disarticulation, 4-bar linkage, with hydraulic swing phase control

➥ **L5614** Addition to lower extremity, endoskeletal system, above knee — knee disarticulation, 4-bar linkage, with pneumatic swing phase control

➥ **L5616** Addition to lower extremity, endoskeletal system, above knee, universal multiplex system, friction swing phase control

➥ ☑ **L5617** Addition to lower extremity, quick change self-aligning unit, above or below knee, each

Additions: Test Sockets

➥ **L5618** Addition to lower extremity, test socket, Symes

➥ **L5620** Addition to lower extremity, test socket, below knee

➥ **L5622** Addition to lower extremity, test socket, knee disarticulation

➥ **L5624** Addition to lower extremity, test socket, above knee

➥ **L5626** Addition to lower extremity, test socket, hip disarticulation

➥ **L5628** Addition to lower extremity, test socket, hemipelvectomy

➥ **L5629** Addition to lower extremity, below knee, acrylic socket

Additions: Socket Variations

➥ **L5630** Addition to lower extremity, Symes type, expandable wall socket

➥ **L5631** Addition to lower extremity, above knee or knee disarticulation, acrylic socket

➥ **L5632** Addition to lower extremity, Symes type, "PTB" brim design socket

➥ **L5634** Addition to lower extremity, Symes type, posterior opening (Canadian) socket

➥ **L5636** Addition to lower extremity, Symes type, medial opening socket

PROSTHETIC PROCEDURES

➡ **L5637** Addition to lower extremity, below knee, total contact

➡ **L5638** Addition to lower extremity, below knee, leather socket

➡ **L5639** Addition to lower extremity, below knee, wood socket

➡ **L5640** Addition to lower extremity, knee disarticulation, leather socket

➡ **L5642** Addition to lower extremity, above knee, leather socket

➡ **L5643** Addition to lower extremity, hip disarticulation, flexible inner socket, external frame

➡ **L5644** Addition to lower extremity, above knee, wood socket

➡ **L5645** Addition to lower extremity, below knee, flexible inner socket, external frame

➡ **L5646** Addition to lower extremity, below knee, air cushion socket

➡ **L5647** Addition to lower extremity, below knee, suction socket

➡ **L5648** Addition to lower extremity, above knee, air cushion socket

➡ **L5649** Addition to lower extremity, ischial containment/narrow M-L socket

➡ **L5650** Addition to lower extremity, total contact, above knee or knee disarticulation socket

➡ **L5651** Addition to lower extremity, above knee, flexible inner socket, external frame

➡ **L5652** Addition to lower extremity, suction suspension, above knee or knee disarticulation socket

➡ **L5653** Addition to lower extremity, knee disarticulation, expandable wall socket

Additions: Socket Insert and Suspension

➡ **L5654** Addition to lower extremity, socket insert, Symes (Kemblo, Pelite, Aliplast, Plastazote or equal)

➡ **L5655** Addition to lower extremity, socket insert, below knee (Kemblo, Pelite, Aliplast, Plastazote or equal)

➡ **L5656** Addition to lower extremity, socket insert, knee disarticulation (Kemblo, Pelite, Aliplast, Plastazote or equal)

➡ **L5658** Addition to lower extremity, socket insert, above knee (Kemblo, Pelite, Aliplast, Plastazote or equal)

➡ **L5660** Addition to lower extremity, socket insert, Symes, silicone gel or equal

➡ **L5661** Addition to lower extremity, socket insert, multidurometer, Symes

➡ **L5662** Addition to lower extremity, socket insert, below knee, silicone gel or equal

➡ **L5663** Addition to lower extremity, socket insert, knee disarticulation, silicone gel or equal

➡ **L5664** Addition to lower extremity, socket insert, above knee, silicone gel or equal

➡ **L5665** Addition to lower extremity, socket insert, multidurometer, below knee

➡ **L5666** Addition to lower extremity, below knee, cuff suspension

➡ **L5667** Addition to lower extremity, below knee/above knee, socket insert, suction suspension with locking mechanism

➡ **L5668** Addition to lower extremity, below knee, molded distal cushion

➡ **L5669** Addition to lower extremity, below knee/above knee, socket insert, suction suspension without locking mechanism

➡ **L5670** Addition to lower extremity, below knee, molded supracondylar suspension ("PTS" or similar)

➡ **L5672** Addition to lower extremity, below knee, removable medial brim suspension

➡ **L5674** Addition to lower extremity, below knee, latex sleeve suspension or equal, each

➡ ☑ **L5675** Addition to lower extremity, below knee, latex sleeve suspension or equal, heavy duty, each

➡ ☑ **L5676** Addition to lower extremity, below knee, knee joints, single axis, pair

➡ ☑ **L5677** Addition to lower extremity, below knee, knee joints, polycentric, pair

➡ ☑ **L5678** Addition to lower extremity, below knee joint covers, pair

➡ **L5680** Addition to lower extremity, below knee, thigh lacer, nonmolded

➡ **L5682** Addition to lower extremity, below knee, thigh lacer, gluteal/ischial, molded

➡ **L5684** Addition to lower extremity, below knee, fork strap

➡ **L5686** Addition to lower extremity, below knee, back check (extension control)

➡ **L5688** Addition to lower extremity, below knee, waist belt, webbing

➡ **L5690** Addition to lower extremity, below knee, waist belt, padded and lined

➡ **L5692** Addition to lower extremity, above knee, pelvic control belt, light

➡ **L5694** Addition to lower extremity, above knee, pelvic control belt, padded and lined

PROSTHETIC PROCEDURES

➡ ☑ **L5695** Addition to lower extremity, above knee, pelvic control, sleeve suspension, neoprene or equal, each

➡ **L5696** Addition to lower extremity, above knee or knee disarticulation, pelvic joint

➡ **L5697** Addition to lower extremity, above knee or knee disarticulation, pelvic band

➡ **L5698** Addition to lower extremity, above knee or knee disarticulation, Silesian bandage

➡ **L5699** All lower extremity prostheses, shoulder harness

Replacements

➡ **L5700** Replacement, socket, below knee, molded to patient model

➡ **L5701** Replacement, socket, above knee/knee disarticulation, including attachment plate, molded to patient model

➡ **L5702** Replacement, socket, hip disarticulation, including hip joint, molded to patient model

➡ **L5704** Replacement, custom shaped protective cover, below knee

➡ **L5705** Replacement, custom shaped protective cover, above knee

➡ **L5706** Replacement, custom shaped protective cover, knee disarticulation

➡ **L5707** Replacement, custom shaped protective cover, hip disarticulation

Additions: Exoskeletal Knee-Shin System

➡ **L5710** Addition, exoskeletal knee-shin system, single axis, manual lock

➡ **L5711** Addition, exoskeletal knee-shin system, single axis, manual lock, ultra-light material

➡ **L5712** Addition, exoskeletal knee-shin system, single axis, friction swing and stance phase control (safety knee)

➡ **L5714** Addition, exoskeletal knee-shin system, single axis, variable friction swing phase control

➡ **L5716** Addition, exoskeletal knee-shin system, polycentric, mechanical stance phase lock

➡ **L5718** Addition, exoskeletal knee-shin system, polycentric, friction swing and stance phase control

➡ **L5722** Addition, exoskeletal knee-shin system, single axis, pneumatic swing, friction stance phase control

➡ **L5724** Addition, exoskeletal knee-shin system, single axis, fluid swing phase control

➡ **L5726** Addition, exoskeletal knee-shin system, single axis, external joints, fluid swing phase control

➡ **L5728** Addition, exoskeletal knee-shin system, single axis, fluid swing and stance phase control

➡ **L5780** Addition, exoskeletal knee-shin system, single axis, pneumatic/hydra pneumatic swing phase control

Component Modification

➡ **L5785** Addition, exoskeletal system, below knee, ultra-light material (titanium, carbon fiber or equal)

➡ **L5790** Addition, exoskeletal system, above knee, ultra-light material (titanium, carbon fiber or equal)

➡ **L5795** Addition, exoskeletal system, hip disarticulation, ultra-light material (titanium, carbon fiber or equal)

Additions: Endoskeletal Knee-Shin System

➡ **L5810** Addition, endoskeletal knee-shin system, single axis, manual lock

➡ **L5811** Addition, endoskeletal knee-shin system, single axis, manual lock, ultra-light material

➡ **L5812** Addition, endoskeletal knee-shin system, single axis, friction swing and stance phase control (safety knee)

➡ **L5814** Addition, endoskeletal knee-shin system, polycentric, hydraulic swing phase control, mechanical stance phase lock

➡ **L5816** Addition, endoskeletal knee-shin system, polycentric, mechanical stance phase lock

➡ **L5818** Addition, endoskeletal knee-shin system, polycentric, friction swing and stance phase control

➡ **L5822** Addition, endoskeletal knee-shin system, single axis, pneumatic swing, friction stance phase control

➡ **L5824** Addition, endoskeletal knee-shin system, single axis, fluid swing phase control

➡ **L5826** Addition, endoskeletal knee-shin system, single axis, hydraulic swing phase control, with miniature high activity frame

➡ **L5828** Addition, endoskeletal knee-shin system, single axis, fluid swing and stance phase control

➡ **L5830** Addition, endoskeletal knee-shin system, single axis, pneumatic/swing phase control

➡ **L5840** Addition, endoskeletal knee-shin system, 4-bar linkage or multiaxial, pneumatic swing phase control

L5845 Addition, endoskeletal knee-shin system, stance flexion feature, adjustable

L5846 Addition, endoskeletal knee-shin system, microprocessor control feature, swing phase only

L5850 Addition, endoskeletal system, above knee or hip disarticulation, knee extension assist

L5855 Addition, endoskeletal system, hip disarticulation, mechanical hip extension assist

L5910 Addition, endoskeletal system, below knee, alignable system

L5920 Addition, endoskeletal system, above knee or hip disarticulation, alignable system

▲ **L5925** Addition, endoskeletal system, above knee, knee disarticulation or hip disarticulation, manual lock

L5930 Addition, endoskeletal system, high activity knee control frame

L5940 Addition, endoskeletal system, below knee, ultra-light material (titanium, carbon fiber or equal)

L5950 Addition, endoskeletal system, above knee, ultra-light material (titanium, carbon fiber or equal)

L5960 Addition, endoskeletal system, hip disarticulation, ultra-light material (titanium, carbon fiber or equal)

L5962 Addition, endoskeletal system, below knee, flexible protective outer surface covering system

L5964 Addition, endoskeletal system, above knee, flexible protective outer surface covering system

L5966 Addition, endoskeletal system, hip disarticulation, flexible protective outer surface covering system

▲ **L5968** Addition to lower limb prosthesis, multiaxial ankle with swing phase active dorsiflexion feature

L5970 All lower extremity prostheses, foot, external keel, SACH foot

L5972 All lower extremity prostheses, flexible keel foot (Safe, Sten, Bock Dynamic or equal)

L5974 All lower extremity prostheses, foot, single axis ankle/foot

L5975 All lower extremity prosthesis, combination single axis ankle and flexible keel foot

L5976 All lower extremity prostheses, energy storing foot (Seattle Carbon Copy II or equal)

L5978 All lower extremity prostheses, foot, multi-axial ankle/foot

L5979 All lower extremity prostheses, multi-axial ankle/foot, dynamic response

L5980 All lower extremity prostheses, flex-foot system

L5981 All lower extremity prostheses, flex-walk system or equal

L5982 All exoskeletal lower extremity prostheses, axial rotation unit

L5984 All endoskeletal lower extremity prostheses, axial rotation unit

L5985 All endoskeletal lower extremity prostheses, dynamic prosthetic pylon

L5986 All lower extremity prostheses, multi-axial rotation unit ("MCP" or equal)

L5987 All lower extremity prosthesis, shank foot system with vertical loading pylon

▲ **L5988** Addition to lower limb prosthesis, vertical shock reducing pylon feature

L5999 Lower extremity prosthesis, not otherwise specified
Determine if an alternative national HCPCS Level II or a local HCPCS Level III code better describes the prosthesis being reported. This code should be used only if a more specific code is unavailable.

Upper Limb

The procedures in L6000-L6599 are considered as "base" or "basic procedures" and may be modified by listing procedures from the "addition" sections. The base procedures include only standard friction wrist and control cable systems unless otherwise specified.

Partial Hand

L6000 Partial hand, Robin-Aids, thumb remaining (or equal)

L6010 Partial hand, Robin-Aids, little and/or ring finger remaining (or equal)

L6020 Partial hand, Robin-Aids, no finger remaining (or equal)

Wrist Disarticulation

L6050 Wrist disarticulation, molded socket, flexible elbow hinges, triceps pad

L6055 Wrist disarticulation, molded socket with expandable interface, flexible elbow hinges, triceps pad

Below Elbow

L6100 Below elbow, molded socket, flexible elbow hinge, triceps pad

L6110 Below elbow, molded socket (Muenster or Northwestern suspension types)

➡ **L6120** Below elbow, molded double wall split socket, step-up hinges, half cuff

➡ **L6130** Below elbow, molded double wall split socket, stump activated locking hinge, half cuff

Elbow Disarticulation

➡ **L6200** Elbow disarticulation, molded socket, outside locking hinge, forearm

➡ **L6205** Elbow disarticulation, molded socket with expandable interface, outside locking hinges, forearm

Above Elbow

➡ **L6250** Above elbow, molded double wall socket, internal locking elbow, forearm

Shoulder Disarticulation

➡ **L6300** Shoulder disarticulation, molded socket, shoulder bulkhead, humeral section, internal locking elbow, forearm

➡ **L6310** Shoulder disarticulation, passive restoration (complete prosthesis)

➡ **L6320** Shoulder disarticulation, passive restoration (shoulder cap only)

Interscapular Thoracic

➡ **L6350** Interscapular thoracic, molded socket, shoulder bulkhead, humeral section, internal locking elbow, forearm

➡ **L6360** Interscapular thoracic, passive restoration (complete prosthesis)

➡ **L6370** Interscapular thoracic, passive restoration (shoulder cap only)

Immediate and Early Postsurgical Procedures

➡ **L6380** Immediate postsurgical or early fitting, application of initial rigid dressing, including fitting alignment and suspension of components, and one cast change, wrist disarticulation or below elbow

➡ ☑ **L6382** Immediate postsurgical or early fitting, application of initial rigid dressing including fitting alignment and suspension of components, and one cast change, elbow disarticulation or above elbow

➡ ☑ **L6384** Immediate postsurgical or early fitting, application of initial rigid dressing including fitting alignment and suspension of components, and one cast change, shoulder disarticulation or interscapular thoracic

➡ ☑ **L6386** Immediate postsurgical or early fitting, each additional cast change and realignment

➡ **L6388** Immediate postsurgical or early fitting, application of rigid dressing only

Endoskeletal: Below Elbow

➡ **L6400** Below elbow, molded socket, endoskeletal system, including soft prosthetic tissue shaping

Endoskeletal: Elbow Disarticulation

➡ **L6450** Elbow disarticulation, molded socket, endoskeletal system, including soft prosthetic tissue shaping

Endoskeletal: Above Elbow

➡ **L6500** Above elbow, molded socket, endoskeletal system, including soft prosthetic tissue shaping

Endoskeletal: Shoulder Disarticulation

➡ **L6550** Shoulder disarticulation, molded socket, endoskeletal system, including soft prosthetic tissue shaping

Endoskeletal: Interscapular Thoracic

➡ **L6570** Interscapular thoracic, molded socket, endoskeletal system, including soft prosthetic tissue shaping

➡ **L6580** Preparatory, wrist disarticulation or below elbow, single wall plastic socket, friction wrist, flexible elbow hinges, figure of eight harness, humeral cuff, Bowden cable control, "USMC" or equal pylon, no cover, molded to patient model

➡ **L6582** Preparatory, wrist disarticulation or below elbow, single wall socket, friction wrist, flexible elbow hinges, figure of eight harness, humeral cuff, Bowden cable control, "USMC" or equal pylon, no cover, direct formed

➡ **L6584** Preparatory, elbow disarticulation or above elbow, single wall plastic socket, friction wrist, locking elbow, figure of eight harness, fair lead cable control, "USMC" or equal pylon, no cover, molded to patient model

➡ **L6586** Preparatory, elbow disarticulation or above elbow, single wall socket, friction wrist, locking elbow, figure of eight harness, fair lead cable control, "USMC" or equal pylon, no cover, direct formed

➡ **L6588** Preparatory, shoulder disarticulation or interscapular thoracic, single wall plastic socket, shoulder joint, locking elbow, friction wrist, chest strap, fair lead cable control, "USMC" or equal pylon, no cover, molded to patient model

PROSTHETIC PROCEDURES

➡ **L6590** Preparatory, shoulder disarticulation or interscapular thoracic, single wall socket, shoulder joint, locking elbow, friction wrist, chest strap, fair lead cable control, "USMC" or equal pylon, no cover, direct formed

Additions: Upper Limb

The following procedures/modifications/components may be added to other base procedures. The items in this section should reflect the additional complexity of each modification procedure, in addition to the base procedure, at the time of the original order.

➡ ☑ **L6600** Upper extremity additions, polycentric hinge, pair

➡ ☑ **L6605** Upper extremity additions, single pivot hinge, pair

➡ ☑ **L6610** Upper extremity additions, flexible metal hinge, pair

➡ **L6615** Upper extremity addition, disconnect locking wrist unit

➡ ☑ **L6616** Upper extremity addition, additional disconnect insert for locking wrist unit, each

➡ **L6620** Upper extremity addition, flexion-friction wrist unit

➡ **L6623** Upper extremity addition, spring assisted rotational wrist unit with latch release

➡ **L6625** Upper extremity addition, rotation wrist unit with cable lock

➡ **L6628** Upper extremity addition, quick disconnect hook adapter, Otto Bock or equal

➡ **L6629** Upper extremity addition, quick disconnect lamination collar with coupling piece, Otto Bock or equal

➡ **L6630** Upper extremity addition, stainless steel, any wrist

➡ ☑ **L6632** Upper extremity addition, latex suspension sleeve, each

➡ **L6635** Upper extremity addition, lift assist for elbow

➡ **L6637** Upper extremity addition, nudge control elbow lock

➡ ☑ **L6640** Upper extremity additions, shoulder abduction joint, pair

➡ **L6641** Upper extremity addition, excursion amplifier, pulley type

➡ **L6642** Upper extremity addition, excursion amplifier, lever type

➡ ☑ **L6645** Upper extremity addition, shoulder flexion-abduction joint, each

➡ ☑ **L6650** Upper extremity addition, shoulder universal joint, each

➡ **L6655** Upper extremity addition, standard control cable, extra

➡ **L6660** Upper extremity addition, heavy duty control cable

➡ **L6665** Upper extremity addition, Teflon, or equal, cable lining

➡ **L6670** Upper extremity addition, hook to hand, cable adapter

➡ **L6672** Upper extremity addition, harness, chest or shoulder, saddle type

➡ **L6675** Upper extremity addition, harness, figure of eight type, for single control

➡ **L6676** Upper extremity addition, harness, figure of eight type, for dual control

➡ **L6680** Upper extremity addition, test socket, wrist disarticulation or below elbow

➡ **L6682** Upper extremity addition, test socket, elbow disarticulation or above elbow

➡ **L6684** Upper extremity addition, test socket, shoulder disarticulation or interscapular thoracic

➡ **L6686** Upper extremity addition, suction socket

➡ **L6687** Upper extremity addition, frame type socket, below elbow or wrist disarticulation

➡ **L6688** Upper extremity addition, frame type socket, above elbow or elbow disarticulation

➡ **L6689** Upper extremity addition, frame type socket, shoulder disarticulation

➡ **L6690** Upper extremity addition, frame type socket, interscapular-thoracic

➡ ☑ **L6691** Upper extremity addition, removable insert, each

➡ ☑ **L6692** Upper extremity addition, silicone gel insert or equal, each

▲ **L6693** Upper extremity addition, locking elbow, forearm counterbalance

Terminal Devices

Hooks

? **L6700** Terminal device, hook, Dorrance or equal, model #3
MCM 2133

? **L6705** Terminal device, hook, Dorrance or equal, model #5
MCM 2133

? **L6710** Terminal device, hook, Dorrance or equal, model #5X
MCM 2133

PROSTHETIC PROCEDURES

? **L6715** Terminal device, hook, Dorrance or equal, model #5XA
MCM 2133

? **L6720** Terminal device, hook, Dorrance or equal, model #6
MCM 2133

? **L6725** Terminal device, hook, Dorrance or equal, model #7
MCM 2133

? **L6730** Terminal device, hook, Dorrance or equal, model #7LO
MCM 2133

? **L6735** Terminal device, hook, Dorrance or equal, model #8
MCM 2133

? **L6740** Terminal device, hook, Dorrance or equal, model #8X
MCM 2133

? **L6745** Terminal device, hook, Dorrance or equal, model #88X
MCM 2133

? **L6750** Terminal device, hook, Dorrance or equal, model #10P
MCM 2133

? **L6755** Terminal device, hook, Dorrance or equal, model #10X
MCM 2133

? **L6765** Terminal device, hook, Dorrance or equal, model #12P
MCM 2133

? **L6770** Terminal device, hook, Dorrance or equal, model #99X
MCM 2133

? **L6775** Terminal device, hook, Dorrance or equal, model #555
MCM 2133

? **L6780** Terminal device, hook, Dorrance or equal, model #SS555
MCM 2133

? **L6790** Terminal device, hook, Accu hook or equal
MCM 2133

? **L6795** Terminal device, hook, 2 load or equal
MCM 2133

? **L6800** Terminal device, hook, APRL VC or equal
MCM 2133

? **L6805** Terminal device, modifier wrist flexion unit
MCM 2133

? **L6806** Terminal device, hook, TRS Grip, Grip III, VC, or equal
MCM 2133

? **L6807** Terminal device, hook, Grip I, Grip II, VC, or equal
MCM 2133

? **L6808** Terminal device, hook, TRS Adept, infant or child, VC, or equal
MCM 2133

? **L6809** Terminal device, hook, TRS Super Sport, passive
MCM 2133

? **L6810** Terminal device, pincher tool, Otto Bock or equal
MCM 2133

Hands

? **L6825** Terminal device, hand, Dorrance, VO
MCM 2133

? **L6830** Terminal device, hand, APRL, VC
MCM 2133

? **L6835** Terminal device, hand, Sierra, VO
MCM 2133

? **L6840** Terminal device, hand, Becker Imperial
MCM 2133

? **L6845** Terminal device, hand, Becker Lock Grip
MCM 2133

? **L6850** Terminal device, hand, Becker Plylite
MCM 2133

? **L6855** Terminal device, hand, Robin-Aids, VO
MCM 2133

? **L6860** Terminal device, hand, Robin-Aids, VO soft
MCM 2133

? **L6865** Terminal device, hand, passive hand
MCM 2133

? **L6867** Terminal device, hand, Detroit Infant Hand (mechanical)
MCM 2133

? **L6868** Terminal device, hand, passive infant hand, Steeper, Hosmer or equal
MCM 2133

? **L6870** Terminal device, hand, child mitt
MCM 2133

? **L6872** Terminal device, hand, NYU child hand
MCM 2133

? **L6873** Terminal device, hand, mechanical infant hand, Steeper or equal
MCM 2133

? **L6875** Terminal device, hand, Bock, VC
MCM 2133

? **L6880** Terminal device, hand, Bock, VO
MCM 2133

Gloves for Above Hands

➡ **L6890** Terminal device, glove for above hands, production glove

➡ **L6895** Terminal device, glove for above hands, custom glove

PROSTHETIC PROCEDURES

Hand Restoration

- **L6900** Hand restoration (casts, shading and measurements included), partial hand, with glove, thumb or one finger remaining
- **L6905** Hand restoration (casts, shading and measurements included), partial hand, with glove, multiple fingers remaining
- **L6910** Hand restoration (casts, shading and measurements included), partial hand, with glove, no fingers remaining
- **L6915** Hand restoration (shading and measurements included), replacement glove for above

External Power

Base Devices

- **L6920** Wrist disarticulation, external power, self-suspended inner socket, removable forearm shell, Otto Bock or equal switch, cables, two batteries and one charger, switch control of terminal device
- **L6925** Wrist disarticulation, external power, self-suspended inner socket, removable forearm shell, Otto Bock or equal electrodes, cables, two batteries and one charger, myoelectronic control of terminal device
- **L6930** Below elbow, external power, self-suspended inner socket, removable forearm shell, Otto Bock or equal switch, cables, two batteries and one charger, switch control of terminal device
- **L6935** Below elbow, external power, self-suspended inner socket, removable forearm shell, Otto Bock or equal electrodes, cables, two batteries and one charger, myoelectronic control of terminal device
- **L6940** Elbow disarticulation, external power, molded inner socket, removable humeral shell, outside locking hinges, forearm, Otto Bock or equal switch, cables, two batteries and one charger, switch control of terminal device
- **L6945** Elbow disarticulation, external power, molded inner socket, removable humeral shell, outside locking hinges, forearm, Otto Bock or equal electrodes, cables, two batteries and one charger, myoelectronic control of terminal device
- **L6950** Above elbow, external power, molded inner socket, removable humeral shell, internal locking elbow, forearm, Otto Bock or equal switch, cables, two batteries and one charger, switch control of terminal device
- **L6955** Above elbow, external power, molded inner socket, removable humeral shell, internal locking elbow, forearm, Otto Bock or equal electrodes, cables, two batteries and one charger, myoelectronic control of terminal device
- **L6960** Shoulder disarticulation, external power, molded inner socket, removable shoulder shell, shoulder bulkhead, humeral section, mechanical elbow, forearm, Otto Bock or equal switch, cables, two batteries and one charger, switch control of terminal device
- **L6965** Shoulder disarticulation, external power, molded inner socket, removable shoulder shell, shoulder bulkhead, humeral section, mechanical elbow, forearm, Otto Bock or equal electrodes, cables, two batteries and one charger, myoelectronic control of terminal device
- **L6970** Interscapular-thoracic, external power, molded inner socket, removable shoulder shell, shoulder bulkhead, humeral section, mechanical elbow, forearm, Otto Bock or equal switch, cables, two batteries and one charger, switch control of terminal device
- **L6975** Interscapular-thoracic, external power, molded inner socket, removable shoulder shell, shoulder bulkhead, humeral section, mechanical elbow, forearm, Otto Bock or equal electrodes, cables, two batteries and one charger, myoelectronic control of terminal device
- **L7010** Electronic hand, Otto Bock, Steeper or equal, switch controlled
- **L7015** Electronic hand, System Teknik, Variety Village or equal, switch controlled
- **L7020** Electronic greifer, Otto Bock or equal, switch controlled
- **L7025** Electronic hand, Otto Bock or equal, myoelectronically controlled
- **L7030** Electronic hand, System Teknik, Variety Village or equal, myoelectronically controlled
- **L7035** Electronic greifer, Otto Bock or equal, myoelectronically controlled
- **L7040** Prehensile actuator, Hosmer or equal, switch controlled
- **L7045** Electronic hook, child, Michigan or equal, switch controlled

Elbow

- **L7170** Electronic elbow, Hosmer or equal, switch controlled
- **L7180** Electronic elbow, Boston, Utah or equal, myoelectronically controlled

PROSTHETIC PROCEDURES

➡ **L7185** Electronic elbow, adolescent, Variety Village or equal, switch controlled

➡ **L7186** Electronic elbow, child, Variety Village or equal, switch controlled

➡ **L7190** Electronic elbow, adolescent, Variety Village or equal, myoelectronically controlled

➡ **L7191** Electronic elbow, child, Variety Village or equal, myoelectronically controlled

➡ **L7260** Electronic wrist rotator, Otto Bock or equal

➡ **L7261** Electronic wrist rotator, for Utah arm

➡ **L7266** Servo control, Steeper or equal

➡ **L7272** Analogue control, UNB or equal

➡ **L7274** Proportional control, 6-12 volt, Liberty, Utah or equal

Battery Components

➡ **L7360** Six volt battery, Otto Bock or equal, each

➡ **L7362** Battery charger, six volt, Otto Bock or equal

➡ **L7364** Twelve volt battery, Utah or equal, each

➡ **L7366** Battery charger, twelve volt, Utah or equal

➡ **L7499** Upper extremity prosthesis, not otherwise specified

Repairs

? **L7500** Repair of prosthetic device, hourly rate
MCM 2100.4, MCM 2130D, MCM 2133
Medicare jurisdiction: local carrier if repair or implanted prosthetic device.

? **L7510** Repair of prosthetic device, repair or replace minor parts
MCM 2100.4, MCM 2130D, MCM 2133

➡ ☑ **L7520** Repair prosthetic device, labor component, per 15 minutes

➡ **L7900** Vacuum erection system

General

Breast Prosthesis

? **L8000** Breast prosthesis, mastectomy bra
MCM 2130A

? **L8010** Breast prosthesis, mastectomy sleeve
MCM 2130A

? **L8015** External breast prosthesis garment, with mastectomy form, post-mastectomy
MCM 2130

? **L8020** Breast prosthesis, mastectomy form
MCM 2130A

? **L8030** Breast prosthesis, silicone or equal
MCM 2130A

? **L8035** Custom breast prosthesis, post mastectomy, molded to patient model
MCM 2130

➡ **L8039** Breast prosthesis, not otherwise specified

Elastic Supports

⊘ ☑ **L8100** Gradient compression stocking, below knee, 18-30 mmhg, each
CIM 60-9, MCM 2133

⊘ ☑ **L8110** Gradient compression stocking, below knee, 30-40 mmhg, each
CIM 60-9, MCM 2133

⊘ ☑ **L8120** Gradient compression stocking, below knee, 40-50 mmhg, each
CIM 60-9, MCM 2133

⊘ ☑ **L8130** Gradient compression stocking, thigh length, 18-30 mmhg, each
CIM 60-9, MCM 2133

⊘ ☑ **L8140** Gradient compression stocking, thigh length, 30-40 mmhg, each
CIM 60-9, MCM 2133

⊘ ☑ **L8150** Gradient compression stocking, thigh length, 40-50 mmhg, each
CIM 60-9, MCM 2133

⊘ ☑ **L8160** Gradient compression stocking, full length/chap style, 18-30 mmhg, each
CIM 60-9, MCM 2133

⊘ ☑ **L8170** Gradient compression stocking, full length/chap style, 30-40 mmhg, each
CIM 60-9, MCM 2133

⊘ ☑ **L8180** Gradient compression stocking, full length/chap style, 40-50 mmhg, each
CIM 60-9, MCM 2133

⊘ ☑ **L8190** Gradient compression stocking, waist length, 18-30 mmhg, each
CIM 60-9, MCM 2133

⊘ ☑ **L8195** Gradient compression stocking, waist length, 30-40 mmhg, each
CIM 60-9, MCM 2133

⊘ ☑ **L8200** Gradient compression stocking, waist length, 40-50 mmhg, each
CIM 60-9, MCM 2133

⊘ **L8210** Gradient compression stocking, custom made
CIM 60-9, MCM 2133

⊘ **L8220** Gradient compression stocking, lymphedema
CIM 60-9, MCM 2133

⊘ **L8230** Gradient compression stocking, garter belt
CIM 60-9, MCM 2133

➡ **L8239** Gradient compression stocking, not otherwise specified

Trusses

? **L8300** Truss, single with standard pad
CIM 70-1, CIM 70-2, MCM 2133

PROSTHETIC PROCEDURES

? L8310 Truss, double with standard pads
CIM 70-1, CIM 70-2, MCM 2133

? L8320 Truss, addition to standard pad, water pad
CIM 70-1, CIM 70-2, MCM 2133

? L8330 Truss, addition to standard pad, scrotal pad
CIM 70-1, CIM 70-2, MCM 2133

Prosthetic Socks

? L8400 Prosthetic sheath, below knee, each
MCM 2133

? L8410 Prosthetic sheath, above knee, each
MCM 2133

? L8415 Prosthetic sheath, upper limb, each
MCM 2133

➡ **L8417** Prosthetic sheath/sock, including a gel cushion layer, below knee or above knee, each

? L8420 Prosthetic sock, multiple ply, below knee, each
MCM 2133

? L8430 Prosthetic sock, multiple ply, above knee, each
MCM 2133

▲ **? L8435** Prosthetic sock, multiple ply, upper limb, each
MCM 2133

? L8440 Prosthetic shrinker, below knee, each
MCM 2133

? L8460 Prosthetic shrinker, above knee, each
MCM 2133

? L8465 Prosthetic shrinker, upper limb, each
MCM 2133

? L8470 Prosthetic sock, single ply, fitting, below knee, each
MCM 2133

? L8480 Prosthetic sock, single ply, fitting, above knee, each
MCM 2133

? L8485 Prosthetic sock, single ply, fitting, upper limb, each
MCM 2133

➡ **L8490** Addition to prosthetic sheath/sock, air seal suction retention system

➡ **L8499** Unlisted procedure for miscellaneous prosthetic services
Determine if an alternative national HCPCS Level II, a local HCPCS Level III code, or a CPT code better describes the service being reported. This code should be used only if a more specific code is unavailable.

Prosthetic Implants

? L8500 Artificial larynx, any type
CIM 65-5, MCM 2130

? L8501 Tracheostomy speaking valve
CIM 65-16

? L8600 Implantable breast prosthesis, silicone or equal
CIM 35-47, MCM 2130
Medicare covers implants inserted in post-mastectomy reconstruction in a breast cancer patient. Always report concurrent to the implant procedure. Medicare jurisdiction: local carrier.

? L8603 Collagen implant, urinary tract, per 2.5 cc syringe, includes shipping and necessary supplies
CIM 65-9
Medicare covers up to five separate collagen implant treatments in patients with intrinsic sphincter deficiency. Who have passed a collagen sensitivity test. Medicare jurisdiction: local carrier.

? L8610 Ocular implant
MCM 2130
Medicare jurisdiction: local carrier.

? L8612 Aqueous shunt
MCM 2130
Medicare jurisdiction: local carrier.

? L8613 Ossicula implant
MCM 2130
Medicare jurisdiction: local carrier.

? L8614 Cochlear device/system
CIM 65-14, MCM 2130
A cochlear implant is covered by Medicare when the patient has bilateral sensorineural deafness. Medicare jurisdiction: local carrier.

? L8619 Cochlear implant external speech processor, replacement
CIM 65-14
Medicare jurisdiction: local carrier.

? L8630 Metacarpophalangeal joint implant
MCM 2130
Medicare jurisdiction: local carrier.

? L8641 Metatarsal joint implant
MCM 2130
Medicare jurisdiction: local carrier.

? L8642 Hallux implant
MCM 2130
Medicare jurisdiction: local carrier.

? L8658 Interphalangeal joint implant
MCM 2130
Medicare jurisdiction: local carrier.

? L8670 Vascular graft material, synthetic, implant
MCM 2130
Medicare jurisdiction: local carrier.

PROSTHETIC PROCEDURES

➡ **L8699** Prosthetic implant, not otherwise specified
Determine if an alternative national HCPCS Level II, a local HCPCS Level III code, or a CPT code better describes the service being reported. This code should be used only if a more specific code is unavailable. Medicare jurisdiction: local carrier.

● ➡ **L9900** Orthotic and prosthetic supply, accessory, and/or service component of another HCPCS L code

Medical Services M0000–M0302

M codes fall under the jurisdiction of the local carrier.

Other Medical Services

? M0064 Brief office visit for the sole purpose of monitoring or changing drug prescriptions used in the treatment of mental psychoneurotic and personality disorders
MCM 2476.3

⊘ **M0075** Cellular therapy
CIM 35-5
The therapeutic efficacy of injecting foreign proteins has not been established.

⊘ **M0076** Prolotherapy
CIM 35-13
The therapeutic efficacy of prolotherapy and joint sclerotherapy have not been established.

⊘ **M0100** Intragastric hypothermia using gastric freezing (MNP)
CIM 35-65
Code with caution: This procedure is considered obsolete.

Cardiovascular Services

⊘ **M0300** IV chelation therapy (chemical endarterectomy)
CIM 35-64
Chelation therapy is considered experimental in the United States.

⊘ **M0301** Fabric wrapping of abdominal aneurysm (MNP)
CIM 35-34
Code with caution: This procedure has largely been replaced with more effective treatment modalities. Submit documentation.

⊘ **M0302** Assessment of cardiac output by electrical bioimpedance
CIM 50-54

Pathology and Laboratory Services P0000–P9999

Under certain circumstances, Medicare allows physicians and laboratories a fee for drawing or collecting test specimens. If the test specimen is collected from a homebound patient, physicians and laboratories may also bill for a travel allowance.

P codes fall under the jurisdiction of the local carrier.

Chemistry and Toxicology Tests

? **P2028** Cephalin floculation, blood
CIM 50-34
Code with caution: This test is considered Oobsolete. Submit documentation.

? **P2029** Congo red, blood
CIM 50-34
Code with caution: This test is considered obsolete. Submit documentation.

⊘ **P2031** Hair analysis (excluding arsenic)
CIM 50-24

? **P2033** Thymol turbidity, blood
CIM 50-34
Code with caution: This test is considered obsolete. Submit documentation.

? **P2038** Mucoprotein, blood (seromucoid) (medical necessity procedure)
CIM 50-34
Code with caution: This test is considered obsolete. Submit documentation.

Pathology Screening Tests

? **P3000** Screening Papanicolaou smear, cervical or vaginal, up to three smears, by technician under physician supervision
CIM 50-20
One Pap test is covered by Medicare every three years, unless the physician suspects cervical abnormalities and shortens the interval.

? **P3001** Screening Papanicolaou smear, cervical or vaginal, up to three smears, requiring interpretation by physician
CIM 50-20
One Pap test is covered by Medicare every three years, unless the physician suspects cervical abnormalities and shortens the interval.

Microbiology Tests

⊘ **P7001** Culture, bacterial, urine; quantitative, sensitivity study
Cross-reference CPT

Miscellaneous

? ☑ **P9010** Blood (whole), for transfusion, per unit
MCM 2455A

? ☑ **P9011** Blood (split unit), specify amount
MCM 2455A

? ☑ **P9012** Cryoprecipitate, each unit
MCM 2455B

? **P9013** Fibrinogen unit
MCM 2455B

(P9014 has been deleted. See code J1460)

(P9015 has been deleted. See code J1561)

? ☑ **P9016** Leukocyte poor blood, each unit
MCM 2049, 2455B

? ☑ **P9017** Plasma, single donor, fresh frozen, each unit
MCM 2455B

? ☑ **P9018** Plasma, protein fraction, each unit
MCM 2455B

? ☑ **P9019** Platelet concentrate, each unit
MCM 2455B

? ☑ **P9020** Platelet rich plasma, each unit
MCM 2455B

? ☑ **P9021** Red blood cells, each unit
MCM 2455A

? ☑ **P9022** Washed red blood cells, each unit
MCM 2455A

● ☑ **P9023** Plasma, pooled multiple donor, solvent/detergent treated, frozen, each unit
MCM 2455B

? ☑ **P9603** Travel allowance one way in connection with medically necessary laboratory specimen collection drawn from homebound or nursing home bound patient; prorated miles actually travelled
MCM 5114.1K

? ☑ **P9604** Travel allowance one way in connection with medically necessary laboratory specimen collection drawn from homebound or nursing home bound patient; prorated trip charge
MCM 5114.1K

(P9610 has been deleted. See code P9612)

? **P9612** Catheterization for collection of specimen, single patient, all places of service
MCM 5114.1D

? **P9615** Catheterization for collection of specimen(s) (multiple patients)
MCM 5114.1D

Q Codes (Temporary) Q0000–Q9999

HCFA assigns Q codes to procedures, services and supplies on a temporary basis. When a permanent code is assigned, the Q code is deleted and cross-referenced.

This section contains national codes assigned by HCFA on a temporary basis. The list contains current codes.

Q codes fall under the jurisdiction of the local carrier unless they represent an incidental service or are otherwise specified.

➥ **Q0034** Administration of influenza vaccine to Medicare beneficiaries by participating demonstration sites

? **Q0035** Cardiokymography
CIM 50-50
Covered only in conjunction with electrocardiographic stress testing in male patients with atypical angina or nonischemic chest pain, or female patients with angina.

(Q0068 has been deleted)

? ☑ **Q0081** Infusion therapy, using other than chemotherapeutic drugs, per visit
CIM 60-14

➥ ☑ **Q0082** Activity therapy furnished in connection with partial hospitalization (e.g., music, dance, art or play therapies that are not primarily recreational), per visit

➥ ☑ **Q0083** Chemotherapy administration by other than infusion technique only (e.g., subcutaneous, intramuscular, push), per visit

? ☑ **Q0084** Chemotherapy administration by infusion technique only, per visit
CIM 60-14

➥ ☑ **Q0085** Chemotherapy administration by both infusion technique and other technique(s) (e.g., subcutaneous, intramuscular, push), per visit

? ☑ **Q0086** Physical therapy evaluation/treatment, per visit
MCM 2210

? **Q0091** Screening Papanicolaou smear; obtaining, preparing and conveyance of cervical or vaginal smear to laboratory
CIM 50-20
One Pap test is covered by Medicare every three years, unless the physician suspects cervical abnormalities and shortens the interval. Q0091 can be reported with an E/M code when a separately identifiable E/M service is provided.

? **Q0092** Set-up portable x-ray equipment
MCM 2070.4

➥ **Q0111** Wet mounts, including preparations of vaginal, cervical or skin specimens
AL, FP, GC, GE, Q4

➥ **Q0112** All potassium hydroxide (KOH) preparations
Lab Certification - Mycology

➥ **Q0113** Pinworm examination
Lab Certification - Parasitology

➥ **Q0114** Fern test
Lab Certification - Routine Chemistry

➥ **Q0115** Post-coital direct, qualitative examinations of vaginal or cervical mucous
Lab Certification - Hematology

(Q0132 has been deleted)

? ☑ **Q0136** Injection, epoetin alpha, (for non ESRD use), per 1,000 units
MCM 2049
This code is for EPO used to treat anemia in patients undergoing chemotherapy for non-myeloid malignancies.

⊘ ☑ **Q0144** Azithromycin dihydrate, oral, capsules/powder, 1 gram (Zithromax)
Medicare jurisdiction: DME regional carrier.

➥ ☑ **Q0156** Infusion, albumin (human), 5%, 500 ml
Medicare jurisdiction: DME regional carrier. Use this code for Albumarc.

➥ ☑ **Q0157** Infusion, albumin (human), 25%, 50 ml
Medicare jurisdiction: DME regional carrier. Use this code for Albumarc.

? **Q0160** Factor IX (antihemophilic factor, purified, non-recombinant) per I.U.
MCM 2049

? **Q0161** Factor IX (antihemophilic factor, recombinant) per I.U.
MCM 2049

? **Q0163** Diphenhydramine hydrochloride, 50 mg, oral, FDA approved prescription anti-emetic, for use as a complete therapeutic substitute for an IV anti-emetic at time of chemotherapy treatment not to exceed a 48-hour dosage regimen
Medicare Statute 4557
Medicare covers at the time of chemotherapy if regimen doesn't exceed 48 hours. Submit on the same claim as the chemotherapy.

? **Q0164** Prochlorperazine maleate, 5 mg, oral, FDA approved prescription anti-emetic, for use as a complete therapeutic substitute for an IV anti-emetic at the time of chemotherapy treatment, not to exceed a 48-hour dosage regimen
Medicare Statute 4557
Medicare covers at the time of chemotherapy if regimen doesn't exceed 48 hours. Submit on the same claim as the chemotherapy.

? **Q0165** Prochlorperazine maleate, 10 mg, oral, FDA approved prescription anti-emetic, for use as a complete therapeutic substitute for an IV anti-emetic at the time of chemotherapy treatment, not to exceed a 48-hour dosage regimen
Medicare Statute 4557
Medicare covers at the time of chemotherapy if regimen doesn't exceed 48 hours. Submit on the same claim as the chemotherapy.

Q CODES (TEMPORARY)

? **Q0166** Granisetron hydrochloride, 1 mg, oral, FDA approved prescription anti-emetic, for use as a complete therapeutic substitute for an IV anti-emetic at the time of chemotherapy treatment, not to exceed a 24-hour dosage regimen
Medicare Statute 4557
Medicare covers at the time of chemotherapy if regimen doesn't exceed 48 hours. Submit on the same claim as the chemotherapy.

? **Q0167** Dronabinol, 2.5 mg, oral, FDA approved prescription anti-emetic, for use as a complete therapeutic substitute for an IV anti-emetic at the time of chemotherapy treatment, not to exceed a 48-hour dosage regimen
Medicare Statute 4557
Medicare covers at the time of chemotherapy if regimen doesn't exceed 48 hours. Submit on the same claim as the chemotherapy.

? **Q0168** Dronabinol, 5 mg, oral, FDA approved prescription anti-emetic, for use as a complete therapeutic substitute for an IV anti-emetic at the time of chemotherapy treatment, not to exceed a 48-hour dosage regimen
Medicare Statute 4557

? **Q0169** Promethazine hydrochloride, 12.5 mg, oral, FDA approved prescription anti-emetic, for use as a complete therapeutic substitute for an IV anti-emetic at the time of chemotherapy treatment, not to exceed a 48-hour dosage regimen
Medicare Statute 4557
Medicare covers at the time of chemotherapy if regimen doesn't exceed 48 hours. Submit on the same claim as the chemotherapy.

? **Q0170** Promethazine hydrochloride, 25 mg, oral, FDA approved prescription anti-emetic, for use as a complete therapeutic substitute for an IV anti-emetic at the time of chemotherapy treatment, not to exceed a 48-hour dosage regimen
Medicare Statute 4557
Medicare covers at the time of chemotherapy if regimen doesn't exceed 48 hours. Submit on the same claim as the chemotherapy.

? **Q0171** Chlorpromazine hydrochloride, 10 mg, oral, FDA approved prescription anti-emetic, for use as a complete therapeutic substitute for an IV anti-emetic at the time of chemotherapy treatment, not to exceed a 48-hour dosage regimen
Medicare Statute 4557
Medicare covers at the time of chemotherapy if regimen doesn't exceed 48 hours. Submit on the same claim as the chemotherapy.

? **Q0172** Chlorpromazine hydrochloride, 25 mg, oral, FDA approved prescription anti-emetic, for use as a complete therapeutic substitute for an IV anti-emetic at the time of chemotherapy treatment, not to exceed a 48-hour dosage regimen
Medicare Statute 4557
Medicare covers at the time of chemotherapy if regimen doesn't exceed 48 hours. Submit on the same claim as the chemotherapy.

? **Q0173** Trimethobenzamide hydrochloride, 250 mg, oral, FDA approved prescription anti-emetic, for use as a complete therapeutic substitute for an IV anti-emetic at the time of chemotherapy treatment, not to exceed a 48-hour dosage regimen
Medicare Statute 4557
Medicare covers at the time of chemotherapy if regimen doesn't exceed 48 hours. Submit on the same claim as the chemotherapy.

? **Q0174** Thiethylperazine maleate, 10 mg, oral, FDA approved prescription anti-emetic, for use as a complete therapeutic substitute for an IV anti-emetic at the time of chemotherapy treatment, not to exceed a 48-hour dosage regimen
Medicare Statute 4557
Medicare covers at the time of chemotherapy if regimen doesn't exceed 48 hours. Submit on the same claim as the chemotherapy.

? **Q0175** Perphenzaine, 4 mg, oral, FDA approved prescription anti-emetic, for use as a complete therapeutic substitute for an IV anti-emetic at the time of chemotherapy treatment, not to exceed a 48-hour dosage regimen
Medicare Statute 4557
Medicare covers at the time of chemotherapy if regimen doesn't exceed 48 hours. Submit on the same claim as the chemotherapy.

? **Q0176** Perphenzaine, 8mg, oral, FDA approved prescription anti-emetic, for use as a complete therapeutic substitute for an IV anti-emetic at the time of chemotherapy treatment, not to exceed a 48-hour dosage regimen
Medicare Statute 4557
Medicare covers at the time of chemotherapy if regimen doesn't exceed 48 hours. Submit on the same claim as the chemotherapy.

? **Q0177** Hydroxyzine pamoate, 25 mg, oral, FDA approved prescription anti-emetic, for use as a complete therapeutic substitute for an IV anti-emetic at the time of chemotherapy treatment, not to exceed a 48-hour dosage regimen
Medicare Statute 4557
Medicare covers at the time of chemotherapy if regimen doesn't exceed 48 hours. Submit on the same claim as the chemotherapy.

Q CODES (TEMPORARY)

? Q0178 Hydroxyzine pamoate, 50 mg, oral, FDA approved prescription anti-emetic, for use as a complete therapeutic substitute for an IV anti-emetic at the time of chemotherapy treatment, not to exceed a 48-hour dosage regimen
Medicare Statute 4557
Medicare covers at the time of chemotherapy if regimen doesn't exceed 48 hours. Submit on the same claim as the chemotherapy.

? Q0179 Ondansetron hydrochloride 8 mg, oral, FDA approved prescription anti-emetic, for use as a complete therapeutic substitute for an IV anti-emetic at the time of chemotherapy treatment, not to exceed a 48-hour dosage regimen
Medicare Statute 4557
Medicare covers at the time of chemotherapy if regimen doesn't exceed 48 hours. Submit on the same claim as the chemotherapy.

? Q0180 Dolasetron mesylate, 100 mg, oral, FDA approved prescription anti-emetic, for use as a complete therapeutic substitute for an IV anti-emetic at the time of chemotherapy treatment, not to exceed a 24-hour dosage regimen
Medicare Statute 4557
Medicare covers at the time of chemotherapy if regimen doesn't exceed 24 hours. Submit on the same claim as the chemotherapy.

? Q0181 Unspecified oral dosage form, FDA approved prescription anti-emetic, for use as a complete therapeutic substitute for an IV anti-emetic at the time of chemotherapy treatment, not to exceed a 48-hour dosage regimen
Medicare Statute 4557
Medicare covers at the time of chemotherapy if regimen doesn't exceed 48 hours. Submit on the same claim as the chemotherapy.

Q0183 Dermal tissue, of human origin, with and without other bioengineered or processed elements, but without metabolically active elements, per square centimeter

Q0184 Dermal tissue, of human origin, with or without other bioengineered or processed elements, with metabolically active elements, per square centimeter

Q0185 Dermal and epidermal tissue, of human origin, with or without bioengineered or processed elements, with metabolically active elements, per square centimeter

Q0186 Paramedic intercept, rural area, transport furnished by a volumnteer ambulance company which is prohibited by state law from billing third party payers

? Q0187 Factor VIIa (coagulation factor, recombinant) per 1.2 mg
MCM 2049

? Q1001 New technology intraocular lens category 1 as defined in *Federal Register* notice

? Q1002 New technology intraocular lens category 2 as defined in *Federal Register* notice

? Q1003 New technology intraocular lens category 3 as defined in *Federal Register* notice

? Q1004 New technology intraocular lens category 4 as defined in *Federal Register* notice

? Q1005 New technology intraocular lens category 5 as defined in *Federal Register* notice

Injection Codes for Epoetin Alpha (EPO)

? Q9920 Injection of EPO, per 1000 units, at patient HCT of 20 or less
MCM 4273.1
Medicare jurisdiction: DME regional carrier when self-administered.

? Q9921 Injection of EPO, per 1000 units, at patient HCT of 21
MCM 4273.1
Medicare jurisdiction: DME regional carrier when self-administered.

? Q9922 Injection of EPO, per 1000 units, at patient HCT of 22
MCM 4273.1
Medicare jurisdiction: DME regional carrier when self-administered.

? Q9923 Injection of EPO, per 1000 units, at patient HCT of 23
MCM 4273.1
Medicare jurisdiction: DME regional carrier when self-administered.

? Q9924 Injection of EPO, per 1000 units, at patient HCT of 24
MCM 4273.1
Medicare jurisdiction: DME regional carrier when self-administered.

? Q9925 Injection of EPO, per 1000 units, at patient HCT of 25
MCM 4273.1
Medicare jurisdiction: DME regional carrier when self-administered.

? Q9926 Injection of EPO, per 1000 units, at patient HCT of 26
MCM 4273.1
Medicare jurisdiction: DME regional carrier when self-administered.

? Q9927 Injection of EPO, per 1000 units, at patient HCT of 27
MCM 4273.1
Medicare jurisdiction: DME regional carrier when self-administered.

? Q9928 Injection of EPO, per 1000 units, at patient HCT of 28
MCM 4273.1
Medicare jurisdiction: DME regional carrier when self-administered.

? Q9929 Injection of EPO, per 1000 units, at patient HCT of 29
MCM 4273.1
Medicare jurisdiction: DME regional carrier when self-administered.

Q9930 Injection of EPO, per 1000 units, at patient HCT of 30
MCM 4273.1
Medicare jurisdiction: DME regional carrier when self-administered.

Q9931 Injection of EPO, per 1000 units, at patient HCT of 31
MCM 4273.1
Medicare jurisdiction: DME regional carrier when self-administered.

Q9932 Injection of EPO, per 1000 units, at patient HCT of 32
MCM 4273.1
Medicare jurisdiction: DME regional carrier when self-administered.

Q9933 Injection of EPO, per 1000 units, at patient HCT of 33
MCM 4273.1
Medicare jurisdiction: DME regional carrier when self-administered.

Q9934 Injection of EPO, per 1000 units, at patient HCT of 34
MCM 4273.1
Medicare jurisdiction: DME regional carrier when self-administered.

Q9935 Injection of EPO, per 1000 units, at patient HCT of 35
MCM 4273.1
Medicare jurisdiction: DME regional carrier when self-administered.

Q9936 Injection of EPO, per 1000 units, at patient HCT of 36
MCM 4273.1
Medicare jurisdiction: DME regional carrier when self-administered.

Q9937 Injection of EPO, per 1000 units, at patient HCT of 37
MCM 4273.1
Medicare jurisdiction: DME regional carrier when self-administered.

Q9938 Injection of EPO, per 1000 units, at patient HCT of 38
MCM 4273.1
Medicare jurisdiction: DME regional carrier when self-administered.

Q9939 Injection of EPO, per 1000 units, at patient HCT of 39
MCM 4273.1
Medicare jurisdiction: DME regional carrier when self-administered.

Q9940 Injection of EPO, per 1000 units, at patient HCT of 40 or above
MCM 4273.1
Medicare jurisdiction: DME regional carrier when self-administered.

Diagnostic Radiology Services R0000–R5999
R codes fall under the jurisdiction of the local carrier.

? ☑ R0070 Transportation of portable x-ray equipment and personnel to home or nursing home, per trip to facility or location, one patient seen
MCM 5244B, MCM 2070.4
Only a single, reasonable transportation charge is allowed for each trip the portable x-ray supplier makes to a location. When more than one patient is x-rayed at the same location, prorate the single allowable transport charge among all patients.

? ☑ R0075 Transportation of portable x-ray equipment and personnel to home or nursing home, per trip to facility or location, more than one patient seen, per patient
MCM 5244B, MCM 2070.4
Only a single, reasonable transportation charge is allowed for each trip the portable x-ray supplier makes to a location. When more than one patient is x-rayed at the same location, prorate the single allowable transport charge among all patients.

? ☑ R0076 Transportation of portable EKG to facility or location, per patient
CIM 50-15, MCM 2070.1, MCM 2070.4
Only a single, reasonable transportation charge is allowed for each trip the portable EKG supplier makes to a location. When more than one patient is tested at the same location, prorate the single allowable transport charge among all patients.

Temporary National Codes (Non-Medicare) (S0009–S9999)

- ⊘ ☑ **S0009** Injection, butorphanol tartrate, 1mg
- ⊘ ☑ **S0010** Injection, somatrem, 5 mg
- ⊘ ☑ **S0011** Injection, somatropin, 5 mg
- ⊘ ☑ **S0012** Butorphanol tartrate, nasal spray, 25 mg
- ⊘ ☑ **S0014** Tacrine hydrochloride, 10 mg
- ⊘ ☑ **S0016** Injection, amikacin sulfate, 500 mg
- ⊘ ☑ **S0017** Injection, aminocaproic acid, 5 grams
- ⊘ ☑ **S0020** Injection, bupivicaine hydrochloride, 30 ml
- ⊘ ☑ **S0021** Injection, ceftoperazone sodium, 1 gram
- ⊘ ☑ **S0023** Injection, cimetidine hydrochloride, 300 mg
- ⊘ ☑ **S0024** Injection, ciprofloxacin, 200 mg
- ⊘ ☑ **S0028** Injection, famotidine, 20 mg
- ⊘ ☑ **S0029** Injection, fluconazole, 400 mg
- ⊘ ☑ **S0030** Injection, metronidazole, 500 mg
- ⊘ ☑ **S0032** Injection, nafcillin sodium, 2 grams
- ⊘ ☑ **S0034** Injection, ofloxacin, 400 mg
- ⊘ ☑ **S0039** Injection, sulfamethoxazole and trimethoprim, 10 ml
- ⊘ ☑ **S0040** Injection, ticarcillin disodium and clavulanate potassium, 3.1 grams
- ⊘ ☑ **S0071** Injection, acyclovir sodium, 50 mg
- ⊘ ☑ **S0072** Injection, amikacin sulfate, 100 mg
- ⊘ ☑ **S0073** Injection, aztreonam, 500 mg
- ⊘ ☑ **S0074** Injection, cefotetan disodium, 500 mg
- ⊘ ☑ **S0077** Injection, clindamycin phosphate, 300 mg
- ⊘ ☑ **S0078** Injection, fosphenytoin sodium, 750 mg
- ⊘ ☑ **S0080** Injection, pentamidine isethionate, 300 mg
- ⊘ ☑ **S0081** Injection, piperacillin sodium, 500 mg
- ⊘ ☑ **S0090** Sildenafil citrate, 25 mg
- ⊘ ☑ **S0096** Injection, itraconazole, 200 mg
- ⊘ ☑ **S0097** Injection, ibutilide fumarate, 1 mg
- ⊘ ☑ **S0098** Injection, sodium ferric gluconate complex in sucrose, 62.5 mg
- ⊘ **S0601** Screening proctoscopy
- ⊘ **S0605** Digital rectal examination, annual
- ⊘ **S0610** Annual gynecological examination, new patient
- ⊘ **S0612** Annual gynecological examination, established patient
- ⊘ **S0620** Routine ophthalmological examination including refraction; new patient
- ⊘ **S0621** Routine ophthalmological examination including refraction; established patient
- ⊘ **S0800** Laser in situ keratomileusis (LASIK)
- ⊘ **S0810** Photorefractive keratectomy (PRK)
- ⊘ **S2050** Donor enterectomy, with preparation and maintenance of allograft; from cadaver donor
- ⊘ **S2052** Transplantation of small intestine allograft
- ⊘ **S2053** Transplantation of small intestine and liver allografts
- ⊘ **S2054** Transplantation of multivisceral organs
- ⊘ **S2055** Harvesting of donor multivisceral organs, with preparation and maintenance of allografts; from cadaver donor
- ⊘ **S2109** Autologous chondrocyte transplantation (preparation of autologous cultured chondrocytes)
- ⊘ **S2190** Subcutaneous implantation of medication pellet(s)
- ⊘ **S2204** Transmyocardial laser revascularization
- ⊘ **S2205** Minimally invasive direct coronary artery bypass surgery involving mini-thoracotomy or mini-sternotomy surgery, performed under direct vision; using arterial graft(s), single coronary arterial graft
- ⊘ **S2206** Minimally invasive direct coronary artery bypass surgery involving mini-thoracotomy or mini-sternotomy surgery, performed under direct vision; using arterial graft(s), two coronary arterial grafts
- ⊘ **S2207** Minimally invasive direct coronary artery bypass surgery involving mini-thoracotomy or mini-sternotomy surgery, performed under direct vision; using venous graft only, single coronary venous graft
- ⊘ **S2208** Minimally invasive direct coronary artery bypass surgery involving mini-thoracotomy or mini-sternotomy surgery, performed under direct vision; using single arterial and venous graft(s), single venous graft
- ⊘ **S2209** Minimally invasive direct coronary artery bypass surgery involving mini-thoracotomy or mini-sternotomy surgery, performed under direct vision; using two arterial grafts and single venous graft
- ⊘ **S2210** Cryosurgical ablation (in situ destruction) of tumorous tissue, one or more lesions; liver

TEMPORARY NATIONAL CODES (NON-MEDICARE)

- ⊘ **S2300** Arthroscopy, shoulder, surgical; with thermally-induced capsulorrhaphy
- ⊘ **S2350** Diskectomy, anterior, with decompression of spinal cord and/or nerve root(s), including osteophytectomy; lumbar, single interspace
- ⊘ **S2351** Diskectomy, anterior, with decompression of spinal cord and/or nerve root(s), including osteophytectomy; lumbar, each additional interspace (list separately in addition to code for primary procedure)
- ⊘ **S3645** HIV-1 antibody testing of oral mucosal transudate
- ⊘ **S3650** Saliva test, hormone level; during menopause
- ⊘ **S3652** Saliva test, hormone level; to assess preterm labor risk
- ⊘ **S8035** Magnetic source imaging
- ⊘ **S8040** Topographic brain mapping
- ⊘ **S8048** Isolated limb perfusion
- ⊘ **S8049** Intraoperative radiation therapy (single administration)
- ⊘ **S8060** Supply of contrast material for use in echocardiography (use in addition to echocardiography code)
- ⊘ **S8092** Electron beam computed tomography (also known as ultrafast CT, cine CT)
- ⊘ **S8095** Wig (for medically-induced hair loss)
- ⊘ **S8096** Portable peak flow meter
- ⊘ **S8110** Peak expiratory flow rate (physician services)
- ⊘ **S8200** Chest compression vest
- ⊘ **S8205** Chest compression system generator and hoses (for use with chest compression vest — S8200)
- ⊘ **S8260** Oral orthotic for treatment of sleep apnea, includes fitting, fabrication, and materials
- ⊘ **S8300** Sacral nerve stimulation test lead kit
- ⊘ **S8950** Complex lymphedema therapy, each 15 minutes
- ⊘ **S9001** Home uterine monitor with or without associated nursing services
- ⊘ **S9022** Digital subtraction angiography (use in addition to CPT code for the procedure for further identification)
- ⊘ **S9023** Xenon regional cerebral blood flow studies
- ⊘ **S9024** Paranasal sinus ultrasound
- ⊘ **S9033** Gait analysis
- ⊘ **S9055** Procuren or other growth factor preparation to promote wound healing
- ⊘ **S9056** Coma stimulation per diem
- ⊘ **S9075** Smoking cessation treatment
- ⊘ **S9085** Meniscal allograft transplantation
- ⊘ **S9090** Vertebral axial decompression, per session
- ⊘ ☑ **S9122** Home health aide or certified nurse assistant, providing care in the home; per hour
- ⊘ ☑ **S9123** Nursing care, in the home; by registered nurse, per hour
- ⊘ ☑ **S9124** Nursing care, in the home; by licensed practical nurse, per hour
- ⊘ ☑ **S9125** Respite care, in the home, per diem
- ⊘ ☑ **S9126** Hospice care, in the home, per diem
- ⊘ ☑ **S9127** Social work visit, in the home, per diem
- ⊘ ☑ **S9128** Speech therapy, in the home, per diem
- ⊘ ☑ **S9129** Occupational therapy, in the home, per diem
- ⊘ **S9140** Diabetic management program, follow-up visit to non-MD provider
- ⊘ **S9141** Diabetic management program, follow-up visit to MD provider
- ⊘ **S9455** Diabetic management program, group session
- ⊘ ☑ **S9460** Diabetic management program, nurse visit
- ⊘ ☑ **S9465** Diabetic management program, dietitian visit
- ⊘ ☑ **S9470** Nutritional counseling, dietitian visit
- ⊘ ☑ **S9472** Cardiac rehabilitation program, non-physician provider, per diem
- ⊘ ☑ **S9473** Pulmonary rehabilitation program, non-physician provider, per diem
- ⊘ ☑ **S9474** Enterostomal therapy by a registered nurse certified in enterostomal therapy, per diem
- ⊘ ☑ **S9475** Ambulatory setting substance abuse treatment or detoxification services, per diem
- ⊘ ☑ **S9480** Intensive outpatient psychiatric services, per diem
- ⊘ ☑ **S9485** Crisis intervention mental health services, per diem
- ⊘ ☑ **S9524** Nursing services related to home IV therapy, per diem
- ⊘ **S9527** Insertion of a peripherally inserted central venous catheter (PICC), including nursing services and all supplies
- ⊘ **S9528** Insertion of midline central venous catheter, including nursing services and all supplies

☑ Quantity Alert   ● New Code   ▲ Revised Code

- ⊘ ☑ **S9543** Administration of medication, intramuscularly, epidurally or subcutaneously, in the home setting, including all nursing care, equipment, and supplies; per diem
- ⊘ **S9990** Services provided as part of a phase II clinical trial
- ⊘ **S9991** Services provided as part of a phase III clinical trial
- ⊘ **S9992** Transportation costs to and from trial location and local transportation costs (e.g., fares for taxicab or bus) for clinical trial participant and one caregiver/companion
- ⊘ **S9994** Lodging costs (e.g., hotel charges) for clinical trial participant and one caregiver/companion
- ⊘ **S9996** Meals for clinical trial participant and one caregiver/companion
- ⊘ **S9999** Sales tax

Vision Services V0000–V2999

V codes fall under the jurisdiction of the DME regional carrier, unless incident to other services or otherwise noted.

Frames

? **V2020** Frames, purchases
MCM 2130

⊘ **V2025** Deluxe frame
MCM 3045.4

Spectacle Lenses

If procedure code 92390 or 92395 is reported, recode with the specific lens type listed below. For aphakic temporary spectacle correction, see 92358.

Single Vision, Glass, or Plastic

- **V2100** Sphere, single vision, plano to plus or minus 4.00, per lens
- **V2101** Sphere, single vision, plus or minus 4.12 to plus or minus 7.00d, per lens
- **V2102** Sphere, single vision, plus or minus 7.12 to plus or minus 20.00d, per lens
- **V2103** Spherocylinder, single vision, plano to plus or minus 4.00d sphere, 0.12 to 2.00d cylinder, per lens
- **V2104** Spherocylinder, single vision, plano to plus or minus 4.00d sphere, 2.12 to 4.00d cylinder, per lens
- **V2105** Spherocylinder, single vision, plano to plus or minus 4.00d sphere, 4.25 to 6.00d cylinder, per lens
- **V2106** Spherocylinder, single vision, plano to plus or minus 4.00d sphere, over 6.00d cylinder, per lens
- **V2107** Spherocylinder, single vision, plus or minus 4.25 to plus or minus 7.00 sphere, 0.12 to 2.00d cylinder, per lens
- **V2108** Spherocylinder, single vision, plus or minus 4.25d to plus or minus 7.00d sphere, 2.12 to 4.00d cylinder, per lens
- **V2109** Spherocylinder, single vision, plus or minus 4.25 to plus or minus 7.00d sphere, 4.25 to 6.00d cylinder, per lens
- **V2110** Spherocylinder, single vision, plus or minus 4.25 to 7.00d sphere, over 6.00d cylinder, per lens
- **V2111** Spherocylinder, single vision, plus or minus 7.25 to plus or minus 12.00d sphere, 0.25 to 2.25d cylinder, per lens
- **V2112** Spherocylinder, single vision, plus or minus 7.25 to plus or minus 12.00d sphere, 2.25d to 4.00d cylinder, per lens
- **V2113** Spherocylinder, single vision, plus or minus 7.25 to plus or minus 12.00d sphere, 4.25 to 6.00d cylinder, per lens
- **V2114** Spherocylinder, single vision sphere over plus or minus 12.00d, per lens
- **V2115** Lenticular (myodisc), per lens, single vision
- **V2116** Lenticular lens, nonaspheric, per lens, single vision
- **V2117** Lenticular, aspheric, per lens, single vision
- **V2118** Aniseikonic lens, single vision
- **V2199** Not otherwise classified, single vision lens

Bifocal, Glass, or Plastic

- **V2200** Sphere, bifocal, plano to plus or minus 4.00d, per lens
- **V2201** Sphere, bifocal, plus or minus 4.12 to plus or minus 7.00d, per lens
- **V2202** Sphere, bifocal, plus or minus 7.12 to plus or minus 20.00d, per lens
- **V2203** Spherocylinder, bifocal, plano to plus or minus 4.00d sphere, 0.12 to 2.00d cylinder, per lens
- **V2204** Spherocylinder, bifocal, plano to plus or minus 4.00d sphere, 2.12 to 4.00d cylinder, per lens
- **V2205** Spherocylinder, bifocal, plano to plus or minus 4.00d sphere, 4.25 to 6.00d cylinder, per lens
- **V2206** Spherocylinder, bifocal, plano to plus or minus 4.00d sphere, over 6.00d cylinder, per lens
- **V2207** Spherocylinder, bifocal, plus or minus 4.25 to plus or minus 7.00d sphere, 0.12 to 2.00d cylinder, per lens
- **V2208** Spherocylinder, bifocal, plus or minus 4.25 to plus or minus 7.00d sphere, 2.12 to 4.00d cylinder, per lens
- **V2209** Spherocylinder, bifocal, plus or minus 4.25 to plus or minus 7.00d sphere, 4.25 to 6.00d cylinder, per lens
- **V2210** Spherocylinder, bifocal, plus or minus 4.25 to plus or minus 7.00d sphere, over 6.00d cylinder, per lens
- **V2211** Spherocylinder, bifocal, plus or minus 7.25 to plus or minus 12.00d sphere, 0.25 to 2.25d cylinder, per lens
- **V2212** Spherocylinder, bifocal, plus or minus 7.25 to plus or minus 12.00d sphere, 2.25 to 4.00d cylinder, per lens
- **V2213** Spherocylinder, bifocal, plus or minus 7.25 to plus or minus 12.00d sphere, 4.25 to 6.00d cylinder, per lens

- ☑ **V2214** Spherocylinder, bifocal, sphere over plus or minus 12.00d, per lens
- ☑ **V2215** Lenticular (myodisc), per lens, bifocal
- ☑ **V2216** Lenticular, nonaspheric, per lens, bifocal
- **V2217** Lenticular, aspheric lens, bifocal
- ☑ **V2218** Aniseikonic, per lens, bifocal
- ☑ **V2219** Bifocal seg width over 28mm
- ☑ **V2220** Bifocal add over 3.25d
- **V2299** Specialty bifocal (by report)
  Pertinent documentation to evaluate medical appropriateness should be included when this code is reported.

Trifocal, Glass, or Plastic

- ☑ **V2300** Sphere, trifocal, plano to plus or minus 4.00d, per lens
- ☑ **V2301** Sphere, trifocal, plus or minus 4.12 to plus or minus 7.00d per lens
- ☑ **V2302** Sphere, trifocal, plus or minus 7.12 to plus or minus 20.00, per lens
- ☑ **V2303** Spherocylinder, trifocal, plano to plus or minus 4.00d sphere, 0.12 to 2.00d cylinder, per lens
- ☑ **V2304** Spherocylinder, trifocal, plano to plus or minus 4.00d sphere, 2.25 to 4.00d cylinder, per lens
- ☑ **V2305** Spherocylinder, trifocal, plano to plus or minus 4.00d sphere, 4.25 to 6.00 cylinder, per lens
- ☑ **V2306** Spherocylinder, trifocal, plano to plus or minus 4.00d sphere, over 6.00d cylinder, per lens
- ☑ **V2307** Spherocylinder, trifocal, plus or minus 4.25 to plus or minus 7.00d sphere, 0.12 to 2.00d cylinder, per lens
- ☑ **V2308** Spherocylinder, trifocal, plus or minus 4.25 to plus or minus 7.00d sphere, 2.12 to 4.00d cylinder, per lens
- ☑ **V2309** Spherocylinder, trifocal, plus or minus 4.25 to plus or minus 7.00d sphere, 4.25 to 6.00d cylinder, per lens
- ☑ **V2310** Spherocylinder, trifocal, plus or minus 4.25 to plus or minus 7.00d sphere, over 6.00d cylinder, per lens
- ☑ **V2311** Spherocylinder, trifocal, plus or minus 7.25 to plus or minus 12.00d sphere, 0.25 to 2.25d cylinder, per lens
- ☑ **V2312** Spherocylinder, trifocal, plus or minus 7.25 to plus or minus 12.00d sphere, 2.25 to 4.00d cylinder, per lens
- ☑ **V2313** Spherocylinder, trifocal, plus or minus 7.25 to plus or minus 12.00d sphere, 4.25 to 6.00d cylinder, per lens
- ☑ **V2314** Spherocylinder, trifocal, sphere over plus or minus 12.00d, per lens
- ☑ **V2315** Lenticular (myodisc), per lens, trifocal
- ☑ **V2316** Lenticular nonaspheric, per lens, trifocal
- **V2317** Lenticular, aspheric lens, trifocal
- **V2318** Aniseikonic lens, trifocal
- ☑ **V2319** Trifocal seg width over 28 mm
- ☑ **V2320** Trifocal add over 3.25d
- **V2399** Specialty trifocal (by report)
  Pertinent documentation to evaluate medical appropriateness should be included when this code is reported.

Variable Asphericity Lens, Glass, or Plastic

- ☑ **V2410** Variable asphericity lens, single vision, full field, glass or plastic, per lens
- ☑ **V2430** Variable asphericity lens, bifocal, full field, glass or plastic, per lens
- **V2499** Variable sphericity lens, other type

Contact Lens

If procedure code 92391 or 92396 is reported, recode with specific lens type listed below (per lens).

- ☑ **V2500** Contact lens, PMMA, spherical, per lens
- ☑ **V2501** Contact lens, PMMA, toric or prism ballast, per lens
- ☑ **V2502** Contact lens, PMMA, bifocal, per lens
- ☑ **V2503** Contact lens, PMMA, color vision deficiency, per lens
- ☑ **V2510** Contact lens, gas permeable, spherical, per lens
- ☑ **V2511** Contact lens, gas permeable, toric, prism ballast, per lens
- ☑ **V2512** Contact lens, gas permeable, bifocal, per lens
- ☑ **V2513** Contact lens, gas permeable, extended wear, per lens
- ? ☑ **V2520** Contact lens, hydrophilic, spherical, per lens
  CIM 45-7, CIM 65-1
  Hydrophilic contact lenses are covered by Medicare only for aphakic patients.
- ? ☑ **V2521** Contact lens, hydrophilic, toric, or prism ballast, per lens
  CIM 45-7, CIM 65-1
  Hydrophilic contact lenses are covered by Medicare only for aphakic patients.
- ? ☑ **V2522** Contact lens, hydrophilic, bifocal, per lens
  CIM 45-7, CIM 65-1
  Hydrophilic contact lenses are covered by Medicare only for aphakic patients.

VISION SERVICES

? ☑ V2523 Contact lens, hydrophilic, extended wear, per lens
CIM 45-7, CIM 65-1
Hydrophilic contact lenses are covered by Medicare only for aphakic patients.

➡ ☑ **V2530** Contact lens, scleral, gas impermeable, per lens (for contact lens modification, see CPT Level I code 92325)
CIM 45-7, CIM 65-1

? ☑ V2531 Contact lens, scleral, gas permeable, per lens (for contact lens modification, see CPT Level I code 92325)
CIM 65-3

➡ **V2599** Contact lens, other type

Vision Aids

If procedure code 92392 is reported, recode with specific systems below.

➡ **V2600** Hand held low vision aids and other nonspectacle mounted aids

➡ **V2610** Single lens spectacle mounted low vision aids

➡ **V2615** Telescopic and other compound lens system, including distance vision telescopic, near vision telescopes and compound microscopic lens system

Prosthetic Eye

? V2623 Prosthetic eye, plastic, custom
MCM 2133

➡ **V2624** Polishing/resurfacing of ocular prosthesis

➡ **V2625** Enlargement of ocular prosthesis

➡ **V2626** Reduction of ocular prosthesis

? V2627 Scleral cover shell
CIM 65-3
A scleral shell covers the cornea and the anterior sclera. Medicare covers a scleral shell when it is prescribed as an artificial support to a shrunken and sightless eye or as a barrier in the treatment of severe dry eye.

➡ **V2628** Fabrication and fitting of ocular conformer

➡ **V2629** Prosthetic eye, other type

Intraocular Lenses

? V2630 Anterior chamber intraocular lens
MCM 2130
The IOL must be FDA-approved for reimbursement. Medicare payment for an IOL is included in the payment for ASC facility services. Medicare jurisdiction: local carrier.

? V2631 Iris supported intraocular lens
MCM 2130
The IOL must be FDA-approved for reimbursement. Medicare payment for an IOL is included in the payment for ASC facility services. Medicare jurisdiction: local carrier.

? V2632 Posterior chamber intraocular lens
MCM 2130
The IOL must be FDA-approved for reimbursement. Medicare payment for an IOL is included in the payment for ASC facility services. Medicare jurisdiction: local carrier.

Miscellaneous

➡ ☑ **V2700** Balance lens, per lens

➡ ☑ **V2710** Slab off prism, glass or plastic, per lens

➡ ☑ **V2715** Prism, per lens

➡ ☑ **V2718** Press-on lens, Fresnell prism, per lens

➡ ☑ **V2730** Special base curve, glass or plastic, per lens

? ☑ V2740 Tint, plastic, rose 1 or 2, per lens
MCM 2130B
LT, RT, VP

? ☑ V2741 Tint, plastic, other than rose 1 or 2, per lens
MCM 2130B

? ☑ V2742 Tint, glass, rose 1 or 2, per lens
MCM 2130B

? ☑ V2743 Tint, glass, other than rose 1 or 2, per lens
MCM 2130B

? ☑ V2744 Tint, photochromatic, per lens
MCM 2130B

? ☑ V2750 Antireflective coating, per lens
MCM 2130B

? ☑ V2755 U-V lens, per lens
MCM 2130B

➡ ☑ **V2760** Scratch resistant coating, per lens

➡ ☑ **V2770** Occluder lens, per lens

➡ ☑ **V2780** Oversize lens, per lens

➡ ☑ **V2781** Progressive lens, per lens

➡ **V2785** Processing, preserving and transporting corneal tissue
Medicare jurisdiction: local carrier.

➡ **V2799** Vision service, miscellaneous
Determine if an alternative national HCPCS Level II, a local HCPCS Level III code, or a CPT code better describes the service being reported. This code should be used only if a more specific code is unavailable.

Hearing Services V5000–V5999

Routine physical checkups for the purpose of prescribing, fitting or changing hearing aids and examinations for hearing aids are not covered by Medicare. These codes are for nonphysician services.

Hearing services fall under the jurisdiction of the local carrier unless incidental or otherwise noted.

⊘ **V5008** Hearing screening
MCM 2320

⊘ **V5010** Assessment for hearing aid
Medicare statute 1862.A7

⊘ **V5011** Fitting/orientation/checking of hearing aid
Medicare statute 1862.A7

⊘ **V5014** Repair/modification of a hearing aid
Medicare statute 1862.A7

⊘ **V5020** Conformity evaluation
Medicare statute 1862.A7

⊘ **V5030** Hearing aid, monaural, body worn, air conduction
Medicare statute 1862.A7

⊘ **V5040** Hearing aid, monaural, body worn, bone conduction
Medicare statute 1862.A7

⊘ **V5050** Hearing aid, monaural, in the ear
Medicare statute 1862.A7

⊘ **V5060** Hearing aid, monaural, behind the ear
Medicare statute 1862.A7

⊘ **V5070** Glasses, air conduction
Medicare statute 1862.A7

⊘ **V5080** Glasses, bone conduction
Medicare statute 1862.A7

⊘ **V5090** Dispensing fee, unspecified hearing aid
Medicare statute 1862.A7

⊘ **V5100** Hearing aid, bilateral, body worn
Medicare statute 1862.A7

⊘ **V5110** Dispensing fee, bilateral
Medicare statute 1862.A7

⊘ **V5120** Binaural, body
Medicare statute 1862.A7

⊘ **V5130** Binaural, in the ear
Medicare statute 1862.A7

⊘ **V5140** Binaural, behind the ear
Medicare statute 1862.A7

⊘ **V5150** Binaural, glasses
Medicare statute 1862.A7

⊘ **V5160** Dispensing fee, binaural
Medicare statute 1862.A7

⊘ **V5170** Hearing aid, CROS, in the ear
Medicare statute 1862.A7

⊘ **V5180** Hearing aid, CROS, behind the ear
Medicare statute 1862.A7

⊘ **V5190** Hearing aid, CROS, glasses
Medicare statute 1862.A7

⊘ **V5200** Dispensing fee, CROS
Medicare statute 1862.A7

⊘ **V5210** Hearing aid, BICROS, in the ear
Medicare statute 1862.A7

⊘ **V5220** Hearing aid, BICROS, behind the ear
Medicare statute 1862.A7

⊘ **V5230** Hearing aid, BICROS, glasses
Medicare statute 1862.A7

⊘ **V5240** Dispensing fee, BICROS
Medicare statute 1862.A7

? **V5299** Hearing service, miscellaneous
MCM 2320
Determine if an alternative national HCPCS Level II, a local HCPCS Level III code, or a CPT code better describes the service being reported. This code should be used only if a more specific code is unavailable.

Speech-Language Pathology Services

⊘ **V5336** Repair/modification of augmentative communicative system or device (excludes adaptive hearing aid)
Medicare statute 1862.A7
Medicare jurisdiction: DME regional carrier.

? **V5362** Speech screening
MCM 2320
Medicare jurisdiction: local carrier.

? **V5363** Language screening
MCM 2320
Medicare jurisdiction: local carrier.

? **V5364** Dysphagia screening
MCM 2320
Medicare jurisdiction: local carrier.

Table of Drugs

INTRODUCTION AND DIRECTIONS

The HCPCS 2000 Table of Drugs is designed to quickly and easily direct the user to drug names and their corresponding codes. Both generic and brand or trade names are alphabetically listed in the "Drug Name" column of the table. The associated J, K, or Q code is given only for the generic name of the drug. Brand or trade name drugs are cross-referenced to the appropriate generic drug name.

The "Amount" column lists the stated amount for the referenced generic drug as provided by the Health Care Financing Administration (HCFA). "Up to" listings are inclusive of all quantities up to and including the listed amount. All other listings are for the amount of the drug as listed. The editors recognize that the availability of some drugs in the quantities listed is dependent on many variables beyond the control of the clinical ordering clerk. The availability in your area of regularly used drugs in the most cost-effective quantities should be relayed to your third-party payers.

The "Route of Administration" column addresses the most common methods of delivering the referenced generic drug as described in current pharmaceutical literature. The official definitions for Level II drug codes generally describe administration other than by oral method. Therefore, with a handful of exceptions, oral-delivered options for most drugs are omitted from the Route of Administration column. The following abbreviations and listings are used in the Route of Administration column:

IA — Intra-arterial administration

IV — Intravenous administration

IM — Intramuscular administration

IT — Intrathecal

SC — Subcutaneous administration

INH — Administration by inhaled solution

INJ — Injection not otherwise specified

VAR — Various routes of administration

OTH — Other routes of administration

ORAL — Administered orally

Intravenous administration includes all methods, such as gravity infusion, injections, and timed pushes. When several routes of administration are listed, the first listing is simply the first, or most common, method as described in current reference literature. The "VAR" posting denotes various routes of administration and is used for drugs that are commonly administered into joints, cavities, tissues, or topical applications, in addition to other parenteral administrations. Listings posted with "OTH" alert the user to other administration methods, such as suppositories or catheter injections.

A dash (—) in a column signifies that no information is available to post for that particular listing.

Please be reminded that the Table of Drugs, as well as all HCPCS Level II National definitions and listings, constitutes a post-treatment medical reference for billing purposes only. Although the editors have exercised all normal precautions to ensure the accuracy of the table and related material, the use of any of this information to select medical treatment is entirely inappropriate.

A

Drug	Dose	Route	Code
Abbokinase, see Urokinase			
Abbokinase, Open Cath, see Urokinase			
Abciximab	10 mg	IV	J0130
Abelcet, see Amphotericin B, any lipid formulation			
Acetazolamide sodium	up to 500 mg	IM, IV	J1120
Acetylcysteine	10%, per ml	INH	J7610
	20%, per ml	INH	J7615
Acetylcysteine, inhalation solution, unit dose form	per gram	INH	J7608
Achromycin, see Tetracycline			
ACTH, see Corticotropin			
Acthar, see Corticotropin			
Actimmune, see Interferon gamma 1-B			
Activase, see Alteplase recombinant			
Acyclovir sodium	50 mg	INJ	S0071
Adenocard, see Adenosine			
Adenosine	6 mg	IV	J0150
	90 mg	IV	J0151
Adrenalin Chloride, see Adrenalin, epinephrine			
Adrenalin, epinephrine	up to 1 ml ampule	SC, IM	J0170
Adriamycin PFS, see Doxorubicin HCl			
Adriamycin RDF, see Doxorubicin HCl			
Adrucil, see Fluorouracil			
A-hydroCort, see Hydrocortisone sodium phosphate			
Akineton, see Biperiden			
Albumin Human, 5%	500 ml	IV	Q0156
Albumin Human, 25%	50 ml	IV	Q0157
Albumarc, see Albumin Human			
Albuterol sulfate	0.083%, per ml	INH	J7620
	0.5%, per ml	INH	J7625
Albuterol, inhalation solution, concentrated form	per mg	INH	J7618
Albuterol, inhalation solution, unit dose form	per mg	INH	J7619
Aldesleukin	per single use vial	IM, IV	J9015
Aldomet, see Methyldopate HCl			
Alferon N, see Interferon alfa-n3			
Alglucerase	per 10 units	IV	J0205
Alkaban-AQ, see Vinblastine sulfate			
Alkeran, see Melphalan, oral			
Alpha 1-proteinase inhibitor, human	per 10 mg	IV	J0256
Alprostadil	per 1.25 mcg	IV	J0270
Alprostadil, urethral suppository	—	OTHER	J0275
Alteplase recombinant	per 10 mg	IV	J2996
Alupent, see Metaproterenol sulfate or Metaproterenol, compounded			
Amcort, see Triamcinolone diacetate			
A-methaPred, see Methylprednisolone sodium succinate			
Amikacin sulfate	100 mg	INJ	S0072
	500 mg	INJ	S0016
Aminocaproic acid	5 g	INJ	S0017
Amifostine	500 mg	IV, INJ	J0207
Aminophylline/Aminophyllin	up to 250 mg	IV	J0280
Amitriptyline HCl	up to 20 mg	IM	J1320
Amobarbital	up to 125 mg	IM, IV	J0300
Amphotec, see Amphotericin B, any lipid formulation			
Amphotericin B	50 mg	IV	J0285
Amphotericin B, any lipid formulation	50 mg	IV	J0286

Ampicillin	500 mg	IM, IV	**J0290**
Ampicillin sodium/sulbactam sodium	1.5 gm	IM, IV	**J0295**

Amygdalin, *see* Laetrile, Amygdalin, vitamin B-17
Amytal, *see* Amobarbital
Anabolin LA 100, *see* Nandrolone decanoate
Ancef, *see* Cefazolin sodium
Andrest 90-4, *see* Testosterone enanthate and estradiol valerate
Andro-Cyp, *see* Testosterone cypionate
Andro-Cyp 200, *see* Testosterone cypionate
Andro L.A. 200, *see* Testosterone enanthate
Andro-Estro 90-4, *see* Testosterone enanthate and estradiol valerate
Andro/Fem, *see* Testosterone cypionate and estradiol cypionate
Androgyn L.A., *see* Testosterone enanthate and estradiol valerate
Androlone-50, *see* Nandrolone phenpropionate
Androlone-D 100, *see* Nandrolone decanoate
Andronaq-50, *see* Testosterone suspension
Andronaq-LA, *see* Testosterone cypionate
Andronate-200, *see* Testosterone cypionate
Andronate-100, *see* Testosterone cypionate
Andropository 100, *see* Testosterone enanthate
Andryl 200, *see* Testosterone enanthate
Anectine, *see* Succinylcholine chloride
Anergan 25, *see* Promethazine HCl
Anergan 50, *see* Promethazine HCl

Anistreplase	30 units	IV	**J0350**
Anti-inhibitor	per IU		**J7198**

Antispas, *see* Dicyclomine HCl

Antithrombin III (human)	per IU	IV	**J7197**

A.P.L., *see* Chorionic gonadotropin
Apresoline, *see* Hydralazine HCl
AquaMEPHYTON, *see* Phytonadione
Aralen, *see* Chloroquine HCl
Aramine, *see* Metaraminol

Arbutamine HCl	1 mg	IV	**J0395**

Aredia, *see* Pamidronate disodium
Arfonad, *see* Trimethaphan camsylate
Aristocort Forte, *see* Triamcinolone diacetate
Aristocort Intralesional, *see* Triamcinolone diacetate
Aristospan Intra-Articular, *see* Triamcinolone hexacetonide
Aristospan Intralesional, *see* Triamcinolone hexacetonide
Arrestin, *see* Trimethobenzamide HCl

Asparaginase	10,000 units	IV, IM	**J9020**

Astramorph PF, *see* Morphine sulfate
Astromorph, *see* Morphine sulfate
Atgam, *see* Lymphocyte immune globulin
Ativan, *see* Lorazepam

Atropine sulfate	up to 0.3 mg	IV, IM, SC	**J0460**
Atropine, inhalation solution, concentrated form	per mg	INH	**J7635**
Atropine, inhalation solution, unit dose form	per mg	INH	**J7636**

Atrovent, *see* Ipratropium bromide

Aurothioglucose	up to 50 mg	IM	**J2910**

Autoplex T, *see* Hemophilia clotting factors

Azathioprine	50 mg	ORAL	**J7500, K0119**
Azathioprine, parenteral	100 mg	IV	**J7501, K0120**

Azithromycin	500 mg	INJ	J0456
Azithromycin dihydrate	1g	ORAL	Q0144
Aztreonam	500 mg	INJ	S0073

B

Baclofen	10 mg	IT	J0475
	50 mcg	IT	J0476

Bactocill, see Oxacillin sodium
BAL in oil, see Dimercaprol
Banflex, see Orphenadrine citrate

BCG (Bacillus Calmette and Guérin), live	per vial	IV	J9031

Bena-D 10, see Diphenhydramine HCl
Bena-D 50, see Diphenhydramine HCl
Benadryl, see Diphenhydramine HCl
Benahist 10, see Diphenhydramine HCl
Benahist 50, see Diphenhydramine HCl
Ben-Allergin-50, see Diphenhydramine HCl
Benoject-10, see Diphenhydramine HCl
Benoject-50, see Diphenhydramine HCl
Bentyl, see Dicyclomine

Benzquinamide HCl	up to 50 mg	IM, IV	J0510
Benztropine mesylate	per 1 mg	IM, IV	J0515

Berubigen, see Vitamin B-12 cyanocobalamin
Betalin 12, see Vitamin B-12 cyanocobalamin
Betameth, see Betamethasone sodium phosphate

Betamethasone acetate & betamethasone sodium phosphate	3 mg of each	IM	J0702
Betamethasone sodium phosphate	4 mg	IM, IV	J0704

Betaseron, see Interferon beta-1b

Bethanechol chloride	up to 5 mg	SC	J0520

Bicillin L-A, see Penicillin G benzathine
Bicillin C-R 900/300, see Penicillin G procaine and penicillin G benzathine
Bicillin C-R, see Penicillin G benzathine and penicillin G procaine
BiCNU, see Carmustine

Biperiden lactate	per 5 mg	IM, IV	J0190
Bitolterol mesylate 0.2%	per 10 ml	INH	J7627
Bitolterol mesylate, inhalation solution, concentrated form	per mg	INH	J7628
Bitolterol mesylate, inhalation solution, unit dose form	per mg	INH	J7629

Blenoxane, see Bleomycin sulfate

Bleomycin sulfate	15 units	IM, IV, SC	J9040
Botulinum toxin type A	per unit	IM	J0585

Brethine, see Terbutaline sulfate or Terbutaline, compounded
Bricanyl Subcutaneous, see Terbutaline sulfate

Brompheniramine maleate	per 10 mg	IM, SC, IV	J0945

Bronkephrine, see Ethylnorepinephrine HCl
Bronkosol, see Isoetharine HCl

Bupivicaine HCl	30 ml	INJ	S0020
Butorphanol tartrate	25 mg	INH	S0012

C

Caine-1, see Lidocaine HCl
Caine-2, see Lidocaine HCl
Calcijex, see Calcitriol
Calcimar, see Calcitonin-salmon

Drug	Dose	Route	Code
Calcitonin-salmon	up to 400 units	SC, IM	J0630
Calcitriol	1 mcg ampule	IM	J0635
Calcium Disodium Versenate, *see* Edetate calcium disodium			
Calcium EDTA, *see* edetate calcium disodium			
Calcium gluconate	per 10 ml	IV	J0610
Calcium glycerophosphate and calcium lactate	per 10 ml	IM, SC	J0620
Capecitabine	150 mg	Oral	J8520
	500 mg	Oral	J8521
Calphosan, *see* Calcium glycerophosphate and calcium lactate			
Carbocaine, *see* Mepivacaine			
Carboplatin	50 mg	IV	J9045
Carmustine	100 mg	IV	J9050
Carnitor, *see* Levocarnitine			
Cefadyl, *see* Cephapirin Sodium			
Cefazolin sodium	500 mg	IV, IM	J0690
Cefizox, *see* Ceftizoxime soduim			
Cefonicid sodium	1 g	IV	J0695
Cefotaxime sodium	per 1 g	IV, IM	J0698
Cefotetan disodium	500 mg	INJ	S0074
Cefoxitin sodium	1 g	IV, IM	J0694
Ceftazidime	per 500 mg	IM, IV	J0713
Ceftizoxime soduim	per 500 mg	IV, IM	J0715
Ceftriaxone sodium	per 250 mg	IV, IM	J0696
Ceftoperazone sodium	1 g	INJ	S0021
Cefuroxime sodium, sterile	per 750 mg	IM, IV	J0697
Celestone Phosphate, *see* Betamethasone sodium phosphate			
Celestone Soluspan, *see* Betamethasone acetate and betamethasone sodium phosphate			
CellCept, *see* Mycophenolate mofetil			
Cel-U-Jec, *see* Betamethasone sodium phosphate			
Cenacort Forte, *see* Triamcinolone diacetate			
Cenacort A-40, *see* Triamcinolone acetonide			
Cephalothin sodium	up to 1 g	IM, IV	J1890
Cephapirin Sodium	up to 1 g	IV, IM	J0710
Ceredase, *see* Alglucerase			
Cerezyme, *see* Imiglucerase			
Cerubidine, *see* Daunorubicin HCl			
Chlor-100, *see* Chlorpheniramine maleate			
Chloramphenicol sodium succinate	up to 1 g	IV	J0720
Chlordiazepoxide HCl	up to 100 mg	IM, IV	J1990
Chloromycetin Sodium Succinate, *see* Chloramphenicol sodium succinate			
Chlor-Pro, *see* Chlorpheniramine maleate			
Chlor-Pro 10, *see* Chlorpheniramine maleate			
Chloroprocaine HCl	per 30 ml	VAR	J2400
Chloroquine HCl	up to 250 mg	IM	J0390
Chlorothiazide sodium	per 500 mg	IV	J1205
Chlorpheniramine maleate	per 10 mg	IV, IM, SC	J0730
Chlorpromazine HCl	10 mg	ORAL	Q0171
	25 mg	ORAL	Q0172
	up to 50 mg	IM, IV	J3230
Chlorprothixene	up to 50 mg	IM	J3080
Chlortrimeton, *see* Chlorpheniramine maleate			
Chorex-5, *see* Chorionic gonadotropin			
Chorex-10, *see* Chorionic gonadotropin			
Chorignon, *see* Chorionic gonadotropin			
Chorionic gonadotropin	per 1,000 USP units	IM	J0725
Choron 10, *see* Chorionic gonadotropin			

Drug	Dose	Route	Code
Cidofovir	375 mg	IV	J0740
Cimetidine HCl	300 mg	INJ	S0077
Ciprofloxacin	200 mg	INJ	S0024
Cilastatin sodium, imipenem	per 250 mg	IV, IM	J0743
Cisplatin, powder or solution	per 10 mg	IV	J9060
Cisplatin	50 mg	IV	J9062
Cladribine	per mg	IV	J9065
Claforan, see Cefotaxime sodium			
Clindamycin phosphate	300 mg	INJ	S0077
Clonidine HCl	1 mg	VAR, ORAL	J0735
Cobex, see Vitamin B-12 cyanocobalamin			
Codeine phosphate	per 30 mg	IM, IV, SC	J0745
Cogentin, see Benztropine mesylate			
Colchicine	per 1 mg	IV	J0760
Colistimethate sodium	up to 150 mg	IM, IV	J0770
Coly-Mycin M, see Colistimethate sodium			
Compa-Z, see Prochlorperazine			
Compazine, see Prochlorperazine			
Cophene-B, see Brompheniramine maleate			
Copper contraceptive, intrauterine	—	OTH	J7300
Corgonject-5, see Chorionic gonadotropin			
Corticotropin	up to 40 units	IV, IM, SC	J0800
Cortisone acetate, see Cortisone			
Cortisone	up to 50 mg	IM	J0810
Cortrosyn, see Cosyntropin			
Cosmegen, see Dactinomycin			
Cosyntropin	per 0.25 mg	IM, IV	J0835
Cotranzine, see Prochlorperazine			
Cromolyn sodium	per 20 mg	INH	J7630
Cromolyn sodium, inhalation solution	10 mg	INH	J7631
Crysticillin 300 A.S., see Penicillin G procaine			
Crysticillin 600 A.S., see Penicillin G procaine			
Cyclophosphamide	100 mg	IV	J9070
	200 mg	IV	J9080
	500 mg	IV	J9090
	1 g	IV	J9091
	2 g	IV	J9092
Cyclophosphamide, lyophilized	100 mg	IV	J9093
	200 mg	IV	J9094
	500 mg	IV	J9095
	1 g	IV	J9096
	2 g	IV	J9097
Cyclophosphamide, oral	25 mg	ORAL	J8530
Cyclosporine, oral	25 mg	ORAL	J7515
	100 mg	ORAL	J7502
	per 100 mg	ORAL	K0418
	25 mg	ORAL	K0121
Cyclosporine, parenteral	250 mg	IV	J7516
Cytarabine	100 mg	SC, IV	J9100
Cytarabine	500 mg	SC, IV	J9110
Cytomegalovirus immune globulin intravenous (human)	per vial	IV	J0850
Cytosar-U, see Cytarabine			
Cytovene, see Ganciclovir sodium			
Cytoxan, see Cyclophosphamide; cyclophosphamide, lyophilized; and cyclophosphamide, oral			

D

D-5-W, infusion	1000 cc	IV	J7070
Dacarbazine	100 mg	IV	J9130
	200 mg	IV	J9140
Daclizumab	25 mg	OTH	J7513
Dactinomycin	0.5 mg	IV	J9120

Dalalone, see Dexamethasone sodium phosphate
Dalalone L.A., see Dexamethasone acetate

Dalteparin Sodium	per 2500 IU	SC	J1645
Daunorubicin citrate, liposomal formula	10 mg	IV	J9151
Daunorubicin HCl	10 mg	IV	J9150

Daunoxome, see Daunorubicin citrate
DDAVP, see Desmopressin acetate
Decadron Phosphate, see Dexamethasone sodium phosphate
Decadron, see Dexamethasone sodium phosphate
Decadron-LA, see Dexamethasone acetate
Deca-Durabolin, see Nandrolone decanoate
Decaject, see Dexamethasone sodium phosphate
Decaject-L.A., see Dexamethasone acetate
Decolone-50, see Nandrolone decanoate
Decolone-100, see Nandrolone decanoate
De-Comberol, see Testosterone cypionate and estradiol cypionate

Deferoxamine mesylate	500 mg per 5 cc	IM, SC, IV	J0895

Dehist, see Brompheniramine maleate
Deladumone OB, see Testosterone enanthate and estradiol valerate
Deladumone, see Testosterone enanthate and estradiol valerate
Delatest, see Testosterone enanthate
Delatestadiol, see Testosterone enanthate and estradiol valerate
Delatestryl, see Testosterone enanthate
Delta-Cortef, see Prednisolone, oral
Delestrogen, see Estradiol valerate
Delta-Cortef, see Prednisone
Deltasone, see Prednisone
Demadex, see Torsemide
Demerol HCl, see Meperidine HCl
DepAndro 100, see Testosterone cypionate
DepAndro 200, see Testosterone cypionate
DepAndrogyn, see Testosterone cypionate and estradiol cypionate
DepGynogen, see Depo-estradiol cypionate
DepMedalone 40, see Methylprednisolone acetate
DepMedalone 80, see Methylprednisolone acetate

Depo-estradiol cypionate	up to 5 mg	IM	J1000

Depogen, see Depo-estradiol cypionate
Depoject, see Methylprednisolone acetate
Depo-Medrol, see Methylprednisolone acetate
Depopred-40, see Methylprednisolone acetate
Depopred-80, see Methylprednisolone acetate
Depo-Provera, see Medroxyprogesterone acetate
Depotest, see Testosterone cypionate
Depo-Testadiol, see Testosterone cypionate and estradiol cypionate
Depotestogen, see Testosterone cypionate and estradiol cypionate
Depo-Testosterone, see Testosterone cypionate
Desferal Mesylate, see Deferoxamine mesylate

Desmopressin acetate	1 mcg	IV, SC	J2597

Dexacen-4, see Dexamethasone sodium phosphate

Drug	Dosage	Route	Code
Dexamethasone acetate	8mg per ml	VAR	J1095
Dexamethosone sodium phosphate	up to 4 mg/ml	IM, IV, OTH	J1100
Dexasone, see Dexamethasone sodium phosphate			
Dexasone L.A., see Dexamethasone acetate			
Dexone, see Dexamethasone sodium phosphate			
Dexone LA, see Dexamethasone acetate			
Dexamethasone, inhalation solution, concentrated form	per mg	INH	J7637
Dexamethasone, inhalation solution, unit dose form	per mg	INH	J7638
Dexrazoxane HCl	per 250 mg	IV	J1190
Dextran 40	500 ml	IV	J7100
Dextran 75	500 ml	IV	J7110
Dextrose/normal saline solution (5%)	500 ml = 1 unit	IV	J7042
Dextrose/water (5%)	500 ml = 1 unit	IV	J7060
D.H.E. 45, see Dihydroergotamine			
Diamox, see Acetazolamide sodium			
Diazepam	up to 5 mg	IM, IV	J3360
Diazoxide	up to 300 mg	IV	J1730
Dibent, see Dicyclomine HCl			
Dicyclomine HCl	up to 20 mg	IM	J0500
Didronel, see Etidronate disodium			
Diethylstilbestrol diphosphate	250 mg	IV	J9165
Digoxin	up to 0.5 mg	IM, IV	J1160
Dihydrex, see Diphenhydramine HCl			
Dihydroergotamine mesylate	per 1 mg	IM, IV	J1110
Dilantin, see Phenytoin sodium			
Dilaudid, see Hydromorphone HCl			
Dilocaine, see Lidocaine HCl			
Dilomine, see Dicyclomine HCl			
Dilor, see Dyphylline			
Dimenhydrinate	up to 50 mg	IM, IV	J1240
Dimercaprol	per 100 mg	IM	J0470
Dimethyl sulfoxide, see DMSO, Dimethylsulfoxide			
Dinate, see Dimenhydrinate			
Dioval, see Estradiol valerate			
Dioval 40, see Estradiol valerate			
Dioval XX, see Estradiol valerate			
Diphenacen-50, see Diphenhydramine HCl			
Diphenhydramine HCl	up to 50 mg	IV, IM	J1200
	50 mg	ORAL	Q0163
Dipyridamole	per 10 mg	IV	J1245
Disotate, see Endrate ethylenediamine-tetra-acetic acid			
Di-Spaz, see Dicyclomine HCl			
Ditate-DS, see Testosterone enanthate and estradiol valerate			
Diuril Sodium, see Chlorothiazide sodium			
D-Med 80, see Methylprednisolone acetate			
DMSO, Dimethyl sulfoxide	50%, 50 ml	OTH	J1212
Dobutamine HCl	per 250 mg	IV	J1250
Dobutrex, see Dobutamine HCl			
Docetaxel	20 mg		J9170
Dolasetron mesylate	100 mg	ORAL	Q0180
	10 mg	INJ	J1260
Dolophine HCl, see Methadone HCl			
Dommanate, see Dimenhydrinate			
Dornase alpha, inhalation solution, unit dose form	per mg	INH	J7639
Doxorubicin HCl	10 mg	IV	J9000
Doxorubicin HCl, all lipid formulations	10 mg		J9001

Dramamine, see Dimenhydrinate
Dramanate, see Dimenhydrinate
Dramilin, see Dimenhydrinate
Dramocen, see Dimenhydrinate
Dramoject, see Dimenhydrinate

Dronabinol	2.5 mg	ORAL	Q0167
	5 mg	ORAL	Q0168
Droperidol	up to 5 mg	IM, IV	J1790
Drug administered through a metered dose inhaler	—	INH	J3535
Droperidol and fentanyl citrate	up to 2 ml ampule	IM, IV	J1810

DTIC-Dome, see Dacarbazine
Dua-Gen L.A., see Testosterone enanthate and estradiol valerate cypionate
Duoval P.A., see Testosterone enanthate and estradiol valerate
Durabolin, see Nandrolone phenpropionate
Dura-Estrin, see Depo-estradiol cypionate
Duracillin A.S., see Penicillin G procaine
Duragen-10, see Estradiol valerate
Duragen-20, see Estradiol valerate
Duragen-40, see Estradiol valerate
Duralone-40, see Methylprednisolone acetate
Duralone-80, see Methylprednisolone acetate
Duralutin, see Hydroxyprogesterone Caproate
Duramorph, see Morphine sulfate
Duratest-100, see Testosterone cypionate
Duratest-200, see Testosterone cypionate
Duratestrin, see Testosterone cypionate and estradiol cypionate
Durathate-200, see Testosterone enanthate
Dymenate, see Dimenhydrinate

Dyphylline	up to 500 mg	IM	J1180

E

Edetate calcium disodium	up to 1000 mg	IV, SC, IM	J0600
Edetate Disodium		IV	

Elavil, see Amitriptyline HCl
Elspar, see Asparaginase
Eminase, see Anistreplase
Emete-Con, see Benzquinamide

Endrate ethylenediamine-tetra-acetic acid EDTA	—	IV	J3520

Enovil, see Amitriptyline HCl

Enoxaparin sodium,	10 mg	SC	J1650
Epinephrine, adrenalin	up to 1 ml amp	SC, IM	J0170
Epinephrine, via DME	2.25%, per ml	INH	J7640
Epoetin alpha, for non ESRD use	per 1,000 units	IV, SC	Q0136
Epoprostenol	0.5 mg		J1325
Eptifibatide	5 mg	INJ	J1327
Ergonovine maleate	up to 0.2 mg	IM, IV	J1330
Erythromycin gluceptate	250 mg	IV	J1362
Erythromycin lactobionate	500 mg	IV	J1364

Estra-D, see Depo-estradiol cypionate
Estra-L 20, see Estradiol valerate
Estra-L 40, see Estradiol valerate
Estra-Testrin, see Testosterone enanthate and estradiol valerate
Estradiol Cypionate, see Depo-estradiol cypionate
Estradiol L.A., see Estradiol valerate
Estradiol L.A. 20, see Estradiol valerate

Estradiol L.A. 40, see Estradiol valerate			
Estradiol valerate	up to 10 mg	IM	**J1380**
	up to 20 mg	IM	**J1390**
	up to 40 mg	IM	**J0970**
Estro-Cyp, see Depo-estradiol cypionate			
Estrogen, conjugated	per 25 mg	IV, IM	**J1410**
Estroject L.A., see Depo-estradiol cypionate			
Estrone	per 1 mg	IM	**J1435**
Estrone 5, see Estrone			
Estrone Aqueous, see Estrone			
Estronol, see Estrone			
Estronol-L.A., see Depo-estradiol cypionate			
Etanercept	25 mg	INJ	**J1438**
Ethylnorepinephrine HCl	1 ml	SC, IM	**J0590**
Etidronate disodium	per 300 mg	IV	**J1436**
Etoposide	10 mg	IV	**J9181**
	100 mg	IV	**J9182**
Etoposide, oral	50 mg	ORAL	**J8560**
Everone, see Testosterone Enanthate			

F

Factor, hemophilia clotting, not otherwise specified		INJ	**J7199**
Factor VIIIa (coagulation-factor, recombinant)	per 1.2 mg	IV	**Q0187**
Factor VIII	per IU	IV	**J7190**
Factor VIII (anti-hemophilic factor (porcine))	per IU	IV	**J7191**
Factor VIII, recombinant	per IU	IV	**J7192**
Factor IX, complex	per IU	IV	**J7194**
Factor IX, non-recombinant	per IU		**Q0160**
Factor IX, recombinant	per IU		**Q0161**
Factrel, see Gonadorelin HCl			
Famotidine	20 mg	INJ	**S0028**
Feiba VH Immuno, see Factors, other hemophilia clotting			
Fentanyl citrate	up to 2 ml	IM, IV	**J3010**
Feostat, see Iron dextran			
Feronim, see Iron dextran			
Filgrastim (G-CSF)	300 mcg	SC, IV	**J1440**
	480 mcg	SC, IV	**J1441**
Flexoject, see Orphenadrine citrate			
Flexon, see Orphenadrine citrate			
Fluconazole	200 mg	INJ	**J1450**
	400 mg	INJ	**S0029**
Floxuridine	500 mg	IV	**J9200**
Fludara, see Fludarabine phosphate			
Fludarabine phosphate	50 mg	IV	**J9185**
Fluorouracil	500 mg	IV	**J9190**
Fluphenazine decanoate	up to 25 mg	IM, SC	**J2680**
Folex, see Methotrexate sodium			
Folex PFS, see Methotrexate sodium			
Follutein, see Chorionic gonadotropin			
Fortaz, see Ceftazidime			
Foscarnet sodium	per 1,000 mg	IV	**J1455**
Foscavir, see Foscarnet sodium			
Fosphenytoin sodium	750 mg	INJ	**S0078**
Fragmin, see Dalteparin			

FUDR, *see* Floxuridine
Furomide M.D., *see* Furosemide
Furosemide up to 20 mg IM, IV **J1940**

G

Gamma globulin

1 cc	IM	**J1460**
2 cc	IM	**J1470**
3 cc	IM	**J1480**
4 cc	IM	**J1490**
5 cc	IM	**J1500**
6 cc	IM	**J1510**
7 cc	IM	**J1520**
8 cc	IM	**J1530**
9 cc	IM	**J1540**
10 cc	IM	**J1550**
over 10 cc	IM	**J1560**

Gamulin RH, *see* Rho(D) immune globulin
Ganciclovir 4.5 mg OTH **J7310**
Ganciclovir sodium 500 mg IV **J1570**
Ganisetron HCl 1 mg ORAL **Q0166**
Garamycin, gentamicin up to 80 mg IM, IV **J1580**
Gemcitabine HCl 200 mg **J9201**
GenESA, *see* Arbutumine HCL
Gentamicin Sulfate, *see* Garamycin, gentamicin
Gentran, *see* Dextran 40
Gentran 75, *see* Dextran 75
Gesterol 50, *see* Progesterone
Gesterol L.A. 250, *see* Hydroxyprogesterone Caproate
Glucagon HCl per 1 mg SC, IM, IV **J1610**
Glukor, *see* Chorionic gonadotropin
Glycopyrrolate, inhalation solution, concentrated form per mg INH **J7642**
Glycopyrrolate, inhalation solution, unit dose form per mg INH **J7643**
Gold sodium thiomalate up to 50 mg IM **J1600**
Gonadorelin HCl per 100 mcg SC, IV **J1620**
Gonic, *see* Chorionic gonadotropin
Goserelin acetate implant per 3.6 mg SC **J9202**
Granisetron HCl 1 mg ORAL **Q0166**
 100 mcg **J1626**

Gynogen L.A. "10," *see* Estradiol valerate
Gynogen L.A. "20," *see* Estradiol valerate
Gynogen L.A. "40," *see* Estradiol valerate

H

Haldol, *see* Haloperidol
Haloperidol up to 5 mg IM, IV **J1630**
Haloperidol decanoate per 50 mg IM **J1631**
Hematran, *see* Iron dextran
Hemofil M, *see* Factor VIII
Hemophilia clotting factors (e.g., anti-inhibitors), other per IU IV **J7196**
Hep-Lock, *see* Heparin sodium (heparin lock flush)
Hep-Lock U/P, *see* Heparin sodium (heparin lock flush)
Heparin sodium 1,000 units IV, SC **J1644**

Heparin sodium (heparin lock flush)	10 units	IV	J1642
Hexadrol Phosphate, *see* Dexamethasone sodium phosphate			
Histaject, *see* Brompheniramine maleate			
Histerone 50, *see* Testosterone suspension			
Histerone 100, *see* Testosterone suspension			
Hyaluronidase	up to 150 units	SC, IV	J3470
Hybolin Improved, *see* Nandrolone phenpropionate			
Hybolin Decanoate, *see* Nandrolone decanoate			
Hydeltra-T.B.A., *see* Prednisolone tebutate			
Hydeltrasol, *see* Prednisolone sodium phosphate			
Hydextran, *see* Iron dextran			
Hydralazine HCl	up to 20 mg	IV, IM	J0360
Hydrate, *see* Dimenhydrinate			
Hydrochlorides of opium alkaloids	up to 20 mg	IM, SC	J2480
Hydrocortisone acetate	up to 25 mg	IV, IM, SC	J1700
Hydrocortisone sodium phosphate	up to 50 mg	IV, IM, SC	J1710
Hydrocortisone succinate sodium	up to 100 mg	IV, IM, SC	J1720
Hydrocortone Acetate, *see* Hydrocortisone acetate			
Hydrocortone Phosphate, *see* Hydrocortisone sodium phosphate			
Hydromorphone HCl	up to 4 mg	SC, IM, IV	J1170
Hydroxyprogesterone Caproate	25 mg/ml	IM	J1739
Hydroxyprogesterone Caproate	250 mg/ml	IM	J1741
Hydroxyzine HCl	up to 25 mg	IM	J3410
Hydroxyzine pamoate	25 mg	ORAL	Q0177
	50 mg	ORAL	Q0178
Hylan G-F 20	16 mg	OTH	J7320
Hylutin, *see* Hydroxyprogesterone Caproate			
Hyoscyamine sulfate	up to 0.25 mg	SC, IM, IV	J1980
Hyperstat IV, *see* Diazoxide			
Hyprogest 250, *see* Hydroxyprogesterone Caproate			
Hyrexin-50, *see* Diphenhydramine HCl			
Hyzine-50, *see* Hydroxyzine HCl			

I

Ibutilide fumarate	1 mg	INJ	S0097
Idamycin, *see* Idarubicin HCl			
Idarubicin HCl	5 mg	IV	J9211
Ibutilide fumarate	1 mg		J1742
Ifex, *see* Ifosfamide			
Ifosfamide	per 1 g	IV	J9208
IL-2, *see* Aldesleukin			
Ilotycin, *see* Erythromycin gluceptate			
Imfergen, *see* Iron dextran			
Imferon, *see* Iron dextran			
Imiglucerase	per unit	IV	J1785
Imipramine HCl	up to 25 mg	IM	J3270
Imitrex, *see* Sumatriptan succinate			
Immune globulin	per 500 mg	IV	J1561
Immune globulin intravenous (human) 10%	5 g	IV	J1562
Immunosuppressive drug, not otherwise classified			J7599
Imuran, *see* Azathioprine			
Inapsine, *see* Droperidol			
Infed			
Infliximab	10 mg	INJ	J1745
Inderal, *see* Propranolol HCl			

Innovar, *see* Droperidol with fentanyl citrate			
Insulin	up to 100 units	SC	**J1820**
Intal, *see* Cromolyn sodium or Cromolyn sodium, compounded			
Interferon alfa-2a, recombinant	3 million units	SC, IM	**J9213**
Interferon alfa-2b, recombinant	1 million units	SC, IM	**J9214**
Interferon alfa-n3 (human leukocyte derived)	250,000 IU	IM	**J9215**
Interferon alfacon-1, recombinant	1 mcg	IM	**J9212**
Interferon beta 1a	33 mcg	IM	**J1825**
Interferon beta-1b	0.25 mg	SC	**J1830**
Interferon gamma-1b	3 million units	SC	**J9216**
Intrauterine copper contraceptive, *see* Copper contraceptive, intrauterine			
Ipratropium bromide 0.2%	per ml	INH	**J7645**
Ipratropium bromide, inhalation solution, unit dose form	per mg	INH	**J0518**
Irinotecan	20 mg		**J9206**
Irodex, *see* Iron dextran			
Iron dextran	50 mg	INJ	**J1750**
Isocaine HCl, *see* Mepivacaine			
Isoetharine HCl	0.1% per ml	INH	**J7650**
	0.125% per ml	INH	**J7651**
	0.167% per ml	INH	**J7652**
	0.2% per ml	INH	**J7653**
	0.25% per ml	INH	**J7654**
	1.0% per ml	INH	**J7655**
Isoetharine HCl, inhalation solution, concentrated form	per mg	INH	**J7648**
Isoetharine HCl, inhalation solution, unit dose form	per mg	INH	**J7649**
Isoproterenol HCl	0.5% per ml	INH	**J7660**
	1.0%, per ml	INH	**J7665**
Isoproterenol HCl, inhalation solution, concentrated form	per mg	INH	**J7658**
Isoproterenol HCl, inhalation solution, unit dose form	per mg	INH	**J7659**
Isuprel, *see* Isoproterenol HCl			

J

Jenamicin, *see* Garamycin, gentamicin

K

Kabikinase, *see* Streptokinase			
Kanamycin sulfate	up to 75 mg	IM, IV	**J1850**
Kanamycin sulfate	up to 500 mg	IM, IV	**J1840**
Kantrex, *see* Kanamycin sulfate			
Keflin, *see* Cephalothin sodium			
Kefurox, *see* Cufuroxime sodium			
Kefzol, *see* Cefazolin sodium			
Kenaject-40, *see* Triamcinolone acetonide			
Kenalog-10, *see* Triamcinolone acetonide			
Kenalog-40, *see* Triamcinolone acetonide			
Kestrone 5, *see* Estrone			
Ketorolac tromethamine	per 15 mg	IM, IV	**J1885**
Key-Pred 25, *see* Prednisolone acetate			
Key-Pred 50, *see* Prednisolone acetate			
Key-Pred-SP, *see* Prednisolone sodium phosphate			
K-Feron, *see* Iron dextran			
K-Flex, *see* Orphenadrine citrate			
Klebcil, *see* Kanamycin sulfate			

Koate-HP, see Factor VIII
Kogenate, see Factor VIII
Konakion, see Phytonadione
Konyne-80, see Factor IX, complex

Kutapressin	up to 2 ml	SC, IM	**J1910**

L

L.A.E. 20, see Estradiol valerate

Laetrile, Amygdalin, vitamin B-17	—	—	**J3570**

Lanoxin, see Digoxin
Largon, see Propiomazine HCl
Lasix, see Furosemide
L-Caine, see Lidocaine HCl

Leucovorin calcium	per 50 mg	IM, IV	**J0640**

Leukine, see Sargramostim (GM-CSF)

Leuprolide acetate (for depot suspension)	3.75 mg	IM	**J1950**
	7.5 mg	IM	**J9217**
Leuprolide acetate	per 1 mg	IM	**J9218**

Leustatin, see Cladribine
Levaquin, see Levofloxacin

Levocarnitine	per 1 gm	IV	**J1955**

Levo-Dromoran, see Levorphanol tartrate

Levofloxacin	250 mg	IV	**J1956**

Levoprome, see Methotrimeprazine

Levorphanol tartrate	up to 2 mg	SC, IV	**J1960**

Levsin, see Hyoscyamine sulfate
Librium, see Chlordiazepoxide HCl

Lidocaine HCl	50 cc	VAR	**J2000**

Lidoject-1, see Lidocaine HCl
Lidoject-2, see Lidocaine HCl
Lincocin, see Lincomycin HCl

Lincomycin HCl	up to 300 mg	IV	**J2010**

Liquaemin Sodium, see Heparin sodium
Lioresal, see Baclofen
LMD (10%), see Dextran 40
Lovenox, see Enoxaparin sodium

Lorazepam	2 mg	IM, IV	**J2060**

Lufyllin, see Dyphylline

Luminal Sodium	up to 120 mg	IM, IV	**J2560**

Lupron, see Leuprolide acetate

Lymphocyte immune globulin, anti-thymocyte globulin	50 mg/ml, 5 ml ea	IV	**J7504**
	250 mg	IV	**K0123**

Lyophilized, see Cyclophosphamide, lyophilized

M

Magnesium sulfate	500 mg	IM, IV	**J3475**
Mannitol	25% in 50 ml	IV	**J2150**

Marmine, see Dimenhydrinate

Mechlorethamine HCl (nitrogen mustard), HN2	10 mg	IV	**J9230**

Medralone 40, see Methylprednisolone acetate
Medralone 80, see Methylprednisolone acetate
Medrol, see Methylprednisolone

Medroxyprogesterone acetate	100 mg	IM	J1050
	150 mg	IM	J1055

Mefoxin, see Cefoxitin sodium

Melphalan HCl	50 mg	IV	J9245
Melphalan, oral	2 mg	ORAL	J8600

Menoject LA, see Testosterone cypionate and estradiol cypionate
Mepergan Injection, see Meperdine and promethazine HCl

Meperidine HCl	per 100 mg	IM, IV, SC	J2175
Meperidine and promethazine HCl	up to 50 mg	IM, IV	J2180
Mephentermine sulfate	up to 30 mg	IM, IV	J3450
Mepivacaine	per 10 ml	VAR	J0670
Mesna	200 mg	IV	J9209

Mesnex, see Mesna
Metaprel, see Metaproterenol sulfate

Metaproterenol, inhalation solution, concentrated form	per 10 mg	INH	J7668
Metaproterenol, inhalation solution, unit dose form	per 10 mg	INH	J7669
Metaproterenol sulfate	0.4%, per 2.5 ml	INH	J7670
	0.6%, per 2.5 ml	INH	J7672
	5.0%, per ml	INH	J7675
Metaraminol bitartrate	per 10 mg	IV, IM, SC	J0380
Methadone HCl	up to 10 mg	IM, SC	J1230

Methergine, see Methylergonovine maleate

Methicillin sodium	up to 1 g	IM, IV	J2970
Methocarbamol	up to 10 ml	IV, IM	J2800
Methotrexate, oral	2.5 mg	ORAL	J8610
Methotrexate sodium	5 mg	IV, IM, IT, IA	J9250
	50 mg	IV, IM, IT, IA	J9260

Methotrexate LPF, see Methotrexate sodium

Methotrimeprazine	up to 20 mg	IM	J1970
Methoxamine HCl	up to 20 mg	IM, IV	J3390
Methyldopate HCl	up to 250 mg	IV	J0210
Methylergonovine maleate	up to 0.2 mg		J2210
Methylprednisolone, oral	per 4 mg	ORAL	J7509
Methylprednisolone acetate	20 mg	IM	J1020
	40 mg	IM	J1030
	80 mg	IM	J1040
Methylprednisolone sodium succinate	up to 40 mg	IM, IV	J2920
	up to 125 mg	IM, IV	J2930
Metoclopramide HCl	up to 10 mg	IV	J2765
Metronidazole	500 mg	INJ	S0030
Metocurine iodide	up to 2 mg	IV	J2240

Metubine iodine, see Metocurine iodide
Miacalcin, see Calcitonin-salmon

Midazolam HCl	per 1 mg	IM, IV	J2250
Milrinone lactate	per 5 ml	IV	J2260

Mithracin, see Plicamycin

Mitomycin	5 mg	IV	J9280
	20 mg	IV	J9290
	40 mg	IV	J9291
Mitoxantrone HCl	per 5 mg	IV	J9293

Monarc-M, see Factor VIII
Monocid, see Cefonicic sodium
Monoclate-P, see Factor VIII

Monoclonal antibodies, parenteral	amp, 5 mg/5 ml, 5 ml ea	IV	J7505
Morphine sulfate	up to 10 mg	IM, IV, SC	J2270
	100 mg	IT, IV, SC	J2271

Drug	Dose	Route	Code
Morphine sulfate, preservative-free	per 10 mg	SC, IM, IV	J2275
M-Prednisol-40, *see* Methylprednisolone acetate			
M-Prednisol-80, *see* Methylprednisolone acetate			
Mucomyst, *see* Acetylcysteine or Acetylcysteine, compounded			
Mucosol, *see* Acetylcysteine			
Mustargen, *see* Mechlorethamine HCl			
Mutamycin, *see* Mitomycin			
Mycophenolate mofetil	250 mg	ORAL	J7517
Myochrysine, *see* Gold sodium thiomalate			
Myolin, *see* Orphenadrine citrate			

N

Drug	Dose	Route	Code
Nafcillin sodium	2 g	INJ	S0032
Nalbuphine HCl	per 10 mg	IM, IV, SC	J2300
Naloxone HCl	per 1 mg	IM, IV, SC	J2310
Nandrobolic, *see* Nandrolone phenpropionate			
Nandrobolic L.A., *see* Nandrolone decanoate			
Nandrolone decanoate	up to 50 mg	IM	J2320
	up to 100 mg	IM	J2321
	up to 200 mg	IM	J2322
Nandrolone phenpropionate	up to 50 mg	IM	J0340
Narcan, *see* Naloxone HCl			
Nasahist B, *see* Brompheniramine maleate			
Nasal vaccine inhalation	—	INH	J3530
Navane, *see* Thiothixene			
Navelbine, *see* Vinorelbine tartrate			
ND Stat, *see* Brompheniramine maleate			
Nebcin, *see* Tobramycin sulfate			
NebuPent, *see* Pentamidine isethionate			
Nembutal Sodium Solution, *see* Pentobarbital sodium			
Neocyten, *see* Orphenadrine citrate			
Neo-Durabolic, *see* Nandrolone decanoate			
Neoquess, *see* Dicyclomine HCl			
Neoral, *see* Cyclosporine, for microemulsion			
Neosar, *see* Cyclophosphamide			
Neostigmine methylsulfate	up to 0.5 mg	IM, IV, SC	J2710
Neo-Synephrine, *see* Phenylephrine HCl			
Neupogen, *see* Filgrastim (G-CSF)			
Neutrexin, *see* Trimetrexate glucuronate			
Nervocaine 1%, *see* Lidocaine HCl			
Nervocaine 2%, *see* Lidocaine HCl			
Nesacaine, *see* Chloroprocaine HCl			
Nesacaine-MPF, *see* Chloroprocaine HCl			
Niacinamide, niacin	up to 100 mg	IV, SC, IM	J2350
Nicotinic Acid, *see* Niacinamide, niacin			
Nicotinamide, *see* Niacinamide, niacin			
Nipent, *see* Pentostatin			
Nordryl, *see* Diphenhydramine HCl			
Nor-Feran, *see* Iron dextran			
Norflex, *see* Orphenadrine citrate			
Norzine, *see* Thiethylperazine maleate			
Not otherwise classified drugs	—	—	J3490
	—	other than INH	J7799
	—	INH	J7699

Not otherwise classified drugs, anti-emetic	—	ORAL	Q0181
Not otherwise classified drugs, anti-neoplastic	—	—	J9999
Not otherwise classified drugs, chemotherapeutic	—	ORAL	J8999
Not otherwise classified drugs, immunosuppressive	—	—	J7599
Not otherwise classified drugs, nonchemotherapeutic	—	ORAL	J8499

Novantrone, see Mitoxantrone HCl
NPH, see Insulin
Nubain, see Nalbuphine HCl
Nulicaine, see Lidocaine HCl
Numorphan, see Oxymorphone HCl
Numorphan H.P., see Oxymorphone HCl

O

Octreotide acetate	1 mg	INJ	J2352
Oculinum, see Botulinum toxin type A			
Odansetron HCl	1 mg	IV	J2405
Ofloxacin	400 mg	INJ	S0034
O-Flex, see Orphenadrine citrate			
Omnipen-N, see Ampicillin			
Oncaspar, see Pegaspargase			
Oncovin, see Vincristine sulfate			
Ondansetron HCl	8 mg	ORAL	Q0179
Oprelvekin	5mg	INJ	J2355
Oraminic II, see Brompheniramine maleate			
Ormazine, see Chlorpromazine HCl			
Orphenadrine citrate	up to 60 mg	IV, IM	J2360
Orphenate, see Orphenadrine citrate			
Or-Tyl, see Dicyclomine			
Oxacillin sodium	up to 250 mg	IM, IV	J2700
Oxymorphone HCl	up to 1 mg	IV, SC, IM	J2410
Oxytetracycline HCl	up to 50 mg	IM	J2460
Oxytocin	up to 10 units	IV, IM	J2590

P

Paclitaxel	30 mg	IV	J9265
Pamidronate disodium	per 30 mg	IV	J2430
Panglobulin, see Immune globulin intravenous			
Pantopon, see Hydrochlorides of opium alkaloids			
Papaverine HCl	up to 60 mg	IV, IM	J2440
Paricalcitrol	5 mcg	INJ	J2500
Paragard T 380 A, see Copper contraceptive, intrauterine			
Paraplatin, see Carboplatin			
Pegaspargase	per single dose vial	IM, IV	J9266
Peg-L-asparaginase, see Pegaspargase			
Penicillin G benzathine	up to 600,000 units	IM	J0560
	up to 1,200,000 units	IM	J0570
	up to 2,400,000 units	IM	J0580
Penicillin G benzathine and penicillin G procaine	up to 600,000 units	IM	J0530
	up to 1,200,000 units	IM	J0540
	up to 2,400,000 units	IM	J0550
Penicillin G potassium	up to 600,000 units	IM, IV	J2540
Penicillin G procaine, aqueous	up to 600,000 units	IM	J2510
Pentagastrin	per 2 ml	SC	J2512

Drug	Dose	Route	Code
Pentamidine isethionate	per 300 mg	INH	J2545
	per 300 mg	INJ	S0080
Pentazocine HCl	up to 30 mg	IM, SC, IV	J3070
Pentobarbital sodium	per 50 mg	IM, IV	J2515
Pentostatin	per 10 mg	IV	J9268
Peptavlon, see Pentagastrin			
Permapen, see Penicillin G benzathine			
Perphenazine	up to 5 mg	IM, IV	J3310
	4 mg	ORAL	Q0175
	8 mg	ORAL	Q0176
Persantine IV, see Dipyridamole			
Pfizerpen, see Penicillin G potassium			
Pfizerpen A.S., see Penicillin G procaine			
PGE$_1$, see Alprostadil			
Phenazine 25, see Promethazine HCl			
Phenazine 50, see Promethazine HCl			
Phenergan, see Promethazine HCl			
Phenobarbital sodium	up to 120 mg	IM, IV	J2560
Phentolamine mesylate	up to 5 mg	IM, IV	J2760
Phenylephrine HCl	up to 1 ml	SC, IM, IV	J2370
Phenytoin sodium	per 50 mg	IM, IV	J1165
Phytonadione	per 1mg	IM, SC, IV	J3430
Piperacillin sodium	500 mg	INJ	S0081
Piperacillin sodium/tazobactam sodium	1.125 g	INJ	J2543
Pitocin, see Oxytocin			
Plantinol AQ, see Cisplatin			
Platinol, see Cisplatin			
Plicamycin	2,500 mcg	IV	J9270
Polocaine, see Mepivacaine			
Polycillin-N, see Ampicillin			
Porfimer sodium	75 mg		J9600
Potassium chloride	per 2 mEq	IV	J3480
Pralidoxime chloride	up to 1 g	IV, IM, SC	J2730
Predalone T.B.A., see Prednisolone tebutate			
Predalone-50, see Prednisolone acetate			
Predcor-25, see Prednisolone acetate			
Predcor-50, see Prednisolone acetate			
Predicort-50, see Prednisolone acetate			
Prednisone	any dose, 100 tabl	ORAL	J7506
Prednisone	tab, 5 mg	ORAL	K0125
Prednisol TBA, see Prednisolone tebutate			
Prednisolone, oral	5 mg	ORAL	J7510
Prednisolone acetate	up to 1 ml	IM	J2650
Prednisolone sodium phosphate	up to 20 mg	IV, IM	J2640
Prednisolone tebutate	up to 20 mg	VAR	J1690
Predoject-50, see Prednisolone acetate			
Pregnyl, see Chorionic gonadotropin			
Premarin Intravenous, see Estrogen, conjugated			
Prescription, chemotherapeutic, not otherwise specified	—	ORAL	J8999
Prescription, nonchemotherapeutic, not otherwise specified	—	ORAL	J8499
Primacor, see Milrinone lactate			
Primaxin I.M., see Cilastatin sodium, imipenem			
Primaxin I.V., see Cilastatin sodium, imipenem			
Priscoline HCl, see Tolazoline HCl			
Pro-Depo, see Hydroxyprogesterone Caproate			
Procainamide HCl	up to 1 g	IM, IV	J2690

Prochlorperazine	up to 10 mg	IM, IV	J0780
Prochlorperazine maleate	10 mg	ORAL	Q0165
	5 mg	ORAL	Q0164

Profasi HP, see Chorionic gonadotropin
Proferdex, see Iron dextran
Profilnine Heat-Treated, see Factor IX
Progestaject, see Progesterone

Progesterone	per 50 mg	IM	J2675

Prograf, see Tacrolimus, oral
Prokine, see Sargramostim (GM-CSF)
Prolastin, see Alpha 1-proteinase inhibitor, human
Proleukin, see Aldesleukin
Prolixin Decanoate, see Fluphenazine decanoate

Promazine HCl	up to 25 mg	IM	J2950
Promethazine HCl	12.5 mg	ORAL	Q0169
	25 mg	ORAL	Q0170
	up to 50 mg	IM, IV	J2550

Pronestyl, see Procainamide HCl

Propiomazine HCl	up to 20 mg	IV, IM	J1930

Proplex T, see Factor IX
Proplex SX-T, see Factor IX

Propranolol HCl	up to 1 mg	IV	J1800

Prorex-25, see Promethazine HCl
Prorex-50, see Promethazine HCl
Prostaglandin E_1, see Alprostadil
Prostaphlin, see Procainamide HCl
Prostigmin, see Neostigmine methylsulfate
Prostin VR Pediatric, see Alprostadil

Protamine sulfate	per 10 mg	IV	J2720
Protirelin	per 250 mcg	IV	J2725

Prothazine, see Promethazine HCl
Protopam Chloride, see Pralidoxime chloride
Proventil, see Albuterol sulfate, compounded
Prozine-50, see Promazine HCl

Q

Quelicin, see Succinylcholine chloride

R

Rantidine HCl	25 mg	INJ	J2780

Recombinate, see Factor VIII
Redisol, see Vitamin B-12 cyanocobalamin
Regitine, see Phentolamine mesylate
Reglan, see Metoclopramide HCl
Regular, see Insulin
Relefact TRH, see Protirelin
Rep-Pred 40, see Methylprednisolone acetate
Rep-Pred 80, see Methylprednisolone acetate

Respiratory syncytial virus immune globulin	50 mg	IV	J1565

Retavase, see Retaplase

Reteplase	37.6 mg	IV	J2994

Rheomacrodex, see Dextran 40
Rhesonativ, see Rho(D) immune globulin, human

Drug	Dose	Route	Code
Rheumatrex Dose Pack, see Methotrexate, oral			
Rho(D) immune globulin	100 IU	IV	J2792
Rho(D) immune globulin, human	1 dose package	IM	J2790
RhoGAM, see Rho(D) immune globulin, human			
Ringer's lactate infusion	up to 1,000 cc	IV	J7120
Rituximab	100 mg		J9310
Robaxin, see Methocarbamol			
Rocephin, see Ceftriaxone sodium			
Roferon-A, see Interferon alfa-2A, recombinant			
Rubex, see Doxorubicin HCl			
Rubramin PC, see Vitamin B-12 cyanocobalamin			

S

Drug	Dose	Route	Code
Saline solution	5% dextrose, 500 ml	IV	J7042
	infusion, 250 cc	IV	J7050
	infusion, 1,000 cc	IV	J7030
Saline solution, sterile	500 ml = 1 unit	IV, OTH	J7040
	up to 5 cc	IV, OTH	J7051
Sandimmune, see Cyclosporine			
Sargramostim (GM-CSF)	50 mcg	IV	J2820
Secobarbital sodium	up to 250 mg	IM, IV	J2860
Seconal, see Secobarbital sodium			
Sildenafil citrte	25 mg		S0090
Selestoject, see Betamethasone sodium phosphate			
Sinusol-B, see Brompheniramine maleate			
Sodium chloride, 0.9%	per 2 ml	IV	J2912
Sodium ferric gluconate complex in sucrose	62.5 mg	INJ	S0098
Sodium hyaluronate	20 mg	OTH	J7315
Solganal, see Aurothioglucose			
Solu-Cortef, see Hydrocortisone sodium phosphate			
Solu-Medrol, see Methylprednisolone sodium succinate			
Solurex, see Dexamethasone sodium phosphate			
Solurex LA, see Dexamethasone acetate			
Somatrem	5 mg	INJ	S0010
Somatropin	5 mg	INJ	S0011
Sparine, see Promazine HCl			
Spasmoject, see Dicyclomine HCl			
Spectinomycin HCl	up to 2 g	IM	J3320
Staphcillin, see Methicillin sodium			
Stilphostrol, see Diethylstilbestrol diphosphate			
Streptase, see Streptokinase			
Streptokinase	per 250,000 IU	IV	J2995
Streptomycin Sulfate, see Streptomycin			
Streptomycin	up to 1 g	IM	J3000
Streptozocin	1 gm	IV	J9320
Sublimaze, see Fentanyl citrate			
Succinylcholine chloride	up to 20 mg	IV, IM	J0330
Sucostrin, see Succinycholine chloride			
Sulfamethoxazole and trimethoprim	10 ml	INJ	S0039
Sumatriptan succinate	6 mg	SC	J3030
Sus-Phrine, see Adrenalin, epinephrine			
Syntocionon, see Oxytocin			
Sytobex, see Vitamin B-12 cyanocobalamin			

T

Drug	Dose	Route	Code
Tacrine HCl	10 mg	INJ	S0014
Tacrolimus, oral	per 1 mg	ORAL	J7507
	per 5 mg	ORAL	J7508
Talwin, see Pentazocine HCl			
Taractan, see Chlorprothixene			
Taxol, see Paclitaxel			
Tazidime, see Ceftazidime			
Technetium TC Sestambi	per dose		A9500
TEEV, see Testosterone enanthate and estradiol valerate			
Terbutaline sulface, inhalation solution, concentrated form	per mg	INH	J7680
Terbutaline sulface, inhalation solution, unit dose form	per mg	INH	J7681
Terbutaline sulfate	up to 1 mg	SC	J3105
Terramycin IM, see Oxytetracycline HCl			
Testa-C, see Testosterone cypionate			
Testadiate, see Testosterone enanthate and estradiol valerate			
Testadiate-Depo, see Testosterone cypionate			
Testaject-LA, see Testosterone cypionate			
Testaqua, see Testosterone suspension			
Test-Estro Cypionates, see Testosterone cypionate and estradiol cypionate			
Test-Estro-C, see Testosterone cypionate and estradiol cypionate			
Testex, see Testosterone propionate			
Testoject-50, see Testosterone suspension			
Testoject-LA, see Testosterone cypionate			
Testone LA 200, see Testosterone enanthate			
Testone LA 100, see Testosterone enanthate			
Testosterone Aqueous, see Testosterone suspension			
Testosterone enanthate and estradiol valerate	up to 1 cc	IM	J0900
Testosterone enanthate	up to 100 mg	IM	J3120
	up to 200 mg	IM	J3130
Testosterone cypionate			
	1 cc, 50 mg	IM	J1090
	up to 100 mg	IM	J1070
	1 cc, 200 mg	IM	J1080
Testosterone cypionate and estradiol cypionate	up to 1 ml	IM	J1060
Testosterone propionate	up to 100 mg	IM	J3150
Testosterone suspension	up to 50 mg	IM	J3140
Testradiol 90/4, see Testosterone enanthate and estradiol valerate			
Testrin PA, see Testosterone enanthate			
Tetanus immune globulin, human	up to 250 units	IM	J1670
Tetracycline	up to 250 mg	IM, IV	J0120
Thallous Chloride TL 201	per MCI		A9505
Theelin Aqueous, see Estrone			
Theophylline	per 40 mg	IV	J2810
TheraCys, see BCG live			
Thiethylperazine	10 mg	ORAL	Q0174
Thiethylperazine maleate	up to 10 mg	IM	J3280
Thiotepa	15 mg	IV	J9340
Thiothixene	up to 4 mg	IM	J2330
Thorazine, see Chlorpromazine HCl			
Thypinone, see Protirelin			
Thyrotropin	0.9 mg	IM, SC	J3240
Thytropar, see Thyrotropin			
Ticarcillin disodium and clarulanate potassium	3.1 g	INJ	S0040
Tice BCG, see BCG live			

HCPCS 2000

Ticon, see Trimethobenzamide HCl
Tigan, see Trimethobenzamide HCl
Tiject-20, see Trimethobenzamide HCl

Tirofiban HCl	12.5 mg	INJ	J3245
Tobramycin	300 mg	INH	J7681
Tobramycin sulfate	up to 80 mg	IM, IV	J3260

Tofranil, see Imipramine HCl

Tolazoline HCl	up to 25 mg	IV	J2670
Topotecan	4 mg		J9350

Toradol, see Ketorolac tromethamine
Torecan, see Thiethylperazine maleate
Tornalate, see Bitolterol mesylate

Torsemide	10 mg/ml	IV	J3265

Totacillin-N, see Ampicillin

Trastuzumab	10 mg		J9355

Tri-Kort, see Triamcinolone acetonide
Triam-A, see Triamcinolone acetonide

Triamcinolone acetonide	per 10 mg	IM	J3301
Triamcinolone diacetate	per 5 mg	IM	J3302
Triamcinolone hexacetonide	per 5 mg	VAR	J3303
Triamcinolone, inhalation solution, concetrated form	per mg	INH	J7683
Triamcinolone, inhalation solution, unit dose form	per mg	INH	J7684
Triflupromazine HCl	up to 20 mg	IM, IV	J3400

Trilafon, see Perphenazine
Trilog, see Triamcinolone acetonide
Trilone, see Triamcinolone diacetate

Trimethaphan camsylate	up to 500 mg	IV	J0400
Trimethobenzamide HCl	up to 200 mg	IM	J3250
	250 mg	ORAL	Q0173
Trimetrexate glucuronate	per 25 mg	IV	J3305

Trobicin, see Spectinomycin HCl

U

Ultrazine-10, see Prochlorperazine
Unasyn, see Ampicillin sodium/sulbactam sodium

Unclassified drugs (see also Not elsewhere classified)	—	—	J3490
Urea	up to 40 g	IV	J3350

Ureaphil, see Urea
Urecholine, see Bethanechol chloride

Urokinase	5,000 IU vial	IV	J3364
	250,000 IU vial	IV	J3365

V

V-Gan 25, see Promethazine HCl
V-Gan 50, see Promethazine HCl
Valergen 10, see Estradiol valerate
Valergen 20, see Estradiol valerate
Valergen 40, see Estradiol valerate
Valertest No. 1, see Testosterone enanthate and estradiol valerate
Valertest No. 2, see Testosterone enanthate and estradiol valerate
Valium, see Diazepam

Valrubicin	200 mg	Intravesical	J9357

Vancocin, see Vancomycin HCl

Vancoled, see Vancomycin HCl
Vancomycin HCl 500 mg IV, IM **J3370**
Vasoxyl, see Methoxamine HCl
Velban, see Vinblastine sulfate
Velsar, see Vinblastine sulfate
Ventolin, see Albuterol sulfate
VePesid, see Etoposide and Etoposide, oral
Versed, see Midazolam HCl
Vesprin, see Triflupromazine HCl
Vinblastine sulfate 1 mg IV **J9360**
Vincasar PFS, see Vincristine sulfate
Vincristine sulfate 1 mg IV **J9370**
2 mg IV **J9375**
5 mg IV **J9380**
Vinorelbine tartrate per 10 mg IV **J9390**
Vistaject-25, see Hydroxyzine HCl
Vistaril, see Hydroxyzine HCl
Vitamin K, see Phytonadione
Vitamin B-12 cyanocobalamin up to 1,000 mcg IM, SC **J3420**
Vitrasert, see Ganciclovir

W

Wehamine, see Dimenhydrinate
Wehdryl, see Diphenhydramine HCl
Wellcovorin, see Leucovorin calcium
Wyamine Sulfate, see Mephentermine sulfate
Wycillin, see Penicillin G procaine
Wydase, see Hyaluronidase

X

Xylocaine HCl, see Lidocaine HCl

Z

Zanosar, see Streptozocin
Zetran, see Diazepam
Zinacef, see Cefuroxime sodium
Zinecard, see Dexrazoxane
Zithromax, see Azithromycin
Zofran, see Ondansetron HCl
Zoladex, see Goserelin acetate implant
Zolicef, see Cefazolin sodium

Appendix A
Coverage Issues Manual (CIM) References

35-10 Hyperbaric Oxygen Therapy

For purposes of coverage under Medicare, hyperbaric oxygen (HBO) therapy is a modality in which the entire body is exposed to oxygen under increased atmospheric pressure.

A. *Covered Conditions* — Program reimbursement for HBO therapy will be limited to that which is administered in a chamber (including the one man unit) and is limited to the following conditions:

1. Acute carbon monoxide intoxication, (ICD-9-CM diagnosis 986).

2. Decompression illness, (ICD-9-CM diagnosis 993.2, 993.3).

3. Gas embolism, (ICD-9-CM diagnosis 958.0, 999.1).

4. Gas gangrene, (ICD-9-CM diagnosis 0400).

5. Acute traumatic peripheral ischemia. HBO therapy is a valuable adjunctive treatment to be used in combination with accepted standard therapeutic measures when loss of function, limb, or life is threatened. (ICD-9-CM diagnosis 902.53, 903.01, 903.1, 904.0, 904.41.)

6. Crush injuries and suturing of severed limbs. As in the previous conditions, HBO therapy would be an adjunctive treatment when loss of function, limb, or life is threatened. (ICD-9-CM diagnosis 927.00-927.03, 927.09-927.11, 927.20-927.21, 927.8-927.9, 928.00-928.01, 928.10-928.11, 928.20-928.21, 928.3, 928.8-928.9, 929.0, 929.9, 996.90-996.99.)

7. Progressive necrotizing infections (necrotizing fasciitis), (ICD-9-CM diagnosis 728.86).

8. Acute peripheral arterial insufficiency (ICD-9-CM diagnosis 444.21, 444.22, 444.81).

9. Treatment of compromised skin grafts, (ICD-9-CM diagnosis 996.52; excludes artificial skin graft).

10. Chronic refractory osteomyelitis, unresponsive to conventional medical and surgical management, (ICD-9-CM diagnosis 730.10-730.19).

11. Osteoradionecrosis as an adjunct to conventional treatment, (ICD-9-CM diagnosis 526.89).

12. Soft tissue radionecrosis as an adjunct to conventional treatment, (ICD-9-CM diagnosis 990).

13. Cyanide poisoning,(ICD-9-CM diagnosis 987.7, 989.0).

14. Actinomycosis, only as an adjunct to conventional therapy when the disease process is refractory to antibiotics and surgical treatment, (ICD-9-CM diagnosis 039.0-039.4, 039.8, 039.9).

B. *Noncovered Conditions* — All other indications not specified under §35-10 (A) are not covered under the Medicare program. No program payment may be made for any conditions other than those listed in §35-10 (A).

C. *Reasonable Utilization Parameters* — Make payment where HBO therapy is clinically practical. HBO therapy should not be a replacement for other standard successful therapeutic measures. Depending on the response of the individual patient and the severity of the original problem, treatment may range from less than 1 week to several months duration, the average being 2 to 4 weeks. Review and document the medical necessity for use of hyperbaric oxygen for more than 2 months, regardless of the condition of the patient, before further reimbursement is made.

D. *Topical Application of Oxygen* — This method of administering oxygen does not meet the definition of HBO therapy as stated above. Also, its clinical efficacy has not been established. Therefore, no Medicare reimbursement may be made for the topical application of oxygen. (Cross refer: §35-31.)

E. *Physician Supervision Requirement* — For HBO therapy to be covered under the Medicare program, the physician must be in constant attendance during the entire treatment. This is a professional activity that cannot be delegated in that it requires independent medical judgement by the physician. The physician must be present, carefully monitoring the patient during the hyperbaric oxygen therapy session and be immediately available should a complication occur. This requirement applies in all settings: no payment will be made under Part A or Part B, unless the physician is in constant attendance during the HBO therapy procedure.

F. *Credentials* — A physician qualified in HBO therapy treatment is defined by Medicare for this purpose to be credentialed by the hospital in which HBO therapy is being performed specifically in hyperbaric medicine and the management of acute cardiopulmonary emergencies, including placement of chest tube. Credentialing includes, at a minimun, the following:

- Training, experience and privileges within the institution to manage acute cardiopulmonary emergencies, including advanced cardiac life support, and emergency myringotomy;
- Completion of a recognized hyperbaric medicine training program as established by either the American College of Hyperbaric Medicine or the Undersea and Hyperbaric Medical Society (UHMS) with a minimum of 60 hours of training and documented by a certificate of completion or an equivalent program; and
- Continuing medical education in hyperbaric medicine of a minimum of 16 hours every 2 years after initial credentialing.

An additional requirement that must be met for Medicare's payment for hyperbaric medical therapy is that cardiopulmonary resuscitation team coverage must be immediately available during the hours of the hyperbaric chamber operations.

35-13   Prolotherapy, Joint Sclerotherapy, and Ligamentous Injections with Sclerosing Agents — Not Covered

The medical effectiveness of the above therapies has not been verified by scientifically controlled studies. Accordingly, reimbursement for these modalities should be denied on the ground that they are not reasonable and necessary as required by §1862(a)(1) of the law.

35-20   Treatment of Motor Function Disorders with Electric Nerve Stimulation — Not Covered

While electric nerve stimulation has been employed to control chronic intractable pain for some time, its use in the treatment of motor function disorders, such as multiple sclerosis, is a recent innovation, and the medical effectiveness of such therapy has not been verified by scientifically controlled studies. Therefore, where electric nerve stimulation is employed to treat motor function disorders, no reimbursement may be made for the stimulator or for the services related to its implantation since this treatment cannot be considered reasonable and necessary.

See §§35-27 and 65-8.

NOTE: Medicare coverage of deep brain stimulation by implantation of a stimulator device is not prohibited. Therefore, coverage of deep brain stimulation provided by an implanted deep brain stimulator is at the carrier's discretion.

35-27   Biofeedback Therapy

Biofeedback therapy provides visual, auditory or other evidence of the status of certain body functions so that a person can exert voluntary control over the functions, and thereby alleviate an abnormal bodily condition. Biofeedback therapy often uses electrical devices to transform bodily signals indicative of such functions as heart rate, blood pressure, skin temperature, salivation, peripheral vasomotor activity, and gross muscle tone into a tone or light, the loudness or brightness of which shows the extent of activity in the function being measured.

Biofeedback therapy differs from electromyography, which is a diagnostic procedure used to record and study the electrical properties of skeletal muscle. An electromyography device may be used to provide feedback with certain types of biofeedback.

Biofeedback therapy is covered under Medicare only when it is reasonable and necessary for the individual patient for muscle re-education of specific muscle groups or for treating pathological muscle abnormalities of spasticity, incapacitating muscle spasm, or weakness, and more conventional treatments (heat, cold, massage, exercise, support) have not been successful. This therapy is not covered for treatment of ordinary muscle tension states or for psychosomatic conditions.

(See HCFA-Pub. 14-3, §§2200ff, 2215, and 4161; HCFA-Pub. 13-3, §§3133.3, 3148, and 3149; HCFA- Pub. 10, §§242 and 242.5 for special physical therapy requirements. See also §35-20 and 65-8.)

35-34   Fabric Wrapping of Abdominal Aneurysms — Not Covered

Fabric wrapping of abdominal aneurysms is not a covered Medicare procedure. This is a treatment for abdominal aneurysms which involves wrapping aneurysms with cellophane or fascia lata. This procedure has not been shown to prevent eventual rupture. In extremely rare instances, external wall reinforcement may be indicated when the current accepted treatment (excision of the aneurysm and reconstruction with synthetic materials) is not a viable alternative, but external wall reinforcement is not fabric wrapping. Accordingly, fabric wrapping of abdominal aneurysms is not considered reasonable and necessary within the meaning of §1862(a)(1) of the Act.

35-46   Assessing Patient's Suitability for Electrical Nerve Stimulation Therapy

Electrical nerve stimulation is an accepted modality for assessing a patient's suitability for ongoing treatment with a transcutaneous or an implanted nerve stimulator. Accordingly, program payment may be made for the following techniques when used to determine the potential therapeutic usefulness of an electrical nerve stimulator:

A. *Transcutaneous Electrical Nerve Stimulation (TENS)* — This technique involves attachment of a transcutaneous nerve stimulator to the surface of the skin over the peripheral nerve to be stimulated. It is used by the patient on a trial basis and its effectiveness in modulating pain is monitored by the physician, or physical therapist. Generally, the physician or physical therapist is able to determine whether the patient is likely to derive a significant therapeutic benefit from continuous use of a transcutaneous stimulator within a trial period of 1 month; in a few cases this determination may take longer to make. Document the medical necessity for such services which are furnished beyond the first month. (See §45-25 for an explanation of coverage of medically necessary supplies for the effective use of TENS.)

If TENS significantly alleviates pain, it may be considered as primary treatment; if it produces no relief or greater discomfort than the original pain electrical nerve stimulation therapy is ruled out. However, where TENS produces incomplete relief, further evaluation with percutaneous electrical nerve stimulation may be considered to determine whether an implanted perifpheral nerve stimulator would provide significant relief from pain. (See §35-46B.)

Usually, the physician or physical therapist providing the services will furnish the equipment necessary for assessment. Where the physician or physical therapist advises the patient to rent the TENS from a supplier during the trial period rather than supplying it himself/herself, program payment may be made for rental of the TENS as well as for the services of the physician or physical therapist who is evaluating its use. However, the combined program payment which is made for the physician's or physical therapist's services and the rental of the stimulator from a supplier should not exceed the amount which would be payable for the total service, including the stimulator, furnished by the physician or physical therapist alone.

B. *Percutaneous Electrical Nerve Stimulation (PENS)* — This diagnostic procedure which involves stimulation of peripheral nerves by a needle electrode inserted through the skin is performed only in a physician's office, clinic, or hospital outpatient department. Therefore, it is covered only when performed by a physician or incident to physician's service. If pain is effectively controlled by percutaneous stimulation, implantation of electrodes is warranted.

As in the case of TENS (described in subsection A), generally the physician should be able to determine whether the patient is likely to derive a significant therapeutic benefit from continuing use of an implanted nerve stimulator within a trial period of 1 month. In a few cases, this determination may take longer to make. The medical necessity for such diagnostic services which are furnished beyond the first month must be documented.

NOTE: Electrical nerve stimulators do not prevent pain but only alleviate pain as it occurs. A patient can be taught how to employ the stimulator, and once this is done, can use it safely and effectively without direct physician supervision. Consequently, it is inappropriate for a patient to visit his/her physician, physical therapist, or an outpatient clinic on a continuing basis for treatment of pain with electrical nerve stimulation. Once it is determined that electrical nerve stimulation should be continued as therapy and the patient has been trained to use the stimulator, it is expected that a stimulator will be implanted or the patient will employ the TENS on a continual basis in his/her home. Electrical nerve stimulation treatments furnished by a physician in his/her office, by a physical therapist or outpatient clinic are excluded from coverage by §1862(a)(1) of the Act. (See §65-8 for an explanation of coverage of the therapeutic use of implanted peripheral nerve stimulators under the prosthetic devices benefit. See §60-20 for an explanation of coverage of the therapeutic use of TENS under the durable medical equipment benefit.)

35-47 Breast Reconstruction Following Mastectomy (Effective for services performed on and after May 15, 1980.)

During recent years, there has been a considerable change in the treatment of diseases of the breast such as fibrocystic disease and cancer. While extirpation of the disease remains of primary importance, the quality of life following initial treatment is increasingly recognized as of great concern. The increased use of breast reconstruction procedures is due to several factors:

- A change in epidemiology of breast cancer, including an apparent increase in incidence;
- Improved surgical skills and techniques;
- The continuing development of better prostheses; and
- Increasing awareness by physicians of the importance of postsurgical psychological adjustment.

Reconstruction of the affected and the contralateral unaffected breast following a medically necessary mastectomy is considered a relatively safe and effective noncosmetic procedure. Accordingly, program payment may be made for breast reconstruction surgery following removal of a breast for any medical reason.

Program payment may not be made for breast reconstruction for cosmetic reasons. (Cosmetic surgery is excluded from coverage under §l862(a)(l0) of the Social Security Act.)

35-48 Osteogenic Stimulation (Effective for services performed on and after September 15, 1980.)

Electrical stimulation to augment bone repair can be attained either invasively or noninvasively. Invasive devices provide electrical stimulation directly at the fracture site either through percutaneously placed cathodes or by implantation of a coiled cathode wire into the fracture site. The power pack for the latter device is implanted into soft tissue near the fracture site and subcutaneously connected to the cathode, creating a self-contained system with no external components.

The power supply for the former device is externally placed and the leads connected to the inserted cathodes. With the noninvasive device, opposing pads, wired to an external power supply, are placed over the cast. An electromagnetic field is created between the pads at the fracture site.

1. *Noninvasive Stimulator* — The noninvasive stimulator device is covered only for the following indications:

Nonunion of long bone fractures;

Failed fusion, where a minimum of nine months has elapsed since the last surgery;

Congenital pseudarthroses; and As an adjunct to spinal fusion surgery for patients at high risk of pseudarthrosis due to previously failed spinal fusion at the same site or for those undergoing multiple level fusion. A multiple level fusion involves 3 or more vertebrae (e.g., L3-L5, L4-S1, etc).

2. *Invasive (Implantable) Stimulator* — The invasive stimulator device is covered only for the following indications:

Nonunion of long bone fractures;

As an adjunct to spinal fusion surgery for patients at high risk of pseudarthrosis due to previously failed spinal fusion at the same site or for those undergoing muliple level fusion. A multiple level fusion involves 3 or more vertebrae (e.g., L3-L5, L4-S1, etc).

Nonunion, for all types of devices, is considered to exist only after six or more months have elapsed without healing of the fracture.

B. *Ultrasonic Osteogenic Stimulators* — An ultrasonic osteogenic stimulator is a non-invasive device that emits low intensity, pulsed ultrasound. The ultrasound signal is applied to the skin surface at the fracture location via ultrasound, conductive, coupling gel in order to accelerate the healing time of the fracture. The device is intended for use with cast immobilization.

There is insufficient evidence to support the medical necessity of using an ultrasonic osteogenic stimulator. Therefore, the device is not covered, because it is not considered reasonable and necessary.

35-5   Cellular Therapy — Not Covered

Cellular therapy involves the practice of injecting humans with foreign proteins like the placenta or lungs of unborn lambs. Cellular therapy is without scientific or statistical evidence to document its therapeutic efficacy and, in fact, is considered a potentially dangerous practice. Accordingly, cellular therapy is not considered reasonable and necessary within the meaning of section 1862 (a) (1) of the law.

35-64   Chelation Therapy for Treatment of Atherosclerosis

Chelation therapy is the application of chelation techniques for the therapeutic or preventive effects of removing unwanted metal ions from the body. The application of chelation therapy using ethylenediamine-tetra-acetic acid (EDTA) for the treatment and prevention of atherosclerosis is controversial. There is no widely accepted rationale to explain the beneficial effects attributed to this therapy. Its safety is questioned and its clinical effectiveness has never been established by well designed, controlled clinical trials. It is not widely accepted and practiced by American physicians. EDTA chelation therapy for atherosclerosis is considered experimental. For these reasons, EDTA chelation therapy for the treatment or prevention of atherosclerosis is not covered. Some practitioners refer to this therapy as chemoendarterectomy and may also show a diagnosis other than atherosclerosis, such as arteriosclerosis or calcinosis. Claims employing such variant terms should also be denied under this section. Cross-refer: §45-20

35-65   Gastric Freezing

Gastric freezing for chronic peptic ulcer disease is a non-surgical treatment which was popular about 20 years ago but now is seldom done. It has been abandoned due to a high complication rate, only temporary improvement experienced by patients, and lack of effectiveness when tested by double-blind, controlled clinical trials. Since the procedure is now considered obsolete, it is not covered.

35-74   Enhanced External Counterpulsation (EECP) for Severe Angina — Covered (Effective for services performed on or after July 1, 1999).

Enhanced external counterpulsation (EECP) is a non-invasive outpatient treatment for coronary artery disease refractory to medical and/or surgical therapy. Although these and similar devices are cleared by the Food and Drug Administration (FDA) for use in treating a variety of conditions, including stable or unstable angina pectoris, acute myocardial infarction and cardiogenic shock, Medicare coverage is limited to its use in patients with stable angina pectoris, since only that use has developed sufficient evidence to demonstrate its medical effectiveness. Other uses of this device and similar devices remain non-covered. In addition, the non-coverage of hydraulic versions of these types of devices remains in force.

Coverage is further limited to those enhanced external counterpulsation systems that have sufficiently demonstrated their medical effectiveness in treating patients with severe angina in well-designed clinical trials. Note that a 510(k) clearance by the Food and Drug Administration does not, by itself, satisfy this requirement.

Coverage is provided for the use of EECP for patients who have been diagnosed with disabling angina (Class III or Class IV, Canadian Cardiovascular Society Classification or equivalent classification) who, in the opinion of a cardiologist or cardiothoracic surgeon, are not readily amenable to surgical intervention, such as PTCA or cardiac bypass because: (1) their condition is inoperable, or at high risk of operative complications or post-operative failure; (2) their coronary anatomy is not readily amenable to such procedures; or (3) they have co-morbid states which create excessive risk.

A full course of therapy usually consists of 35 one-hour treatments, which may be offered once or twice daily, usually 5 days per week). The patient is placed on a treatment table where their lower extremities are wrapped in a series of three compressive air cuffs which inflate and deflate in synchronization with the patient's cardiac cycle.

During diastole the three sets of air cuffs are inflated sequentially (distal to proximal) compressing the vascular beds within the muscles of the calves, lower thighs and upper thighs. This action results in an increase in diastolic pressure, generation of retrograde arterial blood flow and an increase in venous return. The cuffs are deflated simultaneously just prior to systole, which produces a rapid drop in vascular impedance, a decrease in ventricular workload and an increase in cardiac output.

The augmented diastolic pressure and retrograde aortic flow appear to improve myocardial perfusion, while systolic unloading appears to reduce cardiac workload and oxygen requirements. The increased venous return coupled with enhanced systolic flow appears to increase cardiac output. As a result of this treatment, most patients experience increased time until onset of ischemia, increased exercise tolerance, and a reduction in the number and severity of anginal episodes. Evidence was presented that this effect lasted well beyond the immediate post-treatment phase, with patients symptom-free for several months to two years.

This service should be billed using CPT code 97016, Application of a modality to one or more areas; vasopneumatic devices, until a specific code for EECP is established.

35-77 Neuromuscular Electrical Stimulation (NMES) in the Treatment of Disuse Atrophy (Effective for services performed on and after 11-5-84.)

Neuromuscular electrical stimulation (NMES) involves the use of a device which transmits an electrical impulse to the skin over selected muscle groups by way of electrodes. Coverage of NMES is limited to the treatment of disuse atrophy where nerve supply to the muscle is intact, including brain, spinal cord and peripheral nerves, and other non-neurological reasons for disuse are causing atrophy. Some examples would be casting or splinting of a limb, contracture due to scarring of soft tissue as in burn lesions, and hip replacement surgery (until orthotic training begins). (See §45-25 for an explanation of coverage of medically necessary supplies for the effective use of NMES.)

35-93 Lung Volume Reduction Surgery (Reduction Pneumoplasty, Pneumoplasty, aslo called Lung Shaving or Lung Contouring) Unilateral or Bilateral by Open or Thoracoscopic Approcach for Treatment of Emphysema or Chronic Obstructive Pulmonary Disease — Not Generally Covered

Lung volume reduction surgery (LVRS) or reduction pneumoplasty, also referred to as lung shaving or lung contouring, is performed on patients with emphysema and chronic obstructive pulmonary disease (COPD) in order to allow the underlying compressed lung to expand, and thus, establish improved respiratory function. The goal of this procedure is to offer a better quality of life for patients with emphysema and COPD. In addition, LVRS may be offered as a "bridge to transplant" for patients who otherwise may not have been considered candidates for lung transplantation.

Unilateral or bilateral LVRS by open or thoracoscopic approach is not generally covered, because there is insufficient medical evidence available to base a determination that this procedure is generally safe and effective. Therefore, LVRS generally cannot be considered reasonable and necessary under §1862(a)(1)(A) of the Act in most cases.

When this policy was first established in December 1995, HCFA committed Medicare to reviewing the scientific literature as it was published in order to modify coverage policy as clinical data were developed. HCFA has reviewed data that suggest the need for a randomized clinical trial regarding the safety and effectiveness of LVRS. On April 24, 1996, the Health Care Financing Administration (HCFA) and the National Heart, Lung and Blood Institute (NHLBI) of the National Institutes of Health announced their intention to collaborate on a multi-center, randomized clinical study evaluating the effectiveness of LVRS. On December 20, 1996, HCFA and NHLBI announced the clinical centers and the data coordinating center that will be participating in the study. HCFA has determined that LVRS is reasonable and necessary when it is provided under the conditions detailed by the protocol of the HCFA/NHLBI clinical study. Therefore, Medicare will cover LVRS in those limited circumstances when it is provided to a Medicare beneficiary under the protocols established for the study. Coverage will be provided where the care is furnished in facilities that are approved as meeting the criteria established by HCFA and NHLBI for this study.

This study will consist of a registry of all patients referred to the participating clinical centers for LVRS. In addition, a subset of patients from the registry who meet specific inclusion criteria will be invited to participate in the randomized trial. All randomized patients will receive intensive medical therapy and pulmonary rehabilitation. Half will be selected randomly to undergo LVRS, which will be performed via median sternotomy or video-assisted thoracoscopy.

Medicare will provide coverage to those beneficiaries who may participate in the randomized trial for all services integral to the study and for which the Medicare statute does not prohibit. This includes tests performed to determine whether a beneficiary qualifies for randomization, LVRS, and follow-up tests that are necessary during participation in the randomized study. However, Medicare will not provide coverage for those services that are prohibited by the Act. For example, Medicare will provide coverage for pulmonary rehabilitation and pulmonary function testing, but will not provide coverage for oral steroids provided as part of a physician's service under §1862(s)(2) of the Act because they are self-administrable and thus statutorily excluded from coverage.

Payment for these services will be provided under the usual payment systems. For example, Part A services will be paid for according to the DRG system, and Part B physician services will be paid for according to the physician fee schedule.

The data from the randomized phase of the study will be analyzed and monitored continuously in order to determine any appropriate changes in Medicare coverage. These determinations will include if and how coverage will be continued.

35-96 Cryosurgery of Prostate (Effective for services performed on or after July 1, 1999)

Cryosurgery of the prostate gland, also known as cryosurgical ablation of the prostate (CSAP), destroys prostate tissue by applying extremely cold temperatures in order to reduce the size of the prostate gland. It is safe and effective, as well as medically necessary and appropriate, as primary treatment for patients with clinically localized prostate cancer, Stages T1-T3.

45-10 Laetrile and Related Substances — Not Covered

Laetrile (and the other drugs called by the various terms mentioned below) have been used primarily in the treatment or control of cancer. Although the terms "Laetrile," "laetrile," "amygdalin," "Sarcarcinase," "vitamin B-17," and "nitriloside" have been used interchangeably, the chemical identity of the substances to which these terms refer has varied.

The FDA has determined that neither Laetrile nor any other drug called by the various terms mentioned above, nor any other product which might be characterized as a "nitriloside" is generally recognized (by experts qualified by scientific training and experience to evaluate the safety and effectiveness of drugs) to be safe and effective for any therapeutic use. Therefore, use of this drug cannot be considered to be reasonable and necessary within the meaning of §1862(a)(1) of the Act and program payment may not be made for its use or any services furnished in connection with its administration.

A hospital stay only for the purpose of having laetrile (or any other drug called by the terms mentioned above) administered is not covered. Also, program payment may not be made for laetrile (or other drug noted above) when it is used during the course of an otherwise covered hospital stay, since the FDA has found such drugs to not be safe and effective for any therapeutic purpose.

45-16 Certain Drugs Distributed by the National Cancer Institute

(Effective for services furnished on or after October 1, 1980.)

Under its Cancer Therapy Evaluation, the Division of Cancer Treatment of the National Cancer Institute (NCI), in cooperation with the Food and Drug Administration, approves and distributes certain drugs for use in treating terminally ill cancer patients. One group of these drugs, designated as Group C drugs, unlike other drugs distributed by the NCI, are not limited to use in clinical trials for the purpose of testing their efficacy. Drugs are classified as Group C drugs only if there is sufficient evidence demonstrating their efficacy within a tumor type and that they can be safely administered.

A physician is eligible to receive Group C drugs from the Divison of Cancer Treatment only if the following requirements are met:

- A physician must be registered with the NCI as an investigator by having completed an FD-Form 1573;
- A written request for the drug, indicating the disease to be treated, must be submitted to the NCI;
- The use of the drug must be limited to indications outlined in the NCI's guidelines; and
- All adverse reactions must be reported to the Investigational Drug Branch of the Division of Cancer Treatment.

In view of these NCI controls on distribution and use of Group C drugs, intermediaries may assume, in the absence of evidence to the contrary, that a Group C drug and the related hospital stay are covered if all other applicable coverage requirements are satisfied.

If there is reason to question coverage in a particular case, the matter should be resolved with the assistance of the local PSRO, or if there is none, the assistance of your medical consultants.

Information regarding those drugs which are classified as Group C drugs may be obtained from:

> Office of the Chief, Investigational Drug Branch
> Division of Cancer Treatment, CTEP, Landow Building
> Room 4C09, National Cancer Institute
> Bethesda, Maryland 20205

45-20 Ethylenediamine-Tetra-Acetic (EDTA) Chelation Therapy for Treatment of Atherosclerosis

The use of EDTA as a chelating agent to treat atherosclerosis, arteriosclerosis, calcinosis, or similar generalized condition not listed by the FDA as an approved use is not covered. Any such use of EDTA is considered experimental.

See §35-64 for an explanation of this conclusion.

45-22 Lymphocyte Immune Globulin, Anti-thymocyte Globulin (EQUINE)

The lymphocyte immune globulin preparations are biologic drugs not previously approved or licensed for use in the management of renal allograft rejection. A number of other lymphocyte immune globulin products of equine, lapine, and murine origin are currently under investigation for their potential usefulness in controlling allograft rejections in human transplantation. These biologic drugs are viewed as adjunctive to traditional immunosuppressive products such as steroids and anti- metabolic drugs. At present, lymphocyte immune globulin preparations are not recommended to replace conventional immunosuppressive drugs, but to supplement them and to be used as alternatives to elevated or accelerated dosing with conventional immunosuppressive agents.

The FDA has approved one lymphocyte immune globulin preparation for marketing, lymphocyte immune globulin, anti-thymocyte globulin (equine). This drug is indicated for the management of allograft rejection episodes in renal transplantation. It is covered under Medicare when used for this purpose. Other forms of lymphocyte globulin preparation which the FDA approves for this indication in the future may be covered under Medicare.

45-24 Anti-Inhibitor Coagulant Complex (AICC)

Anti-inhibitor coagulant complex, AICC, is a drug used to treat hemophilia in patients with factor VIII inhibitor antibodies. AICC has been shown to be safe and effective and has Medicare coverage when furnished to patients with hemophilia A and inhibitor antibodies to factor VIII who have major bleeding episodes and who fail to respond to other, less expensive therapies.

45-25 Supplies used in the Delivery of Transcutaneous Electrical Nerve Stimulation (TENS) and Neuromuscular Electrial Stimulations (NMES) — (Effective for services rendered (i.e., items rented or purchased) on or after July 14, 1988.)

Transcutaneous Electrical Nerve Stimulation (TENS) and/or Neuromuscular Electrical Stimulation (NMES) can ordinarily be delivered to patients through the use of conventional electrodes, adhesive tapes and lead wires. There may be times, however, where it might be medically necessary for certain patients receiving TENS or NMES treatment to use, as an alternative to conventional electrodes, adhesive tapes and lead wires, a form-fitting conductive garment (i.e., a garment with conductive fibers which are separated from the patients' skin by layers of fabric).

A form-fitting conductive garment (and medically necessary related supplies) may be covered under the program only when:

1. It has received permission or approval for marketing by the Food and Drug Administration;

2. It has been prescribed by a physician for use in delivering covered TENS or NMES treatment; and

3. One of the medical indications outlined below is met:

    The patient cannot manage without the conductive garment because there is such a large area or so many sites to be stimulated and the stimulation would have to be delivered so frequently that it is not feasible to use conventional electrodes, adhesive tapes and lead wires;

    The patient cannot manage without the conductive garment for the treatment of chronic intractable pain because the areas or sites to be stimulated are inaccessible with the use of conventional electrodes, adhesive tapes and lead wires;

    The patient has a documented medical condition such as skin problems that preclude the application of conventional electrodes, adhesive tapes and lead wires;

    The patient requires electrical stimulation beneath a cast either to treat disuse atrophy, where the nerve supply to the muscle is intact, or to treat chronic intractable pain; or

    The patient has a medical need for rehabilitation strengthening (pursuant to a written plan of rehabilitation) following an injury where the nerve supply to the muscle is intact.

    A conductive garment is not covered for use with a TENS device during the trial period specified in §35-46 unless:

4. The patient has a documented skin problem prior to the start of the trial period; and

5. The carrier's medical consultants are satisfied that use of such an item is medically necessary for the patient.

    (See conditions for coverage of the use of TENS in the diagnosis and treatment of chronic intractable pain in §§35-46 and 60-20 and the use of NMES in the treatment of disuse atrophy in §35-77.)

45-4 Vitamin B12 Injections to Strengthen Tendons, Ligaments, etc., of the Foot — Not Covered

Vitamin B12 injections to strengthen tendons, ligaments, etc., of the foot are not covered under Medicare because (1) there is no evidence that vitamin B12 injections are effective for the purpose of strengthening weakened tendons and ligaments, and (2) this is nonsurgical treatment under the subluxation exclusion. Accordingly, vitamin B12 injections are not considered reasonable and necessary within the meaning of §1862(a)(1) of the Act.

See Intermediary Manual, §§3101.3 and 3158 and Carriers Manual, §§2050.5 and 2323.

45-7 Hydrophilic Contact Lens for Corneal Bandage

Some hydrophilic contact lenses are used as moist corneal bandages for the treatment of acute or chronic corneal pathology, such as bullous keratopathy, dry eyes, corneal ulcers and erosion, keratitis, corneal edema, descemetocele, corneal ectasis, Mooren's ulcer, anterior corneal dystrophy, neurotrophic keratoconjunctivitis, and for other therapeutic reasons.

Payment may be made under §1861(s)(2) of the Act for a hydrophilic contact lens approved by the Food and Drug Administration (FDA) and used as a supply incident to a physician's service. Payment for the lens is included in the payment for the physician's service to which the lens is incident. Contractors are authorized to accept an FDA letter of approval or other FDA published material as evidence of FDA approval. (See §65-1 for coverage of a hydrophilic contact lens as a prosthetic device.)

See Intermediary Manual, §3112.4 and Carriers Manual, §§2050.1 and 15010.

50-1 Cardiac Pacemaker Evaluation Services (Effective for services rendered on or after October 1, 1984.)

Medicare covers a variety of services for the post-implant follow-up and evaluation of implanted cardiac pacemakers. The following guidelines are designed to assist contractors in identifying and processing claims for such services.

NOTE: These new guidelines are limited to lithium battery-powered pacemakers, because mercury-zinc battery-powered pacemakers are no longer being manufactured and virtually all have been replaced by lithium units. Contractors still receiving claims for monitoring such units should continue to apply the guidelines published in 1980 to those units until they are replaced.

There are two general types of pacemakers in current use—single-chamber pacemakers, which sense and pace the ventricles of the heart, and dual-chamber pacemakers which sense and pace both the atria and the ventricles. These differences require different monitoring patterns over the expected life of the units involved. One fact of which contractors should be aware is that many dual-chamber units may be programmed to pace only the ventricles; this may be done either at the time the pacemaker is implanted or at some time afterward. In such cases, a dual-chamber unit, when programmed or reprogrammed for ventricular pacing, should be treated as a single-chamber pacemaker in applying screening guidelines.

50-15 Electrocardiographic Services

Reimbursement may be made under Part B for electrocardiographic (EKG) services rendered by a physician or incident to his/her services or by an approved laboratory or an approved supplier of portable X-ray services. Since there is no coverage for EKG services of any type rendered on a screening basis or as part of a routine examination, the claim must indicate the signs and symptoms or other clinical reason necessitating the services.

A separate charge by an attending or consulting physician for EKG interpretation is allowed only when it is the normal practice to make such charge in addition to the regular office visit charge. No payment is made for EKG interpretations by individuals other than physicians.

On a claim involving EKG services furnished by a laboratory or a portable X-ray supplier, identify the physician ordering the service and, when the charge includes both the taking of the tracing and its interpretation, include the identity of the physician making the interpretation. No separate bill for the services of a physician is paid unless it is clear that he/she was the patient's attending physician or was acting as a consulting physician. The taking of an EKG in an emergency, i.e., when the patient is or may be experiencing what is commonly referred to as a heart attack, is covered as a laboratory service or a diagnostic service by a portable X-ray supplier only when the evidence shows that a physician was in attendance at the time the service was performed or immediately thereafter.

Where EKG services are rendered in the patient's home and the laboratory's or portable X-ray supplier's charge is higher than that imposed for the same service when performed in the laboratory or portable X-ray supplier's office, the medical need for home service should be documented. In the absence of such justification, reimbursement for the service if otherwise medically necessary should be based on the reasonable charge applicable when performed in the laboratory or X-ray supplier's office.

The documentation required in the various situations mentioned above must be furnished not only when the laboratory or portable X-ray supplier bills the patient or carrier for its service, but also when such a facility bills the attending physician who, in turn, bills the patient or carrier for the EKG services. (In addition to the evidence required to document the claim, the laboratory or portable X-ray supplier must maintain in its records the referring physician's written order and the identity of the employee taking the tracing.)

Long Term EKG Monitoring, also referred to as long-term EKG recording, Holter recording, or dynamic electrocardiography, is a diagnostic procedure which provides a continuous record of the electrocardiographic activity of a patient's heart while he is engaged in his daily activities.

The basic components of the long-term EKG monitoring systems are a sensing element, the design of which may provide either for the recording of electrocardiographic information on magnetic tape or for detecting significant variations in rate or rhythm as they occur, and a component for either graphically recording the electrocardiographic data or for visual or computer assisted analysis of the information recorded on magnetic tape. The long-term EKG permits the examination in the ambulant or potentially ambulant patient of as many as 70,000 heartbeats in a 12-hour recording while the standard EKG which is obtained in the recumbent position, yields information on only 50 to 60 cardiac cycles and provides only a limited data base on which diagnostic judgments may be made.

Many patients with cardiac arrhythmias are unaware of the presence of an irregularity in heart rhythm. Due to the transient nature of many arrhythmias and the short intervals in which the rhythm of the heart is observed by conventional standard EKG techniques, the offending arrhythmias can go undetected. With the extended examination provided by the long-term EKG, the physician is able not only to detect but also to classify various types of rhythm disturbances and waveform abnormalities and note the frequency of their occurrence. The knowledge of the reaction of the heart to daily activities with respect to rhythm, rate, conduction disturbances, and ischemic changes are of great assistance in directing proper therapy and rehabilitation.

This modality is valuable in both inpatient and outpatient diagnosis and therapy. Long-term monitoring of ambulant or potentially ambulant inpatients provides significant potential for reducing the length of stay for post-coronary infarct patients in the intensive care setting and may result in earlier discharge from the hospital with greater assurance of safety to the patients. The indications for the use of this technique, noted below, are similar for both inpatients and outpatients.

The long-term EKG has proven effective in detecting transient episodes of cardiac dysrhythmia and in permitting the correlation of these episodes with cardiovascular symptomatology. It is also useful for patients who have symptoms of obscure etiology suggestive of cardiac arrhythmia.Examples of such symptoms include palpitations, chest pain, dizziness, light-headedness, near syncope, syncope, transient ischemic episodes, dyspnea, and shortness of breath.

This technique would also be appropriate at the time of institution of any arrhythmic drug therapy and may be performed during the course of therapy to evaluate response.It is also appropriate for evaluating a change of dosage and may be indicated shortly before and after the discontinuation of anti-arrhythemic medication.The therapeutic response to a drug whose duration of action and peak of effectiveness is defined in hours cannot be properly assessed by examining 30-40 cycles on a standard EKG rhythm strip.The knowledge that all patients placed on anti-arrhythmic medication do not respond to therapy and the known toxicity of anti-arrhythmic agents clearly indicate that proper assessment should be made on an individual basis to determine whether medication should be continued and at what dosage level.

The long-term EKG is also valuable in the assessment of patients with coronary artery disease.It enables the documentation of etiology of such symptoms as chest pain and shortness of breath.Since the standard EKG is often normal during the intervals between the episodes of precordial pain, it is essential to obtain EKG information while the symptoms are occurring.The long-term EKG has enabled the correlation of chest symptoms with the objective evidence of ST-segment abnormalities.It is appropriate for patients who are recovering from an acute mycardial infarction or coronary insufficiency before and after discharge from the hospital, since it is impossible to predict which of these patients is subject to ventricular arrhythmias on the basis of the presence or absence of rhythm disturbances during the period of initial coronary care.The long-term EKG enables the physician to identify patients who are at a higher risk of dying suddenly in the period following an accute myocardial infarction.It may also be reasonable and necessary where the high-risk patient with known cardiovascular disease advances to a substantially higher level of activity which might trigger increased or new types of arrhythmias necessitating treatment.Such a high-risk case would be one in which there is documentation that acute phase arrhythmias have not totally disappeared during the period of convalesence.

In view of recent developments in cardiac pacemaker monitoring techniques (see CIA 50-1), the use of the long-term EKG for routine assessment of pacemaker functioncan no longer be justified.Its use for the patient with an internal pacemaker would be covered only when he has symptoms suggestive of arrhythmia not revealed by the standard EKG or rhythm strip.

These guidelines are intended as a general outline of the circumstances under which the use of this diagnostic procedure would be warranted.Each patient receiving a long-term EKG should be evaluated completely, prior to performance of this diagnostic study.A complete history and physical examination should be obtained and the indications for use of the long-term EKG should be reviewed by the referring physician.

The performance of a long-term EKG does not necessarily require the prior performance of a standard EKG.Nor does the demonstration of a normal standard EKG preclude the need for a long-term EKG.Finally, the demonstration of an abnormal standard EKG does not obviate the need for a long-term EKG if there is suspicion that the dysrhythmia is transient in nature.

A period of recording of up to 24 hours would normally be adequate to detect most transient arrhythmias and provide essential diagnostic information.The medical necessity for longer periods of monitoring must be documented.

Medical documentation for adjudicating claims for the use of the long-term EKG should be similar to other EKG services, X-ray services, and laboratory procedures.Generally, a statement of the diagnostic impression of the referring physician with an indication of the patient's relevant signs and symptoms should be sufficient for purposes of making a determination regarding the reasonableness and medical necessity for the use of this procedure.However, the intermediaries or carriersshould require whatever additional documentation their medical consultants deem necessary to properly adjudicate the individual claim where the information submitted is not adequate.

It should be noted that the recording device furnished to the patient is simply one component of the diagnostic system and a separate charge for it will not be recognized under the durable medical equipment benefit.

Patient-Activated EKG Recorders, distributed under a variety of brand names, permit the patient to record an EKG upon manifestation of symptoms, or in response to a physician's order (e.g., immediately following strong exertion).Most such devices also permit the patient to simultaneously voice-record in order to describe symptoms and/or activity.In addition, some of these devices permit transtelephonic transmission of the recording to a physician's office, clinic, hospital, etc., having a decoder/recorder for review and analysis, thus eliminating the need to physically transport the tape.Some of these devices also permit a "time sampling" mode of operation.However, the "time sampling" mode is not covered—only the patient-activated mode of operation, when used for the indications described below, is covered at this time.

Services in connection with patient-activated EKG recorders are covered when used as an alternative to the long-term EKG monitoring (described above) for similar indications—detecting and characterizing symptomatic arrhythmias, regulation of anti-arrhythmic drug therapy, etc.Like long-term EKG monitoring, use of these devices is covered for evaluating patients with symptoms of obscure etiology suggestive of cardiac arrhythmia such as palpitations, chest pain, dizziness, lightheadedness, near syncope, syncope, transient ischemic episodes, dyspnea and shortness of breath.

As with long-term EKG monitors, patient-activated EKG recorders may be useful for both inpatient and outpatient diagnosis and therapy. While useful for assessing some post-coronary infarct patients in the hospital setting, these devices should not, however, be covered for outpatient monitoring of recently discharged post-infarct patients.

Computer Analyzed Electrocardiograms — Computer interpretation of EKG's is recognized as a valid and effective technique which will improve the quality and availability of cardiology services. Reimbursement may be made for such computer service when furnished in the setting and under the circumstances required for coverage of other electrocardiographic services. Where either a laboratory's or a portable x-ray supplier's charge for EKG services includes the physician review and certification of the printout as well as the computer interpretation, the certifying physician must be identified on the HCFA-1490 before the entire charge can be considered a reimbursable charge. Where the laboratory's (or portable x-ray supplier's) reviewing physician is not identified, the carrier should conclude that no professional component is involved and make its charge determination accordingly. If the supplying laboratory (or portable x-ray supplier when supplied by such a facility) does not include professional review and certification of the hard copy, a charge by the patient's physician may be recognized for the service. In any case the charge for the physician component should be substantially less than that for physician interpretation of the conventional EKG tracing in view of markedly reduced demand on the physician's time where computer interpretation is involved. Considering the unit cost reduction expected of this innovation, the total charge for the complete EKG service (taking of tracing and interpretation) when computer interpretation is employed should never exceed that considered reasonable for the service when physician interpretation is involved.

Transtelephonic Electrocardiographic Transmissions (Formerly Referred to as EKG Telephone Reporter Systems) — Effective for services furnished on and after March 1, 1980, coverage is extended to include the use of transtelephonic electrocardiographic (EKG) transmissions as a diagnostic service for the indications described below, when performed with equipment meeting the standards described below, subject to the limitations and conditions specified below. Coverage is further limited to the amounts payable with respect to the physician's service in interpreting the results of such transmissions, including charges for rental of the equipment. The device used by the beneficiary is part of a total diagnostic system and is not considered durable medical equipment.

1. *Covered Uses* — The use of transtelephonic EKGs is covered for the following uses:

    a. To detect, characterize, and document symptomatic transient arrhythmias;

    b. To overcome problems in regulating antiarrhythmic drug dosage;

    c. To carry out early posthospital monitoring of patients discharged after myocardial infarction; (only if 24-hour coverage is provided, see 4. below).

    Since cardiology is a rapidly changing field, some uses other than those specified above may be covered if, in the judgment of the contractor's medical consultants, such a use was justifiable in the particular case. The enumerated uses above represent uses for which a firm coverage determination has been made, and for which contractors may make payment without extensive claims development or review.

2. *Specifications for Devices* — The devices used by the patient are highly portable (usually pocket-sized) and detect and convert the normal EKG signal so that it can be transmitted via ordinary telephone apparatus to a receiving station. At the receiving end, the signal is decoded and transcribed into a conventional EKG. There are numerous devices available which transmit EKG readings in this fashion. For purposes of Medicare coverage, however, the transmitting devices must meet at least the following criteria:

    a. They must be capable of transmitting EKG Leads, I, II, or III;

    b. These lead transmissions must be sufficiently comparable to readings obtained by a conventional EKG to permit proper interpretation of abnormal cardiac rhythms.

3. *Potential for Abuse — Need for Screening Guidelines* — While the use of these devices may often compare favorably with more costly alternatives, this is the case only where the information they contribute is actively utilized by a knowledgeable practitioner as part of overall medical management of the patient. Consequently, it is vital that contractors be aware of the potential for abuse of these devices, and adopt necessary screening and physician education policies to detect and halt potentially abusive situations. For example, use of these devices to diagnose and treat suspected arrhythmias as a routine substitute for more conventional methods of diagnosis, such as a careful history, physical examination, and standard EKG and rhythm strip would not be appropriate. Moreover, contractors should require written justification for use of such devices in excess of 30 consecutive days in cases involving detection of transient arrhythmias.

    Contractors may find it useful to review claims for these devices with a view toward detecting patterns of practice which may be useful in developing schedules which may be adopted for screening such claims in the future.

4. *Twenty-four Hour Coverage* — No payment may be made for the use of these devices to carry out early posthospital monitoring of patients discharged after myocardial infarction unless provision is made for 24 hour coverage in the manner described below.

Twenty-four hour coverage means that there must be, at the monitoring site (or sites) an experienced EKG technician receiving calls; tape recording devices do not meet this requirement.Further, such technicians should have immediate access to a physician, and have been instructed in when and how to contact available facilities to assist the patient in case of emergencies.

Cross-refer:HCFA-Pub. 13-3, §§3101.5, 3110, 3112.3, HCFA-Pub. 14-3, §§2070, 2255, 2050.1

50-16   Hemorheograph

The hemorheograph is a diagnostic instrument which is safe and effective for determining the adequacy of skin perfusion prior to the performance of minor surgical procedures on the extremities, including minor podiatric procedures, and as an adjunct to the evaluation of patients suspected of having peripheral vascular disease.

Program payment may be made only for those services employing the hemorheograph which are performed for preoperative and postoperative diagnostic evaluation of suspected peripheral artery disease.

NOTE: This instrument is not a plethysmograph and is not considered as such. A plethysmograph measures and records changes in the size of a body part as modified by the circulation of blood in that part. The hemorheograph, on the other hand, measures surface blood flow in the skin; it does not measure total blood flow in a digit or limb. (See §50-6.)

50-20   Diagnostic Pap Smears

A diagnostic papa smear and related medically necessary services are covered under Medicare Part B when ordered by a physician under one of the following conditions: previous cancer of the cervix, uterus, or vagina that has been or is presently being treated; previous abnormal pap smear; any abnormal findings of the vagina, cervix, uterus, ovaries, or adnexa; any significant complaint by the patient referable to the female reproductive system; or any signs or symptoms that might in the physician's judgment reasonably be related to a gynecologic disorder.

In respect to the last item, the contractor's medial staff must determine whether in a particular case a previous malignancy at another site is an indication for a diagnostic pap smear or whether the test must be considered a screening pap smear as described in 50-20.1 Use the following CPT codes for indicating diagnostic pap smears:]

> *88141 Cytopathology, cervical or vaginal (any reporting system); requiring interpretation by physician (List separately in addition to code for technical service)*
>
> *88150 Cytopathology, slides, cervical or vaginal; manual screening under physician supervision*

50-20.1   Screening Pap Smears and Pelvic Examination for Early Detection of Cervical or Vaginal Cancer

(For screening pap smears, effective for services performed on or after July 1, 1990. For pelvic examinations, including clinical breast examination, effective for services furnished on or after January 1, 1998.)

A screening pap smear (use HCPCS code P3000 Screening Papanicolaou smear, cervical or vaginal, up to three smears; by technical under physician supervision or P3001 Screening Papanicolaou smear, cervical or vaginal up to three smears requiring interpreation by physician).

(Use HCPCS codes G0123 Screening Cytopathology, cervical or vaginal (any reporting system), collected preservative fluid, automated thin layer preparation, screening by cytotechnologist under physician supervision or G0124 Screening Cytopathology, cervical or vaginal (any reporting system), collected in preservative fluid, automated thin layer preparation, requiring interpretation by physician) and related medically necessary services provided to a woman for the early detection of cervical cancer (including collection of the sample of cells and a physician's interpretation of the test results) and Pelvic examination (including clinical breast examination) (use HCPCS code G0101 Cervical or vaginal cancer screening; pelvic and clinical breast examination) are covered under Medicare Part B when ordered by a physician (or authorized practitioner) under one of the following conditions: 1) She has not had such a test during the preceding 3 years or is a woman of childbearing age (1861(nn) of the Act) 2) There is evidence (on the basis of her medical history or other findings) that she is at high risk of developing cervical cancer and her physician (or authorized practitioner) recommends that she have the test performed more frequently than every 3 years.

High risk factors for cervical and vaginal cancer are: 1) Early onset of sexual activity (under age 16) 2) Multiple sexual partners (five or more in a lifetime) 3) History of sexually transmitted disease (including HIV infection) 4) Fewer than three negative or any pap smears within the previous 7 years; and 5) DES (diethylistilbestrol) - exposed daughters of women who took DES during pregnancy.

Note: Claims for pap smears must indicate the beneficiary's low or high risk status by including the appropriate ICD-9-CM on the line item (Item 24E of the HCFA-1500 form).

> *V76.2   special screening for malignant neoplasms of the cervix,* **indicates low risk**;
>
> *V15.89   other specified personal history presenting hazards to health,* **indicate high risk**

If pap smear of pelvic exam claims do not point to one of these diagnosis codes, the claim will reject in the Common Working File. Claims can contain up to four diagnosis codes, but the one pointed to one the line must be either V76.2 or V15.89.

Definitions:

A woman as described in 1861 (nn) of the Act is a woman who is of childbearing age and has had a pap smear test during any of the preceding 3 years that indicated the presence of cervical or vaginal cancer or her abnormality, or is at high risk of developing cervical or vaginal cancer.

A woman of childbearing age is one who is premenopausal and has been determined by a physician or other qualified practitioner to be of childbearing age, based upon the medial history or other findings.

Other qualified practitioner", as defined in 42 CFR 410.56(a) includes a certified nurse midwife (as defined in 1861 (gg) of the Act), or a physician assistant, nurse practitioner, or clinical nurse specialist (as defined in 1861 (aa) of the Act) who is authorized under State law to perform the examination.

Screening Pelvic Examination
Section 4102 of the Balanced Budget Act of 1997 provides for coverage of screening pelvic examination (including a clinical breast examination) for all female beneficiaries, effective January 1, 1998, subject to certain frequency and other limitations. A screening pelvic examination (including a clinical breast examination) should include at least seven of the following 11 elements: 1) Inspection and palpation of breasts for masses or lumps, tenderness, symmetry, or nipple discharge; 2) Digital rectal examination including sphincter tone, presence of hemorrhoids, and rectal masses. Pelvic examination (with or without specimen collection for smears and cultures) including:

- External genitalia (for example, general appearance, hair distribution, or lesions)
- Urethral maetus (for example, size, location, lesions, or prolapse)
- Urethra (for example, masses, tenderness, or scarring)
- Bladder (for example, fullness, masses, or tenderness)
- Vagina (for example, general appearance, estrogen effect, discharge lesions, pelvic support, cystocele, or rectocele)
- Cervix (for example, general appearance, lesions, or discharge)
- Uterus (for example, size, contour, position, mobility, tenderness, consistency, descent, or support)
- Adnexa/parametria (for example, masses, tenderness, organomegaly, or nodularity)
- Anus and perineum

This description is from Documentation Guidelines for Evaluation and Management Services, published in May 1997 and was developed by the Health Care Financing Administration and the American Medical Association.

50-24   Hair Analysis — Not Covered
Hair analysis to detect mineral traces as an aid in diagnosing human disease is not a covered service under Medicare.

The correlation of hair analysis to the chemical state of the whole body is not possible at this time, and therefore this diagnostic procedure cannot be considered to be reasonable and necessary under §1862(a)(1) of the law.

50-26   Dental Examination Prior to Kidney Transplantation
Despite the "dental services exclusion" in §1862(a)(12) of the Act (see Intermediary Manual,§3162; Carriers Manual, §2336), an oral or dental examination performed on an inpatient basis as part of a comprehensive workup prior to renal transplant surgery is a covered service. This is because the purpose of the examination is not for the care of the teeth or structures directly supporting the teeth. Rather, the examination is for the identification, prior to a complex surgical procedure, of existing medical problems where the increased possibility of infection would not only reduce the chances for successful surgery but would also expose the patient to additional risks in undergoing such surgery.

Such a dental or oral examination would be covered under Part A of the program if performed by a dentist on the hospital's staff, or under Part B if performed by a physician. (When performing a dental or oral examination, a dentist is not recognized as a physician under §1861(r) of the law.)(See Carriers Manual §2020.3.)

50-34   Obsolete or unreliable Diagnostic Tests
A. *Diagnostic Tests (Effective for Services Performed On or After May 15, 1980* — Do not routinely pay for the following diagnostic tests because they are obsolete and have been replaced by more advanced procedures. The listed tests may be paid for only if the medical need for the procedure is satisfactorily justified by the physician who performs it. When the services are subject to PRO review, the PRO is responsible for determining that satisfactory medical justification exists. When the services are not subject to PRO review, the intermediary or carrier is responsible for determining that satisfactory medical justification exists. This includes:

Amylase, blood isoenzymes, electrophoretic,
Chromium, blood,
Guanase, blood,
Zinc sulphate turbidity, blood,
Skin test, cat scratch fever,
Skin test, lymphopathia venereum,
Circulation time, one test,
Cephalin flocculation,
Congo red, blood,
Hormones, adrenocorticotropin quantitative animal tests,
Hormones, adrenocorticotropin quantitative bioassay,
Thymol turbidity, blood,
Skin test, actinomycosis,
Skin test, brucellosis,
Skin test, psittacosis,
Skin test, trichinosis,
Calcium, feces, 24-hour quantitative,
Starch, feces, screening,

Chymotrypsin, duodenal contents,

Gastric analysis, pepsin,

Gastric analysis, tubeless,

Calcium saturation clotting time,

Capillary fragility test (Rumpel-Leede),

Colloidal gold,

Bendien's test for cancer and tuberculosis,

Bolen's test for cancer,

Rehfuss test for gastric acidity, and

Serum seromucoid assay for cancer and other diseases.

B. *Cardiovascular Tests (Effective For Services Performed On or After January 1, 1997)* — Do not pay for the following phonocardiography and vectorcardiography diagnostic tests because they have been determined to be outmoded and of little clinical value. They include:

CPT code 93201, Phonocardiogram with or without ECG lead; with supervision during recording with interpretation and report (when equipment is supplied by the physician),

CPT code 93202, Phonocardiogram; tracing only, without interpretation and report (e.g., when equipment is supplied by the hospital, clinic),

CPT code 93204, Phonocardiogram; interpretation and report,

CPT code 93205, Phonocardiogram with ECG lead, with indirect carotid artery and/or jugular vein tracing, and/or apex cardiogram; with interpretation and report,

CPT code 93208, Phonocardiogram; without interpretation and report,

CPT code 93209, Phonocardiogram; interpretation and report only,

CPT code 93210, Intracardiac,

CPT code 93220, Vectorcardiogram (VCG), with or without ECG; with interpretation and report,

CPT code 93221, Vectorcardiogram; tracing only, without interpretation and report, and

CPT code 93222, Vectorcardiogram; interpretation and report only.

50-36 Positron Emission Tomography (PET) Scans

I. General Description

Positron emission tomography (PET) also known as positron emission transverse tomography (PETT), or positron emission coincident imaging (PECI), is a noninvasive imaging procedure that assesses perfusion and the level of metabolic activity in various organ systems of the human body. A positron camera (tomograph) is used to produce cross-sectional tomographic images by detecting radioactivity from a radioactive tracer substance (radiopharmaceutical) that is injected into the patient.

Medicare has been continuously reviewing the scientific literature regarding PET scans, and has established coverage for three uses—one in 1995 and two in 1998 (see below). As with other new or evolving technologies, we will continue to review the progress of this technology, with a view toward modifying our policy, based upon the best evidence available as to the medical effectiveness of such scans. This instruction adds coverage of PET for evaluation of recurrent colorectal cancer in patients with rising levels of carcinoembryonic antigen (CEA), for staging of lymphoma (both Hodgkins and non-Hodgkins) when the PET scan substitutes for a Gallium scan, and for the detection of recurrent melanoma. All other uses of PET scans remain not covered by Medicare.

II. Conditions Applicable to All Covered Uses of PET Scans:

Regardless of any other terms or conditions, all uses of PET scans, in order to be covered by the Medicare program, must meet the following conditions:

1. Such scans must be performed using a camera that has either been approved or cleared for marketing by the FDA to image radionuclides in the body.

2. Submission of claims for payment must include any information Medicare requires to assure that the PET scans performed were: (a) medically necessary; (b) did not unnecessarily duplicate other covered diagnostic tests, and (c) did not involve investigational drugs or procedures using investigational drugs, as determined by the Food and Drug Administration (FDA).

3. The PET scan entity submitting claims for payment must keep such patient records as Medicare requires on file for each patient for whom a PET scan claim is made.

III. Coverage of PET Scans Using Rubidium 82 (Rb 82) and Related Tests—Effective for Services Performed on or After March 14, 1995:

PET scans done at rest or with pharmacological stress used for noninvasive imaging of the perfusion of the heart for the diagnosis and management of patients with known or suspected coronary artery disease using the FDA-approved radiopharmaceutical Rubidium 82 (Rb 82) are covered, provided such scans meet either one of the two following conditions:

1. The PET scan, whether rest alone, or rest with stress, is used in place of, but not in addition to, a single photon emission computed tomography (SPECT); or

2. The PET scan, whether rest alone or rest with stress, is used following a SPECT that was found inconclusive. In these cases, the PET scan must have been considered necessary in order to determine what medical or surgical intervention is required to treat the patient. (For purposes of this requirement, an inconclusive test is a test(s) whose results are equivocal, technically uninterpretable, or discordant with a patient's other clinical data.)

NOTE: PET scans using Rubidium 82, whether rest or stress are not covered by Medicare for screening of asymptomatic patients, regardless of the number and severity of risk factors applicable to such patients.

Submission of Claims Data — All claims for PET scans with Rb 82 for imaging of perfusion of the heart must include the following information. Failure to submit this information may result in denial of a claim.

For any PET scan for which Medicare payment is claimed, the claimant must submit additionalspecified information on the claim form (including proper codes and modifiers) to indicate the results of the PET scan, as well as information as to whether the PET scan was done after an inconclusive noninvasive cardiac test. The information submitted with respect to the previous noninvasive cardiac test must specify the type of test done prior to the PET scan and whether it was inconclusive or unsatisfactory. These explanations are in the form of special G codes used for billing PET scans using Rb 82.

Maintenance of Patient Record Data Onsite — As with any claim, but particularly in view of the limitations on this coverage, Medicare may decide to conduct post-payment reviews to determine that the use of PET scans is consistent with this instruction. PET scanning facilities must keep patient record information on file for each Medicare patient for whom such a PET scan claim is made. These medical records will be used in any post-payment reviews and must include the information necessary to substantiate the need for the PET scan. These records must include standard information (e.g., age, sex, and height) along with any annotations regarding body size or type which indicated a need for a PET scan to determine that patient's condition (i.e., any reason the nature of the patient's body size or type mandated the use of a PET scan in order to continue treatment).

IV. Coverage of PET Scans Using FDG in Characterization of Solitary Pulmonary Nodules (SPNs)—Effective for Services Performed on or After January 1, 1998.

Background: HCFA has carefully examined a wide range of uses of PET with FDG in detecting, staging and monitoring non-central nervous system (CNS) cancers. Currently, these uses do not appear to be sufficiently developed to allow HCFA to determine their medical effectiveness to a degree sufficient to make a conclusive coverage determination under the Medicare program. However, there is some research data indicating that, in the case of characterization of single pulmonary nodules (SPNs), regional PET chest scans may offer, at least for some patients, an effective method of determining the proper course of management for their disease. It is not yet clear how effective this procedure will be in everyday use. Therefore, Medicare will begin paying for PET scans on an interim basis in accords with the terms of this instruction. During the period of this interim coverage, we will continue to seek and review information on the clinical effectiveness of this procedure. We will also encourage researchers to continue to refine and expand the knowledge base necessary to assure that such scans are fully and properly utilized.

HCFA intends to closely monitor not only the provision of services furnished under this coverage, but also the development of additional information developed by non-HCFA studies. We believe that a full understanding of the clinical effectiveness of PET for the characterization of SPNs will be found after additional clinical research. We will collect and analyze our claims data on this service, and we expect and encourage others to continue their study of the use of PET for characterization of SPNs, including randomized clinical trials. HCFA will continue to review the medical literature, as well as studies, assessments, and other information developed by the medical and scientific community to assure that its coverage of these scans is appropriate.

Coverage of PET scans for characterization of solitary pulmonary nodules (SPNs)—PET scans using the glucose analog 2-[fluorine-18]-fluoro-2-deoxy-D-glucose (FDG) are covered, subject to the conditions and limitations described below, when used for the characterization of suspected solitary pulmonary nodules (SPNs). The primary purpose of such characterization should be to determine the likelihood of malignancy in order to plan future management and treatment for the patient.

The procedure consists of the glucose analog FDG being injected into the patient intravenously, with image acquisition usually beginning 30-60 minutes later, and continuing for a period of 10-20 minutes. The FDG is metabolized by both normal and cancerous tissue in proportion to the rate of glucolysis. Since tumor cells have shown an increased utilization of glucose, those regions observed to have an increased FDG uptake relative to background indicate areas of cancerous tissue.

The coverage of PET scans using FDG for the purpose of characterizing SPNs is limited to situations in which the patient has been tested and evaluated in accordance with the provisions outlined below. These provisions were developed using models for clinical practice developed in collaboration with the PET community as well as professional opinions from several sources familiar with the proper use of PET scans. These provisions are designed to limit coverage of this service to those situations in which it is effective in determining the course of future patient treatment. This criterion, the medical effectiveness of a service based on its utility in determining the course of treatment, is generally applied by Medicare to diagnostic modalities that substitute for, or are intended to replace, other diagnostic modalities for the same medical purpose. As with any other Medicare claim, claims for PET scans may be reviewed to determine whether the provisions below were followed, and contractors may request additional information and clarification prior to making payment, or on post-payment review of claims. In addition, PET scan facilities must maintain sufficient documentation on-site to answer inquiries from contractors as to the performance of PET scans for which they make claims for payment.

Requirements for Payment of Claims for Characterizing Solitary Pulmonary Nodules (SPNs) with PET using FDG:

1. Evidence of primary tumor—Claims for regional PET chest scans for characterizing SPNs should include evidence of the initial detection of a primary lung tumor, usually by computed tomograhy (CT). This should include, but is not restricted to, a report on the results of such CT or other detection method, indicating an indeterminate or possibly malignant lesion, not exceeding four centimeters (cm.) in diameter. Such report should be included with the claim for payment, along with the result of the PET scan, using the appropriate code.

   NOTE: PET scans are not covered by Medicare for screening of asymptomatic patients, regardless of the number and severity of risk factors applicable to such patients.

2. PET scan results and results of concurrent computed tomography (CT)—In order to ensure that the PET scan is properly coordinated with other diagnostic modalities, PET scan claims must include the results of concurrent thoracic CT (as noted above), which is necessary for anatomic information.

   NOTE: A Tissue Sampling Procedure (TSP) should not be routinely covered in the case of a negative PET scan for characterization of SPNs, since the patient is presumed not to have a malignant lesion, based upon the PET scan results. Claims for a TSP after a negative PET must be submitted with documentation for review by the Medicare contractor to determine if the TSP is reasonable and necessary in spite of a negative PET. Physicians should discuss with their patients the implications of this decision, both with respect to the patient's responsibility for payment for such a biopsy if desired, as well as the confidence the physician has in the results of such PET scans, prior to ordering such scans for this purpose.

   This physician-patient decision should occur with a clear discussion and understanding of the sensitivity and specificity trade-offs between CT and PET scans. In cases where a TSP is performed, it is the responsibility of the physician ordering the TSP to provide sufficient documentation of the medical necessity for such procedure or procedures. Such documentation should include, but is not necessarily limited to, a description of the features of the PET scan that call into question whether it is an accurate representation of the patient's condition, the existence of other factors in the patient's condition that call into question the accuracy of the PET scan, and such other information as the contractor processing the claim deems necessary to determine whether the claim for the TSP should be covered and paid.

   In cases of serial evaluation of SPNs using both CT and regional PET chest scanning, such PET scans will not be covered if repeated within 90 days following a negative PET scan.

3. Completion of all items requested on claim form—As with any other Medicare claim, the PET scan facility must complete all required information on the claim form, including any codes or modifiers required by HCFA or its contractors.

4. Maintenance of patient record data onsite — As with any other Medicare claim, but particularly in view of the limitations on this coverage, Medicare may decide to conduct post-payment reviews to determine that the use of PET scans is consistent with this instruction. Those claiming payment for PET scans must keep patient record information on file for each Medicare patient for whom a PET scan claim is made. These medical records will be used in any post-payment reviews and must include the information necessary to substantiate the need for the PET scan. These records must include standard information (e.g., age, sex, and height) along with sufficient patient histories to allow determination that the steps required in this instruction were followed. Such information must include, but is not limited to, the date, place and results of previous diagnostic tests (e.g., pertinent chest X-rays, CT, etc.), as well as the results and reports of the PET scan(s) performed by the claimant. If available, such records should include the prognosis derived from the PET scan, together with information regarding the physician or institution to which the patient proceeded following the scan for treatment or evaluation. The ordering physician is responsible for forwarding appropriate clinical data to the PET scan facility.

   Evaluation of Claims and Other Data After One Year — As noted above, this coverage is predicated upon the use of PET scans with FDG to develop proper treatment plans for patients with SPNs. HCFA will evaluate both the data produced by claims for this service, as well as data obtained from other sources, to determine whether, and to what extent, it should make modifications in this coverage policy to assure that the services covered are medically effective for the treatment of Medicare beneficiaries.

V. Coverage of PET Scans Using FDG to Initially Stage Lung Cancer—Effective for Services Performed on or after January 1, 1998:

Background: HCFA has carefully examined a wide range of uses of PET with FDG in detecting, staging and monitoring non-central nervous system (CNS) cancers. Currently, these uses do not appear to be sufficiently developed to allow HCFA to determine their medical effectiveness to a degree sufficient to make a conclusive coverage determination under the Medicare program. However, there is some research data indicating that, in the case of the initial staging of non-small-cell lung carcinoma (NSCLC), whole body PET scans may offer, at least for some patients, an effective method of determining the proper course of management for their disease. It is not yet clear how effective this procedure will be in everyday use. Therefore, Medicare will begin paying for PET scans on an interim basis in accords with the terms of this instruction. During the period of this interim coverage, we will continue to seek and review information on the clinical effectiveness of this procedure. We will also encourage researchers to continue to refine and expand the knowledge base necessary to assure that such scans are fully and properly utilized.

HCFA intends to closely monitor not only the provision of services furnished under this coverage, but also the development of additional information developed by non-HCFA studies. We believe that a full understanding of the clinical effectiveness of PET for the staging of cancer, including NSCLC, will be found after additional clinical research. We will be collecting and analyzing our claims data on this service, but we expect and encourage others to continue their study on the use of PET with FDG for the staging of lung cancer, including randomized clinical trials. HCFA will continue to review the medical literature, as well as studies, assessments, and other information developed by the medical and scientific community to assure that its coverage of these scans is appropriate.

Coverage of PET scans for staging non-small cell lung carcinoma—PET scans using the glucose analog 2-[fluorine-18]-fluoro-2-deoxy-D-glucose (FDG) are covered, subject to the conditions and limitations described below, only when used for the initial staging of suspected metastatic NSCLC in thoracic (mediastinal) lymph nodes in patients who have a confirmed primary lung tumor, but whose extent of disease has not yet been established. The primary purpose of such staging should be to determine the progress and extent of the disease, as well as the probable rate of its progression, in order to plan future management for the patient. (Note: This instruction covers only the initial staging of NSCLC. Multiple stagings using PET is considered monitoring of the progress of the disease, rather than staging, and is not covered at this time.)

The procedure consists of the glucose analog FDG being injected into the patient intravenously, with image acquisition usually beginning 30-60 minutes later, and continuing for a period of 10-20 minutes. The FDG is metabolized by both normal and cancerous tissue in proportion to the rate of glucolysis. Since tumor cells have shown an increased utilization of glucose, those regions observed to have an increased FDG uptake relative to background indicate areas of cancerous tissue.

The coverage of PET scans using FDG for the purpose of staging NSCLC is limited to situations in which the patient has been tested and evaluated in accordance with the provisions outlined below. These provisions were developed using models for clinical practice developed in collaboration with the PET industry, as well as professional opinion from several sources familiar with the proper use of PET scans. These provisions are designed to limit coverage of this service to those situations in which it is effective in determining the course of future patient treatment. This criterion, the medical effectiveness of a service in determining the course of treatment, is generally applied by Medicare to diagnostic modalities that substitute for, or are intended to replace, other diagnostic modalities for the same medical purpose. As with any other Medicare claim, claims for PET scans may be reviewed to determine whether these provisions were followed, and contractors may request additional information and clarification prior to making payment, or on post-payment review of claims. In addition, PET scan facilities must maintain sufficient documentation on-site to answer inquiries from contractors as to the performance of PET scans for which they make claims for payment.

Requirements for Payment of Claims for Staging Metastatic NSCLC Lung Cancer with PET using FDG:

1. Evidence of primary tumor—Since this service is covered only in those cases in which a primary cancerous lung tumor has been confirmed, claims for PET should include a statement or other evidence of the detection of such primary lung tumor. This should include, but is not restricted to, a surgical pathology report which documents the presence of an NSCLC.

2. Whole body PET scan results and results of concurrent computed tomography (CT) and follow-up lymph node biopsy—In order to ensure that the PET scan is properly coordinated with other diagnostic modalities, claims must include both (1) the results of concurrent thoracic CT, which is necessary for anatomic information, and (2) the results of any lymph node biopsy performed to finalize whether the patient will be a surgical candidate. The ordering physician is responsible for providing this biopsy result to the PET facility.

NOTE: A lymph node biopsy will not be covered in the case of a negative CT and negative PET, where the patient is considered a surgical candidate, given the presumed absence of metastatic NSCLC unless medical review supports a determination of medical necessity of a biopsy. A lymph node biopsy will be covered in all other cases, i.e., positive CT+ positive PET; negative CT+ positive PET; positive CT+ negative PET. Physicians should discuss with their patients the implications of these points, both with respect to the patient's responsibility for payment for such a biopsy if desired (in the case of a negative CT+ negative PET), as well as the confidence the physician has in the results of such PET scans, prior to ordering such scans for this purpose. This physician-patient decision should occur with a clear discussion and understanding of the sensitivity and specificity trade-offs between CT and PET scans. In cases where a lymph node biopsy is performed, it is the responsibility of the physician ordering the lymph node biopsy to provide sufficient documentation of the medical necessity for such procedure or procedures. Such documentation should include, but is not necessarily limited to, a description of the features of the PET scan that call into question whether it is an accurate representation of the patient's condition, the existence of other factors in the patient's condition that call into question the accuracy of the PET scan, and such other information as the contractor processing the claim deems necessary to determine whether the claim for the lymph node biopsy should be covered and paid.

3. Completion of all items requested on claim form—As with any other Medicare claim, the PET facility must complete all required information on the claim form, including any codes or modifiers required by HCFA or its contractors.

4. Maintenance of patient record data onsite — As with any claim, but particularly in view of the limitations on this coverage, Medicare may decide to conduct post-payment reviews to determine that the use of PET scans is consistent with this instruction. PET scan facilities must keep patient record information on file for each Medicare patient for whom a PET scan claim is made. These medical records will be used in any post-payment reviews and must include the information necessary to substantiate the need for the PET scan. These records must include standard information (e.g., age, sex, and height) along with sufficient patient histories to allow determination that the steps required in this instruction were followed. Such information must include, but is not limited to, the date, place and results of previous diagnostic tests (e.g., cytopathology and surgical pathology reports, CT, etc.), as well as the results and reports of the PET scan(s) performed at the center. If available, such records should include the prognosis derived from the PET scan, together with information regarding the physician or institution to which the patient proceeded following the scan for treatment or evaluation. The ordering physician is responsible for forwarding appropriate clinical data to the PET scan facility.

Evaluation of Claims and Other Data After One Year — As noted above, this coverage is predicated upon the use of PET scans with FDG to develop proper treatment plans for patients with NSCLC. HCFA will evaluate both the data produced by claims for this service, as well as data obtained from other sources, to determine whether, and to what extent, it should make modifications in this coverage policy to assure that the services covered are medically effective for the treatment of Medicare beneficiaries.

VI. Coverage of PET Scan Using FDG to Determine the Location of Recurrent Colorectal Tumor as Evidence by Rising Levels of Carcinoembryonic Antigen (CEA).

Background: HCFA has carefully examined a wide range of uses of PET with FDG in detecting, staging and monitoring non-central nervous system cancers. Multiple applications are under active review by the Medicare program. However, there is research data indicating that, in the case of patients with recurrent colorectal carcinomas, which are demonstrated by rising levels of the biochemical tumor marker CEA, PET offers a useful tool in determining the location(s) of these recurrent tumors. The medical effectiveness of this use rests primarily upon its ability to determine whether surgical intervention would be medically effective in treating the patient. Therefore, Medicare will begin paying for PET scans using FDG for this indication, provided all the terms and conditions set forth in this instruction (both general and specific) are met.

Coverage of PET Scans for the Location of Recurrent Colorectal Carcinomas — PET scans using the glucose analog 2[fluorine-18]-fluoro-2-deoxy-D-glucose (FDG) are covered, subject to the conditions and limitations described below, when used for determining the location of recurrent colorectal tumors when such tumors are indicated by rising levels of CEA. This use is limited to locating such tumors for the purpose of making a decision as to whether surgical intervention is warranted. Further, the use of PET with FDG to stage colorectal carcinoma is not covered under this policy.

The procedure consists of the glucose analog FDG being injected into the patient intravenously, with image acquisition usually beginning 30-60 minutes later, and continuing for a period of 10-20 minutes. The FDG is metabolized by both normal and cancerous tissue in proportion to the rate of glycolysis. Since tumor cells have shown an increased utilization of glucose, those regions observed to have an increased FDG uptake relative to background indicate areas of cancerous tissue.

The coverage of PET scans using FDG for the purpose of locating recurrent colorectal tumors is limited to situations in which the patient has been tested and evaluated in accordance with the provisions outlined below. These provisions are designed to limit coverage of this service to those situations in which it is effective in determining the course of future patient treatment. This criterion, the medical effectiveness of the service based on its utility in determining the course of treatment, is generally applied by Medicare to diagnostic modalities that substituted for, or are intended to replace, other diagnostic modalities for the same purpose. As with any other Medicare claim, claims for PET scans may be reviewed to determine whether the provisions below were followed, and contractors may request additional information and clarification prior to making payment, or on post-payment review of claims. In addition, PET scan facilities must maintain sufficient documentation on-site to answer inquiries from contractors as to the performance of PET scans for which they make claims for payment.

Requirements for Payment of Claims for Locating Recurrent Colorectal Tumors with PET using FDG:

1. Evidence of Previous Disease — Since this service is covered only in those cases in which there has been a

recurrence of colorectal tumor, claims for PET should include a statement or other evidence of previous colorectal tumor.

2. Whole Body PET Scan Results and Results of Concurrent Imaging Techniques — In order to ensure that the PET scan is properly coordinated with other diagnostic modalities, claims must include the results of concurrent computed tomography (CT) and/or other diagnostic modalities when they are necessary for additional anatomic information.

3. Assurance PET Scan Is Alternative to a Gallium Scan — Gallium studies, including immunoscintigraphy such as an Oncoscint scan, will not be covered in the case of a PET scan done for locating recurrent colorectal cancer, when performed by the same facility within 50 days of each other.

4. Frequency Limitation — Whole body PET scans cannot be ordered more frequently than once every 12 months, unless medical necessity documentation supports a separate re-elevation of CEA within this period.

5. Completion of All Items Requested on Claim Form — As with any other Medicare claim, the PET facility must complete all required information on the claim form, including any codes or modifiers required by HCFA or its contractors.

6. Maintenance of Patient Record Data Onsite — As with any claim, but particularly in view of the limitations on this coverage, Medicare may decide to conduct post-payment reviews to determine that the use of PET scans is consistent with this instruction. PET scan facilities must keep patient record information on file for each Medicare patient for whom a PET scan claim is made. These medical records will be used in any post-payment reviews and must include the information necessary to substantiate the need for the PET scan. These records must include standard information (e.g., age, sex, and height) along with sufficient patient histories to allow determination that the steps required in this instruction were followed. Such information must include, but is not limited to, the date, place and results of previous diagnostic tests (e.g., cytopathology and surgical pathology reports, computed tomography, etc.), as well as the results and reports of the PET scan(s) performed at the center. If available, such records should include the prognosis derived from the PET scan, together with information regarding the physician or institution to which the patient proceeded following the scan for treatment or evaluation. The ordering physician is responsible for forwarding appropriate clinical data to the PET scan facility. The Medicare program also reserves the right to ensure that the quality of clinical information obtained from a PET scan does not vary among specific types of scanning devices.

VII. Coverage of PET Scan Using FDG to Stage and Re-Stage Lymphoma When Used as an Alternative to a Gallium Scan.

Background: HCFA has carefully examined a wide range of uses of PET with FDG in detecting, staging and monitoring non-central nervous system cancers. Multiple applications are under active review by the Medicare program. However, there is research data indicating that, in the case of patients diagnosed with lymphomas, PET offers a useful tool in tumor staging. Therefore, Medicare will begin paying for PET scans using FDG for this indication, provided all the terms and conditions set forth in this instruction (both general and specific) are met.

Coverage of PET Scans for the Staging of Lymphomas as an Alternative to Gallim Scans — PET scans using the glucose analog 2[fluorine-18]-fluoro-2-deoxy-D-glucose (FDG) are covered, subject to the conditions and limitations described below, when used for staging lymphomas as an alternative to a Gallium scan.

The procedure consists of the glucose analog FDG being injected into the patient intravenously, with image acquisition usually beginning 30-60 minutes later, and continuing for a period of 10-20 minutes. The FDG is metabolized by both normal and cancerous tissue in proportion to the rate of glycolysis. Since tumor cells have shown an increased utilization of glucose, those regions observed to have an increased FDG uptake relative to backgound indicate areas of cancerous tissue.

The coverage of PET scans using FDG for the purpose of staging lymphomas is limited to situations in which the patient has been tested and evaluated in accordance with the provisions outlined below. These provisions are designed to limit coverage of this service to those situations in which it is effective in determining the course of future patient treatment. This criterion, the medical effective- ness of the service based on its utility in determining the course of treatment, is generally applied by Medicare to diagnostic modalities that substituted for, or are intended to replace other diagnostic modalities for the same purpose. As with any other Medicare claim, claims applied by Medicare to diagnostic modalities that substituted for, or are intended to replace for PET scans may be reviewed to determine whether the provisions below were followed, and contractors may request additional information and clarification prior to making payment, or on post-payment review of claims. In addition, PET scan facilities must maintain sufficient documentation on-site to answer inquiries from contractors as to the performance of PET scans for which they make claims for payment.

Requirements for Payment of Claims for Staging and Re-Staging Lymphoma When Used as an Alternative to a Gallium Scan

1. Evidence of Disease — Since this service is covered only for staging or follow-up restaging of lymphoma,

claims for PET should include a statement or other evidence of previously-made diagnosis of lymphoma.

2. Whole Body PET Scan Results and Results of Concurrent Imaging Techniques — In order to ensure that the PET scan is properly coordinated with other diagnostic modalities, claims must include the results of concurrent computed tomography (CT) and/or other diagnostic modalities when they are necessary for additional anatomic information.

3. Assurance PET Scan is Alternative to a Gallium Scan — In order to ensure that the PET scan is covered only as an alternative to a Gallium scan, no PET scan may be covered in cases where it is done within 50 days of a Gallium scan done by the same PET facility where the patient has remained under the care of the same facility during the 50-day period. Gallium scans done by another facility less than 50 days prior to the PET scan will not be counted against this screen. The purpose of this screen is to assure that PET scans are covered only when done as an alternative to a Gallium scan within the same facility. We are aware that, in order to assure proper patient care, the treating physician may conclude that previously-performed. Gallium scans are either inconclusive or not sufficiently reliable to make the staging covered by this provision. Therefore, we will apply this 50-day rule only to PET scans done by the same facility that performed the Gallium scan.

4. Limitation on Re-Staging — PET scans will be allowed for re-staging no sooner than 50 days following the last staging PET scan or Gallium scan, unless sufficient evidence is presented to convince the Medicare contractor that the re-staging at an earlier date is medically necessary. Since PET scans for re-staging are generally done following cycles of chemotherapy, and since such cycles usually take at least 8 weeks, we believe this screen will adequately prevent medically unnecessary scans while allowing some adjustments for unusual cases. In all cases, the determination of the medical necessity for a PET scan for re-staging lymphoma is the responsbility of the local Medicare contractor.

5. Completion of All Items Requested on Claim Form — As with any other Medicare claim, the PET facility must complete all required information on the claim form, including any codes or modifiers required by HCFA or its contractors.

6. Maintenance of Patient Record Data Onsite — As with any claim, but particularly in view of the limitations on this coverage, Medicare may decide to conduct post-payment reviews to determine that the use of PET scans is consistent with this instruction. PET scan facilities must keep patient record information on file for each Medicare patient for whom a PET scan claim is made. These medical records will be used in any post-payment reviews and must include the information necessary to substantiate the need for the PET scan. These records must include standard information (e.g., age, sex, and height) along with sufficient patient histories to allow determination that the steps required in this instruction were followed. Such information must include, but is not limited to, the date, place and results of previous diagnostic tests (e.g., cytopathology and surgical pathology reports, computed tomography, etc.), as well as the results and reports of the PET scan(s) performed at the center. If available, such records should include the prognosis derived from the PET scan, together with information regarding the physician or institution to which the patient proceeded following the scan for treatment or evaluation. The ordering physician is responsible for forwarding appropriate clinical data to the PET scan facility. The Medicare program also reserves the right to ensure that the quality of clinical information obtained from a PET scan does not vary among specific types of scanning devices.

VIII. Coverage of PET Scan Using FDG to Evaluate Recurrence of Melanoma Prior to Surgery (Including Limitation as Alternative to Gallium Scan).

Background: HCFA has carefully examined a wide range of uses of PET with FDG in detecting, staging and monitoring non-central nervous system cancers. Multiple applications are under active review by the Medicare program. However, there is research data indicating that, in the case of patients with recurrent melanoma, PET offers a useful tool in tumor evaluation. The medical effectiveness of this use rests primarily upon its ability to determine whether surgical intervention would be medically effective in treating the patient. Therefore, Medicare will begin paying for PET scans using FDG for this indication, provided all the terms and conditions set forth in this instruction (both general and specific) are met.

Coverage of PET Scans for the Evaluation of Recurrent Melanoma Prior to Surgery — PET scans using the glucose analog 2[fluorine-18]-fluoro-2-deoxy-D-glucose (FDG) are covered, subject to the conditions and limitations described below, when used for evaluation of melanoma prior to scheduling surgical intervention.

The procedure consists of the glucose analog FDG being injected into the patient intravenously, with image acquisition usually beginning 30-60 minutes later, and continuing for a period of 10-20 minutes. The FDG is metabolized by both normal and cancerous tissue in proportion to the rate of glycolysis. Since tumor cells have shown an increased utilization of glucose, those regions observed to have an increased FDG uptake relative to background indicate areas of cancerous tissue.

The coverage of PET scans using FDG for the purpose of evaluating recurrent melanoma is limited to situations in which the patient has been tested and evaluated in accordance with the provisions outlined below. These provisions are designed to limit coverage of this service to those situations in which it is effective in determining the course of future patient treatment. This criterion, the medical effectiveness of the service based on its utility in determining the course of treatment, is generally applied by Medicare to diagnostic modalities that substituted for, or are intended to replace, other diagnostic modalities for the same purpose. As with any other Medicare claim, claims for PET scans may be reviewed to determine whether the provisions below were followed, and contractors may request additional information and clarification prior to making payment, or on post-payment review of claims. In addition, PET scan facilities must maintain sufficient documentation on-site to answer inquiries from contractors as to the performance of PET scans for which they make claims for payment.

Requirements for Payment of Claims for Evaluation of Recurrent Melanoma Prior to Surgical Intervention (Including Limitation as Alternative to Gallium Scan)

1. Evidence of Disease — Since this service is covered only for recurrent melanoma, claims for PET should include a statement or other evidence of previous melanoma.

2. Whole Body PET Scan Results and Results of Concurrent Imaging Techniques — In order to ensure that the PET scan is properly coordinated with other diagnostic modalities, claims must include the results of concurrent computed tomography (CT) and/or other diagnostic modalities when they are necessary for additional anatomic information.

3. Assurance PET Scan Is Alternative to Gallium Scan — In order to ensure that the PET scan is covered only as an alternative to a Gallium scan, no PET scan may be covered in cases where it is done within 50 days of a Gallium scan done by the same PET facility where the patient has remained under the care of the same facility during the 50-day period. Gallium scans done by another facility less than 50 days prior to the PET scan will not be counted against this screen. The purpose of this screen is to assure that PET scans are covered only when done as an alternative to a Gallium scan within the same facility. We are aware that, in order to assure proper patient care, the treating physician may conclude that previously-performed Gallium scans are either inconclusive or not sufficiently reliable to make the determination covered by this provision. Therefore, we will apply this 50-day rule only to PET scans done by the same facility that performed the Gallium scan.

4. Frequency Limitation — Whole body PET scans cannot be ordered more frequently than once every 12 months, unless medical necessity documentation supports the specific need for anatomic localization of possible recurrent tumor within this period.

5. Completion of All Items Requested on Claim Form — As with any other Medicare claim, the PET facility must complete all required information on the claim form, including any codes or modifiers required by HCFA or its contractors.

Maintenance of Patient Record Data Onsite — As with any claim, but particularly in view of the limitations on this coverage, Medicare may decide to conduct post-payment reviews to determine that the use of PET scans is consistent with this instruction. PET scan facilities must keep patient record information on file for each Medicare patient for whom a PET scan claim is made. These medical records will be used in any post-payment reviews and must include the information necessary to substantial the need for the PET scan. These records must include standard information (e.g., age, sex, and height) along with sufficient patient histories to allow determination that the steps required in this instruction were followed. Such information must include, but is not limited to, the date, place and results of previous diagnostic tests (e.g., cytopathology and surgical pathology reports, computed tomography, etc.), as well as the results and reports of the PET scan(s) performed at the center. If available, such records should include the prognosis derived from the PET scan, together with information regarding the physician or institution to which the patient proceeded following the scan for treatment or evaluation. The ordering physician is responsible for forwarding appropriate clinical data to the PET scan facility. The Medicare program also reserves the right to ensure that the quality of clinical information obtained from a PET scan does not vary among specific types of scanning devices.

50-4 Gravlee Jet Washer

The Gravlee Jet Washer is a sterile, disposable, diagnostic device for detecting endometrial cancer. The use of this device is indicated where the patient exhibits clinical symptoms or signs suggestive of endometrial disease, such as irregular or heavy vaginal bleeding.

Program payment cannot be made for the washer or the related diagnostic services when furnished in connection with the examination of an asymptomatic patient. Payment for routine physical checkups is precluded under the statute. (See §1862(a)(7) of the Act.)

(See Intermediary Manual, §3157 and Carriers Manual, §2320.)

50-42 Ambulatory Blood Pressure Monitoring with Fully and Semi-automatic (Patient-activated) Portable Monitors — Not Covered

While ambulatory blood pressure monitoring in hypertensive patients using fully and semi-automatic (patient-activated) portable monitors is a safe and accurate means of measuring blood pressure, the clinical usefulness of the data obtained from such devices is not clearly established. Researchers and clinicians cite the need for standardization of instrumentation and further study of this technology to better ascertain its role in hypertensive therapy. Accordingly, program payment may not be made for the use of such devices at this time.

50-44 Bone (Mineral) Density Studies

Effective for services rendered on or after March 4, 1983.

Bone (mineral) density studies are used to evaluate diseases of bone and/or the responses of bone diseases to treatment. The studies assess bone mass or density associated with such diseases as osteoporosis, osteomalacia, and renal osteodystrophy. Various single or combined methods of measurement may be required to: (a) diagnose bone disease, (b) monitor the course of bone changes with disease progression, or (c) monitor the course of bone changes with therapy. Bone density is usually studied by using photodensitometry, single or dual photon absorptiometry, or bone biopsy.

The following bone (mineral) density studies are covered under Medicare:

A. Single Photon Absorptiometry — A non-invasive radiological technique that measures absorption of amonochromatic photon beam by bone material. The device is placed directly on the patient, uses a low dose of radionuclide, and measures the mass absorption efficiency of the energy used. It provides a quantitative measurement of the bone mineral of cortical and trabecular bone, and is used in assessing an individual's treatment response at appropriate intervals.

Single photon absorptiometry is covered under Medicare when used in assessing changes in bone density of patients with osteodystrophy or osteoporosis when performed on the same individual at intervals of 6 to 12 months.

B. Bone Biopsy — A physiologic test which is a surgical, invasive procedure. A small sample of bone (usually from the ilium) is removed, generally by a biopsy needle. The biopsy sample is then examined histologically, and provides a qualitative measurement of the bone mineral of trabecular bone. This procedure is used in ascertaining a differential diagnosis of bone disorders and is used primarily to differentiate osteomalacia from osteoporosis.

Bone biopsy is covered under Medicare when used for the qualitative evaluation of bone no more than four times per patient, unless there is special justification given. When used more than four times on a patient, bone biopsy leaves a defect in the pelvis and may produce some patient discomfort.

C. Photodensitometry — (radiographic absorptiometry) — A noninvasive radiological procedure that attempts to assess bone mass by measuring the optical density of extremity radiographs with a photodensitometer, usually with a reference to a standard density wedge placed on the film at the time of exposure. This procedure provides a quantitative measurement of the bone mineral of cortical bone, and is used for monitoring gross bone change.

The following bone (mineral) density study is not covered under Medicare:

A. Dual Photon Absorptiometry — A noninvasive radiological technique that measures absorption of a dichromatic beam by bone material. This procedure is not covered under Medicare because it is still considered to be in the investigational stage.

50-54 Cardiac Output Monitoring by Electrical Bioimpedance — Covered (Effective for services performed on or after July 1, 1999)

Cardiac monitoring using electrical bioimpedance, a form of plethysmography, is covered, effective for services furnished on or after July 1, 1999, for the uses and conditions described below. Contractors should be aware that this technology is in the process of being proven for additional uses. Therefore, the uses below represent the current situation. Contractors may cover additional uses when they believe there is sufficient evidence of the medical effectiveness of such uses.

These devices utilize electrical bioimpedance to noninvasively produce hemodynamic measurements of cardiac output, specifically, stroke volume, contractility, systemic vascular resistance and thoracic fluid content. These devices are covered for the following uses:

1. Noninvasive diagnosis or monitoring of hemodynamics in patients with suspected or known cardiovascular disease;
2. Differentiation of cardiogenic from pulmonary causes of acute dyspnea;
3. Optimization of atrioventricular interval for patient with A/V sequential cardiac pacemakers;
4. Patients with need of determination for intravenous inotropic therapy;
5. Post heart transplant myocardial biopsy patients; and,
6. Patients with a need for fluid management.

Not covered at this time are the use of such devices for any monitoring of patients with proven or suspected disease involving severe regurgitation of the aorta, or for patients with minute ventilation (MV) sensor function pacemakers, since the device may adversely affect the functioning of that type of pacemaker. Also, these devices do not render accurate measurements in cardiac bypass patients while on a cardiolpulmonary bypass machine, but do provide accurate measurements prior to and post bypass pump.

Covered uses of cardiac output monitoring by electrical bioimpedance should be billed using HCPCS code M0302.

50-55 Prostate Cancer Screening Tests — Covered (Effective for services furnished on or after January 1, 2000)

A. General — Section 4103 of the Balanced Budget Act of 1997 provides for coverage of certain prostate cancer screening tests subject to certain coverage, frequency, and payment limitations. Effective for services furnished on or after January 1, 2000. Medicare will cover prostate cancer screening tests/procedures for the early detection of prostate cancer. Coverage of prostate cancer screening tests includes the following procedures furnished to an individual for the early detection of prostate cancer:

- Screening digital rectal examination; and
- Screening prostate specific antigen blood test.

B. Screening Digital Rectal Examinations — Screening digital rectal examinations (HCPCS code G0102) are covered at a frequency of once every 12 months for men who have attained age 50 (at least 11 months have passed following the month in which the last Medicare-covered screening digital rectal examination was performed). Screening digital rectal examination means a clinical examination of an individual's prostate for nodules or other abnormalities of the prostate. This screening must be performed by a doctor of medicine or osteopathy (as defined in §1861(r)(1) of the Act), or by a physician assistant, nurse practitioner, clinical nurse specialist, or certified nurse midwife (as defined in §1861(aa) and §1861(gg) of the Act) who is authorized under State law to perform the examination, fully knowledgeable about the beneficiary's medical condition, and would be responsible for using the results of any examination performed in the overall management of the beneficiary's specific medical problem.

Screening Prostate Specific Antigen Tests — Screening prostate specific antigen tests (code G0103) are covered at a frequency of once every 12 months for men who have attained age 50 (at least 11 months have passed following the month in which the last Medicare-covered screening prostate specific antigen test was performed). Screening prostate specific antigen tests (PSA) means a test to detect the marker for adenocarcinoma of prostate. PSA is a reliable immunocytochemical marker for primary and metastatic adenocarcinoma of prostate. This screening must be ordered by the beneficiary's physician or by the beneficiary's physician assistant, nurse practitioner, clinical nurse specialist, or certified nurse midwife (the term "attending physician" is defined in §1861(r)(1) of the Act to mean a doctor of medicine or osteopathy and the terms "physician assistant, nurse practitioner, clinical nurse specialist, or certified nurse midwife" are defined in §1861(aa) and §1861(gg) of the Act) who is fully knowledgeable about the beneficiary's medical condition, and who would be responsible for using the results of any examination (test) performed in the overall management of the beneficiary's specific medical problem.

55-1 Water Purification and Softening Systems Used in Conjuction with Home Dialysis

A. Water Purification Systems — Water used for home dialysis should be chemically free of heavy trace metals and/or organic contaminants which could be hazardous to the patient. It should also be as free of bacteria as possible but need not be biologically sterile. Since the characteristics of natural water supplies in most areas of the country are such that some type of water purification system is needed, such a system used in conjunction with a home dialysis (either peritoneal or hemodialysis) unit is covered uner Medicare.

There are two types of water purification systems which will satisfy these requirements:

Deionization—The removal of organic substances, mineral salts of magnesium and calcium (causing hardness), compounds of fluoride and chloride from tap water using the process of filtration and ion exchange; or

Reverse Osmosis—The process used to remove impurities from tap water utilizing pressure to force water through a porous membrane.

Use of both a deionization unit and reverse osmosis unit in series, theoretically to provide the advantages of both systems, has been determined medically unnecessary since either system can provide water which is both chemically and bacteriologically pure enough for acceptable use in home dialysis. In addition, spare deionization tanks are not covered since they are essentially a precautionary supply rather than a current requirement for treatment of the patient.

Activated carbon filters used as a component of water purification systems to remove unsafe concentrations of chlorine and chloramines are covered when prescribed by a physician.

B. Water Softening System — Except as indicated below, a water softening system used in conjunction with home dialysis is excluded from coverage under Medicare as not being reasonable and necessary within the meaning of §l862(a)(1) of the law. Such a system, in conjunction with a home dialysis unit, does not adequately remove the hazardous heavy metal contaminants (such as arsenic) which may be present in trace amounts.

A water softening system may be covered when used to pretreat water to be purified by a reverse osmosis (RO) unit for home dialysis where:

- The manufacturer of the RO unit has set standards for the quality of water entering the RO (e.g., the water to be purified by the RO must be of a certain quality if the unit is to perform as intended);
- The patient's water is demonstrated to be of a lesser quality than required; and
- The softener is used only to soften water entering the RO unit, and thus, used only for dialysis. (The softener need not actually be built into the RO unit, but must be an integral part of the dialysis system.)

C. Developing Need When a Water Softening System is Replaced with a Water Purification Unit in an Existing Home Dialysis System — The medical necessity of water purification units must be carefully developed when they replace water softening systems in existing home dialysis systems. A purification system may be ordered under these circumstances for a number of reasons. For example, changes in the medical community's opinions regarding the quality of water necessary for safe dialysis may lead the physician to decide the quality of water previously used should be improved, or the water quality itself may have deteriorated. Patients may have dialyzed using only an existing water softener previous to Medicare ESRD coverage because of inability to pay for a purification system. On the other hand, in some cases, the installation of a purification system is not medically necessary. Thus, when such a case comes to your attention, ask the physician to furnish the reason for the changes. Supporting documentation, such as the supplier's recommendations or water analysis, may be required. All such cases should be reviewed by your medical consultants.

Cross-refer: Intermediary Manual, §§3113, 3643 (item 1c); Carriers Manual, §§2100, 2100.2 2130, 2105 (item 1c); Hospital Manual, §235.

60-11   Home Blood Glucose Monitors

There are several different types of blood glucose monitors which use reflectance meters to determine blood glucose levels. Medicare coverage of these devices varies, both with respect to the type of device and the medical condition of the patient for whom the device is prescribed.

Reflectance colorimeter devices used for measuring blood glucose levels in clinical settings are not covered as durable medical equipment for use in the home because their need for frequent professional recalibration makes them unsuitable for home use. However, some types of blood glucose monitors which use a reflectance meter specifically designed for home use by diabetic patients may be covered as durable medical equipment, subject to the conditions and limitations described below.

Blood glucose monitors are meter devices which read color changes produced on specially treated reagent strips by glucose concentrations in the patient's blood. The patient, using a disposable sterile lancet, draws a drop of blood, places it on a reagent strip and, following instructions which may vary with the device used, inserts it into the device to obtain a reading. Lancets, reagent strips, and other supplies necessary for the proper functioning of the device are also covered for patients for whom the device is indicated. Home blood glucose monitors enable certain patients to better control their blood glucose levels by frequently checking and appropriately contacting their attending physician for advice and treatment. Studies indicate that the patient's ability to carefully follow proper procedures is critical to obtaining satisfactory results with these devices. In addition, the cost of the devices, with their supplies, limits economical use to patients who must make frequent checks of their blood glucose levels. Accordingly, coverage of home blood glucose monitors is limited to patients meeting the following conditions:

- The patient must be an insulin-treated diabetic;
- The patient's physician states that the patient is capable of being trained to use the particular device prescribed in an appropriate manner. In some cases, the patient may not be able to perform this function, but a responsible individual can be trained to use the equipment and monitor the patient to assure that the intended effect is achieved. This is permissible if the record is properly documented by the patient's physician; and
- The device is designed for home rather than clinical use.

There is also a blood glucose monitoring system designed especially for use by those with visual impairments. The monitors used in such systems are identical in terms of reliability and sensitivity to the standard blood glucose monitors described above. They differ by having such features as voice synthesizers, automatic timers, and specially designed arrangements of supplies and materials to enable the visually impaired to use the equipment without assistance.

These special blood glucose monitoring systems are covered under Medicare if the following conditions are met:

- The patient and device meet the four conditions listed above for coverage of standard home blood glucose monitors; and
- The patient's physician certifies that he or she has a visual impairment severe enough to require use of this special monitoring system.

The additional features and equipment of these special systems justify a higher reimbursement amount than allowed for standard blood glucose monitors. Separately identify claims for such devices and establish a separate reimbursement amount for them. For those carriers using HCPCS, the procedure code and definition is: EO609—Blood Glucose Monitor—with special features (e.g., voice synthesizers, automatic timer).

60-14   Infusion Pumps

The following indications for treatment using infusion pumps are covered under Medicare:

A. External Infusion Pumps —

1. Iron Poisoning (Effective for Services Performed On or After 9/26/84) — When used in the administration of deferoxamine for the treatment of acute iron poisoning and iron overload, only external infusion pumps are covered.

2. Thromboembolic Disease (Effective for Services Performed On or After 9/26/84) — When used in the administration of heparin for the treatment of thromboembolic disease and/or pulmonary embolism, only external infusion pumps used in an institutional setting are covered.

3. Chemotherapy for Liver Cancer (Effective for Services Performed On or After 1/29/85) — The external chemotherapy infusion pump is covered when used in the treatment of primary hepatocellular carcinoma or colorectal cancer where this disease is unresectable or where the patient refuses surgical excision of the tumor.

4. Morphine for Intractable Cancer Pain (Effective for Services Performed On or After 4/22/85).- -Morphine infusion via an external infusion pump is covered when used in the treatment of intractable pain caused by cancer (in either an inpatient or outpatient setting, including a hospice).

   Other uses of external infusion pumps are covered if the contractor's medical staff verifies the appropriateness of the therapy and of the prescribed pump for the individual patient.

   NOTE: Payment may also be made for drugs necessary for the effective use of an external infusion pump as long as the drug being used with the pump is itself reasonable and necessary for the patient's treatment.

B. Implantable Infusion Pumps —

   1. Chemotherapy for Liver Cancer (Effective for Services Performed On or After 9/26/84) — The implantable infusion pump is covered for intra-arterial infusion of 5-FUdR for the treatment of liver cancer for patients with primary hepatocellular carcinoma or Duke's Class D colorectal cancer, in whom the metastases are limited to the liver, and where (1) the disease is unresectable or (2) where the patient refuses surgical excision of the tumor.

   2. Anti-Spasmodic Drugs for Severe Spasticity — An implantable infusion pump is covered when used to administer anti-spasmodic drugs intrathecally (e.g., baclofen) to treat chronic intractable spasticity in patients who have proven unresponsive to less invasive medical therapy as determined by the following criteria:

      As indicated by at least a 6-week trial, the patient cannot be maintained on noninvasive methods of spasm control, such as oral anti-spasmodic drugs, either because these methods fail to control adequately the spasticity or produce intolerable side effects, and

      Prior to pump implantation, the patient must have responded favorably to a trial intrathecal dose of the anti-spasmodic drug.

   3. Opioid Drugs for Treatment of Chronic Intractable Pain — An implantable infusion pump is covered when used to administer opioid drugs (e.g., morphine) intrathecally or epidurally for treatment of severe chronic intractable pain of malignant or nonmalignant origin in patients who have a life expectancy of at least 3 months and who have proven unresponsive to less invasive medical therapy as determined by the following criteria:

      The patient's history must indicate that he/she would not respond adequately to non- invasive methods of pain control, such as systemic opioids (including attempts to eliminate physical and behavioral abnormalities which may cause an exaggerated reaction to pain); and

      A preliminary trial of intraspinal opioid drug administration must be undertaken with a temporary intrathecal/epidural catheter to substantiate adequately acceptable pain relief and degree of side effects (including effects on the activities of daily living) and patient acceptance.

   4. Coverage of Other Uses of Implanted Infusion Pumps — Determinations may be made on coverage of other uses of implanted infusion pumps if the contractor's medical staff verifies that:

      The drug is reasonable and necessary for the treatment of the individual patient;

      It is medically necessary that the drug be administered by an implanted infusion pump; and

      The FDA approved labelling for the pump must specify that the drug being administered and the purpose for which it is administered is an indicated use for the pump.

   5. Implantation of Infusion Pump Is Contraindicated — The implantation of an infusion pump is contraindicated in the following patients:

      Patients with a known allergy or hypersensitivity to the drug being used (e.g., oral baclofen, morphine, etc.);

      Patients who have an infection;

      Patients whose body size is insufficient to support the weight and bulk of the device; and

      Patients with other implanted programmable devices since crosstalk between devices may inadvertently change the prescription.

      NOTE: Payment may also be made for drugs necessary for the effective use of an implantable infusion pump as long as the drug being used with the pump is itself reasonable and necessary for the patient's treatment.

The following indications for treatment using fusion pumps are not covered under Medicare:

A. External Infusion Pumps —

   1. Diabetes (Effective for Services Performed On or After 1/29/85).-The use of an external infusion pump for the subcutaneous infusion of insulin in the treatment of diabetes is not covered.

   2. Vancomycin (Effective for Services Beginning On or After September 1, 1996) — Medicare coverage of vancomycin as a durable medical equipment infusion pump benefit is not covered. There is insufficient evidence to support the necessity of using an external infusion pump, instead of a disposable elastomeric pump or the gravity drip method, to administer vancomycin in a safe and appropriate manner.

B. Implantable Infusion Pump —
   1. Thromboembolic Disease (Effective for Services Performed On or After 9/26/84) — According to the Public Health Service, there is insufficient published clinical data to support the safety and effectiveness of the heparin implantable pump. Therefore, the use of an implantable infusion pump for infusion of heparin in the treatment of recurrent thromboembolic disease is not covered.
   2. Diabetes—Implanted infusion pumps for the infusion of insulin to treat diabetes is not covered. The data do not demonstrate that the pump provides effective administration of insulin.

60-15 Safety Roller (Effective for Claims Adjudicated On or After 6/3/85)

"Safety roller" is the generic name applied to devices for patients who cannot use standard wheeled walkers. They may be appropriate, and therefore covered, for some patients who are obese, have severe neurological disorders, or restricted use of one hand, which makes it impossible to use a wheeled walker that does not have the sophisticated braking system found on safety rollers.

In order to assure that payment is not made for a safety roller when a less expensive standard wheeled walker would satisfy the patient's medical needs, carriers refer safety roller claims to their medical consultants. The medical consultant determines whether some or all of the features provided in a safety roller are necessary, and therefore covered and reimbursable. If it is determined that the patient could use a standard wheeled walker, the charge for the safety roller is reduced to the charge of a standard wheeled walker.

Some obese patients who could use a standard wheeled walker if their weight did not exceed the walker's strength and stability limits can have it reinforced and its wheel base expanded. Such modifications are routine mechanical adjustments and justify a moderate surcharge. In these cases the carrier reduces the charge for the safety roller to the charge for the standard wheeled walker plus the surcharge for modifications.

In the case of patients with medical documentation showing severe neurological disorders or restricted use of one hand which makes it impossible for them to use a wheeled walker that does not have a sophisticated braking system, a reasonable charge for the safety roller may be determined without relating it to the reasonable charge for a standard wheeled walker. (Such reasonable charge should be developed in accordance with the instructions in Medicare Carriers Manual §§5010 and 5205.)

Cross Refer: Carriers Manual §§2100ff., §60-9.

60-16 Pneumatic Compression Devices (Used for Lymphedema)

Lymphedema is the swelling of subcutaneous tissues due to the accumulation of excessive lymph fluid. The accumulation of lymph fluid results from an impairment to the normal clearing function of the lymphatic system and/or from an excessive production of lymph. It is a relatively uncommon, chronic condition which may be due to many causes, e.g., surgical removal of lymph nodes, post radiation fibrosis, scarring of lymphatic channel, onset of puberty (Milroy's Disease), and congenital anomalies. In the home setting, both the segmental and nonsegmental pneumatic compression devices are covered only for the treatment of generalized, refractory lymphedema.

Pneumatic compression devices are only covered as a treatment of last resort, i.e., other less intensive treatments must have been tried first and found inadequate. Such treatments would include leg or arm elevation and custom fabricated gradient pressure stockings or sleeves. Pneumatic compression devices may be covered only when prescribed by a physician and when they are used with appropriate physician oversight, i.e., physician evaluation of the patient's condition to determine medical necessity of the device, suitable instruction in the operation of the machine, a treatment plan defining the pressure to be used and the frequency and duration of use, and ongoing monitoring of use and response to treatment.

The determination by the physician of the medical necessity of a pneumatic compression device must include (1) the patient's diagnosis and prognosis; (2) symptoms and objective findings, including measurements which establish the severity of the condition; (3) the reason the device is required, including the treatments which have been tried and failed; and (4) the clinical response to an initial treatment with the device. The clinical response includes the change in pre-treatment measurements, ability to tolerate the treatment session and parameters, and ability of the patient (or caregiver) to apply the device for continued use in the home.

In general, the nonsegmented (HCPCS code E0650) or segmented (HCPCS code E0651) compression device without manual control of pressure in each chamber is considered the least costly alternative that meets the clinical needs of the individual. Therefore, when a claim for a segmented pneumatic compression device which allows for manual control in each chamber is received, payment must be made for the least expensive medically appropriate device. If the patient medically needs a segmented device but does not need manual controls, payment must be made for HCPCS code E0651. The segmented device with manual control (HCPCS code E0652) is covered only when there are unique characteristics that prevent the individual from receiving satisfactory pneumatic treatment using a less costly device, e.g., significant sensitive skin scars or the presence of contracture or pain caused by a clinical condition that requires the more costly manual control device.

The use of pneumatic compression devices may be medically appropriate only for those patients with generalized, refractory edema from venous insufficiency with lymphatic obstruction (i.e., recurrent cellulitis with secondary scarring of the lymphatic system) with significant ulceration of the lower extremity(ies) who have received repeated, standard treatment from a physician using such methods as a compression bandage system or its equivalent, but fail to heal after 6 months of continuous treatment. The exact nature of the medical problem must be clear from the medical evidence submitted. If, after obtaining this information, a question of medical necessity remains, the contractor's medical staff resolves the issue.

Cross Refer: §60-9.

60-17 Continuous Positive Airway Pressure (CPAP) (Effective for Claims Adjudicated on and After January 12, 1987)

CPAP is a non-invasive technique for providing low levels of air pressure from a flow generator, via a nose mask, through the nares. The purpose is to prevent the collapse of the oropharyngeal walls and the obstruction of airflow during sleep, which occurs in obstructive sleep apnea (OSA). The diagnosis of OSA requires documentation of at least 30 episodes of apnea, each lasting a minimum of 10 seconds, during 6-7 hours of recorded sleep. The use of CPAP is covered under Medicare when used in adult patients with moderate or severe OSA for whom surgery is a likely alternative to CPAP.

Initial claims must be supported by medical documentation (separate documentation where electronic billing is used), such as a prescription written by the patient's attending physician, that specifies: a diagnosis of moderate or severe obstructive sleep apnea, and surgery is a likely alternative.

The claim must also certify that the documentation supporting a diagnosis of OSA (described above) is available.

Cross Refer: §60-9.

60-18 Hospital beds

A. General Requirements for Coverage of Hospital Beds — A physician's prescription, and such additional documentation as the contractors' medical staffs may consider necessary, including medical records and physicians' reports, must establish the medical necessity for a hospital bed due to one of the following reasons:

The patient's condition requires positioning of the body; e.g., to alleviate pain, promote good body alignment, prevent contractures, avoid respiratory infections, in ways not feasible in an ordinary bed; or

The patient's condition requires special attachments that cannot be fixed and used on an ordinary bed.

B. Physician's Prescription — The physician's prescription, which must accompany the initial claim, and supplementing documentation when required, must establish that a hospital bed is medically necessary. If the stated reason for the need for a hospital bed is the patient's condition requires positioning, the prescription or other documentation must describe the medical condition, e.g., cardiac disease, chronic obstructive pulmonary disease, quadriplegia or paraplegia, and also the severity and frequency of the symptoms of the condition, that necessitates a hospital bed for positioning.

If the stated reason for requiring a hospital bed is the patient's condition requires special attachments, the prescription must describe the patient's condition and specify the attachments that require a hospital bed.

C. Variable Height Feature

In well documented cases, the contractors' medical staffs may determine that a variable height feature of a hospital bed, approved for coverage under subsection A above, is medically necessary and, therefore, covered, for one of the following conditions:

Severe arthritis and other injuries to lower extremities; e.g., fractured hip. The condition requires the variable height feature to assist the patient to ambulate by enabling the patient to place his or her feet on the floor while sitting on the edge of the bed;

Severe cardiac conditions. For those cardiac patients who are able to leave bed, but who must avoid the strain of "jumping" up or down;

Spinal cord injuries, including quadriplegic and paraplegic patients, multiple limb amputee and stroke patients. For those patients who are able to transfer from bed to a wheelchair, with or without help; or

Other severely debilitating diseases and conditions, if the variable height feature is required to assist the patient to ambulate.

D. Electric Powered Hospital Bed Adjustments — Electric powered adjustments to lower and raise head and foot may be covered when the contractor's medical staff determines that the patient's condition requires frequent change in body position and/or there may be an immediate need for a change in body position (i.e., no delay can be tolerated) and the patient can operate the controls and cause the adjustments. Exceptions may be made to this last requirement in cases of spinal cord injury and brain damaged patients.

E. Side Rails — If the patient's condition requires bed side rails, they can be covered when an integral part of, or an accessory to, a hospital bed.

Cross refer: Carriers Manual, §5015.4

60-3 White Cane for use by a Blind Person — Not Covered

A white cane for use by a blind person is more an identifying and self-help device than an item which makes a meaningful contribution in the treatment of an illness or injury.

60-4 Home use of oxygen

A. General

Medicare coverage of home oxygen and oxygen equipment under the durable medical equipment (DME) benefit (see §1861(s)(6)of the Act) is considered reasonable and necessary only for patients with significant hypoxemia who meet the medical documentation, laboratory evidence, and health conditions specified in subsections B, C, and D. This section also includes special coverage criteria for portable oxygen systems. Finally, a statement on the absence of coverage of the professional services of a respiratory therapist under the DME benefit is included in subsection F.

B. Medical documentation

Initial claims for oxygen services must include a completed Form HCFA-484 (Certificate of Medical Necessity: Oxygen)to establish whether coverage criteria are met and to ensure that the oxygen services provided are consistent with the physician's prescription or other medical documentation. The treating physician's prescription or other medical documentation must indicate that other forms of treatment (e.g., medical and physical therapy directed at secretions, bronchospasm and infection) have been tried, have not been sufficiently successful, and oxygen therapy is still required. While there is no substitute for oxygen therapy, each patient must receive optimum therapy before long-term home oxygen therapy is ordered. Use Form HCFA-484 for recertifications. (See Medicare Carriers Manual §3312 for completion of Form HCFA-484.)

The medical and prescription information in section B of Form HCFA-484 can be completed only by the treating physician, the physician's employee, or another clinician (e.g., nurse, respiratory therapist, etc.) as long as that person is not the DME supplier. Although hospital discharge coordinators and medical social workers may assist in arranging for physician-prescribed home oxygen, they do not have the authority to prescribe the services. Suppliers may not enter this information. While this section may be completed by nonphysician clinician or a physician employee, it must be reviewed and the form HCFA-484 signed by the attending physician.

A physician's certification of medical necessity for oxygen equipment must include the results of specific testing before coverage can be determined.

Claims for oxygen must also be supported by medical documentation in the patient's record. Separate documentation is used with electronic billing. (See Medicare Carriers Manual, Part 3,§4105.5.) This documentation may be in the form of a prescription written by the patient's attending physician who has recently examined the patient (normally within a month of the start of therapy) and must specify:

A diagnosis of the disease requiring home use of oxygen;

The oxygen flow rate; and

An estimate of the frequency, duration of use (e.g., 2 liters per minute, 10 minutes per hour, 12 hours per day), and duration of need (e.g., 6 months or lifetime).

NOTE: A prescription for "Oxygen PRN" or "Oxygen as needed" does not meet this last requirement. Neither provides any basis for determining if the amount of oxygen is reasonable and necessary for the patient.

A member of the carrier's medical staff should review all claims with oxygen flow rates of more than 4 liters per minute before payment can be made.

The attending physician specifies the type of oxygen delivery system to be used (i.e., gas, liquid, or concentrator) by signing the completed form HCFA-484. In addition the supplier or physician may use the space in section C for written confirmation of additional details of the physician's order. The additional order information contained in section C may include the means of oxygen delivery (mask, nasal, cannula, etc.), the specifics of varying flow rates, and/or the noncontinuous use of oxygen as appropriate. The physician confirms this order information with their signature in section D.

New medical documentation written by the patient's attending physician must be submitted to the carrier in support of revised oxygen requirements when there has been a change in the patient's condition and need for oxygen therapy.

Carriers are required to conduct periodic, continuing medical necessity reviews on patients whose conditions warrant these reviews and on patients with indefinite or extended periods of necessity as described in Medicare Carriers Manual, Part 3, §4105.5. When indicated, carriers may also request documentation of the results of a repeat arterial blood gas or oximetry study.

NOTE: Section 4152 of OBRA 1990 requires earlier recertification and retesting of oxygen patients who begin coverage with an arterial blood gas result at or above a partial pressure of 55 or an arterial oxygen saturation percentage at or above 89. (See Medicare Carriers Manual §4105.5 for certification and retesting schedules.)

C. Laboratory Evidence — Initial claims for oxygen therapy must also include the results of a blood gas study that has been ordered and evaluated by the attending physician. This is usually in the form of a measurement of the partial pressure of oxygen (PO2) in arterial blood. (See Medicare Carriers Manual, Part 3, §2070.1 for instructions on clinical laboratory tests.) A measurement of arterial oxygen saturation obtained by ear or pulse oximetry, however, is also acceptable when ordered and evaluated by the attending physician and performed under his or her supervision or when performed by a qualified provider or supplier of laboratory services. When the arterial blood gas and the oximetry studies are both used to document the need for home oxygen therapy and the results are conflicting, the arterial blood gas study is the preferred source of documenting medical need. A DME supplier is not considered a qualified provider or supplier of laboratory services for purposes of these guidelines. This prohibition does not extend to the results of blood gas test conducted by a hospital certified to do such tests. The conditions under which the laboratory tests are performed must be specified in writing and submitted with the initial claim, i.e., at rest, during exercise, or during sleep.

The preferred sources of laboratory evidence are existing physician and/or hospital records that reflect the patient's medical condition. Since it is expected that virtually all patients who qualify for home oxygen coverage for the first time under these guidelines have recently been discharged from a hospital where they submitted to arterial blood gas tests, the carrier needs to request that such test results be submitted in support of their initial claims for home oxygen. If more than one arterial blood gas test is performed during the patient's hospital stay, the test result obtained closest to, but no earlier than 2 days prior to the hospital discharge date is required as evidence of the need for home oxygen therapy.

For those patients whose initial oxygen prescription did not originate during a hospital stay, blood gas studies should be done while the patient is in the chronic stable state, i.e., not during a period of an acute illness or an exacerbation of their underlying disease."

Carriers may accept an attending physician's statement of recent hospital test results for a particular patient, when appropriate, in lieu of copies of actual hospital records.

A repeat arterial blood gas study is appropriate when evidence indicates that an oxygen recipient has undergone a major change in their condition relevant to home use of oxygen. If the carrier has reason to believe that there has been a major change in the patient's physical condition, it may ask for documentation of the results of another blood gas or oximetry study.

D. Health Conditions

Coverage is available for patients with significant hypoxemia in the chronic stable state if: (1) the attending physician has determined that the patient has a health condition outlined in subsection D.1, (2) the patient meets the blood gas evidence requirements specified in subsection D.3, and (3) the patient has appropriately tried other alternative treatment measures without complete success. (See subsection B.)

1. Conditions for Which Oxygen Therapy May Be Covered

   A severe lung disease, such as chronic obstructive pulmonary disease, diffuse interstitial lung disease, whether of known or unknown etiology; cystic fibrosis bronchiectasis; widespread pulmonary neoplasm; or

   Hypoxia-related symptoms or findings that might be expected to improve with oxygen therapy. Examples of these symptoms and findings are pulmonary hypertension, recurring congestive heart failure due to chronic cor pulmonale, erythrocytosis, impairment of the cognitive process, nocturnal restlessness, and morning headache.

2. Conditions for Which Oxygen Therapy Is Not Covered

   Angina pectoris in the absence of hypoxemia. This condition is generally not the result of a low oxygen level in the blood, and there are other preferred treatments;

   Breathlessness without cor pulmonale or evidence of hypoxemia. Although intermittent oxygen use is sometimes prescribed to relieve this condition, it is potentially harmful and psychologically addicting;

   Severe peripheral vascular disease resulting in clinically evident desaturation in one or more extremities. There is no evidence that increased PO2 improves the oxygenation of tissues with impaired circulation; or

   Terminal illnesses that do not affect the lungs.

3. Covered Blood Gas Values — If the patient has a condition specified in subsection D.1, the carrier must review the medical documentation and laboratory evidence that has been submitted for a particular patient (see subsections B and C) and determine if coverage is available under one of the three group categories outlined below.

   a. Group I — Except as modified in subsection d, coverage is provided for patients with significant hypoxemia evidenced by any of the following:

      (1) An arterial PO2 at or below 55 mm Hg, or an arterial oxygen saturation at or below 88 percent, taken at rest, breathing room air.

      (2) An arterial PO2 at or below 55 mm Hg, or an arterial oxygen saturation at or below 88 percent, taken during sleep for a patient who demonstrates an arterial PO2 at or above 56 mm Hg, or an arterial oxygen saturation at or above 89 percent, while awake; or a greater than normal fall in oxygen level during sleep (a decrease in arterial PO2 more than 10 mm Hg, or decrease in arterial oxygen saturation more than 5 percent) associated with symptoms or signs reasonably attributable to hypoxemia (e.g., impairment of cognitive processes and nocturnal restlessness or insomnia). In either of these cases, coverage is provided only for use of oxygen during sleep, and then only one type of unit will be

covered. Portable oxygen, therefore, would not be covered in this situation.

(3) An arterial PO2 at or below 55 mm Hg or an arterial oxygen saturation at or below 88 percent, taken during exercise for a patient who demonstrates an arterial PO2 at or above 56 mm Hg, or an arterial oxygen saturation at or above 89 percent, during the day while at rest. In this case, supplemental oxygen is provided for during exercise if there is evidence the use of oxygen improves the hypoxemia that was demonstrated during exercise when the patient was breathing room air.

b. Group II

Except as modified in subsection d, coverage is available for patients whose arterial PO2 is 56-59 mm Hg or whose arterial blood oxygen saturation is 89 percent, if there is evidence of:

(1) Dependent edema suggesting congestive heart failure;

(2) Pulmonary hypertension or cor pulmonale, determined by measurement of pulmonary artery pressure, gated blood pool scan, echocardiogram, or "P" pulmonale on EKG (P wave greater than 3 mm in standard leads II, III, or AVFL; or

(3) Erythrocythemia with a hematocrit greater than 56 percent.

c. Group III

Except as modified in subsection d, carriers must apply a rebuttable presumption that a home program of oxygen use is not medically necessary for patients with arterial PO2 levels at or above 60 mm Hg, or arterial blood oxygen saturation at or above 90 percent. In order for claims in this category to be reimbursed, the carrier's reviewing physician needs to review any documentation submitted in rebuttal of this presumption and grant specific approval of the claims. HCFA expects few claims to be approved for coverage in this category.

d. Variable Factors That May Affect Blood Gas Values — In reviewing the arterial PO2 levels and the arterial oxygen saturation percentages specified in subsections D. 3. a, b and c, the carrier's medical staff must take into account variations in oxygen measurements that may result from such factors as the patient's age, the altitude level, or the patient's decreased oxygen carrying capacity.

E. Portable Oxygen Systems

A patient meeting the requirements specified below may qualify for coverage of a portable oxygen system either (1) by itself or (2) to use in addition to a stationary oxygen system. A portable oxygen system is covered for a particular patient if:

The claim meets the requirements specified in subsections A-D, as appropriate; and

The medical documentation indicates that the patient is mobile in the home and would benefit from the use of a portable oxygen system in the home. Portable oxygen systems are not covered for patients who qualify for oxygen solely based on blood gas studies obtained during sleep.

F. Respiratory Therapists

Respiratory therapists' services are not covered under the provisions for coverage of oxygen services under the Part B durable medical equipment benefit as outlined above. This benefit provides for coverage of home use of oxygen and oxygen equipment, but does not include a professional component in the delivery of such services.

(See §60-9; Intermediary Manual, Part 3, §3113ff; and Medicare Carriers Manual, Part 3, §2100ff.)

60-5 Power-operated vehicles that may be appropriately used as wheelchairs are covered under the durable medical equipment provision

Power-operated vehicles that may be appropriately used as wheelchairs are covered under the durable medical equipment provision.

These vehicles have been appropriately used in the home setting for vocational rehabilitation and to improve the ability of chronically disabled persons to cope with normal domestic, vocational and social activities. They may be covered if a wheelchair is medically necessary and the patient is unable to operate a wheelchair manually.

A specialist in physical medicine, orthopedic surgery, neurology, or rheumatology must provide an evaluation of the patient's medical and physical condition and a prescription for the vehicle to assure that the patient requires the vehicle and is capable of using it safely. When an intermediary determines that such a specialist is not reasonably accessible, e.g., more than 1 day's round trip from the beneficiary's home, or the patient's condition precludes such travel, a prescription from the beneficiary's physician is acceptable.

The intermediary's medical staff reviews all claims for a power-operated vehicle, including the specialists' or other physicians' prescriptions and evaluations of the patient's medical and physical conditions, to insure that all coverage requirements are met. (See §60-9 and Intermediary Manual, Part 3, §3629.)

60-6 Specially sized wheelchairs

Payment may be made for a specially sized wheelchair even though it is more expensive than a standard wheelchair. For example, a narrow wheelchair may be required because of the narrow doorways of a patient's home or because of a patient's slender build. Such difference in the size of the wheelchair from the standard model is not considered a deluxe feature.

A physician's certification or prescription that a special size is needed is not required where you can determine from the information in file or other sources that a specially sized wheelchair (rather than a standard one) is needed to accommodate the wheelchair to the place of use or the physical size of the patient.

To determine the reasonable charge in these cases, use the criteria set out in Carriers Manual, §§5022, 5022.1, 5200, and 5205, as necessary.

Cross-refer: Intermediary Manual, §§3113.2C, 3642.1, 3643 (item 3); Carriers Manual, §§2100.2c, 2105, 4105.2, 5107; Hospital Manual, §§235.2c, 420.1 (item 13).

60-7 Self-Contained Pacemaker Monitors

Self-contained pacemaker monitors are accepted devices for monitoring cardiac pacemakers. Accordingly, program payment may be made for the rental or purchase of either of the following pacemaker monitors when it is prescribed by a physician for a patient with a cardiac pacemaker:

A. Digital Electronic Pacemaker Monitor — This device provides the patient with an instantaneous digital readout of his pacemaker pulse rate. Use of this device does not involve professional services until there has been a change of five pulses (or more) per minute above or below the initial rate of the pacemaker; when such change occurs, the patient contacts his physician.

B. Audible/Visible Signal Pacemaker Monitor — This device produces an audible and visible signal which indicates the pacemaker rate. Use of this device does not involve professional services until a change occurs in these signals; at such time, the patient contacts his physician.

NOTE: The design of the self-contained pacemaker monitor makes it possible for the patient to monitor his pacemaker periodically and minimizes the need for regular visits to the outpatient department of the provider.

Therefore, documentation of the medical necessity for pacemaker evaluation in the outpatient department of the provider should be obtained where such evaluation is employed in addition to the self-contained pacemaker monitor used by the patient in his home.

Cross-refer: §50-1

60-8 Seat Lift

Reimbursement may be made for the rental or purchase of a medically necessary seat lift when prescribed by a physician for a patient with severe arthritis of the hip or knee and patients with muscular dystrophy or other neuromuscular diseases when it has been determined the patient can benefit therapeutically from use of the device. In establishing medical necessity for the seat lift, the evidence must show that the item is included in the physician's course of treatment, that it is likely to effect improvement, or arrest or retard deterioration in the patient's condition, and that the severity of the condition is such that the alternative would be chair or bed confinement.

Coverage of seat lifts is limited to those types which operate smoothly, can be controlled by the patient, and effectively assist a patient in standing up and sitting down without other assistance. Excluded from coverage is the type of lift which operates by a spring release mechanism with a sudden, catapult-like motion and jolts the patient from a seated to a standing position. Limit the payment for units which incorporate a recliner feature along with the seat lift to the amount payable for a seat lift without this feature.

Cross Refer: Carriers Manual, § 5107

60-9 Durable Medical Equipment Reference List

The durable medical equipment (DME) list which follows is designed to facilitate your processing of DME claims. This section is designed to be used as a quick reference tool for determining the coverage status of certain pieces of DME and especially for those items which are commonly referred to by both brand and generic names. The information contained herein is applicable (where appropriate) to all DME coverage determinations discussed in the DME portion of this manual. The list is organized into two columns. The first column lists alphabetically various generic categories of equipment on which national coverage decisions have been made by HCFA; and the second column notes the coverage status of each equipment category.

In the case of equipment categories that have been determined by HCFA to be covered under the DME benefit, the list outlines the conditions of coverage that must be met if payment is to be allowed for the rental or purchase of the DME by a particular patient, or cross-refers to another section of the manual where the applicable coverage criteria are described in more detail. With respect to equipment categories that cannot be covered as DME, the list includes a brief explanation of why the equipment is not covered. This DME list will be updated periodically to reflect any additional national coverage decisions that HCFA may make with regard to other categories of equipment.

When you receive a claim for an item of equipment which does not appear to fall logically into any of the generic categories listed, you have the authority and responsibility for deciding whether those items are covered under the DME benefit. These decisions must be made by each contractor based on the advice of its medical consultants, taking into account:

The general DME coverage instructions in the Carriers Manual, §2100ff and Intermediary Manual, §3113ff (see below for brief summary);

Whether the item has been approved for marketing by the Food and Drug Administration (FDA) (see Carriers Manual, §2303.1 and Intermediary Manual, §3151.1) and is otherwise generally considered to be safe and effective for the purpose intended; and

Whether the item is reasonable and necessary for the individual patient.

As provided in the Carriers Manual, § 2100.1, and Intermediary Manual, §3113.1, the term DME is defined as equipment which

Can withstand repeated use; i.e., could normally be rented, and used by successive patients;

Is primarily and customarily used to serve a medical purpose;

Generally is not useful to a person in the absence of illness or injury; and

Is appropriate for use in a patient's home.

Air Cleaners
Deny — environmental control equipment; not primarily medical in nature (§l861 (n) of the Act)

Air Conditioners
Deny — environmental control equipment; not primarily medical in nature (§l861(n) of the Act)

Air-Fluidized Bed
See §60-19

Alternating Pressure Pads
Covered if patient has, or is highly susceptible to, and Matresses and decubitus ulcers and patient's physician has Lambs Wool Pads specified that he will be supervising its use in connection with his course of treatment.

Audible/Visible Signal
See Self-Contained Pacemaker Monitor

Augmentative Communication
See Communicator Device

Bathtub Lifts
Deny — convenience item; not primarily medical in nature (§l861(n) of the Act)

Bathtub Seats
Deny — comfort or convenience item; hygienic equipment; not primarily medical in nature (§l861(n) of the Act)

Bead Bed
See §60-19

Bed Baths (home type)
Deny — hygienic equipment; not primarily medical in nature (§l861(n) of the Act)

Bed Lifter (bed elevator)
Deny — not primarily medical in nature (§1861(n) of the Act.

Bedboards
Deny — not primarily medical in nature (§ 1861(n) n) of the Act)

Bed Pans (autoclavable hospital type)
Covered if patient is bed confined

Bed Side Rails
See Hospital Beds, §60-l8

Beds-Lounge (power or manual)
Deny — not a hospital bed; comfort or convenience item; not primarily medical in nature (§l861(n) of the Act)

Beds-Oscillating
Deny — institutional equipment; inappropriate for home use

Bidet Toilet Seat
See Toilet Seats

Blood Glucose Analyzer
Deny — unsuitable for home use (See §60-11.)

Reflectance Colorimeter

Blood Glucose Monitor
Covered if patient meets certain conditions (See §60-11.)

Braille Teaching Texts
Deny — educational equipment; not primarily medical in nature (§1861(n) of the Act)

Canes
Covered if patient's condition impairs ambulation (See §60-3.)

Carafes
Deny — convenience item; not primarily medical in nature (§l861(n) of the Act)

Catheters
Deny — nonreusable disposable supply (§1861(n) of the Act)

Commodes
Covered if patient is confined to bed or room

NOTE: The term "room confined" means that the patient's condition is such that leaving the room is medically contraindicated. The accessibility of bathroom facilities generally would not be a factor in this determination. However, confinement of a patient to his home in a case where there are no toilet facilities in the home may be equated to room confinement. Moreover, payment may also be made if a patient's medical condition confines him to a floor of his home and there is no bathroom located on that floor (See Hospital Beds in § 60-18 for definition of "bed confinement".)

Communicator
Deny — convenience item; not primarily medical in nature (§1861(n) of the Act)

Continuous Passive Motion
Continuous Passive Motion devices are (CPM) Devices covered for patients who have received a totalknee replacement. To qualify for coverage, use of the device must commence within two days following surgery. In addition, coverage is limited to that portion of the three week period following surgery during which the device is used in the patient's home. There is insufficient evidence to justify coverage of these devices for longer periods of time or for other applications.

Continuous Positive Airway Pressure (CPAP)
See §60-17

Crutches
Covered if patient's condition impairs ambulation

Cushion Lift Power Seat
See Seat Lifts

Dehumidifiers (room or central heating system type)
Deny — environmental control equipment; not primarily medical in nature (§l861(n) of the Act)

Diathermy Machines (standard wave types)
Deny — inappropriate for home use (See and pulses §35-41.)

Digital Electronic Pacemaker Monitor
See Self-Contained Pacemaker Monitor

Disposable Sheets and Bags
Deny — nonreusable disposable supplies (§l861(n) of the Act)

Elastic Stockings
Deny — nonreusable supply; not rental-type items (§l861(n) of the Act)

Electric Air Cleaners
Deny — (See Air Cleaners.) (§l861(n) of the Act)

Electric Hospital Beds
See Hospital Beds §60-18

Electrostatic Machines
Deny — See Air Cleaners and Air Conditioners (§l861(n) of the Act)

Elevators
Deny — convenience item; not primarily medical in nature (§l861(n) of the Act)

Emesis Basins
Deny — convenience item; not primarily medical in nature (§l861(n) of the Act)

Esophageal Dilator
Deny — physician instrument; inappropriatefor patient use

Exercise Equipment
Deny — not primarily medical in nature (§l861(n) n) of the Act)

Fabric Supports
Deny — nonreusable supplies; not rental-type it (§l861(n) of the Act)

Face Masks (oxygen)
Covered if oxygen is covered (See § 60-4.)

Face Masks (surgical)
Deny — nonreusable disposable items (§l861(n) n) of the Act)

Flowmeter
See Medical Oxygen Regulators

Fluidic Breathing Assister
See IPPB Machines

Fomentation Device
See Heating Pads

Gel Flotation Pads and Mattresses
See Alternating Pressure Pads and Mattresses

Grab Bars
Deny — self-help device; not primarily medical in nature (§l861(n) of the Act)

Heat and Massage Foam Cushion Pad
Deny — not primarily medical in nature; personal comfort item (§§l861(n) and l862(a)(6) of the Act)

Heating and Cooling Plants
Deny — environmental control equipment not primary; medical in nature (§l861(n) of the Act)

Heating Pads
Covered if the contractor's medical staff determines patient's medical condition is one for which the application of heat in the form of a heating pad is therapeutically effective.

Heat Lamps
Covered if the contractor's medical staff determines patient's medical condition is one for which the application of heat in the form of a heat lamp is therapeutically effective.

Hospital Beds
See §60-18

Hot Packs
See Heating Pads

Humidifiers (oxygen)
See Oxygen Humidifiers

Humidifiers (room or central heating system types)
Deny — environmental control equipment; not medical in nature (§l861(n) of the Act)

Hydraulic Lift
See Patient Lifts

Incontinent Pads
Deny — nonreusable supply; hygienic item (§ l861(n) of the Act.)

Infusion Pumps
For external and implantable pumps, see §60-14. If the pump is used with an enteral or parenteral nutritional therapy system, see §§65-10 - 65.10.2 for special coverage rules.

Injectors (hypodermic jet for injection of insulin)
Deny — noncovered self-administered drug supply; pressure powered devices   (§1861(s)(2)(A) of the Act)

IPPB Machines
Covered if patient's ability to breathe is severely impaired

Iron Lungs
See Ventilators

Irrigating Kit
Deny — nonreusable supply; hygienic equipment (§l861(n) of the Act)

Lambs Wool Pads
Covered under same conditions as alternating pressure pads and mattresses

Leotards
Deny — See Pressure Leotards (§l861(n) of the Act)

Lymphedema Pumps
Covered (See §60-16.) (segmental and non-segmental therapy types)

Massage Devices
Deny — personal comfort items; not primarily medical in nature (§§l861(n) and l862(a)(6) of the Act)

Mattress
Covered only where hospital bed is medically necessary (Separate Charge for replacement mattress should not be allowed where hospital bed with mattress is rented.) (See §60-18.)

Medical Oxygen Regulators
Covered if patient's ability to breathe is severely impaired (See §60-4.)

Mobile Geriatric Chair
See Rolling Chairs

Motorized Wheelchairs
See Wheelchairs (power operated)

Muscle Stimulators
Covered for certain conditions (See §35-77.)

Nebulizers
Covered if patient's ability to breathe is severely impaired

Oscillating Beds
Deny — institutional equipment — inappropriate for home use

Overbed Tables
Deny — convenience item; not primarily medicalin nature (§l861(n) of the Act)

Oxygen
Covered if the oxygen has been prescribed for use in connection with medically necessary durable medical equipment (See §60-4.)

Oxygen Humidifiers
Covered if a medical humidifier has been prescribed for use in connection with medically necessary durable medical equipmentfor purposes of moisturizing oxygen (See §60-4.)

Oxygen Regulators (Medical)
See Medical Oxygen Regulators

Oxygen Tents
See § 60-4

Paraffin Bath Units (Portable)
See Portable Paraffin Bath Units

Paraffin Bath Units (Standard)
Deny — institutional equipment; inappropriateor home use

Parallel Bars
Deny — support exercise equipment; primarily for institutional use; in the home setting other devices (e.g., a walker) satisfy the patient's need

Patient Lifts
Covered if contractor's medical staff determines patient's condition is such that periodic movement is necessary to effect improvement or to arrest or retard deterioration in his condition.

Percussors
Covered for mobilizing respiratory tract secretions in patients with chronic obstructive lung disease, chronic bronchitis, or emphysema, when patient or operator of powered percussor has received appropriate training by a physician or therapist, and no one competent to administer manual therapy is available.

Portable Oxygen Systems:
1. Regulated (adjustable flow rate)
   Covered under conditions specified in §60-4. Refer all claims to medical staff for this determination.
2. Preset (flow rate or not adjustable)
   Deny — emergency, first-aid, precautionary equipment; essentially not therapeutic in nature.

Portable Paraffin Bath Units
Covered when the patient has undergone a successful trial period of paraffin therapy ordered by a physician and the patient's condition is expected to be relieved by long term use of this modality.

Portable Room Heaters
Deny — environmental control equipment; not primarily medical in nature (§l861(n) of the Act)

Portable Whirlpool Pumps
Deny — not primarily medical in nature; personal comfort items (§§l861(n) and 1862(a)(6) of the Act)

Postural Drainage Boards
Covered if patient has a chronic pulmonary condition

Preset Portable Oxygen Units
Deny — emergency, first-aid, or precautionaryequipment; essentially not therapeutic in nature

Pressure Leotards
Deny — nonreusable supply, not rental-type item (§l861(n) of the Act)

Pulse Tachometer
Deny — not reasonable or necessary for monitoring pulse of homebound patient with or without a cardiac pacemaker

Quad-Canes
See Walkers

Raised Toilet Seats
Deny — convenience item; hygienic equipment; not primarily medical in nature (§l861(n) of the Act)

Reflectance Colorimeters
See Blood Glucose Analyzers

Respirators
See Ventilators

Rolling Chairs
Covered if the contractor's medical staff determines that the patient's condition is such that there is a medical need for this item and it has been prescribed by the patient's physician in lieu of a wheelchair. Coverage is limited to those rollabout chairs having casters of at least 5 inches in diameter and specifically designed to meet the needs of ill, injured, or otherwise impaired individuals.

Coverage is denied for the wide range of chairs with smaller casters as are found in general use in homes, offices, and institutions for many purposes not related to the care or treatment of ill or injured persons. This type is not primarily medical in nature. (§l861(n) of the Act)

Safety Roller
See §60-15

Sauna Baths
Deny — not primarily medical in nature; personal comfort items (§§l861(n) and (l862(a)(6) of the Act)

Seat Lift
Covered under the conditions specified in §60-8. Refer all to medical staff for this determination.

Self-Contained Pacemaker Monitor
Covered when prescribed by a physician for a patient with a cardiac pacemaker (See §§50-1C and 60-7.)

Sitz Bath
Covered if the contractor's medical staff determines patient has an infection or injury of the perineal area and the item has been prescribed by the patient's physician as a part of his planned regimen of treatment in the patient's home.

Spare Tanks of Oxygen
Deny — convenience or precautionary supply

Speech Teaching Machine
Deny — education equipment; not primarily medical in nature (§l861(n) of the Act)

Stairway Elevators
Deny — See Elevators (§1861(n) of the Act)

Standing Table
Deny — convenience item; not primarily medical in nature (§1861(n) of the Act)

Steam Packs
These packs are covered under the same condition as a heating pad (See Heating Pads.)

Suction Machine
Covered if the contractor's medical staff determines that the machine specified in the claim is medically required and appropriate for home use without technical or professional supervision.

Support Hose
Deny — See Fabric Supports (§1861(n) of the Act)

Surgical Leggings
Deny — nonreusable supply; not rental-type item (§1861(n) of the Act)

Telephone Alert Systems
Deny — these are emergency communications systems and do not serve a diagnostic or therapeutic purpose

Telephone Arms
Deny — convenience item; not medical in nature (§1861(n) of the Act)

Toilet Seats
Deny — not medical equipment (§1861(n) of the Act)

Traction Equipment
Covered if patient has orthopedic impairment requiring traction equipment which prevents ambulation during the period of use (Consider covering devices usable during ambulation; e.g., cervical traction collar, under the brace provision)

Trapeze Bars
Covered if patient is bed confined and the patient needs a trapeze bar to sit up because of respiratory condition, to change body positionfor other medical reasons, or to get in and out of bed.

Treadmill Exerciser
Deny — exercise equipment;not primarily medical in nature (§1861(n) of the Act)

Ultraviolet Cabinet
Covered for selected patients with generalized intractable psoriasis. Using appropriate consultation, the contractor should determine whether medical and other factors justify treatment at home rather than at alternative sites, e.g., outpatient department of a hospital.

Urinals (autoclavable hospital type)
Covered if patient is bed confined

Vaporizers
Covered if patient has a respiratory illness

Ventilators
Covered for treatment of neuromuscular diseases, thoracic restrictive diseases, and chronic respiratory failure consequent to chronic obstructive pulmonary disease. Includes both positive and negative pressure types.

Walkers
Covered if patient's condition impairs ambulation (See also §60-15.)

Water and Pressure Pads and Mattresses
See Alternating Pressure Pads and Mattresses.)

Wheelchairs
Covered if patient's condition is such that without the use of a wheelchair he would otherwise be bed or chair confined. An individual may qualify for a wheelchair and still be considered bed confined.

Wheelchairs (power operated)
Covered if patient's condition is such and wheelchairs with other that a wheelchair is medically necessary special features and the patient is unable to operate the wheelchair manually. Any claim involving a power wheelchair or a wheelchair with other special features should be referred for medical consultation since payment for the special features is limited to those which are medical llyrequired because of the patient's condition. (See §60-5 for power operated and §60-6 for specially sized wheelchairs.)

NOTE:A power-operated vehicle that may appropriately be used as a wheelchair can be covered. (See §60-5 for coverage details.)

Whirlpool Bath Equipment (standard)
Covered if patient is homebound and has a condition for which the whirlpool bath can be expected to provide substantial therapeutic benefit justifying its cost. Where patient is not homebound but has such a condition, payment is restricted to the cost of providing the services elsewhere; e.g., an outpatient department of a participating hospital, if that alternative is less costly. In all cases, refer claim to medical staff for a determination.

Whirlpool Pumps
Deny — See Portable Whirlpool Pumps (§1861(n) of the Act)

White Cane
Deny — See §60-3

65-1 Hydrophilic Contact Lenses

Hydrophilic contact lenses are eyeglasses within the meaning of the exclusion in §l862(a)(7) of the law and are not covered when used in the treatment of nondiseased eyes with spherical ametropia, refractive astigmatism, and/or corneal astigmatism. Payment may be made under the prosthetic device benefit, however, for hydrophilic contact lenses when prescribed for an aphakic patient.

Contractors are authorized to accept an FDA letter of approval or other FDA published material as evidence of FDA approval.

(See §45-7 for coverage of a hydrophilic lens as a corneal bandage.)

Cross-refer: Intermediary Manual, §§3110.3, 3110.4, 3151, and 3157; Carriers Manual, §§2130, 2320; Hospital Manual, §§228.3, 228.4, 260.1 and 260.7.

65-10 Enteral and Pareneteral Nutritional Therapy Covered as Prosthetic Device (Effective for items and services furnished on or after 07-11-84.)

There are patients who, because of chronic illness or trauma, cannot be sustained through oral feeding. These people must rely on either enteral or parenteral nutritional therapy, depending upon the particular nature of their medical condition.

Coverage of nutritional therapy as a Part B benefit is provided under the prosthetic device benefit provision, which requires that the patient must have a permanently inoperative internal body organ or function thereof. (See Intermediary Manual, §3110.4.) Therefore, enteral and parenteral nutritional therapy are not covered under Part B in situations involving temporary impairments. Coverage of such therapy, however, does not require a medical judgment that the impairment giving rise to the therapy will persist throughout the patient's remaining years. If the medical record, including the judgment of the attending physician, indicates that the impairment will be of long and indefinite duration, the test of permanence is considered met.

If the coverage requirements for enteral or parenteral nutritional therapy are met under the prosthetic device benefit provision, related supplies, equipment and nutrients are also covered under the conditions in the following paragraphs and Intermediary Manual, §3110.4.

65-10.1 Parenteral Nutrition Therapy

Daily parenteral nutrition is considered reasonable and necessary for a patient with severe pathology of the alimentary tract which does not allow absorption of sufficient nutrients to maintain weight and strength commensurate with the patient's general condition.

Since the alimentary tract of such a patient does not function adequately, an indwelling catheter is placed percutaneously in the subclavian vein and then advanced into the superior vena cava where intravenous infusion of nutrients is given for part of the day. The catheter is then plugged by the patient until the next infusion. Following a period of hospitalization, which is required to initiate parenteral nutrition and to train the patient in catheter care, solution preparation, and infusion technique, the parenteral nutrition can be provided safely and effectively in the patient's home by nonprofessional persons who have undergone special training. However, such persons cannot be paid for their services, nor is payment available for any services furnished by nonphysician professionals except as services furnished incident to a physician's service.

For parenteral nutrition therapy to be covered under Part B, the claim must contain a physician's written order or prescription and sufficient medical documentation to permit an independent conclusion that the requirements of the prosthetic device benefit are met and that parenteral nutrition therapy is medically necessary. An example of a condition that typically qualifies for coverage is a massive small bowel resection resulting in severe nutritional deficiency in spite of adequate oral intake. However, coverage of parenteral nutrition therapy for this and any other condition must be approved on an individual, case- by-case basis initially and at periodic intervals of no more than 3 months by the carrier's medical consultant or specially trained staff, relying on such medical and other documentation as the carrier may require. If the claim involves an infusion pump, sufficient evidence must be provided to support a determination of medical necessity for the pump. Program payment for the pump is based on the reasonable charge for the simplest model that meets the medical needs of the patient as established by medical documentation.

Nutrient solutions for parenteral therapy are routinely covered. However, Medicare pays for no more than one month's supply of nutrients at any one time. Payment for the nutrients is based on the reasonable charge for the solution components unless the medical record, including a signed statement from the attending physician, establishes that the beneficiary, due to his/her physical or mental state, is unable to safely or effectively mix the solution and there is no family member or other person who can do so. Payment will be on the basis of the reasonable charge for more expensive pre-mixed solutions only under the latter circumstances.

65-10.2 Enteral Nutrition Therapy

Enteral nutrition is considered reasonable and necessary for a patient with a functioning gastrointestinal tract who, due to pathology to or nonfunction of the structures that normally permit food to reach the digestive tract, cannot maintain weight and strength commensurate with his or her general condition. Enteral therapy may be given by nasogastric, jejunostomy, or gastrostomy tubes and can be provided safely and effectively in the home by nonprofessional persons who have undergone special training. However, such persons cannot be paid for their services, nor is payment available for any services furnished by nonphysician professionals except as services furnished incident to a physician's service.

Typical examples of conditions that qualify for coverage are head and neck cancer with reconstructive surgery and central nervous system disease leading to interference with the neuromuscular mechanisms of ingestion of such severity that the beneficiary cannot be maintained with oral feeding. However, claims for Part B coverage of enteral nutrition therapy for these and any other conditions must be approved on an individual, case-by-case basis. Each claim must contain a physician's written order or prescription and sufficient medical documentation (e.g., hospital records, clinical findings from the attending physician) to permit an independent conclusion that the patient's condition meets the requirements of the prosthetic device benefit and that enteral nutrition therapy is medically necessary. Allowed claims are to be reviewed at periodic intervals of no more than 3 months by the contractor's medical consultant or specially trained staff, and additional medical documentation considered necessary is to be obtained as part of this review.

Medicare pays for no more than one month's supply of enteral nutrients at any one time.

If the claim involves a pump, it must be supported by sufficient medical documentation to establish that the pump is medically necessary, i.e., gravity feeding is not satisfactory due to aspiration, diarrhea, dumping syndrome, etc. Program payment for the pump is based on the reasonable charge for the simplest model that meets the medical needs of the patient as established by medical documentation.

65-10.3   Nutritional Supplementation
Some patients require supplementation of their daily protein and caloric intake. Nutritional supplements are often given as a medicine between meals to boost protein-caloric intake or the mainstay of a daily nutritional plan. Nutritional supplementation is not covered under Medicare Part B.

65-11   Bladder Stimulators (Pacemakers) — Not Covered
There are a number of devices available to induce emptying of the urinary bladder by using electrical current which forces the muscles of the bladder to contract. These devices (commonly known as bladder stimulators or pacemakers) are characterized by the implantation of electrodes in the wall of the bladder, the rectal cones, or the spinal cord. While these treatments may effectively empty the bladder, the issue of safety involving the initiation of infection, erosion, placement, and material selection has not been resolved. Further, some facilities previously using electronic emptying have stopped using this method due to the pain experienced by the patient.

The use of spinal cord electrical stimulators, rectal electrical stimulators, and bladder wall stimulators is not considered reasonable and necessary. Therefore, no program payment may be made for these devices or for their implantation.

65-14   Cochlear Implantation
A cochlear implant device is an electronic instrument, part of which is implanted surgically to stimulate auditory nerve fibers, and part of which is worn or carried by the individual to capture, analyze and code sound. Cochlear implant devices are available in single channel and multi-channel modes. The purpose of implanting the device is to provide an awareness and identification of sounds and to facilitate communication for persons who are profoundly hearing impaired.

Medicare coverage is provided only for those patients who meet all of the following selection guidelines.

General: 1) Diagnosis of bilateral severe-to-profound sensorineural hearing impairment with limited benefit from appropriate hearing (or vibrotactile) aids; 2) Cognitive ability to use auditory clues and a willingness to undergo an extended program of rehabilitation; 3) Freedom from middle ear infection, an accessible cochlear lumen that is structurally suited to implantation, and freedom from lesions in the auditory nerve and acoustic areas of the central nervous system; 4) No contraindications to surgery; and 5) The device must be used in accordance with the FDA-approved labeling.

Adults: Cochlear implants may be covered for adults (over age 18) for prelinguistically, perilinguistically, and postlinguistically deafened adults. Postlinguistically deafened adults must demonstrate test scores of 30 percent or less on sentence recognition scores from tape recorded tests in the patient's best listening condition.

Children: cochlear implants may be covered for prelinguisticaly and postlinguistically deafened children aged 2 through 17. Bilateral profound sensorineural deafness must be demonstrated by the inability to improve on age appropriate closed-set word identification tasks with amplification.

65-8   Electrical Nerve Stimulators
Two general classifications of electrical nerve stimulators are employed to treat chronic intractable pain: peripheral nerve stimulators and central nervous system stimulators.

A. Implanted Peripheral Nerve Stimulators

   Payment may be made under the prosthetic device benefit for implanted peripheral nerve stimulators. Use of this stimulator involves implantation of electrodes around a selected peripheral nerve. The stimulating electrode is connected by an insulated lead to a receiver unit which is implanted under the skin at a depth not greater than 1/2 inch. Stimulation is induced by a generator connected to an antenna unit which is attached to the skin surface over the receiver unit. Implantation of electrodes requires surgery and usually necessitates an operating room.

   NOTE: Peripheral nerve stimulators may also be employed to assess a patient's suitability for continued treatment with an electric nerve stimulator. Such use of the stimulator is covered as part of the total diagnostic service furnished to the beneficiary rather than as a prosthesis.

B. Central Nervous System Stimulators (Dorsal Column and Depth Brain Stimulators)

The implantation of central nervous system stimulators may be covered as therapies for the relief of chronic intractable pain, subject to the following conditions conditions for coverage:

a. The implantation of the stimulator is used only as a late resort (if not a last resort) for patients with chronic intractable pain;

b. With respect to item a, other treatment modalities (pharmacological, surgical, physical, or psychological therapies) have been tried and did not prove satisfactory, or are judged to be unsuitable or contraindicated for the given patient;

c. Patients have undergone careful screening, evaluation and diagnosis by a multidisciplinary team prior to implantation. (Such screening must include psychologi cal, as well as physical evaluation);

d. All the facilities, equipment, and professional and support personnel required for the proper diagnosis, treatment training, and follow-up of the patient (including that required to satisfy item c) must be available; and

e. Demonstration of pain relief with a temporarily implanted electrode precedes permanent implantation. Contractors may find it helpful to work with PROs to obtain the information needed to apply these conditions to claims.

65-16 Tracheostomy Speaking Valve

A trachea tube has been determined to satisfy the definition of a prosthetic device, and the tracheostomy speaking valve is an add on to the trachea tube which may be considered a medically necessary accessory that enhances the function of the tube. In other words, it makes the system a better prosthesis. As such, a tracheostomy speaking valve is covered as an element of the trachea tube which makes the tube more effective.

65-3 Scleral Shell

Scleral shell (or shield) is a catchall term for different types of hard scleral contact lenses.

A scleral shell fits over the entire exposed surface of the eye as opposed to a corneal contact lens which covers only the central non-white area encompassing the pupil and iris. Where an eye has been rendered sightless and shrunken by inflammatory disease, a scleral shell may, among other things, obviate the need for surgical enucleation and prosthetic implant and act to support the surrounding orbital tissue.

In such a case, the device serves essentially as an artificial eye. In this situation, payment may be made for a scleral shell under §1861(s)(8) of the law.

Scleral shells are occasionally used in combination with artificial tears in the treatment of "dry eye" of diverse etiology. Tears ordinarily dry at a rapid rate, and are continually replaced by the lacrimal gland. When the lacrimal gland fails, the half-life of artificial tears may be greatly prolonged by the use of the scleral contact lens as a protective barrier against the drying action of the atmosphere. Thus, the difficult and sometimes hazardous process of frequent installation of artificial tears may be avoided. The lens acts in this instance to substitute, in part, for the functioning of the diseased lacrimal gland and would be covered as a prosthetic device in the rare case when it is used in the treatment of "dry eye."

Cross-refer: HCFA-Pub. 13-3, §§3110.4, 3110.5; HCFA-Pub. 14-3, §§2130, 2133; HCFA- Pub. 10, §§210.4, 211

65-5 Electronic Speech Aids

Electronic speech aids are covered under Part B as prosthetic devices when the patient has had a laryngectomy or his larynx is permanently inoperative. There are two types of speech aids. One operates by placing a vibrating head against the throat; the other amplifies sound waves through a tube which is inserted into the user's mouth. A patient who has had radical neck surgery and/or extensive radiation to the anterior part of the neck would generally be able to use only the "oral tube" model or one of the more sensitive and more expensive "throat contact" devices.

Cross-refer: HCFA-Pub. 13-3, §3110.4; HCFA-Pub. 14-3, §2130; HCFA-Pub. 10, §228.4

65-8 Electrical Nerve Stimulators

Two general classifications of electrical nerve stimulators are employed to treat chronic intractable pain: peripheral nerve stimulators and central nervous system stimulators.

A. Implanted Peripheral Nerve Stimulators — Payment may be made under the prosthetic device benefit for implanted peripheral nerve stimulators. Use of this stimulator involves implantation of electrodes around a selected peripheral nerve. The stimulating electrode is connected by an insulated lead to a receiver unit which is implanted under the skin at a depth not greater than 1/2 inch. Stimulation is induced by a generator connected to an antenna unit which is attached to the skin surface over the receiver unit. Implantation of electrodes requires surgery and usually necessitates an operating room.

NOTE: Peripheral nerve stimulators may also be employed to assess a patient's suitability for continued treatment with an electric nerve stimulator. As explained in §35-46, such use of the stimulator is covered as part of the total diagnostic service furnished to the beneficiary rather than as a prosthesis.

B. Central Nervous System Stimulators (Dorsal Column and Depth Brain Stimulators) — The implantation of central nervous system stimulators may be covered as therapies for the relief of chronic intractable pain, subject to the following conditions:

1. Types of Implantations — There are two types of implantations covered by this instruction:
   a. Dorsal Column (Spinal Cord) Neurostimulation — The surgical implantation of neurostimulator electrodes within the dura mater (endodural) or the percutaneous insertion of electrodes in the epidural space is covered.
   b. Depth Brain Neurostimulation — The stereotactic implantation of electrodes in the deep brain (e.g., thalamus and periaqueductal gray matter) is covered.
2. Conditions for Coverage — No payment may be made for the implantation of dorsal column or depth brain stimulators or services and supplies related to such implantation, unless all of the conditions listed below have been met:
   a. The implantation of the stimulator is used only as a late resort (if not a last resort) for patients with chronic intractable pain;
   b. With respect to item a, other treatment modalities (pharmacological, surgical, physical, or psychological therapies) have been tried and did not prove satisfactory, or are judged to be unsuitable or contraindicated for the given patient;
   c. Patients have undergone careful screening, evaluation and diagnosis by a multidisciplinary team prior to implantation. (Such screening must include psychological, as well as physical evaluation);
   d. All the facilities, equipment, and professional and support personnel required for the proper diagnosis, treatment training, and followup of the patient (including that required to satisfy item c) must be available; and
   e. Demonstration of pain relief with a temporarily implanted electrode precedes permanent implantation.

Contractors may find it helpful to work with PROs to obtain the information needed to apply these conditions to claims.

See Intermediary Manual, §3110.4 and §§35-20 and 35-27.

65-9 Incontinence Control Devices
A. Mechanical/Hydraulic Incontinence Control Devices — Mechanical/hydraulic incontinence control devices are accepted as safe and effective in the management of urinary incontinence in patients with permanent anatomic and neurologic dysfunctions of the bladder. This class of devices achieves control of urination by compression of the urethra. The materials used and the success rate may vary somewhat from device to device. Such a device is covered when its use is reasonable and necessary for the individual patient.

B. Collagen Implant — A collagen implant, which is injected into the submucosal tissues of the urethra and/or the bladder neck and into tissues adjacent to the urethra, is a prosthetic device used in the treatment of stress urinary incontinence resulting from intrinsic sphincter deficiency (ISD). ISD is a cause of stress urinary incontinence in which the urethral sphincter is unable to contract and generate sufficient resistance in the bladder, especially during stress maneuvers.

Prior to collagen implant therapy, a skin test for collagen sensitivity must be administered and evaluated over a 4 week period.

In male patients, the evaluation must include a complete history and physical examination and a simple cystometrogram to determine that the bladder fills and stores properly. The patient then is asked to stand upright with a full bladder and to cough or otherwise exert abdominal pressure on his bladder. If the patient leaks, the diagnosis of ISD is established.

In female patients, the evaluation must include a complete history and physical examination (including a pelvic exam) and a simple cystometrogram to rule out abnormalities of bladder compliance and abnormalities of urethral support. Following that determination, an abdominal leak point pressure (ALLP) test is performed. Leak point pressure, stated in cm H2O, is defined as the intra-abdominal pressure at which leakage occurs from the bladder (around a catheter) when the bladder has been filled with a minimum of 150 cc fluid. If the patient has an ALLP of less than 100 cm H2O, the diagnosis of ISD is established.

To use a collagen implant, physicians must have urology training in the use of a cystoscope and must complete a collagen implant training program.

Coverage of a collagen implant, and the procedure to inject it, is limited to the following types of patients with stress urinary incontinence due to ISD:

- Male or female patients with congenital sphincter weakness secondary to conditions such as myelomeningocele or epispadias;
- Male or female patients with acquired sphincter weakness secondary to spinal cord lesions;
- Male patients following trauma, including prostatectomy and/or radiation; and
- Female patients without urethral hypermobility and with abdominal leak point pressures of 100 cm H2O or less.

Patients whose incontinence does not improve with 5 injection procedures (5 separate treatment sessions) are considered treatment failures, and no further treatment of urinary incontinence by collagen implant is covered. Patients who have a reoccurrence of incontinence following successful treatment with collagen implants in the past (e.g., 6-12 months previously) may benefit from additional treatment sessions. Coverage of additional sessions may be allowed but must be supported by medical justification.

C. Electronic Stimulators — Pelvic floor electrical stimulators, whether inserted into the vaginal canal or rectum or implanted in the pelvic area, used as a treatment for urinary incontinence, e.g., as a bladder pacer or a retraining mechanism, are not covered. The effectiveness of these devices is unproven. (See §65-11.)

See Intermediary Manual, §3110.4.

70 BRACES — TRUSSES — ARTIFICIAL LIMBS AND EYES

70-1 Corset Used as Hernia Support

A hernia support (whether in the form of a corset or truss) which meets the definition of a brace is covered under Part B under §1861(s)(9) of the Act.

See Intermediary Manual, §3110.5; Medicare Carriers Manual, §2133; and Hospital Manual, §228.5.

70-2 Sykes Hernia Control

Based on professional advice, it has been determined that the sykes hernia control (a spring-type, U- shaped, strapless truss) is not functionally more beneficial than a conventional truss. Make program reimbursement for this device only when an ordinary truss would be covered. (Like all trusses, it is only of benefit when dealing with a reducible hernia). Thus, when a charge for this item is substantially in excess of that which would be reasonable for a conventional truss used for the same condition, base reimbursement on the reasonable charges for the conventional truss.

See Intermediary Manual, §3110.5; Medicare Carriers Manual, §2133; and Hospital Manual, §228.5.

70-3 Prosthetic Shoe

A prosthetic shoe (a device used when all or a substantial portion of the front part of the foot is missing) can be covered as a terminal device; i.e., a structural supplement replacing a totally or substantially absent hand or foot. The coverage of artificial arms and legs includes payment for terminal devices such as hands or hooks even though the patient may not require an artificial limb. The function of the prosthetic shoe is quite distinct from that of excluded orthopedic shoe and supportive foot devices which are used by individuals whose feet, although impaired, are essentially intact. (Section l862(a)(8) of the Act excludes payment for orthopedic shoes or other supportive devices for the feet.)

See Intermediary Manual, §3110.5; Medicare Carriers Manual, §2133; and Hospital Manual, §228.5.

Appendix B
Medicare Carriers Manual (MCM) References

15022. PAYMENT CONDITIONS FOR RADIOLOGY SERVICES

A. Professional Component (PC) — Pay for the PC of radiology services furnished by a physician to an individual patient in all settings under the fee schedule for physician services regardless of the specialty of the physician who performs the service. For services furnished to hospital patients, pay only if the services meet the conditions for fee schedule payment in §15014.C.1 and are identifiable, direct, and discrete diagnostic or therapeutic services to an individual patient, such as an interpretation of diagnostic procedures and the PC of therapeutic procedures. The interpretation of a diagnostic procedure includes a written report.

B. Technical Component (TC)

1. Hospital Patients — Do not pay for the TC of radiology services furnished to hospital patients. Payment for physicians' radiological services to the hospital, e.g., administrative or supervisory services, and for provider services needed to produce the radiology service is made by the intermediary as provider services through various payment mechanisms.

2. Services Not Furnished in Hospitals — Pay under the fee schedule for the TC of radiology services furnished to beneficiaries who are not patients of any hospital in a physician's office, a freestanding imaging or radiation oncology center, or other setting that is not part of a hospital.

3. Services Furnished in Leased Departments — In the case of procedures furnished in a leased hospital radiology department to a beneficiary who is neither an inpatient nor an outpatient of any hospital, e.g., the patient is referred by an outside physician and is not registered as a hospital outpatient, both the PC and the TC of the services are payable under the fee schedule.

4. Purchased TC Services — Apply the purchased services limitation as set forth in §15048 to the TC of radiologic services other than screening mammography procedures.

5. Computerized Axial Tomography (CT) Procedures — Do not reduce or deny payment for medically necessary multiple CT scans of different areas of the body that are performed on the same day.

The TC RVUs for CT procedures that specify "with contrast" include payment for high osmolar contrast media. When separate payment is made for low osmolar contrast media under the conditions set forth in subsection F.1, reduce payment for the contrast media as set forth in subsection F.2.

6. Magnetic Resonance Imaging (MRI) Procedures — Do not make additional payments for 3 or more MRI sequences. The RVUs reflect payment levels for 2 sequences.

The TC RVUs for MRI procedures that specify "with contrast" include payment for paramagnetic contrast media. Do not make separate payment under code A4647.

A diagnostic technique has been developed under which an MRI of the brain or spine is first performed without contrast material, then another MRI is performed with a standard (0.1mmol/kg) dose of contrast material and, based on the need to achieve a better image, a third MRI is performed with an additional double dosage (0.2mmol/kg) of contrast material. When the high-dose contrast technique is utilized:

- Do not pay separately for the contrast material used in the second MRI procedure;
- Pay for the contrast material given for the third MRI procedure through supply code A4643 when billed with CPT codes 70553, 72156, 72157, and 72158;
- Do not pay for the third MRI procedure. For example, in the case of an MRI of the brain, if CPT code 70553 (without contrast material, followed by with contrast material(s) and further sequences) is billed, make no payment for CPT code 70551 (without contrast material(s)), the additional procedure given for the purpose of administering the double dosage, furnished during the same session. Medicare does not pay for the third procedure (as distinguished from the contrast material) because the CPT definition of code 70553 includes all further sequences; and

- Do not apply the payment criteria for low osmolar contrast media in subsection F to billings for code A4643.

7. Stressing Agent — Make separate payment under code J1245 for pharmacologic stressing agents used in connection with nuclear medicine and cardiovascular stress testing procedures furnished to beneficiaries in settings in which TCs are payable. Such an agent is classified as a supply and covered as an integral part of the diagnostic test. However, pay for code J1245 under the policy for determining payments for "incident to" drugs.

C. Nuclear Medicine (CPT 78000 Through 79999)

1. Payments for Radionuclides — The TC RVUs for nuclear medicine procedures (CPT codes 78XXX for diagnostic nuclear medicine, and codes 79XXX for therapeutic nuclear medicine) do not include the radionuclide used in connection with the procedure. These substances are separately billed under codes A4641 and A4642 for diagnostic procedures and code 79900 for therapeutic procedures and are paid on a "By Report" basis depending on the substance used. In addition, CPT code 79900 is separately payable in connection with certain clinical brachytherapy procedures. (See subsection D.3.)

2. Application of Multiple Procedure Policy (CPT Modifier 51) — Apply the multiple procedure reduction as set forth in §15038 to the following nuclear medicine diagnostic procedures: codes 78306, 78320, 78802, 78803, 78806, and 78807.

3. Generation and Interpretation of Automated Data — Payment for CPT codes 78890 and 78891 is bundled into payments for the primary procedure.

4. Positron Emission Tomography (PET) Scans (HCPCS Codes G0030–G0047) — For procedures furnished on or after March 14, 1995, pay for PET procedure of the heart under the limited coverage policy set forth in §50-36 of the Coverage Issues Manual (HCFA Pub. 6) using the billing instructions in §4173 of the Medicare Carriers Manual.

D. Radiation Oncology (Therapeutic Radiology) (CPT 77261–77799)

1. Weekly Radiation Therapy Management (CPT 77419–77430) — Pay for a physician's weekly treatment management services under codes 77419, 77420, 77425, and 77430. Instruct billing entities to indicate on each claim the number of fractions for which payment is sought.

    A weekly unit of treatment management is equal to five fractions or treatment sessions. A week for the purpose of making payments under these codes is comprised of five fractions regardless of the actual time period in which the services are furnished. It is not necessary that the radiation therapist personally examine the patient during each fraction for the weekly treatment management code to be payable. Multiple fractions representing two or more treatment sessions furnished on the same day may be counted as long as there has been a distinct break in therapy sessions, and the fractions are of the character usually furnished on different days. If, at the final billing of the treatment course, there are three or four fractions beyond a multiple of five, those three or four fractions are paid for as a week. If there are one or two fractions beyond a multiple of five, consider payment for these services as having been made through prior payments.

    EXAMPLE: 18 fractions = 4 weekly services

    62 fractions = 12 weekly services

    8 fractions = 2 weekly services

    6 fractions = 1 weekly service

    If billings have occurred which indicate that the treatment course has ended (and, therefore, the number of residual fractions has been determined), but treatments resume, adjust your payments for the additional services consistent with the above policy.

    EXAMPLE: 8 fractions = payment for 2 weeks

    2 additional fractions are furnished by the same physician. No additional Medicare payment is made for the 2 additional fractions.

    There are situations in which beneficiaries receive a mixture of simple (code 77420), intermediate (code 77425), and complex (code 77430) treatment management services during a course of treatment. In such cases, pay under the weekly treatment management code that represents the more frequent of the fractions furnished during the five-fraction week. For example, an inter-mediate weekly treatment management service is payable when, in a grouping of five fractions, a beneficiary receives three intermediate and two simple fractions.

2. Services Bundled Into Treatment Management Codes — Make no separate payment for any of the following services rendered by the radiation oncologists or in conjunction with radiation therapy:

11920	*Tattooing, intradermal introduction of insoluble opaque pigments to correct color defects of skin; 6.0 sq. cm or less*
11921	*6.1 to 20.0 sq. cm*
11922	*each additional 20.0 sq. cm*
16000	*Initial treatment, first degree burn, when no more than local treatment is required*
16010	*Dressings and/or debridement, initial or subsequent; under anesthesia, small*

16015	under anesthesia, medium or large, or with major debridement
16020	without anesthesia, office or hospital, small
16025	without anesthesia, medium (e.g., whole face or whole extremity)
16030	without anesthesia, large (e.g., more than one extremity)
36425	Venipuncture, cut down age 1 or over
53670	Catheterization, urethra; simple
53675	complicated (may include difficult removal of balloon catheter)
99211	Office or other outpatient visit, established patient; Level I
99212	Level II
99213	Level III
99214	Level IV
99215	Level V
99238	Hospital discharge day management
99281	Emergency department visit, new or established patient; Level I
99282	Level II
99283	Level III
99284	Level IV
99285	Level V
90780	IV infusion therapy, administered by physician or under direct supervision of physician; up to one hour
90781	each additional hour, up to eight (8) hours
90841	Individual medical psychotherapy by a physician, with continuing medical diagnostic evaluation, and drug management when indicated, including psychoanalysis, insight oriented, behavior modifying or supportive psychotherapy; time un-specified
90843	approximately 20 to 30 minutes
90844	approximately 45 to 50 minutes
90847	Family medical psychotherapy (conjoint psychotherapy) by a physician, with continuing medical diagnostic evaluation, and drug management when indicated
99050	Services requested after office hours in addition to basic service
99052	Services requested between 10:00 PM and 8:00 AM in addition to basic service
99054	Services requested on Sundays and holidays in addition to basic service
99058	Office services provided on an emergency basis
99071	Educational supplies, such as books, tapes, and pamphlets, provided by the physician for the patient's education at cost to physician
99090	Analysis of information data stored in computers (e.g., ECG, blood pressures, hematologic data)
99150	Prolonged physician attendance requiring physician detention beyond usual service (e.g., operative standby, monitoring ECG, EEG, intrathoracic pressures, intravascular pressures, blood gases during surgery, standby for newborn care following caesarean section); 30 minutes to one hour
99151	more than one hour
99180	Hyperbaric oxygen therapy initial
99182	Subsequent
99185	Hypothermia; regional
99371	Telephone call by a physician to patient or for consultation or medical management or for coordinating medical management with other health care professionals; simple or brief(e.g., to report on tests and/or laboratory results, to clarify or alter previous instructions, to integrate new information from other health professionals into the medical treatment plan, or to adjust therapy)
99372	intermediate (e.g., to provide advice to an established patient on a new problem, to initiate therapy that can be handled by telephone, to discuss test results in detail, to coordinate medical management of a new problem in an established patient, to discuss and evaluate new information and details, or to initiate a new plan of care)
99373	complex or lengthy (e.g., lengthy counseling session with anxious or distraught patient, detailed or prolonged discussion with family members regarding seriously ill patient, lengthy communication necessary to coordinate complex services or several different health professionals working on different aspects of the total patient care plan)

- Anesthesia (whatever code billed)
- Care of Infected Skin (whatever code billed)
- Checking of Treatment Charts Verification of Dosage, As Needed (whatever code billed)
- Continued Patient Evaluation, Examination, Written Progress Notes, As Needed (whatever code billed)
- Final Physical Examination (whatever code billed)
- Medical Prescription Writing (whatever code billed
- Nutritional Counseling (whatever code billed)

- Pain Management (whatever code billed)
- Review & Revision of Treatment Plan (whatever code billed)
- Routine Medical Management of Unrelated Problem (whatever code billed)
- Special Care of Ostomy (whatever code billed)
- Written Reports, Progress Note (whatever code billed)
- Follow-up Examination and Care for 90 Days After Last Treatment (whatever code billed)

3. Radiation Treatment Delivery (CPT 77401–77417) — Pay for these TC services on a daily basis under CPT codes 77401–77416 for radiation treatment delivery. Do not use local codes and RVUs in paying for the TC of radiation oncology services. Multiple treatment sessions on the same day are payable as long as there has been a distinct break in therapy services, and the individual sessions are of the character usually furnished on different days. Pay for CPT code 77417 (Therapeutic radiology port film(s)) on a weekly (5 fractions) basis.

4. Clinical Brachytherapy (CPT Codes 77750–77799) — Apply the bundled services policy in §15022.D.2. to procedures in this family of codes other than CPT code 77776. For procedures furnished in settings in which you make TC payments, pay separately for the expendable source associated with these procedures under CPT code 79900 except in the case of remote afterloading high intensity brachytherapy procedures (CPT codes 77781–77784). In the 4 codes cited, the expendable source is included in the RVUs for the TC of the procedures.

5. Radiation Physics Services (CPT Codes 77300–77399) — Until further notice, pay for the PC and TC of CPT codes 77300–77334 and 77739 on the same basis as you pay for radiologic services generally. For PC billings in all settings, presume that the radiologist participated in the provision of the service, e.g., reviewed/validated the physicist's calculation. CPT codes 77336 and 77370 are technical services only codes that are payable by carriers only in settings in which TCs are payable.

E. Supervision and Interpretation (S&I) Codes and Interventional Radiology

1. Physician Presence — Radiologic S&I codes are used to describe the personal supervision of the performance of the radiologic portion of a procedure by one or more physicians and the interpretation of the findings. In order to bill for the supervision aspect of the procedure, the physician must be present during its performance. This kind of personal supervision of the performance of the procedure is a service to an individual beneficiary and differs from the type of general supervision of the radiologic procedures performed in a hospital for which intermediaries pay the costs as physician services to the hospital. The interpretation of the procedure may be performed later by another physician. In situations in which a cardiologist, for example, bills for the supervision (the "S") of the S&I code, and a radiologist bills for the interpretation (the "I") of the code, both physicians should use a -52 modifier indicating a reduced service, e.g., the interpretation only. Pay no more for the fragmented S&I code than you would if a single physician furnished both aspects of the procedure.

2. Multiple Procedure Reduction — Make no multiple procedure reductions in the S&I or primary nonradiologic codes in these types of procedures, or in any procedure codes for which the descriptor and RVUs reflect a multiple service reduction. For additional procedure codes that do not reflect such a reduction, apply the multiple procedure reductions set forth in §15038.

F. Low Osmolar Contrast Media (LOCM) (HCPCS Codes A4644–A4646)

1. Payment Criteria — Make separate payments for LOCM (HCPCS codes A4644, A4645, and A4646) in the case of all medically necessary intrathecal radiologic procedures furnished to nonhospital patients. In the case of intraarterial and intravenous radiologic procedures, pay separately for LOCM only when it is used for nonhospital patients with one or more of the following characteristics:

- A history of previous adverse reaction to contrast material, with the exception of a sensation of heat, flushing, or a single episode of nausea or vomiting;
- A history of asthma or allergy;
- Significant cardiac dysfunction including recent or imminent cardiac decompensation, severe arrhythmia, unstable angina pectoris, recent myocardial infarction, and pulmonary hypertension;
- Generalized severe debilitation; or
- Sickle cell disease.

If the beneficiary does not meet any of these criteria, the payment for contrast media is considered to be bundled into the TC of the procedure, and the beneficiary may not be billed for LOCM.

2. Payment Level — A LOCM pharmaceutical is considered to be a supply which is an integral part of the diagnostic test. However, determine payment in the same manner as for a drug furnished incident to a physician's service with the following additional requirement. Reduce the lower of the estimated actual acquisition cost or the national average wholesale price by 8 percent to take into account the

fact that the TC RVUs of the procedure codes reflect less expensive contrast media.

G. Services of Portable X-Ray Suppliers — Services furnished by portable X-ray suppliers (see §2070.4) may have as many as four components.

1. Professional Component — Pay the PC of radiologic services furnished by portable X-ray suppliers on the same basis as other physician fee schedule services.

2. Technical Component — Pay the TC of radiology services furnished by portable X-ray suppliers under the fee schedule on the same basis as TC services generally.

3. Transportation Component (HCPCS Codes R0070–R0076) — This component represents the transportation of the equipment to the patient. Establish local RVUs for the transportation R codes based on your knowledge of the nature of the service furnished. Allow only a single transportation payment for each trip the portable X-ray supplier makes to a particular location. When more than one Medicare patient is X-rayed at the same location, e.g., a nursing home, prorate the single fee schedule transportation payment among all patients receiving the services. For example, if two patients at the same location receive X-rays, make one-half of the transportation payment for each.

Use any information regarding the number of patients X-rayed in each location that the supplier visits during each trip that the supplier of the X-ray may volunteer on the bill or claim for payment. If such information is not indicated, assume that at least four patients were X-rayed at the same location, and pay only one-fourth of the fee schedule payment amount for any one patient. Advise the suppliers in your area regarding the way in which you use this information.

NOTE: No transportation charge is payable unless the portable X-ray equipment used was actually transported to the location where the X-ray was taken. For example, do not allow a transportation charge when the X-ray equipment is stored in a nursing home for use as needed. However, a set-up payment (see subsection G.4) is payable in such situations. Further, for services furnished on or after January 1, 1997, make no separate payment under HCPCS code R0076 for the transportation of EKG equipment by portable X-ray suppliers or any other entity.

4. Set-Up Component (HCPCS Code Q0092) — Pay a set-up component for each radiologic procedure (other than retakes of the same procedure) during both single patient and multiple patient trips under Level II HCPCS code Q0092. Do not make the set-up payment for EKG services furnished by the portable X-ray supplier.

15030. SUPPLIES

Make a separate payment for supplies furnished in connection with a procedure only when one of the two following conditions exists:

A. HCPCS codes A4550, A4200, and A4263 are billed in conjunction with the appropriate procedure in the Medicare Physician Fee Schedule Data Base (place of service is physician's office); or

B. The supply is a pharmaceutical or radiopharmaceutical diagnostic imaging agent (including codes A4641 through A4647); pharmacologic stressing agent (code J1245); or therapeutic radionuclide (CPT code 79900). The procedures performed are:

- Diagnostic radiologic procedures (including diagnostic nuclear medicine) requiring pharmaceutical or radiopharmaceutical contrast media and/or pharmacological stressing agent,
- Other diagnostic tests requiring a pharmacological stressing agent,
- Clinical brachytherapy procedures (other than remote afterloading high intensity brachytherapy procedures (CPT codes 77781 through 77784) for which the expendable source is included in the TC RVUs), or
- Therapeutic nuclear medicine procedures.

2049. DRUGS AND BIOLOGICALS

Generally, drugs and biologicals are covered only if all of the following requirements are met:

- They meet the definition of drugs or biologicals (see §2049.1);
- They are of the type that cannot be self-administered (see §2049.2);
- They meet all the general requirements for coverage of items as incident to a physician's services (see §§2050.1 and 2050.3);
- They are reasonable and necessary for the diagnosis or treatment of the illness or injury for which they are administered according to accepted standards of medical practice (see §2049.4);
- They are not excluded as immunizations (see §2049.4.B); and
- They have not been determined by the FDA to be less than effective. (See §2049.4 D.)

Drugs that can be self-administered, such as those in pill form, or are used for self-injection, are generally not covered by Part B. However, the statute provides for the coverage of some self-administered drugs. Examples of self-administered drugs that are covered include blood clotting factors, drugs used in immunosuppressive therapy, erythropoietin for dialysis patients, osteoporosis drugs for certain homebound patients, and certain oral cancer drugs. (See §§2100.5 and 2130.D for coverage of drugs which are necessary to the effective use of DME or prosthetic devices.)

2049.1   Definition of Drug or Biological

Drugs and biologicals must be determined to meet the statutory definition. Under the statute, payment may be made for a drug or biological only where it is included, or approved for inclusion, in the latest official edition of the United States Pharmacopoeia, the National Formulary, or the United States Homeopathic Pharmacopoeia, except for those unfavorably evaluated in AMA Drug Evaluations (successor publication to New Drugs) or Accepted Dental Therapeutics (successor publication to Accepted Dental Remedies). Combination drugs are also included in the definition of drugs if the combination itself or all of the therapeutic ingredients of the combination are included, or approved for inclusion, in any of the above drug compendia.

Drugs and biologicals are considered approved for inclusion in a compendium if approved under the established procedure by the professional organization responsible for revision of the compendium.

2049.2   Determining Self-Administration of Drug or Biological

Whether a drug or biological is of a type which cannot be self-administered is based on the usual method of administration of the form of that drug or biological as furnished by the physician. Thus, where a physician gives a patient pills or other oral medication, these are excluded from coverage since the form of the drug given to the patient is usually self-administered. Similarly, if a physician gives a patient an injection which is usually self-injected (e.g., insulin or calcitonin), this drug is excluded from coverage, unless administered to the patient in an emergency situation (e.g., diabetic coma). Where, however, a physician injects a drug which is not usually self-injected, this drug is not subject to the self-administrable drug exclusion (regardless of whether the drug may also be available in oral form) since it is not self-administrable in the form in which it was furnished to the patient.

Whole blood is a biological which cannot be self-administered and is covered when furnished incident to a physician's services. Payment may also be made for blood fractions if all coverage requirements are satisfied. (See §2455 on Part B blood deductible.)

2049.3   Incident-to Requirements

In order to meet all the general requirements for coverage under the incident-to provision, an FDA approved drug or biological must be of a form that cannot be self-administered and must be furnished by a physician and administered by him/her or by auxiliary personnel employed by him/her under his/her personal supervision. The charge, if any, for the drug or biological must be included in the physician's bill, and the cost of the drug or biological must represent an expense to the physician. Drugs and biologicals furnished by other health professionals may also meet these requirements. (See §§2154, 2156, 2158 and 2160 for specific instructions.)

2049.4   Reasonableness and Necessity

Use of the drug or biological must be safe and effective and otherwise reasonable and necessary. (See §2303.) Drugs or biologicals approved for marketing by the Food and Drug Administration (FDA) are considered safe and effective for purposes of this requirement when used for indications specified on the labeling. Therefore, you may pay for the use of an FDA approved drug or biological, if:

- It was injected on or after the date of the FDA's approval;
- It is reasonable and necessary for the individual patient; and
- All other applicable coverage requirements are met.

Deny coverage for drugs and biologicals which have not received final marketing approval by the FDA unless you receive instructions from HCFA to the contrary. For specific guidelines on coverage of Group C cancer drugs, see the Coverage Issues Manual.

If there is reason to question whether the FDA has approved a drug or biological for marketing, obtain satisfactory evidence of FDA's approval. Acceptable evidence includes a copy of the FDA's letter to the drug's manufacturer approving the new drug application (NDA); or listing of the drug or biological in the FDA's Approved Drug Products or FDA Drug and Device Product Approvals; or a copy of the manufacturer's package insert, approved by the FDA as part of the labeling of the drug, containing its recommended uses and dosage, as well as possible adverse reactions and recommended precautions in using it. When necessary, the RO may be able to help in obtaining information.

An unlabeled use of a drug is a use that is not included as an indication on the drug's label as approved by the FDA. FDA approved drugs used for indications other than what is indicated on the official label may be covered under Medicare if the carrier determines the use to be medically accepted, taking into consideration the major drug compendia, authoritive medical literature and/or accepted standards of medical practice. In the case of drugs used in an anti-cancer chemotherapeutic regimen, unlabeled uses are covered for a medically accepted indication as defined in §2049.4.C.

Determinations as to whether medication is reasonable and necessary for an individual patient should be made on the same basis as all other such determinations (i.e., with the advice of medical consultants and with reference to accepted standards of medical practice and the medical circumstances of the individual case). The following guidelines identify three categories with specific examples of situations in which medications would not be reasonable and necessary according to accepted standards of medical practice.

1. Not for Particular Illness — Medications given for a purpose other than the treatment of a particular condition, illness, or injury are not covered (except for certain immunizations). Exclude the charge for medications, e.g., vitamins, given simply for the general good and welfare of the patient and not as accepted therapy for a particular illness.

2. Injection Method Not Indicated — Medication given by injection (parenterally) is not covered if standard medical practice indicates that the administration of the medication by mouth (orally) is effective and is an accepted or preferred method of administration. For example, the accepted standards of medical practice for the treatment of certain diseases is to initiate therapy with parenteral penicillin and to complete therapy with oral penicillin. Exclude the entire charge for penicillin injections given after the initiation of therapy if oral penicillin is indicated unless there are special medical circumstances which justify additional injections.

3. Excessive Medications — Medications administered for treatment of a disease which exceed the frequency or duration of injections indicated by accepted standards of medical practice are not covered. For example, the accepted standard of medical practice in the maintenance treatment of pernicious anemia is one vitamin B-12 injection per month. Exclude the entire charge for injections given in excess of this frequency unless there are special medical circumstances which justify additional injections.

Supplement the guidelines as necessary with guidelines concerning appropriate use of specific injections in other situations. Use the guidelines to screen out questionable cases for special review, further development or denial when the injection billed for would not be reasonable and necessary. Coordinate any type of drug treatment review with the PRO.

If a medication is determined not to be reasonable and necessary for diagnosis or treatment of an illness or injury according to these guidelines, exclude the entire charge (i.e., for both the drug and its administration). Also exclude from payment any charges for other services (such as office visits) which were primarily for the purpose of administering a noncovered injection (i.e., an injection that is not reasonable and necessary for the diagnosis or treatment of an illness or injury).

A. Antigens — Payment may be made for a reasonable supply of antigens that have been prepared for a particular patient if: (1) the antigens are prepared by a physician who is a doctor of medicine or osteopathy, and (2) the physician who prepared the antigens has examined the patient and has determined a plan of treatment and a dosage regimen. Antigens must be administered in accordance with the plan of treatment and by a doctor of medicine or osteopathy or by a properly instructed person (who could be the patient) under the supervision of the doctor. The associations of allergists that HCFA consulted advised that a reasonable supply of antigens is considered to be not more than a 12-week supply of antigens that has been prepared for a particular patient at any one time. The purpose of the reasonable supply limitation is to assure that the antigens retain their potency and effectiveness over the period in which they are to be administered to the patient. (See §§2005.2 and 2050.2.)

B. Immunizations — Vaccinations or inoculations are excluded as immunizations unless they are directly related to the treatment of an injury or direct exposure to a disease or condition, such as antirabies treatment, tetanus antitoxin or booster vaccine, botulin antitoxin, antivenin sera, or immune globulin. In the absence of injury or direct exposure, preventive immunization (vaccination or inoculation) against such diseases as smallpox, polio, diphtheria, etc., is not covered. However, pneumococcal, hepatitis B, and influenza virus vaccines are exceptions to this rule. (See items 1, 2 and 3.) In cases where a vaccination or inoculation is excluded from coverage, deny the entire charge.

1. Pneumococcal Pneumonia Vaccinations — Part B of Medicare pays 100 percent of the/ reasonable charge for pneumococcal pneumonia vaccine and its administration to a patient if it is ordered by a physician who is a doctor of medicine or osteopathy. This includes revaccination of patients at highest risk of pneumococcal infection.

A physician does not have to be present to meet the physician order requirement if a previously written physician order (standing order) is on hand and it specifies that for any person receiving the vaccine (1) the person's age, health, and vaccination status must be determined; (2) a signed consent must be obtained; (3) an initial vaccine may be administered only to persons at high risk (see below) of pneumococcal disease; (4) revaccination may be administered only to persons at highest risk of serious pneumococcal infection and those likely to have a rapid decline in pneumococcal antibody levels, provided that at least 5 years have passed since receipt of a previous dose of pneumococcal vaccine; and (5) a record indicating the date the vaccine was given must be presented to each patient.

Persons at high risk for whom an initial vaccine may be administered include all people age 65 and older; immunocompetent adults who are at increased risk of pneumococcal disease or its complications because of chronic illness (e.g., cardiovascular disease, pulmonary disease, diabetes mellitus, alcoholism, cirrhosis, or cerebrospinal fluid leaks); and individuals with compromised immune systems (e.g., splenic dysfunction or anatomic asplenia, Hodgkin's disease, lymphoma, multiple myeloma, chronic renal failure, HIV infection, nephrotic syndrome, sickle cell disease, or organ transplantation).

Persons at highest risk and those most likely to have rapid declines in antibody levels are those for whom revaccination may be appropriate. This group includes persons with functional or anatomic asplenia (e.g., sickle cell disease, splenectomy), HIV infection, leukemia, lymphoma, Hodgkin's disease, multiple myeloma, generalized malignancy, chronic renal failure, nephrotic syndrome, or other conditions associated with immunosuppression such as organ or bone marrow transplantation, and those receiving immunosuppressive chemotherapy. Routine revaccination of people age 65 or older who are not at highest risk is not appropriate.

To help avoid potentially unnecessary doses, every patient should be given a record of their vaccination. Nevertheless, those administering the vaccine should not require the patient to present an immunization record prior to administering the pneumococcal vaccine, nor should they feel compelled to review the patient's complete medical record if it is not available. Instead, provided that the patient is competent, it is acceptable for them to rely on the patient's verbal history to determine prior vaccination status. If the patient is uncertain about their vaccination history in the past 5 years, the vaccine should be given. However, if the patient is certain he/she was vaccinated in the last 5 years, the vaccine should not be given. If the patient is certain that the vaccine was given and that more than 5 years have passed since receipt of the previous dose, revaccination is not appropriate unless the patient is at highest risk.

2. Hepatitis B Vaccine — With the enactment of P.L. 98-369, coverage under Part B was extended to hepatitis B vaccine and its administration, furnished to a Medicare beneficiary who is at high or intermediate risk of contracting hepatitis B. This coverage is effective for services furnished on or after September 1, 1984.

High-risk groups currently identified include (see exception below):

- End stage renal disease (ESRD) patients;
- Hemophiliacs who receive Factor VIII or IX concentrates;
- Clients of institutions for the mentally retarded;
- Persons who live in the same household as an Hepatitis B Virus (HBV) carrier;
- Homosexual men; and
- Illicit injectable drug abusers.

Intermediate risk groups currently identified include:

- Staff in institutions for the mentally retarded; and
- Workers in health care professions who have frequent contact with blood or blood-derived body fluids during routine work.

EXCEPTION: Persons in the above-listed groups would not be considered at high or intermediate risk of contracting hepatitis B, however, if there is laboratory evidence positive for antibodies to hepatitis B. (ESRD patients are routinely tested for hepatitis B antibodies as part of their continuing monitoring and therapy.)

For Medicare program purposes, the vaccine may be administered upon the order of a doctor of medicine or osteopathy by home health agencies, skilled nursing facilities, ESRD facilities, hospital outpatient departments, persons recognized under the incident to physicians' services provision of law, and doctors of medicine and osteopathy.

A charge separate from the ESRD composite rate will be recognized and paid for administration of the vaccine to ESRD patients.

For ESRD laboratory tests, see Coverage Issues Manual, §50-17.

3. Influenza Virus Vaccine — Effective for services furnished on or after May 1, 1993, the Medicare Part B program covers influenza virus vaccine and its administration when furnished in compliance with any applicable State law by any provider of services or any entity or individual with a supplier number. Typically, these vaccines are administered once a year in the fall or winter. Medicare does not require for coverage purposes that the vaccine must be ordered by a doctor of medicine or osteopathy. Therefore, the beneficiary may receive the vaccine upon request without a physician's order and without physician supervision.

C. Unlabeled Use For Anti-Cancer Drugs — Effective January 1, 1994, unlabeled uses of FDA approved drugs and biologicals used in an anti-cancer chemotherapeutic regimen for a medically accepted indication are evaluated under the conditions described in this paragraph. A regimen is a combination of anti-cancer agents which has been clinically recognized for the treatment of a specific type of cancer. An example of a drug regimen is: Cyclophosphamide + vincristine + prednisone (CVP) for non-Hodgkin's lymphoma.

In addition to listing the combination of drugs for a type of cancer, there may be a different regimen or combinations which are used at different times in the history of the cancer (induction, prophylaxis of CNS involvement, post remission, and relapsed or refractory disease). A protocol may specify the combination of drugs, doses, and schedules for administration of the drugs. For purposes of this provision, a cancer treatment regimen includes drugs used to treat toxicities or side effects of the cancer treatment regimen when the drug is administered incident to a chemotherapy treatment. Contractors must not deny coverage based solely on the absence of FDA approved labeling for the use, if the use is supported by one of the following and the use is not listed as "not indicated" in any of the three compendia. (See note at the end of this subsection.)

1. American Hospital Formulary Service Drug Information — Drug monographs are arranged in alphabetical order within therapeutic classifications. Within the text of the monograph, information concerning indications is provided, including both labeled and unlabeled uses. Unlabeled uses are identified with daggers. The text must be analyzed to make a determination whether a particular use is supported.

2. American Medical Association Drug Evaluations — Drug evaluations are organized into sections and chapters that are based on therapeutic classifications. The evaluation of a drug provides information concerning indications, including both labeled and unlabeled uses. Unlabeled uses are not specifically identified as such. The text must be analyzed to make a determination whether a particular use is supported. In making these determinations, also refer to the AMA Drug Evaluations Subscription, Volume III, section 17 (Oncolytic Drugs), chapter 1 (Principles of Cancer Chemotherapy), tables 1 and 2.

    Table 1, Specific Agents Used In Cancer Chemotherapy, lists the anti-neoplastic agents which are currently available for use in various cancers. The indications presented in this table for a particular anti-cancer drug include labeled and unlabeled uses (although they are not identified as such). Any indication appearing in this table is considered to be a medically accepted use.

    Table 2, Clinical Responses To Chemotherapy, lists some of the currently preferred regimens for various cancers. The table headings include (1) type of cancer, (2) drugs or regimens currently preferred, (3) alternative or secondary drugs or regimens, and (4) other drugs or regimens with reported activity.

    A regimen appearing under the preferred or alternative/secondary headings is considered to be a medically accepted use.

    A regimen appearing under the heading "Other Drugs or Regimens With Reported Activity" is considered to be for a medically accepted use provided:

    - The preferred and alternative/secondary drugs or regimens are contraindicated; or
    - A preferred and/or alternative/secondary drug or regimen was used but was not tolerated or was ineffective; or
    - There was tumor progression or recurrence after an initial response.

3. United States Pharmacopoeia Drug Information (USPDI) — Monographs are arranged in alphabetic order by generic or family name. Indications for use appear as accepted, unaccepted, or insufficient data. An indication is considered to be a medically accepted use only if the indication is listed as accepted. Unlabeled uses are identified with brackets. A separate indications index lists all indications included in USPDI along with the medically accepted drugs used in treatment or diagnosis.

4. A Use Supported by Clinical Research That Appears in Peer Reviewed Medical Literature — This applies only when an unlabeled use does not appear in any of the compendia or is listed as insufficient data or investigational. If an unlabeled use of a drug meets these criteria, contact the compendia to see if a report regarding this use is forthcoming. If a report is forthcoming, use this information as a basis for your decision making. The compendium process for making decisions concerning unlabeled uses is very thorough and continuously updated. Peer reviewed medical literature includes scientific, medical, and pharmaceutical publications in which original manuscripts are published, only after having been critically reviewed for scientific accuracy, validity, and reliability by unbiased independent experts. This does not include in-house publications of pharmaceutical manufacturing companies or abstracts (including meeting abstracts).

    In determining whether there is supportive clinical evidence for a particular use of a drug, your medical staff (in consultation with local medical specialty groups) must evaluate the quality of the evidence in published peer reviewed medical literature. When evaluating this literature, consider (among other things) the following:

    - The prevalence and life history of the disease when evaluating the adequacy of the number of subjects and the response rate. While a 20 percent response rate may be adequate for highly prevalent disease states, a lower rate may be adequate for rare diseases or highly unresponsive conditions.
    - The effect on the patient's well-being and other responses to therapy that indicate effectiveness, e.g., a significant increase in survival rate or life expectancy or an objective and significant decrease in the size of the tumor or a reduction in symptoms related to the tumor. Stabilization is not considered a response to therapy.

- The appropriateness of the study design. Consider:

1. Whether the experimental design in light of the drugs and conditions under investigation is appropriate to address the investigative question. (For example, in some clinical studies, it may be unnecessary or not feasible to use randomization, double blind trials, placebos, or crossover.);

2. That nonrandomized clinical trials with a significant number of subjects may be a basis for supportive clinical evidence for determining accepted uses of drugs; and

3. That case reports are generally considered uncontrolled and anecdotal information and do not provide adequate supportive clinical evidence for determining accepted uses of drugs.

Use peer reviewed medical literature appearing in the following publications:

- American Journal of Medicine;
- Annals of Internal Medicine;
- The Journal of the American Medical Association;
- Journal of Clinical Oncology;
- Blood;
- Journal of the National Cancer Institute;
- The New England Journal of Medicine;
- British Journal of Cancer;
- British Journal of Hematology;
- British Medical Journal;
- Cancer;
- European Journal of Cancer (formerly the European Journal of Cancer and Clinical Oncology);
- Lancet; or
- Leukemia.

You are not required to maintain copies of these publications. If a claim raises a question about the use of a drug for a purpose not included in the FDA approved labeling or the compendia, ask the physician to submit copies of relevant supporting literature.

4. Unlabeled uses may also be considered medically accepted if determined by you to be medically accepted generally as safe and effective for the particular use.

   NOTE: If a use is identified as not indicated by HCFA or the FDA or if a use is specifically identified as not indicated in one or more of the three compendia mentioned or if you determine based on peer reviewed medical literature that a particular use of a drug is not safe and effective, the off-label usage is not supported and, therefore, the drug is not covered.

5. Less Than Effective Drug — This is a drug that has been determined by the Food and Drug Administration (FDA) to lack substantial evidence of effectiveness for all labeled indications. Also, a drug that has been the subject of a Notice of an Opportunity for a Hearing (NOOH) published in the Federal Register before being withdrawn from the market, and for which the Secretary has not determined there is a compelling justification for its medical need, is considered less than effective. This includes any other drug product that is identical, similar, or related. Payment may not be made for a less than effective drug.

   Because the FDA has not yet completed its identification of drug products that are still on the market, existing FDA efficacy decisions must be applied to all similar products once they are identified.

6. Denial of Medicare Payment for Compounded Drugs Produced in Violation of Federal Food, Drug, and Cosmetic Act — The Food and Drug Administration (FDA) has found that, from time to time, firms established as retail pharmacies engage in mass production of compounded drugs, beyond the normal scope of pharmaceutical practice, in violation of the Federal Food, Drug, and Cosmetic Act (FFDCA). By compounding drugs on a large scale, a company may be operating as a drug manufacturer within the meaning of the FFDCA, without complying with requirements of that law. Such companies may be manufacturing drugs which are subject to the new drug application (NDA) requirements of the FFDCA, but for which FDA has not approved an NDA or which are misbranded or adulterated. If the manufacturing and processing procedures used by these facilities have not been approved by the FDA, the FDA has no assurance that the drugs these companies are producing are safe and effective. The safety and effectiveness issues pertain to such factors as chemical stability, purity, strength, bioequivalency, and biovailability.

   Section 1862(a)(1)(A) of the Act requires that drugs must be reasonable and necessary in order to by covered under Medicare. This means, in the case of drugs, they must have been approved for marketing by the FDA. Section 2049.4 instructs carriers to deny coverage for drugs that have not received final marketing approval by the FDA, unless instructed otherwise by HCFA. Section 2300.1 instructs carriers to deny coverage of services related to the use of noncovered drugs as well. Hence, if DME or a prosthetic device is used to administer a noncovered drug, coverage is denied for both the nonapproved drug and the DME or prosthetic device.

In those cases in which the FDA has determined that a company is producing compounded drugs in violation of the FFDCA, Medicare does not pay for the drugs because they do not meet the FDA approval requirements of the Medicare program. In addition, Medicare does not pay for the DME or prosthetic device used to administer such a drug if FDA determines that a required NDA has not been approved or that the drug is misbranded or adulterated.

HCFA will notify you when the FDA has determined that compounded drugs are being produced in violation of the FFDCA. Do not stop Medicare payment for such a drug unless you are notified that it is appropriate to do so through a subsequent instruction. In addition, if you or ROs become aware that other companies are possibly operating in violation of the FFDCA, notify:

Health Care Financing Administration
Bureau of Policy Development
Office of Physician and Ambulatory Care Policy
7500 Security Blvd.
Baltimore, MD 21244-1850

2049.5   Self-Administered Drugs and Biologicals

Drugs that are self-administered are not covered by Medicare Part B unless the statute provides for such coverage. This includes blood clotting factors, drugs used in immunosuppressive therapy, erythropoietin for dialysis patients, certain oral anti-cancer drugs, and oral anti-nausea drugs when used in certain situations.

A. Immunosuppressive Drugs — Until January 1, 1995, immunosuppressive drugs are covered under Part B for a period of one year following discharge from a hospital for a Medicare covered organ transplant. HCFA interprets the 1-year period after the date of the transplant procedure to mean 365 days from the day on which an inpatient is discharged from the hospital. Beneficiaries are eligible to receive additional Part B coverage within 18 months after the discharge date for drugs furnished in 1995; within 24 months for drugs furnished in 1996; within 30 months for drugs furnished in 1997; and within 36 months for drugs furnished after 1997.

Covered drugs include those immunosuppressive drugs that have been specifically labeled as such and approved for marketing by the FDA, as well as those prescription drugs, such as prednisone, that are used in conjunction with immunosuppressive drugs as part of a therapeutic regimen reflected in FDA approved labeling for immunosuppressive drugs. Therefore, antibiotics, hypertensives, and other drugs that are not directly related to rejection are not covered. The FDA had identified and approved for marketing five specifically labeled immunosuppressive drugs. They are Sandimmune (cyclosporine), Sandoz Pharmaceutical; Imuran (azathioprine), Burroughs Wellcome; Atgam (antithymocyte globulin), Upjohn; and Orthoclone OKT3 (Muromonab-CD3), Ortho Pharmaceutical and, Prograf (tacrolimus), Fujisawa USA, Inc. You are expected to keep informed of FDA additions to the list of the immunosuppressive drugs.

B. Erythropoietin (EPO) — The statute provides that EPO is covered for the treatment of anemia for patients with chronic renal failure who are on dialysis. Coverage is available regardless of whether the drug is administered by the patient or the patient's caregiver. EPO is a biologically engineered protein which stimulates the bone marrow to make new red blood cells.

NOTE: Non-ESRD patients who are receiving EPO to treat anemia induced by other conditions such as chemotherapy or the drug zidovudine (commonly called AZT) must meet the coverage requirements in §2049.

EPO is covered for the treatment of anemia for patients with chronic renal failure who are on dialysis when:

- It is administered in the renal dialysis facility; or
- It is self-administered in the home by any dialysis patient (or patient caregiver) who is determined competent to use the drug and meets the other conditions detailed below.

NOTE: Payment may not be made for EPO under the incident to provision when EPO is administered in the renal dialysis facility. (See §5202.4.)

Medicare covers EPO and items related to its administration for dialysis patients who use EPO in the home when the following conditions are met.

1. Patient Care Plan — A dialysis patient who uses EPO in the home must have a current care plan (a copy of which must be maintained by the designated back-up facility for Method II patients) for monitoring home use of EPO which includes the following:

    a. Review of diet and fluid intake for aberrations as indicated by hyperkalemia and elevated blood pressure secondary to volume overload;

    b. Review of medications to ensure adequate provision of supplemental iron;

    c. Ongoing evaluations of hematocrit and iron stores;

    d. Reevaluation of the dialysis prescription taking into account the patient's increased appetite and red blood cell volume;

    e. Method for physician and facility (including back-up facility for Method II patients) follow-up on blood tests and a mechanism (such as a patient log) for keeping the physician informed of the results;

    f. Training of the patient to identify the signs and symptoms of hypotension and hypertension; and

g. The decrease or discontinuance of EPO if hypertension is uncontrollable.

2. Patient Selection — The dialysis facility, or the physician responsible for all dialysis-related services furnished to the patient, must make a comprehensive assessment that includes the following:

   a. Pre-selection monitoring. The patient's hematocrit (or hemoglobin), serum iron, transferrin saturation, serum ferritin, and blood pressure must be measured.

   b. Conditions the patient must meet. The assessment must find that the patient meets the following conditions:

      (1) Is a dialysis patient;

      (2) Has a hematocrit (or comparable hemoglobin level) that is as follows:

         (a) For a patient who is initiating EPO treatment, no higher than 30 percent unless there is medical documentation showing the need for EPO despite a hematocrit (or comparable hemoglobin level) higher than 30 percent. Patients with severe angina, severe pulmonary distress, or severe hypotension may require EPO to prevent adverse symptoms even if they have higher hematocrit or hemoglobin levels.

         (b) For a patient who has been receiving EPO from the facility or the physician, between 30 and 36 percent; and

      (3) Is under the care of:

         (a) A physician who is responsible for all dialysis-related services and who prescribes the EPO and follows the drug labeling instructions when monitoring the EPO home therapy; and

         (b) A renal dialysis facility that establishes the plan of care and monitors the progress of the home EPO therapy.

   c. The assessment must find that the patient or a caregiver meets the following conditions:

      (1) Is trained by the facility to inject EPO and is capable of carrying out the procedure;

      (2) Is capable of reading and understanding the drug labeling; and

      (3) Is trained in, and capable of observing, aseptic techniques.

   d. Care and storage of drug. The assessment must find that EPO can be stored in the patient's residence under refrigeration and that the patient is aware of the potential hazard of a child's having access to the drug and syringes.

3. Responsibilities of Physician or Dialysis Facility — The patient's physician or dialysis facility must:

   a. Develop a protocol that follows the drug label instructions;

   b. Make the protocol available to the patient to ensure safe and effective home use of EPO;

   c. Through the amounts prescribed, ensure that the drug on hand at any time does not exceed a 2-month supply; and

   d. Maintain adequate records to allow quality assurance for review by the network and State survey agencies. For Method II patients, current records must be provided to and maintained by the designated back-up facility.

   See §5202.4 for information on EPO payment.

   Submit claims for EPO in accordance with §§4273.1 and 4273.2.

C. Oral Anti-Cancer Drugs — Effective January 1, 1994, Medicare Part B coverage is extended to include oral anti-cancer drugs that are prescribed as anti-cancer chemotherapeutic agents providing they have the same active ingredients and are used for the same indications as anti-cancer chemotherapeutic agents which would be covered if they were not self administered and they were furnished incident to a physician's service as drugs and biologicals.

This provision applies only to the coverage of anti-neoplastic chemotherapeutic agents. It does not apply to oral drugs and/or biologicals used to treat toxicity or side effects such as nausea or bone marrow depression. Medicare will cover anti-neoplastic chemotherapeutic agents, the primary drugs which directly fight the cancer, and self-administered antiemetics which are necessary for the administration and absorption of the anti-neoplastic chemotherapeutic agents when a high likelihood of vomiting exists. The substitution of an oral form of an anti-neoplastic drug requires that the drug be retained for absorption. The antiemetics drug is covered as a necessary means for administration of the oral drug (similar to a syringe and needle necessary for injectable administration). Oral drugs prescribed for use with the primary drug which enhance the anti-neoplastic effect of the primary drug or permit the patient to tolerate the primary anti-neoplastic drug in higher doses for longer periods are not covered. Self-administered antiemetics to reduce the side effects of nausea and vomiting brought on by the primary drug are not included beyond the administration necessary to achieve drug absorption.

In order to assure uniform coverage policy, regional carriers and FIs must be apprised of local carriers' anti-cancer drug medical review policies which may impact on future medical review policy development. Local carrier's current and proposed anti-cancer drug medical review polices should be provided by local carrier medical directors to regional carrier or FI medical directors, upon request.

For an oral anti-cancer drug to be covered under Part B, it must:

- Be prescribed by a physician or other practitioner licensed under State law to prescribe such drugs as anti-cancer chemotherapeutic agents;
- Be a drug or biological that has been approved by the Food and Drug Administration (FDA);
- Have the same active ingredients as a non-self-administrable anti-cancer chemotherapeutic drug or biological that is covered when furnished incident to a physician's service. The oral anti-cancer drug and the non-self-administrable drug must have the same chemical/generic name as indicated by the FDA's Approved Drug Products (Orange Book), Physician's Desk Reference (PDR), or an authoritative drug compendium; — or, effective January 1, 1999, be a prodrug — an oral drug ingested into the body that metabolizes into the same active ingredient that is found in the non-self-administrable form of the drug;
- Be used for the same indications, including unlabeled uses, as the non-self-administrable version of the drug; and
- Be reasonable and necessary for the individual patient.

D. Oral Anti-Nausea Drugs — Section 4557 of the Balanced Budget Act of 1997 amends §1861(s)(2) by extending the coverage of oral anti-emetic drugs under the following conditions:

- Coverage is provided only for oral drugs approved by FDA for use as anti-emetics;
- The oral anti-emetic(s) must either be administered by the treating physician or in accordance with a written order from the physician as part of a cancer chemotherapy regimen;
- Oral anti-emetic drug(s) administered with a particular chemotherapy treatment must be initiated within 2 hours of the administration of the chemotherapeutic agent and may be continued for a period not to exceed 48 hours from that time.
- The oral anti-emetic drug(s) provided must be used as a full therapeutic replacement for the intravenous anti-emetic drugs that would have otherwise been administered at the time of the chemotherapy treatment.

Only drugs pursuant to a physician's order at the time of the chemotherapy treatment qualify for this benefit. The dispensed number of dosage units may not exceed a loading dose administered within 2 hours of that treatment, plus a supply of additional dosage units not to exceed 48 hours of therapy. However, more than one oral anti-emetic drug may be prescribed and will be covered for concurrent usage within these parameters if more than one oral drug is needed to fully replace the intravenous drugs that would otherwise have been given.

Oral drugs that are not approved by the FDA for use as anti-emetics and which are used by treating physicians adjunctively in a manner incidental to cancer chemotherapy are not covered by this benefit and are not reimbursable within the scope of this benefit.

It is recognized that a limited number of patients will fail on oral anti-emetic drugs. Intravenous anti-emetics may be covered (subject to the rules of medical necessity) when furnished to patients who fail on oral anti-emetic therapy.

This coverage, effective for services on or after January 1, 1998, is subject to regular Medicare Part B coinsurance and deductible provisions.

NOTE: Existing coverage policies authorizing the administration of suppositories to prevent vomiting when oral cancer drugs are used are unchanged by this new coverage.

E. Hemophilia Clotting Factors — Section 1861(s)(2)(I) of the Act provides Medicare coverage of blood clotting factors for hemophilia patients competent to use such factors to control bleeding without medical supervision, and items related to the administration of such factors. Hemophilia, a blood disorder characterized by prolonged coagulation time, is caused by deficiency of a factor in plasma necessary for blood to clot. (The discovery in 1964 of a cryoprecipitate rich in antihemophilic factor activity facilitated management of acute bleeding episodes.) For purposes of Medicare Part B coverage, hemophilia encompasses the following conditions:

- Factor VIII deficiency (classic hemophilia);
- Factor IX deficiency (also termed plasma thromboplastin component (PTC) or Christmas factor deficiency); and
- Von Willebrand's disease.

Claims for blood clotting factors for hemophilia patients with these diagnoses may be covered if the patient is competent to use such factors without medical supervision.

The amount of clotting factors determined to be necessary to have on hand and thus covered under this provision is based on the historical utilization pattern or profile developed by the carrier for each patient. It is expected that the treating source; e.g., a family physician or comprehensive hemophilia diagnostic and treatment center, has such information. From this data, the contractor is able to make reasonable projections concerning the quantity of clotting factors anticipated to be needed by the patient over a specific period of time. Unanticipated occurrences involving extraordinary events, such as automobile accidents of inpatient hospital stays, will change this base line data and should be appropriately considered. In addition, changes in a patient's medical needs over a period of time require adjustments in the profile. (See §5245 for payment policies.)

2050. SERVICES AND SUPPLIES

Services and supplies (including drugs and biologicals which cannot be self-administered) are those furnished incident to a physician's professional services. (Certain hospital services may also be covered as incident to physicians' services when rendered to hospital outpatients. Payment for these services is made under Part B to a hospital by the hospital's intermediary.)

To be covered incident to the services of a physician, services and supplies must be:

- An integral, although incidental, part of the physician's professional service (see §2050.1);
- Commonly rendered without charge or included in the physician's bill (see §2050.1A);
- Of a type that are commonly furnished in physician's offices or clinics (see §2050.1A);
- Furnished under the physician's direct personal supervision (see §2050.1B); and
- Furnished by the physician or by an individual who qualifies as an employee of the physician. (See §2050.1C.)

2050.1 Incident to Physician's Professional Services

Incident to a physician's professional services means that the services or supplies are furnished as an integral, although incidental, part of the physician's personal professional services in the course of diagnosis or treatment of an injury or illness.

A. Commonly Furnished in Physicians' Offices — Services and supplies commonly furnished in physicians' offices are covered under the incident to provision. Where supplies are clearly of a type a physician is not expected to have on hand in his/her office or where services are of a type not considered medically appropriate to provide in the office setting, they would not be covered under the incident to provision.

Supplies usually furnished by the physician in the course of performing his/her services, e.g., gauze, ointments, bandages, and oxygen, are also covered. Charges for such services and supplies must be included in the physicians' bills. (See §2049 regarding coverage of drugs and biologicals under this provision.) To be covered, supplies, including drugs and biologicals, must represent an expense to the physician. For example, where a patient purchases a drug and the physician administers it, the cost of the drug is not covered.

B. Direct Personal Supervision — Coverage of services and supplies incident to the professional services of a physician in private practice is limited to situations in which there is direct personal physician supervision. This applies to services of auxiliary personnel employed by the physician and working under his/her supervision, such as nurses, nonphysician anesthetists, psychologists, technicians, therapists, including physical therapists, and other aides. Thus, where a physician employs auxiliary personnel to assist him/her in rendering services to patients and includes the charges for their services in his/her own bills, the services of such personnel are considered incident to the physician's service if there is a physician's service rendered to which the services of such personnel are an incidental part and there is direct personal supervision by the physician.

This does not mean, however, that to be considered incident to each occasion of service by a nonphysician (or the furnishing of a supply) need also always be the occasion of the actual rendition of a personal professional service by the physician. Such a service or supply could be considered to be incident to when furnished during a course of treatment where the physician performs an initial service and subsequent services of a frequency which reflect his/her active participation in and management of the course of treatment. (However, the direct personal supervision requirement must still be met with respect to every nonphysician service.)

Direct personal supervision in the office setting does not mean that the physician must be present in the same room with his or her aide. However, the physician must be present in the office suite and immediately available to provide assistance and direction throughout the time the aide is performing services.

If auxiliary personnel perform services outside the office setting, e.g., in a patient's home or in an institution, their services are covered incident to a physician's service only if there is direct personal supervision by the physician. For example, if a nurse accompanied the physician on house calls and administered an injection, the nurse's services are covered. If the same nurse made the calls alone and administered the injection, the services are not covered (even when billed by the physician) since the physician is not providing direct personal supervision. Services provided by auxiliary personnel in an institution (e.g., skilled nursing facility, nursing, or convalescent home) present a special problem in determining whether direct physician supervision exists. The availability of the physician by telephone and the presence of the physician somewhere in the institution does not constitute direct personal supervision. (See §45-15 of the Coverage Issues Manual for instructions used if a physician maintains an office in an institution.) For hospital patients, there is no Medicare coverage of the services of physician-employed auxiliary personnel as services incident to physicians' services under §1861(s)(2)(A) of the Social Security Act. Such services can be covered only under the hospital outpatient or inpatient benefit and payment for such services can be made to only the hospital by a Medicare intermediary. For services in a hospital, see §2390. (See §2070 concerning physician supervision of technicians performing diagnostic X-ray procedures in a physician's office.)

C. Employment — To be considered an employee for purposes of this section, the nonphysician performing an incident to service may be a part-time, full-time, or leased employee of the supervising physician, physician group practice, or of the legal entity that employs the physician (hereafter referred to collectively as the physician or other entity) who provides direct personal supervision (as described below). A leased employee is a nonphysician working under a written employee leasing agreement which provides that:

- The nonphysician, although employed by the leasing company, provides services as the leased employee of the physician or other entity; and
- The physician or other entity exercises control over all actions taken by the leased employee with regard to the rendering of medical services to the same extent as the physician or other entity would exercise such control if the leased employee were directly employed by the physician or other entity.

In order to satisfy the employment requirement, the nonphysician (either leased or directly employed) must be considered an employee of the supervising physician or other entity under the common law test of an employer/employee relationship specified in §210(j)(2) of the Act, 20 CFR404.1007, and §RS 2101.020 of the Retirement and Survivors Insurance part of the Social Security Program Operations Manual System.

Services provided by auxiliary personnel not in the employ of the physician, physician group practice, or other legal entity, even if provided on the physician's order or included in the physician's bill are not covered as incident to a physician's service since the law requires that the services be of kinds commonly furnished in physicians' offices and commonly either rendered without charge or included in physicians' bills. As with the physicians' personal professional service, the patient's financial liability for the incidental services is to the physician, physician group practice, or other legal entity. Therefore, the incidental service must represent an expense incurred by the physician, physician group practice, or other legal entity responsible for providing the professional service.

2050.2 Services of Nonphysician Personnel Furnished Incident to Physician's Services

In addition to coverage being available for the services of such nonphysician personnel as nurses, technicians, and therapists when furnished incident to the professional services of a physician (as discussed in §2050.1), a physician may also have the services of certain nonphysician practitioners covered as services incident to a physician's professional services. These nonphysician practitioners, who are being licensed by the States under various programs to assist or act in the place of the physician, include, for example, certified nurse midwives, certified registered nurse anesthetists, clinical psychologists, clinical social workers, physician assistants, nurse practitioners, and clinical nurse specialists. (See §§2150 through 2160 for coverage instructions for various allied health/nonphysician practitioners' services.)

Services performed by these nonphysician practitioners incident to a physician's professional services include not only services ordinarily rendered by a physician's office staff person (e.g., medical services such as taking blood pressures and temperatures, giving injections, and changing dressings) but also services ordinarily performed by the physician himself or herself such as minor surgery, setting casts or simple fractures, reading x-rays, and other activities that involve evaluation or treatment of a patient's condition.

Nonetheless, in order for services of a nonphysician practitioner to be covered as incident to the services of a physician, the services must meet all of the requirements for coverage specified in §§2050 through 2050.1. For example, the services must be an integral, although incidental, part of the physician's personal professional services, and they must be performed under the physician's direct personal supervision.

A nonphysician practitioner such as a physician assistant or a nurse practitioner may be licensed under State law to perform a specific medical procedure and may be able (see §§2156 or 2158, respectively) to perform the procedure without physician supervision and have the service separately covered and paid for by Medicare as a physician assistant's or nurse practitioner's service. However, in order to have that same service covered as incident to the services of a physician, it must be performed under

the direct personal supervision of the physician of the physician as an integral part of the physician's

personal in-office service. As explained in §2050.1, this does not mean that each occasion of an incidental service performed by a nonphysician practitioner must always be the occasion of a service actually rendered by the phyysician. It does mean that there must have been a direct, personal, professional service furnished by the physician to initiate the course of treatment of which the service being performed by the nonphysician practitioner is an incidental part, and there must be subsequent services by the physician if a frequency that reflects his or her continuing active participation in and management of the course of treatment. In addition, the physician must be physically present in the same office suite and be immediately available to render assistance if that becomes necessary.

Note also that a physician might render a physician's service that can be covered even though another service furnished by a nonphysician practitioner as incident to the physician's service might not be covered. For example, an office visit during which the physician diagnoses a medical problem and established a course of treatment could be covered even if, during the same visit, a nonphysician practitioner performs a noncovered service such as an acupuncture.

2050.3 Incident to Physician's Service in Clinic

Services and supplies incident to a physician's service in a physician directed clinic or group association are generally the same as those described above.

A physician directed clinic is one where (a) a physician (or a number of physicians) is present to perform medical (rather than administrative) services at all times the clinic is open; (b) each patient is under the care of a clinic physician; and (c) the nonphysician services are under medical supervision.

In highly organized clinics, particularly those that are departmentalized, direct personal physician supervision may be the responsibility of several physicians as opposed to an individual attending physician. In this situation, medical management of all services provided in the clinic is assured. The physician ordering a particular service need not be the physician who is supervising the service. Therefore, services performed by therapists and other aided are covered even though they are performed in another department of the clinic.

Supplies provided by the clinic during the course of treatment are also covered. When the auxiliary personnel perform services outside the clinic premises, the services are covered only if performed under the direct personal supervision of a clinic physician. If the clinic refers a patient for auxiliary services performed by personnel who are not employed by the clinic, such services are not incident to a physician's service.

2070. DIAGNOSTIC X-RAY, DIAGNOSTIC LABORATORY, AND OTHER DIAGNOSTIC TESTS

Diagnostic X-ray, diagnostic laboratory, and other diagnostic tests, including materials and the services of technicians, are covered. Other diagnostic tests include basal metabolism readings, electroencephalograms, electrocardiograms, respiratory function tests, cardiac evaluations, allergy tests, psychological tests, and otologic evaluations. For diagnostic X-ray services and other diagnostic tests (except as provided below and in §§2070.2 through 2070.5), payment may be made only if the services are furnished by a physician (or as incident to a physician's services as defined in §2050.1).

Some diagnostic clinical laboratory procedures or tests require Food and Drug Administration (FDA) approval before coverage is provided.

Diagnostic X-ray services performed in a facility directed by a physician or group of physicians are covered if they are performed under the direct supervision of a physician.

Certain diagnostic X-ray procedures are also covered when performed by technicians without direct personal physician supervision if the technicians' general supervision and training, as well as the maintenance of the necessary equipment and supplies, are the continuing responsibility of a physician. Such covered procedures include skeletal films involving the extremities, pelvis, vertebral column or skull and chest, or abdominal films which do not involve the use of contrast media.

2070.4 Coverage of Portable X-ray Services Not Under the Direct Supervision of a Physician

A. Diagnostic X-ray Tests — Diagnostic x-ray services furnished by a portable x-ray supplier are covered under Part B when furnished in a place or residence used as the patient's home and in nonparticipating institutions. These services must be performed under the general supervision of a physician and certain conditions relating to health and safety (as prescribed by the Secretary) must be met.

Diagnostic portable x-ray services are also covered under Part B when provided in participating SNFs and hospitals, under circumstances in which they cannot be covered under hospital insurance, i.e., the services are not furnished by the participating institution either directly or under arrangements that provide for the institution to bill for the services. (See §2255 for reimbursement for Part B services furnished to inpatients of participating and nonparticipating institutions.)

B. Applicability of Health and Safety Standards — The health and safety standards apply to all suppliers of portable x-ray services, except physicians who provide immediate personal supervision during the administration of diagnostic x-ray services. Payment is made only for services of approved suppliers who have been found to meet the standards. Notice of the coverage dates for services of approved suppliers are given to carriers by the RO.

When the services of a supplier of portable x-ray services no longer meet the conditions of coverage, physicians having an interest in the supplier's certification status must be notified. The notification action regarding suppliers of portable x-ray equipment is the same as required for decertification of independent laboratories, and the procedures explained in §2070.1C should be followed.

C. Scope of Portable X-Ray Benefit — In order to avoid payment for services which are inadequate or hazardous to the patient, the scope of the covered portable X-ray benefit is defined as:

- skeletal films involving arms and legs, pelvis, vertebral column, and skull;
- chest films which do not involve the use of contrast media (except routine screening procedures and tests in connection with routine physical examinations); and
- abdominal films which do not involve the use of contrast media.

D. Exclusions From Coverage as Portable X-Ray Services — Procedures and examinations which are not covered under the portable X-ray provision include the following:
- procedures involving fluoroscopy;
- procedures involving the use of contrast media;
- procedures requiring the administration of a substance to the patient or injection of a substance into the patient and/or special manipulation of the patient;
- procedures which require special medical skill or knowledge possessed by a doctor of medicine or doctor of osteopathy or which require that medical judgment be exercised;
- procedures requiring special technical competency and/or special equipment or materials;
- routine screening procedures; and
- procedures which are not of a diagnostic nature.

E. Reimbursement Procedure

1. Name of Ordering Physician — Assure that portable X-ray tests have been provided on the written order of a physician. Accordingly, if a bill does not include the name of the physician who ordered the service, that information must be obtained before payment may be made.

2. Reason Chest X-Ray Ordered — Because all routine screening procedures and tests in connection with routine physical examinations are excluded from coverage under Medicare, all bills for portable X-ray services involving the chest contain, in addition to the name of the physician who ordered the service, the reason an X-ray test was required. If this information is not shown, it is obtained from either the supplier or the physician. If the test was for an excluded routine service, no payment may be made.

See also §§4110 ff. for additional instructions on reviewing bills involving portable X-ray.

F. Electrocardiograms — The taking of an electrocardiogram tracing by an approved supplier of portable X-ray services may be covered as an "other diagnostic test." The health and safety standards referred to in §2070.4B are thus also applicable to such diagnostic EKG services, e.g., the technician must meet the personnel qualification requirements in the Conditions for Coverage of Portable X-ray Services. (See §50-15 (Electrocardiographic Services) in the Coverage Issues Manual.)

2079. SURGICAL DRESSINGS, AND SPLINTS, CASTS AND OTHER DEVICES USED FOR REDUCTIONS OF FRACTURES AND DISLOCATIONS

Surgical dressings are limited to primary and secondary dressings required for the treatment of a wound caused by, or treated by, a surgical procedure that has been performed by a physician or other health care professional to the extent permissible under State law. In addition, surgical dressings required after debridement of a wound are also covered, irrespective of the type of debridement, as long as the debridement was reasonable and necessary and was performed by a health care professional who was acting within the scope of his or her legal authority when performing this function. Surgical dressings are covered for as long as they are medically necessary.

Primary dressings are therapeutic or protective coverings applied directly to wounds or lesions either on the skin or caused by an opening to the skin. Secondary dressing materials that serve a therapeutic or protective function and that are needed to secure a primary dressing are also covered. Items such as adhesive tape, roll gauze, bandages, and disposable compression material are examples of secondary dressings. Elastic stockings, support hose, foot coverings, leotards, knee supports, surgical leggings, gauntlets, and pressure garments for the arms and hands are examples of items that are not ordinarily covered as surgical dressings. Some items, such as transparent film, may be used as a primary or secondary dressing.

If a physician, certified nurse midwife, physician assistant, nurse practitioner, or clinical nurse specialist applies surgical dressings as part of a professional service that is billed to Medicare, the surgical dressings are considered incident to the professional services of the health care practitioner. (See §§2050.1, 2154, 2156, 2158, and 2160.) When surgical dressings are not covered incident to the services of a health care practitioner and are obtained by the patient from a supplier (e.g., a drugstore, physician, or other health care practitioner that qualifies as a supplier) on an order from a physician or other health care professional authorized under State law or regulation to make such an order, the surgical dressings are covered separately under Part B.

2100. DURABLE MEDICAL EQUIPMENT — GENERAL

Expenses incurred by a beneficiary for the rental or purchase of durable medical equipment (DME) are reimbursable if the following three requirements are met. The decision whether to rent or purchase an item of equipment resides with the beneficiary.

A. The equipment meets the definition of DME (§2100.1); and

B. The equipment is necessary and reasonable for the treatment of the patient's illness or injury or to improve the functioning of his malformed body member (§2100.2); and

C. The equipment is used in the patient's home (§2100.3).

Payment may also be made under this provision for repairs, maintenance, and delivery of equipment as well as for expendable and nonreusable items essential to the effective use of the equipment subject to the conditions in §2100.4.

See §2105 and its appendix for coverage guidelines and screening list of DME. See §4105.3 for models of payment: decisions as to rental or purchase, lump sum and periodic payments, etc. Where covered DME is furnished to a beneficiary by a supplier of services other than a provider of services, reimbursement is made by the carrier on the basis of the reasonable charge. If the equipment is furnished by a provider of services, reimbursement is made to the provider by the intermediary on a reasonable cost basis; see Coverage Issues Appendix 25-1 for hemodialysis equipment and supplies.

2100.1   Definition of Durable Medical Equipment

Durable medical equipment is equipment which (a) can withstand repeated use, and (b) is primarily and customarily used to serve a medical purpose, and (c) generally is not useful to a person in the absence of an illness or injury; and (d) is appropriate for use in the home.

All requirements of the definition must be met before an item can be considered to be durable medical equipment.

A. Durability — An item is considered durable if it can withstand repeated use, i.e., the type of item which could normally be rented. Medical supplies of an expendable nature such as, incontinent pads, lambs wool pads, catheters, ace bandages, elastic stockings, surgical face masks, irrigating kits, sheets and bags are not considered "durable" within the meaning of the definition. There are other items which, although durable in nature, may fall into other coverage categories such as braces, prosthetic devices, artificial arms, legs, and eyes.

B. Medical Equipment — Medical equipment is equipment which is primarily and customarily used for medical purposes and is not generally useful in the absence of illness or injury. In most instances, no development will be needed to determine whether a specific item of equipment is medical in nature. However, some cases will require development to determine whether the item constitutes medical equipment. This development would include the advice of local medical organizations (hospitals, medical schools, medical societies) and specialists in the field of physical medicine and rehabilitation. If the equipment is new on the market, it may be necessary, prior to seeking professional advice, to obtain information from the supplier or manufacturer explaining the design, purpose, effectiveness and method of using the equipment in the home as well as the results of any tests or clinical studies that have been conducted.

  1. Equipment Presumptively Medical — Items such as hospital beds, wheelchairs, hemodialysis equipment, iron lungs, respirators, intermittent positive pressure breathing machines, medical regulators, oxygen tents, crutches, canes, trapeze bars, walkers, inhalators, nebulizers, commodes, suction machines and traction equipment presumptively constitute medical equipment. (Although hemodialysis equipment is a prosthetic device (§ 2130), it also meets the definition of DME, and reimbursement for the rental or purchase of such equipment for use in the beneficiary's home will be made only under the provisions for payment applicable to DME. See 25-1 and 25-2 of the Coverage Issues Appendix for coverage of home use of hemodialysis.)

      NOTE: There is a wide variety in type of respirators and suction machines. The carrier's medical staff should determine whether the apparatus specified in the claim is appropriate for home use.

  2. Equipment Presumptively Nonmedical — Equipment which is primarily and customarily used for a nonmedical purpose may not be considered "medical" equipment for which payment can be made under the medical insurance program. This is true even though the item has some remote medically related use. For example, in the case of a cardiac patient, an air conditioner might possibly be used to lower room temperature to reduce fluid loss in the patient and to restore an environment conducive to maintenance of the proper fluid balance. Nevertheless, because the primary and customary use of an air conditioner is a nonmedical one, the air conditioner cannot be deemed to be medical equipment for which payment can be made.

      Other devices and equipment used for environmental control or to enhance the environmental setting in which the beneficiary is placed are not considered covered DME. These include, for example, room heaters, humidifiers, dehumidifiers, and electric air cleaners. Equipment which basically serves comfort or convenience functions or is primarily for the convenience of a person caring for the patient, such as elevators, stairway elevators, and posture chairs do not constitute medical equipment. Similarly, physical fitness equipment, e.g., an exercycle; first-aid or precautionary-type equipment, e.g., present portable oxygen units; self-help devices, e.g., safety grab bars; and training equipment, e.g., speech teaching machines and braille training texts, are considered nonmedical in nature.

  3. Special Exception Items — Specified items of equipment may be covered under certain conditions even though they do not meet the definition of DME because they are not primarily and customarily used to serve a medical purpose and/or are generally useful in the absence of illness or injury. These items would be covered when it is clearly established that they serve a therapeutic purpose in an individual case and would include:

      a. Gel pads and pressure and water mattresses (which generally serve a preventive purpose) when prescribed for a patient who had bed sores or there is medical evidence indicating that he is highly susceptible to such ulceration; and

b. Heat lamps for a medical rather than a soothing or cosmetic purpose, e.g., where the need for heat therapy has been established.

In establishing medical necessity (§2100.2) for the above items, the evidence must show that the item is included in the physician's course of treatment and a physician is supervising its use. (See also Appendix to § 2105.)

NOTE: The above items represent special exceptions and no extension of coverage to other items should be inferred.

2120. AMBULANCE SERVICE.

Reimbursement may be for expenses incurred for ambulance service provided the conditions specified in the following subsections are met. (See §§4115 and 2125 concerning instructions for processing ambulance service claims.)

2120.1 Vehicle and Crew Requirement

A. The Vehicle — The vehicle must be a specially designed and equipped automobile or other vehicle (in some areas of the United States this might be a boat or plane) for transporting the sick or injured. It must have customary patient care equipment including a stretcher, clean linens, first aid supplies, oxygen equipment, and it must also have such other safety and lifesaving equipment as is required by State or local authorities.

B. The Crew — The ambulance crew must consist of at least two members. Those crew members charged with the care or handling of the patient must include one individual with adequate first aid training, i.e., training at least equivalent to that provided by the standard and advanced Red Cross first aid courses. Training "equivalent" to the standard and advanced Red Cross first aid training courses included ambulance service training and experience acquired in military service, successful completion by the individual of a comparable first aid course furnished by or under the sponsorship of State or local authorities, an educational institution, a fire department, a hospital, a professional organization, or other such qualified organization. On-the-job training involving the administration of first aid under the supervision of or in conjunction with trained first aid personnel for a period of time sufficient to assure the trainee's proficiency in handling the wide range of patient care services that may have to be performed by a qualified attendant can also be considered as "equivalent training."

C. Verification of Compliance — In determining whether the vehicles and personnel of each supplier meet all of the above requirements, carriers may accept the supplier's statement (absent information to the contrary) that its vehicles and personnel meet all of the requirements if (l) the statement describes the first aid, safety, and other patient care items with which the vehicles are equipped, (2) the statement shows the extent of first aid training acquired by the personnel assigned to those vehicles, (3) the statement contains the supplier's agreement to notify the carrier of any change in operation which could affect the coverage of his ambulance services, and (4) the information provided indicates that the requirements are met. The statement must be accompanied by documentary evidence that the ambulance has the equipment required by State and local authorities. Documentary evidence could include a letter from such authorities, a copy of a license, permit certificate, etc., issued by the authorities. The statement and supporting documentation would be kept on file by the carrier.

When a supplier does not submit such a statement or whenever there is a question about a supplier's compliance with any of the above requirements for vehicle and crew (including suppliers who have completed the statement), carriers should take appropriate action including, where necessary, on-site inspection of the vehicles and verification of the qualifications of personnel to determine whether the ambulance service qualifies for reimbursement under Medicare. Since the requirements described above for coverage of ambulance services are applicable to the overall operation of the ambulance supplier's service, it is not required that information regarding personnel and vehicles be obtained on an individual trip basis.

D. Ambulance of Providers of Services — The Part A intermediary is responsible for the processing of claims for ambulance service furnished by participating hospitals, skilled nursing facilities and home health agencies and has the responsibility to determine the compliance of provider's ambulance and crew. Since provider ambulance services furnished "under arrangements" with suppliers can be covered only if the supplier meets the above requirements, the Part A intermediary may ask the carrier to identify those suppliers who meet the requirements.

E. Equipment and Supplies — As mentioned above, the ambulance must have customary patient care equipment and first aid supplies. Reusable devices and equipment such as backboards, neckboards and inflatable leg and arm splints are considered part of the general ambulance service and would be included in the charge for the trip. On the other hand, separate reasonable charge based on actual quantities used may be recognized for nonreusable items and disposable supplies such as oxygen, gauze and dressings required in the care of the patient during his trip.

2120.2 Necessity and Reasonableness — To be covered, ambulance service must be medically necessary and reasonable.

A. Necessity for the Service — Medical necessity is established when the patient's condition is such that use of any other method of transportation is contraindicated. In any case, in which some means of transportation other than an ambulance could be utilized without endangering the individual's health, whether or not such other transportation is actually available, no payment may be made for ambulance service.

B. Reasonableness of the Ambulance Trip — A claim may be denied on the ground that the use of ambulance service was unreasonable in the treatment of the illness or injury involved (§2303) notwithstanding the fact that the patient's condition may have contraindicated the use of other means of transportation. The carrier should use discretion when applying this principle. It is expected that generally its application will be limited to those instances where a supplier or provider repeatedly demonstrates a pattern of uneconomical practice and to those individual claims where the excess cost is large.

2120.3   The Destination

As a general rule, only local transportation by ambulance is covered. This means that the patient must have been transported to a hospital or a skilled nursing home as defined in § 2125 item 3(a) whose locality (see paragraph E below) encompasses the place where the ambulance transportation of the patient began and which would ordinarily be expected to have the appropriate facilities for the treatment of the injury or illness involved. In exceptional situations where the ambulance transportation originates beyond the locality of the institution to which the beneficiary was transported, full payment may be made for such services only if the evidence clearly establishes that such institution is the nearest one with appropriate facilities (see F below). The institution to which a patient is transported need not be a participating institution but must meet at least the requirements of 1861(e)(1) or 1861(j)(1) of the Act. (See §2100.3 A and B for an explanation of these requirements.) A claim for ambulance service to a participating hospital or skilled nursing facility should not be denied on the grounds that there is a nearer nonparticipating institution having appropriate facilities. (See C below for destination exceptions.)

A. Institution to Beneficiary's Home — Ambulance service from an institution to the beneficiary's home is covered when the home is within the locality of such institution or where the beneficiary's home is outside of the locality of such institution and the institution, in relation to the home, is the nearest one with appropriate facilities.

B. Institution to Institution — Occasionally, the institution to which the patient is initially taken is found to have inadequate facilities to provide the required care and the patient is then transported to a second institution having appropriate facilities. In such cases, transportation by ambulance to both institutions would be covered provided the institution to which the patient is being transferred is determined to be the nearest one with appropriate facilities. In these cases, transportation from such second institution to the patient's home could be covered if the home is within the locality served by that institution, or by the first institution to which the patient was taken.

C. Round-Trip for Specialized Services — Round-trip ambulance service is covered for a hospital or participating skilled nursing facility inpatient to the nearest hospital or nonhospital treatment facility, i.e., a clinic, therapy center of physician's office to obtain necessary diagnostic and/or therapeutic services (such as a CT scan or cobalt therapy) not available at the institution where the beneficiary is an inpatient. (See §4168.)

The round-trip ambulance service benefit is subject to all existing coverage requirements and is limited to those cases where the transportation of the patient is less costly than bringing the service to the patient.

Carriers will monitor this by performing a periodic postpayment review with appropriate medical staff assistance to determine whether the frequency of such ambulance services for a particular patient, together with the medical condition, indicates there is another preferred medical course of treatment. The carrier should not request transfer of hospital inpatients to another hospital capable of providing the required service but should deny such ambulance service claims in the future. For patients in SNFs and those residing at home, the attending physician should be asked to furnish additional information supporting the need for ambulance service relative to the option of admission to a treatment facility.

D. Partial Payment — Where ambulance service exceeds the limits defined in A, B and C above, refer to §2125 item #5 for instructions on partial payment.

E. Locality — The term "locality" with respect to ambulance service means the service area surrounding the institution from which individuals normally come or are expected to come for hospital or skilled nursing services.

Example: Mr. A becomes ill at home and requires ambulance service to the hospital. The small community in which he lives has a 35 bed hospital. Two large metropolitan hospitals are located some distance from Mr. A's community but they regularly provide hospital services to the community's residents. The community is within the "locality" of the metropolitan hospital and direct ambulance service to either of these (as well as to the local community hospital) is covered.

F. Appropriate Facilities — The term "appropriate facilities" means that the institution is generally equipped to provide the needed hospital or skilled nursing care for the illness or injury involved. In the case of a hospital, it also means that a physician or a physician specialist is available to provide the necessary care required to treat the patient's condition. However, the fact that a particular physician does or does not have staff privileges in a hospital is not a consideration in determining whether the hospital has appropriate facilities. Thus, ambulance service to a more distant hospital solely to avail a patient of the service of a specific physician or physician specialist does not make the hospital in which the physician has staff privileges the nearest hospital with appropriate facilities.

The fact that a more distant institution is better equipped, either qualitatively or quantitatively, to care for the patient does not warrant a finding that a closer institution does not have "appropriate facilities." However, a legal impediment barring a patient's admission would permit a finding that the institution did not have "appropriate facilities." For example, the nearest tuberculosis hospital may be in another State and that State's law precludes admission of nonresidents.

An institution is also not considered an appropriate facility if there is no bed available.

The carrier, however, will presume that there are beds available at the local institutionsunless the claimant furnished evidence that none of these institutions had a bed availableat the time the ambulance service was provided.

EXAMPLE: A becomes ill at home and requires ambulance service to the hospital. The hospitals servicing the community in which he lives are capable of providing general hospital care. However, Mr. A requires immediate kidney dialysis and the needed equipment is not available in any of these hospitals. The service area of the nearest hospital having dialysis equipment does not encompass the patient's home. Nevertheless, in this case, ambulance service beyond the locality to the hospital with the equipment is covered since it is the nearest one with appropriate facilities.

G. Ambulance Service to Physician's Office — These trips are covered only under the following circumstances:
- The trips meet the criteria of §2120.3C, or
- While transporting a patient to a hospital, the ambulance stops at a physician's office because of a patient's dire need for professional attention, and immediately thereafter, the ambulance continues to the hospital.

H. Transportation Requested by Home Health Agency — Where a home health agency finds it necessary to have a beneficiary transported by ambulance to a hospital or skilled nursing facility to obtain home health services not otherwise available to the individual, the trip is covered as a Part B service only if the above coverage requirements are met. Such transportation is not covered as a home health service.

I. Coverage of Ambulance Service Furnished Deceased Beneficiary — An individual is considered to have expired as of the time he is pronounced dead by a person who is legally authorized to make such a pronouncement, usually a physician. Therefore, if the beneficiary was pronounced dead by a legally authorized individual before the ambulance was called, no program payment is made.

Where the beneficiary was pronounced dead after the ambulance was called but before pickup, the service to the point of pickup is covered. If otherwise covered ambulance services were furnished to a beneficiary who was pronounced dead while enroute to or upon arrival at the destination, the entire ambulance services are covered.

J. Ambulance Transportation to Renal Dialysis Facility Located on Premises of Hospital — A renal dialysis facility may be approved to participate in the end-stage renal disease program as a part of a hospital or as a nonprovider. Where the facility has been approved as a part of a hospital, it meets the destination requirements of an institution. Even where the facility has been approved as a nonprovider, it may be determined to meet the destination requirements for purposes of ambulance service coverage under the following circumstances:
- The facility is located on or adjacent to the premises of a hospital;
- The facility furnishes services to patients of the hospital, e.g., on an outpatient or emergency basis, even though the facility is primarily in operation to furnish dialysis services to its own patients; and
- There is an ongoing professional relationship between the two facilities. For example, the hospital and the facility have an agreement that provides for physician staff of the facility to abide by the bylaws and regulations of the hospital's medical staff.

Do not reopen or change a prior determination that the facility is a nonprovider for approval purposes, even though it is found to be sufficiently related to the hospital, to meet the destination requirement for ambulance service coverage, unless there has been a significant change in the relationship between the hospital and the facility since the facility's certification.

A beneficiary receiving maintenance dialysis on an outpatient basis is not ordinarily ill enough to require ambulance transportation for dialysis treatment. This is so whether the facility is an independent enterprise or part of a hospital. Thus, if a claim for ambulance services furnished to a maintenance dialysis patient does not show that the patient's condition requires ambulance services, disallow it. However, if the documentation submitted with the claim shows that ambulance services is required, determine whether the facility meets the destination requirements under the ambulance service benefit described.

2120.4 Air Ambulance Services

Medically appropriate air ambulance transportation is a covered service regardless of the State or region in which it is rendered. However, approve claims only if the beneficiary's medical condition is such that transportation by either basic or advanced life support land ambulance is not appropriate.

A. Coverage Requirements — Air ambulance transportation services, either by means of a helicopter or fixed wing aircraft, may be determined to be covered only if

- The vehicle and crew requirements described in §2120.1 are met;
- The beneficiary's medical condition required immediate and rapid ambulance transportation that could not have been provided by land ambulance; and either
  - The point of pick-up is inaccessible by land vehicle (this condition could be met in Hawaii, Alaska, and in other remote or sparsely populated areas of the continental United States), or
  - Great distances or other obstacles (for example, heavy traffic) are involved in getting the patient to the nearest hospital with appropriate facilities as described in subsection D.

B. Medical Appropriateness — Medical appropriateness is only established when the beneficiary's condition is such that the time needed to transport a beneficiary by land, or the instability of transportation by land, poses a threat to the beneficiary's survival or seriously endangers the beneficiary's health. Following is an advisory list of examples of cases for which air ambulance could be justified. The list is not inclusive of all situations that justify air transportation, nor is it intended to justify air transportation in all locales in the circumstances listed.

- Intracranial bleeding — requiring neurosurgical intervention;
- Cardiogenic shock;
- Burns requiring treatment in a Burn Center;
- Conditions requiring treatment in a Hyperbaric Oxygen Unit;
- Multiple severe injuries; or
- Life-threatening trauma.

C. Time Needed for Land Transport — Differing Statewide Emergency Medical Services (EMS) systems determine the amount and level of basic and advanced life support land transportation available. However, there are very limited emergency cases where land transportation is available but the time required to transport the patient by land as opposed to air endangers the beneficiary's life or health. As a general guideline, when it would take a land ambulance 30-60 minutes or more to transport an emergency patient, consider air transportation appropriate.

D. Appropriate Facility — It is required that the beneficiary be transported to the nearest hospital with appropriate facilities for treatment. The term "appropriate facilities" refers to units or components of a hospital that are capable of providing the required level and type of care for the patient's illness and that have available the type of physician or physician specialist needed to treat the beneficiary's condition. In determining whether a particular hospital has appropriate facilities, take into account whether there are beds or a specialized treatment unit immediately available and whether the necessary physicians and other relevant medical personnel are available in the hospital at the time the patient is being transported. The fact that a more distant hospital is better equipped does not in and of itself warrant a finding that a closer hospital does not have appropriate facilities. Such a finding is warranted, however, if the beneficiary's condition requires a higher level of trauma care or other specialized service available only at the more distant hospital.

E. Hospital to Hospital Transport — Air ambulance transport is covered for transfer of a patient from one hospital to another if the medical appropriateness criteria are met, that is, transportation by ground ambulance would endanger the beneficiary's health and the transferring hospital does not have adequate facilities to provide the medical services needed by the patient. Examples of such services include burn units, cardiac care units, and trauma units. A patient transported from one hospital to another hospital is covered only if the hospital to which the patient is transferred is the nearest one with appropriate facilities. Coverage is not available for transport from a hospital capable of treating the patient because the patient and/or his or her family prefers a specific hospital or physician.

F. Special Coverage Rule — Air ambulance services are not covered for transport to a facility that is not an acute care hospital, such as a nursing facility, physician's office or a beneficiary's home.

G. Special Payment Limitations — If a determination is made that transport by ambulance was necessary, but land ambulance service would have sufficed, payment for the air ambulance service is based on the amount payable for land transport, if less costly.

If the air transport was medically appropriate (that is, land transportation was contraindicated and the beneficiary required air transport to a hospital), but the beneficiary could have been treated at a nearer hospital than the one to which he or she was transported, the air transport payment is limited to the rate for the distance from the point of pickup to that nearer hospital.

H. Documentation — Obtain adequate documentation of the determination of medical appropriateness for the air ambulance service. All claims for air ambulance services are to be reviewed by your medical staff.

2125. COVERAGE GUIDELINES FOR AMBULANCE SERVICE CLAIMS.

Reimbursement may be made for expenses incurred by a patient for ambulance service provided conditions 1, 2, and 3 in the left-hand column have been met. The right-hand column indicates the documentation needed to establish that the condition has been met.

Conditions

1. Patient was transported by an approved supplier of ambulance services.
2. The patient was suffering from an illness or injury which contraindicated transportation by other means. (§2120.2A)

3. The patient was transported from and to points listed below. (§ 2120.3)
   (a) From patient's residence (or other place where need arose) to hospital or skilled nursing home.

Review Action

1. Ambulance supplier is listed in the carriers table of approved ambulance companies. (§2120.1C)
2. (a) Presume the requirement was met if file shows the patient:
   (i) was transported in an emergency situation, e.g., as a result of an accident, injury, or acute illness, or
   (ii) Need to restrained, or
   (iii) Was unconscious or in shock, or
   (iv) Required oxygen or other emergency treatment on the way to his destination, or
   (v) Had to remain immobile because of a fracture that had not been set or the possibility of a fracture, or
   (vi) Sustained an acute stroke or myocardial infarction,
   (vii) Was experiencing severe hemorrhage, or
   (viii) Was bed confined before and after the ambulance trip, or
   (ix) Could be moved only by stretcher.
   (b) In the absence of any of the conditions listed in (a) above additional documnetation should be obtained to establish medical need where the evidene indicates the existence of the circumstanes listed below:
   (i) Patient's condition would not ordinarily require movement by stretcher, or
   (ii) The individual was not admitted as a hospital inpatient (except in accident cases), or
   (iii) The ambulance was used solely because other means of transportation were unavailable, or
   (iv) The individual merely needed assistance in getting from his room or home to a vehicle.
   (c) Where the information indicates a situation not listed in 2(a) or 2 (b) above, refer the case to your supervisor.
3. Claims should show points of pickup and destination
   (a)
   (i) Condition met if trip began within the institution's service area as shown in the carrier's locality guide.
   (ii) Condition med where the trip began outside the institution's service area if the institution was the nearest one with appropriate facilities. Refer to supervisor for determination.

NOTE: A patient's residence is the place where he makes his home and dwells permanently, or for an extended period of time. A skilled nursing home is one which is listed in the Directory of Medical Facilities as a participating SNF or as an institution which meets section 1861(j)(1) of the law.

    (b) Skilled nursing home to a hospital or hospital to a skilled nursing home.

    (c) Hospital to hospital or skilled nursing home to skilled nursing home

    (d) Form a hospital or skilled nursing home to patient's residence

    (e) Round trip for hospital or participating skilled nursing facility inpatients to the nearest hospital or nonhospital treatment facility.

4. Ambulance services involving hospital admissions in Canada or Mexico are covered (§§ 2312 ff.) if the following conditions are met:
    (a) The foreign hospitalization has been determined to be covered; and
    (b) The ambulance service meets the coverage requirements set forth in §§ 2120-2120.3. If the foreign hospitalization has been determined to be covered on the basis of emergency services (§ 2312.2A) the necessity requirement (§ 2120.2) and the destination requirement (§ 2120.3) are considered met.

5. Make partial payment for otherwise covered ambulance service which exceeded limits defined in item 3. (Claims supervisors are to make all partial payment determinations.) Base the payment on the amount payable had the patient been transported: (1) from the pickup point to the nearest appropriate facility, or (2) from the nearest appropriate facility to his/her residence where he/she is being returned home from a distant institution. (See §5215.2.)

NOTE: A claim for ambulance service to a participating hospital or skilled nursing facility should not be denied on the grounds that there is a nearer nonparticipating institution having appropriate facilities.

    (b)

        (i) Condition met if pickup point is within the service area of the destination as shown in the carrier's locality guide.

        (ii) Condition med where the pickup point is outside the service area of the destination if the destination institution was the nearest one with appropriate facilities. Refer to supervisor for determination.

    (c) Condition met if the discharging institution was not an appropriate facility and the admitting institution was the nearest one with appropriate facilities.

    (d)

        (i) Condition met if patient's residence is within the institution's service area as shown in the carriers's locality guide.

        (ii) Condition met where the patient's residence is outside the institution's service area if the institution was the nearest one with appropriate facilities. Refer to supervisor for determination.

    (e) Condition met if the medically necessary diagnostic or therapeutic service required by the patient's condition is not available at the institution where the beneficiary is an inpatient.

NOTE: Ambulance service to a physician's office or a physician-directed clinic is not covered. (See §2120.3G where a stop is made at a physician's office enroute to a hospital and 2120.3C for additional exceptions.)

2130. PROSTHETIC DEVICES

A. General — Prosthetic devices (other than dental) which replace all or part of an internal body organ (including contiguous tissue), or replace all or part of the function of a permanently inoperative or malfunctioning internal body organ are covered when furnished on a physician's order. This does not require a determination that there is no possibility that the patient's condition may improve sometime in the future. If the medical record, including the judgment of the attending physician, indicates the condition is of long and indefinite duration, the test of permanence is considered met. (Such a device may also be covered under §2050.1 as a supply when furnished incident to a physician's service.)

Examples of prosthetic devices include cardiac pacemakers, prosthetic lenses (see subsection B), breast prostheses (including a surgical brassiere) for postmastectomy patients, maxillofacial devices and devices which replace all or part of the ear or nose. A urinary collection and retention system with or without a tube is a prosthetic device replacing bladder function in case of permanent urinary incontinence. The Foley catheter is also considered a prosthetic device when ordered for a patient with permanent urinary incontinence. However, chucks, diapers, rubber sheets, etc., are supplies that are not covered under this provision. (Although hemodialysis equipment is a prosthetic device, payment for the rental or purchase of such equipment for use in the home is made only under the provisions for payment applicable to durable medical equipment (see §4105ff) or the special rules that apply to the ESRD program.)

NOTE: Medicare does not cover a prosthetic device dispensed to a patient prior to the time at which the patient undergoes the procedure that makes necessary the use of the device. For example, do not make a separate Part B payment for an intraocular lens (IOL) or pacemaker that a physician, during an office visit prior to the actual surgery, dispenses to the patient for his/her use. Dispensing a prosthetic device in this manner raises health and safety issues. Moreover, the need for the device cannot be clearly established until the procedure that makes its use possible is successfully performed. Therefore, dispensing a prosthetic device in this manner is not considered reasonable and necessary for the treatment of the patient's condition.

Colostomy (and other ostomy) bags and necessary accouterments required for attachment are covered as prosthetic devices. This coverage also includes irrigation and flushing equipment and other items and supplies directly related to ostomy care, whether the attachment of a bag is required.

Accessories and/or supplies which are used directly with an enteral or parenteral device to achieve the therapeutic benefit of the prosthesis or to assure the proper functioning of the device are covered under the prosthetic device benefit subject to the additional guidelines in the Coverage Issues Manual §§ 65-10 - 65-10.3.

Covered items include catheters, filters, extension tubing, infusion bottles, pumps (either food or infusion), intravenous (I.V.) pole, needles, syringes, dressings, tape, Heparin Sodium (parenteral only), volumetric monitors (parenteral only), and parenteral and enteral nutrient solutions. Baby food and other regular grocery products that can be blenderized and used with the enteral system are not covered. Note that some of these items, e.g., a food pump and an I.V. pole, qualify as DME. Although coverage of the enteral and parenteral nutritional therapy systems is provided on the basis of the prosthetic device benefit, the payment rules relating to rental or purchase of DME apply to such items. (See §4105.3.) Code claims in accordance with the HCFA Common Procedure Coding System (HCPCS).

The coverage of prosthetic devices includes replacement of and repairs to such devices as explained in subsection D.

B. Prosthetic Lenses — The term "internal body organ" includes the lens of an eye. Prostheses replacing the lens of an eye include post-surgical lenses customarily used during convalescence from eye surgery in which the lens of the eye was removed. In addition, permanent lenses are also covered when required by an individual lacking the organic lens of the eye because of surgical removal or congenital absence. Prosthetic lenses obtained on or after the beneficiary's date of entitlement to supplementary medical insurance benefits may be covered even though the surgical removal of the crystalline lens occurred before entitlement.

1. Prosthetic Cataract Lenses — Make payment for one of the following prosthetic lenses or combinations of prosthetic lenses when determined to be medically necessary by a physician (see §2020.25 for coverage of prosthetic lenses prescribed by a doctor of optometry) to restore essentially the vision provided by the crystalline lens of the eye:

    - prosthetic bifocal lenses in frames;
    - prosthetic lenses in frames for far vision, and prosthetic lenses in frames for near vision; or
    - when a prosthetic contact lens(es) for far vision is prescribed (including cases of binocular and monocular aphakia), make payment for the contact lens(es) and prosthetic lenses in frames for near vision to be worn at the same time as the contact lens(es), and prosthetic lenses in frames to be worn when the contacts have been removed.

    Make payment for lenses which have ultraviolet absorbing or reflecting properties, in lieu of payment for regular (untinted) lenses, if it has been determined that such lenses are medically reasonable and necessary for the individual patient.

Do not make payment for cataract sunglasses obtained in addition to the regular (untinted) prosthetic lenses since the sunglasses duplicate the restoration of vision function performed by the regular prosthetic lenses.

2. Payment for IOLs Furnished in Ambulatory Surgical Centers (ASCs).

Effective for services furnished on or after March 12, 1990, payment for IOLs inserted during or subsequent to cataract surgery in a Medicare certified ASC is included with the payment for facility services that are furnished in connection with the covered surgery. Section 5243.3 explains payment procedures for ASC facility services and the IOL allowance.

3. Limitation on Coverage of Conventional Lenses — Make payment for no more than one pair of conventional eyeglasses or conventional contact lenses furnished after each cataract surgery with insertion of an IOL.

C. Dentures — Dentures are excluded from coverage. However, when a denture or a portion thereof is an integral part (built-in) of a covered prosthesis (e.g., an obturator to fill an opening in the palate), it is covered as part of that prosthesis.

D. Supplies, Repairs, Adjustments, and Replacement — Make payment for supplies that are necessary for the effective use of a prosthetic device (e.g., the batteries needed to operate an artificial larynx). Adjustment of prosthetic devices required by wear or by a change in the patient's condition is covered when ordered by a physician. To the extent applicable, follow the provisions relating to the repair and replacement of durable medical equipment in §2100.4 for the repair and replacement of prosthetic devices. (See §2306.D in regard to payment for devices replaced under a warranty.) Regardless of the date that the original eyewear was furnished (i.e., whether before, on, or after January 1, 1991), do not pay for replacement of conventional eyeglasses or contact lenses covered under subsection B.3.

Necessary supplies, adjustments, repairs, and replacements are covered even when the device had been in use before the user enrolled in Part B of the program, so long as the device continues to be medically required.

2133. LEG, ARM, BACK AND NECK BRACES, TRUSSES AND ARTIFICIAL LEGS, ARMS AND EYES

These appliances are covered when furnished incident to physicians' services or on a physician's order. A brace includes rigid and semi-rigid devices which are used for the purpose of supporting a weak or deformed body member or restricting or eliminating motion in a diseased or injured part of the body. Elastic stockings, garter belts, and similar devices do not come within the scope of the definition of a brace. Back braces include, but are not limited to, special corsets, e.g., sacroiliac, sacrolumbar, dorsolumbar corsets and belts. A terminal device (e.g., hand or hook) is covered under this provision whether an artificial limb is required by the patient. (See §2323.) Stump stockings and harnesses (including replacements) are also covered when these appliances are essential to the effective use of the artificial limb.

Adjustments to an artificial limb or other appliance required by wear or by a change in the patient's condition are covered when ordered by a physician. To the extent applicable, follow the provisions in §2100.4 relating to the repair and replacement of durable medical equipment for the repair and replacement of artificial limbs, braces, etc. Adjustments, repairs and replacements are covered even when the item had been in use before the user enrolled in Part B of the program so long as the device continues to be medically required.

2134. PRESCRIPTION OF DIABETIC SHOES

Payment for the certification of diabetic shoes and for the prescription of the shoes is considered to be included in the payment for the visit or consultation during which these services are provided. If the sole purpose of an encounter with the beneficiary is to dispense or fit the shoes, then no payment may be made for a visit or consultation provided on the same day by the same physician. Thus, a separate payment is not made for certification of the need for diabetic shoes, the prescribing of diabetic shoes, or the fitting of diabetic shoes unless the physician documents that these services were not the sole purpose of the visit or consultation.

2136. DENTAL SERVICES

As indicated under the general exclusions from coverage, items, and services in connection with the care, treatment, filling, removal, or replacement of teeth or structures directly supporting the teeth are not covered. Structures directly supporting the teeth means the periodontium, which includes the gingivae, dentogingival junction, periodontal membrane, cementum of the teeth, and alveolar process.

In addition to the following, see §2020.3 and Coverage Issues Manual, §50-26 for specific services which may be covered when furnished by a dentist. If an otherwise noncovered procedure or service is performed by a dentist as incident to and as an integral part of a covered procedure or service performed by him/her, the total service performed by the dentist on such an occasion is covered.

EXAMPLE 1: The reconstruction of a ridge performed primarily to prepare the mouth for dentures is a noncovered procedure. However, when the reconstruction of a ridge is performed as a result of and at the same time as the surgical removal of a tumor (for other than dental purposes), the totality of surgical procedures is a covered service.

EXAMPLE 2: Make payment for the wiring of teeth when this is done in connection with the reduction of a jaw fracture.

The extraction of teeth to prepare the jaw for radiation treatment of neoplastic disease is also covered. This is an exception to the requirement that to be covered, a noncovered procedure or service performed by a dentist must be an incident to and an integral part of a covered procedure or service performed by him/her. Ordinarily, the dentist extracts the patient's teeth, but another physician, e.g., a radiologist, administers the radiation treatments.

When an excluded service is the primary procedure involved, it is not covered, regardless of its complexity or difficulty. For example, the extraction of an impacted tooth is not covered. Similarly, an alveoplasty (the surgical improvement of the shape and condition of the alveolar process) and a frenectomy are excluded from coverage when either of these procedures is performed in connection with an excluded service, e.g., the preparation of the mouth for dentures. In a like manner, the removal of a torus palatinus (a bony protuberance of the hard palate) may be a covered service. However, with rare exception, this surgery is performed in connection with an excluded service, i.e., the preparation of the mouth for dentures. Under such circumstances, do not pay for this procedure.

Whether such services as the administration of anesthesia, diagnostic X-rays, and other related procedures are covered depends upon whether the primary procedure being performed by the dentist is itself covered. Thus, an X-ray taken in connection with the reduction of a fracture of the jaw or facial bone is covered. However, a single X-ray or X-ray survey taken in connection with the care or treatment of teeth or the periodontium is not covered.

Make payment for a covered dental procedure no matter where the service is performed. The hospitalization or nonhospitalization of a patient has no direct bearing on the coverage or exclusion of a given dental procedure.

Payment may also be made for services and supplies furnished incident to covered dental services. For example, the services of a dental technician or nurse who is under the direct supervision of the dentist or physician are covered if the services are included in the dentist's or physician's bill.

2210. PAYABLE PHYSICAL THERAPY (PT)

A. General — To be covered PT services, the services must relate directly and specifically to an active written treatment regimen established by the physician after any needed consultation with the qualified physical therapist and must be reasonable and necessary to the treatment of the individual's illness or injury. Effective July 18, 1984, a plan of treatment for OPT services may be established by either the physician or the qualified physical therapist providing such services. Services related to activities for the general good and welfare of patients, e.g., general exercises to promote overall fitness and flexibility and activities to provide diversion or general motivation, do not constitute PT services for Medicare purposes.

Services furnished beneficiaries must constitute PT where entitlement to benefits is at issue. Since the OPT benefit under Part B provides coverage only of PT services, payment can be made only for those services which constitute PT.

B. Reasonable and Necessary — To be considered reasonable and necessary the following conditions must be met:

- The services must be considered under accepted standards of medical practice to be a specific and effective treatment for the patient's condition.
- The services must be of such a level of complexity and sophistication or the condition of the patient must be such that the services required can be safely and effectively performed only by a qualified physical therapist or under his supervision. Services which do not require the performance or supervision of a physical therapist are not considered reasonable or necessary PT services, even if they are performed or supervised by a physical therapist. (When you determine the services furnished were of a type that could have been safely and effectively performed only by a qualified physical therapist or under his supervision, presume that such services were properly supervised. However, this assumption is rebuttable, and, if in the course of processing claims you find that PT services are not being furnished under proper supervision, deny the claim and bring this matter to the attention of the Division of Survey and Certification of the RO.)
- The development, implementation, management, and evaluation of a patient care plan constitute skilled physical therapy services when, because of the beneficiary's condition, those activities require the skills of a physical therapist to meet the beneficiary's needs, promote recovery, and ensure medical safety. Where the skills of a physical therapist are needed to manage and periodically reevaluate the appropriateness of a maintenance program because of an identified danger to the patient, those reasonable and necessary management and evaluation services could be covered, even if the skills of a therapist are not needed to carry out the activities performed as part of the maintenance program.
- While a beneficiary's particular medical condition is a valid factor in deciding if skilled physical therapy services are needed, a beneficiary's diagnosis or prognosis should never be the sole factor in deciding that a service is or is not skilled. The key issue is whether the skills of a physical therapist are needed to treat the illness or injury, or whether the services can be carried out by nonskilled personnel.

- A service that ordinarily would be performed by nonskilled personnel could be considered a skilled physical therapy service in cases in which there is clear documentation that, because of special medical complications, a skilled physical therapist is required to perform or supervise the service. However, the importance of a particular service to a beneficiary or the frequency with which it must be performed does not, by itself, make a nonskilled service into a skilled service.
- There must be an expectation that the patient's condition will improve significantly in a reasonable (and generally predictable) period of time, or the services must be necessary for the establishment of a safe and effective maintenance program required in connection with a specific disease state.
- The amount, frequency, and duration of the services must be reasonable.

NOTE: Claims for PT services denied because they are not considered reasonable and necessary are excluded by §1862(a)(1) of the Act and are thus subject to consideration under the waiver of liability provision in §1879 of the Act. (See §7300.10.)

2210.1 Restorative Therapy

To constitute physical therapy a service must, among other things, be reasonable and necessary to the treatment of the individual's illness. If an individual's expected restoration potential would be insignificant in relation to the extent and duration of physical therapy services required to achieve such potential, the physical therapy would not be considered reasonable and necessary. In addition, there must be an expectation that the patient's condition will improve significantly in a reasonable (and generally predictable) period of time. However, if at any point in the treatment of an illness it is determined that the expectations will not materialize the services will no longer be considered reasonable and necessary; and they, therefore, should be excluded from coverage under §1862(a)(l) of the Act.

Skilled physical therapy may be needed, and improvement in a patient's condition may occur, even where a patient's full or partial recovery is not possible. For example, a terminally ill patient may begin to exhibit self care, mobility, and/or safety dependence requiring skilled physical therapy services. The fact that full or partial recovery is not possible does not necessarily mean that skilled physical therapy is not needed to improve the patient's condition. The deciding factors are always whether the services are considered reasonable, effective treatments for the patient's condition and require the skills of a physical therapist, or whether they can be safely and effecively carried out by nonskilled personnel without physical therapy supervision.

2210.2 Maintenance Programs

The repetitive services required to maintain function generally do not involve complex and sophisticated physical therapy procedures, and, consequently, the judgment and skill of a qualified physical therapist are not required for safety and effectiveness.

However, in certain instances, the specialized knowledge and judgment of a qualified physical therapist may be required to establish a maintenance program intended to prevent or minimize deterioration caused by a medical condition, if the program is to be safely carried out and the treatment aims of the physician achieved. Establishing such a program is a skilled service. For example, a Parkinson patient who has not been under a restorative physical therapy program may require the services of a physical therapist to determine what type of exercises will contribute the most to maintain the patient's present functional level. In such situations, the initial evaluation of the patient's needs, the designing by the qualified physical therapist of a maintenance program which is appropriate to the capacity and tolerance of the patient and the treatment objectives of the physician, the instruction of the patient or family members in carrying out the program, and such infrequent reevaluations as may be required would constitute physical therapy.

While a patient is under a restorative physical therapy program, the physical therapist should reevaluate his/her condition when necessary and adjust any exercise program the patient is expected to carry out himself/herself or with the aid of supportive personnel to maintain the function being restored. Consequently, by the time it is determined that no further restoration is possible, i.e., by the end of the last restorative session, the physical therapist will have already designed the maintenance program required and instructed the patient or supportive personnel in the carrying out of the program. Therefore, where a maintenance program is not established until after the restorative physical therapy program has been completed, it would not be considered reasonable and necessary for the treatment of the patient's condition and would be excluded from coverage under §1862(a)(l) of the Act.

The repetitive services required to maintain function sometimes involve the use of complex and sophisticated therapy procedures, and, consequently, the judgment and skill of a physical therapist might be required for the safe and effective rendition of such services.

EXAMPLE: Where there is an unhealed, unstable fracture which requires regular exercise to maintain function until the fracture heals, the skills of a physical therapist would be needed to ensure that the fractured extremity is maintained in proper position and alignment during maintenance range of motion exercises.

2210.3 Application of Guidelines

The following discussion illustrates the application of the above guidelines to some of the more common physical therapy modalities and procedures utilized in the treatment of patients:

1. Hot Pack, Hydrocollator, Infra-Red Treatments, Paraffin Baths and Whirlpool Baths - Heat treatments of this type and whirlpool baths do not ordinarily require the skills of a qualified physical therapist. However, in a particular case the skills, knowledge, and judgment of a qualified physical therapist might be required in such treatments or baths, e.g., where the patient's condition is complicated by circulatory deficiency, areas of desensitization, open wounds, or other complications. Also, if such treatments are given prior to but as an integral part of a skilled physical therapy procedure, they would be considered part of the physical therapy service.

2. Gait Training - Gait evaluation and training furnished a patient whose ability to walk has been impaired by neurological, muscular, or skeletal abnormality require the skills of a qualified physical therapist. However, if gait evaluation and training cannot reasonably be expected to improve significantly the patient's ability to walk, such services would not be considered reasonable and necessary. Repetitive exercises to improve gait or maintain strength and endurance, and assistive walking, such as provided in support for feeble or unstable patients, are appropriately provided by supportive personnel, e.g., aides or nursing personnel and do not require the skills of a qualified physical therapist.

3. Ultrasound, Shortwave, and Microwave Diathermy Treatments - These modalities must always be performed by or under the supervision of a qualified physical therapist, and therefore, such treatments constitute physical therapy.

4. Range of Motion Tests - Only the qualified physical therapist may perform range of motion tests and, therefore, such tests would constitute physical therapy.

5. Therapeutic Exercises - Therapeutic exercises which must be performed by or under the supervision of a qualified physical therapist due either to the type of exercise employed or to the condition of the patient would constitute physical therapy. Range of motion exercises require the skills of a qualified physical therapist only when they are part of the active treatment of a specific disease which has resulted in a loss or restriction of mobility (as evidenced by physical therapy notes showing the degree of motion lost and the degree to be restored) and such exercises, either because of their nature or the condition of the patient, may only be performed safely and effectively by or under the supervision of a qualified physical therapist. Generally, range of motion exercises which are not related to the restoration of a specific loss of function but rather are related to the maintenance of function (see §2210.2) do not require the skills of a qualified physical therapist.

2300. GENERAL EXCLUSIONS.

No payment can be made under either the hospital insurance or supplementary medical insurance programs for certain items and services.

A. Not reasonable and necessary (§2303);
B. No legal obligation to pay for or provide services (§2306);
C. Furnished or paid for by government instrumentalities (§2309);
D. Not provided within United States (§2312);
E. Resulting from war (§2315);
F. Personal comfort (§2318);
G. Routine services and appliances (§2320);
H. Supportive devices for feet (§2323);
I. Custodial care (§2326);
J. Cosmetic surgery (§2329);
K. Charges by immediate relatives or members of household (§2332);
L. Dental services (§2336);
M. Paid or expected to be paid under worker's compensation (§2370).
N. Nonphysician services provided to a hospital inpatient which were not provided directly or arranged for by the hospital (§2390).

2300.1 Services Related to and Required as a Result of Services Which Are Not Covered Under Medicare

Medical and hospital services are sometimes required to treat a condition that arises as a result of services which are not covered because they are determined to be not reasonable and necessary or because they are excluded from coverage for other reasons. Services "related to" noncovered services (e.g., cosmetic surgery, noncovered organ transplants, noncovered artificial organ implants, etc.), including services related to followup care and complications of noncovered services which require treatment during a hospital stay in which the noncovered service was performed, are not covered services under Medicare. Services "not related to" noncovered services are covered under Medicare.

2320. ROUTINE SERVICES AND APPLIANCES

Routine physical checkups; eyeglasses, contact lenses, and eye examinations for the purpose of prescribing, fitting or changing eyeglasses; eye refractions; hearing aids and examinations for hearing aids; and immunizations are not covered.

The routine physical checkup exclusion applies to (a) examinations performed without relationship to treatment or diagnosis for a specific illness, symptom, complaint, or injury, and (b) examinations required by third parties such as insurance companies, business establishments, or Government agencies.

(If the claim is for a diagnostic test or examination performed solely for the purpose of establishing a claim under title IV of Public Law 91-173 (Black Lung Benefits), advise the claimant to contact his/her Social Security office regarding the filing of a claim for reimbursement under that program.)

The exclusions apply to eyeglasses or contact lenses and eye examinations for the purpose of prescribing, fitting, or changing eyeglasses or contact lenses for refractive errors. The exclusions do not apply to physician services (and services incident to a physician's service) performed in conjunction with an eye disease (e.g., glaucoma or cataracts) or to postsurgical prosthetic lenses which are customarily used during convalescence from eye surgery in which the lens of the eye was removed or to permanent prosthetic lenses required by an individual lacking the organic lens of the eye, whether by surgical removal or congenital disease. Such prosthetic lens is a replacement for an internal body organ (the lens of the eye). (See §2130.)

The coverage of services rendered by an ophthalmologist is dependent on the purpose of the examination rather than on the ultimate diagnosis of the patient's condition. When a beneficiary goes to an ophthalmologist with a complaint or symptoms of an eye disease or injury, the ophthalmologist's services (except for eye refractions) are covered regardless of the fact that only eyeglasses were prescribed. However, when a beneficiary goes to his/her ophthalmologist for an eye examination with no specific complaint, the expenses for the examination are not covered even though as a result of such examination the doctor discovered a pathologic condition.

In the absence of evidence to the contrary, you may carrier may assume that an eye examination performed by an ophthalmologist on the basis of a complaint by the beneficiary or symptoms of an eye disease was not for the purpose of prescribing, fitting, or changing eyeglasses.

Expenses for all refractive procedures, whether performed by an ophthalmologist (or any other physician) or an optometrist and without regard to the reason for performance of the refraction, are excluded from coverage. (See §§4125 and 5217 for claims review and reimbursement instructions concerning refractive services.)

With the exception of vaccinations for pneumococcal pneumonia, hepatitis B, and influenza, which are specifically covered under the law, vaccinations or inoculations are generally excluded as immunizations unless they are directly related to the treatment of an injury or direct exposure such as antirabies treatment, tetanus antitoxin or booster vaccine, botulin antitoxin, antivenin, or immune globulin.

A. Indigency — This exclusion does not apply when items and services are furnished an indigent individual without charge because of his inability to pay, if the physician or supplier bills other patients to the extent that they are able to pay.

B. Physician or Supplier Bills Only Insured Patients — Some physicians and suppliers waive their charges for individuals of limited means, but they also expect to be paid if the patient has insurance which covers the items or services they furnish. In such a situation, because it is clear that a patient would be charged if insured, a legal obligation to pay exists and benefits are payable for services rendered to patients with medical insurance if the physician or supplier customarily bills all insured patients--not just Medicare patients--even though noninsured patients are not charged.

Individuals with conditions which are the subject of a research project may receive treatment financed by a private research foundation. The foundation may establish its own clinic to study certain diseases or it may make grants to various other organizations. In most cases, the patient is not expected to pay for his treatment out-of-pocket, but if he has insurance, the parties expect that the insurer will pay for the services. In this situation, a legal obligation is considered to exist in the case of a Medicare patient even though other patients may not have insurance and are not charged.

C. Medicare Patient Has Other Health Insurance — Except as provided in §§3335ff., 3336ff., and 3340ff., payment is not precluded under Medicare even though the patient is covered by another health insurance plan or program which is obligated to provide or pay for the same services. This plan may be the type which pays money toward the cost of the services, such as a health insurance policy, or it may be the type which organizes and maintains its own facilities and professional staff. Examples of this latter type are employer and union sponsored plans which furnish services to special groups of employees or retirees or to union members and group practice prepayment plans.

The exceptions to this rule are services covered by automobile medical or no-fault insurance (§3338ff.), services rendered during a specified period of up to 12 months to individuals entitled solely on the basis of end stage renal disease who are insured under an employer group health plan (§3335ff.), services rendered employed individuals age 65 or over and spouses age 65 or over of employed individuals of any age who are insured under an employer group health plan (§3336ff.), and services covered by workers' compensation (§§3330ff.). In these cases the other plan pays primary benefits and if the other plan doesn't pay the entire bill, secondary Medicare benefits may be payable. Medicare is also secondary to the extent that services have been paid for by a liability insurer (§3340ff.).

D. Items Covered Under a Warranty — When a defective medical device such as a cardiac pacemaker is replaced under a warranty, hospital or other provider services rendered by parties other than the warrantor are covered despite the warrantor's liability. However, consider recovering Medicare payment for such services under the liability insurance provisions in §§3340ff.

With respect to payment for the device itself, in the case of services reimbursed on the basis of cost, the following rules apply: If the device is replaced free of charge by the warrantor, no program payment may be made, since there was no charge involved. If, however, a replacement device from another manufacturer had to be substituted because the replacement device offered under the warranty was not acceptable to the beneficiary or his physician, payment may be made for the replaced device. Also, if the warrantor supplied the replaced device, but some charge or pro rata payment was imposed, program payment may be made for the partial payment imposed for the device furnished by the warrantor.

If a provider could have obtained an acceptable device free of charge under a warranty but chose to purchase one instead, payment cannot be made for the purchased device under the prudent buyer rules. (See Provider Reimbursement Manual Part 1, §2103.) Also, if an acceptable device could have been purchased at a reduced price under a warranty but the provider did not take advantage of the warranty (i.e., it paid the full price to the original manufacturer or purchased the replacement device from a different manufacturer), the most the provider can receive as reimbursement for the purchased device is the amount it would have had to pay if it had pursued the warranty.

E. Ambulance Services — There are numerous methods of financing ambulance companies. For example, some volunteer organizations do not charge the patient or any other person but ask the recipient of services for a donation to help offset the cost of the service. Although the recipients may be under considerable moral and social pressure to donate, they are not required to do so, and there is no enforceable legal obligation on the part of the individual or anyone else to pay for the services. Thus, Medicare benefits would not be payable. However, services of volunteer ambulance corps are not categorically excluded. Many such companies regularly charge for their services and these services are covered by Medicare.

Some ambulance companies provide services without charge to residents of specific geographical areas but charge non-residents to the extent they are able to pay (e.g., through private health insurance). Under those circumstances, the free services provided the residents would be excluded from coverage, while the services furnished non-residents would be covered.

Ambulance companies which charge membership fees generally do not charge additional fees for services covered under the membership plan, although they may charge for certain other services (e.g., additional trips or mileage). Services furnished by such ambulance companies including services for which prepayment is made under the membership plan, are considered to be services for which there is a legal obligation to pay. Therefore such services are reimbursable provided the ambulance company bills all third party payers. The ambulance company's charges to nonmembers and to other third parties would be considered in determining the reasonable charge. Membership fees and insurance premiums are not incurred expenses under Medicare (see §2000) and are not reimbursable.

F. Members of Religious Orders — A legal obligation to pay exists where a religious order either pays for or furnishes services to members of the order. Although medical services furnished in such a setting are not ordinarily expressed in terms of a legal obligation, the order has an obligation to care for its members who have rendered lifelong services, similar to that existing under an employer's prepayment plan. Thus, pay for such services whether they are furnished by the order itself or by independent sources that customarily charge for their services.

2323. FOOT CARE AND SUPPORTIVE DEVICES FOR FEET

A. Exclusion of Coverage.--The following foot care services are generally excluded from coverage under both Part A and Part B. Exceptions to this general exclusion for limited treatment of routine foot care services are described in subsections A.2 and B. (See §4120 for procedural instructions in applying foot care exclusions.)

1. Treatment of Flat Foot.--The term "flat foot" is defined as a condition in which one or more arches of the foot have flattened out. Services or devices directed toward the care or correction of such conditions, including the prescription of supportive devices, are not covered.

2. Treatment of Subluxation of Foot.--Subluxations of the foot are defined as partial dislocations or displacements of joint surfaces, tendons ligaments, or muscles of the foot. Surgical or nonsurgical treatments undertaken for the sole purpose of correcting a subluxated structure in the foot as an isolated entity are not covered.

This exclusion does not apply to medical or surgical treatment of subluxation of the ankle joint (talo-crural joint). In addition, reasonable and necessary medical or surgical services, diagnosis, or treatment for medical conditions that have resulted from or are associated with partial displacement of structures is covered. For example, if a patient has osteoarthritis that has resulted in a partial displacement of joints in the foot, and the primary treatment is for the osteoarthritis, coverage is provided.

3. Routine Foot Care.--Except as provided in subsection B, routine foot care is excluded from coverage. Services that normally are considered routine and not covered by Medicare include the following:

- The cutting or removal of corns and calluses;
- The trimming, cutting, clipping, or debriding of nails; and
- Other hygienic and preventive maintenance care, such as cleaning and soaking the feet, the use of skin creams to maintain skin tone of either ambulatory or bedfast patients, and any other service performed in the absence of localized illness, injury, or symptoms involving the foot.

B. Exceptions to Routine Foot Care Exclusion.--

1. Necessary and Intergral Part of Otherwise Covered Services-- In certain circumstances, services ordinarily considered to be routine may be covered if they are performed as a necessary and integral part of otherwise covered services, such as diagnosis and treatment of ulcers, wounds, or infections.

2. Treatment of Warts on Foot.--The treatment of warts (including plantar warts) on the foot is covered to the same extent as services provided for the treatment of warts located elsewhere on the body.

3. Presence of Systemic Condition.--The presence of a systemic condition such as metabolic, neurologic, or peripheral vascular disease may require scrupulous foot care by a professional that in the absence of such condition(s) would be considered routine (and, therefore, excluded from coverage). Accordingly, foot care that would otherwise be considered routine may be covered when systemic condition(s) result in severe circulatory embarrassment or areas of diminished sensation in the individual's legs or feet. (See subsection C.)

In these instances, certain foot care procedures that otherwise are considered routine (e.g., cutting or removing corns and calluses, or trimming, cutting, clipping, or debriding nails) may pose a hazard when performed by a nonprofessional person on patients with such systemic conditions. (See §4120 for procedural instructions.)

4. Mycotic Nails.--In the absence of a systemic condition, treatment of mycotic nails may be covered.

The treatment of mycotic nails for an ambulatory patient is covered only when the physician attending the patient's mycotic condition documents that (1) there is clinical evidence of mycosis of the toenail, and (2) the patient has marked limitation of ambulation, pain, or secondary infection resulting from the thickening and dystrophy of the infected toenail plate.

The treatment of mycotic nails for a nonambulatory patient is covered only when the physician attending the patient's mycotic condition documents that (1) there is clinical evidence of mycosis of the toenail, and (2) the patient suffers from pain or secondary infection resulting from the thickening and dystrophy of the infected toenail plate.

For the purpose of these requirements, documentation means any written information that is required by the carrier in order for services to be covered. Thus, the information submitted with claims must be substantiated by information found in the patient's medical record. Any information, including that contained in a form letter, used for documentation purposes is subject to carrier verification in order to ensure that the information adequately justifies coverage of the treatment of mycotic nails. (See §4120 for claims processing criteria.)

C. Systemic Conditions.--Although not inte nded as a comprehensive list, the following metabolic, neurologic, and peripheral vascular diseases (with synonyms in parentheses) most commonly represent the underlying conditions that might justify coverage for routine foot care.

*Diabetes mellitus

Arteriosclerosis obliterans (A.S.O., arteriosclerosis of the extremities, occlusive peripheral arteriosclerosis)

Buerger's disease (thromboangiitis obliterans)

*Chronic thrombophlebitis

Peripheral neuropathies involving the feet -

*Associated with malnutrition and vitamin deficiency

Malnutrition (general, pellagra)

Alcoholism

Malabsorption (celiac disease, tropical sprue)

Pernicious anemia

*Associated with carcinoma

*Associated with diabetes mellitus

*Associated with drugs and toxins

*Associated with multiple sclerosis

*Associated with uremia (chronic renal disease)

Associated with traumatic injury

Associated with leprosy or neurosyphilis

Associated with hereditary disorders -

Hereditary sensory radicular neuropathy

Angiokeratoma corporis diffusum (Fabry's)

Amyloid neuropathy

When the patient's condition is one of those designated by an asterisk (*), routine procedures are covered only if the patient is under the active care of a doctor of medicine or osteopathy who documents the condition.

2323D Supportive Devices for Feet

Orthopedic shoes and other supportive devices for the feet generally are not covered. However, this exclusion does not apply to such a shoe if it is an integral part of a leg brace (see §2133), and its expense is included as part of the cost of the brace. Also, this exclusion does not apply to therapeutic shoes furnished to diabetics. (See §2134.)

2336. DENTAL SERVICES AND EXCLUSION.

Items and services in connection with the care, treatment, filling, removal, or replacement of teeth, or structures directly supporting the teeth are not covered. "Structures directly supporting the teeth" means the periodontium, which includes the gingivae, dentogingival junction, periodontal membrane, cementum, and alveolar process. However, payment may be made for other services of a dentist. (See §§2020.3, 2136 and Coverage Issues Manual §50-26.)

The hospitalization or nonhospitalization of a patient has no direct bearing on the coverage or exclusion of a given dental procedure. (See also §§2020.3 and 2136 for additional information on dental services.)

2455. MEDICAL INSURANCE BLOOD DEDUCTIBLE

A. General — Program payment under Part B may not be made for the first three units of whole blood, or packed red cells, received by a beneficiary in a calendar year. For purpose of the blood deductible, a unit of whole blood means a pint of whole blood. The term whole blood means human blood from which none of the liquid or cellular components has been removed. Where packed red cells are furnished, a unit of packed red cells is considered equivalent to a pint of whole blood. After the three unit deductible has been satisfied, payment may be made for all blood charges, subject to the normal coverage and reasonable charge criteria.

NOTE: Blood is a biological and can be covered under Part B only when furnished incident to a physician's services. (See §§2050.1ff. for a more complete explanation of services rendered "incident to a physician's services.")

B. Application of the Blood Deductible — The blood deductible applies only to whole blood or packed red cells. Other components of blood such as platelets, fibrinogen, plasma, gamma globulin, and serum albumin are not subject to the blood deductible. These components of blood are covered biologicals.

The blood deductible involves only the charges for the blood (or packed red cells). Charges for the administration of blood or packed cells are not subject to the blood deductible. Accordingly, although payment may not be made for the first three pints of blood and/or units of packed red cells furnished to a beneficiary in a calendar year, payment may be made (subject to the cash deductible) for the administration charges for all covered pints or units including the first three furnished in a calendar year.

The blood deductible applies only to the first three pints and/or units furnished in a calendar year, even though more than one physician or clinic furnished blood. Furthermore, to count toward the deductible, the blood must be covered with respect to all applicable criteria (i.e., it must be medically necessary, it must be furnished incident to a physician's services, etc.). (See §2050.5.)

3045. FILING THE REQUEST - ASSIGNMENTS

If the patient and the physician or supplier agree to an assignment of benefits, the patient signs Item 12 of Form HCFA-1500. The physician or supplier completes the claim form and checks yes in Item 26 to show acceptance of the assignment.

Itemized information relating to medical services or supplies are furnished in Item 24 of Form HCFA-1500 by the physician or supplier accepting the assignment.

Physicians (and suppliers) accepting assignment may find it advisable to either:

- Make sure any bill sent to the patient clearly indicates that the physician has accepted assignment in order to forestall a possible claim by the patient or confusion in your operation; or
- Delay billing the patient until receipt of your payment determination notice to ensure that the allowed charges or remaining balance are accurately shown.

Form HCFA-1500 is used by physicians, clinics, or suppliers claiming payment under the assignment method for services furnished to an enrollee. If this procedure is used, the physician, clinic, or supplier must agree to accept the reasonable charge as the full charge. With few exceptions, pay the physician, clinic, or supplier 80 percent of the Medicare approved charge over and above the deductible. The physician, clinic, or supplier can collect no more than the 20 percent balance and the deductible from the patient.

3045.4 Effect of Assignment Upon Purchase of Cataract Glasses from Participating Physician or Supplier

A pair of cataract glasses is comprised of two distinct products: a professional product (the prescribed lenses) and a retail commercial product (the frames). The frames serve not only as a holder of lenses but also as an article of personal apparel. As such, they are usually selected on the basis of personal taste and style. Although Medicare will pay only for standard frames, most patients want deluxe frames. Participating physicians and suppliers cannot profitably furnish such deluxe frames unless they can make an extra (non-covered) charge for the frames even though they accept assignment.

Therefore, a participating physician or supplier (whether an ophthalmologist, optometrist, or optician) who accepts assignment on cataract glasses with deluxe frames may charge the Medicare patient the difference between his usual charge to private pay patients for glasses with standard frames and his usual charge to such patients for glasses with deluxe frames, in addition to the applicable deductible and coinsurance on glasses with standard frames, if all of the following requirements are met:

A. The participating physician or supplier has standard frames available, offers them for sale to the patient, and explains to the patient the price and other differences between standard and deluxe frames.

B. The participating physician or supplier obtains from the patient (or his representative) and keeps on file the following signed and dated statement:

    Name of Patient   Medicare Claim Number

Having been informed that an extra charge is being made by the physician or supplier for deluxe frames, that this extra charge is not covered by Medicare, and that standard frames are available for purchase from the physician or supplier at no extra charge, I have chosen to purchase deluxe frames.

    Signature Date

C. The participating physician or supplier itemizes on his claim his actual charge for the lenses, his actual charge for the standard frames, and his actual extra charge for the deluxe frames (charge differential).

Once the assigned claim for deluxe frames has been processed, the carrier will explain the extra charge for the deluxe frames on the EOMB, as indicated in the following example.

	BILLED	APPROVED
CATARACT LENSES JULY 20, 1985	$200.00	$175.00
APPROVED AMOUNT LIMITED BY ITEM 5C ON BACK		
STANDARD FRAMES JULY 20, 1985	$20.00	$15.00
APPROVED AMOUNT LIMITED BY ITEM 5C ON BACK		
DR. JONES AGREED TO CHARGE NO MORE FOR THE ABOVE SERVICES THAN THE AMOUNT APPROVED BY MEDICARE.		
EXTRA CHARGE DELUXE JULY 20, 1985	$35.00	$00.00
MEDICARE DOES NOT PAY THE EXTRA CHARGE FOR DELUXE FRAMES.		
TOTAL APPROVED AMOUNT		$190.00
MEDICARE PAYMENT (80% OF THE APPROVED AMOUNT)		$152.00

WE ARE PAYING A TOTAL OF $152.00 TO DR. JONES FOR THE ABOVE SERVICES. YOU ARE RESPONSIBLE FOR THE DIFFERENCE OF $38.00 BETWEEN THE APPROVED AMOUNT AND THE MEDICARE PAYMENT, PLUS THE EXTRA CHARGE OF $35.00 FOR DELUXE FRAMES.

3312. EVIDENCE OF MEDICAL NECESSITY FOR DURABLE MEDICAL EQUIPMENT

For certain items or services billed to the DME Regional Carrier (DMERC), the supplier must receive a signed Certificate of Medical Necessity (CMN) from the treating physician. The supplier must retain the original copy of the signed CMN in their records. CMNs communicate, either on paper or in an electronic record, required medical necessity information and have a DMERC form number (e.g., 01, 02, 03) and a revision number (e.g., .01, .02). Some DMERC forms also have an alpha suffix (e.g., A, B, C).

All CMNs have a HCFA form number in addition to the DMERC form number. (See the following listing of CMN form numbers.) The HCFA form number is in the bottom left corner of the form. CMNs are referred to by their HCFA form numbers. DMERC form numbers identify the CMN on electronic claims submitted to the DMERC in the National Standard Format (NSF). Form HCFA 484 serves as the CMN for home oxygen therapy.

The orginial CMN must be retained in the supplier's file and be available to the DMERCs on request. When CMNs are submitted hardcopy, the supplier must include a copy of only the front side. When CMNs are submitted electronically, only information from sections A, B, and D is required.

The following is a list of the currently approved CMNs:

DMERC FORM	HCFA FORM	ITEMS ADDRESSED
484.2	484	Home oxygen therapy
01.02A	841	Hospital beds
01.02B	842	Support surfaces
02.02A	843	Motorized wheelchairs
02.02B	844	Manual wheelchairs
03.02	845	Continuous positive airway pressure (CPAP) devices
04.02B	846	Lymphedema pumps (pneumatic compression devices)
04.02C	847	Osteogenesis stimulators
06.02	848	Transcutaneous electrical nerve stimulators (TENS)
07.02A	849	Seat lift mechanisms
07.02B	850	Power operated vehicles
09.02	851	Infusion pumps
10.02A	852	Parenteral nutrition
10.02B	853	Enteral nutrition
11.01	854	Section C continuation (manual and motorized wheelchairs - ONLY)

The CMN sent to the physician must be two-sided with instructions on the back. Because these forms have been approved by the Office of Management and Budget (OMB), when a CMN is submitted with a paper claim, the hard copy must be an exact reproduction of the HCFA form. However, when the CMN is submitted electronically, the font on the hard copy CMN, which the supplier retains in their files, may be modified as follows:

- Pitch may vary from 10 characters per inch (cpi) to 17.7 cpi.;
- Line spacing must be 6 lines per inch;
- Each CMN must have a minimum 1/4 inch margin on all four sides;
- Without exception, these modified hard copy forms must contain identical questions/wording to the HCFA forms, in the same sequence, with the same pagination, and identicaltructions/definitions printed on the back; and

- CMN question sets may not be combined.

The CMN can serve as the physician order if the narrative description is sufficiently detailed. This would include quantities needed and frequency of replacement on accessories, supplies, nutrients, and drugs. For items requiring a written order on hand prior to delivery (air fluidized beds, TENS, POVs, seat lift mechanisms), suppliers may utilize a completed and physician-signed CMN for this purpose. Otherwise, a separate order in addition to a subsequently completed and signed CMN is necessary.

The information in section B of the CMN may not be completed by the supplier. A supplier who knowingly and willfully completes section B of the form is subject to a civil money penalty up to $1,000 for each form or document so distributed. Any supplier who remains in non-compliance after repeated attempts by the contractor to get the supplier into compliance, refer to your RO as a potential civil money penalty case.

The information in section C of the CMN (fee schedule amount and the supplier's charge for the medical equipment or supplies being furnished) must be completed on the form by the supplier prior to it being furnished to the physician. A supplier who knowingly and willfully fails to include this information may be subject to a civil money penalty up to $1,000 for each form or document so distributed. Any supplier who remains in non-compliance, after repeated attempts by the contractor to get the supplier into compliance, refer to your RO as a potential civil money penalty case.

Do not modify the language or content when reprinted. Also, do not accept any CMN that has been modified in any way by any other party. In addition, do not accept any other certifications of medical necessity by other insurers or government agencies.

A. Completion of Certificate of Medical Necessity Forms

1. SECTION A: (This may be completed by supplier.)

    a. Certification Type/Date — If this is an initial certification for this patient, the date (MM/DD/YY) is indicated in the space marked "INITIAL." If this is a revised certification (to be completed when the physician changes the order, based on the patient's changing clinical needs), the initial date is indicated in the space marked "INITIAL," and the revision date is indicated in the space marked "REVISED." If this is a recertification, the initial date is indicated in the space marked "INITIAL," and the recertification date is indicated in the space marked "RECERTIFICATION." Whether a REVISED or RECERTIFIED CMN is submitted, the INITIAL date as well as the REVISED or RECERTIFICATION date is always furnished.

b. Patient Information — This indicates the patient's name, permanent legal address, telephone number, and his/her health insurance claim number (HICN) as it appears on his/her Medicare card and on the claim form.

c. Supplier Information — This indicates the name of the company (supplier name), address, telephone number, and the Medicare supplier number assigned by the National Supplier Clearinghouse (NSC).

d. Place of Service — This indicates the place in which the item is being used, i.e., patient's home is 12, skilled nursing facility (SNF) is 31, or end stage renal disease (ESRD) facility is 65. See §4030.5 for a complete list.

e. Facility Name — This indicates the name and complete address of the facility, if the place of service is a facility.

f. HCPCS Codes — This is a list of all HCPCS procedure codes for items ordered that require a CMN. Procedure codes that do not require certification are not listed on the CMN.

g. Patient Date of Birth (DOB), Height, Weight, and Sex — This indicates patient's DOB (MM/DD/YY), height in inches, weight in pounds, and sex (male or female).

h. Physician Name and Address — This indicates the treating physician's name and complete mailing address.

i. UPIN — This indicates the treating physician's unique physician identification number (UPIN).

j. Physician's Telephone Number — This indicates the telephone number where the treating physician can be contacted (preferably where records would be accessible pertaining to this patient) if additional information is needed.

2. SECTION B: (This may not be completed by the supplier. While this section may be completed by a non-physician clinician, or a physician employee, it must be reviewed by the treating physician. Publish this requirement about section B in your bulletins at least annually.)

a. Estimated Length of Need — This indicates the estimated length of need (the length of time (in months) the physician expects the patient to require use of the ordered item). If the treating physician expects that the patient will require the item for the duration of his/her life, 99 is entered. For recertification and revision CMNs, the cumulative length of need (the total length of time in months from the initial date of need) is entered.

b. Diagnosis Codes — Listed in the first space is the ICD-9 code that represents the primary reason for ordering this item. Additional ICD-9 codes that would further describe the medical need for the item (up to 3 codes) are also listed. A given CMN may have more than one item billed, and for each item, the primary reason for ordering may be different. For example, a CMN is submitted for a manual wheelchair (K0001) and elevating legrests (K0195). The primary reason for K0001 is stroke, and the primary reason for K0195 is edema.

c. Question Section — This section is used to gather clinical information regarding the patient's condition, the need for the DME, and supplies.

d. Name of Person Answering Section B Questions — If a clinical professional other than the treating physician (e.g., home health nurse, physical therapist, dietician, or a physician employee) answers the questions in section B, he/she must print his/her name, give his/her professional title, and the name of his/her employer, where indicated. If the treating physician answered the questions, this space may be left blank.

3. SECTION C: (This is completed by the supplier.)

a. Narrative Description of Equipment and Cost — The supplier indicates (1) a narrative description of the item(s) ordered, as well as all options, accessories, supplies, and drugs; (2) the supplier's charge for each item, option, accessory, supply, and drug; and (3) the Medicare fee schedule allowance for each item, option, accessory, supply, or drug, if applicable.

4. SECTION D: (This is completed by the treating physician.)

a. Physician Attestation — The treating physician's signature certifies the CMN which he/she is reviewing includes sections A, B, C, and D, the answers in section B are correct, and the self-identifying information in section A is correct.

b. Physician Signature and Date — After completion and/or review by the treating physician of sections A, B, and C, the treating physician must sign and date the CMN in section D, verifying the attestation appearing in this section. The treating physician's signature also certifies the items ordered are medically necessary for this patient. Signature and date stamps are not acceptable.

B. Development of Incomplete Data — Claims that require development for missing or incomplete information are nonclean claims for purposes of processing timeliness standards. Develop the missing information directly with the DME supplier.

When written development is necessary, advise the supplier (or in nonassigned claims, the beneficiary) and stress to the claimant that no payment can be made unless the treating physician provides satisfactory evidence of medical necessity within 45 days.

4107. DURABLE MEDICAL EQUIPMENT - BILLING AND PAYMENT CONSIDERATIONS UNDER THE FEE SCHEDULE

The Omnibus Budget Reconciliation Act of 1987 requires that payment for DME, prosthetics and orthotics be made under fee schedules effective January 1, 1989. The allowable charge is limited to the lower of the actual charge for the equipment, or the fee schedule amount. The equipment is categorized into one of six classes:

- Inexpensive or other routinely purchased DME;
- Items requiring frequent and substantial servicing;
- Customized items;
- Prosthetic and orthotic devices;
- Capped rental items; or
- Oxygen and oxygen equipment.

The fee schedule allowances for each class are determined in accord with §§5102ff.

4107.6 WRITTEN ORDER PRIOR TO DELIVERY

Ensure that your system will pay for the equipment listed below only when the supplier has a written order in hand prior to delivery. Otherwise, do not pay for that item even if a written order is subsequently furnished. However, you can pay for a similar item if it is subsequently provided by an unrelated supplier which has a written order in hand prior to delivery. The HCPCS codes for the equipment requiring a written order are:

- E0180
- E0181
- E0182
- E0183
- E0184
- E0185
- E0188
- E0189
- E0190
- E0192
- E0195
- E0620
- E0720
- E0730
- E1230

4107.8 EOMB Messages

The following EOMB messages are suggested: (See §§7012ff. for other applicable messages.)

A. General. "This is the maximum approved amount for this item." (Use when payment is reduced for a line item.)

B. Inexpensive/Frequently Purchased Equipment

- "The total approved amount for this item is _____ whether this item is purchased or rented." (Use in first month.)
- "This is your next to last rental payment."
- "This is your last rental payment."
- "This item has been rented up to the Medicare payment limit."
- "The approved amount has been reduced by the previously approved rental amounts."

C. Items Requiring Frequent and Substantial Servicing — Use the general rental messages in §4107.8A, if applicable. If the beneficiary has purchased the item prior to June 1, 1989, follow §7014.6. If the beneficiary purchase an item in this category on or after June 1, 1989, use the following message:

- "This equipment can only be paid for on a rental basis."

D. Customized Items and Other Prosthetic and Orthotic Devices

- "The total approved amount for this item is _____."

E. Capped Rental Items

- "Under a provision of Medicare law, monthly rental payments for this item can continue for up to 15 months from the first rental month or until the equipment is no longer needed, whichever comes first."
- "If you no longer are using this equipment or have recently moved and will rent this item from a different supplier, please contact our office." (Use on beneficiary's EOMB.)
- "This is your next to last rental payment."
- "This is your last rental payment."
- "This item has been rented up to the 15 month Medicare payment limit."
- "Your equipment supplier must supply and service this item for as long as you continue to need it."
- "Medicare cannot pay for maintenance and/or servicing of this item until 6 months have elapsed since the end of the 15th paid rental month."

If the beneficiary purchased a capped rental item prior to June 1, 1989, follow §7014.6. If the beneficiary purchased a capped rental item on or after June 1, 1989, use the following denial message:

- "This equipment can only be paid for on a rental basis."

F. Oxygen and Oxygen Equipment

- "The monthly allowance includes payment for all covered oxygen contents and supplies."
- "Payment for the amount of oxygen supplied has been reduced or denied based on the patient's medical condition." (To supplier after medical review.)
- "The approved amount has been reduced to the amount allowable for medically necessary oxygen therapy." (To beneficiary.)

- "Payment denied because the allowance for this item is included in the monthly payment amount."
- "Payment denied because Medicare oxygen coverage requirements are not met."

If the beneficiary purchased an oxygen system prior to June 1, 1989, follow §7014.6. If the beneficiary purchased an oxygen system on or after June 1, 1989, use the following denial message:

- "This item can only be paid for on a rental basis."

G. Items Requiring a Written Order Prior to Delivery

- "Payment is denied because the supplier did not obtain a written order from your doctor prior to the delivery of this item."

4107.9 Oxygen HCPCS Codes Effective 1/1/89

NEW	OLD	DEFINITION
Q0036 See notes (1) and (8)	E1377-E1385, E1397	Oxygen concentrator, High humidity
Q0038 See note (2)	E0400, E0405	Oxygen contents, gaseous, per unit (for use with owned gaseous stationary systems or when both a stationary and portable gaseous system are owned; 1 unit = 50 cubic ft.)
Q0039 See note (2)	E0410, E0415O	Oxygen contents, liquid, per unit, (for use with owned stationary liquid systems or when both a stationary and portable liquid system are owned; 1 unit = 10 lbs.)
Q0040 See note (2)	E0416	Portable oxygen contents, per unit (for use only with portable gaseous systems when no stationary gas system is used; 1 unit = 5 cubic ft.)
Q0041 See note (2)	None	Portable oxygen contents, liquid, per unit (for use only with portable liquid systems when no stationary liquid system is used; 1 unit = 1 lb.)
Q0042 See note (3)	E0425	Stationary compressed gas system rental, includes contents (per unit), regulator with flow gauge, humidifier, nebulizer, cannula or mask & tubing; 1 unit = 50 cubic ft.
E0425 See notes (4) and (8)	Same	No change
E0430 See notes (8) and (9)	Same	No change
E0435 See notes (7) and (8)	Same	No change in terminology, but see note (7).
Q0043	E0440	Stationary liquid (see note (3) oxygen system rental), includes contents (per unit), use of reservoir, contents indicator, flowmeter, humidifier, nebulizer, cannula or mask and tubing; 1 unit of contents = 10 lbs.
0440 See note (4)	Same	No change
E0455 See note (6)	Same	No change
E0555 See note (6)	Same	No change
E0580 See note (6)	Same	No change
E1351 See note (6)	Same	No change

E1352 See note (6)	Same	No change	E1406	Q0037	Combine the fee schedule amounts for the stationary oxygen system and the nebulizer with only a compressor (i.e., without a heater, code E0570) to determine the fee schedule amount to apply to oxygen without a heater (code E1406)
E1353 See notes (6) and (8)	Same	No change			
E1354 See note (6)	Same	No change			
E1371 See note (6)	Same	No change			
E1374 See note (6)	Same	No change			
E1400 See note (1) and (8)	E1388-E1396	Same as Q0014			
E1401 See notes (1) and (8)	E1388-E1396	Same as Q0015			
E1402	Same	No change			
E1403	Same	No change			
E1404	Same	No change			
E1405 See note (10)	Q0037	Combine the fee schedule amounts for the stationary oxygen system and the nebulizer with a compressor and heater (code E0585) to determine the fee schedule amount to apply to oxygen enrichers with a heater (code E1405)			

NOTES:

(1) For billing concentrator rentals or purchases

(2) For monthly billing of contents used with purchased gas or liquid oxygen delivery systems (i.e., no stationary system is being rented)

(3) For billing gas or liquid system rentals only

(4) For billing of purchased stationary gas or liquid systems

(5) For billing the portable add-on for liquid systems

(6) For billing of replacement items for oxygen delivery systems purchased prior to 6/1/89

(7) For services furnished on or after 6/1/89, use E0435 when only portable liquid is prescribed (i.e., no stationary liquid system prescribed) or both stationary and portable oxygen were prescribed but the patient uses a stationary system other than a liquid system (e.g., stationary system is concentrator)

(8) Do not pay for oxygen systems purchased on or after 6/1/89

(9) For billing the portable add-on for gas systems

(10) For billing of rental oxygen and water vapor enriching systems only.

4120. APPLICATION OF FOOT CARE EXCLUSIONS TO PHYSICIANS' SERVICES.

The exclusion of foot care is determined by the nature of the service (§ 2323). Thus, reimbursement for an excluded service should be denied whether performed by a podiatrist, osteopath, or a doctor of medicine, and without regard to the difficulty or complexity of the procedure.

When an itemized bill shows both covered services and noncovered services not integrally related to the covered service, the portion of charges attributable to the noncovered services should be denied. (For example, if an itemized bill shows surgery for an ingrown toenail and also removal of calluses not necessary for the performance of toe surgery, any additional charge attributable to removal of the calluses should be denied.)

In reviewing claims involving foot care, the carrier should be alert to the following exceptional situations:

1. Payment may be made for incidental noncovered services performed as a necessary and integral part of, and secondary to, a covered procedure. (For example, if trimming of toenails is required for application of a cast to a fractured foot, the carrier need not allocate and deny a portion of the charge for the trimming of the nails. However, a separately itemized charge for such excluded service should be disallowed. When the primary procedure is covered the administration of anesthesia necessary for the performance of such procedure is also covered.

2. Payment may be made for initial diagnostic services performed in connection with a specific symptom or complaint if it seems likely that its treatment would be covered even though the resulting diagnosis may be one requiring only noncovered care.

3. Payment may be made for routine-type foot care such as cutting or removal of corns, calluses, or nails when the patient has a systemic disease of sufficient severity that unskilled performance of such procedure would be hazardous (§2323C.).

   a. Claims for such routine services would show in item 7D of the SSA-1490 the complicating systemic disease. Where these services were rendered by a podiatrist this item should also include the name of the M.D. or D.O. who diagnosed the complicating condition. In those cases where active care is required, the approximate date the beneficiary was last seen by such physician must also be indicated.

   NOTE: Section 939 of P.L. 96-499 removed "warts" from the routine foot care exclusion effective July 1, 1981.

   b. Relatively few claims for routine-type care are anticipated considering the severity of conditions contemplated as the basis for this exception. Claims for this type of foot care should not be paid in the absence of convincing evidence that nonprofessional performance of the service would have been hazardous for the beneficiary because of an underlying systemic disease. The mere statement of a diagnosis such as those mentioned in §2323C does not of itself indicate the severity of the condition. Where development is indicated to verify diagnosis and/or severity the carrier should follow existing claims processing practices which may include review of carrier's history and medical consultation as well as physician contacts.

   c. A presumption of coverage may be made by the carrier where the claim or other evidence available discloses certain physical and/or clinical findings consistent with the diagnosis and indicative of severe peripheral involvement. For purposes of applying this presumption, the following findings are pertinent:

   Class A Findings
   - Nontraumatic amputation of foot or integral skeletal portion thereof

   Class B Findings
   - Absent posterior tibial pulse
   - Advanced trophic changes as (three required): hair growth (de-crease or absence); nail changes (thickening); pigmentary changes (discoloration); skin texture (thin, shiny); skin color (rubor or redness)
   - Absent dorsalis pedis pulse

   Class C Findings
   - Claudication
   - Temperature changes (e.g., cold feet)
   - Edema
   - Paresthesia (abnormal spontaneous sensations in the feet)

Burning

The presumption of coverage may be applied when the physician rendering the routine foot care has identified: (1) a Class A finding; (2) two of the Class B findings; or (3) one Class B and two Class C findings. Case evidencing findings falling short of these alternatives may involve podiatric treatment that may constitute covered care and should be reviewed by the carrier's medical staff and developed as necessary.

For purposes of applying the coverage presumption where the routine services have been rendered by a podiatrist, the carrier may deem the active care requirement met if the claim or other evidence available discloses that the patient has seen an M.D. or D.O. for treatment and/or evaluation of the complicating disease process during the 6-month period prior to the rendition of the routine-type service or had come under such care shortly after the services were furnished usually as a result of a referral.

4173. POSITRON EMISSION TOMOGRAPHY (PET) SCANS BACKGROUND:

For dates of service on or after March 14, 1995, Medicare covers one use of PET scans, imaging of the perfusion of the heart using Rubidium 82 (Rb 82).

For dates of service on or after January 1, 1998, Medicare expanded coverage of PET scans for the characterization of solitary pulmonary nodules and for the initial staging of lung cancer, conditioned upon its ability to effect the management and treatment of patients with either suspected or demonstrated lung cancer. All other uses of PET scans remain not covered by Medicare.

Beginning for dates of service on or after July 1, 1999, Medicare will cover PET scans for evaluation of recurrent colorectal cancer in patients with levels of carinoembryonic antigen (CEA), staging lymphoma (both Hodgkins and non-Hodgkins) in place of a Gallium study or lymphangiogram, and for the staging of recurrent melanoma prior to surgery.

See Coverage Issues Manual §50-36 for specific coverage criteria for PET scans.

Regardless of any other terms or conditions, all uses of PET scans, in order to be covered by Medicare program, must meet the following conditions:

- Scans must be performed using PET scanners that have either been approved or cleared for marketing by the FDA as PET scanners;
- Submission of claims for payment must include any information Medicare requires to assure that the PET scans performed were: (a) reasonable and necessary; (b) did not unnecessarily duplicate other covered diagnostic tests, and (c) did not involve investigational drugs or procedures using investigational drugs, as determined by the Food and Drug Administration (FDA); and
- The PET scan entity submitting claims for payment must keep such patient records as Medicare requires on file for each patient for whom a PET scan claim is made.

4173.1 Conditions for Medicare Coverage of PET Scans for Noninvasive Imaging of the Perfusion of the Heart

Pet scans done at rest or with pharmacological stress used for noninvasive imaging of the perfusion of the heart for the diagnosis management of patients with known or suspected coronary artery disease using the FDA-approved radiopharmaceutical Rubidium 82 (Rb 82) are covered for services performed on or after March 15, 1995, provided such scans meet either of the two following conditions:

- The PET scan, whether rest alone or rest with stress, is used in place of, but not in addition to, a single photon emission computed tomography (SPECT); or
- The PET scan, whether rest alone or rest with stress, is used following a SPECT that was found inconclusive. In these cases, the PET scan must have been considered necessary in order to determine what medical or surgical intervention is required to treat the patient. (For purposes of this requirement, an inconclusive test is a test whose results are equivocal, technically uninterpretable, or discordant with a patient's other clinical data.)

NOTE: PET scans using Rubidium 82, whether rest or stress are not covered by Medicare for routine screening of asymptomatic patients, regardless of the level of risk factors applicable to such patients.

4173.2 Conditions of Coverage of PET Scans for Characterization of Solitary Pulmonary Nodules (SPNs) and PET Scans Using FDG to Initially Stage Lung Cancer

PET scans using the glucose analog 2-[fluorine-18]-fluoro-2-deoxy-D-glucose(FDG) are covered for services on or after January 1, 1998, subject to the condition and limitations described in CIM 50-36.

NOTE: A Tissue Sampling Procedure (TSP) should not be routinely covered in the case of a negative PET scan for characterization of SPNs, since the patient is presumed not to have a malignant lesion, based upon the PET scan results. Claims for a TSP after a negative PET must be submitted with documentation in order to determine if the TSP is reasonable and necessary in spite of a negative PET. Claims submitted for a TSP after a negative PET without documentation should be denied. Physicians should discuss with their patients the implications of this decision, both with respect to the patient's responsibility for payment for such a biopsy if desired, as well as the confidence the physician has in the results of such PET scans, prior to ordering such scans for this purpose. This physician-patient decision should occur with a clear discussion and understanding of the sensitivity and specificity trade-offs between a computerized tomography (CT) and PET scans. In cases where a TSP is performed, it is the responsibility of the physician ordering the TSP to provide sufficient documentation of the reasonableness and necessity for such procedure or procedures. Such documentation should include, but is not necessarily limited to, a description of the features of the PET scan that call into question whether it is an accurate representation of the patient's condition, the existence of other factors in the patient's condition that call into question the accuracy of the PET scan, and such other information as the contractor deems necessary to determine whether the claim for the TSP should be covered and paid.

In cases of serial evaluation of SPNs using both CT and regional PET chest scanning, such PET scans will not be covered if repeated within 90 days following a negative PET scan.

4173.3 Conditions of Coverage of PET Scans for Recurrence of Colorectal Cancer, Staging and Characterization of Lymphoma, and Recurrence of Melanoma

Medicare adds coverage for these three new indications for PET, one for evaluation of recurrent colorectal cancer in patients with rising levels of carcinoembryonic antigen (CEA), one for staging of lymphoma (both Hodgkins and non-Hodgkins) when the PET scan substitutes for a Gallium scan, and one for the detection of recurrent melanoma, provided certain conditions are met. All three indications are covered only when using the radiopharmaceutical FDA (2-[flourine-18]-fluoro-2-deoxy-D-glucose), and are further predicated on the legal availability of FDG for use in such scans.

4173.4 Billing Requirements for PET Scans

A. Effective for Services on or After January 1, 1998, Claims for Characterizing SPNs Should Includ

- Evidence of the initial detection of a primary lung tumor, usually by CT. This should include an indication of the results of such CT or other detection method, indicating an indeterminate or possibly malignant lesion, not exceeding four centimeters (cm.) in diameter. This indication should be included with the claim, along with the result of the PET scan, using the appropriate modifiers. For example, you should not get a claim showing G0125 with modifier N; if you do, deny the claim.
- In order to ensure that the PET scan is properly coordinated with other diagnostic modalities, PET scan claims must include the results of concurrent thoracic CT, which is necessary for anatomic information.
- In view of the limitations on this coverage, you may consider conducting pre- or post-payment reviews to determine that the use of PET scans is consistent with Medicare instructions. Providers must keep patient record information on file for each Medicare patient for whom a PET scan claim is made. These medical records may be used in any review and must include information necessary to substantiate the need for the PET scan.

NOTE: PET scans are not covered by Medicare for routine screening of asymptomatic patients, regardless of the level of risk factors applicable to such patients.

B. Effective for Services on or After January 1, 1998, Claims for Staging Metastatic Non-Small-Cell Lung Carcinoma (NSCLC) Must Include:

- Since this service is covered only in those cases in which a primary cancerous lung tumor has been confirmed, claims for PET must show evidence of the detection of such primary lung tumor. For example, a diagnosis code indicating the existence of a primary tumor or any other evidence you deem appropriate. A surgical pathology report which documents the presence of an NSCLC must be kept on file with the provider. If you deem it necessary, contact the provider for a copy of this documentation.
- Whole body PET scan results and results of concurrent CT and follow-up lymph node biopsy. In order to ensure that the PET scan is properly coordinated with other diagnostic modalities, claims must include both (1) the results of concurrent thoracic CT, which is necessary for anatomic information, and (2) the results of any lymph node biopsy performed to finalize whether the patient will be a surgical candidate.

NOTE: A lymph node biopsy is not covered in the case of a negative CT and negative PET where the patient is considered a surgical candidate, given the presumed absence of metastatic NSCLC.

C. Effective for Dates of Service on or After July 1, 1999 PET Claims For the Following Conditions Must Include:

- Recurring colorectal cancer with rising CEA:
  - A statement or other evidence of previous colorectal tumor;
  - The results of the concurrent CT, which is necessary for anatomic information; and
  - The necessary procedure codes and/or modifiers.
- Staging or restaging of lymphoma in place of a Gallium study or lymphangiogram:
  - A statement or other evidence of previously-made diagnosis of lymphoma;
  - The results of the concurrent CT, which is necessary for anatomic information; and
  - The date of the last Gallium scan or lymphangiogram when done in the same facility as the PET scan.
- Recurrent Melanoma prior to surgery:
  - A statement or other evidence of previous melanoma;
  - The results of the concurrent CT, which is necessary for anatomic information; and
  - The date of the last Gallium scan when done in the same facility as the PET scan.

As with any claim but particularly in view of the limitations on this coverage, you may decide to conduct post-payment reviews to determine that the use of PET scans is consistent with this instruction. PET scan facilities must keep patient record information on file for each Medicare patient for whom a PET scan claim is made. These medical records will be used in any post-payment reviews and must include the information necessary to substantial the need for the PET scan.

4173.5 HCPCS and Modifiers for PET Scans

Providers should use HCPCS codes G0030 through G0047 to indicate the conditions under which a PET scan was done for imaging of the perfusion of the heart. These codes represent the global service, so providers performing just the technical or professional component of the test should use modifier TC or 26, respectively. The following codes should be reported for PET scans used for the imaging of the lungs:

- G0125--PET lung imaging of solitary pulmonary nodules using 2-[fluorine-18]-fluoro-2-deoxy-D-glucose (FDG), following CT (71250/71260 or 71270); or
- G0126--PET lung imaging of solitary pulmonary nodules using 2-[fluorine-18]-fluoro-2-deoxy-D-glucose (FDG), following CT (71250/71260 or 71270); for initial staging of pathologically diagnosed NSCLC.
- G0163--Positron Emission Tomography (PET), whole body, for recurrence of colorectal or colorectal metastatic cancer; or
- G0164--Positron Emission Tomography (PET), whole body, for staging and characterization of lymphoma; or
- G0165--Positron Emission Tomography (PET), whole body, for recurrence of melanoma or melanoma metastic cancer

NOTE: The payment for the radio tracer, or radio pharmaceutical is included in the relative value units of the technical components of the above procedure codes. Do not make any separate payments for these agents for PET scans.

In addition, providers must indicate the results of the PET scan and the previous test using a two digit modifier. (The modifier is not required for technical component-only billings or billings to the intermediary.) The first character should indicate the result of the PET scan; the second character should indicate the results of the prior test. Depending on the procedure codes with which the modifiers are used, the meaning of the modifier will be apparent. The test result modifiers and their descriptions are as follows:

Modifier	Description
N	Negative;
E	Equivocal;
P	Positive, but not suggestive of , extensive ischemia or not suggestive of malignant single pulmonary nodule; and
S	Positive and suggestive of; extensive ischemia (greater than 20 percent of the left ventricle) or malignant single pulmonary nodule.

These modifiers may be used in any combination.

4173.6 Claims Processing Instructions for PET Scan Claims

A. FDA Approval — PET scans are covered only when performed at a PET imaging center with a PET scanner that has been approved or cleared by the FDA. When submitting the claim, the provider is certifying this and must be able to produce a copy of this approval upon request. An official approval letter need not be submitted with the claim.

You may consider conducting a review on a post-payment basis to verify, based on a sample of PET scan claims, that the PET scan was performed at a center with a PET scanner which was approved or cleared for marketing.

B. EOMB and Remittance Messages — Providers must indicate the results of the PET scan and the previous test using a two-digit modifier as specified in §4173.4. Deny assigned claims received prior to April 1, 1996 without such modifier, using the following EOMB message:

"Your service was denied because information required to make payment was missing. We have asked your provider to resubmit a claim with the missing information so that it may be reprocessed." (Message 9.33)

Deny unassigned claims received prior to April 1, 1996, without the two-digit modifier using the following EOMB message:

"Medicare cannot pay for this service because the claim is missing information/documentation. Please ask your provider to submit a new, complete claim to us." (Messages 9.8 and 9.15)

Claims received on or after April 1, 1996 without the two-digit modifier must be returned as unprocessable. (See §3005.)

Use the following remittance message for assigned claims:

"The procedure code is inconsistent with the modifier used, or a required modifier is missing." (Reason Code 4)

Assigned claims for dates of service on or after January 1, 1998 without the proper documentation must be denied using the following EOMB message:

"Your service was denied because information required to make payment was missing. We have asked your provider to resubmit a claim with the missing information so that it may be reprocessed." (Message 9.33)

C. Type of Service — The type of service for the PET scan codes in the "G" range is 4, Diagnostic Radiology.

NEW PROCEDURES--EFFECTIVE DATE: Dates of Service on and after January 1, 1998

Section 4173, Positron Emission Tomography (PET) Scans, has been updated to include coverage of PET Scans for the characterization of solitary pulmonary nodules and for the initial staging of lung cancer, conditioned upon its ability to effect the management and treatment of patients with either suspected or demonstrated lung cancer.

Section 4173.1, Conditions for Medicare Coverage of PET Scans for Noninvasive Imaging of the Perfusion of the Heart, provides specific conditions for PET Scans for noninvasive imaging of the perfusion of the heart for the diagnosis and management of patients with known or suspected coronary artery disease.

Section 4173.2, Conditions of Coverage of PET Scans for Characterization of Solitary Pulmonary Nodules (SPNs) and PET Scans Using FDG to Initially Stage Lung Cancer, provides that the conditions and limitations of this coverage are contained in CIM §50-36.

Section 4173.3, Billing requirements for PET Scans, provides specific instructions for providers to use when billing for PET Scans. Submission of claims data/documentation is necessary.

Section 4173.4, HCPCS and Modifiers for PET Scans, lists the new HCPCS codes for providers to use when reporting PET Scans for the imaging of the lungs. Previous PET Scan modifiers have been revised so that they can also be used for lung PET Scans.

Section 4173.5, Claims Processing Instructions for PET Scan Claims, has been revised to include processing instructions for lung PET scans.

4182. PROSTATE CANCER SCREENING TESTS AND PROCEDURES

The following sections summarize coverage requirements and detail claims processing procedures for prostate cancer screening tests and procedures.

4182.1 Coverage Summary

Sections 1861(s)(2)(P) and 1861(oo) of the Social Security Act (as added by §4103 of the Balanced Budget Act of 1997), provide for coverage of certain prostate cancer screening tests and procedures subject to certain coverage, frequency, and payment limitations. Effective for services furnished on or after January 1, 2000, Medicare will cover prostate cancer screening tests and procedures for the early detection of prostate cancer. Coverage currently consists of the following tests and procedures furnished to an individual for the early detection of prostate cancer:

A. Screening Digital Rectal Examination — This test is a clinical examination of an individual's prostate for nodules or other abnormalities of the prostate; and

B. Screening Prostate Specific Antigen (PSA) Blood Test — This test detects the marker for adenocarcinoma of the prostate.

For more information regarding coverage of prostate cancer screening tests and procedures, refer to §50-55 of the Coverage Issues Manual.

4182.2 Requirements for Submitting Claims

Submit claims for prostate cancer screening tests on Health Insurance Claim Form HCFA-1500 or electronic equivalent. Follow the general instructions in §2010, Purpose of Health Insurance Claim Form HCFA-1500, Medicare Carriers Manual, Part 4, Chapter 2.

4182.3 HCPCS Codes and Payment Requirements

The following table lists coverable codes and services for prostate cancer screening tests and procedures. Pay for these services according to the appropriate fee schedule when all of the requirements noted are met.

4182.4 Calculating the Frequency

Once a beneficiary has received any (or all) of the covered prostate cancer screening test/procedures, he may receive another (or all) of such test/procedures after 11 full months have passed. To determine the 11-month period, start your count beginning with the month after the month in which any (or all) of the previous covered screening test/procedures was performed.

EXAMPLE: The beneficiary received a screening PSA test in January 2000. Start your count beginning February 2000. The beneficiary is eligible to receive another screening PSA test in January 2001 (the month after 11 months have passed.)

4182.5 CWF Edits

Effective for dates of service January 1, 2000, and later, CWF will edit prostate cancer screening tests and procedures for age, frequency, sex, and valid HCPCS code.

4273. CLAIMS FOR PAYMENT FOR EPOETIN ALFA (EPO)

Effective June 1, 1989, the drug EPO is covered under Part B if administered incident to a physician's services. EPO is used to treat anemia associated with chronic renal failure, including patients on dialysis and those who are not on dialysis.

4273.1 Completion of Initial Claim for EPO

The following information is required. Due to space limitations, some items must be documented on a separate form. Therefore, initial claims are generally submitted on paper unless your electronic billers are able to submit supplemental documentation with EMC claims. Return incomplete assigned claims in accordance with §3311. Develop incomplete unassigned claims.

A. Diagnoses — The diagnoses must be submitted according to ICD-9-CM and correlated to the procedure. This information is in Items 23A and 24D, of the Form HCFA-1500.

B. Hematocrit (HCT)/Hemoglobin (Hgb) — There are special HCPCS codes for reporting the injection of EPO. These allow the simultaneous reporting of the patient's latest HCT or Hgb reading before administration of EPO.

Instruct the physician and/or staff to enter a separate line item for injections of EPO at different HCT/Hgb levels. The Q code for each line items is entered in Item 24C.

1. Code Q9920 - Injection of EPO, per 1,000 units, at patient HCT of 20 or less/Hgb of 6.8 or less.

2. Codes Q9921 through Q9939 - Injection of EPO, per 1,000 units, at patient HCT of 21 to 39/Hgb of 6.9 to 13.1. For HCT levels of 21 or more, up to a HCT of 39/Hgb of 6.9 to 13.1, a Q code that includes the actual HCT levels is used. To convert actual Hgb to corresponding HCT values for Q code reporting, multiply the Hgb value by 3 and round to the nearest whole number. Use the whole number to determine the appropriate Q code.

EXAMPLES: If the patient's HCT is 25/Hgb is 8.2-8.4, Q9925 must be entered on the claim. If the patient's HCT is 39/Hgb is 12.9-13.1, Q9939 is entered.

3. Code Q9940 - Injection of EPO, per 1,000 units at patient HCT of 40 or above.

A single line item may include multiple doses of EPO administered while the patient's HCT level remained the same.

C. Units Administered — The standard unit of EPO is 1,000. The number of 1,000 units administered per line item is included on the claim. The physician's office enters 1 in the units field for each multiple of 1,000 units. For example, if 12,000 units are administered, 12 is entered. This information is shown in Item 24F (Days/Units) on Form HCFA-1500.

In some cases, the dosage for a single line item does not total an even multiple of 1,000. If this occurs, the physician's office rounds down supplemental dosages of 0 to 499 units to the prior 1,000 units. Supplemental dosages of 500 to 999 are rounded up to the next 1,000 units.

EXAMPLES: A patient's HCT reading on August 6 was 22/Hgb was 7.3. The patient received 5,000 units of EPO on August 7, August 9 and August 11, for a total of 15,000 units. The first line of Item 24 of Form HCFA-1500 shows:

Dates of Service	Procedure Code	Days or Units
8/7-8/11	Q9922	15

On September 13, the patient's HCT reading increased to 27/Hgb increased to 9. The patient received 5,100 units of EPO on September 13, September 15, and September 17, for a total of 15,300 units. Since less than 15,500 units were given, the figure is rounded down to 15,000. This line on the claim form shows:

Dates of Service	Procedure Code	Days or Units
8/7-8/11	Q9922	15
9/13-9/17	Q9927	15

On October 16, the HCT level increased to 33/Hgb increased to 11. The patient received doses of 4,850 units on October 16, October 18, and October 20 for a total of 14,550 units. Since more than 14,500 units were administered, the figure is rounded up to 15,000. Form HCFA-1500 shows:

Dates of Service	Procedure Code	Days or Units
10/16-10/20	Q9933	15

D. Date of the patient's most recent HCT or Hgb.

E. Most recent HCT or Hgb level prior to initiation of EPO therapy.

F. Date of most recent HCT or Hgb level prior to initiation of EPO therapy.

G. Patient's most recent serum creatinine, within the last month, prior to initiation of EPO therapy.

H. Date of most recent serum creatinine prior to initiation of EPO therapy.

I. Patient's weight in kilograms.

J. Patient's starting dose per kilogram. (The usual starting dose is 50-100 units per kilogram.)

When a claim is submitted on Form HCFA-1500, these items are submitted on a separate document. It is not necessary to enter them into your claims processing system. This information is used in utilization review.

4450. PARENTERAL AND ENTERAL NUTRITION (PEN)

PEN coverage is determined by information provided by the attending physician and the PEN supplier. A certification of medical necessity (CMN) contains pertinent information needed to ensure consistent coverage and payment determinations nationally. A completed CMN must accompany and support the claims for PEN to establish whether coverage criteria are met and to ensure that the PEN provided is consistent with the attending physician's prescription.

The medical and prescription information on a PEN CMN can be completed most appropriately by the attending physician, or from information in the patient's records by an employee of the physician for the physician's review and signature. Although PEN suppliers may assist in providing PEN items they cannot complete the CMN since they do not have the same access to patient information needed to properly enter medical or prescription information.

A. Scheduling and Documenting Certifications and Recertifications of Medical Necessity for PEN — A PEN CMN must accompany the initial claim submitted. The initial certification is valid for three months. Establish the schedule on a case-by-case basis for recertifying the need for PEN therapy. A change in prescription for a beneficiary past the initial certification period does not restart the certification process. A period of medical necessity ends when PEN is not medically required for two consecutive months. The entire certification process, if required, begins after the period of two consecutive months have elapsed.

B. Initial Certifications — In reviewing the claim and the supporting data on the CMN, compare certain items, especially pertinent dates of treatment. For example, the start date of PEN coverage cannot precede the date of physician certification. The estimated duration of therapy must be contained on the CMN. Use this information to verify that the test of permanence is met. Once coverage is established, the estimated length of need at the start of PEN services will determine the recertification schedule. (See §4450 A.)

Verify that the information shown on the certification supports the need for PEN supplies as billed. A diagnosis must show a functional impairment that precludes the enteral patient from swallowing and the parenteral patient from absorbing nutrients.

The attending physician and/or his/her designated employee are in a position to accurately complete the patient's medical information including:

- The patient's general condition, estimated duration of therapy, and other treatments or therapies (see §3329 B.2.);
- The patient's clinical assessment relating to the need for PEN therapy (see §3329 B.3.); and
- The nutritional support therapy (i.e., the enteral or parenteral formulation). (See §3329 B.4.)

Initial assigned claims with the following conditions can be denied without development:

- Inappropriate or missing diagnosis or functional impairment;
- Estimated duration of therapy is less than 90 consecutive days;
- Duration of therapy is not listed;
- Supplies have not been provided;
- Supplies were provided prior to onset date of therapy; and
- Stamped physician's signature.

Develop unassigned claims for missing or incomplete information. (See §3329 C.)

Review all claims with initial certifications and recertifications before payment is authorized.

C. Revised Certifications/Change in Prescription — Remind suppliers to submit revised certifications if the attending physician changes the PEN prescription. A revised certification is appropriate when:

- There is a change in the attending physician's orders in the category of nutrients and/or calories prescribed;
- There is a change by more than one liter in the daily volume of parenteral solutions;
- There is a change from home-mix to pre-mix or pre-mix to home-mix parenteral solutions;
- There is a change from enteral to parenteral or parenteral to enteral therapy; or
- There is a change in the method of infusion (e.g., from gravity-fed to pump-fed).

Do not adjust payments on PEN claims unless a revised or renewed certification documents the necessity for the change. Adjust payments timely, if necessary, for supplies since the PEN prescription was changed.

Do not exceed payment levels for the most current certification or recertification if a prescription change is not documented by a new recertification.

Adjust your diary for scheduled recertifications. When the revised certification has been considered, reschedule the next recertification according to the recertification schedule. (See § 4450 A.)

D. Items Requiring Special Attention

1. Nutrients — Category IB of enteral nutrients contains products that are natural intact protein/protein isolates commonly known as blenderized nutrients. Additional documentation is required to justify the necessity of Category IB nutrients. The attending physician must provide sufficient information to indicate that the patient:

- Has an intolerance to nutritionally equivalent (semi-synthetic) products;
- Had a severe allergic reaction to a nutritionally equivalent (semi-synthetic) product; or
- Was changed to a blenderized nutrient to alleviate adverse symptoms expected to be of permanent duration with continued use of semi-synthetic products.

Also, enteral nutrient categories III through VI require additional medical justification for coverage.

Parenteral nutrition may be either "self-mixed" (i.e., the patient is taught to prepare the nutrient solution aseptically) or "pre-mixed" (i.e., the nutrient solution is prepared by trained professionals employed or contracted by the PEN supplier). The attending physician must provide information to justify the reason for "pre-mixed" parenteral nutrient solutions.

2. Prospective Billing — Pay for no more than a one-month supply of parenteral or enteral nutrients for any one prospective billing period. Claims submitted retroactively may include multiple months.

3. Pumps — Enteral nutrition may be administered by syringe, gravity, or pump. The attending physician must specify the reason that necessitates the use of an enteral feeding pump. Ensure that the equipment for which payment is claimed is consistent with that prescribed (e.g., expect a claim for an I.V. pole, if a pump is used).

Effective April 1, 1990, claims for parenteral and enteral pumps are limited to rental payments for a total of 15 months during a period of medical need. A period of medical need ends when enteral or parenteral nutrients are not medically necessary for two consecutive months.

Do not allow additional rental payments once the 15-month limit is reached, unless the attending physician changes the prescription between parenteral and enteral nutrients.

Do not continue rental payments after a pump is purchased unless the attending physician changes the prescription between parenteral and enteral nutrients.

Do not begin a new 15-month rental period when a patient changes suppliers. The new supplier is entitled to the balance remaining on the 15-month rental period.

Effective October 1, 1990, necessary maintenance and servicing of pumps after the 15-month rental limit is reached, includes repairs and extensive maintenance that involves the breaking down of sealed components or performing tests that require specialized testing equipment not available to the beneficiary or nursing home.

    4. Supplies — Enteral care kits contain all the necessary supplies for the enteral patient using the syringe, gravity, or pump method of nutrient administration. Parenteral nutrition care kits and their components are considered all inclusive items necessary to administer therapy during a monthly period.

Compare the enteral feeding care kits on the claim with the method of administration indicated on the CMN.

- Reduce the allowance to the amount paid for a gravity-fed care kit when billed for a pump feeding kit in the absence of documentation or unacceptable documentation for a pump.
- Limit payment to a one-month supply.
- Deny payment for additional components included as part of the PEN supply kit.

    5. Attending Physician Identification — A CMN must contain the attending physician's Unique Physician Identification Number (UPIN) and be signed and dated by the attending physician. A stamped signature is unacceptable.

Deny certifications and recertifications altered by "whiting out" or "pasting over" and entering new data. Consider suppliers that show a pattern of altering CMNs for educational contact and/or audit.

Be alert to certifications from suppliers who have questionable utilization or billing practices or who are under sanction. Consider an audit of any such situations.

5114. PAYMENT FOR DIAGNOSTIC LABORATORY SERVICES

This section sets out payment rules for diagnostic laboratory services, i.e., (1) outpatient clinical diagnostic laboratory tests subject to the fee schedule, and (2) other diagnostic laboratory tests. Regardless of whether a diagnostic laboratory test is performed in a physician's office, by an independent laboratory, or by a hospital laboratory for its outpatients or nonpatients, it is considered a laboratory service. When a hospital laboratory performs diagnostic laboratory tests for nonhospital patients, the laboratory is functioning as an independent laboratory. Also, when physicians and laboratories perform the same test, whether manually or with automated equipment, the services are deemed similar.

The laboratory services for which this instruction applies are those listed in §2070.1.D. The tests are not subject to the economic index under the guidelines in §5020.3.A. Any test not listed in §2070.1.D is considered a physicians' service, is subject to the economic index as described in §5020.3.A, and is not considered in implementing this instruction. The only exceptions are as specified in §5020.3.A. For example, the taking of an EKG is a laboratory service when billed separately; but an EKG interpretation alone, as well as the taking of an EKG billed with interpretation, is a physician service subject to the economic index. Similarly, clinical laboratory services not subject to the fee schedule (see §5114.1) included in office visits for which a single prevailing charge screen is maintained are subject to the economic index.

Clinical diagnostic laboratory tests subject to the fee schedule are specifically delineated in §5114.1.B.

Other diagnostic laboratory tests are laboratory tests other than clinical diagnostic laboratory tests subject to fee schedule reimbursement. Such tests include EKGs and physiological testing.

Payment for clinical diagnostic laboratory tests subject to the fee schedule is made in accordance with the instructions in §5114.1.

Generally, payment for other diagnostic laboratory tests is made in accordance with the reasonable charge methodology. Special payment rules for physicians who do not personally perform or supervise other diagnostic laboratory tests but who bill for such tests are referenced in §5258. In accordance with §5262, payment for diagnostic radiology tests is made on a fee schedule basis.

5114.1 Payment for Outpatient Clinical Diagnostic Laboratory Tests Using Fee Schedules and for Specimen Collection

Under Part B, for services rendered on or after July 1, 1984, clinical diagnostic laboratory tests performed in a physician's office, by an independent laboratory, or by a hospital laboratory for its outpatients are reimbursed on the basis of fee schedules.

The fee schedules are established on a carrierwide basis (not to exceed a statewide basis). National fee schedules may be established beginning

January 1, 1990.

The lowest charge level provisions no longer apply to clinical diagnostic laboratory tests. In addition, §5100.2.C no longer applies. This section provides that laboratory tests furnished to CAPD End Stage Renal Disease (ESRD) patients dialyzing at home are billed in the same way as any other test furnished home patients. The reasonable charge criteria were used for tests performed by an independent laboratory for the home patient. Since clinical diagnostic laboratory tests are no longer paid in accordance with the reasonable charge criteria, the fee schedule now applies to laboratory tests performed for the home ESRD dialysis patient described in §5100.2.C when the tests are not covered under the ESRD composite rate.

    A. Application of Fee Schedule — The fee schedule applies to all clinical diagnostic laboratory tests except:

- laboratory tests furnished to a hospital inpatient whose stay is covered under Part A. Laboratory tests provided by a hospital for an inpatient of such hospital that are payable under Part B (due to lack of Part A coverage) continue to be reimbursed on a reasonable cost basis.
- laboratory tests performed by a SNF for its own SNF inpatients and reimbursed under Part A or Part B; and any laboratory tests furnished under arrangements to a SNF inpatient with Part A coverage. Continue to reimburse such tests on a reasonable cost basis. All other tests furnished by a laboratory other than the SNF's own are reimbursable only to the laboratory under the fee schedule. Therefore, laboratory tests for SNF inpatients without Part A coverage are no longer reimbursed to the SNF under arrangements.
- laboratory tests furnished by hospital-based or independent ESRD dialysis facilities that are included under the ESRD composite rate payment. (See §4270 for discussion of laboratory tests included in composite rate payment.) These tests are reimbursed only through this payment and you never pay anyone else for these tests. Laboratory tests that are not included under the ESRD composite rate payment and are performed by an independent laboratory for dialysis patients of independent dialysis facilities are billed to you and paid at the fee schedule. This procedure applies to all laboratory tests furnished to home dialysis patients who have selected payment Method II. (See §4271.)
- laboratory tests furnished by hospitals in States or areas which have been granted demonstration waivers of Medicare reimbursement principles for outpatient services. The State of Maryland has been granted such demonstration waivers. This also may apply to hospitals in States granted approval for alternative payment methods for paying for hospital outpatient services under §1886(c) of the Act.
- laboratory tests furnished to inpatients of a hospital with a waiver under §602(k) of the 1983 Amendments to the Act. (See §2255.) This section of the Act provides that an outside supplier may bill under Part B for laboratory and other nonphysician services furnished to inpatients that are otherwise paid only though the hospital. Part B payment to the outside supplier for laboratory tests furnished to inpatients under the 602(k) waiver is made at 80 percent of the reasonable charge if the claim is unassigned or at 100 percent of the reasonable charge if the claim is assigned. The fee schedule does apply to any tests furnished by the outside supplier to hospital outpatients and to nonhospital patients.
- laboratory tests furnished to patients of rural health clinics under an all inclusive rate.
- laboratory tests provided by a participating health maintenance organization (HMO) or health care prepayment plan (HCPP) to an enrolled member of the plan.
- laboratory test furnished by a hospice.

B. Clinical Diagnostic Laboratory Services Subject to Fee Schedule — For purposes of the fee schedule, clinical diagnostic laboratory services include laboratory tests listed in codes 80002-89399 of the Current Procedural Terminology, Fourth Edition (CPT-4), 1991 printing. Certain tests, however, are required to be performed by a physician and are therefore exempt from the fee schedule. These tests include:

80500-80502	Clinical pathology consultation
85095-85109	Codes dealing with bone marrow smears and biopsies
86077-86079	Blood bank services
88000-88125	Certain cytopathology services
88160-88199	Certain cytopathology services
88300-88399	Surgical pathology services

Some CPT-4 codes in the 80000 series are not clinical diagnostic laboratory tests. Such codes include codes for procedures, services, blood products and autotransfusions. Other codes for tests primarily associated with the provision of blood products are also not considered clinical diagnostic tests.

These codes include the various blood crossmatching techniques. The following codes are never subject to fee schedule limitations:

85060	86070	86595
86012	86100	89100–89105
86013	86120	89130–89141
86016–86019	86128	89350
86024	86130	89360
86034	86265–86267	86068
86455–86585		

The following codes are not subject to fee schedule limitations when they are submitted for payment on the same bill with charges for blood products:

86011	86080	86014
86082–86095	86031–86033	86105

If no blood product is provided and billed on the same claim, these codes are subject to the fee schedule.

The following codes that delineate allergy, organ or disease oriented panels/profiles are not currently subject to the national limitation amounts because laboratories do not always utilize the same array or number of tests in a particular panel. However, the national limitation amount applies to each test included in the panel/profile. (See §§5114.1.F and 5114.1.G.)

80050–80099   86421–86422

Know which individual tests have been performed when claims are received using panel/profile codes. This does not need to be reported on each bill as long as you are confident that every laboratory reporting a panel or profile uses a consistent set of tests. If there is variation in content of the panel or profile, establish a uniform definition and require laboratories that do not comply with this definition to identify the individual tests when billing the panel or profile.

The following codes for unlisted or not otherwise classified clinical diagnostic laboratory tests are not subject to the national limitation amounts.

81099	87999	84999
88299	85999	89399
86999		

Please note that for purposes of the fee schedule, clinical diagnostic laboratory tests include some services described as anatomic pathology services in CPT-4 (i.e., certain cervical, vaginal, or peripheral blood smears). Use the CPT-4 code 85060 only when a physician interprets an abnormal peripheral blood smear for a hospital inpatient or a hospital outpatient, and the hospital is responsible for the technical component. When a physician interpretation of an abnormal peripheral blood smear is billed by an independent laboratory, it is considered a complete or global service, and the service is not billed under the CPT-4 code 85060. A physician interpretation of an abnormal peripheral blood smear performed by an independent laboratory is considered a routine part of the ordered hematology service (i.e., those tests that include a different white blood count).

HCPCS code 88150 (cervical or vaginal smears) included both screening and interpretation in CPT-4 1986 terminology while the CPT-4 1987 terminology includes only screening. A new code, 88151, was added for those smears which require physician interpretation. Code 88151 is treated and priced in the same manner as you previously treated code 88150. Code 88151 with a "26" modifier is paid when a physician performs an interpretation of an abnormal smear for a hospital inpatient or outpatient, and the hospital is responsible for the technical component. No longer recognize the "26" modifier for code 88150. Price code 88151(26) as you would have priced code 88150(26) if the coding terminology had not been revised. Independent laboratories bill under code 88150 for normal smears and under code 88151 for abnormal smears. However, the fee schedule amount is equivalent.

Certain blood gas levels are determined either by invasive means through use of a blood specimen for a clinical diagnostic laboratory test or by noninvasive means through ear or pulse oximetry which is not considered a clinical diagnostic laboratory test. Use CPT-4 code 82792 for invasive oximetry. Use HCPCS code M0592 for ear and pulse oximetry. Code M0592 is not subject to fee schedules. (See Coverage Issues Manual, §60-4C, for coverage requirements and Medicare Carriers Manual §5246.6 for pricing consideration.)

Services excluded from the fee schedule when billed by an independent laboratory are reimbursable under existing reasonable charge rules and assignment may be taken on a case-by-case basis unless the laboratory enrolls as a participating supplier in which event assignment is mandatory. Where a service is performed by a physician for a hospital inpatient or outpatient and meets the definition of a physician service under §8318-B, the service is subject to the Medicare Economic Index and the limitation on physician fees under §9331 of the Omnibus Budget Reconciliation Act of 1986. Such service, however, when billed by an independent laboratory as a laboratory service for a nonhospital patient (e.g., surgical pathology) is not considered a physician service for purposes of the Medicare Economic Index or the limitation on physician fees.

C. Calculation of Fee Schedule Amounts — Set the fee schedule amounts at 60 percent of the prevailing charges for laboratory tests performed in physicians' offices by independent laboratories and for laboratory tests performed by hospital laboratories for nonhospital patients for the fee screen year beginning July 1, 1984. For hospital outpatient laboratory tests, the fee schedule amount is established at 62 percent of the prevailing charges. Beginning January 1, 1987, the fee schedule amount of 62 percent is paid for outpatient laboratory services only if provided by a qualified hospital laboratory, as described below. Beginning April 1, 1988, the fee schedule amount of 62 percent is payable only in a qualified hospital laboratory located in a sole community hospital. For this purpose, a qualified hospital laboratory is one which provides some clinical diagnostic laboratory tests 24 hours a day, 7 days a week, in order to serve a hospital's emergency room which is available to provide services 24 hours a day, 7 days week. To meet this requirement, a hospital must have physicians physically present or available within 30 minutes through a medical staff call roster to handle emergencies 24 hours a day, 7 days a week. Hospital laboratory personnel must be on duty or on call at all times to provide testing for the emergency room.

The prevailing charge is calculated as the 75th percentile of the customary charges, weighted by frequency, that were determined for the fee screen year beginning on July 1, 1984, for both physicians and independent laboratories (including hospital laboratories acting as independent laboratories) in (1) your existing service area or (2) no more than one State where your service area includes more than one entire State. In several instances, e.g., Kansas City and Washington, D.C. metropolitan areas, the area of a carrier includes portions of more than one State and that area is used in determining the prevailing charge.

Effective April 1, 1988, the fee schedules for certain automated tests, and for tests (with the exception of cytopathology) that were subject to the lowest charge level (LCL) provision prior to July 1, 1984, are adjusted in accordance with §5114.1.F.

Any rounding of initial fee schedule amounts is handled in the same manner as rounding for the application of the Medicare Economic Index. (See §5021.)

Where a hospital laboratory acts as an independent laboratory, i.e., performs tests for persons who are nonhospital patients or, where, commencing January 1, 1987, the hospital laboratory is not a qualified hospital laboratory, the services are reimbursed using the 60 percent of prevailing charge fee schedule or the adjusted fee schedule (see §5114.1.F), as appropriate. A hospital outpatient is a person who has not been admitted by the hospital as an inpatient but is registered on the hospital records as an outpatient and receives services (rather than supplies alone) from the hospital. Where a tissue sample, blood sample, or specimen is taken by personnel who are not employed by the hospital and is sent to the hospital for performance of tests, the tests are not outpatient hospital services since the patient does not directly receive services from the hospital. Where the hospital uses the category "day patient," i.e., an individual who receives hospital services during the day and is not expected to be lodged in the hospital at midnight, the individual is classified as an outpatient.

The fee schedule amounts are adjusted annually to reflect changes in the Consumer Price Index (CPI) for all Urban Consumers (U.S. city average). For laboratory tests performed on or after July 1, 1985 through December 31, 1986, the fee schedules are increased 4.1 percent. Beginning January 1, 1987, CPI adjustments are made January 1 of each year instead of July 1. The annualized index changes are as follows:

FSY	Annual Adjustment by Percent
1986	4.1
1987	5.4
1988	0
1989	4.0
1990	4.7
1991	2.0
1992	2.0
1993	2.0

Information regarding the index changes for subsequent periods is furnished to you in time to make the necessary adjustments. In applying the annual adjustment, round calculations to the nearest penny.

The provisions in §5020.3.A provide for using the economic index to limit the prevailing charges for office visits combined with clinical laboratory tests for which you maintained a single prevailing charge screen. Since clinical diagnostic laboratory tests are no longer paid on the basis of the customary and prevailing charge criteria, do not allow the combination of laboratory tests with the physician's office visit in one prevailing charge. The fee schedule is used in determining the payment amount allowed for the laboratory tests, and the regular reasonable charge criteria and economic index are used for the office visit.

The codes and terminology in HCPCS are used in the fee schedule to identify and describe the laboratory tests. If you have not yet converted your coding systems to HCPCS, identify the equivalent tests in your own systems and use HCPCS codes for those services in establishing the fee schedules.

D. Specimen Collection Fee — Separate charges made by physicians (except for services furnished to dialysis patients as indicated below), independent laboratories (except for services furnished to dialysis patients as indicated below), or hospital laboratories for drawing or collecting specimens are allowed up to $3 whether the specimens are referred to physicians or other laboratories for testing. This fee is not paid to anyone who has not actually extracted the specimen from the patient. Only one collection fee is allowed for each patient encounter, regardless of the number of specimens drawn. When a series of specimens is required to complete a single test (e.g., glucose tolerance test), the series is treated as a single encounter. A specimen collection fee is allowed in circumstances such as drawing a blood sample through venipuncture (i.e., inserting into a vein a needle with syringe or vacutainer to draw the specimen) or collecting a urine sample by catheterization.

A specimen collection fee for physicians is allowed only when (1) it is the accepted and prevailing practice among physicians in the locality to make separate charges for drawing or collecting a specimen, and (2) it is the customary practice of the physician performing such services to bill separate charges for them.

A specimen collection fee is not allowed when the cost of collecting the specimen is minimal, such as a throat culture or a routine capillary puncture for clotting or bleeding time. Stool specimen collection for an occult blood test is usually done by the patients at home, and a fee for such collection is not allowed. When a stool specimen is collected during a rectal examination, the collection is an incidental byproduct of that examination. Costs such as gloves are related to the rectal examination and compensated for in the payment for the visit. Payment for performing the test is separate from the specimen collection fee. Costs such as media (e.g., the slides) and labor are included in the payment for the test.

You no longer have authority to make payment for routine handling charges where a specimen is referred by one laboratory to another. Preparatory services, e.g., where a referring laboratory prepares a specimen before transfer to a reference laboratory, are considered an integral part of the testing process, and the costs of such services are included in the charge for the total testing service.

A specimen collection fee is allowed when it is medically necessary for a laboratory technician to draw a specimen from either a nursing home patient or homebound patient. The technician must personally draw the specimen, e.g., venipuncture or urine sample by catheterization. A specimen collection fee is not allowed in situations where a patient is not in a nursing facility or confined to his or her home. When a laboratory performs the specimen collection, it may receive payment both for the draw and for the associated travel to obtain the specimen(s) for testing. Payment may be made to the laboratory even if the nursing facility has on-duty personnel qualified to perform the specimen collection. When the nursing home performs the specimen collection, it may only receive payment for the draw. Specimen collection performed by nursing home personnel for patients covered under Part A is paid for as part of the facility's payment for its reasonable costs, not on the basis of the specimen collection fee.

Special rules apply when services are furnished to dialysis patients. ESRD facilities are only paid by intermediaries. Therefore, never pay a specimen collection fee to an ESRD facility. The specimen collection fee is not allowed when a physician or one of the physician's employees draws the specimen from the dialysis patient because it is included in the Monthly Capitation Payment (MCP). (See §5037.) Independent laboratories are not paid the specimen collection fee for specimens collected that are used in performing a laboratory test reimbursed under the composite rate. If a home dialysis patient selects reimbursement Method II (see §4271) and all other criteria for payment are met, pay an independent laboratory the specimen collection fee for specimens collected from the patient.

The coinsurance and deductible provisions do not apply to the specimen collection fee where 100 percent of the fee schedule amount is payable on the basis of an assignment to the persons or entities drawing the specimen. For services (including specimen collection) rendered on or after January 1, 1987, payment to laboratories or physicians is only made on the basis of an assignment. For services rendered prior to January 1, 1987, acceptance of an assignment is optional for physicians. However, the coinsurance and deductible is applied to the specimen collection fee where a physician collects the specimen and does not accept assignment.

Complex vascular injection procedures, such as arterial punctures and venesections, are not subject either to this specimen collection policy or to the assignment provisions.

E. Who Can Bill and Receive Payment for Clinical Laboratory Tests

1. General

It is your responsibility to determine whether the laboratory services were performed in the office of the physician or by another laboratory. If they were performed by another laboratory, payment may be made only if the laboratory performed tests in the specialties for which it is certified under the program. (See §2070.1.D.)

When Part B payment for clinical laboratory tests is subject to the fee schedule, payment is only made to the person or entity which performed or supervised the performance of the tests, except as follows:

- Payment may be made to an independent laboratory (if it meets the special conditions below) or hospital laboratory for tests performed by another laboratory on specimens referred to it by the first laboratory. Section 3102.F describes the guidelines regarding jurisdiction for payment of independent laboratory services.

- Payment may be made to one physician for tests performed or supervised by another physician with whom he shares his practice, i.e., where the two physicians are members of a medical group whose physicians bill in their own names rather than in the name of the group. Where the medical group bills in the name of the group for the services of the physician who performed or supervised the performance of these tests, payment is made to the group if the claim is assigned or, for services rendered on or before December 31, 1986, to the beneficiary if the claim is not assigned. See §2070.1 regarding the determination of when a laboratory is considered independent.

- Payment may only be made to the beneficiary, including home dialysis patients under Method II (see §4271), when:

    - For services rendered on or before December 31, 1986, on the basis of an itemized bill of a physician or medical group for tests performed or supervised by that physician or group, where the physician or group is not required to meet the conditions of coverage of an independent laboratory because during any calendar year the physician or medical group performs the tests on less than 100 specimens in any particular category on referral from other physicians not in the same practice; and neither the physician or group has entered into an agreement to be a participating physician or supplier; or

    - On the basis of an itemized bill of a rural health clinic for tests performed for a nonpatient of the clinic where the rural health clinic is not required to meet the conditions of coverage of an independent laboratory because, during any calendar year, the clinic performs tests on less than 100 specimens in a particular category on referral from outside physicians.

Except as noted above, unless a laboratory, physician or medical group accepts assignment, no Part B payment may be made for laboratory tests. Laboratories, physicians or medical groups that have entered into a participation agreement must accept assignment. Effective January 1, 1988, sanctions of double the violative charges, civil money penalties (up to $2,000 per violation) and/or disbarment from the program for a period of up to 5 years may be imposed upon physicians and laboratories with the exception of rural health clinic laboratories who knowingly, willfully, and repeatedly bill patients on an unassigned basis. However, sole community physicians and physicians who are the sole source of an essential specialty in a community are not excluded from the program. Whenever you are notified of a sanction action, follow the procedures contained in §4165 regarding processing of claims after the imposition of a sanction.

For purposes of this section, the term assignment includes assignment in the strict sense of the term as well as the procedure under which payment is made, after the death of the beneficiary, to the person or entity which furnished the service, on the basis of that person's or entity's agreement to accept the approved charge or fee you determine as the full charge or fee for the service.

When payment is made under the above rules to the beneficiary but the beneficiary is deceased, follow §7201 and §A7201. If the beneficiary has a legal guardian or representative payee, follow §7050. If an approved health benefits plan pays for the test on behalf of the beneficiary, follow §7065.

Ordinarily a physician or laboratory does not bill the Medicare program for noncovered tests. However, if the beneficiary (or his representative) contends that a clinical diagnostic laboratory test which a physician or laboratory believes is noncovered may be covered, the physician or laboratory must file a claim that includes the test, to effectuate the beneficiary's right to a determination. The physician or laboratory notes on the claim that he or it believes that the test is noncovered and is including it at the beneficiary's insistence.

Before furnishing a beneficiary a test which the physician or laboratory believes is excluded from coverage as not reasonable and necessary (rather than excluded from coverage as part of a routine physical checkup), the physician or laboratory obtains a statement from the beneficiary (or his representative) that the physician or laboratory has informed him of the noncoverage of the test and that there is a charge for the test. This is needed to protect the physician or laboratory against possible liability for the test under the limitation of liability provision.

2. Special Conditions for Referring Laboratories

In accordance with §6111(b) of OBRA of 1989 as amended by §4154 of OBRA of 1990, a referring laboratory may bill for tests for Medicare beneficiaries performed on or after May 1, 1990, by a reference laboratory only if it meets any one of the following three exceptions:

- The rural hospital exception. The referring laboratory is located in, or is part of, a rural hospital;
- The ownership related exception (formerly, the subsidiary related exception). The referring laboratory and reference laboratory are ownership related. That is:
  - The referring laboratory is wholly-owned by the reference laboratory; or
  - The referring laboratory wholly owns the reference laboratory; or
  - Both the referring laboratory and the reference laboratory are wholly-owned subsidiaries of the same entity; or
- The 30 percent exception
  - For services rendered from May 1, 1990 through April 30, 1991, no more than 30 percent of the clinical diagnostic laboratory tests billed annually by the referring laboratory may be performed by another laboratory other than an ownership related laboratory.
  - For services rendered on or after January 1, 1991, no more than 30 percent of the clinical diagnostic laboratory tests for which the referring laboratory receives requests annually may be performed by another laboratory, other than an ownership related laboratory described above.

  EXAMPLE: A laboratory receives requests for 200 tests, performs 70 tests, and refers 130 tests to a non-related laboratory. The laboratory bills Medicare for the 70 tests it performed and 30 of the tests it referred. Before January 1, 1991, the laboratory would have met the 30 percent exception. Since only the referred tests that the laboratory billed itself would have been counted, no more than 30 percent of the tests (30/100) are counted, and the laboratory may receive Medicare payment for the tests for which it bills. However, under the amended rule, all referred tests are counted. Thus, 65 percent (130/200) of the tests are considered referred tests and, since this exceeds the 30 percent standard, the laboratory may not bill for any referred tests for Medicare beneficiaries.

  Effective with services rendered on or after January 1, 1991, deny bills from a referring laboratory for tests performed by a reference laboratory unless you are informed in writing by the referring laboratory that it meets one of the exceptions.

  If it is later found that a referring laboratory does not, in fact, meet an exception criterion recoup payment for the referred tests improperly billed. For services rendered between January 1, 1991 and April 30, 1991, there is a date overlap in the criteria for a referring laboratory to meet the 30 percent exception. Therefore, payments made to referring laboratories for referred tests performed between January 1, 1991 and April 30, 1991 are subject to recoupment if the referring laboratory fails to meet either of the 30 percent criteria.

  NOTE: This provision of §6111(b) of OBRA of 1989 has no effect on hospitals that are paid under §1833(h)(5)(A)(iii).

F. Adjusted Fee Schedule — Beginning April 1, 1988, the 1987 fee schedules for automated tests, and for tests (with the exception of cytopathology) that were subject to the LCL provision prior to July 1, 1984, are reduced by 8.3 percent. To determine the adjusted fee schedules, multiply the 1987 fee schedules by .9170 (100 percent of the 1987 fee schedule minus 8.3 percent).

The automated tests subject to the adjusted fee schedules tests are listed in codes 80002-80019 of the 1990 printing of the CPT-4.

The adjusted fee schedules also apply to the following tests that were subject to the LCL provision prior to the establishment of the fee schedule methodology. The current CPT-4 codes are provided.

Test	1989 CPT-4 Code
Cholesterol, Serum	82465
Complete Blood Count	85022
	85031
Hemoglobin	85018
Hematocrit	85014
Prothrombin Time	85610
Sedimentation Rate (ESR)	85650
	85651
Glucose	82947
	82948
Urinalysis	81000*
Blood Uric Acid	84550
Blood Urea Nitrogen	84520
White Blood Cell Count	85048

*If 81002 and 81015 are both billed, pay as though the combined service (81000) had been billed.

Where these adjusted fee schedule tests are part of allergy, disease or organ panels/profiles, you must assure that your fee for the panel/profile does not exceed the sum of the fees for the individual components after accounting for the reductions due to the adjustment.

G. National Limitation Amount — The Consolidated Omnibus Budget Reconciliation Act (COBRA) requires national limitation amounts to be applied to the payments for outpatient clinical diagnostic laboratory services. For services rendered on or after July 1, 1986 and before April 1, 1988, the national limitation amount is 115 percent of the median of all the fee schedules established for a test for each laboratory code (separately calculated for 60 and 62 percent fee schedules). HCFA furnished you a tape file of these initial national limitation amounts for each HCPCS code for both the 60 and 62 percent fee schedules. For laboratory tests performed on or after January 1, 1987 through March 31, 1988, the initial national limitation amounts are increased by 5.4 percent and the result is the 1987 national limitation amount.

For laboratory tests performed on or after April 1, 1988 and before January 1, 1990, the national limitation amount is 100 percent of the median of all the fee schedules established for a test for each laboratory code (separately calculated for 60 and 62 percent fee schedules). The 100 percent national limitation amount for automated tests and tests formerly subject to the LCL limit, is determined by reducing the current national limitation amount by 8.3 percent (i.e., by multiplying the national limitation by .9170) and multiplying this result by .8696 (100 percent divided by 115 percent). In a single step computation, the 1987 national limitation amount is multiplied by .7974 (.9170 x .8696). For all other tests, the 100 percent national limitation amount is determined by multiplying the 1987 national limitation amount by .8696 (100 percent divided by 115 percent). Each HCFA regional office has a listing of the computed 1988 national limitation amounts which is available to you.

For laboratory tests performed on or after January 1, 1990 and before January 1, 1991, the national limitation amount is 93 percent of the median of all the fee schedules established for a test for each laboratory code (separately calculated for 60 and 62 percent fee schedules).

For laboratory tests performed on or after January 1, 1991, the national limitation amount is 88 percent of the median of all the fee schedules established for a test for each laboratory code (separately calculated for 60 and 62 percent fee schedules).

Currently, no specific national limitation amounts apply to allergy, organ, or disease oriented panels/profiles. However, the individual tests that comprise such panels are subject to the national limitation and where applicable, to the adjusted fee schedule. Ensure that the payment allowance for the panel/profile, therefore, does not exceed the lower of (1) the sum of the applicable fee schedule amounts (or national limitation amounts, if lower) for the individual tests included in the panel/profile, or (2) the sum of the fee schedule amount you have established for the panel/profile.

You are responsible for applying the national limitations in calculating your payment allowances. The national limitation amounts are computed to the nearest cent. Do not round in applying these limits. Do not use the national limitation amounts to fill gaps in your prevailing charge screens for clinical laboratory tests. Establish a fee schedule for each HCPCS code that requires gap filling and then apply the national limitation amount.

H. Summary of Payment Rules for Clinical Diagnostic Laboratory Tests — The following rules apply in determining the amount of Part B payment for clinical laboratory tests:

- For tests performed by an independent laboratory, by a hospital or SNF laboratory (for a nonpatient of the hospital or SNF), or by a physician or medical group, the payment is the lesser of the actual charge, the fee schedule amount or the national limitation amount and the Part B deductible and coinsurance do not apply.

- If payment is made to a hospital for tests furnished for an outpatient of that hospital, the payment is the lesser of the actual charge, the fee schedule amount, or the national limitation amount and Part B deductible and coinsurance do not apply.

- For tests performed by a reference laboratory, the payment is the lesser of the actual charge by the billing laboratory, the fee schedule amount or the national limitation amount. Existing carrier jurisdiction rules apply. Part B deductible and coinsurance do not apply.
- If payment is made to a beneficiary for services prior to January 1, 1987 (see §5114.1.E.3) on the basis of an unassigned itemized bill from a physician, medical group or rural health clinic, the payment is 80 percent of the lesser of the fee schedule, the actual charge or the national limitation amount and Part B deductible and coinsurance applies.
- If payment is made to a participating hospital for tests performed for an inpatient of that hospital without Part A coverage, payment is made on a cost basis and is subject to Part B deductible and coinsurance.
- If payment is made to a participating SNF for tests performed by that SNF for an inpatient of the SNF, payment is made on a cost basis and is subject to Part B deductible and coinsurance.
- If payment is made to a hospital-based or independent dialysis facility for laboratory tests included under the composite rate payment and performed for a patient of that facility, the facility's composite rate payment includes payment for these tests and is subject to the Part B deductible and coinsurance.
- If payment is made to a rural health clinic for laboratory tests performed for a patient of that clinic, payment is made as part of the all-inclusive rate and is subject to Part B deductible and coinsurance.
- If payment is made to a hospital which has been granted a waiver of Medicare reimbursement principles for outpatient services, Part B deductible and coinsurance apply unless otherwise waived as part of an approved waiver.
- If payment is made to a participating HMO or HCPP for laboratory tests performed for a patient who is not a member, payment is the lesser of the actual charge, the national limitation amount or the fee schedule amount and the Part B deductible and coinsurance do not apply.

I. Coordination Between Intermediaries, Carriers, and the Railroad Retirement Board (RRB) — Furnish copies of fee schedules and updates (including national limitation amounts where applicable) to Medicare fiscal intermediaries and to the appropriate Travelers RRB office. (See §4540.) Provide updates at least 30 days prior to the scheduled implementation. The fiscal intermediaries and the RRB use the fee schedules in paying for hospital laboratory tests performed for outpatients of the hospital and for persons who are not patients of the hospital. The Travelers RRB offices use the fee schedules in paying for outpatient clinical diagnostic laboratory tests. Fiscal intermediaries and the Travelers RRB consult with carriers on filling gaps in fee schedules for certain tests. If intermediaries or the Travelers RRB offices have bills for payment on laboratory tests that are not in the fee schedule, they consult with the carriers that gave them the fee schedules. If those carriers are unable to help the intermediaries, the carriers consult with other nearby carriers. HCPCS contains the American Medical Association's CPT-4 (Physician's Current Procedural Terminology). For those entities which are not familiar with HCPCS but have used the CPT-4, the coding and terminology for laboratory tests are the same in both HCPCS and the CPT-4. The CPT-4 may be used before receipt of the HCPCS.

J. Application of Fee Schedules to Medicaid — Furnish copies of the fee schedules and the annual update (including national limitation amounts where applicable) to State agencies. Provide updates at least 30 days prior to the scheduled implementation. To obtain Federal matching funds for clinical diagnostic laboratory services, State Medicaid agencies may not pay more for the services and specimen collections than are paid for them under Medicare. This applies to payments for calendar quarters beginning on or after October 1, 1984.

Since the fee schedule provisions have been implemented on a carrierwide basis, a State may have more than one carrier servicing Medicare beneficiaries residing there. A Medicaid agency for such a State may, if it deems necessary, use the fee schedules of either one or both of the carriers to meet the Federal fund matching requirement. State Medicaid agencies may consult with ROs concerning the fee schedule, the national limitation amounts and specimen collection provisions.

K. Travel Allowance — In addition to a specimen collection fee allowed under §5114.1.D, a travel allowance can also be made to cover the costs of travel to collect a specimen from a nursing home or homebound patient. The additional allowance can be made only where a specimen collection fee is also payable, i.e., no travel allowance is made where the technician merely performs a messenger service to pick up a specimen drawn by a physician or nursing home personnel. The travel allowance may not be paid to a physician unless the trip to the home or nursing home was solely for the purpose of drawing a specimen. Otherwise travel costs are considered to be associated with the other purposes of the trip. Since a travel allowance can now be paid routinely, the differential specimen collection amount formerly allowed when a specimen is collected from a single patient rather than multiple patients (i.e., $5 rather than $3) is discontinued.

The allowance is intended to cover the estimated travel costs of collecting a specimen and is an allowance reflecting the technician's salary and travel costs. The following HCPCS codes are used for travel allowances:

P9603--Travel allowance - one way, in connection with medically necessary laboratory specimen collection drawn from homebound or nursing home bound patient;

prorated miles actually traveled (carrier allowance on per mile basis); or

P9604--Travel allowance - one way, in connection with medically necessary laboratory specimen collection drawn from homebound or nursing home bound patient; prorated trip charge (carrier allowance on flat fee basis).

Identify round trip travel by use of modifier LR.

If you determine that it results in equitable payment, you may extend your former payment allowances for additional travel (such as to a distant rural nursing home) to all circumstances where travel is required. This might be appropriate, for example, if your former payment allowance was on a per mile basis. Otherwise you must establish an appropriate allowance. If you decide to establish a new allowance, one method is to consider developing a travel allowance consisting of:

- The current Federal mileage allowance for operating personal automobiles, plus
- A personnel allowance per mile to cover personnel costs based on an estimate of average hourly wages and average driving speed.

For your convenience, a chronology of mileage rates from July 1, 1984 to date is listed below:

Mileage Rate	From	To
20.5 cents	July 1, 1984	July 31, 1987
21 cents	August 1, 1987	August 13, 1988
22.5 cents	August 14, 1988	September 16, 1989
24 cents	September 17, 1989	June 29, 1991
25 cents		June 30, 1991

Travel allowance amounts claimed by suppliers are prorated by the total number of patients (including Medicare and non Medicare patients) from whom specimens are drawn or picked up on a given trip.

EXAMPLE 1: On October 1, 1989, a carrier determines that the average technician is paid $9 per hour and estimates 45 miles per hour as the average speed driven or $.20 per mile. This amount plus the Federal mileage allowance of $0.24 per mile results in a total allowance of $0.44 per mile. A laboratory technician makes a trip to two nursing homes involving a total mileage of 20 miles and draws specimens from three patients, Medicare as well as non- Medicare patients. In addition, specimens that were not drawn by the technician are picked up from two patients. A travel allowance per Medicare claim of $1.76 can be made (20 miles round trip x $0.44 per mile divided by 5). The supplier bills 4 miles (20 miles _ 5) under code P9603LR.

EXAMPLE 2: The carrier, through a review of the laboratory records, estimates that on average four specimens are drawn or picked up each trip, and that the average trip is 30 miles including both round trips and one way trips. Assuming the same facts as Example 1 (i.e., $9 per hour and 45 miles per hour), the carrier establishes a flat travel allowance of $3.30. Suppliers bill code P9604 and are paid $3.30 regardless of actual distance or number of patients served.

In keeping with the principles of §5024 and §5200, a payment in addition to the routine travel allowance determined under this section may be allowed to cover the additional costs of travel to collect a specimen from a nursing home or homebound patient when clinical diagnostic laboratory tests are needed on an emergency basis outside the general business hours of the laboratory making the collection.

L. Laboratory Tests Utilizing Automated Equipment — Because of the numerous technological advances and innovations in the clinical laboratory field and the increased availability of automated testing equipment to all entities that perform clinical diagnostic laboratory tests, no distinction is generally made in determining payment allowances (i.e., the lower of the respective fee schedules or the national limitations) for such tests between (1) the sites where the service is performed, i.e., physician's office or other laboratory, or (2) the method of the testing process used, whether manual or automated.

When physicians and laboratories perform the same test, whether manually or with automated equipment, the services are considered similar.

1. Determining Payment for Automated Tests — The common automated tests comprise specific groupings of blood chemistries which enable physicians to more accurately diagnose their patients' medical problems.

   The following list contains some of the tests which can be and are frequently done as groups and combinations on automated profile equipment.

Alanine Aminotransferase (ALT,SGPT)	Albumin
Alkaline phosphatase	Aspartate aminotransferase
Bilirubin, direct	(AST, SGOT)
Bilirubin, total	Carbon dioxide content
Calcium	Chloride
Creatinine	Cholesterol
Glucose(sugar)	Creatine kinase (CK, CPK)
GammaGlutamylTransferase (GGT)	Lactate dehydrogenase (LDH, LD)
Phosphorus	Potassium
Protein, total	Sodium
Triglyceride	Urea nitrogen (BUN)
Uric Acid	

While the component tests in automated profiles may vary somewhat from one laboratory to another, or from one physician's office or clinic to another, group together those profile tests which can be performed at the same time on the same equipment for purposes of developing appropriate payment allowances. For Medicare payment purposes, the tests on this list must be grouped together when billed separately and considered automated profile tests. While laboratory entities may bill additional tests using automated profile codes and be paid according to §5114.1, the above listed 22 tests are the only tests that you may group into automated profiles if they are billed separately. Future revisions to this list will be made through manual revisions.

Payment is made only for those tests in an automated profile that meet Medicare coverage rules. Where only some of the tests in a profile of tests are covered, payment cannot exceed the amount that would have been paid if only the covered tests had been ordered. For example, the use of the 12-channel serum chemistry test to determine the blood sugar level in a proven case of diabetes is unreasonable because the results of a blood sugar test performed separately provides the essential information. Normally, the payment allowance for a blood sugar test is lower than the payment allowance for the automated profile of tests. In no event, however, may payment for the covered tests exceed the payment allowance for the profile.

Periodically, at least annually, remind physicians and suppliers that you will review claims for patterns of high utilization of automated profiles with large number of tests and if your review shows that the documentation does not support Medicare coverage that you will pursue recoupment. Encourage physicians to target their test ordering to only those tests that are related to specific symptoms or disease conditions. Remind physicians of Medicare coverage rules that require that payment may be made only for medically necessary tests and that payment is not made for routine screening tests. As a general rule, you may assume that where a physician orders automated profile tests on a test-by-test basis (i.e., not as part of a profile or custom panel), each of the tests is covered. (See §7517.1.) If, after analysis, you find that a pattern of overutilization exists, even if tests were individually ordered, follow the procedures of §7517.2 to aid you in ameliorating the problems.

2. Separately Billed Tests That Are Commonly Part of Automated Test Profiles — If you receive claims for laboratory services in which the physician or laboratory has separately billed for tests that are available as part of an automated profile test, make the following determinations:

- If the sum of the payment allowance for the separately billed tests exceeds the payment allowance for the profile that includes these tests, make payment at the lesser amount for the profile. Conversely, the payment allowance for a profile cannot exceed the payment allowances for the individual tests.

- The limitation that payment for individual tests not exceed the payment allowance for an automated profile is applied whether or not a particular laboratory has the automated equipment. A higher amount may be paid in unusual circumstances where justified or where individual tests are unavailable on automated equipment. (See §5024.) Suppliers are to provide a detailed explanation to you of the justification for a higher level of payment. Review to determine if unusual circumstances exist and warrant a higher payment amount.

- When one or more automated profile tests are performed for a patient on the same day, determine whether to base payment on an automated profile that includes such tests rather than to base payment on the individual or separately billed tests. For example, compare the allowance for code 80002 of the Current Procedural Terminology - Fourth Edition (CPT-4) for the above determination when one or two tests from the commonly performed automated tests are included on a claim.

M. Organ or Disease Oriented Panels — The American Medical Association (AMA) is responsible for the nomenclature of codes in the Current Procedural Terminology (CPT). The AMA has developed codes for panels of tests commonly ordered together and related through their use to diagnose a disease state or to evaluate an organ system. The tests listed in the CPT with each panel code are the defined components of that code for Medicare purposes.

Payment for panels is the same as found in subsection L. Payment for the total panel cannot exceed the allowance for individual tests. All Medicare coverage rules apply.

Appendix C
Medicare Statutes

SEC. 1833. [42 U.S.C. 1395l] (a) Except as provided in section 1876, and subject to the succeeding provisions of this section, there shall be paid from the Federal Supplementary Medical Insurance Trust Fund, in the case of each individual who is covered under the insurance program established by this part and incurs expenses for services with respect to which benefits are payable under this part, amounts equal to-- (1) in the case of services described in section 1832(a)(1)--80 percent of the reasonable charges for the services; except that (A) an organization which provides medical and other health services (or arranges for their availability) on a prepayment basis (and either is sponsored by a union or employer, or does not provide, or arrange for the provision of, any inpatient hospital services)[95] may elect to be paid 80 percent of the reasonable cost of services for which payment may be made under this part on behalf of individuals enrolled in such organization in lieu of 80 percent of the reasonable charges for such services if the organization undertakes to charge such individuals no more than 20 percent of such reasonable cost plus any amounts payable by them as a result of subsection (b),[96] (B) with respect to items and services described in section 1861(s)(10)(A), the amounts paid shall be 100 percent of the reasonable charges for such items and services, (C) with respect to expenses incurred for those physicians' services for which payment may be made under this part that are described in section 1862(a)(4), the prosthetic devices and orthotics and prosthetics (as defined in section 1834(h)(4)), the amounts paid shall be the amounts described in section 1834(h)(1), the amounts paid shall be subject to such limitations as may be prescribed by regulations, (D) with respect to clinical diagnostic laboratory tests for which payment is made under this part (i) on the basis of a fee schedule under subsection (h)(1) or section 1834(d)(1)[97], the amount paid shall be equal to 80 percent (or 100 percent, in the case of such tests for which payment is made on an assignment-related basis) of the lesser of the amount determined under such fee schedule, the limitation amount for that test determined under subsection (h)(4)(B), or the amount of the charges billed for the tests, or (ii) on the basis of a negotiated rate established under subsection (h)(6), the amount paid shall be equal to 100 percent of such negotiated rate, (E) with respect to services furnished to individuals who have been determined to have end stage renal disease, the amounts paid shall be determined subject to the provisions of section 1881, (F) with respect to clinical social worker services under section 1861(s)(2)(N), the amounts paid shall be 80 percent of the lesser of (i) the actual charge for the services or (ii) 75 percent of the amount determined for payment of a psychologist under clause (L), [(G) Stricken.[98]] (H) with respect to services of a certified registered nurse anesthetist under section 1861(s)(11), the amounts paid shall be 80 percent of the least of the actual charge, the prevailing charge that would be recognized (or, for services furnished on or after January 1, 1992, the fee schedule amount provided under section 1848) if the services had been performed by an anesthesiologist, or the fee schedule for such services established by the Secretary in accordance with subsection (1), (I) with respect to covered items (described in section 1834(a)(13)), the amounts paid shall be the amounts described in section 1834(a)(1), and (J) with respect to expenses incurred for radiologist services (as defined in section 1834(b)(6)), subject to section 1848, the amounts paid shall be 80 percent of the lesser of the actual charge for the services or the amount provided under the fee schedule established under section 1834(b), (K) with respect to certified nurse-midwife services under section 1861(s)(2)(L), the amounts paid shall be 80 percent of the lesser of the actual charge for the services or the amount determined by a fee schedule established by the Secretary for the purposes of this subparagraph (but in no event shall such fee schedule exceed 65 percent of the prevailing charge that would be allowed for the same service performed by a physician, or, for services furnished on or after January 1, 1992, 65 percent of the fee schedule amount provided under section 1848 for the same service performed by a physician), (L) with respect to qualified psychologist services under section

1861(s)(2)(M)

The amounts paid shall be 80 percent of the lesser of the actual charge for the services or the amount determined by a fee schedule established by the Secretary for the purposes of this subparagraph, (M) with respect to prosthetic devices and orthotics and (N) with respect to expenses incurred for physicians' services (as defined in section 1848(j)(3)), the amounts paid shall be 80 percent of the payment basis determined under section 1848(a)(1), (O) with respect to services described in section 1861(s)(2)(K)[99] (relating to services furnished by physicians assistants, nurse practitioners, or clinical nurse specialists[100]), the amounts paid shall be equal to 80 percent of (i) the lesser of the actual charge or 85 percent of the fee schedule amount provided under section 1848, or (ii) in the case of services as an assistant at surgery, the lesser of the actual charge or 85 percent of the amount that would otherwise be recognized if performed by a physician who is serving as an assistant at surgery;[101], (P)[102] with respect to surgical dressings, the amounts paid shall be the amounts determined under section 1834(i), (Q) with respect to items or services for which fee schedules are established pursuant to section 1842(s), the amounts paid shall be 80 percent of the lesser of the actual charge or the fee schedule established in such section[103], (R) with respect to ambulance service, the amounts paid shall be 80 percent of the lesser of the actual charge for the services or the amount determined by a fee schedule established by the Secretary under section 1834(l)[104], and (S) with respect to drugs and biologicals not paid on a cost or prospective payment basis as otherwise provided in this part (other than items and services described in subparagraph (B)), the amounts paid shall be 80 percent of the lesser of the actual charge or the payment amount established in section 1842(o);[105]

(2) in the case of services described in section 1832(a)(2) (except those services described in subparagraphs (C),[106] (D), (E), (F), (G), (H), and (I) of such section and unless otherwise specified in section 1881)--

(A) with respect to home health services (other than a covered osteoporosis drug) (as defined in section 1861(kk)), the amount determined under the prospective payment system under section 1895;[107]

(B) with respect to other items and services (except those described in subparagraph (C), (D), or (E) of this paragraph and except as may be provided in section 1886 or section 1888(e)(9)[108])--

(i) furnished before January 1, 1999,[109] the lesser of--

(I) the reasonable cost of such services, as determined under section 1861(v), or

(II) the customary charges with respect to such services, less the amount a provider may charge as described in clause (ii) of section 1866(a)(2)(A), but in no case may the payment for such other services exceed 80 percent of such reasonable cost, or

(ii) if such services are furnished before January 1, 1999,[110] by a public provider of services, or by another provider which demonstrates to the satisfaction of the Secretary that a significant portion of its patients are low-income (and requests that payment be made under this clause), free of charge or at nominal charges to the public, 80 percent of the amount determined in accordance with section 1814(b)(2), or[111]

(iii) if such services are furnished on or after January 1, 1999, the amount determined under subsection (t), or[112]

(iv)[113] if (and for so long as) the conditions described in section 1814(b)(3) are met, the amounts determined under the reimbursement system described in such section;

(C) with respect to services described in the second sentence of section 1861(p), 80 percent of the reasonable charges for such services;

(D) with respect to clinical diagnostic laboratory tests for which payment is made under this part (i) on the basis of a fee schedule determined under subsection (h)(1) or section 1834(d)(1)[114], the amount paid shall be equal to 80 percent (or 100 percent, in the case of such tests for which payment is made on an assignment-related basis or to a provider having an agreement under section 1866 of the lesser of the amount determined under such fee schedule, the limitation amount for that test determined under subsection (h)(4)(B), or the amount of the charges billed for the tests, or (ii) on the basis of a negotiated rate established under subsection (h)(6), the amount paid shall be equal to 100 percent of such negotiated rate for such tests;

(E) with respect to--

(i) outpatient hospital radiology services (including diagnostic and therapeutic radiology, nuclear medicine and CAT scan procedures, magnetic resonance imaging, and ultrasound and other imaging services, but excluding screening mammography), and

(ii) effective for procedures performed on or after October 1, 1989, diagnostic procedures (as defined by the Secretary) described in section 1861(s)(3) (other than diagnostic x-ray tests and diagnostic laboratory tests), the amount determined under subsection (n) or, for services or procedures performed on or after January 1, 1999, subsection (t)[115]; [116]

(F) with respect to a covered osteoporosis drug (as defined in section 1861(kk)) furnished by a home health agency, 80 percent of the reasonable cost of such service, as determined under section 1861(v); and[117] (G) with respect to items and services described in section 1861(s)(10)(A), the lesser of--

(i) the reasonable cost of such services, as determined under section 1861(v), or

(ii) the customary charges with respect to such services, or, if such services are furnished by a public provider of services, or by another provider which demonstrates to the satisfaction of the Secretary that a significant portion of its patients are low-income (and requests that payment be made under this provision), free of charge or at nominal charges to the public, the amount determined in accordance with section 1814(b)(2);[118]

(3) in the case of services described in section 1832(a)(2)(D)[119], the costs which are reasonable and related to the cost of furnishing such services or which are based on such other tests of reasonableness as the

Secretary may prescribe in regulations, including those authorized under section 1861(v)(1)(A), less the amount a provider may charge as described in clause (ii) of section 1866(a)(2)(A), but in no case may the payment for such services (other than for items and services described in section 1861(s)(10)(A)) exceed 80 percent of such costs;

(4) in the case of facility services described in section 1832(a)(2)(F), and outpatient hospital facility services furnished in connection with surgical procedures specified by the Secretary pursuant to section 1833(i)(1)(A), the applicable amount as determined under paragraph (2) or (3) of subsection (i) or subsection (t)[120];

(5) in the case of covered items (described in section 1834(a)(13)) the amounts described in section 1834(a)(1);

(6) in the case of outpatient critical access[121] hospital services, the amounts described in section 1834(g);

(7) in the case of prosthetic devices and orthotics and prosthetics (as described in section 1834(h)(4)), the amounts described in section 1834(h);[123]

(8) in the case of--

(A) outpatient physical therapy services (which includes outpatient speech-language pathology services) and outpatient occupational therapy services furnished--

(i) by a rehabilitation agency, public health agency, clinic, comprehensive outpatient rehabilitation facility, or skilled nursing facility,

(ii) by a home health agency to an individual who is not homebound, or

(iii) by another entity under an arrangement with an entity described in clause (i) or (ii); and

(B) outpatient physical therapy services (which includes outpatient speech-language pathology services) and outpatient occupational therapy services furnished--

(i) by a hospital to an outpatient or to a hospital inpatient who is entitled to benefits under part A but has exhausted benefits for inpatient hospital services during a spell of illness or is not so entitled to benefits under part A, or

(ii) by another entity under an arrangement with a hospital described in clause (i), the amounts described in section 1834(k); and

(9) in the case of services described in section 1832(a)(2)(E) that are not described in paragraph (8), the amounts described in section 1834(k).[124]

DEFINITIONS OF SERVICES, INSTITUTIONS, ETC.

SEC. 1861. [42 U.S.C. 1395x] For purposes of this title--

Physician

(r) The term "physician", when used in connection with the performance of any function or action, means (1) a doctor of medicine or osteopathy legally authorized to practice medicine and surgery by the State in which he performs such function or action (including a physician within the meaning of section 1101(a)(7)), (2) a doctor of dental surgery or of dental medicine who is legally authorized to practice dentistry by the State in which he performs such function and who is acting within the scope of his license when he performs such functions, (3) a doctor of podiatric medicine for the purposes of subsections (k), (m), (p)(1), and (s) of this section and sections 1814(a), 1832(a)(2)(F)(ii), and 1835 but only with respect to functions which he is legally authorized to perform as such by the State in which he performs them, (4) a doctor of optometry, but only with respect to the provision of items or services described in subsection (s) which he is legally authorized to perform as a doctor of optometry by the State in which he performs them, or (5) a chiropractor who is licensed as such by the State (or in a State which does not license chiropractors as such, is legally authorized to perform the services of a chiropractor in the jurisdiction in which he performs such services), and who meets uniform minimum standards promulgated by the Secretary, but only for the purpose of sections 1861(s)(1) and 1861(s)(2)(A) and only with respect to treatment by means of manual manipulation of the spine (to correct a subluxation [352]) which he is legally authorized to perform by the State or jurisdiction in which such treatment is provided. For the purposes of section 1862(a)(4) and subject to the limitations and conditions provided in the previous sentence, such term includes a doctor of one of the arts, specified in such previous sentence, legally authorized to practice such art in the country in which the inpatient hospital services (referred to in such section 1862(a)(4)) are furnished.

EXCLUSIONS FROM COVERAGE AND MEDICARE AS SECONDARY PAYER

SEC. 1862. [42 U.S.C. 1395y] (a) Notwithstanding any other provision of this title, no payment may be made under part A or part B for any expenses incurred for items or services--

(1)(A) which, except for items and services described in a succeeding subparagraph, are not reasonable and necessary for the diagnosis or treatment of illness or injury or to improve the functioning of a malformed body member,

(B) in the case of items and services described in section 1861(s)(10), which are not reasonable and necessary for the prevention of illness,

(C) in the case of hospice care, which are not reasonable and necessary for the palliation or management of terminal illness,

(D) in the case of clinical care items and services provided with the concurrence of the Secretary and with respect to research and experimentation conducted by, or under contract with, the Medicare Payment Advisory Commissionfn466[466] or the

Secretary, which are not reasonable and necessary to carry out the purposes of section 1886(e)(6),

(E) in the case of research conducted pursuant to section 1142, which is not reasonable and necessary to carry out the purposes of that section, fn467[467]

(F) in the case of screening mammography, which is performed more frequently than is covered under section 1834(c)(2) or which is not conducted by a facility described in section 1834(c)(1)(B), and, in the case of screening pap smear and screening pelvic examfn468[468], which is performed more frequently than is provided under section 1861(nn),fn469[469]

(G) in the case of prostate cancer screening tests (as defined in section 1861(oo)), which are performed more frequently than is covered under such section,fn470[470]

(H) in the case of colorectal cancer screening tests, which are performed more frequently than is covered under section 1834(d), andfn471[471]

(I) the frequency and duration of home health services which are in excess of normative guidelines that the Secretary shall establish by regulation;fn472[472]

(2) for which the individual furnished such items or services has no legal obligation to pay, and which no other person (by reason of such individual's membership in a prepayment plan or otherwise) has a legal obligation to provide or pay for, except in the case of Federally qualified health center services;

(3) which are paid for directly or indirectly by a governmental entity (other than under this Act and other than under a health benefits or insurance plan established for employees of such an entity), except in the case of rural health clinic services, as defined in section 1861(aa)(1),fn473[473] in the case of Federally qualified health center services, as defined in section 1861(aa)(3), and in such other cases as the Secretary may specify;

(4) which are not provided within the United States (except for inpatient hospital services furnished outside the United States under the conditions described in section 1814(f) and, subject to such conditions, limitations, and requirements as are provided under or pursuant to this title, physicians' services and ambulance services furnished an individual in conjunction with such inpatient hospital services but only for the period during which such inpatient hospital services were furnished);

(5) which are required as a result of war, or of an act of war, occurring after the effective date of such individual's current coverage under such part;

(6) which constitute personal comfort items (except, in the case of hospice care, as is otherwise permitted under paragraph (1)(C));

(7) where such expenses are for routine physical checkups, eyeglasses (other than eyewear described in section 1861(s)(8)) or eye examinations for the purpose of prescribing, fitting, or changing eyeglasses, procedures performed (during the course of any eye examination) to determine the refractive state of the eyes, hearing aids or examinations therefor, or immunizations (except as otherwise allowed under section 1861(s)(10) and subparagraphs (B), (F), (G), or (H)fn474[474] of paragraph (1)fn475[475]);

(8) where such expenses are for orthopedic shoes or other supportive devices for the feet, other than shoes furnished pursuant to section 1861(s)(12);

(9) where such expenses are for custodial care (except, in the case of hospice care, as is otherwise permitted under paragraph (1)(C));

(10) where such expenses are for cosmetic surgery or are incurred in connection therewith, except as required for the prompt repair of accidental injury or for improvement of the functioning of a malformed body member;

(11) where such expenses constitute charges imposed by immediate relatives of such individual or members of his household;

(12) where such expenses are for services in connection with the care, treatment, filling, removal, or replacement of teeth or structures directly supporting teeth, except that payment may be made under part A in the case of inpatient hospital services in connection with the provision of such dental services if the individual, because of his underlying medical condition and clinical status or because of the severity of the dental procedure, requires hospitalization in connection with the provision of such services;

(13) where such expenses are for--

(A) the treatment of flat foot conditions and the prescription of supportive devices therefor,

(B) the treatment of subluxations of the foot, or

(C) routine foot care (including the cutting or removal of corns or calluses, the trimming of nails, and other routine hygienic care);

(14) which are other than physicians' services (as defined in regulations promulgated specifically for purposes of this paragraph), services described by section 1861(s)(2)(K)fn476[476], certified nurse-midwife services, qualified psychologist services, and services of a certified registered nurse anesthetist, and which are furnished to an individual who is a patient of a hospital or critical accessfn477[477] hospital by an entity other than the hospital or critical accessfn478[478] hospital, unless the services are furnished under arrangements (as defined in section 1861(w)(1)) with the entity made by the hospital or critical accessfn479[479] hospital; fn480[480]

(15)(A) which are for services of an assistant at surgery in a cataract operation (including subsequent insertion of an intraocular lens) unless, before the surgery is performed, the appropriate utilization and quality control peer review organization (under part B of title XI) or a carrier under section 1842 has approved of the use of such an assistant in the surgical procedure based on the existence of a complicating medical condition, orfn481[481]

(B) which are for services of an assistant at surgery to which section 1848(i)(2)(B) applies;fn482[482]

(16) in the case in which funds may not be used for such items and services under the Assisted Suicide Funding Restriction Act of 1997;fn483[483]

(17) where the expenses are for an item or service furnished in a competitive acquisition area (as established by the Secretary under section 1847(a)) by an entity other than an entity with which the Secretary has entered into a contract under section 1847(b) for the furnishing of such an item or service in that area, unless the Secretary finds that the expenses were incurred in a case of urgent need, or in other circumstances specified by the Secretary;fn484[484]

(18) which are covered skilled nursing facility services described in section 1888(e)(2)(A)(i) and which are furnished to an individual who is a resident of a skilled nursing facility or of a part of a facility that includes a skilled nursing facility (as determined under regulations), by an entity other than the skilled nursing facility, unless the services are furnished under arrangements (as defined in section 1861(w)(1)) with the entity made by the skilled nursing facility; orfn485[485]

(19) which are for items or services which are furnished pursuant to a private contract described in section 1802(b);fn486[486]

(20) in the case of outpatient occupational therapy services or outpatient physical therapy services furnished as an incident to a physician's professional services (as described in section 1861(s)(2)(A)), that do not meet the standards and conditions (other than any licensing requirement specified by the Secretary) under the second sentence of section 1861(p) (or under such sentence through the operation of section 1861(g)) as such standards and conditions would apply to such therapy services if furnished by a therapist; orfn487[487]

(21) where such expenses are for home health services furnished to an individual who is under a plan of care of the home health agency if the claim for payment for such services is not submitted by the agency.fn488[488]

Paragraph (7) shall not apply to Federally qualified health center services described in section 1861(aa)(3)(B).

Appendix D

Payer Directory For HCPCS Level II Codes

COMPANIES ACCEPTING HCPCS LEVEL II CODES

Note: These companies have indicated that they process HCPCS Level II codes. Companies are listed in alphabetic order.

ACS CLAIMS SERVICE
PO BOX 296
DALLAS, TX 75221
TEL: (214) 826-8148
FAX: (214) 826-8239
TOLL FREE: (800) 456-9653

ADMINISTRATION SYSTEMS RESEARCH CORP
3033 ORCHARD VISTA DR SE
GRAND RAPIDS, MI 49546-7000
TEL: (616) 957-1751
FAX: (616) 957-8986
TOLL FREE: (800) 968-2449

ADMINISTRATIVE CONSULTANTS, INC
92 BROOKSIDE RD
PO BOX 1471
WATERBURY, CT 06721
TEL: (203) 756-8061
FAX: (203) 754-3941

ADMINISTRATIVE SERVICE CONSULTANTS
3301 E ROYALTON RD
BROADVIEW HEIGHTS, OH 44147
TEL: (440) 526-2730
FAX: (440) 526-1608
TOLL FREE: (800) 634-8816

ADMINISTRATIVE SERVICES, INC
7990 SW 117TH AVE
PO BOX 839000
MIAMI, FL 33283
TEL: (305) 595-4040
FAX: (305) 596-6820
TOLL FREE: (800) 749-1858

ADMIRAL INSURANCE CO
1255 CALDWELL RD
PO BOX 5725
CHERRY HILL, NJ 08034-3220
TEL: (609) 429-9200
FAX: (609) 428-3390

ADVANCED BENEFIT ADMINISTRATORS
6420 SW MACADAM AVE, STE 380
PORTLAND, OR 97201-3519
TEL: (503) 245-3770
FAX: (503) 245-4122
TOLL FREE: (800) 443-6531

ADVANCED INSURANCE SERVICES
600 JEFFERSON AVE
PO BOX 19
MEMPHIS, TN 38101-0019
TEL: (901) 544-2344
FAX: (901) 544-2328
TOLL FREE: (800) 772-1352

AETNA / U.S. HEALTHCARE
151 FARMINGTON AVE
PO BOX 150417
HARTFORD, CT 06156
TEL: (860) 273-0123
TOLL FREE: (800) 872-3862

6795 N PALM AVE
FRESNO, CA 93704
TEL: (209) 241-1000
FAX: (209) 241-1226
TOLL FREE: (800) 756-7039

1000 MIDDLE ST
MIDDLETOWN, CT 06457-4621
TEL: (860) 636-8300
FAX: (860) 638-6599
TOLL FREE: (800) 445-3184

4300 W CYPRESS ST
PO BOX 31450
TAMPA, FL 33631-3450
TEL: (813) 870-6670
TOLL FREE: (800) 872-3862

PO BOX 30167
TAMPA, FL 33630-3167
TEL: (813) 870-7940
FAX: (813) 878-7839
TOLL FREE: (800) 323-9930
IN-STATE: (800) 282-3517

400-1 TOTTEN POND RD
WALTHAM, MA 02154
TEL: (781) 273-5600
FAX: (781) 902-3871
TOLL FREE: (800) 448-8742

55 LANE RD
FAIRFIELD, NJ 07004
TEL: (973) 575-5600
FAX: (973) 244-3911
TOLL FREE: (800) 852-0629

1425 UNION MEETING RD
PO BOX 1125
BLUE BELL, PA 19422
TEL: (215) 775-4800
TOLL FREE: (800) 233-3105

7600 A LEESBURG PIKE, STE 300
FALLS CHURCH, VA 22043-2413
TEL: (703) 903-7100
FAX: (703) 903-0316
TOLL FREE: (800) 231-8415

AETNA / U.S. HEALTHCARE CO
7601 ORA GLEN DR
GREENBELT, MD 20770-3647
TEL: (301) 441-1600
FAX: (301) 489-5284
TOLL FREE: (800) 635-3121
IN-STATE: (800) 635-3121

AIG CLAIM SERVICES, INC
70 PINE ST
NEW YORK, NY 10270-0002
TEL: (212) 770-7000
FAX: (212) 943-1125

PO BOX 25477
TAMPA, FL 33622-5477
TEL: (813) 218-3000
FAX: (813) 272-1122
IN-STATE: (800) 647-4767

120 S CENTRAL AVE, STE 300
CLAYTON, MO 63105
TEL: (314) 719-4000
FAX: (314) 863-5939
TOLL FREE: (888) 745-7819

1700 CNG TWR, 625 LIBERTY AVE
PITTSBURGH, PA 15222
TEL: (412) 393-3960
FAX: (412) 288-5959
TOLL FREE: (800) 892-9779
IN-STATE: (800) 258-7152

HCPCS 2000   233

ALL RISK ADMINISTRATORS
PO BOX 66237
SAINT PETERSBURG BEACH, FL 33736-6210
TEL: (727) 367-3315
FAX: (727) 367-4510
TOLL FREE: (800) 338-4485

ALLIED GROUP INSURANCE CO
PO BOX 1420
MINNEAPOLIS, MN 55440-1420
TEL: (612) 896-1774
FAX: (612) 896-6640
TOLL FREE: (800) 862-6024

ALPHA DATA SYSTEMS, INC
1545 W MOCKINGBIRD LN, STE 6000
DALLAS, TX 75235
TEL: (214) 638-1485
TOLL FREE: (800) 342-5248

AMERICAN COMMERCIAL LINES
1701 E MARKET ST
PO BOX 610
JEFFERSONVILLE, IN 47131-0610
TEL: (812) 288-0100
FAX: (812) 288-1720
TOLL FREE: (800) 548-7689

AMERICAN FAMILY INSURANCE
PO BOX 59173
MINNEAPOLIS, MN 55459
TEL: (612) 933-4446
FAX: (612) 933-7268
TOLL FREE: (800) 374-1111

AMERICAN HEALTH CARE
PO BOX 7000
RICHTON, IL 60471
TEL: (630) 916-8400
FAX: (630) 261-7988
TOLL FREE: (800) 624-8568

AMERICAN HEALTH CARE PROVIDERS, INC
900 S SHACKLEFORD RD, STE 110
LITTLE ROCK, AR 72211-3845
TEL: (501) 221-3534
FAX: (501) 221-3049
TOLL FREE: (800) 333-3534

4601 SAUK TRAIL
PO BOX 7000
RICHTON PARK, IL 60471
TEL: (708) 503-5000
FAX: (708) 503-5001
TOLL FREE: (800) 242-7460

AMERICAN HERITAGE LIFE INSURANCE CO
1776 AMERICAN HERITAGE LIFE DR
JACKSONVILLE, FL 32224-3492
TEL: (904) 992-1776
FAX: (904) 992-2695
TOLL FREE: (800) 535-8086

AMERICAN LIFE INSURANCE CO
208 S LA SALLE ST, STE 2070
CHICAGO, IL 60604
TEL: (312) 372-5722
FAX: (312) 372-5727

AMERICAN MEDICAL & LIFE INSURANCE CO
35 N BROADWAY
HICKSVILLE, NY 11801-4236
TEL: (516) 822-8700
FAX: (516) 931-1010
TOLL FREE: (800) 822-0004

AMERICAN MINING INSURANCE CO, INC
550 MONTGOMERY HWY
PO BOX 660847
BIRMINGHAM, AL 35266-0847
TEL: (205) 823-4496
FAX: (205) 823-6177
TOLL FREE: (800) 448-5621

AMERICAN NATIONAL INSURANCE CO
1 MOODY PLZ
PO BOX 1520
GALVESTON, TX 77550-1520
TEL: (409) 763-4661
FAX: (409) 766-6694
TOLL FREE: (800) 899-6805

AMERICAN PIONEER LIFE
11 N BAYLEN ST
PO BOX 130
PENSACOLA, FL 32591-0130
TEL: (850) 469-8220
FAX: (850) 433-1186
TOLL FREE: (800) 999-2224

AMERICAN POSTAL WORKERS UNION HEALTH PLAN
12345 NEW COLUMBIA PIKE
PO BOX 967
SILVER SPRING, MD 20910-0967
TEL: (301) 622-1700
FAX: (301) 622-6074
TOLL FREE: (800) 222-2798
IN-STATE: (800) 222-2798

AMERICAN REPUBLIC INSURANCE CO
601 6TH AVE
PO BOX 10
DES MOINES, IA 50301-0001
TEL: (515) 245-2000
FAX: (515) 245-4282
TOLL FREE: (800) 247-2190

AMERICAN RESOURCES INSURANCE CO
1111 HILLCREST RD
PO BOX 91149
MOBILE, AL 36691
TEL: (334) 639-0985
FAX: (334) 633-2944
TOLL FREE: (800) 826-6570

AMERICAN SERVICE LIFE INSURANCE CO
9151 GRAPEVINE HWY
PO BOX 982017
NORTH RICHLAND HILLS, TX 76182
FAX: (817) 255-8101
TOLL FREE: (800) 733-8880
IN-STATE: (800) 733-1110

AMERICAN TRUST ADMINISTRATORS, INC
7101 COLLEGE BLVD, STE 1505
PO BOX 87
SHAWNEE MISSION, KS 66201
TEL: (913) 451-4900
FAX: (913) 451-0598
TOLL FREE: (800) 843-4121

AMERICAN UNION LIFE INSURANCE CO
303 E WASHINGTON
PO BOX 2814
BLOOMINGTON, IL 61701-2814
TEL: (309) 829-1061
FAX: (309) 827-0303

AMERIHEALTH
10151 DEERWOOD PRK BLVD- BLDG 200, STE 400
PO BOX 40238
JACKSONVILLE, FL 32203
TEL: (904) 998-6700
FAX: (904) 998-5411
TOLL FREE: (800) 274-5466

AMERIHEALTH HMO, INC
919 N MARKET ST
WILMINGTON, DE 19801-3021
FAX: (302) 777-6444
TOLL FREE: (800) 444-6282

AMERITAS LIFE INSURANCE CORP
5900 O ST
PO BOX 81889
LINCOLN, NE 68501
TEL: (402) 467-1122
FAX: (402) 467-7935
TOLL FREE: (800) 487-5553

AMOCO INSURANCE PLANS
4850 STREET RD
TREVOSE, PA 19049-8000
TEL: (215) 953-3000
FAX: (215) 953-3156
TOLL FREE: (800) 626-0038

AMWAY CORP
7575 E FULTON RD
ADA, MI 49355-0001
TEL: (616) 787-6000
FAX: (616) 787-6177
TOLL FREE: (800) 528-5748

ANTHEM BLUE CROSS & BLUE SHIELD
2400 MARKET ST
YOUNGSTOWN, OH 44507
TEL: (330) 492-2151

PO BOX 37180
LOUISVILLE, KY 40233
TEL: (513) 872-8100
FAX: (513) 872-8174
TOLL FREE: (800) 442-1832

ANTHEM BLUE CROSS & BLUE SHIELD OF CONNECTICUT
370 BASSETT RD
HAVEN, CT 06473
TEL: (203) 239-4911
FAX: (203) 985-7834
TOLL FREE: (800) 922-4670

ANTHEM BLUE CROSS & BLUE SHIELD OF SOUTHWEST OHIO
PO BOX 37180
LOUISVILLE, KY 40233
TEL: (513) 872-8100
FAX: (513) 872-8174
TOLL FREE: (800) 442-1832

ARIZONA PHYSICIANS, IPA, INC
3141 N 3RD AVE
PHOENIX, AZ 85013
TEL: (602) 274-6102
FAX: (602) 664-5466
IN-STATE: (800) 348-4058

ARIZONA PUBLIC SERVICE CO
STA 8482
PO BOX 53970
PHOENIX, AZ 85072-3970
TEL: (602) 250-3578
FAX: (602) 250-2453

ARKANSAS BEST CORP
3801 OLD GREENWOOD RD
PO BOX 10048
FORT SMITH, AR 72917-0048
TEL: (501) 785-6178
FAX: (501) 785-6011

ARTHUR J. GALLAGAR & CO
2345 GRAND BLVD, STE 800
KANSAS CITY, MO 64108
TEL: (816) 421-7788
FAX: (816) 472-5517
TOLL FREE: (800) 279-7500

ASH GROVE CEMENT CO
8900 INDIAN CRK PKY
PO BOX 25900
OVERLAND PARK, KS 66225-5900
TEL: (913) 451-8900
FAX: (913) 451-8324
TOLL FREE: (800) 545-1822

ASSOCIATED ADMINISTRATORS, INC
2929 NW 31ST AVE
PO BOX 5096
PORTLAND, OR 97210-1721
TEL: (503) 223-3185
FAX: (503) 727-7444
TOLL FREE: (800) 888-9603

ASSOCIATION & SOCIETY INSURANCE CORP
11300 ROCKVILLE PIKE, STE 500
PO BOX 2510
ROCKVILLE, MD 20852
TEL: (301) 816-0045
FAX: (301) 816-1125
TOLL FREE: (800) 638-2610

ASSUMPTION MUTUAL LIFE INSURANCE CO
770 MAIN ST
PO BOX 160
MONCTON, NB E1C-8L1
TEL: (506) 853-6040
FAX: (506) 853-5459
TOLL FREE: (800) 455-7337

ASSURE CARE
4660 S HAGADORN RD, STE 210
EAST LANSING, MI 48823
TEL: (517) 351-6616
FAX: (517) 351-6633
TOLL FREE: (800) 968-6616

ATLANTIC MUTUAL / CENTENNIAL INSURANCE CO
628 HEBORN AVE- BLDG 2
PO BOX 6510
GLASTONBURY, CT 06033-6510
TEL: (860) 657-9966
FAX: (860) 657-7962
TOLL FREE: (800) 289-2299

AUTOMOBILE MECHANICS LOCAL NO 701
500 W PLAINFIELD RD
COUNTRYSIDE, IL 60525
TEL: (708) 482-0110
FAX: (708) 482-9140
TOLL FREE: (800) 704-6270

AUTOMOTIVE PETROLEUM & ALLIED
300 S GRAND AVE, RM 232
SAINT LOUIS, MO 63103-2430
TEL: (314) 531-3052
FAX: (314) 531-5285

BABB, INC
850 RIDGE AVE
PITTSBURGH, PA 15212
TEL: (412) 237-2020
FAX: (412) 322-1756
TOLL FREE: (800) 245-6102
IN-STATE: (800) 892-1015

BASHAS', INC
22402 S BASHA RD
PO BOX 488
CHANDLER, AZ 85244
TEL: (602) 895-5247
FAX: (602) 802-5497
TOLL FREE: (800) 755-7292

BELLSOUTH ADMINISTRATORS
3616 S I-10 SERVICE RD
PO BOX 8570
METAIRIE, LA 70011-8570
TEL: (504) 849-1459
FAX: (504) 849-1347
TOLL FREE: (800) 366-2475

BENEFIT ADMINISTRATORS, INC
1111 S GLENSTONE, STE 2-203
PO BOX 10868
SPRINGFIELD, MO 65808
TEL: (417) 866-8913
FAX: (417) 866-2103
TOLL FREE: (800) 375-8913

PO BOX 21308
COLUMBIA, SC 29221-1308
TEL: (803) 739-0001
FAX: (803) 739-2200

BENEFIT CLAIMS PAYERS, INC
1717 W NORTHERN AVE, STE 200
PO BOX 37400
PHOENIX, AZ 85069
TEL: (602) 861-6868
FAX: (602) 861-6878
TOLL FREE: (800) 266-6868

BENEFIT COORDINATORS CORP
200 FLEET ST- 5TH FL
PITTSBURGH, PA 15220-2910
TEL: (412) 920-2200
FAX: (412) 920-2279
TOLL FREE: (800) 685-6100

BENEFIT MANAGEMENT, INC
628 W BROADWAY, STE 100
PO BOX 5989
LITTLE ROCK, AR 72119
TEL: (501) 375-5500
FAX: (501) 375-4718

BENEFIT PLAN ADMINISTRATORS, INC
ONE HUNTINGTON QUANDRANGLE, STE 4N
PO BOX 8911
MELVILLE, NY 11747
TEL: (516) 694-4900
FAX: (516) 694-5650

101 S JEFFERSON ST
PO BOX 11746
ROANOKE, VA 24022-1746
TEL: (540) 345-2721
FAX: (540) 342-0282
TOLL FREE: (800) 277-8973

BENEFIT PLANNERS, INC
PO BOX 690450
SAN ANTONIO, TX 78269-0450
TEL: (210) 699-1872
FAX: (210) 697-3108
TOLL FREE: (800) 292-5386

194 S MAIN
BOERNE, TX 78006
TEL: (210) 699-1872
FAX: (210) 697-3108
TOLL FREE: (800) 292-5386

BENEFIT & RISK MANAGEMENT SERVICES
3610 AMERICAN RIVER DR, STE 150
SACRAMENTO, CA 95864
TEL: (916) 974-2626
FAX: (916) 974-2653
TOLL FREE: (800) 476-0218

BENICORP INSURANCE CO
5285 W LAKEVIEW PKY S DR
PO BOX 68917
INDIANAPOLIS, IN 46268-4111
TEL: (317) 290-1205
FAX: (317) 216-7877
TOLL FREE: (800) 837-1205

BERWANGER OVERMYER ASSOCIATES
2245 NORTHBANK DR
PO BOX 20945
COLUMBUS, OH 43220
TEL: (614) 457-7000
FAX: (614) 457-1507
TOLL FREE: (800) 837-0503
IN-STATE: (800) 837-0503

BLUE CROSS & BLUE SHIELD
450 RIVERCHASE PKY E
PO BOX 995
BIRMINGHAM, AL 35298-0001
TEL: (205) 988-2100
FAX: (205) 988-2949

PO BOX 2924
PHOENIX, AZ 85062-2924
TEL: (602) 864-4400
FAX: (602) 864-4242
TOLL FREE: (800) 232-2345

700 BROADWAY
DENVER, CO 80273
TEL: (303) 831-2131
TOLL FREE: (800) 433-5447

ONE BRANDYWINE GTWY
PO BOX 1991
WILMINGTON, DE 19899-1991
TEL: (302) 421-3000
FAX: (302) 421-2089
TOLL FREE: (800) 633-2563
IN-STATE: (800) 292-7865

550 12TH ST SW
WASHINGTON, DC 20065
TEL: (202) 479-8000
FAX: (202) 479-3520
TOLL FREE: (800) 424-7474

532 RIVERSIDE AVE
PO BOX 1798
JACKSONVILLE, FL 32231-0014
TEL: (904) 791-6111
FAX: (904) 791-8738

PO BOX 4445
ATLANTA, GA 30302-4445
TEL: (404) 842-8000
FAX: (404) 842-8010
TOLL FREE: (800) 441-2273

2357 WARM SPRINGS RD
PO BOX 9907
COLUMBUS, GA 31908-9907
TEL: (706) 571-5371
FAX: (706) 571-5487
TOLL FREE: (800) 241-7475

818 KEEAUMOKU ST
PO BOX 860
HONOLULU, HI 96808-0860
TEL: (808) 948-5110
FAX: (808) 948-6555
IN-STATE: (800) 790-4672

PO BOX 1364
CHICAGO, IL 60690-1364
TEL: (312) 653-6000
FAX: (312) 819-1220

9901 LINN STATION RD
LOUISVILLE, KY 40223
TEL: (502) 423-2011
FAX: (502) 423-2627
TOLL FREE: (800) 880-2583

2 GANNETT DR
SOUTH PORTLAND, ME 04106-6911
TEL: (207) 822-7000
FAX: (207) 822-7375
TOLL FREE: (800) 482-0966
IN-STATE: (800) 482-0966

1831 CHESTNUT ST
SAINT LOUIS, MO 63103-2275
TEL: (314) 923-4444
FAX: (417) 888-9075
TOLL FREE: (800) 392-8740

404 FULLER
PO BOX 4309
HELENA, MT 59604-4309
TEL: (406) 444-8200
FAX: (406) 442-6946
TOLL FREE: (800) 447-7828

7261 MERCY RD
PO BOX 3248
OMAHA, NE 68180-0001
TEL: (402) 390-1800
FAX: (402) 392-2141
TOLL FREE: (800) 642-8980

3 PENN PLZ E
NEWARK, NJ 07105
TEL: (973) 466-4000
TOLL FREE: (800) 355-2583

PO BOX 27630
ALBUQUERQUE, NM 87125-7630
TEL: (505) 291-3500
FAX: (505) 291-3541
TOLL FREE: (800) 432-0750

622 3RD AVE
PO BOX 345
NEW YORK, NY 10017
TEL: (212) 476-1000
TOLL FREE: (800) 261-5962

12 RHOADS DR- UTICA BUSINESS PARK
UTICA, NY 13502-6398
TEL: (315) 798-4200
FAX: (315) 792-9752
TOLL FREE: (800) 765-5226

800 S DUKE ST
PO BOX 2291
DURHAM, NC 27702
TEL: (919) 489-7431
FAX: (919) 765-4837
TOLL FREE: (800) 222-2783
IN-STATE: (800) 222-5028

1351 WILLIAM HOWARD TAFT RD
CINCINNATI, OH 45206
TEL: (513) 872-8100
FAX: (513) 872-8174
TOLL FREE: (800) 442-1832

3737 W SALVANIA AVE
PO BOX 943
TOLEDO, OH 43656-0001
TEL: (419) 473-7100
FAX: (419) 473-6200

3530 VELMONT
YOUNGSTOWN, OH 44505
TEL: (330) 759-0771
TOLL FREE: (800) 458-6813

1215 S BOULDER
PO BOX 3283
TULSA, OK 74102-3283
TEL: (918) 560-3500

I-20 E AT ALPINE RD
COLUMBIA, SC 29219-0001
TEL: (803) 788-3860
FAX: (803) 736-3420
TOLL FREE: (800) 868-2500
IN-STATE: (800) 288-2227

2890 E COTTONWOOD PKY
PO BOX 30270
SALT LAKE CITY, UT 84121-0270
TEL: (801) 333-2000
FAX: (801) 333-6523
TOLL FREE: (800) 624-6519

PO BOX 186
MONTPELIER, VT 05601-0186
TEL: (802) 223-6131
FAX: (802) 223-1077
TOLL FREE: (800) 457-6648
IN-STATE: (800) 247-2583

PO BOX 27401
RICHMOND, VA 23279-7401
TEL: (804) 354-7000
FAX: (804) 354-7600
TOLL FREE: (800) 451-1527

1800 9TH AVE
PO BOX 21267
SEATTLE, WA 98111-3267
TEL: (206) 464-3600
FAX: (206) 389-6778
TOLL FREE: (800) 464-3663
IN-STATE: (800) 458-3523

EAST 3900 SPRAGUE
PO BOX 3048
SPOKANE, WA 99220-3048
TEL: (509) 536-4700
TOLL FREE: (800) 835-3510
IN-STATE: (800) 572-0778

401 W MICHIGAN ST
PO BOX 2025
MILWAUKEE, WI 53201-2025
TEL: (414) 226-5000
FAX: (414) 226-5040
TOLL FREE: (800) 558-1584

PO BOX 2266
CHEYENNE, WY 82003-2266
TEL: (307) 634-1393
FAX: (307) 778-8582
TOLL FREE: (800) 442-2376
IN-STATE: (800) 442-2376

165 COURT ST
ROCHESTER, NY 14647-0001
TEL: (716) 454-1700
FAX: (716) 238-4400
TOLL FREE: (800) 847-1200

BLUE PLUS
PO BOX 64179
SAINT PAUL, MN 55164-0179
TEL: (651) 456-8501
FAX: (651) 456-1004
TOLL FREE: (800) 382-2000

BLUE RIDGE ADMINISTRATORS
105 S PANTOPS DR, STE C3
PO BOX 1067
CHARLOTTESVILLE, VA 22902
TEL: (804) 977-3500
FAX: (804) 979-5626
TOLL FREE: (800) 677-1867

BLUE SHIELD OF CALIFORNIA
103 WOOD MERE
PO BOX 272550
FOLSOM, CA 95630
TOLL FREE: (800) 424-6521
IN-STATE: (800) 424-6521

129 N GUILD AVE
PO BOX 241004
LODI, CA 95241-9504
TEL: (209) 367-2800
TOLL FREE: (800) 248-2341

40 NE ST
PO BOX 769028
WOODLAND, CA 95776-9028
TEL: (530) 674-0504
FAX: (530) 668-2801
TOLL FREE: (800) 688-0327

BLUE SHIELD OF NORTHEASTERN NEW YORK
187 WOLF RD
PO BOX 15013
ALBANY, NY 12212
TEL: (518) 453-5700
FAX: (518) 438-1837
TOLL FREE: (800) 888-1238

BOON-CHAPMAN
7600 CHEVY CHASE DR, STE 300
PO BOX 9201
AUSTIN, TX 78766-9201
TEL: (512) 454-2681
FAX: (512) 459-1552
TOLL FREE: (800) 252-9653

BPS INC
145 N CHURCH ST, STE 300
PO BOX 1227
SPARTANBURG, SC 29304-1227
TEL: (864) 585-4338
FAX: (864) 573-7709
TOLL FREE: (800) 868-7526

BROKERAGE CONCEPTS, INC
651 ALLENDALE RD
PO BOX 60608
KING OF PRUSSIA, PA 19406-0608
TEL: (610) 337-2600
FAX: (610) 491-4992
TOLL FREE: (800) 220-2600

BROKERAGE SERVICES, INC
11200 LOOMAS BLVD NE
PO BOX 11020
ALBUQUERQUE, NM 87192-0020
TEL: (505) 292-5533
FAX: (505) 293-7725
TOLL FREE: (800) 274-5533

BUFFALO ROCK CO, INC
103 OXMOOR RD
PO BOX 10048
BIRMINGHAM, AL 35202-0048
TEL: (205) 942-3435
FAX: (205) 940-7768

BUILDERS TRANSPORT, INC
PO BOX 24949
COLUMBIA, SC 29223
TEL: (803) 699-9940
FAX: (803) 699-6673

BUNZL DISTRIBUTION USA, INC
701 EMERSON RD, STE 500
PO BOX 419111
SAINT LOUIS, MO 63141-9111
TEL: (314) 997-5959
FAX: (314) 997-0247

BUSINESS ADMINISTRATORS & CONSULTANTS, INC
6331 E LIVINGSTON AVE
PO BOX 107
REYNOLDSBURG, OH 43068-0107
TEL: (614) 863-8780
FAX: (614) 863-9137
TOLL FREE: (800) 521-2654

C.F.S. HEALTH GROUP
10455 MILL RUN CIR
PO BOX 819
OWINGS MILLS, MD 21117-0819
TEL: (410) 654-9394
FAX: (410) 998-5177
TOLL FREE: (800) 553-3745

C & O EMPLOYEES' HOSPITAL ASSOCIATION
543 CHURCH ST
CLIFTON FORGE, VA 24422-1199
TEL: (540) 862-5728
FAX: (540) 862-3552

CABOT SAFETY CORP
90 MECHANIC ST
SOUTHBRIDGE, MA 01550-2555
TEL: (508) 764-5705
FAX: (508) 764-5648

CALIFORNIA MOTOR CAR DEALERS ASSOCIATION
420 CULVER BLVD
PLAYA DEL REY, CA 90293-7706
TEL: (310) 306-6232
FAX: (310) 822-6733
TOLL FREE: (800) 445-8290
IN-STATE: (800) 262-6232

CAM ADMINISTRATIVE SERVICES, INC
25800 NORTHWESTERN HWY, STE 700
PO BOX 5131
SOUTHFIELD, MI 48086-5131
TEL: (248) 827-1050
FAX: (248) 827-2112
TOLL FREE: (800) 732-8906

CAPITAL BLUE CROSS & PENNSYLVANIA BLUE SHIELD
2500 ELMERTON AVE
HARRISBURG, PA 17110
TEL: (717) 541-7000
FAX: (717) 541-6072
TOLL FREE: (800) 958-5558

CAPITAL DISTRICT PHYSICIANS' HEALTH PLAN, INC
17 COLUMBIA CIR
ALBANY, NY 12203-5190
TEL: (518) 862-3700
FAX: (518) 452-0003
TOLL FREE: (800) 777-CARE

CAPITAL HEALTH PLAN
2140 CENTERVILLE PL
PO BOX 15349
TALLAHASSEE, FL 32317-5349
TEL: (850) 383-3377
FAX: (850) 383-3441

CARE AMERICA HEALTH PLANS
6300 CANOGA AVE
PO BOX 946
WOODLAND HILLS, CA 91365
TEL: (818) 228-5050
FAX: (818) 228-5103
TOLL FREE: (800) 827-2273

CARE CHOICES HEALTH PLANS
522 4TH ST- TERRE CENTRE, STE 250
SIOUX CITY, IA 51101-1748
TEL: (712) 252-2344
FAX: (712) 294-7018
TOLL FREE: (800) 535-6252

CAREMARK MEDICAL & DENTAL PLAN
2211 SANDERS RD
NORTHBROOK, IL 60062-6126
TEL: (847) 559-4700
FAX: (847) 559-3905

CARETON HEALTH CARE
PO BOX 22987
KNOXVILLE, TN 37933
FAX: (423) 778-4620
TOLL FREE: (800) 976-7747

CARILION HEALTH PLANS
110 W CAMPBELL AVE
PO BOX 1531
ROANOKE, VA 24007
TEL: (540) 343-6101
FAX: (540) 343-0748

CARNEGIE-MELLON UNIVERSITY
143 N CRAIG ST
PITTSBURGH, PA 15213
TEL: (412) 268-4747
FAX: (412) 268-1524

CAROLINA BENEFIT ADMINISTRATORS OF SOUTH CAROLINA
291 S PINE ST
PO BOX 3257
SPARTANBURG, SC 29304
TEL: (864) 573-6937
FAX: (864) 582-2265
TOLL FREE: (800) 476-2295

CARPENTERS COMBINED FUNDS
495 MANSFIELD AVE- 1ST FL
PITTSBURGH, PA 15205-4376
TEL: (412) 922-5330
FAX: (412) 922-3420
IN-STATE: (800) 242-2539

CELTIC LIFE INSURANCE CO
200 S WACKER DR, STE 900
PO BOX 06410
CHICAGO, IL 60606-5802
TEL: (312) 332-5401
TOLL FREE: (800) 477-7870

CEMARA ADMINISTRATORS INC
3450 N ROCK RD, STE 605
PO BOX 8902
WICHITA, KS 67208-0902
TEL: (316) 631-3939
FAX: (316) 631-3788
TOLL FREE: (800) 285-1551

CEMETERY WORKERS WELFARE FUND
2409 38TH AVE
LONG ISLAND CITY, NY 11101
TEL: (718) 729-7400
FAX: (718) 729-0253

CENTRAL DATA SERVICES, INC
503 MARTINDALE ST, 5TH FL
PITTSBURGH, PA 15212
TEL: (412) 321-6172
FAX: (412) 237-1444

CENTRAL ILLINOIS CARPENTERS
2400 N MAIN ST, STE 100
EAST PEORIA, IL 61611-1735
TEL: (309) 699-7200
FAX: (309) 699-7032

CENTRAL PENNSYLVANIA TEAMSTERS HEALTH & WELFARE FUND
1055 SPRING ST
PO BOX 15224
READING, PA 19612-5224
TEL: (610) 320-5500
FAX: (610) 320-9209
TOLL FREE: (800) 331-0420
IN-STATE: (800) 422-8330

CENTURY FURNITURE
401 11TH ST NW
PO BOX 608
HICKORY, NC 28603
TEL: (828) 328-1851
FAX: (828) 328-2176

CHAMPUS
PO BOX 202000
FLORENCE, SC 29502-2000
TEL: (843) 665-7822
TOLL FREE: (800) 403-3950

PO BOX 7011
CAMDEN, SC 29020-7011
TOLL FREE: (800) 578-1294

PO BOX 100598
FLORENCE, SC 29501-0598
TEL: (843) 665-7822
TOLL FREE: (800) 403-3950

PO BOX 7021
CAMDEN, SC 29020-7021
TOLL FREE: (800) 613-7124

PO BOX 202000
FLORENCE, SC 29502-2000
TEL: (843) 665-7822
TOLL FREE: (800) 403-3950

1717 W BROADWAY
PO BOX 7985
MADISON, WI 53707-7985
TEL: (608) 259-4848

CHER BUMPS & ASSOCIATES
6100 N ROBINSON, STE 204
PO BOX 548805
OKLAHOMA CITY, OK 73154-8805
TEL: (405) 840-6022
FAX: (405) 858-7361
TOLL FREE: (888) 840-8924

CHOICECARE HEALTH PLANS, INC
655 EDEN PARK DR, STE 400
PO BOX 3188
CINCINNATI, OH 45201
TEL: (513) 784-5200
FAX: (513) 784-5310
TOLL FREE: (800) 543-7158

CHURCHILL ADMINISTRATIVE PLANS, INC
270 SYLVAN AVE
ENGLEWOOD CLIFFS, NJ 07632
TEL: (201) 871-8400

CIGNA CORPORATION
1601 CHESTNUT ST- TWO LIBERTY PL
PHILADELPHIA, PA 19192-1550
TEL: (215) 761-1000

600 E TAYLOR
PO BOX 9328
SHERMAN, TX 75091-9328
TEL: (903) 892-8167
FAX: (903) 892-6271
TOLL FREE: (800) 525-5803
IN-STATE: (800) 238-8801

9740 APPALOOSA DR
PO BOX 85490
SAN DIEGO, CA 92121
TEL: (619) 693-4600
FAX: (619) 693-4881
TOLL FREE: (800) 822-2994

4025 W MINERAL KING
PO BOX 5038
VISALIA, CA 93278-5038
TEL: (209) 738-2000
FAX: (209) 738-2050
TOLL FREE: (800) 272-2471

2220 PARK LAKE DR, STE 100
PO BOX 49400
ATLANTA, GA 30359
TEL: (770) 723-7894
FAX: (770) 723-7890
TOLL FREE: (800) 942-2471
IN-STATE: (800) 526-7431

2 VANTAGE WY
PO BOX 22599
NASHVILLE, TN 37202
TEL: (615) 244-5650
FAX: (615) 782-4651
IN-STATE: (800) 627-2782

21 HERITAGE DR
BOURBONNAIS, IL 60914
TEL: (815) 939-4566
FAX: (815) 935-3499
TOLL FREE: (800) 654-8777

1630 E SHAW AVE, STE 106
PO BOX 24022
FRESNO, CA 93779-4022
TEL: (209) 222-2500
TOLL FREE: (800) 245-2471
IN-STATE: (800) 428-8891

PO BOX 2300
PITTSBURGH, PA 15230
TEL: (412) 562-2960
TOLL FREE: (800) 338-7691

4050 INNSLAKE DR, STE 300
PO BOX 31353
RICHMOND, VA 23294
TEL: (804) 273-1100
FAX: (804) 273-1219
TOLL FREE: (800) 533-1708

5100 N BROOKLINE- 9TH FL
OKLAHOMA CITY, OK 73112
TOLL FREE: (800) 245-2471
IN-STATE: (800) 245-2471

3838 N CSWY BLVD #2800-B
METAIRIE, LA 70002
TEL: (504) 832-1994
FAX: (504) 831-7499
TOLL FREE: (800) 654-3106
IN-STATE: (800) 238-8801

1 BEAVER VALLEY RD
PO BOX 15408
WILMINGTON, DE 19850
TEL: (302) 324-1841
TOLL FREE: (800) 441-7150

ONE CORP CTR DR, STE 500-472-50
PO BOX 9339
SHERMAN, TX 75091
TEL: (903) 892-8167
TOLL FREE: (800) 492-2224

1700 HIGGINS, STE 600
DES PLAINES, IL 60018
TEL: (815) 939-4566
FAX: (815) 939-0473
TOLL FREE: (800) 541-7526

CINCINNATI INSURANCE CO
3150 HOLCOMB BRDIGE RD, STE 350
PO BOX 920338
NORCROSS, GA 30092-0338
TEL: (770) 662-8753
FAX: (770) 417-4635

CITY OF AMARILLO GROUP HEALTH PLAN
909 E 7TH
PO BOX 1971
AMARILLO, TX 79105-1971
TEL: (806) 378-4209
FAX: (806) 378-9488

CITY OF EULESS EMPLOYEE BENEFITS PLAN
201 N ECTOR DR
EULESS, TX 76039-3543
TEL: (817) 685-1475
FAX: (817) 685-1819

CITY PUBLIC SERVICE GROUP HEALTH PLAN
145 NAVARRO
PO BOX 1771
SAN ANTONIO, TX 78296-1771
TEL: (210) 978-2900
FAX: (210) 978-3351

COAST BENEFITS
3850 S VALLEY VIEW BLVD
PO BOX 80040
LAS VEGAS, NV 89180-0040
TEL: (702) 889-1155
FAX: (702) 889-1284

COLLIN COUNTY COURTHOUSE
210 S MCDONALD ST, STE 612
MCKINNEY, TX 75069-5667
TEL: (972) 548-4604

COLUMBIA UNIVERSAL LIFE INSURANCE CO
11211 TAYLOR DRAPER LN
PO BOX 200225
AUSTIN, TX 78720-0225
TEL: (512) 345-3200
FAX: (512) 343-7599
TOLL FREE: (800) 880-1370

COMCAR INDUSTRIES, INC
111 HAVENDALE BLVD
PO BOX 67
AUBURNDALE, FL 33823
TEL: (941) 967-1101
FAX: (941) 551-1442
TOLL FREE: (800) 524-1101

COMMUNITY HEALTH PLAN OF OHIO
1915 TAMARACK RD
NEWARK, OH 43055-1300
TEL: (740) 348-1400
FAX: (740) 348-1500
TOLL FREE: (800) 806-2756

COMPREHENSIVE CARE SERVICES
1200 YANKEE DOODLE RD
PO BOX 64668
EGAN, MN 55122
TEL: (612) 456-5940
FAX: (612) 456-1582
TOLL FREE: (800) 365-2735

COMPREHENSIVE HEALTH SERVICES INC
2875 W GRAND BLVD
DETROIT, MI 48202
TEL: (313) 875-4200
TOLL FREE: (800) 875-9355

COMPUTER SCIENCE CORP
800 N PEARL ST
PO BOX 4444
ALBANY, NY 12204-0444
TEL: (518) 447-9200
FAX: (518) 447-9240
IN-STATE: (800) 522-5518

CONSECO
11815 N PENN ST
PO BOX 1951
CARMEL, IN 46032
TEL: (317) 817-3700
FAX: (317) 817-3345
TOLL FREE: (800) 824-2726

CONSOLIDATED ASSOCIATION OF RAILROAD EMPLOYEES CARE
4912 MIDWAY DR
PO BOX 6130
TEMPLE, TX 76503
TEL: (254) 773-1330
FAX: (254) 774-8029
TOLL FREE: (800) 334-1330

CONTINENTAL GENERAL INSURANCE CO
8901 INDIAN HILLS DR
PO BOX 247007
OMAHA, NE 68124-7007
TEL: (402) 397-3200
FAX: (402) 392-7771
TOLL FREE: (800) 545-8905
IN-STATE: (800) 397-3200

CONTINENTAL LIFE & ACCIDENT
304 N MAIN ST
PO BOX 1300
ROCKFORD, IL 61105-1300
TEL: (815) 987-5000
FAX: (815) 720-2829
TOLL FREE: (800) 221-3770

COOPERATIVE BENEFIT ADMINISTRATORS
PO BOX 6249
LINCOLN, NE 68506-0249
TEL: (402) 483-9200
FAX: (402) 483-9201

CORESOURCE
6100 FAIRVIEW RD, STE 1000
CHARLOTTE, NC 28210-3291
TEL: (704) 552-0900
FAX: (704) 552-8635
TOLL FREE: (800) 327-5462
IN-STATE: (800) 821-0345

CORESOURCE, INC
4940 CAMPBELL BLVD, STE 200
BALTIMORE, MD 21236
TEL: (410) 931-5060
FAX: (410) 931-3653
TOLL FREE: (800) 624-7130

229 HUBER VLG BLVD
PO BOX 6118
WESTERVILLE, OH 43081-6118
TEL: (614) 890-0070
FAX: (614) 794-0736
TOLL FREE: (800) 282-3920

940 W VALLEY RD
PO BOX 6994
WAYNE, PA 19087
TEL: (610) 687-5924
FAX: (610) 687-1959
TOLL FREE: (800) 345-1166

CORESTAR
146 INDUSTRIAL PARK
JACKSON, MN 56143-9511
TEL: (507) 847-5740
FAX: (507) 847-2358
TOLL FREE: (800) 274-6965

146 INDUSTRIAL PARK
JACKSON, MN 56143-9511
TEL: (507) 847-5740
FAX: (507) 847-2358
TOLL FREE: (800) 274-6965

CORPORATE DIVERSIFIED SERVICES
2401 S 73RD ST, STE 1
PO BOX 2835
OMAHA, NE 68103-2835
TEL: (402) 393-3133
FAX: (402) 398-3773
TOLL FREE: (800) 642-4089

CORVEL CORP
10260 SW GREENBERG RD, STE 1165
PORTLAND, OR 97223
TEL: (503) 244-2093
FAX: (503) 244-2189

COUNTY OF LOS ANGELES
1436 GOODRICH BLVD
COMMERCE, CA 90022
TEL: (213) 738-2279

COVENANT ADMINISTRATORS, INC
11330 LAKEFIELD DR, STE 100
PO BOX 740042
ATLANTA, GA 30374
TEL: (770) 242-6100
FAX: (770) 239-3989
TOLL FREE: (800) 374-6101

CPIC LIFE
PO BOX 3007
LODI, CA 95241-1911
TEL: (209) 367-3415
FAX: (209) 367-3450
TOLL FREE: (800) 642-5599
IN-STATE: (800) 537-0666

CRAWFORD & CO
4341 B ST, STE 301
ANCHORAGE, AK 99503
TEL: (907) 561-5222
FAX: (907) 561-7383
IN-STATE: (888) 549-5222

DAKOTACARE
1323 S MINNESOTA AVE
SIOUX FALLS, SD 57105-0624
TEL: (605) 334-4000
FAX: (605) 336-0270
TOLL FREE: (800) 628-3778
IN-STATE: (800) 325-5598

DC CHARTERED HEALTH PLAN, INC
820 FIRST ST NE, STE LL100
WASHINGTON, DC 20002
TEL: (202) 408-4710
FAX: (202) 408-4730
TOLL FREE: (800) 799-4710

DCA HEALTHCARE MANAGEMENT GROUP
13100 WAYZATA BLVD
MINNETONKA, MN 55305-1840
TEL: (612) 541-7500
FAX: (612) 541-5999
TOLL FREE: (800) 284-4464

DCA INC
3405 ANNAPOLIS LN N, STE 100
PLYMOUTH, MN 55447
TEL: (612) 278-4000
FAX: (612) 278-4601
TOLL FREE: (800) 284-4464

DELMARVA HEALTH PLAN, INC
301 BAY ST, STE 401
PO BOX 2410
EASTON, MD 21601
TEL: (410) 822-7223
FAX: (410) 822-8152
TOLL FREE: (800) 334-3427
IN-STATE: (800) 334-3427

DELTA DENTAL PLAN OF NEW JERSEY INC
1639 RT 10
PO BOX 222
PARSIPPANY, NJ 07054
TEL: (973) 285-4000
FAX: (973) 285-4141
TOLL FREE: (800) 321-0142

DISTRICT 6 HEALTH FUND
18 E 31ST ST
NEW YORK, NY 10016-6702
TEL: (212) 696-5545
FAX: (212) 696-5556
TOLL FREE: (800) 331-1070

DIVERSIFIED GROUP ADMINISTRATORS
311 S CENTRAL
PO BOX 330
CANONSBURG, PA 15317-0330
TEL: (724) 746-8700
FAX: (724) 746-8508
TOLL FREE: (800) 221-8490
IN-STATE: (800) 222-2322

EASTERN BENEFIT SYSTEMS OF CENTENNIAL FINANCIAL GROUP
200 FREEWAY DR E
EAST ORANGE, NJ 07018
TEL: (973) 676-6100
FAX: (973) 676-6794
TOLL FREE: (800) 524-0227
IN-STATE: (800) 772-3610

EAU CLAIRE HEALTH PROTECTION PLAN
3430 OAKWOOD MALL DR
PO BOX 1060
EAU CLAIRE, WI 54702
TEL: (715) 835-6174
FAX: (715) 838-0220
TOLL FREE: (800) 835-6174

EDUCATORS MUTUAL LIFE INSURANCE CO
202 N PRINCE ST
PO BOX 83888
LANCASTER, PA 17608-3888
TEL: (717) 397-2751
FAX: (717) 397-1821
TOLL FREE: (800) 233-0307

ELCA BOARD OF PENSIONS
800 MARQUETTE AVE, STE 1050
PO BOX 59093
MINNEAPOLIS, MN 55459-0093
TEL: (612) 333-7651
FAX: (612) 334-5407
IN-STATE: (800) 352-2876

ELECTRONIC DATA SYSTEMS
PO BOX 15508
SACRAMENTO, CA 95852
TEL: (916) 636-1100
FAX: (916) 636-1056
IN-STATE: (800) 541-5555

EMERALD HEALTH NETWORK, INC
1100 SUPERIOR AVE- 16TH FL
PO BOX 94808
CLEVELAND, OH 44101-4808
TEL: (216) 479-2030
FAX: (216) 241-4158
TOLL FREE: (800) 683-6830

EMPIRE BLUE CROSS & BLUE SHIELD
11 CORPORATE WOODS BLVD
PO BOX 11800
ALBANY, NY 12211-0800
TEL: (518) 367-4737
FAX: (518) 367-5373

EMPIRE MEDICARE SERVICES
PO BOX 4846
SYRACUSE, NY 13221-4846
TEL: (315) 442-4400
FAX: (315) 442-4815
TOLL FREE: (800) 442-8430

EMPLOYEE BENEFIT ASSOCIATION
2858 W MARKET ST, STE N
PO BOX 5427
AKRON, OH 44333
TEL: (330) 867-9050
FAX: (330) 867-7029
TOLL FREE: (800) 624-2564

EMPLOYEE BENEFIT CLAIMS, INC
820 PARISH ST
PITTSBURGH, PA 15220-3405
TEL: (412) 922-0780
FAX: (412) 922-3071
TOLL FREE: (800) 922-4966

EMPLOYEE BENEFIT PLAN ADMINISTRATORS
210 MAIN ST
MANCHESTER, CT 06040
TEL: (860) 643-6401
FAX: (860) 643-6818
TOLL FREE: (800) 848-2129

EMPLOYEE BENEFIT SYSTEMS CORP
1701 MT PLEASANT ST, STE 1
PO BOX 1053
BURLINGTON, IA 52601-2799
TEL: (319) 752-3200
FAX: (319) 754-4480
TOLL FREE: (800) 373-1327

EQUITABLE PLAN SERVICES, INC
12312 SAINT ANDREWS DR
PO BOX 770466
OKLAHOMA CITY, OK 73177
TEL: (405) 755-2929
FAX: (405) 755-1185
TOLL FREE: (800) 749-2631

ERISA ADMINISTRATIVE SERVICES, INC
12325 HYMEADOW DR- BLDG 4
AUSTIN, TX 78750-0001
TEL: (512) 250-9397
FAX: (512) 335-7298
TOLL FREE: (800) 933-7472

10520 E BETHANY DR- BLDG 7
AURORA, CO 80014
TEL: (303) 745-0147
FAX: (303) 745-7010

1200 SAN PEDRO NE
ALBUQUERQUE, NM 87110
TEL: (505) 262-1821
FAX: (505) 262-1822

3108 N 24TH ST- BLDG B
PHOENIX, AZ 85016-7313
TEL: (602) 956-3516
FAX: (602) 956-1943

2156 W 2200 S
SALT LAKE CITY, UT 84119-1326
TEL: (801) 973-1001
FAX: (801) 973-1007

1429 SECOND ST
SANTA FE, NM 87505
TEL: (505) 988-4974
FAX: (505) 988-8943

FARM BUREAU MUTUAL INSURANCE CO
194 E COMMERCIAL
WEISER, ID 83672-2511
TEL: (208) 549-1414
FAX: (208) 549-1433

FARM BUREAU MUTUAL INSURANCE CO OF IDAHO
444 E 5TH N
PO BOX 1148
BURLEY, ID 83318-1148
TEL: (208) 678-0431
FAX: (208) 678-5368

345 MAIN
PO BOX 428
GRAND VIEW, ID 83624-0428
TEL: (208) 834-2766
FAX: (208) 834-2526

170 S 2ND E
PO BOX 506
SODA SPRINGS, ID 83276-0506
TEL: (208) 547-3315
FAX: (208) 547-3316

FARMERS AUTO INSURANCE ASSOCIATION
2505 COURT ST
PO BOX 129
PEKIN, IL 61558-0001
TEL: (309) 346-1161
FAX: (309) 346-8265
TOLL FREE: (800) 322-0160

FEDERATED MUTUAL INSURANCE CO
2701 N ROCKY PT DR, STE 1200
PO BOX 31716
TAMPA, FL 33631-3716
TEL: (813) 287-0155
FAX: (813) 287-0785
IN-STATE: (800) 237-8292

FIDELITY SECURITY LIFE INSURANCE CO
PO BOX 418131
KANSAS CITY, MO 64141-9131
TEL: (816) 756-1060
FAX: (816) 968-0560
TOLL FREE: (800) 821-7303

FIRST HEALTH
4411 BUSINESS PARK BLVD, STE 16
ANCHORAGE, AK 99503
TEL: (907) 561-5650
FAX: (907) 563-1082

FIRST INTEGRATED HEALTH
19191 S VERMONT, STE 700
PO BOX 5279
TORRANCE, CA 90510-5279
TEL: (310) 532-8887
FAX: (310) 532-2824
TOLL FREE: (800) 433-3554

FORTIS BENEFITS INSURANCE CO
1950 SPECTRUM CIR, STE B100
MARIETTA, GA 30067-6052
FAX: (770) 916-0905
TOLL FREE: (800) 955-1586

FOX-EVERETT, INC
3780 I-55 N FRONTAGE RD, STE 200
PO BOX 23096
JACKSON, MS 39225-3095
TEL: (601) 981-6000
FAX: (601) 718-5399

FREMONT COMPENSATION INSURANCE CO
255 CALIFORNIA ST
PO BOX 7468
SAN FRANCISCO, CA 94111
TEL: (415) 627-5000
FAX: (415) 296-3099
IN-STATE: (800) 464-0556

FRINGE BENEFIT COORDINATORS
1239 NW 10TH AVE
GAINESVILLE, FL 32601-4154
TEL: (352) 372-2028
FAX: (352) 372-9805
IN-STATE: (800) 654-1452

GALLATIN MEDICAL CLINICS
10720 PARAMOUNT BLVD
PO BOX 868
DOWNEY, CA 90241-3306
TEL: (562) 923-6511
FAX: (562) 861-6884

GARDNER & WHITE
8902 N MERIDIAN ST, STE 202
PO BOX 40619
INDIANAPOLIS, IN 46260-5307
TEL: (317) 581-1580
FAX: (317) 587-0780
TOLL FREE: (800) 347-5737

GEM INSURANCE CO
525 E 100 S
PO BOX 115
PUEBLO, CO 81002-0115
FAX: (888) 359-5304
TOLL FREE: (800) 888-7164

GENERAL AMERICAN LIFE INSURANCE CO
719 TEACO RD
PO BOX 882
KENNETT, MO 63857-3749
TEL: (314) 843-8700
FAX: (314) 525-5740
TOLL FREE: (800) 633-8989

GENERAL INSURANCE EXCHANGE AGENCY, INC
4301 DARROW RD
PO BOX 1849
STOW, OH 44224-0849
TEL: (330) 688-4322
FAX: (330) 688-4904
TOLL FREE: (800) 968-7222

GEORGIA BANKERS ASSOCIATION INSURANCE
50 HURT PLZ, STE 1050
ATLANTA, GA 30303-2916
TEL: (404) 522-1501
FAX: (404) 522-9848

GILBERT-MAGILL CO
920 MAIN ST, STE 1800
PO BOX 410249
KANSAS CITY, MO 64141-0249
TEL: (816) 474-3535
FAX: (816) 842-5795
TOLL FREE: (800) 522-2460

GOLDEN RULE LIFE INSURANCE CO
712 11TH ST
LAWRENCEVILLE, IL 62439-2395
TEL: (618) 943-8000
FAX: (618) 943-8031

7440 WOODLAND DR
INDIANAPOLIS, IN 46278-1719
TEL: (317) 297-4123
FAX: (317) 298-4410
IN-STATE: (800) 265-7791

GOLDEN STATE MUTUAL LIFE INSURANCE CO
1999 W ADAMS BLVD
PO BOX 512332
LOS ANGELES, CA 90051-0332
TEL: (323) 731-1131
TOLL FREE: (800) 225-5476

GOULD MEDICAL FOUNDATION
PO BOX 254708
SACRAMENTO, CA 95865
TEL: (209) 524-2221
FAX: (209) 524-4562
IN-STATE: (800) 564-6853

GRAND VALLEY CORP
829 FOREST HILLS AVE SE
GRAND RAPIDS, MI 49546-2325
TEL: (616) 949-2410
FAX: (616) 949-4978

GRANGE INSURANCE ASSOCIATION
2425 REGENCY RD
PO BOX 8035
LEXINGTON, KY 40533-8035
TEL: (606) 278-5481
FAX: (800) 837-0802
TOLL FREE: (800) 837-0801

GRAY INSURANCE CO
3601 N I-10 SERVICE RD W
PO BOX 6202
METAIRIE, LA 70009-6202
TEL: (504) 888-7790
FAX: (504) 887-5658

GREAT WEST LIFE
1740 TECHNOLOGY DR, STE 300
PO BOX 1120
SAN JOSE, CA 95108
FAX: (408) 453-7963
TOLL FREE: (800) 685-1050

1511 N WEST SHORE BLVD, STE 850
PO BOX 31251
TAMPA, FL 33631-3251
FAX: (813) 281-0019
TOLL FREE: (800) 333-5251

10000 N CENTRAL EXPY, STE 800
DALLAS, TX 75231
FAX: (214) 987-0827
TOLL FREE: (800) 685-3020

1802 DEL RANGE BLVD, STE 200
CHEYENNE, WY 82001
TOLL FREE: (800) 288-9575

GREAT-WEST LIFE & ANNUITY
PO BOX 950
DENVER, CO 80201
FAX: (303) 790-1998
TOLL FREE: (800) 685-2020

1800 S W 1ST AVE, STE 410
PO BOX 429
PORTLAND, OR 97207-0429
FAX: (503) 224-2202
TOLL FREE: (800) 685-1020

GREAT-WEST LIFE ASSURANCE CO
455 MARKET ST, STE 2000
SAN FRANCISCO, CA 94105-2403
TEL: (415) 777-4646
FAX: (415) 957-9842
TOLL FREE: (800) 685-1040

GROCER'S INSURANCE GROUP
6605 SE LAKE RD
PO BOX 22146
PORTLAND, OR 97269
TEL: (503) 833-1600
FAX: (503) 833-1699
TOLL FREE: (800) 777-3602

GROUP BENEFIT SERVICES, INC
6 N PARK, STE 310
HUNT VALLEY, MD 21030
TEL: (410) 832-1300
FAX: (410) 832-1315
TOLL FREE: (800) 638-6085

GROUP BENEFITS UNLIMITED
1000 PLAZA DR, STE 300
CHAMBERG, IL 60173
TEL: (847) 330-6000
FAX: (847) 330-9400
TOLL FREE: (800) 772-0666

GROUP HEALTH MANAGERS
26205 FIVE-MILE RD
REDFORD, MI 48239-3154
TEL: (313) 535-7100
FAX: (313) 535-8472
TOLL FREE: (800) 992-2508

GROUP HEALTH NORTHWEST
CORP CTR- 5615 W SUNSET HWY
PO BOX 204
SPOKANE, WA 99210
TEL: (509) 838-9100
FAX: (509) 838-3292
TOLL FREE: (800) 497-2210
IN-STATE: (800) 377-8853

5615 W SUNSET HIGH
PO BOX 204
SPOKANE, WA 99210-0204
TEL: (509) 838-9100
FAX: (509) 458-0368
TOLL FREE: (800) 767-4670
IN-STATE: (800) 838-9100

GROUP HEALTH PLAN OF ST LOUIS
111 CORPERATE OFFICE DR, STE 400
EARTH CITY, MO 63145
TEL: (314) 453-1700
FAX: (314) 506-1555
TOLL FREE: (800) 743-3901

GROUP HEALTH PLAN OF ST. LOUIS
111 CORPERATE OFFICE DR, STE 400
EARTH CITY, MO 63145
TEL: (314) 453-1700
FAX: (314) 506-1958
TOLL FREE: (800) 743-3901

GROUP INSURANCE PLAN CHATTANOOGA
1500 N DALE MABRY HWY E 6
PO BOX 31601
TAMPA, FL 33631-3601
TEL: (813) 871-4664
FAX: (813) 871-4601

GROUP MAJOR MEDICAL EXPENSE
PO BOX 6614
SAINT LOUIS, MO 63166-6149
TEL: (314) 554-6490

GROUP SERVICES & ADMINISTRATION, INC
3113 CLASSEN BLVD
OKLAHOMA CITY, OK 73118-3818
TEL: (405) 528-4400
FAX: (405) 528-5558
TOLL FREE: (800) 475-4445

GUARANTEE RESERVE LIFE INSURANCE CO
530 RIVER OAKS W
CALUMET CITY, IL 60409
TEL: (708) 868-4232
FAX: (708) 891-8886
TOLL FREE: (800) 323-8764

GUARDIAN LIFE INSURANCE CO OF AMERICA
777 E MAGNESIUM
PO BOX 2467
SPOKANE, WA 99210
TEL: (509) 468-6000
FAX: (509) 468-6420
TOLL FREE: (800) 695-4542

GULF GUARANTY EMPLOYEE BENEFIT SERVICES, INC
4785 I-55 N, STE 106
PO BOX 14977
JACKSON, MS 39236-4977
TEL: (601) 981-9505
FAX: (601) 981-6805
TOLL FREE: (800) 890-7337

GULFCO LIFE INSURANCE CO
660 N MAIN
PO BOX 157
MARKSVILLE, LA 71351-0157
TEL: (318) 253-7564
FAX: (318) 253-4903

H.E.R.E.I.U. WELFARE FUNDS
711 N COMMONS DR
PO BOX 6020
AURORA, IL 60598
TEL: (630) 236-5100
FAX: (630) 236-4394

HARRINGTON BENEFIT SERVICES
3041 MORSE XING
PO BOX 16789
COLUMBUS, OH 43216-6789
TEL: (614) 470-7000
FAX: (614) 470-7171
TOLL FREE: (800) 848-4623
IN-STATE: (800) 848-2664

HARRIS METHODIST HEALTH PLAN
611 RYAN PLZ DR, STE 900
PO BOX 90100
ARLINGTON, TX 76011
TEL: (817) 878-5800
FAX: (817) 462-7235
TOLL FREE: (800) 633-8598

HAWAII MEDICAL SERVICE ASSOCIATION
818 KEEAUMOKU ST
PO BOX 860
HONOLULU, HI 96808
TEL: (808) 948-6111
FAX: (808) 948-6555
TOLL FREE: (800) 776-4672

HEALTH ALLIANCE MEDICAL PLANS
102 MAIN ST
URBANA, IL 61801
TEL: (217) 337-8100
FAX: (217) 337-8008
TOLL FREE: (800) 851-3379

HEALTH ALLIANCE PLAN OF MICHIGAN
2850 W GRAND BLVD
DETROIT, MI 48202-2692
TEL: (313) 872-8100
FAX: (313) 874-7496
TOLL FREE: (800) 422-4641
IN-STATE: (800) 367-3292

HEALTH AMERICA
2575 INTERSTATE DR
HARRISBURG, PA 17110
TEL: (412) 553-7300
FAX: (412) 553-7384
TOLL FREE: (800) 735-2202

HEALTH CARE ADMINISTRATORS
2401 CHANDLER RD, STE 300
PO BOX 1309
MUSKOGEE, OK 74402
TEL: (918) 687-1261
FAX: (918) 682-7984
TOLL FREE: (800) 749-1422

HEALTH CARE ADMINISTRATORS, INC
415 N 26TH ST, STE 101
PO BOX 6108
LAFAYETTE, IN 47903-6108
TEL: (765) 474-5455
FAX: (765) 448-7799
TOLL FREE: (888) 448-7447

HEALTH CARE SERVICE CORP
300 E RANDOLPH ST
PO BOX 1364
CHICAGO, IL 60690
TEL: (312) 938-6000

HEALTH FIRST
278 BARKS RD W
PO BOX 1820
MARION, OH 43301-1820
TEL: (740) 387-6355
FAX: (740) 383-3840
TOLL FREE: (800) 858-1472

HEALTH FIRST, INC
821 E SE LOOP 323, II AMERICAN CTR, STE 200
PO BOX 130217
TYLER, TX 75713
TEL: (903) 581-2600
FAX: (903) 509-5726
TOLL FREE: (800) 477-2287
IN-STATE: (800) 477-2287

HEALTH GUARD
280 GRANITE RUN DR, STE 105
LANCASTER, PA 17601-6810
TEL: (717) 560-9049
FAX: (717) 560-9413
TOLL FREE: (800) 269-4606

HEALTH MANAGEMENT ASSOCIATES
1600 W BROADWAY RD, STE 385
TEMPE, AZ 85282
TEL: (480) 921-8944
FAX: (480) 894-5230
TOLL FREE: (800) 331-9562

HEALTH NET
21600 OXIDE ST
PO BOX 9103
WOODLAND HILLS, CA 91367-9103
TEL: (818) 676-6775
FAX: (818) 676-8755
TOLL FREE: (800) 522-0088

2300 MAIN ST, STE 700
KANSAS CITY, MO 64108
TEL: (816) 221-8400
FAX: (816) 221-7709
TOLL FREE: (800) 468-1442

HEALTH NET HMO, INC
44 VANTAGE WAY, STE 300
PO BOX 20000
NASHVILLE, TN 37202
TEL: (615) 291-7022
FAX: (615) 401-4647
TOLL FREE: (800) 881-9466
IN-STATE: (800) 314-3258

HEALTH PARTNERS
PO BOX 1309
MINNEAPOLIS, MN 55440-1309
TEL: (612) 883-6000
FAX: (612) 883-6100
TOLL FREE: (800) 828-1159

HEALTH PLAN
52160 NATIONAL RD E
ST. CLAIRSVILLE, OH 43950-9306
TEL: (740) 695-7605
FAX: (740) 695-8103
TOLL FREE: (800) 624-6961

HEALTH PLAN OF NEVADA, INC
2724 TENAYA
PO BOX 15645
LAS VEGAS, NV 89114-5645
TEL: (702) 242-7444
FAX: (702) 242-9038

HEALTH PLAN OF THE REDWOODS
3033 CLEVELAND AVE
SANTA ROSA, CA 95403-2126
TEL: (707) 544-2273
FAX: (707) 525-4261
IN-STATE: (800) 248-2070

HEALTH RISK MANAGEMENT
10900 HAMPSHIRE AVE S
PO BOX 226
MINNEAPOLIS, MN 55440-0226
TEL: (612) 829-3500
FAX: (612) 829-3622
TOLL FREE: (800) 642-4456

5250 LOVERS LN
PO BOX 4022
KALAMAZOO, MI 49002-1564
TEL: (616) 381-7995
FAX: (616) 382-1525
TOLL FREE: (800) 253-0966
IN-STATE: (800) 632-5674

HEALTH SERVICES MEDICAL CORP
8278 WILLETT PKY
BALDWINSVILLE, NY 13027
TEL: (315) 638-2133
FAX: (315) 638-0985
TOLL FREE: (800) 388-3264

HEALTHCARE AMERICA PLANS, INC
453 S WEBB RD, STE 200
PO BOX 780467
WICHITA, KS 67278-0467
TEL: (316) 687-1600
FAX: (316) 616-2076
TOLL FREE: (800) 475-4274

HEALTHCARE PARTNERS MEDICAL GROUP, INC
PO BOX 6099
TORRANCE, CA 90504
TEL: (310) 965-1100
FAX: (310) 352-6219

HEALTHFIRST, INC
PO BOX 17709
GREENVILLE, SC 29606
TEL: (864) 289-3000
FAX: (864) 289-3053
TOLL FREE: (800) 832-7713

HEALTHSOURCE
5794 WIDEWATERS PKY- 2ND FL
PO BOX 1498
SYRACUSE, NY 13201-1498
TEL: (315) 449-1100
FAX: (315) 449-2200
TOLL FREE: (800) 999-0874

2 COLLEGE PARK DR
HOOKSETT, NH 03106
TEL: (603) 225-5077
FAX: (603) 268-7981
TOLL FREE: (800) 531-3121
IN-STATE: (800) 531-3121

HELLER ASSOCIATES
2755 BRISTOL ST, STE 250
COSTA MESA, CA 92626-5956
TEL: (714) 549-7052
FAX: (714) 549-4816
IN-STATE: (800) 552-2929

2235 FLAMINGO RD #406
LAS VEGAS, NV 89119
TEL: (714) 549-7052
FAX: (714) 549-4816

8228 MAYFIELD RD, STE 5-B
CHESTERLAND, OH 44026
TEL: (714) 549-7052
FAX: (714) 549-4816

HERITAGE INSURANCE MANAGERS, INC
PO BOX 659570
SAN ANTONIO, TX 78265-9570
TEL: (210) 829-7467
FAX: (210) 822-4113
TOLL FREE: (800) 456-7480

HMA, INC
PO BOX 2069
COTTONWOOD, AZ 86326
TEL: (602) 921-8944
FAX: (602) 894-5230
TOLL FREE: (800) 448-3585

HMO COLORADO, INC
700 BROADWAY
DENVER, CO 80273
TEL: (303) 831-0801
FAX: (303) 861-9018
TOLL FREE: (800) 544-3879
IN-STATE: (800) 533-5643

HMO MONTANA
404 FULLER AVE
PO BOX 5004
GREAT FALLS, MT 59403
TEL: (406) 447-8600
TOLL FREE: (800) 447-7828

HMO NEBRASKA
2401 S 73RD ST, STE 2
PO BOX 241739
OMAHA, NE 68124-5739
TEL: (402) 392-2800
FAX: (402) 392-2761
TOLL FREE: (800) 843-2373

HMO NEW MEXICO, INC
12800 INDIAN SCHOOL NE
PO BOX 11968
ALBUQUERQUE, NM 87112
TEL: (505) 291-6945
TOLL FREE: (800) 423-1630
IN-STATE: (800) 423-1630

HMO REGENCE CARE
1800 9TH AVE
PO BOX 91005
SEATTLE, WA 98111-9105
TEL: (206) 340-6600
FAX: (206) 389-6719
TOLL FREE: (800) 222-6129

HOLY CROSS RESOURCES, INC
ST MARY'S LOURDES HALL, 3575 MOREAU CT
SOUTH BEND, IN 46628-4320
TEL: (219) 283-4600
FAX: (219) 283-4709
TOLL FREE: (800) 348-2616

HOMETOWN HEALTH NETWORK
100 LILLIAN GISH BLVD, STE 301
MASSILLON, OH 44647
TEL: (330) 837-6880
FAX: (330) 837-6869
IN-STATE: (800) 426-9013

HOMETOWN HEALTH PLAN
400 S WELLS AVE
RENO, NV 89502-1823
TEL: (775) 325-3000
FAX: (775) 982-3160
TOLL FREE: (800) 336-0123
IN-STATE: (800) 336-0123

HUMANA
PO BOX 12359
MILWAUKEE, WI 53212-0359
TEL: (414) 223-3300
FAX: (414) 223-7777
TOLL FREE: (800) 289-0260

HUMANA HEALTH CARE PLAN, INC
500 W MAIN
LOUISVILLE, KY 40202
TEL: (502) 580-5251
FAX: (502) 580-3127
TOLL FREE: (800) 448-6262

HUMANA, INC
500 W MAIN ST
LOUISVILLE, KY 40202-1438
TEL: (502) 580-1000
FAX: (502) 580-3127
TOLL FREE: (800) 448-6262
IN-STATE: (800) 486-2620

10450 HOLMES RD, STE 200
KANSAS CITY, MO 64131
TEL: (816) 941-8900
FAX: (816) 942-6782

HUMANA/ WISCONSIN HEALTH ORGANIZATION
111 W PLEASANT ST
MILWAUKEE, WI 53212
TEL: (414) 223-3300
TOLL FREE: (800) 289-0906
IN-STATE: (800) 777-0184

IDAHO FARM BUREAU MUTUAL INSURANCE CO
435 LINCOLN
PO BOX 239
AMERICAN FALLS, ID 83211-0239
TEL: (208) 226-5066
FAX: (208) 226-7929

225 W GRAND
PO BOX 824
ARCO, ID 83213-0824
TEL: (208) 527-3431
FAX: (208) 527-3432

124 N OAK
PO BOX 668
BLACKFOOT, ID 83221-0668
TEL: (208) 785-2410
FAX: (208) 785-2422

6426 KOOTENAI ST
PO BOX 1387
BONNERS FERRY, ID 83805-1387
TEL: (208) 267-5502
FAX: (208) 267-5503

6912 N GOVERNMENT WY
DALTON GARDENS, ID 83815-8747
TEL: (208) 772-6662
FAX: (208) 772-2553

906 S WASHINGTON
PO BOX 156
EMMETT, ID 83617-0156
TEL: (208) 365-5382
FAX: (208) 365-2465

131 3RD AVE E
GOODING, ID 83330-1101
TEL: (208) 934-8405
FAX: (208) 934-8406

711 N MAIN
PO BOX 609
HAILEY, ID 83333-0609
TEL: (208) 788-3529
FAX: (208) 788-3619

118 W IDAHO
PO BOX 1197
HOMEDALE, ID 83620-1197
TEL: (208) 337-4041
FAX: (208) 337-4042

956 LINCOLN
PO BOX 2948
IDAHO FALLS, ID 83403-2948
TEL: (208) 522-2652
FAX: (208) 522-2675

200 E AVE A
PO BOX C
JEROME, ID 83338-0326
TEL: (208) 324-4378
FAX: (208) 324-4393

2007 14TH AVE
LEWISTON, ID 83501-3019
TEL: (208) 743-5533
FAX: (208) 743-5535

34 N MAIN
MALAD, ID 83252-1247
TEL: (208) 766-2259
FAX: (208) 766-4211

470 WASHINGTON ST
MONTPELIER, ID 83254-1545
TEL: (208) 847-0851
FAX: (208) 847-0856

140 E 2ND N
PO BOX 673
MOUNTAIN HOME, ID 83647-0673
TEL: (208) 587-8484
FAX: (208) 587-8121

1501 26TH ST, STE C
OROFINO, ID 83544
TEL: (208) 476-4722
FAX: (208) 476-7348

235 N MAIN
PAYETTE, ID 83661-2852
TEL: (208) 642-4414
FAX: (208) 642-4415

200 W ALAMEDA
PO BOX 4848
POCATELLO, ID 83205
TEL: (208) 233-9442
FAX: (208) 233-4167

112 CENTER ST
PO BOX 1924
SALMON, ID 83467-1924
TEL: (208) 756-3335
FAX: (208) 756-3357

325 E MAIN
PO BOX 528
SAINT ANTHONY, ID 83445-0528
TEL: (208) 624-3171
FAX: (208) 624-3173

414 MAIN AVE
SAINT MARIES, ID 83861-2059
TEL: (208) 245-5568
FAX: (208) 245-5569

IHC HEALTH PLANS
4646 W LAKE PARK BLVD
SALT LAKE CITY, UT 84120-8212
TEL: (801) 442-5000
FAX: (801) 442-5003
TOLL FREE: (800) 538-5038
IN-STATE: (800) 442-5038

ILLINOIS MASONIC COMMUNITY HEALTH PLAN
836 W WELLINGTON
CHICAGO, IL 60657-5147
TEL: (773) 296-7167
FAX: (773) 296-5598

INSURANCE CO OF THE WEST
11455 EL CAMINO REAL
PO BOX 85563
SAN DIEGO, CA 92186-5563
TEL: (619) 350-2400
FAX: (619) 350-2543
TOLL FREE: (800) 877-1111

INSURANCE MANAGEMENT ADMINISTRATORS OF LOUISIANA
1325 BARKSDALE BLVD, STE 300
PO BOX 71120
BOSSIER, LA 71171
TEL: (318) 868-0600
FAX: (318) 747-5074

INSURANCE MANAGEMENT ASSOCIATES, INC
250 N WATER ST, STE 600
PO BOX 2992
WICHITA, KS 67201
TEL: (316) 267-9221
FAX: (316) 266-6385
TOLL FREE: (800) 288-6732

INSURANCE & PERSONNEL SERVICES
2121 N WEBB RD
PO BOX 2160
GRAND ISLAND, NE 68802-2160
TEL: (308) 384-8700
FAX: (308) 384-8423

INSURERS ADMINISTRATIVE CORP
2101 W PEORIA AVE, STE 100
PO BOX 39119
PHOENIX, AZ 85029-9119
TEL: (602) 870-1400
FAX: (602) 395-0496
TOLL FREE: (800) 843-3106

INSUREX BENEFITS ADMINISTRATORS
1835 UNION AVE, STE 400
PO BOX 41779
MEMPHIS, TN 38174-1779
TEL: (901) 725-6435
FAX: (901) 725-6437

INTEGON CORP
500 W 5TH ST
PO BOX 3199
WINSTON-SALEM, NC 27102-3199
TEL: (336) 770-2000
FAX: (336) 770-2122
TOLL FREE: (800) 642-0506

INTEGRATED HEALTH SERVICES
235 ELM ST NE
PO BOX 30278
ALBUQUERQUE, NM 87190
TEL: (505) 222-8260

INTER VALLEY HEALTH PLAN
300 S PARK AVE
PO BOX 6002
POMONA, CA 91769-6002
TEL: (909) 623-6333
FAX: (909) 622-2907
TOLL FREE: (800) 251-8191

INTERACTIVE MEDICAL SYSTEMS, INC
4505 FALLS OF NEUSE, STE 550
PO BOX 19108
RALEIGH, NC 27619
TEL: (919) 877-9933
FAX: (919) 846-8887

INTERCARE BENEFIT SYSTEMS, INC
5500 GREENWOOD PLZ BLVD
PO BOX 3559
ENGLEWOOD, CO 80111-3559
TEL: (303) 770-5710
FAX: (303) 770-2743
TOLL FREE: (800) 426-7453

INTERCONTINENTAL CORP
135 N PENNSYLVANIA ST, STE 770
INDIANAPOLIS, IN 46204
TEL: (317) 238-5700
FAX: (317) 637-6634
TOLL FREE: (800) 962-6831

INTERGROUP OF ARIZONA
930 N FINANCE CTR DR
TUCSON, AZ 85710
TEL: (520) 751-6111
FAX: (520) 290-5176
TOLL FREE: (800) 289-2818

INTERGROUP OF UTAH, INC
127 S 500 E
SALT LAKE CITY, UT 84102
TEL: (801) 532-7665

INTERMOUNTAIN ADMINISTRATORS, INC
2806 GARFIELD
PO BOX 3018
MISSOULA, MT 59806
TEL: (406) 721-2222
FAX: (406) 721-2252
TOLL FREE: (800) 877-1122

J.P. FARLEY CORP
22021 BROOKPARK RD, STE 100
PO BOX 268000
CLEVELAND, OH 44126-8000
TEL: (440) 734-6800
FAX: (440) 734-1668
TOLL FREE: (800) 634-0173

JARDINE GROUP SERVICES CORP
13 CORNELL RD
LATHAM, NY 12110
TEL: (518) 782-3000
FAX: (518) 782-3157
TOLL FREE: (800) 366-5273

JEFFERSON LIFE INSURANCE CO
9304 FOREST LN N, STE 256
PO BOX 749008
DALLAS, TX 75374-9008
TEL: (214) 340-8995
FAX: (214) 340-6114
TOLL FREE: (800) 343-5542

JEFFERSON-PILOT LIFE INSURANCE CO
100 N GREEN ST
PO BOX 21008
GREENSBORO, NC 27420-1008
TEL: (336) 691-3000
FAX: (336) 691-4500
TOLL FREE: (800) 458-1419
IN-STATE: (800) 792-2268

JENSEN ADMINISTRATIVE SERVICES
4885 S 9TH E, STE 202
SALT LAKE CITY, UT 84117-5725
TEL: (801) 266-3256
FAX: (801) 266-4383
TOLL FREE: (800) 345-3248

JFP BENEFIT MANAGEMENT
100 S JACKSON ST, STE 200
PO BOX 189
JACKSON, MI 49201
TEL: (517) 784-0535
FAX: (517) 784-0821
IN-STATE: (800) 589-7660

JM FAMILY ENTERPRISES
8019 BAYBERRY RD
JACKSONVILLE, FL 32256-7411
TEL: (904) 443-6650
FAX: (904) 443-6670
TOLL FREE: (800) 736-3936

KAISER PERMANENTE
711 KAPIOLANI BLVD
PO BOX 31000
HONOLULU, HI 96849-5086
TEL: (808) 597-5340
FAX: (808) 597-5300
TOLL FREE: (800) 596-5955
IN-STATE: (800) 596-5955

PO BOX 40669
RALEIGH, NC 27629
TEL: (919) 981-6000
FAX: (919) 981-6052
TOLL FREE: (800) 221-5347

500 NE MULTNOMAH, STE 100
PORTLAND, OR 97232-2099
TEL: (503) 813-2800
FAX: (503) 813-2710
TOLL FREE: (800) 813-2000

KEENAN & ASSOCIATES
2105 S BASCOM AVE, STE 310
CAMPBELL, CA 95008-3271
TEL: (408) 377-3338
FAX: (408) 371-1796
TOLL FREE: (800) 334-6554

3610 CENTRAL, STE 400
RIVERSIDE, CA 92506-2405
TEL: (909) 788-0330
FAX: (909) 788-8013
TOLL FREE: (800) 654-8347

KENTUCKY FARM BUREAU MUTUAL INSURANCE CO
2909 RING RD
PO BOX 958
ELIZABETHTOWN, KY 42702-0958
TEL: (270) 765-4400
FAX: (270) 765-7756
TOLL FREE: (800) 782-3811

3036 PARRISH AVE
PO BOX 21369
OWENSBORO, KY 42304-1369
TEL: (502) 684-2165
FAX: (502) 684-4019
TOLL FREE: (800) 538-8655

KEYSTONE MERCY HEALTH PLAN
200 STEVENS DR
LESTER, PA 19113-1570
TEL: (215) 937-7300
FAX: (215) 937-5300
IN-STATE: (800) 521-6007

KITSAP PHYSICIANS SERVICE
400 WARREN AVE
PO BOX 339
BREMERTON, WA 98337
TEL: (360) 377-5576
FAX: (360) 415-6514
TOLL FREE: (800) 552-7114

KLAIS & CO
1867 W MARKET ST
AKRON, OH 44313
TEL: (330) 867-8443
FAX: (330) 867-0827
TOLL FREE: (800) 331-1096

LANCER CLAIM SERVICE CORP
333 CITY BLVD W
PO BOX 7048
ORANGE, CA 92863
TEL: (714) 939-0700
FAX: (714) 978-8023
TOLL FREE: (800) 821-0540
IN-STATE: (800) 645-5324

LANDMARK HEALTH CARE
1750 HOWE AVE, STE 300
SACRAMENTO, CA 95825
TEL: (916) 646-3477
FAX: (916) 929-8350
TOLL FREE: (800) 638-4557

LEWER AGENCY, INC
4534 WORNALL RD
KANSAS CITY, MO 64111-3211
TEL: (816) 753-4390
FAX: (816) 561-6840
TOLL FREE: (800) 821-7715

LIFE INSURANCE CO OF GEORGIA
4850 STREET RD
PO BOX 3013
LANGHORNE, PA 19047-9113
TOLL FREE: (800) 877-7756

LOCALS 302 & 612 INTERNATIONAL
2815 SECOND AVE #300
PO BOX 34684
SEATTLE, WA 98124-1203
TEL: (206) 441-7574
FAX: (206) 441-9110
TOLL FREE: (800) 331-6158
IN-STATE: (800) 732-1121

LOMA LINDA UNIVERSITY ADVENTIST HEALTH SCIENCES CENTER
11161 ANDERSON ST, STE 200
PO BOX 1770
LOMA LINDA, CA 92354-0570
TEL: (909) 824-4386
FAX: (909) 824-4775

M-PLAN
8802 N MERIDIAN ST, STE 100
INDIANAPOLIS, IN 46260-5318
TEL: (317) 571-5300
FAX: (317) 705-3119
TOLL FREE: (800) 878-8802

MANAGED HEALTH, INC
25 BROADWAY, STE 900
NEW YORK, NY 10004
FAX: (212) 801-1799
TOLL FREE: (888) 260-1010

MASSACHUSETTS MUTUAL LIFE INSURANCE CO
1350 MAIN ST
PO BOX 51130
SPRINGFIELD, MA 01151-5130
TOLL FREE: (800) 288-8630

MAYO HEALTH PLAN
21 1ST ST SW, STE 401
ROCHESTER, MN 55902
TEL: (507) 284-8274
FAX: (507) 284-0528
TOLL FREE: (800) 635-6671

MED-PAY, INC
1650 E BATTLEFIELD, STE 300
PO BOX 10909
SPRINGFIELD, MO 65808
TEL: (417) 886-6886
FAX: (417) 886-2276
TOLL FREE: (800) 777-9087

MEDICAID FISCAL AGENTS
PO BOX 5600
JEFFERSON CITY, MO 65102
TEL: (573) 751-2896
TOLL FREE: (800) 392-0938

1460 ANN ST
MONTGOMERY, AL 36107
TEL: (334) 834-3330
FAX: (334) 834-5301
IN-STATE: (800) 688-7989

701 E JEFFERSON
PO BOX 25520
PHOENIX, AZ 85002-9949
TEL: (602) 417-4000
FAX: (602) 253-5472
TOLL FREE: (800) 523-0231

PO BOX 8036
LITTLE ROCK, AR 72203-2501
TEL: (501) 374-6608
FAX: (501) 374-0549
IN-STATE: (800) 457-4454

700 BROADWAY
PO BOX 173300
DENVER, CO 80217-3300
TEL: (303) 831-0504
TOLL FREE: (800) 443-5747
IN-STATE: (800) 443-5747

PO BOX 2941
HARTFORD, CT 06104-2941
TEL: (860) 832-9259
IN-STATE: (800) 842-8440

MANOR BRANCH
PO BOX 908
NEW CASTLE, DE 19720
TEL: (302) 454-7154
FAX: (302) 454-7603
IN-STATE: (800) 999-3371

201 S GRAND AVE E- PRESCOTT BLOOM BLDG
PO BOX 19105
SPRINGFIELD, IL 62794-9105
TEL: (217) 782-5567
FAX: (217) 524-7194

PO BOX 3571
TOPEKA, KS 66601
TOLL FREE: (800) 933-6593

275 E MAIN ST
FRANKFORT, KY 40621-0001
TEL: (502) 564-4321

8591 UNITED PLZ BLVD
PO BOX 91024
BATON ROUGE, LA 70821-9024
TEL: (504) 237-3200
TOLL FREE: (800) 473-2783

BUREAU OF MED SVCS- 249 WESTERN AVE
AUGUSTA, ME 04333-0001
TEL: (207) 287-3081
IN-STATE: (800) 321-5557

201 W PRESTON ST, RM L9
PO BOX 1935
BALTIMORE, MD 21203
TEL: (410) 767-5503
FAX: (410) 333-7118
TOLL FREE: (800) 445-1159

5 MIDDLESEX AVE
PO BOX 9101
SOMMERVILLE, MA 02145-9101
TEL: (617) 625-0120
FAX: (617) 576-4087
TOLL FREE: (800) 325-5231

444 LAFAYETTE
PO BOX 3849
SAINT PAUL, MN 55155-3849
TEL: (612) 296-3598
FAX: (612) 282-6744
TOLL FREE: (800) 366-5411

111 E CAPITOL ST, STE 400
PO BOX 23077
JACKSON, MS 39225-3077
TEL: (601) 960-2800
FAX: (601) 960-2807
TOLL FREE: (800) 884-3222

PO BOX 8000
HELENA, MT 59604-8000
TEL: (406) 442-1837
FAX: (406) 442-4402
IN-STATE: (800) 624-3958

PO BOX 95026
LINCOLN, NE 68509-5026
TEL: (402) 471-9147
FAX: (402) 471-9092
TOLL FREE: (800) 430-3244

7 EAGLE SQ
PO BOX 2001
CONCORD, NH 03302-2001
TEL: (603) 224-1747
FAX: (603) 225-7964
IN-STATE: (800) 423-8303

3705 QUAKERBRIDGE RD, STE 101
TRENTON, NJ 08619-1209
TEL: (609) 584-0200
FAX: (609) 584-8270
TOLL FREE: (800) 776-6334

1720 RANDOLPH RD, STE A
PO BOX 25700
ALBUQUERQUE, NM 87125
TEL: (505) 246-9988
FAX: (505) 246-8485
IN-STATE: (800) 282-4477

600 E BLVD AVE
BISMARCK, ND 58505-0261
TEL: (701) 328-2321
FAX: (701) 328-1544
TOLL FREE: (800) 755-2604

201 NW 63RD, STE 100
OKLAHOMA CITY, OK 73116
TEL: (405) 841-3400
FAX: (405) 841-3510

PO BOX 2675
HARRISBURG, PA 17105-2675
TEL: (717) 787-1870
FAX: (717) 787-4639
TOLL FREE: (800) 537-8862

600 NEW LONDON AVE
CRANSTON, RI 02920-3037
TEL: (401) 464-3575

700 GOVERNORS DR- KNIEP BLDG
PIERRE, SD 57501-2291
TEL: (605) 945-5006
FAX: (605) 773-5246
IN-STATE: (800) 452-7691

PO BOX 143106
SALT LAKE CITY, UT 84114-3106
TEL: (801) 538-6451
FAX: (801) 538-6952
TOLL FREE: (800) 662-9651
IN-STATE: (800) 662-9651

4300 COX RD
PO BOX 3900
GLEN ALLEN, VA 23060
TEL: (804) 965-7400
FAX: (804) 965-7416
TOLL FREE: (800) 884-2822
IN-STATE: (800) 884-2822

4905 WATEREDGE DR
RALEIGH, NC 27606
TEL: (919) 851-8888
FAX: (919) 851-4014
TOLL FREE: (800) 688-6696

5000 CAPITAL BLVD
PO BOX 45080
DUMWATER, WA 98501
TEL: (360) 753-1777
FAX: (360) 586-6787
TOLL FREE: (800) 562-3022
IN-STATE: (800) 321-6787

MEDICAL MUTUAL OF OHIO
PO BOX 6018
CLEVELAND, OH 44101-1355
TEL: (216) 522-8622
FAX: (216) 694-2910
TOLL FREE: (800) 233-2058

MEDICARE PART A
PO BOX 908
CHEYENNE, WY 82003
TEL: (307) 432-2860
FAX: (307) 632-1654
IN-STATE: (800) 442-2376

MEDICARE — PART A HORIZON BLUE CROSS BLUE SHIELD OF NEW JERSEY
33 WASHINGTON ST
PO BOX 1236
NEWARK, NJ 07101-1236
TEL: (973) 456-2112
FAX: (973) 456-2086

MEDICARE — PART A INTERMEDIARIES
4305 13TH AVE SW
FARGO, ND 58103-3309
TEL: (701) 277-2655
FAX: (701) 277-2196

9901 LINN STATION RD
PO BOX 23711
LOUISVILLE, KY 40223-0711
TEL: (502) 425-7776
FAX: (502) 329-8559

1064 FLINT DR
PO BOX 23035
JACKSON, MS 39225-3035
TEL: (601) 936-0105
FAX: (601) 932-9233

3000 GOFF FALLS RD
MANCHESTER, NH 03111-0001
TEL: (603) 695-7204
FAX: (603) 695-7741

444 WESTMINSTER ST
PROVIDENCE, RI 02903
TEL: (401) 455-0177
FAX: (401) 459-1709
TOLL FREE: (800) 662-5170

3000 GOFFS FALLS RD
MANCHESTER, NH 03111-0001
TEL: (603) 695-7204
FAX: (603) 695-7741

PO BOX 57
COLUMBUS, OH 43216-0057
TEL: (614) 249-7111
FAX: (614) 249-4467
IN-STATE: (800) 848-0106

7261 MERCY RD
PO BOX 24563
OMAHA, NE 68124-0563
TEL: (402) 390-1850
FAX: (402) 398-3640

4510 13TH AVE SW
PO BOX 6706
FARGO, ND 58108-6706
TEL: (701) 277-1100
FAX: (701) 282-1002
TOLL FREE: (800) 874-2656

2444 W LAS PAMARITAS DR
PO BOX 13466
PHOENIX, AZ 85002-3466
TEL: (602) 864-4100
FAX: (602) 864-4653

601 GAINES ST
PO BOX 2181
LITTLE ROCK, AR 72203-2181
TEL: (501) 378-2000
FAX: (501) 378-2576
TOLL FREE: (800) 813-8868

21555 OXNARD ST
PO BOX 70000
VAN NUYS, CA 91470
TEL: (818) 703-2345
FAX: (818) 703-2848
TOLL FREE: (800) 234-0111

1800 CENTER ST
PO BOX 890089
CAMP HILL, PA 17089-0089
TEL: (717) 763-3151
FAX: (717) 763-3544

1800 CENTER ST
PO BOX 890089
CAMP HILL, PA 17089-0089
TEL: (717) 763-3151
FAX: (717) 763-3544

532 RIVERSIDE AVENUE- 17TH & 18TH FLS
PO BOX 2711
JACKSONVILLE, FL 32231-0021
TEL: (904) 355-8899
FAX: (904) 791-8296
IN-STATE: (800) 333-7586

2357 WARM SPGS RD
PO BOX 9048
COLUMBUS, GA 31908-9048
TEL: (706) 571-5371
FAX: (706) 571-5431

8115 KNUE RD
INDIANAPOLIS, IN 46250-2804
TEL: (317) 841-4400
FAX: (317) 841-4691
TOLL FREE: (800) 999-7608

636 GRAND AVE, STATION 120
DES MOINES, IA 50309
TEL: (515) 245-4834
FAX: (515) 245-3984

346 HOLMER RD
MENDON, LA 71055
TEL: (318) 377-7387
TOLL FREE: (800) 772-1213

2 GANNETT DR
SOUTH PORTLAND, ME 04106-6911
TEL: (207) 822-8484
FAX: (207) 822-7926
TOLL FREE: (888) 896-4997

PO BOX 64357
SAINT PAUL, MN 55164-0357
TEL: (651) 662-8000
FAX: (651) 662-2745
TOLL FREE: (800) 382-2000

133 S TOPEKA
TOPEKA, KS 66601-1712
TEL: (785) 291-7000
FAX: (785) 291-6924

340 N LAST CHANCE GULCH
PO BOX 4309
HELENA, MT 59604
TEL: (406) 791-4000
FAX: (406) 791-4119
TOLL FREE: (800) 447-7828

1901 MAIN ST
PO BOX 80
BUFFALO, NY 14208
TEL: (716) 887-6900
FAX: (716) 887-8981
TOLL FREE: (800) 252-6550
IN-STATE: (800) 695-2583

ONE WORLD TRADE CENTER
PO BOX 1407
NEW YORK, NY 10048
TEL: (212) 476-1000
TOLL FREE: (800) 442-8430

4361 ERWIN SIMPSON RD
MASON, OH 45050
TEL: (513) 872-8100
FAX: (513) 852-4562

1215 S BOULDER AVE
PO BOX 3404
TULSA, OK 74101
TEL: (918) 560-2090
FAX: (918) 560-3506

1800 CENTER ST
PO BOX 890089
CAMP HILL, PA 17089-0089
TEL: (717) 763-3151
FAX: (717) 763-3544

730 CHESTNUT ST
CHATTANOOGA, TN 37402-1790
TEL: (423) 755-5950

730 CHESTNUT ST
CHATTANOOGA, TN 37402-1790
TEL: (423) 755-5950

450 COLOUMBUS BLVD - 5GB
PO BOX 150450
HARTFORD, CT 06115-0450
TEL: (860) 702-6668
FAX: (860) 702-6587

450 COLOUMBUS BLVD - 5GB
PO BOX 150450
HARTFORD, CT 06115-0450
TEL: (860) 702-6669
FAX: (860) 702-6587

2 GANNETT DR
SOUTH PORTLAND, ME 04106-6911
TEL: (207) 822-8484
FAX: (207) 822-7926
TOLL FREE: (888) 896-4997

4305 13TH AVE SW
FARGO, ND 58103-3309
TEL: (701) 277-2655
FAX: (701) 277-2196

3000 GOFF FALLS RD
MANCHESTER, NH 03111-0001
TEL: (603) 695-7204
FAX: (603) 695-7741

3000 GOFFS FALLS RD
MANCHESTER, NH 03111-0001
TEL: (603) 695-7204
FAX: (603) 695-7741

MEDICARE — PART B CARRIERS

1133 TOPEKA AVE
PO BOX 239
TOPEKA, KS 66601
TEL: (816) 756-1601
FAX: (913) 291-8532

PO BOX 830140
BIRMINGHAM, AL 35283-0140
TEL: (205) 981-4842
FAX: (205) 981-4965
TOLL FREE: (800) 292-8855

1149 SOUTH BROADWAY

PO BOX 54905
LOS ANGELES, CA 90054-0905
TEL: (213) 748-2311
FAX: (213) 741-6803
TOLL FREE:

636 GRAND AVE, STATION 28
DES MOINES, IA 50309
TEL: (515) 245-4618
FAX: (515) 245-3984

444 WESTMINSTER ST
PROVIDENCE, RI 02903
TEL: (401) 272-3131

450 W EAST AVE
CHICO, CA 95926
TEL: (530) 896-7025
FAX: (530) 896-7182

1800 CENTER ST
PO BOX 890101
CAMP HILL, PA 17089-0101
TEL: (717) 731-2333

532 RIVERSIDE AVE
PO BOX 2525
JACKSONVILLE, FL 32231-0019
TEL: (904) 634-4994
FAX: (904) 791-8378
IN-STATE: (800) 333-7586

818 KEEAUMOKU ST
PO BOX 860
HONOLULU, HI 96808
TEL: (808) 948-6247
FAX: (808) 948-6555

8115 KNUE RD
INDIANAPOLIS, IN 46250-2804
TEL: (317) 841-4400
FAX: (317) 841-4691
TOLL FREE: (800) 999-7608

8115 KNUE RD
PO BOX 37630
INDIANAPOLIS, IN 46250-2804
TEL: (317) 841-4400
FAX: (317) 841-4691
TOLL FREE: (800) 999-7608

4305 16TH AVE S
PO BOX 6701
FARGO, ND 58103-3373
TOLL FREE: (800) 444-4606
IN-STATE: (800) 332-6681

1133 SW TOPEKA BLVD
PO BOX 239
TOPEKA, KS 66629
TEL: (785) 291-4003
FAX: (785) 291-8532

1133 TOPEKA AVE
PO BOX 239
TOPEKA, KS 66601
TEL: (785) 291-4155
FAX: (785) 291-8532

1901 MAIN ST
PO BOX 80
BUFFALO, NY 14240-0080
TEL: (716) 887-6900
TOLL FREE: (800) 950-0051

PO BOX 16788 OR 57
COLUMBUS, OH 43216-0057
TEL: (614) 249-7111
FAX: (616) 249-4467
IN-STATE: (800) 282-0530

4510 13TH AVE SW
FARGO, ND 58121-0001
TEL: (701) 277-1100
FAX: (701) 282-1002
TOLL FREE: (800) 874-2656
IN-STATE: (800) 247-2267

300 ARBOR LK DR, STE 1300
COLUMBIA, SC 29223
TEL: (803) 788-5568
FAX: (803) 691-2188

1133 SW TOPEKA BLVD
PO BOX 239
TOPEKA, KS 66629
TEL: (816) 756-1601
FAX: (785) 291-8532

2890 COTTONWOOD PKY
PO BOX 30269
SALT LAKE CITY, UT 84130-0269
TEL: (801) 333-2440
FAX: (801) 333-6505
IN-STATE: (800) 426-3477

PO BOX 57
COLUMBUS, OH 43216-0057
TEL: (614) 249-7111
FAX: (614) 249-4467
IN-STATE: (800) 848-0106

PO BOX 1787
MADISON, WI 53701-1787
TEL: (608) 221-3218
IN-STATE: (800) 944-0051

TWO VANTAGE WAY
PO BOX 1465
NASHVILLE, TN 37228
TEL: (615) 782-4576
FAX: (615) 782-4662
TOLL FREE: (800) 342-8900

4305 16TH AVE S
PO BOX 6704
FARGO, ND 58108-6704
TOLL FREE: (800) 444-4606
IN-STATE: (800) 332-6681

MEMORIAL SISTERS OF CHARITY HEALTH NETWORK INC

9494 SOUTHWEST FWY, STE 300
HOUSTON, TX 77074-1419
TEL: (713) 430-1400
FAX: (713) 778-2375
TOLL FREE: (800) 776-2885

MENNONITE MUTUAL AID ASSOCIATION

1110 N MAIN ST
PO BOX 483
GOSHEN, IN 46526-0483
TEL: (219) 533-9511
FAX: (219) 533-5264
TOLL FREE: (800) 348-7468

MERVYN'S HEALTH CARE PLAN
PO BOX 3108
RANCHO CORDOVA, CA 95741-3108
FAX: (916) 636-2314
TOLL FREE: (800) 873-3039

MICHIGAN FARM BUREAU MUTUAL INSURANCE CO
7373 W SAGINAW
PO BOX 30100
LANSING, MI 48909
TEL: (517) 323-7000
FAX: (517) 323-6793
TOLL FREE: (800) 292-2680

MID AMERICA MUTUAL LIFE INSURANCE CO
11808 GRANT ST
PO BOX 3160
OMAHA, NE 68103-0160
TEL: (605) 886-8363
TOLL FREE: (800) 995-9051
IN-STATE: (800) 786-7557

MID-SOUTH INSURANCE CO
4317 RAMSEY ST
PO BOX 2547
FAYETTEVILLE, NC 28302-2069
TEL: (910) 822-1020
FAX: (910) 822-3018
TOLL FREE: (800) 822-9993

MIDWEST SECURITY ADMINISTRATORS
1150 SPRINGHURST DR, STE 140
PO BOX 19035
GREEN BAY, WI 54307-9035
TEL: (920) 496-2500

MIDWEST SECURITY INSURANCE CO
2700 MIDWEST DR
ONALASKA, WI 54650-8764
TEL: (608) 783-7130
FAX: (608) 783-8581
TOLL FREE: (800) 542-6642

MILLENNIUM CARE ADMINISTRATORS (DBA MCA ADMINISTRATORS)
5900 ROCHE DR- 5TH FL
PO BOX 18245
COLUMBUS, OH 43218-0245
TEL: (614) 888-1212
FAX: (614) 888-2240
TOLL FREE: (800) 229-6786
IN-STATE: (800) 524-4426

MILLETTE ADMINISTRATORS, INC
4619 MAIN ST, STE A
MOSS POINT, MS 39563
TEL: (228) 475-8687
TOLL FREE: (800) 456-8647

MIT HEALTH PLAN
77 MASSACHUSETTS AVE- BLDG E 23, STE 308
PO BOX E23-308 MIT
CAMBRIDGE, MA 02139-4307
TEL: (617) 253-1322
FAX: (617) 253-6558

MMA INSURANCE CO
1110 N MAIN ST
PO BOX 483
GOSHEN, IN 46527
TEL: (219) 533-9511
FAX: (219) 533-5264
TOLL FREE: (800) 348-7468

MUTUAL MED BENEFIT ADMINISTRATORS
3216 E 35TH ST CT
DAVENPORT, IA 52807
TEL: (319) 344-2890
FAX: (319) 344-2891
TOLL FREE: (800) 747-4126

NALC HEALTH BENEFIT PLAN
20547 WAVERLY CT
ASHBURN, VA 20149-0001
TEL: (703) 729-4677
FAX: (703) 729-0076
TOLL FREE: (800) 548-8484

NAPUS HEALTH BENEFIT PLAN
550 12TH ST SW
WASHINGTON, DC 20065-3520
TEL: (202) 479-8000
FAX: (202) 479-3520
TOLL FREE: (800) 424-7474

NATIONAL HEALTH PLANS
1005 W ORANGEBURG, STE B
PO BOX 5356
MODESTO, CA 95352
TEL: (209) 527-3350
FAX: (209) 527-6773
TOLL FREE: (800) 468-8600

NATIONAL TRAVELERS LIFE INSURANCE CO
5700 WESTOWN PKY
PO BOX 9197
WEST DES MOINES, IA 50266-9197
TEL: (515) 221-0101
FAX: (515) 327-5830
TOLL FREE: (800) 232-5818

NATIONWIDE LIFE INSURANCE CO
ONE NATIONWIDE PLZ
PO BOX 2399
COLUMBUS, OH 43216-2399
TEL: (614) 249-7111
FAX: (614) 249-7705
TOLL FREE: (800) 772-9956

NAVISTAR
455 N CITYFRONT PLZ DR
PO BOX 5367
CHICAGO, IL 60611
TEL: (312) 836-2000
FAX: (312) 836-2227

NEW AIR LIFE
PO BOX 4884
HOUSTON, TX 77210-4884
TEL: (281) 368-7200
FAX: (281) 368-7329
TOLL FREE: (800) 552-7879

NORTH DAKOTA WORKERS COMPENSATION BUREAU
500 E FRONT AVE
BISMARCK, ND 58504-5685
TEL: (701) 328-3800
FAX: (701) 328-3820
TOLL FREE: (800) 777-5033

NORTHEAST MEDICAL CENTER
920 CHURCH ST N
CONCORD, NC 28025-2927
TEL: (704) 783-3000
FAX: (704) 783-1487
TOLL FREE: (800) 842-6868

NORTHWEST WASHINGTON MEDICAL BUREAU
3000 NORTHWEST AVE
PO BOX 9753
BELLINGHAM, WA 98227-9753
TEL: (360) 734-8000
FAX: (360) 734-6676
TOLL FREE: (800) 825-5962

NYL CARE
2425 WEST LOOP S, STE 1000
PO BOX 56228
HOUSTON, TX 77027
TEL: (713) 624-5000
FAX: (713) 993-9462
TOLL FREE: (800) 833-5318

O'BRIEN, BOUCK & ASSOCIATES
8340 MISSION RD STE 119
PO BOX 6826
LEAWOOD, KS 66206-0353
TEL: (913) 381-3444
FAX: (913) 381-3953

ODS HEALTH PLAN
315 SW 5TH AVE
PO BOX 40384
PORTLAND, OR 97204
TEL: (503) 228-6554
FAX: (503) 243-5105
TOLL FREE: (800) 852-5195

OLYMPIC BENEFITS
PO BOX 1077
BELLINGHAM, WA 98227-1077
TEL: (360) 734-9888
FAX: (360) 734-6199
TOLL FREE: (800) 533-3941

OMNI HEALTH CARE
1776 W MARCH LN, STE 240
STOCKTON, CA 95207
TEL: (209) 474-6664
FAX: (209) 955-7536
TOLL FREE: (800) 342-8462

PACIFIC INDEMNITY CO
801 S FIGUROA ST
PO BOX 30850
LOS ANGELES, CA 90030-0850
TEL: (213) 612-0880
FAX: (213) 612-5731
TOLL FREE: (800) 262-4459

PACIFICARE HEALTH SYSTEMS, INC
5 CENTER PT DR, STE 600
LAKE OSWEGO, OR 97035
FAX: (503) 533-6335
TOLL FREE: (800) 922-1444

PAN AMERICAN LIFE INSURANCE CO
601 POYDRAS ST
PO BOX 60219
NEW ORLEANS, LA 70130
TEL: (504) 566-1300
FAX: (504) 523-8584
TOLL FREE: (800) 227-3417

PARTNERS NATIONAL HEALTH PLANS
2085 FRONTIS PLZ BLVD
PO BOX 24907
WINSTON-SALEM, NC 27114
TEL: (336) 760-4822
FAX: (336) 760-3198
TOLL FREE: (800) 942-5695
IN-STATE: (800) 942-5695

PAULA INSURANCE CO
1780 E BULLARD, STE 101
PO BOX 40009
FRESNO, CA 93755-0009
TEL: (559) 439-3330
FAX: (559) 439-3505

PEER REVIEW ORGANIZATIONS
818 KEEAUMOKU ST
PO BOX 860
HONOLULU, HI 96808-0860
TEL: (808) 948-5110
FAX: (808) 948-6811

2851 S PARKER RD, STE 200
AURORA, CO 80014
TEL: (303) 695-3300
FAX: (303) 695-3350

57 EXECUTIVE PARK DR S, STE 200
ATLANTA, GA 30329
TEL: (404) 982-0411
FAX: (404) 982-7591
TOLL FREE: (800) 982-7581

40600 ANN ARBOR RD, STE 200
PLYMOUTH, MI 48170-4486
TEL: (734) 459-0900

10700 MERIDIAN AVE N, STE 100
SEATTLE, WA 98133-9075
TEL: (206) 364-9700
FAX: (208) 343-4705

PERSONAL INSURANCE ADMINISTRATORS
PO BOX 5004
WOODLAND HILLS, CA 91359
TEL: (805) 777-0032
FAX: (805) 777-0033
TOLL FREE: (800) 468-4343

PERSONALCARE HEALTH MANAGEMENT
210 BOX DR
CHAMPAIGN, IL 61820-7399
TEL: (217) 366-1226
FAX: (217) 366-5410
TOLL FREE: (800) 431-1211

PFS INSURANCE GROUP
PO BOX 1250
ROCKFORD, IL 61105-1250
TEL: (815) 965-8955
FAX: (815) 720-2990
TOLL FREE: (800) 659-7374

PHARMACIST MUTUAL
808 U.S. HWY 18-W
PO BOX 370
ALGONA, IA 50511-0370
TEL: (515) 295-2461
FAX: (515) 295-9306
TOLL FREE: (800) 247-5930

PHICO
1 PHICO DR
PO BOX 85
MECHANICSBURG, PA 17055-0085
TEL: (717) 691-1600
FAX: (717) 766-2837
TOLL FREE: (800) 627-4626

PHN-HMO
1099 WINTERSAN RD
LINTHICUM HEIGHTS, MD 21090
TEL: (410) 850-7461
TOLL FREE: (800) 422-1996

PHYSICIANS BENEFITS TRUST
150 S WACKER DR, STE 1200
PO BOX 8263
CHICAGO, IL 60680-8263
TEL: (312) 541-2711
FAX: (312) 541-4589
TOLL FREE: (800) 621-0748

PHYSICIANS HEALTH PLAN OF NORTHERN INDIANA, INC
8101 W JEFFERSON BLVD
PO BOX 2359
FT WAYNE, IN 46801
TEL: (219) 432-6690
FAX: (219) 432-0493
TOLL FREE: (800) 982-6257

PHYSICIANS HEALTH SERVICES
1 FARMILL CROSSING
PO BOX 904
SHELTON, CT 06484-0944
TEL: (203) 225-8000
FAX: (203) 225-4001
TOLL FREE: (800) 772-5869
IN-STATE: (800) 848-4747

PREFERRED HEALTH NORTHWEST
100 SW MARKET
PO BOX 1271
PORTLAND, OR 97207-1271
TEL: (503) 274-0761
FAX: (503) 375-4293
TOLL FREE: (800) 452-7390
IN-STATE: (800) 452-7278

PREFERRED HEALTH SYSTEMS INSURANCE CO
355 N WACO
PO BOX 49288
WICHITA, KS 67201-5007
TEL: (316) 268-0345
FAX: (316) 268-0346
TOLL FREE: (800) 660-8114

PO BOX 49218
WICHITA, KS 67202
TEL: (316) 268-0345
FAX: (316) 263-3673
TOLL FREE: (800) 660-8114

PREMERA BLUE CROSS
7001 220TH ST SW
PO BOX 327
MOUNTLAKE TERRACE, WA 98111
TEL: (425) 670-4700
FAX: (425) 670-5457
TOLL FREE: (800) 527-6675

3900 E SPRAGUE
PO BOX 3048
SPOKANE, WA 99220-3048
TEL: (509) 536-4700
FAX: (509) 536-4771
TOLL FREE: (800) 835-3510
IN-STATE: (800) 572-0778

7001 220TH ST SW
PO BOX 327
MOUNTLAKE TERRACE, WA 98111
TEL: (425) 670-4700
FAX: (425) 670-5457
TOLL FREE: (800) 527-6675

PREMIER BLUE
1133 SW TOPEKA AVE
PO BOX 3518
TOPEKA, KS 66601-3518
TEL: (785) 291-4010
FAX: (785) 291-8848
TOLL FREE: (800) 332-0028

PRESBYTERIAN HEALTH PLAN / FHP OF NEW MEXICO
PO BOX 27489
ALBUQUERQUE, NM 87125
TEL: (505) 923-5799
FAX: (505) 923-5277
TOLL FREE: (800) 356-2884
IN-STATE: (800) 356-2219

PRIME HEALTH OF ALABAMA
1400 UNIVERSITY BLVD S
PO BOX 851239
MOBILE, AL 36685-1239
TEL: (334) 342-0022
FAX: (334) 380-3236
TOLL FREE: (800) 544-9449

PRINCIPAL FINANCIAL GROUP
1755 TELSTAR DR, STE 300
PO BOX 39710
COLORADO SPRINGS, CO 80949
TEL: (719) 548-4000
FAX: (719) 548-4001
TOLL FREE: (800) 273-2486

9428 BAYMEADOWS RD, STE 360
JACKSONVILLE, FL 32256-9933
TEL: (904) 731-8159
FAX: (904) 367-8444
TOLL FREE: (800) 445-6133

1245 CORPORATE BLVD, STE 200
AURORA, IL 60504-9955
TEL: (630) 978-5100
FAX: (630) 978-5117

330 N 117TH ST
PO BOX 542060
OMAHA, NE 68154
TEL: (402) 330-0800
FAX: (402) 330-1636
TOLL FREE: (800) 331-9443

620 S GLENSTONE AVE, STE 300
PO BOX 2593
SPRINGFIELD, MO 65801-2593
TEL: (417) 877-0085
TOLL FREE: (800) 422-5002

PRINCIPAL HEALTHCARE OF FLORIDA
2203 N LOIS AVE, STE 900
PO BOX 31298
TAMPA, FL 33631-3298
TEL: (813) 875-3737
FAX: (813) 876-4572
TOLL FREE: (800) 443-5810

PRIORITY HEALTH
1111 E HERNDON, STE 202
PO BOX 25790
FRESNO, CA 93729-5790
TEL: (559) 435-8366
FAX: (559) 435-9718
TOLL FREE: (800) 350-8366

PROFESSIONAL ADMINISTRATION GROUP
PO BOX 13391
OVERLAND PARK, KS 66282-3391
TEL: (913) 327-7104
FAX: (913) 451-4762

PROFESSIONAL ADMINISTRATORS, INC
3751 MAGUIRE BLVD, STE 100
PO BOX 140415-0415
ORLANDO, FL 32803-0415
TEL: (407) 896-0521
FAX: (407) 897-6976
TOLL FREE: (800) 741-0521
IN-STATE: (800) 432-2686

PROFESSIONAL BENEFIT ADMINISTRATORS, INC
15 SPINNING WHEEL RD, STE 210
PO BOX 4687
OAKBROOK, IL 60522
TEL: (630) 655-3755
FAX: (630) 655-3781

PROFESSIONAL RISK MANAGEMENT
2101 WEBSTER ST, STE 900
OAKLAND, CA 94612
TEL: (510) 452-9300
FAX: (510) 452-1479

PROTECTED HOME MUTUAL LIFE INSURANCE CO
30 E STATE ST
SHARON, PA 16146
TEL: (724) 981-1520
FAX: (724) 981-2682
TOLL FREE: (800) 223-8821
IN-STATE: (800) 222-8894

PROVIDENCE HEALTH PLANS
1501 FOURTH AVE, STE 600
SEATTLE, WA 98101
TEL: (206) 215-9000
TOLL FREE: (800) 443-0996

PRUDENTIAL HEALTH CARE PLAN, INC
7912 E 31 CT, STE 200
TULSA, OK 74145-1338
TEL: (918) 624-4600
FAX: (918) 624-5050
TOLL FREE: (800) 345-8310

7700 CHEVY CHASE DR- BLDG 1, STE 500
PO BOX 26699
AUSTIN, TX 78755-0699
TEL: (512) 323-0440
FAX: (713) 663-0731
TOLL FREE: (800) 621-2645

ONE PRUDENTIAL CIR
PO BOX 27718
HOUSTON, TX 77227
TEL: (713) 350-2150
FAX: (713) 663-0731
TOLL FREE: (800) 876-7778

PRUDENTIAL HEALTHCARE OF CALIFORNIA
21261 BURBANK AVE
WOODLAND HILLS, CA 91367
TEL: (818) 992-2000
FAX: (818) 594-4266
TOLL FREE: (800) 433-3150

PUBLIC EMPLOYEES HEALTH PROGRAM
560 E 200 S
SALT LAKE CITY, UT 84102-2020
TEL: (801) 366-7500
FAX: (801) 366-7596
TOLL FREE: (800) 933-7347

PYRAMID LIFE INSURANCE CO
6201 JOHNSON DR
PO BOX 772
MISSION, KS 66202
TEL: (913) 722-1110
FAX: (913) 722-3567
TOLL FREE: (800) 444-0321

QUAL-MED HEALTH PLAN
225 N MAIN ST
PO BOX 640
PUEBLO, CO 81002-0640
TEL: (719) 542-0500
FAX: (719) 585-8333
TOLL FREE: (800) 628-2287

QUEEN'S ISLAND CARE/QUEEN'S HEALTH PLAN
500 ALA MOANA BLVD, STE 200
PO BOX 37549
HONOLULU, HI 96837
TEL: (808) 532-6900
FAX: (808) 522-8642
TOLL FREE: (800) 856-4668

RAYTHEON CO
141 SPRING ST
LEXINGTON, MA 02173
TEL: (781) 862-6600
FAX: (781) 860-2172
TOLL FREE: (800) 843-4121

REGENCE BLUE CROSS & BLUE SHIELD
100 SW MARKET
PO BOX 100
PORTLAND, OR 97207
TEL: (503) 225-5227
TOLL FREE: (800) 452-7278

201 HIGH ST SE
PO BOX 12625
SALEM, OR 97309
TEL: (503) 364-4868
FAX: (503) 588-4350
TOLL FREE: (800) 228-0978

REGENCE BLUE CROSS & BLUE SHIELD OF UTAH
2870 E COTTONWOOD PKY
PO BOX 30270
SALT LAKE CITY, UT 84130-0270
TEL: (801) 333-2320
FAX: (801) 333-6523
TOLL FREE: (800) 662-0876
IN-STATE: (800) 624-6519

REGENCE BLUE SHIELD
1800 NINTH AVE
PO BOX 21267
SEATTLE, WA 98111-3267
TEL: (206) 464-3600
TOLL FREE: (800) 544-4246
IN-STATE: (800) 458-3523

REGENCE BLUE SHIELD OF IDAHO
1602 21ST AVE
PO BOX 1106
LEWISTON, ID 83501-1106
TEL: (208) 746-2671
FAX: (208) 798-2090
TOLL FREE: (800) 632-2022

REGENCE BLUESHIELD
7600 EVERGREEN WAY
EVERETT, WA 98203-6413
TEL: (425) 348-8160
FAX: (425) 348-8167
TOLL FREE: (800) 328-7273
IN-STATE: (800) 548-8385

REGENCY EMPLOYEE BENEFITS
330 SUPERIOR MALL
PO BOX 610609
PORT HURON, MI 48061-0609
TEL: (810) 987-7711
FAX: (810) 987-7603
TOLL FREE: (800) 369-3718

REGIONS BLUE CROSS & BLUE SHIELD OF OREGON
100 SW MARKET ST
PO BOX 900
PORTLAND, OR 97207
TEL: (503) 274-0761
FAX: (503) 375-4293
TOLL FREE: (800) 643-4512
IN-STATE: (800) 228-0978

REINSURANCE MANAGEMENT, INC
9485 REGENCY SQ BLVD, STE 220
JACKSONVILLE, FL 32225
TEL: (904) 727-5088
FAX: (904) 727-7892
TOLL FREE: (800) 830-3856

RESOURCE PARTNER
180 E BROAD ST
PO BOX 189
COLUMBUS, OH 43216-0189
TEL: (614) 220-5001
FAX: (614) 220-5033
TOLL FREE: (800) 848-6181

RIVERBEND GOVERNMENT BENEFITS ADMINISTRATOR
730 CHESTNUT ST
CHATTANOOGA, TN 37402
TEL: (423) 755-5783
FAX: (423) 752-6518

RMSCO, INC
731 JAMES ST
PO BOX 6309
SYRACUSE, NY 13217
TEL: (315) 474-8200
FAX: (315) 476-8440

ROBERT S. WEISS & CO
SILVER HILLS BUS CTR- 500 S BROAD ST
PO BOX 1034
MERIDEN, CT 06450-1034
TEL: (203) 235-6882
FAX: (203) 639-7422
TOLL FREE: (800) 466-7900

ROCKFORD HEALTH PLANS
3401 N PERRYVILLE RD
ROCKFORD, IL 61114
TEL: (815) 654-3600
FAX: (815) 282-0634
TOLL FREE: (800) 331-0424

ROCKY MOUNTAIN HMO
2775 CROSSROADS BLVD
PO BOX 10600
GRAND JUNCTION, CO 81506
TEL: (970) 244-7760
FAX: (970) 244-7880
TOLL FREE: (800) 843-0719
IN-STATE: (800) 843-0719

ROYAL STATE GROUP
819 S BERETANIA ST, STE 100
HONOLULU, HI 96813
TEL: (808) 539-1600
FAX: (808) 538-1458

ROYAL & SUNALLIANCE
801 N BRAND BLVD, STE 500
PO BOX 29035
GLENDALE, CA 91209-9035
TEL: (818) 241-5212
FAX: (818) 543-6393
TOLL FREE: (800) 252-0431

300 E LOMBARD ST, STE 700
BALTIMORE, MD 21202
TEL: (410) 685-5844
FAX: (410) 637-1699
TOLL FREE: (800) 482-4446

25 NEW CHARDEN
PO BOX 8088
BOSTON, MA 02114-4774
TEL: (617) 742-7750
FAX: (617) 557-4252
TOLL FREE: (800) 367-7036
IN-STATE: (800) 367-7036

80 WOLF RD, STE 606
PO BOX 15096
ALBANY, NY 12205
TEL: (518) 489-8331
TOLL FREE: (800) 553-2556

2 JERICHO PLZ
PO BOX 4002
JERICHO, NY 11753-0873
TEL: (516) 939-0600
FAX: (516) 937-3338
TOLL FREE: (800) 523-6273

255 E 5TH ST, STE 2100
CINCINNATI, OH 45202
TEL: (513) 421-2183
FAX: (513) 357-9580
TOLL FREE: (800) 843-5772

25800 NORTHWESTERN HWY, STE 701
PO BOX 5010
SOUTHFIELD, MI 48086-5010
TEL: (248) 746-6180
FAX: (248) 746-6190
IN-STATE: (800) 482-8772

255 E 5TH ST, STE 2100
CINCINNATI, OH 45202
TEL: (513) 421-2183
FAX: (513) 357-9580
TOLL FREE: (800) 843-5772

80 WOLF RD, STE 606
PO BOX 15096
ALBANY, NY 12205
TEL: (518) 489-8331
TOLL FREE: (800) 553-2556

SAFECO INSURANCE CO OF AMERICA
330 N BRAND BLVD, STE 900
PO BOX 29082
GLENDALE, CA 91029-9082
TEL: (818) 956-4200
FAX: (818) 956-4259
TOLL FREE: (800) 826-8921

1551 JULIET RD
PO BOX A
STONE MOUNTAIN, GA 30086
TEL: (770) 469-1111
FAX: (770) 879-3333
TOLL FREE: (800) 241-2279

3637 S GEYER RD
PO BOX 66783
SAINT LOUIS, MO 63127-6783
TEL: (314) 957-4500
FAX: (314) 957-4630
TOLL FREE: (800) 843-1487

5901 E GALBRAITH RD
PO BOX 36177
CINCINNATI, OH 45236-2251
TEL: (513) 745-5861
FAX: (513) 745-5810
TOLL FREE: (800) 543-7138

SAN DIEGO ELECTRICAL HEALTH & WELFARE TRUST
4675 VIEW RDG, STE B
PO BOX 231219
SAN DIEGO, CA 92194-1219
TEL: (619) 569-6322
FAX: (619) 573-0830
TOLL FREE: (800) 632-2569

SEABURY & SMITH
2615 NORTHGATE DR
PO BOX 1520
IOWA CITY, IA 52244-1520
TEL: (319) 351-2667
FAX: (319) 351-0603
TOLL FREE: (800) 562-4023

SECURITY HEALTH PLAN OF WISCONSIN, INC
1000 N OAK AVE
MARSHFIELD, WI 54449-5703
TEL: (715) 387-5621
FAX: (715) 387-9399
TOLL FREE: (800) 472-2363

SEDGWICK
1000 RIDGEWAY LOOP RD
PO BOX 171377
MEMPHIS, TN 38120
TEL: (901) 761-1550
FAX: (901) 684-3858

SELF INSURED SERVICES CO
PO BOX 389
DUBUQUE, IA 52004-0389
TEL: (319) 583-7344
FAX: (319) 583-0439

SENTARA HEALTH PLAN
4417 CORPORATION LN
VIRGINIA BEACH, VA 23462-3114
TEL: (757) 552-7100
FAX: (757) 552-7397
TOLL FREE: (800) 229-1199
IN-STATE: (800) 229-8822

SENTRY INSURANCE A MUTUAL CO
1800 N POINT DR
STEVENS POINT, WI 54481
TEL: (715) 346-6000
FAX: (715) 346-6161
TOLL FREE: (800) 638-8763

SENTRY INSURANCE GROUP
3 CARLISLE RD
PO BOX 584
WESTFORD, MA 01886-0584
TEL: (508) 392-7000
FAX: (978) 392-7033
TOLL FREE: (800) 225-1390

SHELTER INSURANCE COMPANIES
1817 W BROADWAY
COLUMBIA, MO 65218-0001
TEL: (573) 445-8441
FAX: (573) 445-3199
TOLL FREE: (800) 743-5837

SIGMA ADMINISTRATORS
111 E 5600 S, STE 305
PO BOX 57767
SALT LAKE CITY, UT 84157-0767
TEL: (801) 263-3300
FAX: (801) 263-3319

SIGNA HEALTHCARE
100 FRONT ST, STE 300
WORCESTER, MA 01608-1449
TEL: (508) 799-2642
FAX: (508) 849-4299
TOLL FREE: (800) 244-1870
IN-STATE: (800) 922-8380

SILVER STATE MEDICAL ADMINISTRATORS
2085 E SAHARA, STE B
PO BOX 14790
LAS VEGAS, NV 89114
TEL: (702) 732-0292
FAX: (800) 280-3782
TOLL FREE: (800) 230-3904

SOUTHERN BENEFIT ADMINISTRATORS, INC
907 TWO MILE PKY, BLDG C
PO BOX 1449
GOODLETTSVILLE, TN 37070-1449
TEL: (615) 859-0131
FAX: (615) 859-0818
TOLL FREE: (800) 831-4914

SOUTHERN CALIFORNIA PIPE TRADES TRUST FUND
501 SHATTO PL- 5TH FL
LOS ANGELES, CA 90020-1713
TEL: (213) 385-6161
FAX: (213) 487-3640
IN-STATE: (800) 595-7473

SOUTHERN GROUP ADMINISTRATORS, INC
200 S MARSHALL ST
WINSTON-SALEM, NC 27101-5251
TEL: (336) 723-7111
FAX: (336) 722-4748
TOLL FREE: (800) 334-8159

SOUTHERN GUARANTY INSURANCE CO
PO BOX 235004
MONTGOMERY, AL 36123-5004
TEL: (334) 270-6000
FAX: (334) 270-6115
TOLL FREE: (800) 633-5606

SOUTHERN HEALTH PLAN, INC
600 JEFFERSON AVE
PO BOX 97
MEMPHIS, TN 38101-0097
TEL: (901) 544-2636
FAX: (901) 544-2440
TOLL FREE: (800) 527-9206

SOUTHERN HEALTH SERVICES
9881 MAYLAND DR
PO BOX 85603
RICHMOND, VA 23285-5603
TEL: (804) 747-3700
FAX: (804) 747-8723
TOLL FREE: (800) 627-4872

SOUTHERN INSURANCE MANAGEMENT ASSOCIATION
1812 UNIVERSITY BLVD
PO BOX 1250
TUSCALOOSA, AL 35403-1250
TEL: (205) 345-3505
TOLL FREE: (800) 476-9928

SOUTHWEST ADMINISTRATORS
1000 S FREEMONT AVE
PO BOX 1121
ALHAMBRA, CA 91802-1121
TEL: (626) 284-4792

SPECIAL AGENTS MUTUAL BENEFIT ASSOCIATION
11301 OLD GEORGETOWN RD
ROCKVILLE, MD 20852-2800
TEL: (301) 984-1440
FAX: (301) 984-6224
TOLL FREE: (800) 638-6589

SPECTARA
2811 LORD BALTIMORE DR
BALTIMORE, MD 21244-2644
TEL: (410) 265-6033
FAX: (410) 944-5118
TOLL FREE: (800) 638-6265
IN-STATE: (800) 638-6265

ST. FRANCIS HOME CARE
414 PETTIGRU ST
PO BOX 9312
GREENVILLE, SC 29605
TEL: (864) 233-5300
FAX: (864) 233-8473

ST. LOUIS LABOR HEALTH INSTITUTE
300 S GRANDE BLVD
SAINT LOUIS, MO 63103-2430
TEL: (314) 658-5627
FAX: (314) 652-5022
TOLL FREE: (800) 466-5688

STANDARD LIFE & ACCIDENT INSURANCE CO
ONE MOODY PLZ
PO BOX 1800
GALVESTON, TX 77553
TEL: (405) 290-1000
FAX: (409) 766-6663
TOLL FREE: (800) 827-2524

STATE FARM INSURANCE CO
ONE STATE FARM PLZ
PO BOX 2700
BLOOMINGTON, IL 61710
TEL: (309) 766-2311
TOLL FREE: (800) 538-4643

1665 W ALAMEDA DR
TEMPE, AZ 85289-0001
TEL: (602) 784-3000
FAX: (602) 784-3870

8900 STATE FARM WAY
AUSTIN, TX 78729
TEL: (512) 918-4000
FAX: (512) 918-5298

STATE OF NEW YORK INSURANCE DEPARTMENT LIQUIDATION BUREAU
123 WILLIAM ST
NEW YORK, NY 10038-3804
TEL: (212) 341-6400
FAX: (212) 341-6104

TAYLOR EMPLOYEES HEALTH & DENTAL PLAN
1725 ROE CREST
PO BOX 3728
NORTH MANKATO, MN 56002-3728
TEL: (507) 625-2828
FAX: (507) 625-7742
TOLL FREE: (800) 345-6954

TEACHERS PROTECTIVE MUTUAL LIFE INSURANCE CO
116-118 N PRINCE ST
PO BOX 597
LANCASTER, PA 17608-0597
TEL: (717) 394-7156
FAX: (717) 394-7024
TOLL FREE: (800) 555-3122

THE ALLIANCE
650 S CHERRY ST, STE 300
DENVER, CO 80246
TEL: (303) 333-6767
FAX: (303) 322-3830
TOLL FREE: (800) 996-2447

THE WHEELER COMPANIES
200 CAHABA PARK CIR, STE 250
PO BOX 43350
BIRMINGHAM, AL 35243-0350
TEL: (205) 995-8688
FAX: (940) 980-9047
TOLL FREE: (800) 741-8688

TOWER LIFE INSURANCE CO
TOWER LIFE BLDG, 310 S ST MARY ST, STE 400
SAN ANTONIO, TX 78205-3164
TEL: (210) 554-4400
FAX: (210) 554-4401
TOLL FREE: (800) 880-4576

TRAVELERS PROPERTY & CASUALTY
215 SHUMAN BLVD
NAPERVILLE, IL 60563-8458
TOLL FREE: (800) 238-6225

TRIGON
PO BOX 27280
RICHMOND, VA 23261
TEL: (804) 358-1551
FAX: (804) 354-4340
IN-STATE: (800) 451-1527

TRINITY UNIVERSAL INSURANCE CO
PO BOX 655028
DALLAS, TX 75265-5028
TEL: (214) 360-8000
FAX: (214) 360-8076
TOLL FREE: (800) 777-2249

TRUST MARK
10777 SUNSET OFFICE DR, STE 300
SAINT LOUIS, MO 63127-1080
TEL: (314) 984-0666
FAX: (314) 984-9380
IN-STATE: (800) 325-8628

TRUSTMARK INSURANCE
8324 S AVE
BOARDMAN, OH 44512-6417
TEL: (330) 758-2212
FAX: (330) 758-3242
TOLL FREE: (800) 544-7312

TRUSTMARK INSURANCE CO
400 FIELD DR
LAKE FOREST, IL 60045-2586
TEL: (847) 615-1500
FAX: (847) 615-3910

UNICARE
3820 AMERICAN DR
PLANO, TX 75070
TEL: (972) 599-6500
TOLL FREE: (800) 332-2060

UNICARE ASSOCIATION SERVICES
13523 BARRET PKY, STE 250
PO BOX 120
BALLWIN, MO 63022-0120
TEL: (630) 679-4288
TOLL FREE: (800) 332-2060

UNICARE LIFE & HEALTH
PO BOX 833947
RICHARDSON, TX 75083-3947
TEL: (972) 599-6500
TOLL FREE: (800) 332-2060

3200 GREENFIELD RD
PO BOX 4479
DEARBORN, MI 48120
TEL: (313) 336-5550
TOLL FREE: (800) 332-2060
IN-STATE: (800) 843-8184

7025 ALBERTPICK RD- 5TH FL
GREENSBORO, NC 27409
TEL: (336) 665-1888
FAX: (336) 605-6406
TOLL FREE: (800) 597-6735

3179 TEMPLE AVE, STE 200
POMONA, CA 91768
TEL: (909) 444-6000
FAX: (909) 444-6161

24650 CENTER RDG RD, STE 310
WESTLAKE, OH 44145-5680
TEL: (800) 543-4556
TOLL FREE: (800) 437-2277
IN-STATE: (800) 223-9940

UNION LABOR LIFE INSURANCE CO
111 MASSACHUSETTS AVE NW
WASHINGTON, DC 20001
TEL: (202) 682-0900
FAX: (202) 682-8795

161 FORBES RD, STE 204
BRAINTREE, MA 02184-2606
TEL: (781) 848-7474
FAX: (781) 849-6113
TOLL FREE: (800) 248-0029

UNISYS
2525 S MONROE
TALLAHASSEE, FL 32301
TEL: (850) 671-0100
FAX: (850) 671-4528
TOLL FREE: (800) 289-7799

UNITED AMERICAN INSURANCE
3700 S STONEBRIDGE DR
PO BOX 8080
MCKINNEY, TX 75070-8080
TEL: (972) 529-5085
FAX: (972) 569-3688

UNITED CHAMBERS ADMINISTRATORS
1805 HIGH PT DR
PO BOX 3048
NAPERVILLE, IL 60566-7048
TEL: (630) 505-3100
FAX: (630) 577-2915
TOLL FREE: (800) 323-3529

UNITED FARM FAMILY MUTUAL INSURANCE
9135 BROADWAY
MARYVILLE, IN 46410
TEL: (219) 756-9650
FAX: (219) 756-9669
TOLL FREE: (800) 477-6767

UNITED GOVERNMENT SERVICES
401 W MICHIGAN ST
MILWAUKEE, WI 53212
TEL: (414) 226-5000
FAX: (414) 226-5226
TOLL FREE: (800) 558-1584

UNITED HEALTHCARE
11140 N KENDALL DR
MIAMI, FL 33183
TEL: (305) 596-5696
FAX: (305) 275-4050
TOLL FREE: (800) 543-3145
IN-STATE: (888) 716-8787

555 N CARANCAHUA, STE 500
CORPUS CHRISTI, TX 78478
TEL: (512) 887-0101
FAX: (512) 887-8115
TOLL FREE: (800) 580-2247

ONE S WACKER DR
CHICAGO, IL 60606
TEL: (312) 424-4460
FAX: (312) 424-5620
TOLL FREE: (800) 826-9400

969 EXECUTIVE PKY, STE 100
PO BOX 419080
SAINT LOUIS, MO 63141-9080
TOLL FREE: (800) 535-9291

3650 OLENTANGY RIVER RD
PO BOX 182281
COLUMBUS, OH 43219
TEL: (614) 442-7100
FAX: (614) 442-3902
TOLL FREE: (800) 328-8835
IN-STATE: (800) 458-5346

UNITED HEALTHCARE INSURANCE CO
PO BOX 22545
JACKSON, MS 39225-2545
TEL: (601) 977-0208
FAX: (601) 977-5854

UNITED HEALTHCARE INSURANCE CO, PART A INTERMEDIARY
538 PRESTON AVE
PO BOX 1043
MERIDEN, CT 06450-1041
TEL: (203) 639-3230
FAX: (203) 639-3202

UNITED HEALTHCARE INSURANCE CO, PART B CARRIER
538 PRESTON AVE
PO BOX 1043
MERIDEN, CT 06450-1041
TEL: (203) 639-3124
FAX: (203) 639-3018

8120 PENN AVE S
BLOOMINGTON, MN 55431-1394
TEL: (612) 884-3030
FAX: (612) 885-2839

300 ARBORETUM PL- 4TH FL
PO BOX 26463
RICHMOND, VA 23261-3480
TEL: (804) 327-2211
FAX: (804) 327-2101

UNITED HERITAGE MUTUAL LIFE INSURANCE CO
1212 12TH AVE RD
PO BOX 48
NAMPA, ID 83653-0048
TEL: (208) 466-7856
FAX: (208) 466-0825
TOLL FREE: (800) 657-6351

USI ADMINISTRATORS
7402 HODGSON MEMORIAL DR #210
PO BOX 9888
SAVANNAH, GA 31406
TEL: (912) 691-1551
FAX: (912) 352-8935
TOLL FREE: (800) 631-3441

VALERO ENERGY CORP
7990 W IH 10
SAN ANTONIO, TX 78230-4715
TEL: (210) 370-2776
FAX: (210) 370-2861
TOLL FREE: (800) 531-7911
IN-STATE: (800) 292-7816

VALERO HEALTHCARE ADMISSION
2269 S UNIVERSITY DR, STE 308
FT LAUDERDALE, FL 33324
TEL: (210) 370-2100
TOLL FREE: (800) 531-7911
IN-STATE: (800) 292-7816

VIACHRISTI ST. FRANCIS
929 N ST FRANCIS
WICHITA, KS 67214
TEL: (316) 268-5192
FAX: (316) 268-6985
TOLL FREE: (800) 362-0070

VIACHRISTI ST. JOSEPH MEDICAL CENTER
3600 E HARRY ST
WICHITA, KS 67218-3784
TEL: (316) 685-1111
TOLL FREE: (800) 851-0051

VIRGINIA SURETY CO
4850 STREET RD
TREVOSE, PA 19049
TEL: (215) 953-3000
FAX: (215) 953-3156
TOLL FREE: (800) 523-6599
IN-STATE: (800) 523-5758

WARD NORTH AMERICA, INC
3330 ARCTIC BLVD, STE 206
ANCHORAGE, AK 99503
TEL: (907) 561-1725
FAX: (907) 562-6595

WAUSAU INSURANCE CO
200 WESTWOOD DR
PO BOX 8013
WAUSAU, WI 54401-7881
TEL: (715) 845-5211
FAX: (715) 847-7569
TOLL FREE: (800) 826-9781

WEA INSURANCE GROUP
45 NOB HILL RD
PO BOX 7338
MADISON, WI 53707-7330
TEL: (608) 276-4000
FAX: (608) 276-9119
TOLL FREE: (800) 279-4000

WESTCHESTER TEAMSTERS HEALTH & WELFARE
160 S CENTRAL AVE
ELMSFORD, NY 10523-3521
TEL: (914) 592-9330
FAX: (914) 592-1519

WEYCO, INC
PO BOX 30132
LANSING, MI 48909-7632
TEL: (517) 349-7010
FAX: (517) 349-7335
TOLL FREE: (800) 748-0003

WEYERHAEUSER CO
1145 BROADWAY, STE 600
PO BOX TF-C
TACOMA, WA 98402-3527
TEL: (253) 924-7381
FAX: (253) 924-3221
TOLL FREE: (800) 833-0030

WILLSE & ASSOCIATES
100 S CHARLES- TWR 2, STE 9
PO BOX 1196
BALTIMORE, MD 21297-0417
TEL: (410) 347-1925
FAX: (410) 347-1924
TOLL FREE: (800) 423-9791

WISCONSIN PHYSICIANS SERVICE INSURANCE CO (WPS)
1717 W BROADWAY
PO BOX 1890
MADISON, WI 53703
TEL: (608) 221-4711
FAX: (608) 223-3626
TOLL FREE: (800) 828-2837

WISCONSIN SHEETMETAL HEALTH
PO BOX 3500
MADISON, WI 53704
TEL: (608) 277-0477
TOLL FREE: (800) 779-7577

XACT MEDICARE SERVICES — MEDICARE PART B CARRIER
1800 CENTER ST
PO BOX 890089
CAMP HILL, PA 17089-0089
TEL: (717) 763-5700
FAX: (717) 760-9296

ZENITH ADMINISTRATORS, INC
6801 E WASHINGTON BLVD
PO BOX 22041
COMMERCE, CA 90022
TEL: (323) 724-1144

2873 N DIRKSEN PKY, STE 200
SPRINGFIELD, IL 62702
TEL: (217) 753-4531
FAX: (217) 753-3953
TOLL FREE: (800) 538-6466

1320 PATUXTENT PKY, STE 610
PO BOX 1100
COLUMBIA, MD 21044
TEL: (410) 884-1440
FAX: (410) 997-3657
TOLL FREE: (800) 235-5805

3100 BROADWAY, STE 400
KANSAS CITY, MO 64111
TEL: (818) 756-0173
FAX: (816) 531-6518

4380 SW MACADAN AVE, STE 300
PO BOX 1420
PORTLAND, OR 97201
TEL: (503) 226-6753
FAX: (503) 226-7900
TOLL FREE: (800) 547-5900

2100 N MAYFAIR RD, STE 100
MILWAUKEE, WI 53226
TEL: (414) 476-1220
FAX: (414) 476-2997
TOLL FREE: (800) 242-4712

2801 COHO ST, STE 300
MADISON, WI 53713
TEL: (608) 274-4773
FAX: (608) 277-1088
TOLL FREE: (800) 397-3373

Appendix E

Medicare Carriers, Intermediaries, and Contacts

State	Questions	Who To Call	Who Is...	Phone Number
Alabama	Medicare Part B	Medicare Carrier	Blue Cross/Blue Shield of Alabama	1-800-292-8855 or 1-205-988-2244
	Medicare Part A	Fiscal Intermediary (FI)	Mutual of Omaha	1-402-351-9860 or 1-402-351-3825 (Spanish)
	Home Health/Hospice	Regional Home Office	Palmetto Government Benefits Administrators	1-803-788-4660
	Durable Medical Equipment (DME)	DME Regional Carrier	Palmetto Government Benefits Administrators	1-800-213-5452 or (Spanish) 1-800-213-5446
Alaska	Medicare Part B	Medicare Carrier	Noridian Mutual Insurance Co	1-800-444-4606 or 1-303-858-5903 (TDD)
	Medicare Part A	Fiscal Intermediary (FI)	Premera Blue Cross	1-425-670-1010
	Home Health/Hospice	Regional Home Office	Blue Cross of California	1-805-383-2990
	Durable Medical Equipment (DME)	DME Regional Carrier	CIGNA Medicare	1-800-899-7095
American Samoa	Medicare Part B	Medicare Carrier	Noridian Mutual Insurance Co	1-800-444-4606
	Medicare Part A	Fiscal Intermediary (FI)	Blue Cross of California	1-808-942-2400
	Home Health/Hospice	Regional Home Office	Blue Cross of California	1-805-383-2990
	Durable Medical Equipment (DME)	DME Regional Carrier	CIGNA Medicare	1-800-899-7095

State	Questions	Who To Call	Who Is...	Phone Number
Arizona	Medicare Part B	Medicare Carrier	Noridian Mutual Insurance Co	1-800-444-4606 or 1-303-858-5903 (TDD)
	Medicare Part A	Fiscal Intermediary (FI)	Blue Cross of Arizona	1-602-864-4298
	Home Health/Hospice	Regional Home Office	Blue Cross of California	1-805-383-2990
	Durable Medical Equipment (DME)	DME Regional Carrier	CIGNA Medicare	1-800-899-7095
Arkansas	Medicare Part B	Medicare Carrier	Arkansas Blue Cross/ Blue Shield	1-800-482-5525 or 1-501-378-2320
	Medicare Part A	Fiscal Intermediary (FI)	Arkansas Blue Cross/ Blue Shield	1-501-378-2713
	Home Health/Hospice	Regional Home Office	Palmetto Government Benefits Administrators	1-803-788-4660
	Durable Medical Equipment (DME)	DME Regional Carrier	Palmetto Government Benefits Admnistrators	1-800-213-5452
California	Medicare Part B	Medicare Carrier	Transamerica Occidental Life Ins.	Counties of Los Angeles, Orange, San Diego, Ventura, Imperial, San Luis Obispo, Santa Barbara 1-800-675-2266 or 1-213-748-2311 Rest of State: National Heritage Insurance Co 1-800-952-8627 or 1-530-743-1583
	Medicare Part A	Fiscal Intermediary (FI)	Blue Cross of California	1-805-383-2038
	Home Health/Hospice	Regional Home Office	Blue Cross of California	1-805-383-2990
	Durable Medical Equipment (DME)	DME Regional Carrier	CIGNA Medicare	1-800-899-7095

State	Questions	Who To Call	Who Is...	Phone Number
Colorado	Medicare Part B	Medicare Carrier	Noridian Mutual Insurance Co	1-800-332-6681 or 1-303-831-2661
	Medicare Part A	Fiscal Intermediary (FI)	Blue Cross and Blue Shield	1-903-463-4568 (TDD) 1-800-442-2620
	Home Health/Hospice	Regional Home Office	Welmark Or Blue Cross of Iowa	1-515-246-0126
	Durable Medical Equipment (DME)	DME Regional Carrier	Palmetto Government Benefits Administrators	1-800-213-5452
Connecticut	Medicare Part B	Medicare Carrier	United HealthCare	1-800-982-6819 (in CT only) 1-203-237-8592
	Medicare Part A	Fiscal Intermediary (FI)	United HealthCare Insurance Company	1-203-639-3222
	Home Health/Hospice	Regional Home Office	Associated Hospital Service of Maine	1-888-896-4997 1-207-822-8484
	Durable Medical Equipment (DME)	DME Regional Carrier	United HealthCare	1-800-842-2052
Delaware	Medicare Part B	Medicare Customer Service Cntr	Xact Medicare Services	1-800-851-3535
	Medicare Part A	Fiscal Intermediary (FI)	Empire Medicare Services	1-800-442-8430 or 1-800-492-6879 (Spanish)
	Home Health/Hospice	Regional Home Office	Wellmark Blue Cross Blue Shield	1-515-246-0126
	Durable Medical Equipment (DME)	DME Regional Carrier	United HealthCare Insurance Company	1-800-842-2052
District of Columbia	Medicare Part B	Medicare Customer Service Cntr	Xact Medicare Services	1-800-233-1124
	Medicare Part A	Fiscal Intermediary (FI)	Xact Medicare Services	1-800-233-1124
	Home Health/Hospice	Regional Home Office	Xact Medicare Services	1-800-233-1124
	Durable Medical Equipment (DME)	DME Regional Carrier	Adminiastar Federal, Inc.	1-800-270-2313

State	Questions	Who To Call	Who Is...	Phone Number
Florida	Medicare Part B	Medicare Carrier	Blue Cross and Blue Shield of Florida	1-800-333-7586 or 1-904-355-3680
	Medicare Part A	Fiscal Intermediary (FI)	Blue Cross and Blue Shield of Florida	1-904-355-8899
	Home Health/Hospice	Regional Home Office	Palmetto Government Benefits Administrators	1-727-773-9225 or (Spanish) 1-800-213-5446
	Durable Medical Equipment (DME)	DME Regional Carrier	Palmetto Government Benefits Administrators	1-800-727-0827 or (Spanish) 1-912-920-2412
Georgia	Medicare Part B	Medicare Carrier	Cahaba Government Benefits Administrators	1-800-727-0827 or 1-912-920-2412
	Medicare Part A	Fiscal Intermediary (FI)	Blue Cross and Blue Shield of Georgia	1-706-571-5000 (TDD) 1-706-322-4082
	Home Health/Hospice	Regional Home Office	Palmetto Government Benefits Administrators	1-803-788-4660
	Durable Medical Equipment (DME)	DME Regional Carrier	Palmetto Government Benefits Administrators	1-727-773-9225 or (Spanish) 1-800-213-5452
Guam	Medicare Part B	Medicare Carrier	Blue Cross and Blue Shield of North Dakota	1-800-444-4606
	Medicare Part A	Fiscal Intermediary (FI)	Blue Cross of California	1-808-942-2400
	Home Health/Hospice	Regional Home Office	Blue Cross of California	1-805-383-2990
	Durable Medical Equipment (DME)	DME Regional Carrier	CIGNA Medicare	1-800-899-7095
Hawaii	Medicare Part B	Medicare Carrier	Medicare Part B	1-800-444-4606
	Medicare Part A	Fiscal Intermediary (FI)	Blue Cross of California	1-808-942-2400
	Home Health/Hospice	Regional Home Office	Blue Cross of California	1-805-383-2990
	Durable Medical Equipment (DME)	DME Regional Carrier	CIGNA Medicare	1-800-899-7095

State	Questions	Who To Call	Who Is...	Phone Number
Idaho	Medicare Part B	Medicare Carrier	Medicare Part B	1-800-627-2782 or 1-615-244-5650
	Medicare Part A	Fiscal Intermediary (FI)	Blue Cross/Blue Shield Oregon	1-503-721-7000
	Home Health/Hospice	Regional Home Office	Blue Cross of California	1-805-383-2990
	Durable Medical Equipment (DME)	DME Regional Carrier	CIGNA Medicare	1-800-899-7095
Illinois	Medicare Part B	Medicare Carrier	Claims/HealthCare Service Corp.	1-800-642-6930 or 1-312-938-8000 1-800-535-6152 (TTY/TDD)
	Medicare Part A	Fiscal Intermediary (FI)	AdminaStar Federal, Inc.	1-312-938-6266
	Home Health/Hospice	Regional Home Office	Palmetto Government Benefits Administrators	1-803-788-4660
	Durable Medical Equipment (DME)	DME Regional Carrier	AdminiStar Federal Inc.	1-800-270-2313
Indiana	Medicare Part B	Medicare Carrier	AdminiStar Federal Inc.	1-800-622-4792 or 1-317-842-4151
	Medicare Part A	Fiscal Intermediary (FI)	AdminiStar Federal Inc.	1-800-622-4792
	Home Health/Hospice	Regional Home Office	Palmetto Government Benefits Administrators	1-803-788-4660
	Durable Medical Equipment (DME)	DME Regional Carrier	AdminiStar Federal Inc.	1-800-270-2313
Iowa	Medicare Part B	Medicare Carrier	IASD Health Services Corp. Blue Cross/Blue Shield of Iowa	1-515-245-4785 or 1-800-532-1285
	Medicare Part A	Fiscal Intermediary (FI)	Wellmark Blue Cross/Blue Shield of Iowa	1-712-279-8650
	Home Health/Hospice	Regional Home Office	Wellmark Blue Cross/Blue Shield	1-515-246-0126
	Durable Medical Equipment (DME)	DME Regional Carrier	CIGNA Medicare	1-800-899-7095

State	Questions	Who To Call	Who Is...	Phone Number
Kansas	Medicare Part B	Medicare Carrier	Blue Cross and Blue Shield of Kansas	1-800-432-3531 1-913-232-3773
	Medicare Part A	Fiscal Intermediary (FI)	Blue Cross and Blue Shield of Kansas	1-800-445-7170 1-785-291-4001
	Home Health/Hospice	Regional Home Office	Wellmark Blue Cross/ Blue Shied	1-515-246-0126
	Durable Medical Equipment (DME)	DME Regional Carrier	CIGNA Medicare	1-800-899-7095
Kentucky	Medicare Part B	Medicare Carrier	AdminiStar of Kentucky	1-800-999-7608 or 1-502-425-6759
	Medicare Part A	Fiscal Intermediary (FI)	AdminiStar Federal Inc.	1-800-999-7608 or 1-502-425-6759
	Home Health/Hospice	Regional Home Office	Palmetto Government Benefits Administrators	1-803-788-4660
	Durable Medical Equipment (DME)	DME Regional Carrier	Palmetto Government Benefits Administrators	1-800-213-5452 or (Spanish) 1-800-213-5446
Louisiana	Medicare Part B	Medicare Carrier	Medicare Part B	1-800-462-9666 or Baton Rouge 1-504-927-3490
	Medicare Part A	Fiscal Intermediary (FI)	Trispan Health Services	1-800-932-7644 or 1-601-936-0105
	Home Health/Hospice	Regional Home Office	Palmetto Government Benefits Administrators	1-803-788-4660
	Durable Medical Equipment (DME)	DME Regional Carrier	Palmetto Government Benefits Administrators	1-800-213-5452
Maine	Medicare Part B	Medicare Carrier	Natural Heritage Insurance Co.	1-800-492-0919
	Medicare Part A	Fiscal Intermediary (FI)	Associated Hospital Services of Maine	1-888-896-4997 or 1-207-822-8484
	Home Health/Hospice	Regional Home Office	Associated Hospital Services of Maine	1-888-896-4997 or 1-207-822-8484
	Durable Medical Equipment (DME)	DME Regional Carrier	United Health Care Insurance Co.	1-800-842-2052

State	Questions	Who To Call	Who Is...	Phone Number
Maryland	Medicare Part B	Medicare Customer Service Cntr.	Exact Mediare Services (Counties of Montgomery & Prince George) Trail Blazer Enterprises (Rest of State)	1-800-444-4606 1-800-444-4606
	Medicare Part A	Medicare Customer Service Cntr	Trailblazers	1-800-444-4606 or 1-410-822-0697
	Home Health/Hospice	Medicare Customer Service Cntr	Trailblazers	1-800-444-4606 or 1-410-822-0697
	Durable Medical Equipment (DME)	Medicare Customer Service Cntr	AdminaStar Federal Inc.	1-800-270-2313
Massachusetts	Medicare Part B	Medicare Carrier	National Heritage Insurance Co.	1-800-882-1228
	Medicare Part A	Fiscal Intermediary (FI)	Associated Hospital Services of Maine	1-888-896-4997
	Home Health/Hospice	Regional Home Office	Associated Hospital Services of Maine	1-888-896-4997 or 1-207-822-8484
	Durable Medical Equipment (DME)	DME Regional Carrier	United Health Care Insurance Co.	1-800-842-2052 or 1-717-735-7383
Michigan	Medicare Part B	Medicare Carrier	Michigan Medicare Claims	Rest of State 1-800-482-4045 Area code 906: 1-800-562-7802 or 1-313-225-8200
	Medicare Part A	Fiscal Intermediary (FI)	Wisconsin United Government Services	1-313-225-8317 or 1-800-535-6152 (TDD)
	Home Health/Hospice	Regional Home Office	United Government Services	1-414-224-4954 or 1-800-213-1682 (Spanish)
	Durable Medical Equipment (DME)	DME Regional Carrier	AdminiStar Federal Inc.	1-800-270-2313

State	Questions	Who To Call	Who Is...	Phone Number
Minnesota	Medicare Part B	Medicare Carrier	Metra Health Medicare	1-800-352-2762 or 1-612-884-7171
	Medicare Part A	Fiscal Intermediary (FI)	Noridian	1-800-330-5935
	Home Health/Hospice	Regional Home Office	United Government Services	1-414-224-4954 or 1-800-213-1682 (Spanish)
	Durable Medical Equipment (DME)	DME Regional Carrier	AdminiStar Federal Inc.	1-800-270-2313
Mississippi	Medicare Part B	Medicare Carrier	United Health Care Insurance Co.	1-800-682-5417 or 1-601-956-0372
	Medicare Part A	Fiscal Intermediary (FI)	Trispan Health Services	1-601-936-0105 or 1-800-932-7644
	Home Health/Hospice	Regional Home Office	Palmetto Government Benefits Administrators	1-803-788-4660
	Durable Medical Equipment (DME)	DME Regional Carrier	Palmetto Government Benefits Administrators	1-800-213-5452

State	Questions	Who To Call	Who Is...	Phone Number
Missouri	Medicare Part B	Medicare Carrier	Blue Cross and Blue Shield of Kansas for counties of Andrew, Atchison, Bates, Benton, Buchanan, Caldwell, Carroll, Cass, Clay, Clinton, Davies, Dekalb, Gentry, Grundy, Harrison, Henry, Holt, Jackson, Johnson, Lafayette, Livingston, Mercer, Nodaway, Pettis, Platte, Ray, St. Claire, Saline, Vernon, and Worth Rest of State: Medicare General American Life Insurance Company	1-800-892-5900 or 1-816-561-0900 Rest of State 1-800-392-3070 or 1-314-843-8880
	Medicare Part A	Fiscal Intermediary (FI)	Trispan Health Services	1-800-932-7644 or 1-601-936-0105
	Home Health/Hospice	Regional Home Office	Wellmark, Inc. OR Blue Cross of California	1-515-246-0126
	Durable Medical Equipment (DME)	DME Regional Carrier	CIGNA Medicare	1-800-899-7095
Montana	Medicare Part B	Medicare Carrier	Blue Cross and Blue Shield of Montana	1-800-332-6146 or 1-406-444-8350
	Medicare Part A	Fiscal Intermediary (FI)	Blue Cross and Blue Shield of Montana	1-406-791-4086 or 1-800-447-7828 (ext. 4086)
	Home Health/Hospice	Regional Home Office	Wellmark, Inc. OR Blue Cross of Iowa	IA 1-515-246-0126
	Durable Medical Equipment (DME)	DME Regional Carrier	CIGNA Medicare	1-800-899-7095

State	Questions	Who To Call	Who Is...	Phone Number
Nebraska	Medicare Part B	Medicare Carrier	Blue Cross and Blue Shield of Kansas	1-800-633-1113
	Medicare Part A	Fiscal Intermediary (FI)	Blue Cross and Blue Shield of Nebraska	1-402-390-1850
	Home Health/Hospice	Regional Home Office	Wellmark Blue Cross/ Blue Shield	1-515-246-0126
	Durable Medical Equipment (DME)	DME Regional Carrier	CIGNA Medicare	1-800-899-7095
Nevada	Medicare Part B	Medicare Carrier	Medicare Part B	1-800-444-4606
	Medicare Part A	Fiscal Intermediary (FI)	Blue Cross of California	1-805-383-2038
	Home Health/Hospice	Regional Home Office	Blue Cross of California	1-805-383-2990
	Durable Medical Equipment (DME)	DME Regional Carrier	CIGNA Medicare	1-800-899-7095
New Hampshire	Medicare Part B	Medicare Carrier	National Heritage Insurance Co.	1-800-447-1142
	Medicare Part A	Fiscal Intermediary (FI)	New Hampshire-Vermont Health Service	1-603-695-7204 or 1-800-874-9426 (Spanish)
	Home Health/Hospice	Regional Home Office	Associated Hospital Service of Maine	1-207-822-8484 or 1-888-896-4997
	Durable Medical Equipment (DME)	DME Regional Carrier	United Health Care Insurance Co.	1-800-842-2052 or 1-603-749-1641
New Jersey	Medicare Part B	Medicare Carrier	Xact Medicare Service	1-800-462-9306
	Medicare Part A	Fiscal Intermediary (FI)	Horizon Blue Cross and Blue Shield of New Jersey	1-973-456-2112
	Home Health/Hospice	Regional Home Office	United Government Services	1-414-224-4954 or 1-800-213-1682 (Spanish)
	Durable Medical Equipment (DME)	DME Regional Carrier	United Health Care Insurance Co	1-800-842-2052

State	Questions	Who To Call	Who Is...	Phone Number
New Mexico	Medicare Part B	Medicare Carrier	Medicare Services New Mexico	1-800-423-2925 or 1-505-821-3350
	Medicare Part A	Fiscal Intermediary (FI)	Blue Cross and Blue Shield of Texas, Inc.	1-800-442-2620 1-903-463-4658 (TDD)
	Home Health/Hospice	Regional Home Office	Palmetto Government Benefits Administrators	1-803-788-4660
	Durable Medical Equipment (DME)	DME Regional Carrier	Palmetto Government Benefits Administrators	1-800-213-5452
New York	Medicare Part B	Medicare Carrier	Empire: Bronx, Columbia, Delaware, Dutchess, Greene, Kings, Nassau, New York, Orange, Putnam, Richmond, Rockland, Suffolk, Sullivan, Ulster & Westchester Columbia	1-800-442-8430 or 1-516-244-5100
			Group Health: Queens	1-212-721-1770
			Blue Cross and Blue Shield of Western New York	1-800-252-6550 or 1-607-766-6223
	Medicare Part A	Fiscal Intermediary (FI)	Empire Medicare Services	1-800-442-8430 1-800-492-6879 (Spanish)
	Home Health/Hospice	Regional Home Office	United Government Services	1-414-224-4954 or 1-800-213-1682 (Spanish)
	Durable Medical Equipment (DME)	DME Regional Carrier	United Health Insurance Company	1-800-842-2052

State	Questions	Who To Call	Who Is...	Phone Number
North Carolina	Medicare Part B	Medicare Carrier	CIGNA	1-800-672-3071 or 1-910-665-0348
	Medicare Part A	Fiscal Intermediary (FI)	Blue Cross and Blue Shield of North Carolina	1-919-688-5528 or 1-800-685-1512 (NC only)
	Home Health/Hospice	Regional Home Office	Palmetto Government Benefits Administrators	1-803-788-4660
	Durable Medical Equipment	DME Regional Carrier	Palmetto Government Benefits Administrators	1-800-213-5452
North Dakota	Medicare Part B	Medicare Carrier	Blue Cross and Blue Shield of North Dakota	1-800-247-2267 or 1-701-277-2363
	Medicare Part A	Fiscal Intermediary (FI)	Noridian Mutual Insurance Company	1-800-247-2267 or 1-701-277-2363
	Home Health/Hospice	Regional Home Office	Wellmark Blue Cross/ Blue Shield	1-515-246-0126
	Durable Medical Equipment (DME)	DME Regional Carrier	CIGNA Medicare	1-800-899-7095
Ohio	Medicare Part B	Medicare Carrier	Nationwide Mutual Insurance Co.	1-800-282-0530 or 1-614-249-7157
	Medicare Part A	Fiscal Intermediary (FI)	AdminiStar Federal	1-513-852-4314
	Home Health/Hospice	Regional Home Office	Palmetto Government Benefits Administrators	1-803-788-4660
	Durable Medical Equipment (DME)	DME Regional Carrier	AdminiStar Federal Inc.	1-800-270-2313

State	Questions	Who To Call	Who Is...	Phone Number
Oklahoma	Medicare Part B	Medicare Carrier	Medicare Services of Oklahoma	1-800-522-9079 or 1-405-848-7711
	Medicare Part A	Fiscal Intermediary (FI)	Blue Cross and Blue Shield	1-918-560-3367
	Home Health/Hospice	Regional Home Office	Palmetto Government Benefits Administrators	1-803-788-4660
	Durable Medical Equipment (DME)	DME Regional Carrier	Palmetto Government Benefits Administrators	1-800-213-5452
Oregon	Medicare Part B	Medicare Carrier	Medicare Part B	1-800-444-4606
	Medicare Part A	Fiscal Intermediary (FI)	Blue Cross/Blue Shield	1-503-721-7000
	Home Health/Hospice	Regional Home Office	Blue Cross of California	1-805-383-2990
	Durable Medical Equipment (DME)	DME Regional Carrier	CIGNA Medicare	1-800-899-7095
Pennsylvania	Medicare Part B	Medicare Carrier	Xact Medicare Services	1-800-382-1274
	Medicare Part A	Fiscal Intermediary (FI)	Veritus Medicare Services	1-800-853-1419
	Home Health/Hospice	Regional Home Office	Wellmark Blue Cross/ Blue Shield	1-515-246-0126
	Durable Medical Equipment (DME)	DME Regional Carrier	United Health Care Insurance Co	1-800-842-2052
Puerto Rico	Medicare Part B	Medicare Carrier	Triple-S, Inc.	1-800-981-7015 (Puerto Rico) or 1-787-749-4900 (San Juan Metro)
	Medicare Part A	Fiscal Intermediary (FI)	Cooperativa De Seguros De Vida	1-787-758-9733 or 1-800-986-5656 (Puerto Rico only)
	Home Health/Hospice	Regional Home Office	United Government Services	1-414-224-4954 or 1-800-213-1682 (Spanish)
	Durable Medical Equipment (DME)	DME Regional Carrier	Palmetto Government Benefits Administrators	1-800-213-5452

State	Questions	Who To Call	Who Is...	Phone Number
Rhode Island	Medicare Part B	Medicare Carrier	Blue Cross and Blue Shield of Rhode Island	1-800-662-5170 (RI only) or 1-401-861-2273
	Medicare Part A	Fiscal Intermediary (FI)	Blue Cross and Blue Shield of Rhode Island	1-800-662-5170 or 1-401-861-2273
	Home Health/Hospice	Regional Home Office	Associated Hospital Service of Maine	1-888-896-4997 or 1-207-822-8484
	Durable Medical Equipment (DME)	DME Regional Carrier	United Health Care Insurance Co	1-800-842-2052
South Carolina	Medicare Part B	Medicare Carrier	Palmetto Government Benefits Administrators	1-800-868-2522 or 1-803-788-3882
	Medicare Part A	Fiscal Intermediary (FI)	Blue Cross and Blue Shield	1-800-521-3761 or 1-803-788-4660
	Home Health/Hospice	Regional Home Office	Palmetto Government Benefits Administrators	1-803-788-4660
	Durable Medical Equipment (DME)	DME Regional Carrier	Palmetto Government Benefits Administrators	1-800-213-5452
South Dakota	Medicare Part B	Medicare Carrier	Blue Shield of North Dakota	1-800-437-4762 or 1-701-277-2363
	Medicare Part A	Fiscal Intermediary (FI)	Wellmark	1-712-279-8650
	Home Health/Hospice	Regional Home Office	Blue Cross and Blue Shield	1-515-246-0126
	Durable Medical Equipment (DME)	DME Regional Carrier	CIGNA Medicare	1-800-899-7095

State	Questions	Who To Call	Who Is...	Phone Number
Tennessee	Medicare Part B	Medicare Carrier	CIGNA Medicare	1-800-342-8900 or 1-615-244-5650
	Medicare Part A	Fiscal Intermediary (FI)	Blue Cross and Blue Shield of Tennessee	1-423-755-5955
	Home Health/Hospice	Regional Home Office	Palmetto Government Benefits Administrators	1-803-788-4660
	Durable Medical Equipment (DME)	DME Regional Carrier	Palmetto Government Benefits Administrators	1-800-213-5452
Texas	Medicare Part B	Medicare Carrier	Blue Cross and Blue Shield of Texas	1-800-442-2620 or 1-214-235-3433 (TDD)
	Medicare Part A	Fiscal Intermediary (FI)	Blue Cross and Blue Shield of Texas	1-903-463-4658 or 1-800-442-2620
	Home Health/Hospice	Regional Home Office	Palmetto Government Benefits Administrators	1-803-788-4660
	Durable Medical Equipment (DME)	DME Regional Carrier	Palmetto Government Benefits Administrators	1-800-213-5452
Utah	Medicare Part B	Medicare Carrier	Blue Shield of Utah	1-800-426-3477 or 1-801-481-6196
	Medicare Part A	Fiscal Intermediary (FI)	Blue Shield of Utah	1-801-333-2410
	Home Health/Hospice	Regional Home Office	Wellmark Blue Cross Blue Shield	1-515-246-0126
	Durable Medical Equipment (DME)	DME Regional Carrier	CIGNA Medicare	1-800-899-7095

State	Questions	Who To Call	Who Is...	Phone Number
Vermont	Medicare Part B	Medicare Carrier	National Heritage Insurance Co	1-800-447-1142
	Medicare Part A	Fiscal Intermediary (FI)	New Hampshire-Vermont Health Services	1-603-695-7204 or 1-800-874-9426 (Spanish)
	Home Health/Hospice	Regional Home Office	Associated Hospital Service of Maine	1-888-896-4997 or 1-207-822-8484
	Durable Medical Equipment (DME)	DME Regional Carrier	United Health Care Insurance Company	1-800-842-2052
Virgin Islands	Medicare Part B	Medicare Carrier	Triple-S, Inc.	1-800-474-7448
	Medicare Part A	Fiscal Intermediary (FI)	Cooperativa De Seguros De Vida	1-787-758-9733 1-800-986-5656 (VI only)
	Home Health/Hospice	Regional Home Office	Medicare Part A United Government Services	1-414-224-4954
	Durable Medical Equipment (DME)	DME Regional Carrier	Palmetto Government Benefits Administrators	1-800-213-5452
Virginia	Medicare Part B	Medicare Carrier	Xact Medicare Services Arlington, Fairfax counties Metrahealth (rest of state)	1-800-233-1124 or (Rest of State) 1-800-552-3423 1-804-330-4786
	Medicare Part A	Fiscal Intermediary (FI)	Blue Cross and Blue Shield	1-540-985-3931 or 1-540-853-5120 (TDD)
	Home Health/Hospice	Regional Home Office	Wellmark Blue Cross Blue Shield	1-515-246-0126
	Durable Medical Equipment (DME)	DME Regional Carrier	AdminiStar Federal	1-800-270-2313
Washington	Medicare Part B	Medicare Carrier	Medicare Part B	1-800-444-4606
	Medicare Part A	Fiscal Intermediary (FI)	Premera Blue Cross	1-425-670-1010
	Home Health/Hospice	Regional Home Office	Blue Cross of California	1-805-383-2990
	Durable Medical Equipment (DME)	DME Regional Carrier	CIGNA Medicare	1-800-899-7095

State	Questions	Who To Call	Who Is...	Phone Number
West Virginia	Medicare Part B	Medicare Carrier	Nationwide Mutual Insurance Co	1-800-848-0106 or 1-614-249-7157
	Medicare Part A	Fiscal Intermediary (FI)	Blue Cross and Blue Shield	1-540-985-3931 or 1-540-853-5120 (TDD)
	Home Health/Hospice	Regional Home Office	Wellmark Blue Cross Blue Shield	1-515-246-0126
	Durable Medical Equipment (DME)	DME Regional Carrier	AdminiStar Federal Inc.	1-800-270-2313
Wisconsin	Medicare Part B	Medicare Carrier	Medicare/Wisconsin Physicians Service	1-800-944-0051 or 1-608-221-3330
	Medicare Part A	Fiscal Intermediary (FI)	Blue Cross and Blue Shield of Wisconsin	1-414-224-4954 or 1-414-226-2626 (Spanish)
	Home Health/Hospice	Regional Home Office	United Government Services	1-414-224-4954 or 1-800-213-1682 (Spanish)
	Durable Medical Equipment (DME)	DME Regional Carrier	AdminiStar Federal Inc.	1-800-270-2313
Wyoming	Medicare Part B	Medicare Carrier	Blue Cross and Blue Shield of North Dakota	1-800-442-2371 or 1-307-632-9381
	Medicare Part A	Fiscal Intermediary (FI)	Blue Cross and Blue Shield of Wyoming	1-307-634-2860 or 1-800-442-2376
	Home Health/Hospice	Regional Home Office	Wellmark Blue Cross Blue Shield	1-515-246-0126
	Durable Medical Equipment (DME)	DME Regional Carrier	CIGNA Medicare	1-800-899-7095

Index

Abbokinase, J3364, J3365
Abciximab, J0130
Abdomen/abdominal
   dressing holder/binder, A4462
   pad, low profile, L1270
   supports, pendulous, L0920, L0930
Abdominal binder
   elastic, A4462
Abduction
   control, each L2624
   pillow, E1399
   rotation bar, foot, L3140-L3170
Abelcet, J0286
Ablation
   cryosurgical
      tumor tissue, liver, S2210
ABLC, K0433
Absorption dressing, A6251–A6256
Access system, A4301
Accessories
   ambulation devices, E0153–E0159
   artificial kidney and machine (see also ESRD), E1510–E1699
   beds, E0271–E0280, E0305–E0326
   wheelchairs, E0950–E1001, E1050–E1298, K0001–K0108
AccuChek
   blood glucose meter, E0607
   test strips, box of 50, A4253
Accu Hook, prosthesis, L6790
Accurate
   prosthetic sock, L8420–L8435
   stump sock, L8470–L8485
Acetazolamide sodium, J1120
Acetylcysteine, J7610, J7615
   inhalation solution, J7608
Achromycin, J0120
ACTH, J0800
Acthar, J0800
Actimmune, J9216
Action neoprene supports, L1825
Action Patriot manual wheelchair, K0004
Action Xtra, Action MVP, Action Pro-T, manual wheelchair, K0005
Activase, J2996
Active Life
   convex one-piece urostomy pouch, A4421
   flush away, A5051
   one-piece
      drainable custom pouch, A5061
      pre-cut closed-end pouch, A5051
      stoma cap, A5055
Acyclovir sodium, S0071

Adenocard, J0150, J0151
Adenosine, J0150, J0151
Adhesive
   catheter, A4364, K0407
   disc or foam pad, A5126
   liquid, K0450
   medical, A4364
   Nu-Hope
      1 oz bottle with applicator, A4364
      3 oz bottle with applicator, A4364
   ostomy, A4364
   pads, A6203–A6205, A6212–A6214, A6219–A6221, A6237–A6239, A6245–A6247, A6254–A6256
   remover, A4365, A4455, K0451
   support, breast prosthesis, A4280
   tape, A4454, A6265
   tissue, G0168
Adjustabrace™ 3, L2999
Adrenalin, J0170
   chloride, J0170
Adriamycin, J9000
Adrucil, J9190
AdvantaJet, A4210
Aerosol
   compressor, K0269
AFO, E1815, E1830, L1900–L1990, L4392, L4396
Aggrastat, J3245
A-hydroCort, J1720
Aimsco Ultra Thin syringe, 1 cc or 1/2 cc, each, A4206
Air ambulance (see also Ambulance), A0030, A0040
Air bubble detector, dialysis, E1530
Aircast, L4350–L4380
Air fluidized bed, E0194
Airlife Brand Misty-Neb Nebulizer, E0580
Air pressure pad/mattress, E0176, E0186, E0197
Air travel and nonemergency transportation, A0140
Aircast air stirrup ankle brace, L1906
Akineton, J0190
Alarm, pressure, dialysis, E1540
Alatrofloxacin mesylate, J0200
Albecet, J0286
Albumarc, Q0156, Q0157
Albumin, human, Q0156, Q0157
Albuterol
   inhalation solution
      concentrated, J7618
      unit dose, J7619
   sulfate, J7620, J7625

Alcohol, A4244
Alcohol wipes, A4245
Aldesleukin, J9015
Aldomet, J0210
Alferon N, J9215
Algiderm, alginate dressing, A6196–A6199
Alginate dressing, A6196–A6199
Alglucerase, J0205
Algosteril, alginate dressing, A6196–A6199
Alkaban-AQ, J9360
Alkaline battery for blood glucose monitor, A4254
Alkeran, J8600
Allkare protective barrier wipe, box of 100, A5119
Allograft
   small intestine, S2052
   small intestine and liver, S2053
Alpha 1-proteinase inhibitor, human, J0256
Alprostadil, J0270
   injection, J0270
   urethral suppository, J0275
Alteplase recombinant, J2996
Alternating pressure mattress/pad, A4640, E0180, E0181, E0277
   pump, E0182
   replacement pad, A4640
Alupent, J7670, J7672, J7675
Alveoloplasty, D7310–D7320
Amalgam dental restoration, D2110–D2161
Ambulance, A0021–A0999
   air, A0030, A0040
   disposable supplies, A0382–A0398
   oxygen, A0422
Ambulation device, E0100–E0159
Amcort, J3302
A-methaPred, J2920, J2930
Amifostine, J0207
Amikacin sulfate, S0072
Aminaid, enteral nutrition, B4154
Aminocaproic acid, S0017
Aminophylline/Aminophyllin, J0280
Amitriptyline HCl, J1320
Amirosyn-RF, parenteral nutrition, B5000
Ammonia test paper, A4774
Amobarbital, J0300
Amphocin, J0285
Amphotec, J0286
Amphotericin B, J0285
   B lipid complex, J0286
Ampicillin sodium, J0290
   sodium/sulbactam sodium, J0295
Amputee
   adapter, wheelchair, E0959

Amputee — *continued*
   prosthesis, L5000–L7510, L7520, L7900, L8400–L8465
   stump sock, L8470–L8490
   wheelchair, E1170–E1190, E1200, K0100
Amygdalin, J3570
Amytal, J0300
Anabolin LA 100, J2320–J2322
Analgesia, dental, D9230
Ancef, J0690
Andrest 90-4, J0900
Andro-Cyp, J1070–J1090
Andro-Estro 90-4, J0900
Androgyn L.A., J0900
Andro L.A. 200, J3130
Androlone
   -50, J0340
   -D 100, J2321
Andronaq
   -50, J3140
   -LA, J1070
Andronate
   -100, J1070
   -200, J1080
Andropository 100, J3120
Andryl 200, J3130
Anectine, J0330
Anergan (25, 50), J2550
Anesthesia
   dental, D7110–D7130, D7210–D7250, D9210–D9240
   dialysis, A4735
Angiography digital subtraction, S9022
Anistreplase, J0350
Ankle splint, recumbent, K0126–K0130
Ankle-foot orthosis (AFO; *see also*
   Orthopedic shoe, and tibia), L1900-L1990, L2102-L2116
   Dorsiwedge™ Night Splint, L4398 or A4570 or L2999
   Specialist™
     Ankle Foot Orthosis, L1930
     Tibial Pre-formed Fracture Brace, L2116
   Surround™ Ankle Stirrup Braces with Floam™, L1906
Anterior-posterior orthosis, L0320, L0330, L0530
   -lateral orthosis, L0520, L0550–L0565, L0700, L0710
   -lateral-rotary orthosis, L0340–L0440
Antibody testing, HIV-1, S3645
Antiemetic drug, prescription
   oral, Q0163–Q0181
   rectal, K0416
Anti-hemophilic factor (Factor VIII), J7190–J7192
Anti-inhibitors, J7198
Anti-neoplastic drug, NOC, J9999
Antispas, J0500
Antithrombin III, J7197
Antral fistula closure, oral, D7260
Anzemet, J1260
Apexification, dental, D3351–D3353
Apicoectomy, dental, D3410–D3426
A.P.L., J0725
Apnea monitor, E0608
   electrodes, A4556
   lead wires, A4557

Appliance
   cleaner, A5131
   pneumatic, E0655–E0673
Apresoline, J0360
AquaMEPHYTON, J3430
AquaPedic sectional gel flotation, E0196
Aqueous
   shunt, L8612
   sterile, J7051
Aralen, J0390
Aramine, J0380
Arbutamine HCl, J0395
Arch support, L3040–L3100
Aredia, J2430
Arfonad, J0400
Argyle Sentinel Seal chest drainage unit, E0460
Aristocort
   forte, J3302
   intralesional, J3302
Aristospan
   Intra-articular, J3303
   Intralesional, J3303
Arm
   sling
     deluxe, A4565
     mesh cradle, A4565
     universal
       arm, A4565
       elevator, A4565
   wheelchair, E0973
Arm-a-Med Isoetharine HCl, J7654
Arnold apron-front, spinal orthosis, L0340
Arrestin, J3250
Arrow, power wheelchair, K0014
Arthroscopy
   shoulder
     with capsulorrhaphy, S2300
Artificial
   kidney machines and accessories (see also Dialysis), E1510–E1699
   larynx, L8500
Asparaginase, J9020
Assessment
   audiologic, V5008–V5020
   cardiac output, M0302
   speech, V5362–V5364
Astramorph, J2275
Atgam, J7504
Ativan, J2060
Atropine
   inhalation solution
     concentrated, J7635
     unit dose, J7636
   sulfate, J0460
Atrovent, J7645
Attends, adult diapers, A4335
Audiologic assessment, V5008–V5020
Auricular prosthesis, D5914, D5927
Aurothioglucose, J2910
Autoclix lancet device, A4258
Auto-Glide folding walker, E0143
Autolance lancet device, A4258
Autolet lancet device, A4258
Autolet Lite lancet device, A4258
Autolet Mark II lancet device, A4258
Autoplex T, J7196
Avonex, J1825
Azathioprine, J7500, J7501

Azithromycin dihydrate, Q0144
Azithromycin injection, J0456
Aztreonam, S0073

Back supports, L0500–L0960
Baclofen, J0475, J0476
Bacterial sensitivity study, P7001
Bactocill, J2700
Bag
   drainage, A4357
   irrigation supply, A4398
   spacer, for metered dose inhaler, A4627
   urinary, A5112, A4358
Baker, spinal orthosis, L0370
BAL in oil, J0470
Balken, fracture frame, E0946
Bandages, A4460
   Orthoflex™ Elastic Plaster Bandages, A4580
   Specialist™ Plaster Bandages, A4580
Banflex, J2360
Barium enema, G0106
   cancer screening, G0120
Baseball finger splint, A4570
Bathtub
   heat unit, E0249
   stool or bench, E0245
   transfer rail, E0246
   wall rail, E0241, E0242
Battery, K0082–K0087, L7360, L7364
   blood glucose monitor, A4254
   charger, E1066, K0088–K0089, L7362, L7366
   TENS, A4630
   ventilator, A4611–A4613
   wheelchair, A4631
Bayer chemical reagent strips, box of 100 glucose/ketone urine test strips, A4250
BCG live, intravesical, J9031
BCW 600, manual wheelchair, K0007
BCW Power, power wheelchair, K0014
BCW recliner, manual wheelchair, K0007
B-D alcohol swabs, box, A4245
B-D disposable insulin syringes, up to 1cc, per syringe, A4206
B-D lancets, per box of 100, A4258
Bebax, foot orthosis, L3160
Becker, hand prosthesis
   Imperial, L6840
   Lock Grip, L6845
   Plylite, L6850
Bed
   air fluidized, E0194
   accessory, E0315
   cradle, any type, E0280
   drainage bag, bottle, A4357, A5102
   hospital, E0250–E0270
     full electric, home care, without mattress, E0297
     heavy duty, K0456
     manual, without mattress, E0293
     semi-electric, without mattress, E0295
   pan, E0275, E0276
     Moore, E0275
   rail, E0305, E0310
Bell-Horn
   prosthetic shrinker, L8440–L8465
   sacrocinch, L0510, L0610

Belt
  adapter, A4421
  extremity, E0945
  Little Ones Sur-Fit pediatric, A4367
  ostomy, A4367
  pelvic, E0944
  safety, K0031
  support, L0940
  wheelchair, E0978, E0979
Bena-D (10, 50), J1200
Benadryl, J1200
Benahist (10, 50), J1200
Ben-Allergin-50, J1200
Bench, bathtub (*see also* Bathtub), E0245
Benefix, Q0161
Benesch boot, L3212–L3214
Benoject (-10, -50), J1200
Bentyl, J0500
Benzquinamide HCl, J0510
Benztropine, J0515
Berkeley shell, foot orthosis, L3000
Berubigen, J3420
Betadine, A4246
  swabs/wipes, A4247
Betalin 12, J3420
Betameth, J0704
Betamethasone
  acetate and betamethasone sodium
    phosphate, J0702
  sodium phosphate, J0704
Betaseron, J1830
Bethanechol chloride, J0520
Bicarbonate dialysate, A4705
Bicillin, Bicillin C-R, Bicillin C-R 900/300,
  and Bicillin L-A, J0530–J0580
BiCNU, J9050
Bicuspid (excluding final restoration),
  D3320
  retreatment, by report, D3347
  surgery, first root, D3421
Bifocal, glass or plastic, V2200–V2299
Bilirubin (phototherapy) light, E0202
Binder
  abdominal, A4462, L0920, L0930
  nonelastic, A4465
Biofeedback device, E0746
Bio Flote alternating air pressure pump, pad
  system, E0181, E0182
Bioimpedance, electrical, cardiac output,
  M0302
Biperiden lactate, J0190
Bite disposable jaw locks, E0700
Bitewing, D0270–D0274
Bitolterol mesylate, J7627
  inhalation solution
    concentrated, J7628
    unit dose, J7629
Bladder capacity test, ultrasound, G0050
Bleaching tooth, D3960
Blenoxane, J9040
Bleomycin sulfate, J9040
Blood
  Congo red, P2029
  glucose monitor, A4258, E0607, E0609
  glucose test strips, A4253
  leak detector, dialysis, E1560
  leukocyte poor, P9016
  mucoprotein, P2038

Blood — *continued*
  pressure equipment, A4660, A4663,
    A4670
  pump, dialysis, E1620
  strips, A4253
  supply, P9010–P9022
  testing supplies, A4770
  tubing, A4750, A4755
Bock, hand prosthesis, L6875, L6880
Bock Dynamic, foot prosthesis, L5972
Bock, Otto *see* Otto Bock
Body jacket
  lumbar-sacral orthosis (spinal),
    L0500–L0565, L0600, L0610
  scoliosis, L1300, L1310
Body sock, L0984
Body Wrap
  foam positioners, E0191
  therapeutic overlay, E0199
Bond or cement, ostomy, skin, A4364
Boot
  pelvic, E0944
  surgical, ambulatory, L3260
Boston type spinal orthosis, L1200
Botulinum toxin type A, J0585
Brake attachment, wheeled walker, E0159
Breast and pelvic exam, G0101
Breast prosthesis, L8000–L8035, L8600
  adhesive skin support, A4280
Breast pump, all types, E0602
Breathing circuit, A4618
Brethine, J3105
Bricanyl subcutaneous, J3105
Bridge
  recement, D6930
  repair, by report, D6980
Brompheniramine maleate, J0945
Broncho-Cath endobronchial tubes, with
  CPAP system, E0601
Bronkephrine, J0590
Bronkosol, J7655
  Unijet, J7654
Buck's, traction
  frame, E0870
  stand, E0880
Bupivicaine, S0020
Bus, nonemergency transportation, A0110
Butorphanot tartrate nasal spray, S0012

Caine (-1, -2), J2000
Calcijex, J0635
Calcimar, J0630
Calcitonin-salmon, J0630
Calcitriol, J0635
Calcium
  disodium edetate, J0600
  disodium versenate, J0600
  EDTA, J0600
  gluconate, J0610
  glycerophosphate and calcium lactate,
    J0620
  lactate and calcium glycerophosphate,
    J0620
  leucovorin, J0640
Calibrator solution, A4256
Calphosan, J0620

CAMP
  lumbosacral support, L0910, L0920,
    L0940, L0950
  thoracolumbar support, L0300
Camptosar, J9206
Cancer screening
  breast exam, G0101
  barium enema, G0122
  cervical exam, G0101
  colorectal, G0104–G0106, G0120–G0122
Cane, E0100, E0105
  accessory, A4636, A4637
  Easy-Care quad, E0105
  quad canes, E0105
  Quadri-Poise, E0105
  wooden canes, E0100
Canister
  disposable, used with suction pump,
    A7000
  non-disposable, used with suction pump,
    A7001
Cannula
  fistula, set (for dialysis), A4730
  nasal, A4615
  tracheostomy, A4623
Capecitabine, oral, J8520, J8521
Carbo Zinc, A4363
Carbocaine with Neo-Cobefrin, J0670
Carbon filter, A4680
Carboplatin, J9045
Cardia event, recorder implantable, E0616
Cardiokymography, Q0035
Cardiovascular services, M0300–M0302
Carelet safety lancet, A4258
Carex
  adjustable bath/shower stool, E0245
  aluminum crutches, E0114
  cane, E0100
  folding walker, E0135
  shower bench, E0245
Carmustine, J9050
Carnitor, J1955
Carries susceptibility test, D0425
Casec, enteral nutrition, B4155
Cash, spinal orthosis, L0370
Cast
  diagnostic, dental, D0470
  hand restoration, L6900–L6915
  materials, special, A4590
  padding, (not separately reimbursable
    from the casting procedure or
    casting supplies codes)
    Delta-Rol™ Cast Padding
    Sof-Rol™ Cast Padding
    Specialist™ 100 Cotton Cast Padding
    Specialist™ Cast Padding
  plaster, A4580, L2102, L2122
  supplies, A4580, A4590
    Delta-Cast™ Elite™ Casting Material,
      A4590
    Delta-Lite™ Conformable Casting
      Tape, A4590
    Delta-Lite™ C-Splint™ Fibreglass
      Immobilizer, A4590
    Delta-Lite™ "S" Fibreglass Casting
      Tape, A4590
    Flashcast™ Elite™ Casting Material,
      A4590

Cast — *continued*
  supplies — *continued*
    Orthoflex™ Elastic Plaster Bandages. A4580
    Orthoplast™ Splints (and Orthoplast™ II Splints), A4590
    Specialist™ J-Splint™ Plaster Roll Immobilizer
    Specialist™ Plaster Bandages, A4580
    Specialist™ Plaster Roll Immobilizer, A4580
    Specialist™ Plaster Splints, A4580
  synthetic, L2104, L2124
  thermoplastic, L2106, L2126
Caster, wheelchair, E0997, E0998, K0099
Catheter, A4300–A4365, K0410, K0411
  anchoring device, K0407, K0408
    percutaneous, A5200
  cap, disposable (dialysis), A4860
  external collection device, A4327–A4330, A4347, K0410, K0411
    implantable intraspinal, E0785
  indwelling, A4338–A4346
  indwelling, insertion of, G0002
  insertion tray, A4354
  intermittent, with insertion supplies, A4353
  irrigation supplies, A4355, K0409
  lubricant, K0281
  male, external, K0410, K0411
  oropharyngeal suction, A4628
  starter set, A4329
  trachea (suction), A4624
Catheterization, specimen collection, P9612, P9615
Cefadyl, J0710
Cefazolin sodium, J0690
Cefizox, J0715
Cefonicid sodium, J0695
Cefotaxime sodium, J0698
Cefotetan disodium, S0074
Cefoxitin, J0694
Ceftazidime, J0713
Ceftizoxime sodium, J0715
Ceftriaxone sodium, J0696
Ceftoperazone, S0021
Cefuroxime sodium, J0697
Celestone phosphate, J0704
CellCept, K0412
Cellular therapy, M0075
Cel-U-Jec, J0704
Cement, ostomy, A4364
Cenacort
  A-40, J3301
  Forte, J3302
Centrifuge, A4650
Cephalin floculation, blood, P2028
Cephalothin sodium, J1890
Cephapirin sodium, J0710
Cerebral blood flow studies, xenon, S9023
Ceredase, J0205
Cerezyme, J1785
Certified nurse assistant, S9122
Cerubidine, J9150
Cervical
  collar, L0120, L0130, L0140, L0150
  halo, L0810–L0830
  head harness/halter, E0942

Cervical — *continued*
  helmet, L0100, L0110
    Softop, leather protective, L0110
  orthosis, L0100–L0200
  pillow, E0943
  traction equipment, not requiring frame, E0855
Cervical cap contraceptive, A4261
Cervical-thoracic-lumbar-sacral orthosis (CTLSO), L0700, L0710, L1000
Chair
  adjustable, dialysis, E1570
  lift, E0627
  rollabout, E1031
  sitz bath, E0160–E0162
Challenger manual wheelchair, K0009
Champion 1000 manual wheelchair, K0004
Champion 30000, manual wheelchair, K0005
Chealamide, J3520
Chelation therapy, M0300
CheckMate Plus blood glucose monitor, E0607
Chemical endarterectomy, M0300
Chemistry and toxicology tests, P2028–P3001
Chemotherapy
  administration, Q0083–Q0085 (hospital reporting only)
  dental, D4381
  drug, oral, not otherwise classified, J7150, J8999, J9999
  drugs (see also drug by name), J9000–J9999
Chemstrip bG, box of 50 blood glucose test strips, A4253
Chemstrip K, box of 100 ketone urine test strips, A4250
Chemstrip UGK, box of 100 glucose/ketone urine test strips, A4250
Chest compression vest, S8200
  system generator and hoses, S8205
Chest shell (cuirass), E0457
Chest wrap, E0459
Chin
  cup, cervical, L0150
  strap (for CPAP device), K0186
Chlor-100, J0730
Chloramphenicol sodium succinate, J0720
Chlordiazepoxide HCl, J1990
Chloromycetin sodium succinate, J0720
Chloroprocaine HCl, J2400
Chloroquine HCl, J0390
Chlorothiazide sodium, J1205
Chlorpheniramine maleate, J0730
Chlor-Pro (10), J0730
Chlorpromazine HCl, J3230, Q0171–Q0172
Chlorprothixene, J3080
Chlortrimeton, J0730
Chopart prosthetic
  ankle, L5050, L5060
  below knee, L5100
Chorex (-5, -10), J0725
Chorignon, J0725
Chorionic gonadotropin, J0725
Choron 10, J0725

Chronimed Comfort insulin infusion set
  23", A4230
  43", A4230
Chux's, A4554
Cida
  exostatic cervical collar, L0140, L0150
  form fit collar, L0120
Cidofovir, J0740
Cilastatin sodium, imipenem, J0743
Cimetidine hydrochloride, S0023
Ciprofloxacin, S0024
Cisplatin, J9060, J9062
Cladribine, J9065
Claforan, J0698
Clamp
  dialysis, A4910, A4918, A4920
  external urethral, A4356
Clavicle
  splint, L3650, L3660
  support
    2-buckle closure, L3660
    4-buckle closure, L3660
Cleanser, wound, A6260
Cleaning solvent, Nu-Hope
  4 oz bottle, A4455
  16 oz bottle, A4455
Cleansing agent, dialysis equipment, A4790
Clindamycin phosphate, S0077
Clonidine, J0735
Clevis, hip orthosis, L2570, L2600, L2610
Clinical trials
  lodging costs, S9994
  meals, S9996
  phase II, S9990
  phase III, S9991
  transportation costs, S9992
Clotting time tube, A4771
Clubfoot wedge, L3380
Cobex, J3420
Cochlear prosthetic implant, L8614
  replacement, L8619
Codeine phosphate, J0745
Codimal-A, J0945
Cogentin, J0515
Colchicine, J0760
Colistimethate sodium, J0770
Collagen
  implant, urinary tract, L8603
  skin test, G0025
  wound dressing, A6020
Collar, cervical
  contour (low, standard), L0120
  multiple, post, L0180-L0200
  nonadjust (foam), L0120
  Philly™ One-piece™ Extrication collar, L0150
  tracheostomy, A4621
  tracheotomy, L0172
    Philadelphia™ tracheotomy cervical collar, L0172
  traction, E0942
    Turtle Neck safety collars, E0942
Colonoscopy, cancer screening
  patient at high risk, G0105
  patient not at high risk, G0121

Coloplast
  closed pouch, A5051
  drainable pouch, A5061
    closed, A5054
    small, A5063
  skin barrier
    4 x 4, A4362
    6 x 6, A5121
    8 x 8, A5122
  stoma cap, A5055
Coly-Mycin M, J0770
Coma stimulation, S9056
Combo-Seat universal raised toilet seat, E0244
Comfort items, A9190
Commode, E0160–E0179
  "3-in-1" Composite, E0164
  Economy VersaGuard Coated, E0164
  heavy duty, K0457
  lift, E0625
  pail, E0167
  seat, wheelchair, E0968
Compa-Z, J0780
Compazine, J0780
Compleat B, enteral nutrition, B4151
  Modified, B4151
Composite dressing, A6203–A6205
Compressed gas system, E0424–E0480, L3902
Compression bandage, A4460
Compression stockings, L8100–L8239
Compressogrip prosthetic shrinker, L8440–L8465
Compressor, E0565, E0570, E0650–E0652, E1375, K0269, K0501
Concentrator, oxygen, E1377–E1385
Conductive
  garment (for TENS), E0731
  paste or gel, A4558
Conductivity meter (for dialysis), E1550
Congo red, blood, P2029
Contact layer, A6206–A6208
Contact lens, V2500–V2599
Continent device, A5081, A5082
Continuous positive airway pressure (CPAP) device, E0601
  chin strap, K0186
  compressor, K0269
  filter, K0188–K0189
  headgear, K0185
  humidifier, K0268
  nasal application accessories, K0183, K0184
  tubing, K0187
Contraceptive
  cervical cap, A4261
  intrauterine, copper, J7300
  Levonorgestrel, implants and supplies, A4260
Contracts, maintenance, ESRD, A4890
Contrast material
  for echocardiography, S8060
  injection during MRI, A4643
  low osmolar, A4644–A4646
Controlyte, enteral nutrition, B4155
Cophene-B, J0945
Corgonject-5, J0725

Corneal tissue processing, V2785
Coronary artery bypass surgery, direct
  with coronary arterial grafts, only
    single, S2205
    two grafts, S2206
  with coronary arterial and venous grafts
    single, each, S2208
    two arterial and single venous, S2209
  with coronary venous grafts, only
    single, S2207
Corset, spinal orthosis, L0970–L0976
Corticotropin, J0800
Cortisone acetate, J0810
Cortone acetate, J0810
Cortrosyn, J0835
Corvert, J1742
Cosmegen, J9120
Cosyntropin, J0835
Cotranzine, J0780
Counseling for control of dental disease, D1310, D1320
Cover, wound
  alginate dressing, A6196–A6198
  collagen dressing, A6020
  foam dressing, A6209–A6214
  hydrocolloid dressing, A6234–A6239
  hydrogel dressing, A6242–A6248
  specialty absorptive dressing, A6251–A6256
CPAP (continuous positive airway pressure) device, E0601
  chin strap, K0186
  compressor, K0269
  filter, K0188–K0189
  headgear, K0185
  humidifier, K0268
  nasal application accessories, K0183, K0184
  tubing, K0187
Cradle, bed, E0280
Criticare HN, enteral nutrition, B4153
Cromolyn sodium, J7630
  inhalation solution, unit dose, J7631
Crowns, D2710–D2810, D2930–D2933, D4249, D6720–D6792
Crutches, E0110–E0116
  accessories, A4635–A4637, K0102
  aluminum, E0114
  forearm, E0111
    Ortho-Ease, E0111
  underarm, other than wood, pair, E0114
    Quikfit Custom Pack, E0114
    Red Dot, E0114
  underarm, wood, single, E0113
    Ready-for-use, E0113
  wooden, E0112
Cryoprecipitate, each unit, P9012
Cryosurgical ablation
  tumerous tissue, liver, S2210
Cryosurgical probes
  ultrasonic guidance, G0161
Crysticillin (300 A.S., 600 A.S.), J2510
CTLSO, L1000–L1120, L0700, L0710
Cuirass, E0457
Culture sensitivity study, P7001

Cushion, wheelchair, E0962–E0965, E0977
  Geo-Matt, E0964
    High Profile Therapeutic Dry Flotation, 4-inch, E0965
    Low Profile Therapeutic Dry Flotation, 2-inch, E0963
Custom Masterhinge™ Hip Hinge 3, L2999
Curasorb, alginate dressing, A6196–A6199
Cycler dialysis machine, E1594
Cyclophosphamide, J9070–J9092
  lyophilized, J9093–J9097
  oral, J8530
Cyclosporine, J7502, J7515, J7516
Cylinder tank carrier, K0104
Cytarabine, J9110
Cytarabine 100, J9100
CytoGam, J0850
Cytomegalovirus immune globulin (human), J0850
Cytopathology, screening, G0123, G0124, G0141, G0143–G0148
Cytosar-U, J9100
Cytovene, J1570
Cytoxan, J8530, J9070–J9097

Dacarbazine, J9130, J9140
Daclizumab, J7513
Dactinomycin, J9120
Dalalone, J1100
  L.A., J1095
Dalteparin sodium, J1645
Daunorubicin citrate, J9151
  HCl, J9150
DaunoXome, J9151
Day Treads slippers, E0690
DDAVP, J2597
Decadron, J1100
Decadron-LA, J1095
Decadron Phosphate, J1100
Deca-Durabolin, J2320–J2322
Decaject, J1100
Decaject-LA, J1095
Decolone
  -50, J2320
  -100, J2321
De-Comberol, J1060
Decompression, vertebral axial, S9090
Decubitus care equipment, E0180–E0199
  mattress
    AquaPedic Sectional Gel Flotation, E0196
    Iris Pressure Reduction/Relief, dry, E0184
    PressureGuard II, air, E0186
    TenderFlo II, E0187
    TenderGel II, E0196
  pressure pads, overlays, E0197–E0199
    Body Wrap, E0199
    Geo-Matt, E0199
    Iris, E0199
    PressureKair, E0197
    Richfoam Convoluted and Flat, E0199
  pressure pads, with pumps, E0180, E0181
    Bio Flote, E0181
    KoalaKair, E0181

Decubitus care equipment — *continued*
  protectors
    Heel or elbow, E0191
      Body Wrap Foam Positioners, E0191
      Pre-Vent, E0191
  pump, E0182
    Bio Flote, E0182
    Pillo, E0182
    TenderCloud, E0182
  wheelchair cushion, E0964
    Geo-Matt, E0964
    High Profile Therapeutic Dry Flotation, 4-inch, E0965
    Low Profile Therapeutic Dry Flotation, 2-inch, E0963
Deferoxamine mesylate, J0895
Dehist, J0945
Dehydroergotamine mesylate, J1110
Deionizer, water purification system, E1615
Deladumone (OB), J0900
Delatest, J3120
Delatestadiol, J0900
Delatestryl, J3120, J3130
Delestrogen, J0970
Delivery/set-up/dispensing, A9901
Delta-Cortef, J7510
Delta-Cast™ Elite™ Casting Material, A4590
Delta-Lite™ Conformable Casting Tape, A4590
Delta-Lite™ C-Splint™ Fibreglass Immobilizer, A4590
Delta-Lite™ "S" Fibreglass Casting Tape, A4590
Delta-Net™ Orthopaedic Stockinet, (not separately reimbursable from the casting procedure or casting supplies codes)
Delta-Rol™ Cast Padding, (not separately reimbursable from the casting procedure or casting supplies codes)
Deltasone, J7506
Demadex, J3265
Demerol HCl, J2175
Dennis Browne, foot orthosis, L3140, L3150
Dental procedures
  adjunctive general services, D9000–D9999
  alveoloplasty, D7310–D7320
  analgesia, D9230
  chemotherapy, D4381
  diagnostic, D0120–D0999
  endodontics, D3110–D3999
  implant services, D6010–D6199
  maxillofacial, D5911–D5999
  oral and maxillofacial surgery, D7110–D7999
  orthodontic, D8010–D8999
  periodontic, D4210–D4999
  preventive, D1110–D1550
  prosthodontic, fixed, D6210–D6999
  prosthodontic, removable, D5110–D5899
  restorative, D2110–D2999
Dentures, D5110–D5899
DepAndro
  100, J1070
  200, J1080
Dep-Androgyn, J1060

DepMedalone
  40, J1030
  80, J1040
Depo-estradiol cypionate, J1000
Depogen, J1000
Depoject, J1030, J1040
Depo
  -Medrol, J1020, J1030, J1040
  -Provera, J1050, J1055
  -Testadiol, J1060
  -Testosterone, J1070, J1080, J1090
Depopred
  -40, J1030
  -80, J1040
Depotest, J1070, J1080
Depotestogen, J1060
Derata injection device, A4210
Dermal tissue, Q0183–Q0185
Desferal mesylate, J0895
Desmopressin acetate, J2597
Detector, blood leak, dialysis, E1560
Devitalized tissue, removed without anesthesia G0169
Dexacen-4, J1100
Dexamethasone
  acetate, J1095
  inhalation solution
    concentrated, J7637
    unit dose, J7638
  sodium phosphate, J1100
Dexasone, J1100
Dexasone L.A., J1095
Dexferrum (iron dextran), J1750
Dexone, J1100
Dexrazoxane HCl, J1190
Dextran, J7100, J7110
Dextrose
  saline (normal), J7042
  water, J7060, J7070
Dextrostick, A4772
D.H.E. 45, J1110
Diabetes supplies
  alcohol swabs, per box, A4245
  battery for blood glucose monitor, A4254
  bent needle set for insulin pump infusion, A4231
  blood glucose monitor, E0607
  blood glucose test strips, box of 50, A4253
  injection device, needle-free, A4210
  insulin, J1820
  insulin pump, external, E0784
  lancet device, A4258
  lancets, box of 100, A4259
  non needle cannula for insulin infusion, A4232
  syringe, disposable, per syringe, A4206
  urine glucose/ketone test strips, box of 100, A4250
Diagnostic
  dental services, D0100–D0999
  radiology services, R0070–R0076
Dialet lancet device, A4258
Dialysate
  concentrate additives, A4765
  solution, A4700, A4705
  testing solution, A4760

Dialysis
  air bubble detector, E1530
  bath conductivity, meter, E1550
  blood leak detector, E1560
  CAPD supply kit, A4900
  CCPD supply kit, A4901
  equipment, E1510–E1702
  filter, A4680
  fluid barrier, E1575
  forceps, A4910
  graft, for thrombectomy and/or fistula, G0159
  heparin infusion pump, E1520
  home equipment repair, A4890
  kit, A4820, A4900, A4901, A4905, A4914
  measuring cylinder, A4921
  peritoneal, A4300, A4900, A4901, A4905, E1592, E1594, E1630, E1640
  pressure alarm, E1540
  replacement parts for equipment, E1640
  shunt, A4740
  supplies, A4650–A4927
  thermometer, A4910
  tourniquet, A4910
  unipuncture control system, E1580
Dialyzer, artificial kidney, A4690
  holder, A4919
Diamox, J1120
Diabetic management program
  dietitian visit, S946
  follow-up visit to MD provider, S9141
  follow-up visit to non-MD provider, S9140
  group session, S9455
  nurse visit, S9460
Diaper, A4335
Diascan blood glucose monitor, E0609
Diazepam, J3360
Diazoxide, J1730
Dibent, J0500
Didronel, J1436
Diethylstilbestrol diphosphate, J9165
Diflucan injection, J1750
Digital subtraction angiography, S9022
Digi-Voice blood glucose monitor, E0609
Digoxin, J1160
Dihydrex, J1200
Dihydroergotamine mesylate, J1110
Dilantin, J1165
Dilaudid, J1170
Dilocaine, J2000
Dilomine, J0500
Dilor, J1180
Dimenhydrinate, J1240
Dimercaprol, J0470
Dimethyl sulfoxide (DMSO), J1212
Dinate, J1240
Dioval (XX, 40), J0970, J1380, J1390
Diphenacen-50, J1200
Diphenhydramine HCl, J1200, Q0163
Dipyridamole, J1245
Disarticulation
  lower extremities, prosthesis, L5000–L5999
  upper extremities, prosthesis, L6000–L6692

Disetronic
　　glass cartridge syringe for insulin pump, each, A4232
　　insulin infusion set with bent needle, with or without wings, each, A4231
Disetronic H-Tron insulin pump, E0784
Diskard head halter, E0940
Diskectomy, lumbar, S2350, S2351
　　single interspace, S2350
Disotate, J3520
Di-Spaz, J0500
Disposable
　　diapers, A4335
　　supplies, ambulance, A0382–A0398
　　underpads, A4554
Distilled water (for nebulizer), K0182
Ditate-DS, J0900
Diuril sodium, J1205
D-med 80, J1040
DMSO, J1212
Dobutamine HCl, J1250
Dobutrex, J1250
Docetaxel, J9170
Dolasetron mesylate, J1260, Q0180
Dolophine HCl, J1230
Dome, J9130
　　and mouthpiece (for nebulizer), A7016
Dommanate, J1240
Don-Joy
　　cervical support collar, L0150
　　deluxe knee immobilizer, L1830
　　rib belt, L0210
　　wrist forearm splint, L3984
Dornase alpha, inhalation solution, unit dose, J7639
Donor cadaver
　　enterectomy, S2050
　　harvesting multivisceral organs, with allografts, S2055
Dorrance prosthesis
　　hand, L6825
　　hook, L6700–L6780
Dorsiwedge™ Night Splint, L4398 or A4570 or L2999
Double bar
　　"AK," knee-ankle-foot orthosis, L2020, L2030
　　"BK," ankle-foot orthosis, L1990
Doxil, J9001
Doxorubicin HCl, J9000
Drainage
　　bag, A4347, A4357, A4358
　　board, postural, E0606
　　bottle, A5102
　　pouch with adhesive foam pads, A5064
Dramamine, J1240
Dramanate, J1240
Dramilin, J1240
Dramocen, J1240
Dramoject, J1240
Dressing (see also Bandage), A6020–A6406
　　alginate, A6196–A6199
　　collagen, A6020
　　composite, A6200–A6205
　　contact layer, A6206–A6208
　　film, A6257–A6259
　　foam, A6209–A6215
　　gauze, A6216–A6230, A6402–A6406

Dressing — continued
　　holder/binder, A4462
　　hydrocolloid, A6234–A6241
　　hydrogel, A6242–A6249
　　specialty absorptive, A6251–A6256
　　tape, A4454, A6265
　　transparent film, A6257–A6259
Dronabinol, Q0167–Q0168
Droperidol, J1790
　　and fentanyl citrate, J1810
Dropper, A4649
Drugs (see also Table of Drugs)
　　administered through a metered dose inhaler, J3535
　　chemotherapy, J8999–J9999
　　disposable delivery system, 5 ml or less per hour, A4306
　　disposable delivery system, 50 ml or greater per hour, A4305
　　immunosuppressive, J7500–J7599
　　infusion supplies, A4221, A4222, A4230–A4232
　　inhalation solutions, J7610–J7699
　　injections (see also drug name), J0120–J8999
　　not otherwise classified, J3490, J7599, J7699, J7799, J8499, J8999, J9999
　　prescription, oral, J8499, J8999
Dry pressure pad/mattress, E0179, E0184, E0199
DTIC-Dome, J9130
Dunlap
　　heating pad, E0210
　　hot water bottle, E0220
Duo-Gen L.A., J0900
Duolock curved tail closures, A4421
Durable medical equipment (DME), E0100–E1830, K codes
Duracillin A.S., J2510
Duraclon, J0735
Duragen (-10, -20, -40), J0970, J1380, J1390
Durahesive wafer with flange, A5123
Duralone-40, J1030
　　-80, J1040
Duralutin, J1741
Duramorph, J2275
Duratest
　　-100, J1070
　　-200, J1080
Duratestrin, J1060
Durathate-200, J3130
Durr-Fillauer
　　cervical collar, L0140
　　Pavlik harness, L1620
Dymenate, J1240
Dyphylline, J1180

Easy Care
　　folding walker, E0143
　　quad cane, E0105
Economy VersaGuard coated commode, E0164
Economy knee splint, L1830
Edetate
　　calcium disodium, J0600
　　Edetate disodium, J3520
Eggcrate dry pressure pad/mattress, E0179, E0184, E0199

Elastic
　　bandage, A4460
　　gauze, A6263, A6405
　　support, L8100–L8230
Elastoplast adhesive tape, A4454, A6265
Elavil, J1320
Elbow
　　brace, universal rehabilitation, L3720
　　disarticulation, endoskeletal, L6450
　　Masterhinge™ Elbow Brace 3, L3999
　　Neoprene Tennis Elbow Support with Floam™, A4460
　　orthosis (EO), E1800, L3700-L3740
　　protector, E0191
　　support
　　　　elastic or neoprene slip-on, A4460
Electrical work, dialysis equipment, A4870
Electrocardiogram strips
　　monitoring, G0004–G0007
　　physician interpretation, G0016
　　tracing, G0015
　　transmission, G0015, G0016
Electrodes, per pair, A4556
Electron beam computed tomography, S8092
Elevating leg rest, K0195
Elevator, air pressure, heel, E0370
Elspar, J9020
Emergency transporation (see also Ambulance), A0050, A0225, A0302, A0308, A0310, A0322, A0328, A0330, A0342, A0348, A0350, A0362, A0368, A0370
Emete-Con, J0510
EMG, E0746
Eminase, J0350
Enbrel, J1438
Endarterectomy, chemical, M0300
Endodontic procedures, D3110–D3999
　　periapical services, D3410–D3470
　　pulp capping, D3110, D3120
　　root canal therapy, D3310–D3353
Endoscope sheath, A4270
Endoskeletal system, addition, L5925
Enema, barium, G0106
　　cancer screening, G0120
Enovil, J1320
Enoxaparin sodium, J1650
Enrich, enteral nutrition, B4150
Ensure, enteral nutrition, B4150
　　HN, B4150
　　Plus, B4152
　　Plus HN, B4152
　　Powder, B4150
Enteral
　　feeding supply kit (syringe) (pump) (gravity), B4034–B4036
　　formulae, B4150–B4156
　　gastronomy tube, B4084, B4085
　　nutrition infusion pump (with alarm) (without), B9000, B9002
　　supplies, not otherwise classified, B9998
Epinephrine, J0170, J7640
Epoetin alpha, for non-ESRD use, Q0136
Epoprostenol, J1325
　　infusion pump, K0455
Ergonovine maleate, J1330

Erythromycin
    gluceptate, J1362
    lactobionate, J1364
ESRD (End Stage Renal Disease; see also
        Dialysis)
    machines and accessories, E1510–E1699
    plumbing, A4870
    services, E1510–E1699
    supplies, A4650–A4927
Estra-D, J1000
Estradiol, J1000, J1060
    cypionate and testosterone cypionate,
        J1060
    L.A., J0970, J1380, J1390
    L.A. 20, J0970, J1380, J1390
    L.A. 40, J0970, J1380, J1390
    valerate and testosterone enanthate, J0900
Estra-L (20, 40), J0970, J1380, J1390
Estra-Testrin, J0900
Estro-Cyp, J1000
Estrogen conjugated, J1410
Estroject L.A., J1000
Estrone (5, Aqueous), J1435
Estronol, J1435
    -L.A., J1000
Ethylnorepinephrine HCl, J0590
Ethyol, J0207
Etidronate disodium, J1436
Etopophos, J9181, J9182
    oral, J8560
Etoposide, J9181, J9182
    oral, J8560
Everone, J3120, J3130
Exactech lancet device, A4258
Examination
    breast and pelvic, G0101
    oral, D0120–D0160
Exercise equipment, A9300
Exo-Static overdoor traction unit, E0860
External
    ambulatory infusion pump, E0781, E0784
    counterpulsation, G0166
    power, battery components, L7360–L7499
    power, elbow, L7191
    urinary supplies, A4356–A4359
Extractions (see also Dental procedures),
        D7110–D7130, D7250
Extraoral films, D0250, D0260
Extremity belt/harness, E0945
Eye
    lens (contact) (spectacle), V2100–V2615
    prosthetic, V2623–V2629
    safety, E0690
        Vision Tek, E0690
    service (miscellaneous), V2700–V2799
EZ Fit LSO, L0500
E-ZJect Lite Angle Lancets, box of 100,
        A4259
E-ZJect disposable insulin syringes, up to
        1cc, per syringe, A4206
E-Z-lets lancet device, A4258
E-Z Lite Wheelchair, E1250

Faceplate, ostomy, A4361
Face tent, oxygen, A4619
Factor VIII, anti-hemophilic factor,
        J7190–J7192
Factor IX, J7194, Q0160, Q0161

Factrel, J1620
Famotidine, S0028
Fashion-Tread slipper, E0690
Fecal
    leukocyte examination, G0026
    occult blood test, G0107
Fentanyl citrate, J3010
    and droperidol, J1810
Fern test, Q0114
Feronim, J1760-1780
Fibrinogen unit, P9013
Filgrastim (G-CSF), J1440, J1441
Filler, wound
    alginate, A6199
    foam, A6215
    hydrocolloid, A6240–A6241
    hydrogel, A6248
    not elsewhere classified, A6261, A6262
Film
    dressing, A6257–A6259
    radiographic, dental, D0210–D0340
Filter
    carbon, A4680
    CPAP device, K0188, K0189
    dialysis carbon, A4680
    ostomy, A4368
    tracheostoma, A4481
Finger
    baseball splint, A4570
    fold-over splint, A4570
    four-pronged splint, A4570
Fistula cannulation set, A4730
Flashcast™ Elite™ Casting Material, A4590
Flexoject, J2360
Flexon, J2360
Flolan, J1325
Flowmeter, E0440, E0555, E0580
Flow rate meter, peak A4614
Floxuridine, J9200
Fluconazole, injection, J1450, S0029
Fludara, J9185
Fludarabine phosphate, J9185
Fluid barrier, dialysis, E1575
Fluoride treatment, D1201–D1205
Fluorouracil, J9190
Fluphenazine decanoate, J2680
Foam
    dressing, A6209–A6215
    pad adhesive, A5126
Folding walker, E0135, E0143
Fold-over finger splint, A4570
Folex, J9260
    PFS, J9260
Foley catheter, A4312–A4316,
        A4338–A4346
Follutein, J0725
Foot, cast boot
    Specialist™ Closed-Back Cast Boot,
        L3260
    Specialist™ Gaitkeeper™ Boot, L3260
    Specialist™ Open-Back Cast Boot, L3260
    Specialist™ Toe Insert for Specialist™
        Closed-Back Cast Boot and
        Specialist™ Health/Post Operative
        Shoe, A9270
Foot, insoles/heel cups
    Specialist™ Heel Cups, L3485
    Specialist™ Insoles, L3510

Foot, soles
    Masterfoot™ Walking Cast Sole, L3649
    Solo™ Cast Sole, L3540
Footdrop splint, L4398
Footplate, E0175, E0970
Footwear, orthopedic, L3201–L3265
Forceps, dialysis, A4910
Forearm crutches, E0110, E0111
Fortaz, J0713
Fortex, alginate dressing, A6196–A6199
Foscarnet sodium, J1455
Foscavir, J1455
Fosphenytoin sodium, S0078
Four Poster, fracture frame, E0946
Four-pronged finger splint, A4570
Fracture
    bedpan, E0276
    frame, E0920, E0930, E0946-E0948
    orthosis, L2102-L2136, L3980-L3986
    orthotic additions, L2180-L2192, L3995
    Specialist™ Pre-Formed Humeral
        Fracture Brace, L3980
Fragmin, J1645
Frames (spectacles), V2020, V2025
    sales tax, S9999
FreAmine HBC, parenteral nutrition, B5100
Frejka, hip orthosis, L1600
    replacement cover, L1610
FUDR, J9200
Fungizone, J0285
Furomide MD, J1940
Furosemide, J1940

Gadolinium, A4647
Gait analysis, S9033
Gamastan, J1460–J1561
Gamma globulin, J1460–J1561
Gammar, J1460–J1560
Gamulin RH, J2790
Ganciclovir
    implant, J7310
    sodium, J1570
Garamycin, J1580
Gas system
    compressed, E0424, E0425
    gaseous, E0430, E0431, E0441, E0443
    liquid, E0434–E0440, E0442, E0444
Gastrostomy/jejunostomy tubing, B4084
Gastrostomy tube, B4084, B4085
Gauze (see also Bandage), A6216–A6230,
        A6263, A6264, A6266
    elastic, A6263, A6405
    impregnated, A6222–A6230, A6266
    pads, A6216–A6230, A6402–A6404
        Johnson & Johnson, A6402
        Kendall, A6402
        Moore, A6402
    nonelastic, A6264, A6406
    nonimpregnated, A6216, A6221, A6402,
        A6406
Gel
    conductive, A4558
    pressure pad, E0178, E0185, E0196
Gemcitabine HCl, J9201
GemZar, J9201
Generator
    implantable neurostimulator, E0751
    ultrasonic with nebulizer, K0270

Genmould™ Creamy Plaster, A4580
Gentamicin (sulfate), J1580
Gentran, J7100, J7110
Geo-Matt
    therapeutic overlay, E0199
    wheelchair cushion, E0964
Geronimo PR, power wheelchair, K0011
Gerval Protein, enteral nutrition, B4155
Gesterol
    50, J2675
    L.A. 250, J1741
Gingival procedures, D4210–D4240
Glasses
    air conduction, V5070
    binaural, V5120–V5150
    bone conduction, V5080
    frames, V2020, V2025
    hearing aid, V5150, V5190, V5230
    lens, V2100–V2499, V2610, V2718, V2730, V2755, V2770, V2780
Gloves, dialysis, A4927
Glucagon HCl, J1610
Glucometer
    II blood glucose meter, E0607
    II blood glucose test strips, box of 50, A4253
    3 blood glucose meter, E0607
    3 blood glucose test strips, box of 50, A4253
Glucose
    test strips, A4253, A4772
Glukor, J0725
Gluteal pad, L2650
Glycopyrrolate, inhalation solution
    concentrated, J7642
    unit dose, J7643
Gold
    foil dental restoration, D2410–D2430
    sodium thiomalate, J1600
Goldthwaite apron-front, sacroiliac orthosis, L0620
Gomco
    aspirators, E0600
    drain bottle, A4912
Gonadorelin HCl, J1620
Gonic, J0725
Goserelin acetate implant (*see also* Implant), J9202
Grab bar, trapeze, E0910, E0940
Grade-aid, wheelchair, E0974
Granisetron HCl, J1626, Q0166
Gravity traction device, E0941
Gravlee jet washer, A4470
Greissing, foot prosthesis, L5978
Guilford multiple-post collar, cervical orthosis, L0190
Gynogen, J1380, J1390
    L.A. (10, 20, 40), J0970, J1380, J1390

H-Tron Plus insulin pump, E0784
H. Weniger finger orthosis
    cock-up splint, L3914
    combination Oppenheimer
        with
            knuckle bender no. 13, L3950
            reverse knuckle no. 13B, L3952
    composite elastic no. 10, L3946

H. Weniger finger orthosis — *continued*
    dorsal wrist no. 8, L3938
        with outrigger attachment no. 8A, L3940
    finger extension, with clock spring no. 5, L3928
    finger extension, with wrist support no. 5A, L3930
    finger knuckle bender no. 11, L3948
    knuckle bender splint type no. 2, L3918
    knuckle bender, two segment no. 2B, L3922
    knuckle bender with outrigger no. 2, L3920
    Oppenheimer, L3924
    Palmer no. 7, L3936
    reverse knuckle bender no. 9, L3942
        with outrigger no. 9A, L3944
    safety pin, modified no. 6A, L3934
    safety pin, spring wire no. 6, L3932
    spreading hand no. 14, L3954
    Thomas suspension no. 4, L3926
Hair analysis (excluding arsenic), P2031
Haldol, J1630
    decanoate (-50, -100), J1631
Hallus-valgus dynamic splint, L3100
Hallux prosthetic implant, L8642
Haloperidol, J1630
    decanoate, J1631
Halo procedures, L0810–L0860
Halter, cervical head, E0942
Hand restoration, L6900–L6915
    partial prosthesis, L6000–L6020
    orthosis (WHFO), E1805, E1825, L3800–L3805, L3900–L3954
    rims, wheelchair, E0967
Handgrip (cane, crutch, walker), A4636
Harness, E0942, E0944, E0945
Harvard pressure clamp, dialysis, A4920
Harvesting multivisceral organs, cadaver donor, S2055
Harvey arm abduction orthosis, L3960
Headgear (for CPAP device), K0185
Hearing devices, L8614, V5008–V5299
Heat
    application, E0200–E0239
    lamp, E0200, E0205
    pad, E0210, E0215, E0217, E0218, E0238, E0249
    units, E0239
        Hydrocollator, mobile, E0239
        Thermalator T-12-M, E0239
Heater (nebulizer), E1372
Heating pad, Dunlap, E0210
Heel
    elevator, air, E0370
    pad, L3480, L3485
    protector, E0191
    shoe, L3430–L3485
    stabilizer, L3170
Helicopter, ambulance (*see also* Ambulance), A0040
Helmet, cervical, L0100, L0110
Hemalet lancet device, A4258
Hematran, J1760-1780
Hemi-wheelchair, E1083–E1086
Hemipelvectomy prosthesis, L5280, L5340

Hemodialysis
    kit, A4820
    machine, E1590
Hemodialyzer, portable, E1635
Hemofil M, J7190
Hemophilia clotting factor, J7190–J7198
Hemophilia clotting factor, NOC, J7199
Hemostats, A4850
Hemostix, A4773
Heparin
    for dialysis, A4800
    infusion pump (for dialysis), E1520
    lock flush, J1642
    sodium, J1644
HepatAmine, parenteral nutrition, B5100
Hepatic-aid, enteral nutrition, B4154
Hep-Lock (U/P), J1642
Herceptin, J9355
Hexadrol phosphate, J1100
Hexalite, A4590
Hexior power wheelchair, K0014
High Profile therapeutic dry flotation cushion, E0965
Hip
    Custom Masterhinge™ Hip Hinge 3, L2999
    disarticulation prosthesis, L5250, L5270, L5330
    Masterhinge™ Hip Hinge 3, L2999
    orthosis (HO), L1600-L1686
Hip-knee-ankle-foot orthosis (HKAFO), L2040–L2090
Histaject, J0945
Histerone (-50, -100), J3140
HIV-1 antibody testing, S3645
HKAFO, L2040–L2090
HN2, J9230
Hole cutter tool, A4421
Hollister
    belt adapter, A4421
    closed pouch, A5051, A5052
    colostomy/ileostomy kit, A4421, A5061
    drainable pouches, A5061
        with flange, A5063
    medical adhesive, A4364
    pediatric ostomy belt, A4367
    remover, adhesive, A4455
    replacement filters, A4421
    stoma cap, A5055
    skin barrier, A4362, A5122, A5123
    skin cleanser, A4335
    skin conditioning creme, A4335
    skin gel protective dressing wipes, A5119
    stoma cap, A5055
    two-piece pediatric ostomy system, A5054, A5063, A5073, A5123
    urostomy pouch, A5071, A5072
Home health
    aide, S9122
        home health setting, G0156
    services of
        clinical social worker, G0155
        occupational therapist, G0152
        physical therapist, G0151
        skilled nurse, G0154
        speech/language pathologist, G0153

Home health care
    administration of medication, IM
        epidurally or subcutaneously, S9543
    certified nurse assistant, S9122
    home health aide, S9122
    nursing care, S9123, S9124
Home uterine monitor, S9001
Hosmer
    baby mitt, L6870
    child hand, mechanical, L6872
    forearm lift, assist unit only, L6635
    gloves, above hands, L6890, L6895
    hand prosthesis, L6868
    hip orthotic joint, post-op, L1685
    hook
        with
            neoprene fingers, #8X, L6740
            neoprene fingers, #88X, L6745
            plastisol, #10P, L6750
        #5, L6705
        #5X, L6710
        #5XA, L6715
        child, L6755, L6765
        small adult, L6770
        stainless steel #8, L6735
            with neopren, L6780
        work, #3, L6700
            for use with tools, #7, L6725
            with lock, #6, L6720
            with wider opening, L6730
    passive hand, L6868
    soft, passive hand, L6865
Hospice care, S9126
Hot water bottle, E0220
H-Tron insulin pump, E0784
Houdini security suit, E0700
Hoyer patient lifts, E0621, E0625, E0630
Hudson
    adult multi-vent "venturi" style mask, A4620
    nasal cannula, A4615
    oxygen supply tubing, A4616
    UC-BL type shoe insert, L3000
Humalog, J1820
Human insulin, J1820
Humidifier, E0550–E0560, K0268
Humulin insulin, J1820
Hyaluronate, J7315
Hyaluronidase, J3470
Hyate, J7191
Hybolin
    decanoate, J2321
    improved, J0340
Hycamtin, J9350
Hydeltra-TBA, J1690
Hydeltrasol, J2640
Hydextran, J1760-J1780
Hydralazine HCl, J0360
Hydrate, J1240
Hydraulic patient lift, E0630
Hydrochlorides of opium alkaloids, J2480
Hydrocollator, E0225, E0239
Hydrocolloid dressing, A6234–A6241
Hydrocortisone
    acetate, J1700
    sodium phosphate, J1710
    sodium succinate, J1720

Hydrocortone
    acetate, J1700
    phosphate, J1710
Hydrogel dressing, A6242–A6248
Hydromorphone, J1170
Hydroxyprogesterone caproate, J1739, J1741
Hydroxyzine HCl, J3410
    pamoate, Q0177–Q0178
Hylan G-F 20, J7320
Hylutin, J1741
Hyoscyamine sulfate, J1980
Hyperbaric oxygen chamber, topical, A4575
Hyperstat IV, J1730
Hypertonic saline solution, J7130
Hypo-Let lancet device, A4258
HypRho-D, J2790
Hyprogest 250, J1741
Hyrexin-50, J1200
Hyzine-50, J3410

Ibutilide fumarate, J1742
    injection, S0096
Ice cap or collar, E0230
Idamycin, J9211
Idarubicin HCl, J9211
Ifex, J9208
Ifosfamide, J9208
IL-2, J9015
Iletin insulin, J1820
Ilfeld, hip orthosis, L1650
Ilotycin Gluceptate, J1362
Imfergen, J1760-J1780
Imiglucerase, J1785
Imipramine HCl, J3270
Imitrex, J3030
Immune globulin IV, J1561, J1562
Immunosuppressive drug, not otherwise classified, J7599
Implant
    access system, A4301
    aqueous shunt, L8612
    breast, L8600
    cochlear, L8614, L8619
    collagen, urinary tract, L8603
    contraceptive, A4260
    dental, D3460, D5925, D6030–D6999, D7270–D7272, D7850
    ganciclovir, J7310
    goserelin acetate, J9202
    hallux, L8642
    infusion pump, E0782, E0783
    joint, L8630, L8641, L8658
    lacrimal duct, A4262, A4263
    maintenance procedures, D6080, D6100
    maxillofacial, D5913–D5937
    medication pellet(s), subcutaneous, S2190
    metacarpophalangeal joint, L8630
    metatarsal joint, L8641
    neurostimulator, electrodes/leads, E0753
    neurostimulator, pulse generator or receiver, E0751
    not otherwise specified, L8699
    ocular, L8610
    ossicular, L8613
    osteogenesis stimulator, E0749
    percutaneous access system, A4301
    removal, dental, D6100
    repair, dental, D6090

Implant — *continued*
    vascular access portal, A4300
    vascular graft, L8670
    Zoladex, J9202
Impregnated gauze dressing, A6222–A6230
Imuran, J7500, J7501
Inapsine, J1790
Incontinence
    appliances and supplies, A4310–A4421, A5071–A5075, A5102–A5114, K0280, K0281
    treatment system, E0740
Inderal, J1800
Indium/111 capromab pendetide, A9507
Indwelling catheter insertion, G0002
Infergen, J9212
Infliximab injection, J1745
Infusion pump
    ambulatory, with administrative equipment, E0781
    epoprostenol, K0455
    external, K0284
    heparin, dialysis, E1520
    implantable, E0782, E0783
    implantable, refill kit, A4220
    insulin, E0784
    mechanical, reusable, E0779, E0780
    supplies, A4221, A4222, A4230–A4232
    Versa-Pole IV, E0776
    therapy, other than chemotherapeutic drugs, Q0081
Inhalation solution (*see also* drug name), J7610–J7799
Injections (*see also* drug name), J0120–J7506
    contrast material, during MRI, A4643
    dental service, D9610, D9630
    supplies for self-administered, A4211
Inlay/onlay dental restoration, D2510–D2664
Innovar, J1810
Insert, convex, for ostomy, A5093
Insertion
    indwelling catheter, G0002
    midline central venous catheter, S9528
    peripherally inserted central venous catheter (PICC), S9527
    tray, A4310–A4316
Insulin, J1820
Insulin pump, external, E0784
Intal, J7630
Intergrilin injection, J1327
Interferon
    Alfa, J9212–J9215
    Alfacon-1, J9212
    Beta-1a, J1825
    Beta-1b, J1830
    Gamma, J9216
Intermittent
    peritoneal dialysis system, E1592
    positive pressure breathing (IPPB) machine, E0500
Interphalangeal joint, prosthetic implant, L8658
Interscapular thoracic prosthesis
    endoskeletal, L6570
    upper limb, L6350–L6370

Intraocular lenses, V2630–V2632, Q1001–Q1005
  new technology
    category 1, Q1001
    category 2, Q1002
    category 3, Q1003
    category 4, Q1004
    category 5, Q1005
Intraoral radiographs, D0210–D0240
Intrauterine copper contraceptive, J7300
Intron A, J9214
Iodine swabs/wipes, A4247
IPD
  supply kit, A4905
  system, E1592
IPPB machine, E0500
Ipratropium bromide
  0.2%, J7645
  inhalation solution, unit dose, J7644
Irinotecan, J9206
Iris Preventix pressure relief/reduction mattress, E0184
Iris therapeutic overlays, E0199
IRM ankle-foot orthosis, L1950
Irodex, J1750
Iron dextran, J1750
Irrigation/evacuation system, bowel
  control unit, E0350
  disposable supplies for, E0352
Irrigation supplies, A4320, A4322, A4323, A4355, A4397–A4400
  Surfit
    irrigation adapter face plate, A4361
    irrigation sleeve, A4397
    night drainage container set, A5102
  Visi-flow irrigator, A4398, A4399
Isocaine HCl, J0670
Isocal, enteral nutrition, B4150
  HCN, B4152
Isoetharine
  HCl, J7650–J7655
  inhalation solution
    concentrated, J7648
    unit dose, J7649
Isolated limb perfusion, S8048
Isolates, B4150, B4152
Isoproterenol
  HCl, J7660, J7665
  inhalation solution
    concentrated, J7658
    unit dose, J7659
Isotein, enteral nutrition, B4153
Isuprel, J7660, J7665
Itraconazole, S0096
IUD, J7300
IV pole, E0776, K0105

J-cell battery, replacement for blood glucose monitor, A4254
Jace tribrace, L1832
Jacket
  body (LSO) (spinal), L0500–L0565
  scoliosis, L1300, L1310
Jenamicin, J1580
Jewett, spinal orthosis, L0370
Johnson's orthopedic wrist hand cock-up splint, L3914

Johnson's thumb immobilizer, L3800
Joystick, power add-on, K0460

Kabikinase, J2995
Kaleinate, J0610
Kaltostat, alginate dressing, A6196–A6199
Kanamycin sulfate, J1840, J1850
Kantrex, J1840, J1850
Kartop Patient Lift, toilet or bathroom (see also Lift), E0625
Keflin, J1890
Kefurox, J0697
Kefzol, J0690
Kenaject -40, J3301
Kenalog (-10,-40), J3301
Keratectomy photorefractive, S0810
Kestrone-5, J1435
Keto-Diastix, box of 100 glucose/ketone urine test strips, A4250
Ketorolac thomethamine, J1885
Key-Pred
  -SP, J2640
  -25,-50, J2650
K-Feron, J1760-J1780
K-Flex, J2360
Kidney
  ESRD supply, A4650–A4927
  system, E1510
  wearable artificial, E1632
Kingsley gloves, above hands, L6890
Kits
  continuous ambulatory peritoneal dialysis (CAPD), A4900
  continuous cycling peritoneal dialysis (CCPD), A4901
  dialysis, A4820, A4910, A4914
  enteral feeding supply (syringe) (pump) (gravity), B4034–B4036
  fistula cannulation (set), A4730
  intermittent peritoneal dialysis (IPD) supply, A4905
  parenteral nutrition, B4220–B4224
  surgical dressing (tray), A4550
  tracheostomy, A4625
Klebcil, J1840, J1850
Knee
  Adjustabrace™ 3, L2999
  disarticulation, prosthesis, L5150-L5160
  immobilizer, L1830
  joint, miniature, L5826
  Knee-O-Prene™ Hinged Knee Sleeve, L1810
  Knee-O-Prene™ Hinged Wraparound Knee Support, L1810
  orthosis (KO), E1810, L1800-L1885
  locks, L2405-L2425
  Masterbrace™ 3, L2999
  Masterhinge Adjustabrace™ 3, L2999
  Performance Wrap™ (KO), L1825
Knee-ankle-foot orthosis (KAFO), L2000–L2039, L2122–L2136
Knee-O-Prene™ Hinged Knee Sleeve, L1810
Knee-O-Prene™ Hinged Wraparound Knee Support, L1810
Knight apron-front, spinal orthosis, L0330, L0520
Knight-Taylor apron-front, spinal orthosis, L0330

KnitRite
  prosthetic
    sheath, L8400–L8415
    sock, L8420–L8435
    stump sock, L8470–L8485
KoalaKair mattress overlay, with pump, E0180
Kodel clavicle splint, L3660
Kogenate, J7192
Konakion, J3430
Konyne-HT, J7194
Kutapressin, J1910
K-Y Lubricating Jelly, A4402, K0281
Kyphosis pad, L1020, L1025
Kytril, J1626

Laboratory tests
  chemistry, P2028–P2038
  microbiology, P7001
  miscellaneous, P9010–P9615, Q0111–Q0115
  toxicology, P3000–P3001, Q0091
Lacrimal duct implant
  permanent, A4263
  temporary, A4262
Lactated Ringer's infusion, J7120
LAE 20, J0970, J1380, J1390
Laetrile, J3570
Lederle, J8610
Lancet, A4258, A4259
Lanoxin, J1160
Largon, J1930
Larynx, artificial, L8500
Laser
  in situ keratomileusis, S0800
Lasix, J1940
L-Caine, J2000
Lead wires per pair, A4557
Leg
  bag, A4358, S5105, A5112
  extensions for walker, E0158
  Nextep™ Contour™ Lower Leg Walker, L2999
  Nextep™ Low Silhouette™ Lower Leg Walkers, L2999
  rest, elevating, K0195
  rest, wheelchair, E0990
  strap, A5113, A5114, K0038, K0039
Legg Perthes orthosis, L1700–L1755
Lennox, spinal orthosis, L0370
Lens
  aniseikonic, V2118, V2318
  contact, V2500–V2599
  eye, V2100–V2615, V2700–V2799
  intraocular, V2630–V2632
  low vision, V2600–V2615
  progressive, V2781
Lente insulin, J1820
Lerman Minerva spinal orthosis, L0174
Leucovorin calcium, J0640
Leukocyte
  examination, fecal, G0026
  poor blood, each unit, P9016
Leuprolide acetate, J9217, J9218, J1950
Leustatin, J9065
Levaquin I.U., J1956
Levine, stomach tube, B4083
Levocarnitine, J1955

Levo-Dromoran, J1960
Levofloxacin, J1956
Levonorgestrel, contraceptive implants and supplies, A4260
Levoprome, J1970
Levorphanol tartrate, J1960
Levsin, J1980
Librium, J1990
Lidocaine HCl, J2000
Lidoject (-1, -2), J2000
Lifescan lancets, box of 100, A4259
Lifestand manual wheelchair, K0009
Lift
    patient, and seat, E0621–E0635
        Hoyer
            Home Care, E0621
            Partner All-Purpose, hydraulic, E0630
            Partner Power Multifunction, E0625
    shoe, L3300–L3334
Lift-Aid patient lifts, E0621
Lilly insulin, J1820
Lincocin, J2010
Lincomycin HCl, J2010
Lioresal, J0475
Liquaemin sodium, J1644
Lithium battery for blood glucose monitor, A4254
Little Ones
    drainable pouch, A5063
    mini-pouch, A5054
    one-piece custom drainable pouch, A5061
    one-piece custom urostomy pouch, A5071
    pediatric belt, A4367
    pediatric urine collector, A4335
    Sur-Fit flexible wafer, A5123
    urostomy pouch, transparent, A5073
Lively, knee-ankle-foot orthosis, L2038
LMD, 10%, J7100
Lodging, recipient, escort nonemergency transport, A0180, A0200
Lonalac powder, enteral nutrition, B4150
Lorazepam, J2060
Lovenox, J1650
Low Profile therapeutic dry flotation cushion, E0964
Lower limb, prosthesis, addition, L5968
LSO, L0500–L0565
Lubricant, A4402, K0281
Lufyllin, J1180
Lumbar
    criss-cross (LSO), L0500
    EZ Fit LSO, L0500
    flexion, L0540
    pad, L1030, L1040
    -sacral orthosis (LSO), L0500-L0565
Luminal sodium, J2560
Lupron, J9218
    depot, J1950
Lymphedema therapy, S8950
Lymphocyte immune globulin, J7504

Macausland apron-front, spinal orthosis, L0530
Madamist II medication compressor/nebulizer, E0570
Magnacal, enteral nutrition, B4152

Magnesium sulphate, J3475
Magnetic source imaging, S8035
Magnuson apron-front, spinal orthosis, L0340
Maintenance contract, ESRD, A4890
Malibu cervical turtleneck safety collar, L0150
Mannitol, J2150
Mapping, topographic brain, S8040
Marmine, J1240
Mask
    cushion, K0184
    oxygen, A4620, A4621
Mastectomy
    bra, L8000
    form, L8020
    prosthesis, L8015, L8030, L8035, L8600
    sleeve, L8010
Masterbrace™ 3, L2999
Masterfoot™ Walking Cast Sole, L3649
Masterhinge Adjustabrace™ 3, L2999
Masterhinge™ Elbow Brace 3, L3999
Masterhinge™ Hip Hinge 3, L2999
Masterhinge™ Shoulder Brace 3, L3999
Maternity support, L0920, L0930
Mattress
    air pressure, E0176, E0186, E0197
    alternating pressure, E0277
        pad, Bio Flote, E0181
        pad, KoalaKair, E0181
    AquaPedic Sectional, E0196
    decubitus care, E0196
    dry pressure, E0184
    flotation, E0184
    gel pressure, E0196
    hospital bed, E0271, E0272
        non-powered, pressure reducing, E0373
    Iris Preventix pressure relief/reduction, E0184
    Overlay, E0371-E0372
    TenderFlor II, E0187
    TenderGel II, E0196
    water pressure, E0177, E0187, E0198
    powered, pressure reducing, E0277
Maxillofacial dental procedures, D5911–D5999
MCP, multi-axial rotation unit, L5986
MCT Oil, enteral nutrition, B4155
Measuring cylinder, dialysis, A4921
Mechlorethamine HCl, J9230
Medical and surgical supplies, A4206–A6404
Medi-Jector injection device, A4210
MediSense 2 Pen blood glucose monitor, E0607
Medralone 40, J1030
    80, J1040
Medrol, J7509
Medroxyprogesterone acetate, J1050, J1055
Mefoxin, J0694
Melphalan HCl, J9245
    oral, J8600
Mepergan (injection), J2180
Meperidine, J2175
    and promethazine, J2180
Mephentermine sulfate, J3450
Mepivacaine HCl, J0670

Meritene, enteral nutrition, B4150
    Powder, B4150
Mesna, J9209
Mesnex, J9209
Metabolically active tissue, Q0184
Metabolically active D/E tissue, Q0185
Metacarpophalangeal joint prosthesis, L8630
Metaprel, J7675
Metaproterenol
    inhalation solution
        concentrated, J7668
        unit dose, J7669
    sulfate, J7670–J7675
Metaraminol bitartrate, J0380
Metatarsal joint, prosthetic implant, L8641
Meter, bath conductivity, dialysis, E1550
Methadone HCl, J1230
Methergine, J2210
Methicillin sodium, J2970
Methocarbamol, J2800
Methotrexate, oral, J8610
    sodium, J9250, J9260
Methotrimeprazine, J1970
Methoxamine, J3390
Methyldopate HCl, J0210
Methylergonovine maleate, J2210
Methylprednisolone
    acetate, J1020–J1040
    oral, J7509
    sodium succinate, J2920, J2930
Metoclopramide HCl, J2765
Metocurine iodide, J2240
Metronidazole, S0030
Metubine iodide, J2240
Meunster Suspension, socket prosthesis, L6110
Miacalcin, J0630
Microbiology test, P7001
Midazolam HCl, J2250
Micro-Fine
    disposable insulin syringes, up to 1cc, per syringe, A4206
    lancets, box of 100, A4259
Microlipids, enteral nutrition, B4155
Midline central venous catheter insert, S9528
Mileage, ambulance, A0380, A0390
Milrinone lactate, J2260
Milwaukee spinal orthosis, L1000
Minerva, spinal orthosis, L0700, L0710
Mini-bus, nonemergency transportation, A0120
Minimed
    3 cc syringe, A4232
    506 insulin pump, E0784
    insulin infusion set with bent needle wings, each, A4231
    Sof-Set 24" insulin infusion set, each, A4230
Mirage headgear, K0185
Miscellaneous, A9150–A9600
Mitomycin, J9280–J9291
Mitoxantrone HCl, J9293
Mobilite hospital beds, E0293, E0295, E0297
Moducal, enteral nutrition, B4155
Moisture exchanger for use with invasive mechanical ventilation, A4483
Moisturizer, skin, A6250

Monarc-M, J7190
Monitor
  apnea, E0608
  blood glucose, E0607, E0609
    Accu-Check, E0607
    One Touch II, E0609
    Re Flotron Plus Analyzer, E0609
    Tracer II, E0607
  blood pressure, A4670
  pacemaker, E0610, E0615
  ventilator, E0450
Monitoring and recording, EKG, G0004–G0007
Monoclonal antibodies, J7505
Monoject disposable insulin syringes, up to 1cc, per syringe, A4206
Monojector lancet device, A4258
Mononine, Q0160
Morphine sulfate, J2270, J2271
  sterile, preservative-free, J2275
Mouthpiece (for respiratory equipment), A4617
M-Prednisol-40, J1030
  -80, J1040
MRI contrast material, A4643
Mucomyst, J7610, J7615
Mucoprotein, blood, P2038
Mucosol, J7610, J7615
Multiple post collar, cervical, L0180–L0200
Muse, J0275
Mutamycin, J9280
Mycophenolate mofetil, J7517
Myochrysine, J1600
Myolin, J2360

Nafcillin sodium, S0032
Nail trim, G0127
Nalbuphine HCl, J2300
Naloxone HCl, J2310
Nandrobolic, J0340
  L.A., J2321
Nandrolone
  decanoate, J2320–J2322
  phenpropionate, J0340
Narrowing device, wheelchair, E0969
Narcan, J2310
Nasahist B, J0945
Nasal
  application device (for CPAP device), K0183
  pillows/seals (for nasal application device), K0184
  vaccine inhalation, J3530
Nasogastric tubing, B4081, B4082
National Emphysema Treatment Trial (NETT) codes, G0110–G0116
Navane, J2330
Navelbine, J9390
ND Stat, J0945
Nebcin, J3260
Nebulizer, E0570–E0585
  aerosol compressor, K0501
  aerosol mask, A7015
  aerosols, E0580
    Airlife Brand Misty-Neb, E0580
    Power-Mist, E0580
    Up-Draft Neb-U-Mist, E0580
    Up-Mist hand-held nebulizer, E0580

Nebulizer — *continued*
  compressor, with, E0570
    Madamist II medication compressor/nebulizer, E0570
    Pulmo-Aide compressor/nebulizer, E0570
    Schuco Mist nebulizer system, E0570
  corrugated tubing
    disposable, A7010
    non-disposable, A7011
  distilled water, K0182
  drug dispensing fee, E0590
  filter
    disposable, A7013
    non-disposable, A7014
  heater, E1372
  large volume
    disposable, prefilled, A7008
    disposable, unfilled, A7007
  not used with oxygen
    durable glass, A7107
  pneumatic, administration set, A7003, A7005, A7006
  pneumatic, nonfiltered, A7004
  portable, E1375
  small volume, K0270
  ultrasonic, dome and mouthpiece, A7016
  ultrasonic, reservoir bottle
    non-disposable, A7009
  water collection device
    large volume nebulizer, A7012
NebuPent, J2545
Needle, A4215
  dialysis, A4655
  non-coring, A4212
  with syringe, A4206–A4209
Nembutal sodium solution, J2515
Neocyten, J2360
Neo-Durabolic, J2320–J2322
Neomax knee support, L1800
Neonatal transport, ambulance, base rate, A0225
Neoprene Tennis Elbow Support with Floam™, A4460
Neoquess, J0500
Neosar, J9070–J9092
Neostigmine methylsulfate, J2710
Neo-Synephrine, J2370
NephrAmine, parenteral nutrition, B5000
Nervocaine (1%, 2%), J2000
Nesacaine MPF, J2400
NETT pulmonary rehab, G0110–G0116
Neumega, J2355
Neuromuscular stimulator, E0745
Neuro-Pulse, E0720
Neurostimulator
  electrodes, E0753
  leads, E0753
  pulse generator, E0751
  receiver, E0751
Neutrexin, J3305
Newington
  Legg Perthes orthosis L1710
  mobility frame, L1500
Newport Lite hip orthosis, L1685
Nextep™ Contour™ Lower Leg Walker, L2999

Nextep™ Low Silhouette™ Lower Leg Walkers, L2999
Niacin, J2350
Niacinamide, J2350
Nicotinamide, J2350
Nicotinic acid, J2350
Nipent, J9268
Nitrogen mustard, J9230
Nonchemotherapy drug, oral, J8499
Noncovered services, A9160, A9170, A9270
Nonelastic gauze, A6264, A6406
Nonemergency transportation, A0080–A0210
Nonimpregnated gauze dressing, A6216, A6221, A6402, A6404
Nonmetabolic active tissue, Q0183
Nonprescription drug, A9150
Nordryl, J1200
Norflex, J2360
Norplant System contraceptive, A4260
Northwestern Suspension, socket prosthesis, L6110
Norzine, J3280
Not otherwise classified drug, J3490, J7599, J7699, J7799, J8499, J8999, J9999, Q0181
Novantrone, J9293
Novo Nordisk insulin, J1820
Novo Seven, Q0187
NPH insulin, J1820
Nubain, J2300
NuHope
  adhesive, 3 oz bottle with applicator, A4364
  adhesive, 1 oz bottle with applicator, A4364
  carbo zinc, 6 oz jar, A4363
  cleaning solvent, 4 oz bottle, A4455
  cleaning solvent, 16 oz bottle, A4455
  extra long adhering tape strips (100/pkg), A4454
  extra long pink adhering tape strips (100/pkg), A4454
  extra wide adhering tape strips (100/pkg), A4454
  extra wide pink adhering tape strips (100/pkg), A4454
  hole cutter tool, A4421
  regular adhering tape strips (100/pkg), A4454
  regular pink adhering tape strips (100/pkg), A4454
  round post-op drainables, A5064
  round post-op urinary pouches, A5074
  support belt, L0940
  thinning solvent, A4454
Nulicaine, J2000
Numorphan H.P., J2410
Nursing care, in home
  licensed practical nurse, S9124
  registered nurse, S9123
Nutri-Source, enteral nutrition, B4155
Nutrition
  counseling, dental, D1310, D1320
  enteral infusion pump, B9000, B9002
  enteral formulae, B4150–B4156
  guidance, NETT pulmonary rehab
    initial, G0112

Nutrition — *continued*
  guidance — *continued*
    subsequent, G0113
    parenteral infusion pump, B9004, B9006
    parenteral solution, B4164–B5200
Nutritional counseling, dietition visit, S9470
NYU, hand prosthesis, child, L6872

Obturator prosthesis
  definitive, D5932
  interim, D5936
  surgical, D5931
Occipital/mandibular support, cervical, L0160
Occupational therapy, G0129, S9129
Occupational therapist
  home health setting, G0152
Ocular prosthetic implant, L8610
Oculinum, J0585
Office service, M0064
Offobock cosmetic gloves, L6895
O-Flex, J2360
Ofloxacin, S0034
Ohio Willow
  prosthetic sheath
    above knee, L8410
    below knee, L8400
    upper limb, L8415
  prosthetic sock, L8420–L8435
  stump sock, L8470–L8485
Omnipen-N, J0290
Oncaspar, J9266
Oncoscint, A4642
Oncovin, J9370
Ondansetron HCl, J2405, Q0179
One arm drive attachment, K0101
One-Button foldaway walker, E0143
One Touch
  Basic blood glucose meter, E0607
  Basic test strips, box of 50, A4253
  Profile blood glucose meter, E0607
O & P Express
  above knee, L5300, L5210
  ankle-foot orthosis with bilateral uprights, L1990
  anterior floor reaction orthosis, L1945
  below knee, L5105
  elbow disarticulation, L6200
  hip disarticulation, L5250
    endoskeletal, L5330
  hip-knee-ankle-foot orthosis, L2080
  interscapular thoracic, L6370
  Legg Perthes orthosis, Scottish Rite, L1730
  Legg Perthes orthosis, Patten, L1755
  knee-ankle-foot orthosis, L2000, L2010, L2020, L2036
  knee disarticulation, L5150, L5160
  partial foot, L5000, L5020
  plastic foot drop brace, L1960
  supply/accessory/service, L9900
Opium alkaloids, hydrochlorides of, J2480
Oppenheimer, wrist-hand-finger orthosis, L3924
Oprelvekin, J2355
Oral and maxillofacial surgery, D7110–D7999
Oral examination, D0120–D0160

Oral orthotic treatment for sleep apnea, S8260
Oraminic II, J0945
Ormazine, J3230
Oropharyngeal suction catheter, A4628
Orphenadrine, J2360
Orphenate, J2360
Orthodontics, D8010–D8999
Ortho-Ease forearm crutches, E0111
Orthoflex™ Elastic Plaster Bandages, A4580
Orthoguard hip orthosis, L1685
Orthomedics
  ankle-foot orthosis, L1900
  pediatric hip abduction splint, L1640
  plastic foot drop brace, L1960
  single axis shoe insert, L2180
  ultralight airplane arm abduction splint, L3960
  upper extremity fracture orthosis
    combination, L3986
    humeral, L3980
    radius/ulnar, L3982
Orthomerica
  below knee test socket, L5620
  pediatric hip abduction splint, L1640
  plastic foot drop brace, L1960
  single axis shoe insert, L2180
  upper extremity fracture orthosis
    humeral, L3980
    radius/ulnar, L3982
  wrist extension cock-up, L3914
Orthopedic devices, E0910-E0948
  cervical
    Turtle Neck safety collars, E0942
    Diskard head halters, E0942
Orthopedic shoes
  arch support, L3040–L3100
  footwear, L3201–L3265
  insert, L3000–L3030
  lift, L3300–L3334
  miscellaneous additions, L3500–L3595
  positioning device, L3140–L3170
  transfer, L3600–L3649
  wedge, L3340–L3420
Orthoplast™ Splints (and Orthoplast™ II Splints), A4590
Orthotic additions
  carbon graphite lamination, L2755
  fracture, L2180–L2192, L3995
  halo, L0860
  lower extremity, L2200–L2999
  rachet lock, L2430
  scoliosis, L1010–L1120, L1210–L1290
  shoe, L3300–L3595, L3649
  spinal, L0970–L0999
  upper extremity joint, L3956
  upper limb, L3810–L3890, L3970–L3974, L3995
Orthotic devices
  ankle-foot (see also Orthopedic shoes), E1815, E1830, L1900–L1990, L2102–L2116, L3160
  anterior-posterior, L0320, L0330, L0530
  anterior-posterior-lateral, L0520, L0550–L0565, L0700, L0710
  anterior-posterior-lateral-rotary, L0340–L0440
  cervical, L0100–L0200

Orthotic devices — *continued*
  cervical-thoracic-lumbar-sacral, L0700, L0710
  elbow, E1800, L3700–L3740
  fracture, L2102–L2136, L3980–L3986
  halo, L0810–L0830
  hand, E1805, E1825, L3800–L3805, L3900–L3954
  hip, L1600–L1686
  hip-knee-ankle-foot, L2040–L2090
  interface material, E1820
  knee, E1810, L1800–L1885
  knee-ankle-foot, L2000–L2038, L2122–L2136
  Legg Perthes, L1700–L1755
  lumbar flexion, L0540
  lumbar-sacral, L0500–L0565
  lumbar-sacral, hip, femur, L1690
  multiple post collar, L0180–L0200
  not otherwise specified, L0999, L1499, L2999, L3999, L5999, L7499, L8039, L8239
  pneumatic splint, L4350–L4380
  repair or replacement, L4000–L4210
  replace soft interface material, L4392–L4394
  sacroilliac, L0600–L0620
  scoliosis, L1000, L1200, L1300–L1499
  shoe, see Orthopedic shoes
  shoulder, L3650–L3675
  shoulder-elbow-wrist-hand, L3960–L3969
  spinal, cervical, L0100–L0200
  spinal, DME, K0112–K0116
  thoracic, L0210
  thoracic-hip-knee-ankle, L1500–L1520
  thoracic-lumbar-sacral, L0300–L0440
  toe, E1830
  torso supports, L0900–L0690
  transfer (shoe orthosis), L3600–L3640
  wrist-hand-finger, E1805, E1825, L3800–L3805, L3900–L3954
Or-Tyl, J0500
Osgood apron-front, sacroiliac orthosis, L0620
Osmolite, enteral nutrition, B4150
  HN, B4150
Ossicula prosthetic implant, L8613
Osteogenic stimulator, E0747–E0749, E0760
Osteotomy, segmented/subapical, D7944
Ostomy
  accessories, A5093
  adhesive remover wipes, A4365
  appliance belt, A4367
  filter, A4368
  irrigation supply, A4398, A4399
  supplies, A4361–A4421, A5051–A5149
    pediatric one-piece system, A5061, A5062
    pediatric two-piece drainable pouch, A5063
    pediatric two-piece system with cut-to-fit synthetic skin barrier, A5123
Otto Bock prosthesis
  battery, six volt, L7360
  battery charger, six volt, L7362
  electronic greifer, L7020, L7035
  electronic hand, L7010, L7025
  hook adapter, L6628

Otto Bock prosthesis — *continued*
  lamination collar, L6629
  pincher tool, L6810
  wrist, L6629, L7260
Overlay, mattress, E0371–E0373
Owens & Minor
  cervical helmet, L0120
  cervical collar, L0140
Oxacillin sodium, J2700
Oxi-Uni-Pak, E0430
Oxygen
  ambulance, A0422
  chamber, hyperbaric, topical, A4575
  concentrator, E1390
  concentrator, high humidity system, E1377–E1385
  contents, E1400–E1404
  hyperbaric treatment, G0167
  mask, A4620, A4621
  medication supplies, A4611–A4627
  rack/stand, E1355
  regulator, E1353
  respiratory equipment/supplies, A4611–A4627, E0424–E0480
    Argyle Sentinel seal chest drainage unit, E0460
    Oxi-Uni-Pak, E0430
  supplies and equipment, E0425–E0444, E0455, E1353–E1406
  tent, E0455
  tubing, A4616
  water vapor enriching system, E1405, E1406
Oxymorphone HCl, J2410
Oxytetracycline HCl, J2460
Oxytocin, J2590

Pacemaker monitor, E0610, E0615
Pacer manual wheelchair, K0003
Paclitaxel, J9265
Pad
  abdominal, L1270
  adhesive, A6203–A6205, A6212–A6214, A6219–A6221, A6237–A6239, A6245–A6247, A6254–A6256
  air pressure, E0178, E0179
  alginate, A6192–A6199
  alternating pressure, E0180, E0181
  arm, K0019
  asis, L1250
  calf, K0049
  condylar, L2810
  crutch, A4635
  gel pressure, E0178, E0185, E0196
  gluteal L2650
  heating, E0210, E0215, E0217, E0238, E0249
  heel, L3480, L3485
  knee, L1858
  kyphosis, L1020, L1025
  lumbar, L1030, L1040, L1240
  nonadhesive (dressing), A6209–A6211, A6216–A6218, A6222–A6224, A6228–A6230, A6234–A6236, A6242–A6244
  orthotic device interface, E1820
  rib gusset, L1280
  sheepskin, E0188, E0189
  shoe, L3430–L3485

Pad — *continued*
  stabilizer, L3170
  sternal, L1050
  thoracic, L1060, L1260
  torso support, L0960
  triceps, L6100
  trocanteric, L1290
  truss, L8320, L8330
  water circulating, cold, with pump, E0218
  water circulating, heat, with pump, E0217
  water circulating, heat, unit, E0249
  wheelchair, low pressure and positioning, E0192
  water pressure, E0177, E0198
Padden Shoulder Immobilizer, L3670
Pail, for use with commode chair, E0167
Palmer, wrist-hand-finger orthosis, L3936
Pamidronate disodium, J2430
Pan, for use with commode chair, E0167
Panglobulin, J1562
Pantopon, J2480
Papanicolaou (Pap) screening smear, P3000, P3001, Q0091
Papaverine HCl, J2440
Paraffin, A4265
  bath unit, E0235
Paragard T 380 A, IUD, J7300
Paramagnetic contrast material, (Gadolinium), A4647
Paranasal sinus ultrasound, S9024
Paraplatin, J9045
Parapodium, mobility frame, L1500
Parenteral nutrition
  administration kit, B4224
  pump, B9004, B9006
  solution, B4164–B5200
  supplies, not otherwise classified, B9999
  supply kit, B4220, B4222
Parking fee, nonemergency transport, A0170
Paste, conductive, A4558
Pathology and laboratory tests, miscellaneous, P9010–P9615
Patten Bottom, Legg Perthes orthosis, L1755
Pavlik harness, hip orthosis, L1650
Peak expiratory flow meter, S8110
Peak flow meter, portable, S8096
PEFR, peak expiratory flow rate meter, A4614
Pegaspargase, J9266
Peg-L-asparaginase, J9266
Pediatric hip abduction splint
  Orthomedics, L1640
  Orthomerica, L1640
Pelvic and breast exam, G0101
Pelvic belt/harness/boot, E0944
Penicillin G
  benzathine and penicillin G procaine, J0530–J0580
  potassium, J2540
  procaine, aqueous, J2510
Penlet lancet device, A4258
Penlet II lancet device, A4258
Pentagastrin, J2512
Pentamidine isethionate, J2545, S0080
Pentazocine HCl, J3070
Pentobarbital sodium, J2515
Pentostatin, J9268
Peptavlon, J2512
Percussor, E0480

Percutaneous access system, A4301
Performance Wrap™ (KO), L1825
Periapical service, D3410–D3470
Periodontal procedures, D4210–D4999
Peripherally inserted central venous catheter (PICC) insertion, S9527
Perlstein, ankle-foot orthosis, L1920
Permapen, J0560–J0580
Peroneal strap, L0980
Peroxide, A4244
Perphenazine, J3310, Q0175–Q0176
Persantine, J1245
Personal comfort item, A9190
Pessary, A4560
PET
  lung, imaging, G0125, G0126
  myocardial perfusion imaging, G0030–G0047
  whole body
    colorectal metastatic cancer, G0163
    lymphoma, G0164
    melanoma, G0165
    melanoma metastatic cancer, G0165
Pfizerpen, J2540
  A.S., J2510
PGE_1, J0270
Pharmaplast disposable insulin syringes, per syringe, A4206
Phelps, ankle-foot orthosis, L1920
Phenazine (25, 50), J2550
Phenergan, J2550
Phenobarbital sodium, J2560
Phentolamine mesylate, J2760
Phenylephrine HCl, J2370
Phenytoin sodium, J1165
Philadelphia™ tracheotomy cervical collar, L0172
Philly™ One-piece™ Extrication collar, L0150
PHisoHex solution, A4246
Photofrin, J9600
Phototherapy light, E0202
Physical therapy/therapist
  evaluation/treatment, Q0086
  home health setting, G0151
Phytonadione, J3430
Physician services
  peak expiratory flow rate, S8110
Pillo pump, E0182
Pillow
  abduction, E1399
  cervical, E0943
Pin retention, per tooth, D2951
Pinworm examination, Q0113
Piperacillin sodium, S0081
Pitocin, J2590
Plasma
  multiple donor, pooled, frozen, P9023
  protein fraction, P9018
  single donor, fresh frozen, P9017
Plastazote, L3002, L3252, L3253, L3265, L5654–L5658
Plaster
  bandages
    Orthoflex™ Elastic Plaster Bandages, A4580
    Specialist™ Plaster Bandages, A4580
    Genmould™ Creamy Plaster, A4580

Plaster — *continued*
  Specialist™ J-Splint™ Plaster Roll Immobilizer, A4580
  Specialist™ Plaster Roll Immobilizer, A4580
  Specialist™ Plaster Splints, A4580
Platelet
  concentrate, each unit, P9019
  rich plasma, each unit, P9020
Platform, for home blood glucose monitor, A4255
Platform attachment
  forearm crutch, E0153
  walker, E0154
Platinol, J9060, J9062
Plicamycin, J9270
Plumbing, for home ESRD equipment, A4870
Pneumatic
  appliance, E0655–E0673, L4350–L4380
  compressor, E0650–E0652
  splint, L4350–L4380
  tire, wheelchair, E0953
Pneumatic nebulizer
  administration set
    small volume
      filtered, A7006
      non-filtered, A7003
        non-disposable, A7005
    small volume, disposable, A7004
Podiatric service, noncovered, A9160
Polocaine, J0670
Polycillin-N, J0290
Polycose, enteral nutrition,
  liquid, B4155
  powder, B4155
Polygam SD, J1562
Pontics, D5281, D6210–D6252
Porfimer, J9600
Pork insulin, J1820
Portable
  equipment transfer, R0070–R0076
  hemodialyzer system, E1635
  nebulizer, E1375
  x-ray equipment, Q0092
Portagen Powder, enteral nutrition, B4150
Posey restraints, E0700
Post-coital examination, Q0115
Post-voiding residual, ultrasound, G0050
Postural drainage board, E0606
Potassium
  chloride, J3480
  hydroxide (KOH) preparation, Q0112
Pouch
  Active Life convex one-piece urostomy, A4421
  closed, A5052
  drainable, A5061
  fecal collection, A4330
  Little Ones Surfit mini, A5054
  ostomy, A4375–A4378, A5051–A5054, A5061–A5065
  pediatric, drainable, A5061
  post-op urinary, A5074
  Pouchkins pediatric ostomy system, A5061, A5062, A5073
  Sur-Fit, drainable, A5063

Pouch — *continued*
  urinary, A4379–A4383, A5071–A5075
  urosotomy, A5073
Power mist nebulizer, E0580
Pralidoxime chloride, J2730
Precision, enteral nutrition
  HN, B4153
  Isotonic, B4153
  LR, B4156
Predoject-50, J2650
Predalone-50, J2650
  TBA, J1690
Predcor (-25, -50), J2650
Predicort-50, J2650
Prednisolone
  acetate, J2650
  oral, J7506, J7510
  sodium phosphate, J2640
  tebutate, J1690
Prednisol TBA, J1690
Prednisone, J7506
Predoject-50, J2650
Prefabricated crown, D2930–D2933
Pregnyl, J0725
Premarin IV, J1410
Premium knee sleeve, L1830
Preparation kit, dialysis, A4914
Preparatory prosthesis, L5510–L5595
Prescription drug, J3490, J7140, J8499
  chemotherapy, J7150, J8999, J9999
  nonchemotherapy, J8499
Pressure
  alarm, dialysis, E1540
  pad, A4640, E0176–E0199
PressureGuard II, E0186
PressureKair mattress overlay, E0197
Prestige blood glucose monitor, E0607
Pre-Vent heel and elbow protector, E0191
Preventive dental procedures, D1000–D1999
Primacor, J2260
Primaxin, J0743
Priscoline HCl, J2670
Procainamide HCl, J2690
Prochlorperazine, J0780, Q0164–Q0165
Procuren, S9055
Pro-Depo, J1739, J1741
Profasi HP, J0725
Proferdex. J1760-J1780
Profilnine Heat-Treated, J7194
Progestaject, J2675
Progesterone, J2675
Prograf, J7507, J7508
Prolastin, J0256
Proleukin, J9015
Prolixin decanoate, J2680
Prolotherapy, M0076
Promazine HCl, J2950
Promethazine HCl, J2550, Q0169–Q0170
Promethazine and meperdine, J2180
Promix, enteral nutrition, B4155
Pronestyl, J2690
Propac, enteral nutrition, B4155
Propiomazine, J1930
Proplex (-T and SX-T), J7194
Propranolol HCl, J1800
Prorex (-25, -50), J2550
Prostaglandin E_1, J0270
Prostaphlin, J2700

Prosthesis
  adhesive, used for facial
    liquid, K0450
    remover, K0451
  auricular, D5914, K0445
  breast, L8000–L8035, L8600
  dental, fixed, D6210–D6999
  dental, removable, D5110–D5899
  eye, L8610, V2623–V2629
  fitting, L5400–L5460, L6380–L6388
  hand, L6000–L6020
  hemifacial, K0444
  implants, L8600–L8699
  larynx, L8500
  lower extremity, L5700–L5999, L8642
  maxiofacial, provided by a nonphysician, K0440-K0448
  midfacial, K0441
  miscellaneous service, L8499
  nasal, K0440
  nasal septal, K0447
  obturator, D5931–D5933, D5936
  ocular, V2623–V2629
  partial facial, K0446
  repair, K0449, L7520
  socks (shrinker, sheath, stump sock), L8400–L8480
  tracheostomy speaking, L8501
  unspecified maxillofacial, K0448
  upper extremity, L6000–L6915
  upper facial, K0443
  vacuum erection system, L7900
Prosthetic additions
  lower extremity, L5610–L5999
  upper extremity, L6600–L7274
Prosthetic shrinker, L8440-L8465
Prosthodontic procedures
  fixed, D6210–D6999
  removable, D5110–D5899
Prostigmin, J2710
Prostin VR Pediatric, J0270
Protamine sulfate, J2720
Protectant, skin, A6250
Protector, heel or elbow, E0191
Protirelin, J2725
Protopam chloride, J2730
Proventil, J7620, J7625
Prozine-50, J2950
Pulmo-Aide compressor/nebulizer, E0570
Pulp capping, D3110, D3120
Pulpotomy, D3220
  vitality test, D0460
Pump
  alternating pressure pad, E0182
  ambulatory infusion, E0781
  ambulatory insulin, E0874
  Bio Flote alternating pressure pad, E0182
  blood, dialysis, E1620
  Broncho-Cath endobronchial tubes, with CPAP, E0601
  enteral infusion, B9000, B9002
  Gomco lightweight mobile aspirator, E0600
  Gomco portable aspirator, E0600
  heparin infusion, E1520
  implantable infusion, E0782, E0783
  implantable infusion, refill kit, A4220
  infusion, supplies, A4230–A4232

Pump — *continued*
　insulin, external, E0784
　parenteral infusion, B9004, B9006
　Pillo alternating pressure pad, E0182
　suction, CPAP, E0601
　suction, portable, E0600
　TenderCloud alternating pressure pad, E0182
　water circulating pad, E0217, E0218, E0236
Purification system, A4880, E1610, E1615
Purified pork insulin, J1820

Quad cane, E0105
Quadri-Poise canes, E0105
Quelicin, J0330
Quick Check blood glucose test strips, box of 50, A4253
Quick release restraints, E0700
Quikfit crutch, E0114
Quik-Fold Walkers, E0141, E0143

Rack/stand, oxygen, E1355
Radiation therapy, intraoperative, S8049
Radiograph, dental, D0210–D0340
Radiology service, R0070–R0076
Radiopharmaceutical
　diagnostic imaging agent, A4641, A4642, A9500–A9505
　Technetium Tc 99m Apcitide, A9504
　therapeutic, A9600
Rail
　bathtub, E0241, E0242, E0246
　bed, E0305, E0310
　toilet, E0243
Rancho hip action, hip orthosis, L1680
Rascal, power wheelchair, K0010
Re Flotron Plus analyzer, E0609
Ready-For-Use wooden crutches, E0113
Recement
　crown, D2920
　inlay, D2910
Reciprocating peritoneal dialysis system, E1630
Recombinate, J7192
Recombinant
　ankle splints, L4392–L4398
　DNA insulin, J1820
Red blood cells, each unit, P9021, P9022
Red Dot
　crutches, E0114
　folding walkers, E0135, E0143
Redisol, J3420
Regitine, J2760
Reglan, J2765
Regular insulin, J1820
Regulator, oxygen, E1353
Relefact TRH, J2725
Remicade, J1745
RenAmin, parenteral nutrition, B5000
Renu, enteral nutrition, B4150
ReoPro, TRH, J0130
Repair
　contract, ERSD, A4890
　dental, D2980, D3351–D3353, D5510–D5630, D6090, D6980, D7852, D7955
　durable medical equipment, E1340

Repair — *continued*
　hearing aid, V5014, V5336
　home dialysis eqipment, A4890
　orthotic, L4000–L4130
　prosthetic, L7500, L7510, L7520
　skilled technical, E1350
Replacement
　battery, A4254, A4630, A4631
　components, ESRD machine, E1640
　handgrip for cane, crutch, walker A4636
　ostomy filters, A4421
　pad (alternating pressure), A4640
　tanks, dialysis, A4880
　tip for cane, crutch, walker, A4637
　underarm pad for crutch, A4635
Rep-Pred
　40, J1030
　80, J1040
ResCap headgear, K0185
Reservoir
　metered dose inhaler, A4627
Resin dental restoration, D2330–D2387
Resipiradyne II Plus pulmonary function/ventilation monitor, E0450
RespiGam, J1565
Respiratory syncytial virus immune globulin, J1565
Respite care, in home, S9125
Restorative dental procedure, D2110–D2999
Restraint
　any type, E0710
　belts
　　Posey, E0700
　　Secure-All, E0700
　Bite disposable jaw locks, E0700
　body holders
　　Houdini security suit, E0700
　　Quick Release, one piece, E0700
　　Secure-All, one piece, E0700
　　System2 zippered, E0700
　　UltraCare vest-style with sleeves, E0700
　hand
　　Secure-All finger control mit, E0700
　limb holders
　　Posey, E0700
　　Quick Release, E0700
　　Secure-All, E0700
　pelvic
　　Secure-All, E0700
Retavase, J2994
Reteplase, J2994
Revascularization
　laser transmyocardial, S2204
Rhesonativ, J2790
Rheumatrex, J8610
Rho(D) immune globulin, human, J2790, J2792
RhoGAM, J2790
Rib belt
　elastic, A4572
　thoracic, A4572, L0210, L0220
　Don-Joy, L0210
Rice ankle splint, L1904
Richhfoam convoluted & flat overlays, E0199
Ride Lite 200, Ride Lite 9000, manual wheelchair, K0004

Rimso, J1212
Ringer's lactate infusion, J7120
Ring, ostomy, A4404
Rituxan, J9310
Rituximab, J9310
Riveton, foot orthosis, L3140, L3150
Road Savage power wheelchair, K0011
Road Warrior, power wheelchair, K0011
Robaxin, J2800
Robin-Aids, prosthesis
　hand, L6855, L6860
　partial hand, L6000–L6020
Rocephin, J0696
Rocking bed, E0462
Rollabout chair, E1031
Root canal therapy, D3310–D3353
RSV immune globulin, J1565
Rubex, J9000
Rubramin PC, J3420

Sabre power wheelchair, K0011
Sacral nerve stimulation test lead kit, S8300
Sacroiliac orthosis, L0600–L0620
Safe, hand prosthesis, L5972
Safety
　belt/pelvic strap, each, K0031
　equipment, E0700
　slippers, E0690
　　Day Tread, E0690
　　Fashion-Tread, E0690
　　Safe-T-Tread, E0690
　　Terry Tread, E0690
　vest, wheelchair, E0980
Safe-T-Tread slipper, E0690
Saline
　hypertonic, J7130
　solution, J7030–J7051, A4214, A4323
　solution, for use with inhalation drugs, K0283
Saliva test, hormone level
　during menopause, S3650
　preterm labor risk, S3652
Samarium sm153 lexidronamm, A9605
Sam Brown, Legg Perthes orthosis, L1750
Sandostatin Lar Depot, J2352
Sargramostim (GM-CSF), J2820
Satumomab pendetide, A4642
Scale, dialysis, A4910
Schuco
　mist nebulizer system, E0570
　vac aspirator, E0600
Scissors, dialysis, A4910
Scoliosis, L1000, L1200, L1300–L1499
　additions, L1010–L1120, L1210–L1290
Scott ankle splint, canvas, L1904
Scott-Craig, stirrup orthosis, L2260
Scottish-Rite, Legg Perthes orthosis, L1730
Screening examination
　cervical or vaginal, G0101
　colorectal cancer, G0104-G0017, G0120-G0122
　digital rectal, annual, S0605
　gynecological
　　established patient, S0612
　　new patient, S0610
　ophthalmological, including refraction
　　established patient, S0621
　　new patient, S0620

Screening examination — *continued*
  proctoscopy, S0601
  prostate
    digital, rectal, G0102
    prostate specific antigen test (PSA), G0103
Sealant
  skin, A6250
  tooth, D1351
Seat
  attachment, walker, E0156
  insert, wheelchair, E0992
  lift (patient), E0621, E0627–E0629
  upholstery, wheelchair, E0975
Seattle Carbon Copy II, foot prosthesis, L5976
Secobarbital sodium, J2860
Seconal, J2860
Secure-All
  restraints, E0700
  universal pelvic traction belt, E0890
Selestoject, J0704
Semen analysis, G0027
Semilente insulin, J1820
Sensitivity study, P7001
Serum clotting time tube, A4771
SEWHO, L3960–L3974
Sexa, G0130
Sheepskin pad, E0188, E0189
Shoes
  arch support, L3040–L3100
  for diabetics, A5500–A5508
  insert, L3000–L3030
  lift, L3300–L3334
  miscellaneous additions, L3500–L3595
  orthopedic (See also Orthopedic shoes), L3201–L3265
  positioning device, L3140–L3170
  post-operative
    Specialist™ Health/Post Operative Shoe, A9270
    Specialist™ Trainer, L3218 (women), L3223 (men)
  transfer, L3600–L3649
  wedge, L3340–L3485
Shoulder
  abduction positioner, L3999
  braces, L3999
    Masterhinge™ Shoulder Brace 3, L3999
  disarticulation, prosthetic, L6300-L6320, L6550
  orthosis (SO), L3650–L3675
    elastic shoulder immobilizer, L3670
    Padden Shoulder Immobilizer, L3670
    Sling and Swathe, L3670
    Velpeau Sling Immobilizer, L3670
  spinal, cervical, L0100-L0200
Shoulder-elbow-wrist-hand orthosis (SEWHO), L3960–L3969
Shunt accessory for dialysis, A4740
  aqueous, L8612
Sierra wrist flexion unit, L6805
Sigmoidoscopy, cancer screening, G0104, G0106
Sildenafil citrate, S0090
Silicate dental restorations, D2210
Single bar "AK," ankle-foot orthosis, L2000, L2010

Single bar "BK," ankle-foot orthosis, L1980
Sinusol-B, J0945
Sitz bath, E0160–E0162
Skilled nurse
  home health setting, G0154
Skilled nursing, G0128
Skin
  barrier, ostomy, A4362, A4369–A4374, A4385–A4386
  bond or cement, ostomy, A4364
  gel protective dressing wipes, A5119
  grafts, cultured, G0170, G0171
  sealant, protectant, moisturizer, A6250
  test, collagen, G0025
Sling, A4565
  axilla, L1010
  Legg Perthes, L1750
  lumbar, L1090
  patient lift, E0621, E0630, E0635
  pelvic, L2580
  Sam Brown, L1750
  SEWHO, L3969
  trapezius, L1070
Sling and Swathe, orthosis (SO), L3670
Smoking cessation program, S9075
So, vest type abduction retrainer, L3675
Social worker
  home health setting, G0155
  nonemergency transport, A0160
  visit in home, S9127
Sock
  body sock, L0984
  prosthetic sock, L8420–L8435, L8480, L8485
  stump sock, L8470–L8485
Sodium
  chloride injection, J2912
  ferric gluconate in sucrose, S0098
  hyaluronate, J7315
  succinate, J1720
Sof-Rol™ Cast Padding, (not separately reimbursable from the casting procedure or casting supplies codes)
Soft Touch lancets, box of 100, A4259
Softclix lancet device, A4258
Softop helmet, L0110
Soft Touch II lancet device, A4258
Solganal, J2910
Solo, power attachment (for wheelchair), E1065
Solo™ Cast Sole, L3540
Solu-Cortef, J1720
Solu-Medrol, J2920, J2930
Solurex, J1100
Solurex LA, J1095, J1100
Solution
  calibrator, A4256
  dialysate, A4700, A4705, A4760
  enteral formulae, B4150–B4156
  irrigation, A4323
  parenteral nutrition, B4164–B5200
Somatrem, S0010
Somatropin, S0011
S.O.M.I. brace, L0190, L0200
Somi multiple-post collar, cervical orthosis, L0190
Sorbent cartridge, ESRD, E1636
Sorbsan, alginate dressing, A6196–A6198

Sparine, J2950
Spasmoject, J0500
Specialist™ Ankle Foot Orthosis, L1930
Specialist™ Closed-Back Cast Boot, L3260
Specialist™ 100 Cotton Cast Padding, (not separately reimbursable from the casting procedure or casting supplies codes)
Specialist™ Cast Padding, (not separately reimbursable from the casting procedure or casting supplies codes)
Specialist™ Gaitkeeper™ Boot, L3260
Specialist™ Health/Post Operative Shoe, A9270
Specialist™ Heel Cups, L3485
Specialist™ Insoles, L3510
Specialist™ J-Splint™ Plaster Roll Immobilizer, A4580
Specialist™ Open-Back Cast Boot, L3260
Specialist™ Orthopaedic Stockinet, (not separately reimbursable from the casting procedure or casting supplies codes)
Specialist™ Plaster Bandages, A4580
Specialist™ Plaster Roll Immobilizer, A4580
Specialist™ Plaster Splints, A4580
Specialist™ Pre-Formed Humeral Fracture Brace, L3980
Specialist™ Pre-Formed Ulnar Fracture Brace, L3982
Specialist™ Thumb Orthosis, L3800
Specialist™ Tibial Pre-formed Fracture Brace, L2116
Specialist™ Toe Insert for Specialist™ Closed-Back Cast Boot and Specialist™ Health/Post Operative Shoe, A9270
Specialist™ Trainer, shoe, post-operative, L3218 (women), L3223 (men)
Specialist™ Wrist/Hand Orthosis, L3999
Specialist™ Wrist-Hand-Thumb-orthosis, L3999
Specialty absorptive dressing, A6251–A6256
Spectinomycin HCl, J3320
Speech assessment, V5362–V5364
Speech and language pathologist
  home health setting, G0153
Speech communication device, E1900
Speech therapy, S9128
Spenco shoe insert, foot orthosis, L3001
Spinal orthosis,
  anterior-posterior, L0320, L0330, L0530
  anterior-posterior-lateral, L0520, L0550–L0565
  anterior-posterior-lateral-rotary, L0340–L0440
  Boston type, L1200
  cervical, L0100–L0200
  cervical-thoracic-lumbar-sacral (CTLSO), L0700, L0710, L1000
  DME, K0112–K0116
  halo, L0810–L0830
  lumbar flexion, L0540
  lumbar-sacral (LSO), L0500–L0565
  Milkaukee, L1000
  multiple post collar, L0180–L0200
  sacroilliac, L0600–L0620
  scoliosis, L1000, L1200, L1300–L1499
  torso supports, L0900–L0999

Splint, A4570, L3100, L4350–L4380
  ankle, L4392–L4398
  dynamic, E1800, E1805, E1810, E1815
  footdrop, L4398
  Orthoplast™ Splints (and Orthoplast™ II Splints), A4590
  Specialist™ Plaster Splints, A4580
  Thumb-O-Prene™ Splint, L3999
  toad finger, A4570
  Wrist-O-Prene™ Splint, L3800
Spoke protectors, each, K0065
Sports supports hinged knee support, L1832
Staphcillin, J2970
Star Lumen tubing, A4616
Steeper, hand prosthesis, L6868, L6873
Steindler apron-front, spinal orthosis, L0340
Sten, foot prosthesis, L5972
Step 'N Rest folding walker, E0145
Sterile cefuroxime sodium, J0697
Stilphostrol, J9165
Stimulators
  neuromuscular, E0744, E0745
  osteogenesis, electrical, E0747–E0749
  salivary reflex, E0755
  ultrasound, E0760
Stocking
  Delta-Net™ Orthopaedic Stockinet, (not separately reimbursable from the casting procedure or casting supplies codes)
  gradient compression, L8100–L8239
  Specialist™ Orthopaedic Stockinet, (not separately reimbursable from the casting procedure or casting supplies codes)
Stoma
  cap, A5055
  catheter, A5082
  cone, A4399
  plug, A5081
Stomach tube, B4083
Stomahesive
  paste, K0138
  powder, K0139
  skin barrier, A4362, A5122
  sterile wafer, A4362
  strips, A4362
Storm Arrow power wheelchair, K0014
Storm Torque power wheelchair, K0011
Streptase, J2995
Streptokinase, J2995
Streptomycin sulfate, J3000
Streptozocin, J9320
Strip(s)
  blood, A4253
  glucose test, A4253, A4772
  Nu-Hope
    adhesive, 3 oz bottle with applicator, A4364
    adhesive, 1 oz bottle with applicator, A4364
    extra long adhering tape strips (100/pkg), A4454
    extra long pink adhering tape strips (100/pkg), A4454
    extra wide adhering tape strips (100/pkg), A4454

Strip(s) — *continued*
  Nu-Hope — *continued*
    extra wide pink adhering tape strips (100/pkg), A4454
    regular adhering tape strips (100/pkg), A4454
    regular pink adhering tape strips (100/pkg), A4454
  urine reagent, A4250
Strontium-89 chloride, A9600
Stump sock, L8470–L8485
Stylet, A4212
Sublimaze, J3010
Succinylcholine chloride, J0330
Sucostrin, J0330
Suction pump
  portable, E0600
Sulfamethoxazole and trimethoprim, S0039
Sullivan
  V, E0601
  V Elite, E0601
  VPAP II, E0452
  VPAP II ST, E0453
  VPlus, E0601
Sumacal, enteral nutrition, B4155
Sumatriptan succinate, J3030
Supply/accessory/service, A9900
Sunbeam moist/dry heat pad, E0215
Support
  arch, L3040–L3090
  cervical, L0100–L0200
  elastic, L8100–L8239
  maternity, L0920, L0930
  spinal, L0900–L0960
  vaginal, A4560
Supreme bG Meter, E0607
SureStep blood glucose monitor, E0607
Sur-Fit/Active Life tail closures, A4421
Sur-Fit
  closed-end pouch, A5054
  disposable convex inserts, A5093
  drainable pouch, A5063
  flange cap, A5055
  irrigation sleeve, A4397
  urostomy pouch, A5073
Sure-Gait folding walker, E0141, E0143
Sure-Safe raised toilet seat, E0244
Surgery, oral, D7110–D7999
Surgical
  boot, L3208–L3211
  brush, dialysis, A4910
  dressing, A6020–A6406, Q0183–Q0185
  stocking, A4490–A4510
  supplies, miscellaneous, A4649
  tray, A4550
Surround™ Ankle Stirrup Braces with Floam™, 1906
Sus-Phrine, J0170
Sustacal, enteral nutrition, B4150
  HC, B4152
Sus-Phrine, J0170
Sustagen Powder, enteral nutrition, B4150
Swabs, betadine or iodine, A4247
Swanson, wrist-hand-finger orthosis, L3910
Swede Basic F# manual wheelchair, K0004
Swede, ACT, Cross, or Elite manual wheelchair, K0005

Swedish knee orthosis, L1850
Synkayvite, J3430
Syntocinon, J2590
Synvise, J7320
Syringe, A4213
  dialysis, A4655
  with needle, A4206–A4209
System2 zippered body holder, E0700
Sytobex, J3420

2 Load, hook prosthesis, L6795
3-in-1 composite commode, E0164
Tables, bed, E0274, E0315
Tachdijan, Legg Perthes orthosis, L1720
Tacrine hydrochloride, S0014
Tacrolimus, oral, J7507, J7508
Talwin, J3070
Tape, A4454, A6265
Taractan, J3080
Taxi, nonemergency transportation, A0100
Taxotere, J9170
Taylor
  apron-front, spinal orthosis, L0320
Tazidime, J0713
  multiple-post collar, cervical orthosis, L0190
Technetium TC 99 M
  medronate, A9503
  sestamibi, A9500
  tetrofosmin, A9502
Technol
  Colles splint, L3986
  wrist and forearm splint, L3906
TEEV, J0900
Temporomandibular joint, D0320, D0321, L8610
TenderCloud electric air pump, E0182
TenderFlo II, E0187
TenderGel II, E0196
Tenderlet lancet device, A4258
TENS, A4595, E0720–E0749
  Neuro-Pulse, E0720
Tent, oxygen, E0455
Terbutaline
  inhalation solution
    concentrated, J7680
    unit dose, J7681
  sulfate, J3105
Terminal devices, L6700–L6895
Terramycin IM, J2460
Terry Treads slipper, E0690
Terumo disposable insulin syringes, up to 1cc, per syringe, A4206
Testadiate-Depo, J1080
Testaqua, J3140
Testa-C, J1080
Test-Estra-C, J1060
Test-Estro Cypionates, J1060
Testex, J3150
Test lead kit
  sacral nerve stimulation, S8300
Testoject
  -50, J3140
  -LA, J1070, J1080
Testone LA 100, J3120
  LA 200, J3130

Testosterone
　aqueous, J3140
　cypionate and estradiol cypionate, J1060
　enanthate and estradiol valerate, J0900, J3120, J3130
　propionate, J3150
　suspension, J3140
Testradiate, J0900
Testradiol 90/4, J0900
Testrin PA, J3120, J3130
Tetanus immune globulin, human, J1670
Tetracycline, J0120
Thallous chloride TL 201, A9505
Theelin aqueous, J1435
Theophylline, J2810
TheraCys, J9031
Therapeutic agent, A4321
Therapy
　activity, Q0082
　lymphedema, S8950
　physical, evaluation/treatment, Q0086
Thermalator T-12-M, E0239
Thermometer, dialysis, A4910
Thiethylperazine maleate, J3280, Q0174
Thinning solvent, NuHope, 2 oz bottle, A4455
Thiotepa, J9340
Thiothixene, J2330
Thomas
　heel wedge, foot orthosis, L3465, L3470
　suspension, wrist-hand-finger orthosis, L3926
Thoracic-hip-knee-ankle (THKO), L1500–L1520
　Big Hug, L1510
　Chameleon, L1510
　Easy Stand, L1500
　Little Hug, L1510
　Tristander, L1510
Thoracic-lumbar-sacral orthosis (TLSO)
　scoliosis, L1200–L1290
　spinal, L0300–L0440
Thoracic orthosis, L0210
Thorazine, J3230
Thumb
　immobilizer, Johnson's, L3800
　Specialist™ Thumb Orthosis, L3800
Thymoglobulin, J7504
Thumb-O-Prene™ Splint, L3999
Thymol turbidity, blood, P2033
Thypinone, J2725
Thyrotropin (TSH) injection, up to 10 I.U., J3240
Thytropar, J3240
Tibia
　Specialist™ Tibial Pre-formed Fracture Brace, L2116
　Toad finger splint, A4570
Ticarcillin disodium and clavulanate potassium, S0040
Tice BCG, J9031
Ticon, J3250
Tigan, J3250
Tiject-20, J3250
Tiller control, power add-on, K0461
Tip (cane, crutch, walker) replacement, A4637
Tire, wheelchair, E0996, E0999, E1000

Tissue-based surgical dressings, Q0183–Q0185
TLSO, L0300–L0440, L1200–L1290
Tobramycin
　inhalation solution, J7682
　sulfate, J3260
　unit dose, J7682
Toe
　Specialist™ Toe Insert for Specialist™ Closed-Back Cast Boot and Specialist™ Health/Post Operative Shoe, A9270
Tofranil, J3270
Toilet accessories, E0167–E0179, E0243, E0244, E0625
　raised toilet seat, E0244
　　Combo-Seat Universal, E0244
　　Moore, E0244
　　Sure-Safe, E0244
Tolazoline HCl, J2670
Tolerex, enteral nutrition, B4156
Toll, non emergency transport, A0170
Tomographic radiograph, dental, D0322
Tomography, G0132
Tool kit, dialysis, A4910
Topical hyperbaric oxygen chamber, A4575
Topographic brain mapping, S8040
Topotecan, J9350
Toradol, J1885
Torecan, J3280
Tornalate inhalation solution, J7627
Toronto, Legg Perthes orthosis, L1700
Torsemide, J3265
Torso support, L0900–L0960
Totacillin-N, J0290
Total universal buck's boot, E0870
Touch-n-Talk III blood glucose monitor, E0609
Tourniquet, dialysis, A4910
Tracer blood glucose
　meter, E0607
　strips, box of 50, A4253
Tracer II Diabetes Care System, E0607
Tracer Wheelchairs, E1240, E1250, E1260, E1270, E1280, E1285, E1290, E1295
Tracheostomy
　care kit, A4629
　filter, A4481
　speaking valve, L8501
　supplies, A4622–A4626, A4628, A4629
Tracheotomy mask or collar, A4621
Traction equipment, E0840-E0948
　cervical equipment, not requiring frame, E0855
　extremity, E0870, E0880
　　Total universal buck's boot, E0870
　head harness/halter, cervical, E0942
　occipital-pull head halter, E0942
　overdoor, cervical, E0860
　　Exo-Static, E0860
　pelvic, E0890, E0900
　　Secure-All universal, belt, E0890
Training, diabetes, G0108, G0109
Training, NETT pulmonary rehabilitation
　individual, G0110
　group, G0111
Tramacal, enteral nutrition, B4154

Transcutaneous electrical nerve stimulator (TENS), E0720–E0749
Transducer protector, dialysis, E1575
Transfer board or device, E0972
Transfer (shoe orthoses), L3600–L3640
Transparent film (for dressing), A6257–A6259
Transplant
　autologous chondrocyte, S2109
　meniscal allograft, S9085
　multivisceral organs, S2054
　small intestine allograft, S2052
　small intestine and liver allografts, S2053
Transportation
　ambulance, A0021–A0999
　corneal tissue, V2785
　EKG (portable), R0076
　handicapped, A0130
　nonemergency, A0080–A0210
　service, including ambulance, A0021–A0999
　taxi, nonemergency, A0100
　toll, nonemergency, A0170
　volunteer, nonemergency, A0080, A0090
　x-ray (portable), R0070, R0075
Trapeze bar, E0910, E0940
Traum-aid, enteral nutrition, B4154
Travasorb, enteral nutrition, B4150
　Hepatic, B4154
　HN, B4153
　MCT, B4154
　Renal, B4154
　STD, B4156
Traveler manual wheelchair, K0001
Tray
　insertion, A4310–A4316, A4354
　irrigation, A4320
　surgical (see also kits), A4550
　wheelchair, E0950
Treatment program
　partial hospitalization, G0172
Triam-A, J3301
Triamcinolone
　acetonide, J3301
　diacetate, J3302
　hexacetonide, J3303
　inhalation solution
　　concentrated, J7683
　　unit dose, J7684
Triethylperazine maleate, J3280
Trifupromazine HCI, J3400
Trifocal, glass or plastic, V2300–V2399
Trigeminal division block anesthesia, D9212
Tri-Kort, J3301
Trilafon, J3310
Trilog, J3301
Trilone, J3302
Trim nails, G0127
Trimethaphan, J0400
Trimethobenzamide HCl, J3250, Q0173
Trimetrexate glucoronate, J3305
Trismus appliance, D5937
Trobicin, J3320
Trovan, J0200
Truform prosthetic shrinker, L8440-L8465
Truss, L8300–L8330

Tube/Tubing
  anchoring device, A5200
  blood, A4750, A4755
  CPAP device, K0187
  drainage extension, K0280
  gastrostomy, B4084, B4085
  irrigation, A4355
  larynectomy, A4622
  nasogastric, B4081, B4082
  oxygen, A4616
  serum clotting time, A4771
  stomach, B4083
  suction pump, each, A7002
  tire, K0064, K0068, K0078, K0091, K0093, K0095, K0097
  tracheostomy, A4622
  urinary drainage, K0280
Turtle Neck safety collars, E0942

Ultra Blood Glucose
  monitor, E0607
  test strips, box of 50, A4253
UltraCare vest-style body holder, E0700
Ultrafast computed tomography, S8092
Ultrafine disposable insulin syringes, per syringe, A4206
Ultralente insulin, J1820
Ultrasound
  bladder capacity test, G0050
  paranasal sinus, S9024
Ultraviolet cabinet, E0690
Ultrazine-10, J0780
Unasyn, J0295
Unclassified drug, J3490
Undercasting (not separately reimbursable from the casting procedure or casting supplies codes)
  Delta-Net™ Orthopaedic Stockinet
  Delta-Rol™ Cast Padding
  Specialist™ Orthopaedic Stockinet
Underpads, disposable, A4554
Unilet lancet device, A4258
Unipuncture control system, dialysis, E1580
Unistik lancet device, A4258
Universal
  remover for adhesives, A4455
  socket insert
    above knee, L5694
    below knee, L5690
  telescoping versarail bed rail, E0310
Up-Draft Neb-U-Mist, E0580
Upper extremity addition, locking elbow, L6693
Upper extremity fracture orthosis, L3980–L3999
Upper limb prosthesis, L6000–L7499
Urea, J3350
Ureaphil, J3350
Urecholine, J0520
Ureterostomy supplies, A4454–A4590
Urethral suppository, Alprostadil, J0275
Urinal, E0325, E0326
Urinary
  catheter, A4338–A4346, A4351–A4353, K0410, K0411
  catheter irrigation, A4321

Urinary — *continued*
  collection and retention (supplies), A4310–A4359, K0407, K0408, K0410, K0411
  leg bag, A5105, A5112
  tract implant, collagen, L8603
Urine
  collector, A4335
  sensitivity study, P7001
  tests, A4250
Urokinase, J3364, J3365
Urostomy pouch, A5073
USMC
  hinged Swedish knee cage, L1850
  universal knee immobilizer, L1830
U-V lens, V2755

Vabra aspirator, A4480
Vaccination, administration
  hepatitis B, G0010
  influenza virus, G0008
  pneumococcal, G0009
Vacuum erection system, L7900
Valergen (10, 20, 40), J0970, J1380, J1390
Valertest No. 1, 2, J0900
Valium, J3360
Valrubicin, J9357
Valstar, J9357
Vancocin, J3370
Vancoled, J3370
Vancomycin HCl, J3370
Vaporizer, E0605
Vascular
  catheter (appliances and supplies), A4300–A4306
  graft material, synthetic, L8670
Vasoxyl, J3390
Velban, J9360
Velosulin, J1820
Velpeau Sling Immobilizer, L3670
Velsar, J9360
Venipuncture, routine specimen collection, G0001
Venous pressure clamp, dialysis, A4918
Ventilator
  battery, A4611–A4613
  moisture exchanger, disposable, A4483
  negative pressure, E0460
  volume, stationary or portable, E0450
Ventolin, J7620, J7625
VePesid, J8560, J9181, J9182
Versa-Pole IV pole, E0776
Versed, J2250
Vertebral axial decompression, S9090
Vesprin, J3400
Vest, safety, wheelchair, E0980
  chest compression, S8200
    system generator and hoses, S8205
V-Gan (25, 50), J2550
Vinblastine sulfate, J9360
Vincasar PFS, J9370
Vincristine sulfate, J9370–J9380
Vinorelbine tartrate, J9390
Visi wheelchair tray, E0950
Visi-flow
  irrigation, A4367, A4397, A4398, A4399, A4402, A4421, A5123
  stoma cone, A4399

Vision Record wheelchair, K0005
Vision service, V2020–V2799
Vision Tek protective eyewear, E0690
Vistaject, J3410
Vistaril, J3410
Vistide, J0740
Vitajet, A4210
Vital HN, enteral nutrition, B4153
Vitamin B_{12} cyanocobalamin, J3420
Vitamin B_{17}, J3570
Vitamin K, J3430
Vitaneed, enteral nutrition, B4151
Vitrasert, J7310
Vivonex, enteral nutrition
  HN, B4153
  STD, B4156
  T.E.N., B4153
Voice Touch blood glucose monitor, E0609
Von Rosen, hip orthosis, L1630
Vortex power wheelchair, K0014

Wafer, Little Ones Surfit flexible, A5123
Walker, E0130–E0147, K0458, K0459
  accessories, A4636, A4637
  attachments, E0153–E0159
  enclosed with wheels, E0144
  folding
    Auto-Glide, E0143
    Easy Care, E0143, E0146
    framed with wheels, E0144
    One-Button, E0143
    Quik-Fold, E0141, E0143
    Red Dot, E0135, E0143
    Step 'N Rest, E0145
    Sure-Gait, E0141, E0143
  heavy duty
    with wheels, K0459
    without wheels, K0458
Water
  ambulance, A0050
  distilled (for nebulizer), K0182
  for nebulizer, K0529
  pressure pad/mattress, E0177, E0187, E0198
  purification system (ESRD), E1610, E1615
  softening system (ESRD), E1625
  sterile, A4214, A4712, A4714, K0409
  tanks (dialysis), A4880
  treated, A4714
Wedges, shoe, L3340–L3420
Wehamine, J1240
Wehdryl, J1200
Wellcovorin, J0640
Wet mount, Q0111
Wheel attachment, rigid pickup walker, E0155
Wheelchair, E0950–E1298, K0001–K0108
  accessories, E0192, E0950–E1001, E1065–E1069
  cushions, E0963-E0965
    High Profile, 4-inch, E0965
    Low Profile, 2-inch, E0963
  tray, E0950
    Visi, E0950
  amputee, E1170–E1200
  back, fully reclining, manual, K0028
  battery, A4631

Wheelchair — *continued*
- bearings, any type, K0452
- component or accessory, NOS, K0108
- heavy-duty
    - Tracer, E1280, E1285, E1290, E1295
- lightweight, E1240–E1270
    - Ez Lite, E1250
    - Tracer, E1240, E1250, E1260, E1270
- motorized, E1210–E1213
- narrowing device, E0969
- power add-on, K0460–K0461
- specially sized, E1220–E1230
- tire, E0996, E0999, E1000
- transfer board or device, E0972
- tray, K0107
- van, nonemergency, A0130
- youth, E1091

WHFO, with inflatable air chamber, L3807
Whirlpool equipment, E1300–E1310
WHO, wrist extension, L3914
Wig, S8095
Wilcox apron-front, spinal orthosis, L0520
Williams, spinal orthosis, L0540
Win RhoSD, J2792
Wipes, A4245, A4247
- Allkare protective barrier, A5119

WIZZ-ard manual wheelchair, K0006
Wound cleanser, A6260
Wound cover
- alginate dressing, A6196–A6198
- collagen dressing, A6020
- foam dressing, A6209–A6214
- hydrocolloid dressing, A6234–A6239
- hydrogel dressing, A6242–A6248
- specialty absorptive dressing, A6251–A6256

Wound filler
- alginate, A6199
- foam, A6215
- hydrocolloid, A6240–A6241
- hydrogel, A6248–A6249
- not elsewhere classified, A6261–A6262

Wound healing
- other growth factor preparation, S9055
- Procuren, S9055

Wound pouch, A6154
Wrist
- brace, cock-up, L3908
- disarticulation prosthesis, L6050, L6055
- hand/finger orthosis (WHFO), E1805, E1825, L3800-L3954
- Specialist™ Pre-Formed Ulnar Fracture Brace, L3982
- Specialist™ Wrist/Hand Orthosis, L3999
- Specialist™ Wrist-Hand-Thumb-orthosis, L3999
- Splint, lace-up, L3800
- Wrist-O-Prene™ Splint, L3800

Wyamine sulfate, J3450
Wycillin, J2510
Wydase, J3470

Xcaliber power wheelchair, K0014
Xenon regional cerebral blood-flow studies, S9023
Xylocaine HCl, J2000
X-ray equipment, portable, Q0092, R0070, R0075

Zantac, J2780
Zemplar, J2500
Zenapax, J7513
Zetran, J3360
Zinacef, J0697
Zinecard, J1190
Zithromax I.V., J0456
Zofran, J2405
Zoladex, J9202
Zolicef, J0690
Zosyn, J2543